Success in

WORLD HISTORY SINCE 1945

Lowena Eddyvean - New
B

Helen Bowley C

Success Studybooks

Success in

WORLD HISTORY SINCE 1945

Jack B. Watson, M.A.

Consultant editor

Brendan O'Leary B.A., Ph.D.

JOHN MURRAY

Jack Watson wished that this book be dedicated to Bernard (L.C.B.) Seaman

First published 1989
Reprinted 1994

Typeset in 9/11pt and 8/10pt Compugraphic English Times by Colset Private Ltd, Singapore.
Printed in Great Britain by Athenaeum Press, Gateshead, Tyne & Wear.

British Library Cataloguing in Publication Data

Watson, Jack B. (Jack Brierley), *1927-88*
Success in world history since 1945.
1. World, 1900-
I. Title
909.82

ISBN 0-7195-4637-0

Contents

Foreword

This book outlines some of the major developments in world history since 1945. It is designed both for the general reader and for the student who needs a text which provides a frameword for A-level, pre-university or first-year university courses in contemporary history and politics. The extensive cross-referencing throughout should enable readers to follow events which overlap in time or run parallel to each other in different parts of the world. Photographs, maps and cartoons are used liberally, not for entertainment, but to clarify persons, places and political postures.

This book is selective. It has to be. Historians live in the world like everybody else. They never enjoy the privilege of some vantage point which transcends human values, or an objectivity comparable to the detached perspective that visitors from outer space might enjoy. Their intellectual and value judgements are always affected by the human culture(s) within which their texts are planned, produced and read. Moreover, in dealing with the sheer immensity of recorded events and data, and in selecting which themes to focus upon, those dealing with contemporary history have much greater difficulties than their colleagues working on previous eras. The mass-media revolutions of our time have exponentially expanded the quantity of primary information confronting historians; but, as we all know, the growth in the quantity of information has not been matched by comparable increases in its quality and integrity. However, we do know more about the information-processing capacity of human beings than we did; and these limits are especially obvious for writers of books of world history. Indeed books with *World History* in the title often seem too ambitious given the constraints imposed by an individual's mental limits, cultural assumptions, and the scale of the task involved. Yet such books are perhaps increasingly necessary, given the clash of states and cultures in the world, and the depressing levels of ignorance we collectively display about our very recent past.

The book begins in 1945, after the greatest war in human history. The subsequent era cannot be summed up in a phrase, but has been characterized by some incredible contradictions: we have known 'the best of times and the worst of times'. The period since 1945 has been littered with peace treaties, successful and unsuccessful; wars, both cold and hot; and revolutions, both beneficial and catastrophic in their consequences. It has witnessed the greatest growth of economic wealth, economic opportunities and technological progress in human history. More people than ever before have been liberated from traditionalist roles, especially women. However, the period has also been accompanied by the greatest growth ever in the numbers of desperately poor people, the increasing spread and rapidity of impact of major economic depressions, genocide, technologically enhanced torture, and the widespread ravaging of the natural environment. The years since 1945 have seen considerable expansion in international organization, co-operation and interdependence, but they have also exhibited nationalist, chauvinist and ethnic movements of the most varied kind. World religions have declined, but some, notably Islam, have also experienced revivals and expanded the numbers of their enthusiasts. Many see connections between all these contradictory tendencies; others deny that such connections exist anywhere other than in some people's minds.

It is inevitable in a work of this kind that most of the history of the world since 1945 is missing from this book. What is included was governed by three considerations. First, the book attempts to throw light on major political developments since the end of the Second World War. Second, it seeks to avoid the assumption that world history is just the story of the 'West', even if a large part of it necessarily entails examining the history of the 'West' and the impact of (or reaction to) the 'West' on the rest of the planet. Finally, it tries to provoke the reader into further thought and research about the historical sources of many contemporary tensions. If the book provides more questions than answers it will have achieved a great deal.

The book was finished in 1988, when the prospects for relative stability, at least between the powers of East and West, seemed better than they had been since the late 1970s. The subject-matter has no clear end-point, and that is surely a good thing: the history of the world is not yet over. After 1945 the human species developed the ability to put an end to history, if not yet the world. As the sad joke goes: a nuclear war would make historians redundant. Knowledge of world history *might* help us hand on the world to subsequent generations.

* * *

Jack Watson died on 10 June 1988, having put the finishing touches to the typescript of this book a few weeks before. He did not live to see the publication of this book, his seventh and sadly his last. A profoundly learned man, inspiring teacher, and prodigiously industrious author, chief examiner and lecturer, he will be sorely missed by the world of education. His wife Margaret, daughter Lorelei and son Roger – whom he certainly would have thanked had he lived to write this foreword – have lost a loving husband and father. He would also have thanked those of his many regular correspondents and fellow-teachers with whom he discussed the enormous range of issues introduced in this book. Since I cannot be certain of all their names I have decided not to cause difficulties by mentioning some and unfortunately omitting others.

With the approval of Jack's widow, and my mother-in-law, Margaret Watson, I have corrected the proofs of the text of the book, made some minor additions and updated it to the end of 1988. The very considerable assistance of my wife Lorelei Watson was extremely valuable in spotting flaws I would otherwise have missed (or introduced), and Bob Dāvenport and Wendy Reed of John Murray (Publishers) Ltd displayed courtesy and politeness to a family stricken by Jack's loss and thereby aided the completion of the editorial task. Any remaining or newly introduced stylistic infelicities or errors of fact must be my responsibility.

Dr Brendan O'Leary, B.A. (Oxon.), Ph.D. (London)
Government Department
London School of Economics and Political Science
January 1989

Acknowledgements

Photographs and cartoons illustrating the text are reproduced by courtesy of the following (photographers' names are given in parentheses where known):

Imperial War Museum (fig. 1.2); *Punch* Publications Ltd (figs 2.1, 2.3, 6.2, 8.1); Camera Press (figs 2.2, 11.1 (Klaus Weizman), 11.2); Novosti Press Agency (figs 3.1, 10.5); Hulton Deutsch Collection (figs 3.5, 12.2, 13.1, 16.1 (Bert Hardy)); Stanley Gibbons Publications Ltd (figs 4.4, 9.2, 10.4, 14.1); Topham Picture Library (figs 5.1, 5.3, 17.1); Express Newspapers plc (fig. 7.2); Dennis Renault, *The Sacramento Bee* (fig. 9.3); The John Hillelson Agency Ltd (figs 10.2 (Andrew St George), 19.1 (Ernest Cole), 20.1 (Alain Keler/Sygma)); Popperfoto (fig. 14.5 (J. Eggitt)); R.K. Laxman, *The Times of India* (fig. 16.2); Oxfam (fig. 16.3); *Soviet Weekly* (fig. 17.3); UPI/Bettmann Newsphotos (fig. 18.2 (Darryl Heikes)); The Associated Press Ltd (fig. 18.5 (Nguyen Kong)); Les Gibbard (figs 19.3, 20.3, 21.1); Network Photographers (fig. 19.5 (Judah Passow)); Barnaby's Picture Library (fig. 22.2 (Joe Clarke)); RSPCA (fig. 22.3); Solo Syndication & Literary Agency Ltd (fig. 22.5); Frank Spooner Pictures (fig. 23.1 (Françoise Demulder)); Magnum Photos Ltd (fig. 23.2 (Raymond Depardon)).

The Index was compiled by J.D. Lee.

List of maps, diagrams and tables

Maps

Tables

Note

An explanation of words or phrases in the text followed by 'G' will be found in the Glossary towards the end of the book.

UNIT 1

The end of the Second World War: the post-war world

1.1 The defeat of the Axis

Admiral Karl Doenitz authorized Germany's surrender to the Allies on 7 May 1945. The Allies had long since insisted that such surrender must be unconditional; by this time, it was hardly more than a formality. Nazi Germany had been utterly defeated. General Alfred Jodl surrendered the German forces in the West to the American General Dwight Eisenhower and the next day, 8 May, Soviet Marshal Georgi Zhukov accepted the surrender of German forces in the East. Thus the Allies celebrated 8 May 1945 as VE (Victory in Europe) Day.

Adolf Hitler, the *Führer* (leader) of Nazi Germany, had committed suicide among the ruins of Berlin a week earlier, making sure that he would not become a prisoner of the Soviet forces to whom the city was about to capitulate, which it did on 2 May. One of Hitler's last acts was to make Doenitz the President of what was left of Germany. But Doenitz, along with other Nazis, was quickly arrested by the Allies and was imprisoned for ten years for his war crimes. The Nazi Reich had been shattered, surviving for only twelve of the thousand years Hitler had promised. For the last six years of the Reich, Germany had been at war, and fig. 1.1 shows how few European states had been able to remain neutral in this war. Table 1.1 shows the numbers of dead of the main powers involved in the Second World War before Germany and the other Axis powers were beaten.

The term 'Axis' was popularized by Benito Mussolini, the *Duce* (leader) of Fascist Italy, his imagination seizing on a line linking Berlin and Rome, an 'axis' around which would revolve the states of Europe. Germany and Italy became firm allies in the late 1930s, and they forged links with Japan which were strengthened by the Tripartite Axis Pact of 1940. The three became known as the Axis powers, and they had support in Europe from governments sympathetic to Nazism and Fascism. Miklós Horthy, Regent of Hungary, joined the Axis powers in the Second World War, though other sympathizers such as Francisco Franco of Spain and Antonio Salazar of Portugal preferred a

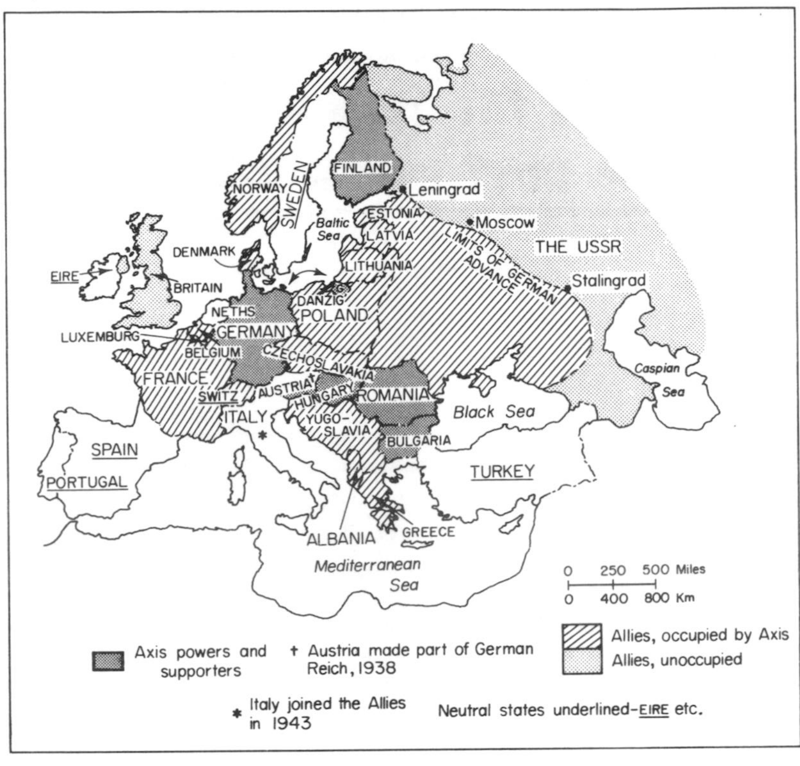

Fig. 1.1 Europe before and during the Second World War

cautious neutrality. For Mussolini, the Axis proved disastrous. He soon lost the Italian Empire in East Africa, and the Allied invasion of Sicily in 1943 led his own people to overthrow him. Italy changed sides, joining the Allies against Nazi Germany, though it took a slow and costly struggle to drive German troops northwards and out of Italy. Mussolini took shelter behind the German lines but his reprieve proved merely temporary. In 1945 he was captured by Italian partisans. When he tried to escape, they shot him, just a couple of days before Hitler's suicide. Horthy was more fortunate. He broke with the Nazis late in the war, and that sufficed for his American captors to refuse the Yugoslav request that he should be handed over to be tried as a war criminal. Horthy was able to live out his life in exile.

Anti-communism had helped to unite the Axis powers, drawing together Germany, Japan and Italy in the Anti-Comintern Pacts of 1936–7. The Comintern was a communist propaganda agency closely linked with the Soviet Union, which before 1945, and along with its satellite Mongolian People's Republic, was the world's only Marxist state. One of Hitler's fanatical

Table 1.1 The dead in the Second World War*

Allies	Millions	Axis powers	Millions
Soviet Union	20.0†	Germany	4.2
Poland	5.8†	Japan	2.0
China	2.2†	Romania	0.5
Yugoslavia	1.7	Hungary	0.4
France	0.6	Italy	0.4§
British Empire and Commonwealth	0.5‡	Austria	0.3
USA	0.4	Finland	0.1
Greece	0.4		
Netherlands	0.2		

* Including civilian casualities

† Calculations vary, especially for civilian deaths. For the Soviet Union and China, military deaths probably slightly outnumbered civilian deaths. In the case of Poland, the great majority of deaths were civilian, especially among the Jewish population: about half of the six million Jews killed by the Nazis were Polish. Poland lost about fifteen per cent of its population. The next greatest losses were those of the Soviet Union and Yugoslavia, each about eleven per cent. Only three in every one hundred Soviet youths aged seventeen in 1941 survived the war.

‡ Mainly UK deaths (over 350 000); Canada 38 000; Australia 25 000; India 25 000

§ Including the period when Italy joined the Allies

ambitions was the destruction of the Soviet Union and he launched his invasion of that country in 1941 in Operation Barbarossa. Nazi intentions seem to have included the occupation and exploitation of all Soviet lands west of the Urals, the elimination of Jews and of communism, and the enslavement of the Slavonic peoples whom the Nazis regarded as inferior to the *Herrenvolk* (the German master race). Operation Barbarossa was a massive miscalculation by the Nazis, however: they failed to take either Moscow or Leningrad and, instead, the Soviet Red Army entered Berlin in 1945. At the same time, Operation Barbarossa had launched in eastern Europe a war of unparalleled fury, its devastation almost beyond comprehension and its casualties horrific (See Table 1.1). The war which ended in Europe in 1945 had therefore been more like two wars – the war of annihilation in eastern Europe where vast areas were laid waste, and the more conventional war in western Europe where the damage, though regionally severe, was less universal and not quite so awesome. Such terms are relative, however, and by 1945 the ambition and ruthlessness of Nazi Germany had led both to the destruction of Germany itself and to such ravaging and upheaval that the entire European continent was in need of restoration and repair. The Soviet Union faced vast problems of reconstruction. Its Western Allies, Britain and France, although they had emerged from the war victorious, teetered on the brink of exhaustion and bankruptcy. Only the USA had not been brought to its knees by the war.

But the Second World War was not yet over. When the war ended in Europe, the Allies had still to defeat Japan in Asia. Like Nazi Germany, Japan had won spectacular successes in the early stages of the war, overrunning much of China and the Pacific as far as the Dutch East Indies. Though the liberation of the Pacific had long since begun, it was not yet certain that Japan's surrender was imminent. In fact the surrender was accomplished only 99 days after VE Day, not so much by following up the 'peace feelers' that Japan was already putting out as by terror. President Truman of the USA decided to use newly invented atomic bombs. 'Little Boy', the first such bomb, was dropped on the Japanese city of Hiroshima early in August 1945. 'Fat Man', a bomb of different design with plutonium instead of uranium, was dropped on Nagasaki three days later. Some 80 000 Japanese were killed by the bomb at Hiroshima, almost 40 000 by the bomb at Nagasaki. Even more horrifying were the larger numbers gravely injured, many condemned to lingering and painful death from radiation and other effects of the new weapons, the full consequences of which were as yet unknown. During the next ten years, the death toll at Hiroshima and Nagasaki rose to around 200 000 as a result of the atomic explosions, and victims continued to suffer and die. Meanwhile, Emperor Hirohito authorized Japan's unconditional surrender on 15 August 1945. The country's formal capitulation was received at the beginning of September by the American General MacArthur aboard the USS *Missouri* lying off Tokyo. Like the Nazi dream of *Lebensraum* - a European sphere for economic exploitation by Germany - Japan's dream of an East Asian Co-prosperity Sphere, stretching from Manchuria to the East Indies for the benefit of the Japanese, had crumbled in defeat. The Japanese were forced to withdraw their troops from the Asian mainland and the Pacific islands they still held at the time of their government's surrender. Here too the war left behind problems of reconstruction and rehabilitation, not least in China, whose soil was at last freed from a Japanese presence which had endured for eight years in many parts of eastern China and longer than that in Manchuria.

1.2 Superpower rivalry and a new balance of power

The Munich Conference in September 1938 had enabled Europe to avoid war in that year. Britain and France succeeded in appeasing Nazi Germany but it turned out to be the last occasion on which western and central Europeans settled alone an issue of grave international importance. The USA at that time sheltered behind its Neutrality Laws, trying to avoid foreign commitments and especially entanglement in Europe. The Soviet Union was simply not invited to Munich by European powers deeply suspicious of communism. In 1939, however, Germany attacked Danzig and Poland, provoking declarations of war by Britain and France at the start of a conflict which spread throughout Europe. This was the second great twentieth-century war to afflict the continent, and when it ended in 1945 such changes had occurred in the world's balance of power that the reputation of European states was much diminished and the post-war world was dominated by the USA and the Soviet Union. Only seven years after the Munich Conference in which they had no direct part, the USA and the Soviet Union had become superpowers whose size and strength had done much to determine the outcome of the Second World War.

The wealth of the USA had grown steadily, outstripping every rival during the first half of the twentieth century. America had not joined the First World War until 1917 and many Americans were anxious to avoid being involved in any such war again. The USA therefore stood aside when Japan launched a full-scale war on China in 1937 and when war began in Europe in 1939. But President Franklin D. Roosevelt made little secret of where his sympathies lay: American supplies stiffened the resistance to the Axis and by 1941 the USA seemed to be involved in war against Nazi Germany in all but name. At the same time the USA was obstructing Japanese expansionism in Asia by imposing economic boycotts which threatened to starve the Japanese war machine of supplies, especially of oil. The upshot was the Japanese attack on Pearl Harbor, Hawaii, in December 1941, in a desperate effort to cripple the USA's capacity to thwart Japanese plans in the Pacific for some time to come. Roosevelt's reply was swift and unsurprising. On 8 December he addressed a message to Congress:

> I ask that Congress declare that since the unprovoked and dastardly attack by Japan on Sunday, December seventh, a state of war has existed between the United States and the Japanese Empire.

Three days later the President addressed Congress again:

> On the morning of December 11 the Government of Germany, pursuing its course of world conquest, declared war against the United States. The long-known and the long-expected has thus taken place. The forces endeavouring to enslave the entire world now are moving toward this hemisphere.

Germany and Italy had honoured the Tripartite Axis Pact, going to war against the USA in support of Japan, but all three Axis powers now had to contend with America's vast resources. Already in 1940 Roosevelt had proclaimed the USA 'the great arsenal of democracy' and stepped up production of foodstuffs, minerals and industrial supplies. Production now increased still further, far beyond that which even Germany could hope to match.

Joseph Stalin, Secretary-General of the Communist Party and the undisputed leader of the USSR (Union of Soviet Socialist Republics, or the Soviet Union, the name by which most of the former Russian Empire has been known since 1923) had meanwhile avoided war in 1939 by agreeing to the Nazi–Soviet Pact:

> Both High Contracting Parties [the Governments of the German Reich and the Union of Soviet Socialist Republics] obligate themselves to desist from any act of violence, any aggressive action, and any attack on each other, either individually or jointly with other Powers. . . . The present Treaty is concluded for a period of ten years.

The Pact caused astonishment in the West, marrying the sworn enemies, Nazis and Communists. But it was a marriage of convenience which meant that when Germany invaded Poland and went to war with Britain and France, the USSR remained neutral. It was therefore useful at the time to both Hitler and Stalin.

Indeed, secret clauses in the Pact gave the Soviets a share of Poland, enabling them to regain former tsarist lands and to push their boundaries westwards for added security. In April 1941 Stalin, still intent on avoiding involvement in the wars then raging while protecting the security of the Soviet Union, made a Neutrality Pact with Japan. Only two months later, however, the Germans tore up the Pact of 1939, launching Operation Barbarossa and plunging the USSR into a furious struggle for survival. Nazi armies penetrated deeply into Russia but they could not achieve a decisive victory. Now Prime Minister, Defence Commissar and a Soviet Marshal as well as Party Secretary, Stalin rallied the Soviet people to the 'Great Patriotic War' and the expulsion of their enemies from Mother Russia. The tide turned during the winter of 1942–3 and from then onwards the Soviet Red Army drove the invaders back, eventually liberating the USSR itself and much of eastern Europe. Stalin remained cautious, however. His country suffered grievously during the war against Nazi Germany and he refused to put victory at risk by fighting a war on two fronts. The Neutrality Pact with Japan lasted into 1945 and only on 6 August, the day the Americans dropped the atomic bomb on Hiroshima, did the USSR declare war on Japan and begin to liberate Manchuria and Korea.

It was not only the major parts they played in the defeat of the Axis powers that gave the USA and USSR superpower status, and made them much more influential in the post-war world than European nation states such as Britain and France. Both the USA and the USSR had a population of around 150 million made up of mixed nationalities occupying millions of square miles. The USA covered an area similar to that of the whole of Europe; the USSR was more than twice that size, the largest country in the world. Such great areas yielded vast and rich resources and, though the USSR did not yet match the USA in output and wealth, both were giants among the nations of the world.

Even as wartime allies they had not been close. Rivals in strength, and in 1945 rivals for influence in the post-war world, the USA and the Soviet Union were also ideological rivals. The USA had long been the champion of capitalism, private enterprise and western democracy, with its emphasis on individual liberties. Since 1917 when the Bolsheviks[G] seized power, Russians had lived under Marxist–Leninist government, eventually consolidated as rule by the Communist Party. Communists believed that the injustices and inequalities of capitalism were bound to be self-destructive, as the philosopher Karl Marx had forecast in the nineteenth century. Lenin, leader of the Bolsheviks, had set up in Russia the 'dictatorship of the proletariat', a system which he hoped would one day lead the country to a utopian sort of communism based on equality and co-operation, free from the tensions and competitiveness commonplace under capitalism. The system set up by Lenin was inherited by Stalin and, at the end of the Second World War, the Soviet Union was still under Stalinist government. This was one-party government, a 'people's democracy' it was claimed, since the Communist Party represented all the people and their interests. Democracy in the West was usually based on two or more parties (in the USA, mainly Democrats and Republicans), so the West alleged that Soviet democracy was not democracy at all. The Soviets in turn saw the 'bourgeois democracy' of the

West as fraudulent, the outcome of elections manipulated by the media, and the parties offering only a narrow choice with no real chance of changing the economic and social system. In the USA, Democrats and Republicans were both strongly pro-capitalist.

Just as the political systems of the superpowers differed, so too did their economies. The USA prided itself on its private enterprise with which government interfered little. In the 1920s the Republicans had put their faith in 'rugged individualism', leaving the economy and society to look after themselves. In the 1930s, faced with the Depression and evidence of gross inequalities between rich and poor, the Democrats under Roosevelt had opted for a 'New Deal'. The use of the powers of the US federal government to try to manipulate the economy and to introduce laws to help the poor, sick and unemployed had brought angry accusations of socialism and even communism, but even the Democrats did little to interfere with economic and social conditions compared with the policies of governments in western Europe.

In the Soviet Union, on the other hand, the government of the Communist Party had brought rigid controls, with strong central planning of the economy and extensive social reform. In 1945 Russian enterprises had long since been nationalized and now operated for the benefit of the community and not of private shareholders. In agriculture, private farms had given way to state farms and to collectives, the latter operating as joint ventures under official supervision, where individuals shared in the joint fortunes and could make only very limited personal gains from the produce of small private plots. The planned economy nevertheless shielded Soviet workers from extreme poverty and from the unemployment widespread in the West in the 1930s. The Soviet state also made great efforts to extend social services, for example health care, education and housing. In return, the Soviet people gave up a good deal of personal freedom, had very few consumer goods compared with Americans and, while Stalin was in control, suffered under a regime which was often brutal and frightening. The country the Bolsheviks had inherited had been backward and underdeveloped, compared with the USA. Stalin's overriding ambition was to close the gap, driving the Soviet people to the limits of their endurance in doing so.

When civil war broke out in Russia soon after the Bolsheviks seized power in 1917, the Americans like the British, French and Japanese sent troops and supplies to encourage the anti-Bolsheviks. Apart from hoping for Lenin's overthrow, the Interventionists no doubt had an eye on Russia's resources which might have continued to be available to capitalist opportunists. The Bolsheviks fought off their enemies, however. Though the USA sent aid to help feed Russians hit by famine, it still refused to recognize Lenin's government or, after Lenin's death in 1924, that of Stalin. Diplomatic recognition was not granted until the Democrats won the US Presidency and Roosevelt took office in 1933. When Nazi Germany attacked the Soviet Union in 1941, Roosevelt went further, sending supplies to Stalin under the system of Lend-Lease. When the two became wartime Allies at the end of 1941, Roosevelt maintained cordial relations with the Soviet leader. The relationship between the two countries changed with Roosevelt's sudden death in April 1945, on the eve of victory in Europe.

Harry S. Truman, the new US President, was quick to adopt a hard line towards the USSR. The atomic bombs used against Japan were a clear demonstration of US power, not just to the Japanese but also to the Soviets with whom the secrets of manufacture were not to be shared. Before the end of August 1945, Truman announced the end of Lend-Lease, disregarding the enormous problems of reconstruction that faced the war-torn Soviet Union, and instantly cutting off aid. The Soviets were also denied any effective part in the settlement of the affairs of Japan, against whom, the Americans argued, the Soviet declaration of war had come too late.

Relations between the superpowers deteriorated rapidly, each looking for support and allies in a post-war world where new alignments were formed quickly. Diplomacy in the 1930s had tended to revolve around the often localized ambitions of Germany, Japan and Italy. Diplomacy after the Second World War was dominated by the global interests of the USA and the USSR. To begin with, however, both paid close attention to the problems of post-war Europe.

1.3 Post-war planning: Yalta and Potsdam

1.3.1 The Yalta Summit

Summit meetings (meetings between heads of government) took place at various times during the Second World War. Roosevelt and Winston Churchill, the British Prime Minister, met quite often from 1941 onwards. Their first joint meeting with Stalin was at Tehran late in 1943 when their main concern was the Allied strategy for winning the war. The 'Big Three' met again in February 1945, this time at Yalta in the Crimea. Victory in Europe was now in sight and it was time to give more urgent attention to problems likely to arise after the war. Roosevelt declared of the meeting at Yalta that the Allies had never been 'more closely united – not only in their war aims but also in their peace aims'. In truth, however, the statesmen painted with a broad brush at this Crimean meeting, avoiding minute detail in favour of generalities. A good many issues were shelved until a later date and the unity between the West and the Soviet Union was not rigorously tested.

Agreements at Yalta nevertheless proved fundamental to developments in post-war Europe. The three leaders confirmed an earlier agreement that, when defeated, Germany would be divided into zones and occupied by the Soviet Union, the USA and Britain, and they now accepted that there would be a fourth zone of occupation administered by the French. Similar divisions would be imposed on Berlin, Germany's capital city. The Red Army had already advanced across much of eastern Europe at the time of this summit meeting and some thought was given to the future of that part of the continent. The Yalta Declaration on Liberated Europe laid down general principles:

> The establishment of order in Europe and the rebuilding of national economic life must be achieved by processes which will enable the liberated peoples to destroy the

> last vestiges of Nazism and Fascism and to create democratic institutions of their own choice. This is a principle of the Atlantic Charter. . . .

The Atlantic Charter, drawn up in 1941 by Roosevelt and Churchill, had, however, affirmed that in their hostility to the Axis powers the USA and Britain stood by democratic principles as they were understood in the West. The 'democratic institutions' Roosevelt and Churchill had in mind at Yalta were such as existed in the USA and Britain. The Declaration on Liberated Europe went on to pledge 'free elections' in each state, and these, in the West's view, were likely to involve a choice of political parties. Stalin, on the other hand, was unlikely to allow on the Soviet doorstep elections so free that they might bring to power capitalist governments unsympathetic to the USSR.

The problem surfaced at Yalta in relation to Poland. The leaders accepted Stalin's general policy concerning Poland's boundaries, namely that Poland should be moved bodily westwards. Poland's eastern frontier with the Soviet Union would follow the Curzon Line, a boundary first put forward in 1920 by Lord Curzon, the then British Foreign Secretary, and more or less the boundary between German and Russian Poland agreed in the Nazi–Soviet Pact of 1939. In compensation, Poland would gain lands to the west from Germany, probably up to the line of the Rivers Oder and Neisse though final details were to await a peace settlement. There remained, however, the question of how this liberated Poland was to be governed, a matter vital to the security of the Soviet Union. More than a quarter of a million Soviet soldiers had died in driving the Nazis from Poland and Stalin was eager that the country should be governed by the friendly Lublin Committee of Polish partisans and communists. The USSR had recognized this new Polish government a month before the meeting at Yalta. But there were other Polish resistance leaders in the West, the London Poles, who claimed a right to share in government. They alleged that the Nazis had managed to crush the pro-West Warsaw Rising in 1944 partly because Soviet troops were slow to go to Warsaw's aid. There were therefore deep suspicions between rival Polish politicians. It was nevertheless agreed at Yalta that Poland's government should be broadened to include those who had been in exile, setting up:

> This Polish Provisional Government of National Unity . . . pledged to the holding of free and unfettered elections as soon as possible on the basis of universal suffrage and secret ballot [in which] all democratic and anti-Nazi parties shall have the right to take part and to put forward candidates.

Similar principles were outlined for the settlement of affairs in Yugoslavia.

The three leaders rounded off their work at Yalta by confirming their intention to co-operate in setting up the United Nations Organization, while Stalin undertook to declare war on Japan 'in two or three months after Germany had surrendered'.

1.3.2 The Potsdam Summit

Germany's surrender was followed by a further summit meeting of the Big Three at Potsdam, near Berlin, in July 1945. Truman represented the USA, having become President on the death of Roosevelt. During the Conference,

Fig. 1.2 The 'Big Three' at Potsdam, July 1945: Attlee (*left*) and Truman (*centre*) were Western leaders who were new to negotiating with Stalin (*right*). From left to right behind the seated leaders stood US Admiral Leahy and Foreign Ministers Bevin, Byrnes and Molotov. The negotiations at Potsdam hardly papered over the East–West divisions which were beginning to surface.

Clement Attlee replaced Churchill as Britain's Prime Minister and so took Churchill's place at Potsdam. Stalin thus had to deal with new colleagues, and his own deep suspicions of the West were to some extent mirrored by the distrust shown towards the Soviet Union by Truman. Ernest Bevin, the new British Foreign Secretary, was also wary of the ambitions of the Kremlin. The powers nevertheless agreed to set up a Council of Foreign Ministers (Bevin, Byrnes of the USA, Molotov of the USSR and ministers from France and China) to begin work on a series of peace treaties with special relevance to Europe (see section 1.5.2). Stalin meanwhile agreed that the time was near for the USSR to join the war against Japan.

The main issues of the Potsdam meeting, however, were the affairs of Germany and Poland. Further details were worked out concerning the occupation of Germany, for the total elimination of Nazism and the encouragement of democracy. Germany's ability to make war was also to be eliminated and the powers agreed that:

> In organising the German economy, primary emphasis shall be given to the development of agriculture and peaceful domestic industries.

They would treat Germany 'as a single economic unit' in spite of its division into zones of occupation, and they accepted the principle that Germany should make some payment to the Allies for the damage and losses the latter had suffered in the war. Such had been the suffering of the USSR that that country was to have the lion's share of these reparations: the Soviets were to be allowed to take reparations not only from the Soviet Zone of occupied Germany but from the Western zones as well. The West nevertheless insisted that the Soviets should send foodstuffs to Western Germany in return for some of the machinery and industrial goods sent eastwards. The East had little food to spare at this time and arguments about reparations seemed highly likely to lead to future East–West disputes. Berlin seemed likely to be a further source of controversy. The city had already been divided into four sectors of occupation, but it lay deep inside the Soviet Zone of Germany so that special arrangements were needed to give the Western powers access to the city.

On the question of Poland, the meeting at Potsdam was not able to move much beyond the position reached at Yalta. The powers confirmed their earlier agreements and looked forward to 'the holding of free and unfettered elections as soon as possible'. Again, final details of Poland's changed boundaries were left to a future peace settlement. But whatever the ideas discussed at Potsdam, in reality the division of Europe between the superpowers had begun. The West was in a weak position to influence events in eastern Europe, just as the USSR could not much influence western Europe. Stalin readily accepted that the West would determine the future of Italy, a former Axis state now within the USA's sphere of influence. Eastern Europe, however, was next to the Soviet Union, and its future was already being moulded by the Soviets.

1.4 Post-war planning: the United Nations Organization

1.4.1 Origins

The League of Nations, the world's first peace-keeping organization founded after the First World War, failed to keep the peace: the League was unable to prevent the Second World War. But almost as soon as the Second World War began so too did discussion about some new international organization which might replace the League when the war ended. Roosevelt avoided pledging the USA to join such an organization when he met Churchill in 1941 and signed the Atlantic Charter. By 1943, however, American attitudes had changed. The USA and the USSR, as well as Britain and China, gave support to the idea of a United Nations Organization when their Foreign Ministers met in Moscow.

It had been a weakness of the League of Nations that its membership was never complete. The USA had not joined the League in case it should entangle Americans in international problems from which they would prefer to stand aside. The USSR had joined the League only in 1934, at that time seeking (though not confidently) collective security against the menace of Nazi Germany. Collective security was not forthcoming and the Soviet government found Britain and France, the main members of the League, unreliable partners for purposes of joint defence. The Soviets sought their own salvation in the Nazi–Soviet Pact, and in a brief war with Finland over frontiers near Leningrad, for which the USSR was expelled from the League at the end of 1939.

The Moscow Conference of Foreign Ministers in October 1943 agreed on:

> the necessity of establishing at the earliest practicable date a general international organisation, based on the principle of the sovereign equality of all peace-loving states, and open to membership by all such states, large or small, for the maintenance of international peace and security.

The four Allies met again at Dumbarton Oaks, Washington, in 1944 for more detailed discussion of the structure of the United Nations Organization (UN). At this stage the planning was the work of the principal Allies, and at Dumbarton Oaks the USA, the USSR, Britain and China reserved to themselves and to France permanent seats on the UN Security Council (see section 1.4.2). At Yalta the Big Three agreed that each permanent member of the Council should have the right to veto its decisions. Though willing to support the new Organization, the major powers were taking care to protect their own authority. A further Conference was arranged to meet at San Francisco in April 1945. Fifty nations, all of them enemies of the Axis powers, drafted the United Nations Charter at this meeting, accepting what had been agreed at Dumbarton Oaks and Yalta and further developing the machinery of the UN. The Charter was signed in June by the UN's founder members, their number raised to 51 by the admission of Poland.

In October 1945 the UN General Assembly met for the first time in temporary premises in London. It was not intended that the Organization should be based in Europe as the League had been, since the League had come to resemble a European club. With their new-found enthusiasm for international co-operation the Americans offered hospitality to the UN, and it was soon decided to locate the UN headquarters in New York.

1.4.2 The Charter and machinery of the United Nations Organization

The aims of the United Nations were set out in the opening words of the Charter, first among them:

> to save succeeding generations from the scourge of war, which twice in our lifetime has brought untold sorrow to mankind.

The UN also intended to promote human rights, respect for international law, and 'social progress and better standards of life in larger freedom'. Its founders designed the UN to be much more than a mere peace-keeping association. They wanted to extend the functions of the former League of Nations, especially in relation to economic and social programmes to improve the well-being of mankind, and they wanted to learn from the League's experiences. Whereas the Covenant of the League had had 26 Articles, the Charter had 111. The statesmen also took care in 1945 to keep the Charter and the Organization separate from the making of a peace settlement with the Axis powers, since they were well aware of the problems that had resulted from writing the Covenant into all the treaties of the Peace of Paris after the First World War. On the surface, however, the machinery of the United Nations Organization was very similar to that of the League of Nations (see fig. 1.3).

All UN members were to be represented in the General Assembly where,

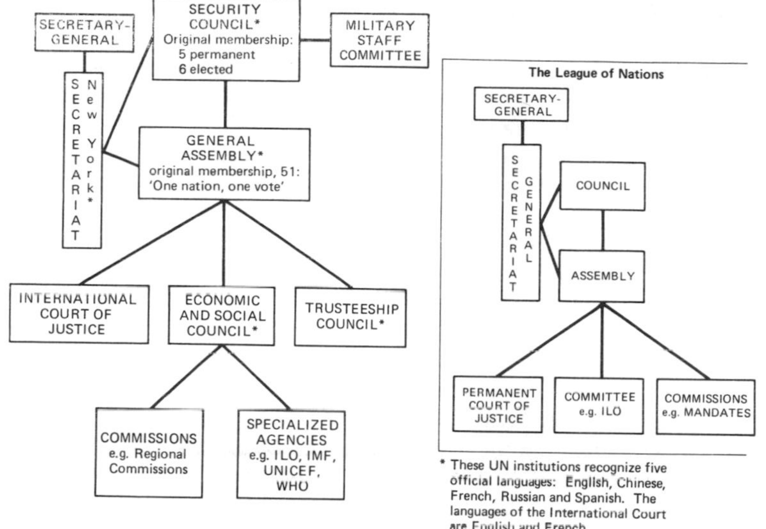

* These UN institutions recognize five official languages: English, Chinese, French, Russian and Spanish. The languages of the International Court are English and French.

Fig. 1.3 The United Nations Organization

Summary of the Charter of the United Nations Organization, 26 June 1945

Articles

1–2: Purposes and principles.

3–6: Membership, admissions, expulsion

7–22: UN institutions – the General Assembly ('may discuss any questions or matters within the scope of the present Charter').

23–32: UN institutions – the Security Council ('Members confer on the Security Council primary responsibility for the maintenance of international peace and security').

33–51: Procedure for the peaceful settlement of disputes by arbitration and, if needed, action against aggression. *Article 41*: 'measures not involving the use of armed force'. *Articles 42–51*: 'such action by air, sea, or land forces as may be necessary' to be undertaken by 'the Security Council with the assistance of the Military Staff Committee'.

52–4: Regional arrangements allowed where in keeping with the aims of the UN.

55–72: UN institutions – the co-ordination of the work of Specialized Agencies; the Economic and Social Council; work for 'the creation of conditions of stability and well-being'.

73–91: UN institutions – the Trusteeship Council ('for the administration of territories whose peoples have not yet attained a full measure of self-government'; 'a sacred trust ... to promote to the utmost ... the well-being of the inhabitants of these territories').

92–6: UN institutions – the International Court of Justice ('the principal judicial organ of the United Nations').

97–101: UN institutions – the Secretariat ('recruiting the staff on as wide a geographical basis as possible', aiming at 'the highest standards of efficiency, competence and integrity').

102–111: Miscellaneous provisions including immunities for UN representatives; transitional arrangements until the Charter came into force; provision for amending the Charter.

'Done at the San Francisco the twenty-sixth day of June, one thousand nine hundred and forty-five'.

regardless of size, each had a vote. Decisions on important issues needed a two-thirds majority; on lesser issues a simple majority would be enough. The General Assembly was to meet annually and, as the heart of the Organization, was to have oversight of virtually all the UN's work, from the admission of new members to the supervision of the budget, from the appointment of the UN Secretary-General to the maintenance of peace. In times of crisis, additional meetings of the General Assembly might be called, though much of the Assembly's routine work was usually carried on through committees.

The Security Council was specially designed for emergencies, however. It was also designed partly to balance the extravagant democracy of the General Assembly and to preserve the influence of the major powers. Originally the Security Council had eleven members, six of whom were elected by the General Assembly for two-year terms. Five seats on the Security Council were permanent, assigned from the outset to the 'Big Five' – the USA, the USSR, Britain, France and China, victorious powers in the Second World War. As decided at Yalta, each permanent member had the right of veto: no decision could be reached if a permanent member voted against it. The number of elected members rose to ten in 1965 but the permanent members remained. The Security Council also remained small enough to be summoned almost immediately in a crisis 'to ensure prompt and effective action by the United Nations'. Such action could include the imposing of sanctions on an offending state if mediation in a dispute failed. The sanctions might be economic, for instance a boycott of trade such as had been imposed by the League of Nations on Italy in 1935 for aggression against Ethiopia. They might also be military. Like the League, the UN possessed no standing army but Article 43 of the Charter made provision for raising troops when necessary:

> All members . . . undertake to make available to the Security Council . . . armed forces, assistance, and facilities, including rights of passage, necessary for the purpose of maintaining international peace and security.

Article 47 of the Charter provided for a Military Staff Committee 'to advise and assist the Security Council', the expertise of this Committee coming mainly from the Big Five. The General Assembly appeared to claim final responsibility for matters of sanctions and peace, however, when it approved the 'Uniting for Peace' Resolution in 1950. This extended the authority of the General Assembly to deal with crises when a veto paralysed proceedings in the Security Council (see section 4.5.2).

A third UN institution was to be the International Court of Justice sitting at the Hague in the Netherlands. This Court descended from the Permanent Court of Arbitration, first set up in 1901, by way of the Permanent Court of International Justice which had functioned under the League of Nations. The International Court was to have fifteen judges jointly chosen by the General Assembly and Security Council, five judges retiring every third year. The Court was to be essentially concerned with 'legal questions', and parties who allowed the Court to rule on their dispute had to agree in advance to accept its judgement as binding.

The Trusteeship Council took over the work of the League of Nations Mandates Commission, its function being to supervise the administration of trust territories. Many of these territories had been known since the end of the First World War as mandated territories (or mandates), having been put under the control of countries such as Britain and France when they were forfeited by the defeated powers of Germany and Turkey. The control of mandates was deemed to be 'a sacred trust' and the administering powers were required to prepare the peoples in the mandated territories for independence. In the meantime they were to promote the peoples' well-being. Some mandates such as Iraq had already become independent. For others such as Tanganyika, which was under British rule, new trusteeship agreements were made. The Trusteeship Council worked efficiently and the trust territories, both former mandates and new ones such as Somaliland assigned to Italy in 1950, moved smoothly towards independence until by the 1980s little remained under the Council's supervision.

There was one former mandate, however, where things ran less smoothly. South Africa refused to take out a trusteeship agreement for South West Africa, a former German colony mandated to South Africa after its capture in 1915. South Africans now declared that the territory was part of South Africa, a view the United Nations disputed. The International Court ruled against South Africa in 1950, but South Africa still rejected the trusteeship and the problem dragged on (see section 19.2.3).

While the work of the Trusteeship Council decreased with passing years, that of the Economic and Social Council (Ecosoc) remained vast. The Council was set up to handle 'international economic, social, cultural, educational, health, and related matters' as directed by the General Assembly. The eighteen members of the Council were increased to 27 in 1965, a third retiring each year. Ecosoc was assisted by Commissions which dealt with specific issues such as trade, drugs, population, human rights and the status of women. There were also regional Commissions for Africa, Asia, Europe and Latin America. Ecosoc was further intended to co-ordinate the work of the Specialized Agencies of the United Nations, concerned with various aspects of the welfare of mankind. Some of these Agencies had their origins within the League of Nations; others were entirely new.

The International Labour Organization (ILO), based in Geneva, was intended to promote the well-being of working people, member states sending on their behalf two representatives of government, one of employers and one of workers. When the League of Nations officially ceased to exist in 1946, the ILO simply went on with its work under the supervision of Ecosoc and the UN. The World Health Organization (WHO) was set up in 1948, taking over from the League's Health Organization and other international agencies, and working from Geneva like the ILO. The United Nations Relief and Rehabilitation Administration (UNRRA) dated from 1943. But UNRRA was short-lived, being wound up in 1949 after dealing with post-war emergencies such as starvation in the Balkans and the relief of refugees. For a time the International Refugee Organization (IRO) helped the latter, but it lasted only from 1948 to

1951 when its work was transferred to the Office of the United Nations High Commissioner for Refugees. Other aspects of UNRRA's work fell to various new Agencies. The United Nations International Children's Emergency Fund (UNICEF) was founded in 1946, at first caring mainly for the welfare of children in the wake of the war but eventually concentrating on children in the world's poorer countries. The Food and Agriculture Organization (FAO), with its headquarters in Rome, dated from 1945 and aimed to monitor and increase world yields of foodstuffs. The United Nations Educational, Scientific and Cultural Organization (UNESCO), based in Paris, was founded in 1946 to promote:

> collaboration among the nations through education, science, and culture in order to further universal respect for justice, for the rule of law, and for . . . human rights and fundamental freedoms.

In particular, UNESCO campaigned against illiteracy and aimed to promote education across the world. Other Specialized Agencies were mainly concerned with communications – the International Telecommunications Union (ITU), the International Civil Aviation Organization (ICAO) and the Universal Postal Union (UPU), which was already 73 years old when it became a Specialized Agency of the UN in 1947. The World Meteorological Organization (WMO), founded in the 1950s, aimed to co-ordinate weather reporting across the world.

A meeting in July 1944 at Bretton Woods, New Hampshire, in the USA, had taken steps to set up the International Monetary Fund (IMF) and the World Bank, both of which became UN Specialized Agencies. Both aimed to promote post-war reconstruction, trade and sound international finance. It was essential to make gold and currency available if trade were to flourish. Loans would also be needed to assist the recovery and development of war-torn and impoverished nations. In 1947 the General Agreement on Tariffs and Trade (GATT) helped international trade by reducing some tariffs. In 1956 a new Specialized Agency came into existence when the World Bank set up the International Finance Corporation (IFC) to make capital available to private enterprise. Increasingly, however, the post-war world grew disenchanted with the world economic order and with the part played in it by the financial institutions of the United Nations (see section 21.1). Nevertheless, the Specialized Agencies of the UN made an immeasurable contribution to the betterment of the lives of millions. In some recognition of this, the Nobel Peace Prize was in 1954 awarded to the UN High Commissioner for Refugees and in 1965 to UNICEF.

As was the League of Nations, the UN is serviced by a Secretariat, an international civil service pledged to serve the world community rather than individual nations and led by the United Nations Secretary-General. The Secretary-General is appointed for a five-year term of office by the General Assembly after recommendation by the Security Council. It is one of the Secretary-General's duties to bring to the attention of the Security Council all threats to international peace. The first Secretary-General was Trygve Lie, a Norwegian, who served from 1946 to his resignation late in 1952. Another Scandinavian, Dag Hammarskjöld of Sweden, succeeded him in 1953 but was killed in an air disaster in the Congo in 1961, part way through his second term of duty. There was argument about Hammarskjöld's successor before U Thant of Burma was installed, the major powers fearing the appointment of a Secretary-General who might be unfriendly to their interests. The USSR therefore proposed a troika system, to divide the office between three Secretaries, one pro-West, one pro-East and one non-aligned. The proposal was eventually dropped and U Thant gave general satisfaction as Secretary-General for ten years, from 1961 to 1971. The burden was such that he refused to serve longer and the office passed to Kurt Waldheim, an Austrian. The superpowers would have agreed a third term for Waldheim in 1981 and he himself was willing. China argued that there should be a new Secretary-General who was not a European, however, and vetoed Waldheim's re-election sixteen times. The USA vetoed Africa's favoured candidate, Salim Ahmed Salim of Tanzania, and after prolonged wrangling Javier Perez de Cuellar, a Peruvian, became the new Secretary-General at the end of 1981. He won general approval and was re-elected in 1986.

1.4.3 Superpower rivalry and UN membership

The UN Secretary-Generalship was not the only subject of scrutiny by the superpowers. Both the USA and the USSR were concerned that the other might muster increased voting support in the General Assembly and so the membership of the UN was slow to grow from the original 51 states. That original membership was advantageous to the USA: 21 founder-members were in the Americas, Britain and five other members of the British Commonwealth usually supported the USA, and there were also other 'Western' states such as France and the Netherlands. The admission of new UN members needed the recommendation of the Security Council and a two-thirds majority in the General Assembly. By 1950, however, of 31 states applying for admission only nine had won acceptance, among them Israel and Indonesia.

Batches of new members were admitted in 1955 and subsequent years as the result of package deals between the major powers, several eastern-European states like Hungary and Romania entering the UN in this way in 1955. But by the early 1960s the number of new states in the world was increasing rapidly, the old colonial empires being fast dismantled. By the time UN membership reached 100 in 1961, it was widely believed that admission to the UN was a badge of a nation's independence and a right which should not be denied. Ten years later the superpowers had a new worry on which to brood: that the many new nations, especially those of Africa and Asia, would build sufficient unity among themselves to use the United Nations Organization to outvote and embarrass both the USA and the USSR.

The China which vetoed Waldheim's re-election as Secretary-General was Communist China. The Chinese Communist Party (CCP) came to power in 1949 (see section 11.1.2). When the UN was founded in 1945, however, the Nationalists of the Kuomintang ruled China and it was they who occupied China's seat on the UN Security Council. In 1949 the Nationalists were driven from the Chinese mainland, taking refuge on the off-shore island of Taiwan

(Formosa), where their independence was in due course safeguarded by the USA. The USA also safeguarded Nationalist China's place in the UN, maintaining the fiction that Chiang Kai-shek, the Kuomintang leader, was one of the Big Five and denying that Communist China, led by Mao Tse-tung, should be allowed into the UN. As they had done with the USSR before 1933, the Americans refused to recognize the legality of Communist rule in China. In spite of Soviet fury and the criticism even of friends, the USA went on blocking any change in China's UN representation for almost a quarter of a century. Communist China did not gain admission and its permanent seat on the Security Council until President Nixon at last softened American policy in 1971 (see section 11.2.3(c)). Taiwan was at that time expelled from the UN, mainly as a result of the lobbying of Albania, a Marxist state firmly aligned with Communist China for most of the 1960s and 1970s.

1.5 Divided nations and a fragmented peace settlement

1.5.1 The meeting of East and West

Advancing from opposite sides against the Axis powers in the closing stages of the Second World War, Soviet and Western forces came face to face on a number of fronts. Their meeting in Germany was quickly followed by the agreed division of that country into zones of occupation (see sections 1.3 and 4.2.1). The Allies made a similar division of Austria, a country which had lost its independence when absorbed into Hitler's Great German Reich in 1938. Vienna, Austria's capital city, lay in the Soviet Zone and was divided into sectors in the same way as Berlin (see fig. 1.4). For some years after 1945 it seemed that the line between the Western and Soviet Zones of Germany and Austria also divided the whole of Europe, one part capitalist, the other communist.

In Asia, Korea was divided. Korea had been ruled by the Japanese for most of the twentieth century but was liberated at the end of the Second World War. The Big Three had agreed at Yalta that there would be temporary occupation and division of Korea, Soviet forces north of the 38th Parallel (38° north latitude), US forces south of it. As was to happen in Germany, Korea ended up with two governments and the nation was divided. Indeed there was war between the two Koreas in 1950 (see section 4.5.2).

Germany and Austria were conquered; Korea was liberated; Iran, meanwhile, was invaded and occupied in 1941 to remove German influence and to secure Iranian oilfields. The invading forces were British and Soviet, the British occupying the south, the Soviets the north. When Nazi Germany was defeated the British withdrew but the Soviets lingered. Stalin showed particular interest in Azerbaijan in the north-west of Iran where the people differed from other Iranians, their culture having more in common with that of their kinsfolk on the Soviet side of the Soviet–Iranian border. The Tudeh Party wanted to make Azerbaijan independent of Iran. The West noted that the Tudeh Party was Marxist and it was assumed that the Soviets were fomenting unrest, aiming

Fig. 1.4 Occupation zones in Germany and Austria and German losses, 1945

to extend Soviet authority. Britain and the USA protested fiercely and referred the matter to the UN. Under such pressure Soviet forces left Iran and some three years later, in 1949, the Tudeh Party was suppressed by the Iranian government.

The Soviet Union was also unsuccessful in trying to set up a joint Soviet–Iranian Oil Company, to exploit oil deposits in northern Iran and to balance the considerable influence the West already had in Iran through the Anglo–Iranian Oil Company and other enterprises. Having rebuffed the Soviets, Iranian opinion began to turn against the West too. Violent anti-British and anti-American agitation helped to install Dr Mohammed Mussadiq as Iran's Prime Minister in 1951. He immediately nationalized the country's oil industry, expelling foreign interests. The mood failed to last and Mussadiq's overthrow in 1954 enabled British Petroleum and other Western companies again to share (with the National Iranian Oil Company) in the exploitation of Iran's oil.

It seemed in 1946 that the West had successfully wrested Iran from the grasp of the Soviets, renewing its own influence there. The early 1950s, on the other hand, revealed a different problem – local nationalism which resented all foreign interference in the affairs of an independent nation. That the West was not wanted in Iran was a message spelt out even more forcefully at the end of the 1970s (see section 20.2).

1.5.2 Peace-making in Europe

A Peace Conference met in Paris in late July 1946 for the wider discussion of the peace proposals being made by the Council of Foreign Ministers set up at Potsdam (see section 1.3.2). Twenty-one nations attended the Conference but, when it broke up in October 1946, only the Council of Foreign Ministers held further meetings to draft a number of treaties, which were finally signed in February 1947. The main decisions were those of the USA, the USSR, Britain and to a lesser extent France. The treaties were imposed on Italy and the former eastern European supporters of the Axis – Bulgaria, Finland, Hungary and Romania. This concluded the first phase of peace-making after the Second World War. Relations between East and West were as yet too unsettled for similar treaties to be made with Germany and Austria, while the USA had begun to treat Japan as a special case, the responsibility of the USA itself rather than of the Allies generally.

The Peace Treaty between the Allies and Italy took account of the fact that Italy had changed sides during the war and fought against Nazi Germany. Italy had nevertheless to make reparations to the Soviet Union and to the victims of Fascism, modest payments to Albania and Ethiopia (Mussolini's conquests, now liberated), and more substantial ones to Greece and Yugoslavia. Greece also received the Dodecanese Islands from Italy, while Yugoslavia gained Fiume and its surrounding district, territories which had been in dispute since the First World War. The port and territory of Trieste were divided, and after Allied occupation were eventually partitioned between Italy and Yugoslavia in 1954. Italy also had to renounce:

> all right and title to the Italian territorial possessions in Africa, i.e. Libya, Eritrea and Italian Somaliland.

This was the Italian colonial empire, which was older than Fascism. It was typical of the piecemeal nature of the peace settlement after the Second World War that, although these ex-colonies were removed from Italy's control, other decisions about their future were postponed. The Peace Treaty with Italy was completed with provisions for eliminating Fascism, limiting the country's armed forces and upholding human rights.

Similar provisions were included in the Treaties with Bulgaria, Finland, Hungary and Romania, all of which were signed on 10 February 1947, the same day as the Treaty with Italy. All these states had to pay reparations, chiefly to the Soviet Union although Czechoslovakia, Greece and Yugoslavia also benefited. Figure 1.5 shows the main territorial changes made by these Treaties. There were in addition minor restorations of territory, some of them undoing changes the Nazis had encouraged. Hungary, for example, restored small areas

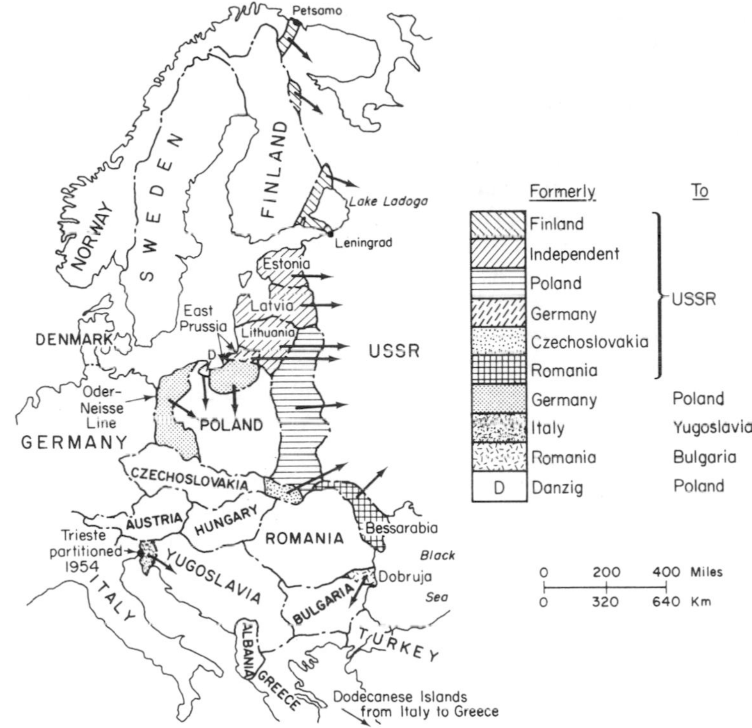

Fig. 1.5 Central and Eastern Europe post-1945

of land to Czechoslovakia and Romania, while Bulgaria made small concessions to Greece and Yugoslavia.

Figure 1.5 also shows the changes to Poland's boundaries and to what before 1940 had been the Baltic states of Estonia, Latvia and Lithuania. These changes resulted not from general peace treaties but from post-war arrangements made by the USSR. Poland was effectively moved westwards as had been discussed at Yalta (see section 1.3.1), so that Germany ceased to include any lands east of the Oder–Neisse Line. By general agreement of the Allies all Germans resident in Czechoslovakia, Hungary and Poland were uprooted and sent west of the Oder–Neisse Line into Germany, in case discontented German minorities in other countries should create further trouble of the sort Hitler had been able to exploit in the 1930s. Many of the territorial changes proved to be in the interests of the Soviet Union, and the Soviets' intention to maintain stability and quiet in eastern Europe was further emphasized when they mediated in the long-standing dispute between Czechoslovakia and Poland about the town of Teschen, the Soviet award favouring Czechoslovakia.

The Council of Foreign Ministers expected to go on with its work and to draft treaties of peace with Austria and Germany. It soon became clear, however, that little common ground existed between the superpowers or between West and East on which to build a settlement. The idea of signing further peace treaties in Europe gradually withered (see Unit 4). In 1955, however, there was suddenly sufficient goodwill for the Allies to fulfil the aim – first set down in 1943 – of recreating a 'free and independent Austria'. Independent Austria was reborn when its full sovereignty was restored in the Austrian State Treaty of May 1955 (see section 4.6). By the end of that year all occupation forces had been withdrawn from Austria.

1.5.3 Peace-making in Asia

A peace treaty with Japan, the Treaty of San Francisco, was eventually signed in September 1951. A Conference of powers which had declared war on Japan was summoned to San Francisco by the USA. The Treaty they signed was drafted by the Americans though influenced by talks the Americans had had with their Allies. The Soviet Union, Czechoslovakia and Poland all refused to sign the Treaty, arguing that there had been too little consultation and that since 1945 the USA had managed Japan's affairs and its occupation almost alone (see section 12.1). The Soviet Union had nevertheless regained the southern half of Sakhalin, earlier lost to Japan in the Russo–Japanese War of 1904–5, and had seized the Kurile Islands, territorial changes to which the Allies had agreed at Yalta.

China was not even represented at San Francisco, in spite of having been longest at war with Japan. In 1949 the mainland of China came under the government of the Chinese Communist Party, much to America's dismay (see sections 1.4.3 and 11.1). The USA solved the problem of whom to invite to San Francisco by inviting neither Chinese Communists nor Chinese Nationalists. It was therefore not until 1978 that a peace treaty was signed between Communist China and Japan.

The Treaty of San Francisco in 1951 treated Japan comparatively leniently, aiming to settle 'questions still outstanding' so that the Allies and Japan might:

> as sovereign equals, co-operate in friendly association to promote their common welfare and to maintain international peace and security.

Japan was obliged to give up its claims to Korea, Taiwan (Formosa), Sakhalin and the Kurile Islands, and to renounce 'all special rights and interests in China'. It was also to forfeit its interests in mandated territories in the Pacific. Although Japan accepted liability for reparations, the details were left to be settled later. Nor did Japan suffer the same military limitations as were imposed on Axis powers in Europe. The USA had already ensured that under its new constitution in 1947 Japan had given up armed forces (see section 12.1.1). By 1951 the Americans wished to avoid international restrictions here. The Korean War had begun in 1950, and in American eyes Japan was now increasingly important as a bulwark against communism in Asia. Indeed, on the same day that the Treaty of San Francisco was signed, the USA made a Security Treaty with Japan which permitted US troops to remain in Japan when the occupation ended as a result of the peace settlement. In only a few years Japan had moved from being the Axis enemy of the USA to being a sort of ally against the Soviet Union and China. Such was the pace of change in the post-war world.

UNIT 2

The superpowers: 1 – the USA, champion of capitalist freedom

2.1 The USA at the end of the Second World War

The United States of America emerged from the Second World War with its industry and farmlands untouched by enemy action and its economy stronger than before the war. In 1945 the USA's gross national product[G] stood at 213 billion dollars, compared with 91 billion on the eve of the Depression some fifteen years earlier. Part of the increase was due to inflation and the fall in the value of money. Nevertheless, it soon became apparent that the average American income was twice the British and some seven times that in the USSR. In 1945 more than half of the world's motor vehicles were to be found in the USA; some 40 million were registered there by 1950. The USA had an even larger proportion of the world's telephones and refrigerators. Although wealth was unevenly distributed and hideous slums and poverty existed in cities like New York, the USA was clearly the world's richest country. Moreover, it had a well-established system of democracy and a generally stable society.

Americans were nevertheless uneasy at the end of the war. They feared that wartime economic growth might not last, and that the USA might return to the Depression years of the 1930s with their high unemployment. The death of Franklin D. Roosevelt in April 1945 seemed to leave a void in the country's leadership. Roosevelt had been the US President since 1933, re-elected in 1936, 1940 and 1944. Since he died in office, he was succeeded by his Vice-President, Harry S. Truman, whose experience was very limited and who was little known to the American people as a whole. It would be Truman's task to convert the USA back to a peacetime economy, demobilizing about twelve million servicemen and steering a course between inflation and unemployment. At the same time, Americans were disturbed about the bombs exploded at Hiroshima and Nagasaki and the dangerous new world which lay ahead. To their deep-rooted suspicions of socialism – which seemed to threaten American traditions of competition and self-help – were now added anxieties about the Soviet Union. Wartime propaganda had played on the idea of two worlds, the light represented by a crusading USA and the dark by the Axis. The image was all too

REUNION DINNER

Fig. 2.1 John Bull and Uncle Sam in 1946: Illingworth's cartoon in *Punch* made its own comment on the contrast between the post-war austerity in Britain and the abundance of the USA.

easily extended: Americans were soon conjuring up a new darkness – the world of Marxism and the Soviet Union.

Some Americans had other problems, however: the blacks and other minority groups such as the Indians formed a disproportionate section of the country's poor, and the war had made many of them more aware of the discrimination from which they suffered. Having fought for freedom against the Axis powers, many servicemen returned home less willing to accept inequalities which had previously been taken for granted in the USA.

The struggle for equality and civil rights was to some extent handicapped by the US constitution with its 'separation of powers' and concern for 'checks and balances'. The constitution dated from 1787, 'amendments' having been added from time to time. It was a federal system: the US federal government was centred on Washington but, in addition, each state such as California and Alabama had its own state government to deal with many of the state's affairs. Republicans, more so than Democrats, were always anxious to safeguard state rights against federal interference. Both at federal and state levels, the system aimed to separate the powers of the executive, legislative and judiciary, using one to check the others – so that none should be too strong – for the good of the American people. At the federal level this meant that the President (the country's chief executive officer) was often checked by Congress (the legislative or law-making body sitting in two houses, the Senate and the House of Representatives). Both were watched by the judiciary, in particular the Supreme Court which, when a case was brought before it, could declare an action 'unconstitutional' and thus illegal. Making new laws was therefore less easy in the USA than in countries such as Britain, where the Prime Minister almost always had support in and control of Parliament.

The President is elected at four-year intervals by a complex process which finally produces an electoral college. This is made up of representatives of the states in proportion to population: for example in 1980, in a college of 538 members, 41 represented New York, 27 Pennsylvania. It is the duty of the electoral college to choose the President. The new President takes office in the January following the election. Thus, Roosevelt was elected in 1932 and took office in 1933. His re-election on three occasions caused unease and, in 1951, an amendment to the constitution known as Article XXII restricted further Presidents to two terms of office.

Congress is comprised of two separately elected houses; the Senate is made up of two senators from each state, serving six-year terms, while the members of the House of Representatives are elected every two years in proportion to population. The President has therefore to deal with a House of Representatives whose members may change in the middle of his term of office in 'mid-term elections'. In 1946, Truman's problems were increased when mid-term elections returned a Republican House of Representatives. When he was elected President in his own right in 1948, his way was eased by a Democrat majority in the House. Even so, Truman still had difficulty persuading Congress to accept his legislation. Although Democrats had more liberal traditions in favouring social reform, Southern Democrats from states such as Alabama were often deeply conservative and likely to join with the Republicans in blocking changes which would involve government spending or curtail white privileges in relation to blacks. Effective laws to extend civil liberties therefore came only slowly (see section 2.3).

2.2 The swings of the political pendulum

Table 2.1 shows how the US Presidency alternated between Democrats and Republicans after the Second World War. It was not unusual for presidential elections to attract far more than the two main candidates, but seldom did any

Table 2.1 Federal elections in the United States

Year of presidential election	President elected			Main candidate defeated			House of Representatives
	Name (Party)	State votes*	Popular vote (millions)	Name (Party)	State votes*	Popular vote (millions)	
1944	Roosevelt (D)‡	432	25.6	Dewey (R)	99	22.0	D
							R†
1948	Truman (D)	303	24.1	Dewey (R)	189	22.0	D
1952	Eisenhower (R)	442	33.9	Stevenson (D)	89	27.3	R
							D†
1956	Eisenhower (R)	457	35.6	Stevenson (D)	73	26.0	D
1960	Kennedy (D)‡	303	34.2	Nixon (R)	219	34.1	D
1964	Johnson (D)	486	43.1	Goldwater (R)	52	27.2	D
1968	Nixon (R)	301	31.8	Humphrey (D)	191	31.3	D
				Wallace (I)	46	9.9	
1972	Nixon (R)§	521	47.2	McGovern (D)	17	29.2	D
1976	Carter (D)	297	40.8	Ford (R)	241	39.1	D
1980	Reagan (R)	489	43.2	Carter (D)	49	34.9	D
1984	Reagan (R)	525	52.8	Mondale (D)	13	36.6	D
1988	Bush (R)	426	48.9	Dukakis (D)	111	41.8	D

D – Democrat
R – Republican
I – Independent

* Votes in electoral college (see section 2.1)
† Mid-term elections (see section 2.1)
‡ Died while in office
§ Resigned from office

except Democrats and Republicans win votes in the electoral college. George Wallace was an exception, standing for election in 1968 as an American Independent, in defence of what he regarded as traditional American values and in fierce opposition to civil liberties for blacks and liberal reform in general. Wallace had become Governor of Alabama in 1963 and he attracted strong support, especially in the American South. Socialist candidates for the Presidency, on the other hand, were lucky to attract even 100 000 popular votes; Norman Thomas fared the best when he won 139 000 votes in 1948.

Truman's election in 1948 was one of the most surprising events of his Presidency. He had succeeded Roosevelt as President in 1945, only four months after becoming Vice-President and with little experience of office. Opinion polls in 1948 suggested that he would be soundly beaten by the Republican, Thomas E. Dewey. Instead, he won a new term in the White House (the official residence of the US President), though his Presidency was clouded by struggles with Congress which obstructed much of his legislation, by the illiberal hysteria of McCarthyism (see section 2.3.2) and by confrontation and conflict overseas (see Unit 4).

When the election of 1952 was held, the USA was still involved in war in Korea (see section 4.5.2). The Democrats had held the Presidency for twenty years, and a swing of the pendulum was overdue. The Republicans enlisted Dwight D. Eisenhower as their candidate though he had shown little interest in politics. His background was that of a soldier, not a politician. He won distinction in the Second World War, rising to the supreme command of Allied forces in Europe, and in 1951 became Supreme Commander of the forces of the North Atlantic Treaty Organization (NATO), charged with the defence of the West against communism. Americans found these reassuring qualifications in 1952 and, with the slogan 'I like Ike', the Republican electoral machine made Eisenhower President.

The Korean War ended, McCarthyism faded, and Eisenhower was re-elected in 1956, winning a second clear victory over the Democrat, Adlai Stevenson. The tide was running with the Republicans. In the 1950s economies generally were recovering from the Second World War: confidence was returning and prosperity spreading. Even in international affairs tension seemed to have eased and Nikita Khrushchev, the Soviet leader, began to talk of 'peaceful co-existence' with the West (see section 3.6). The years of Eisenhower's Presidency were comparatively tranquil. Eisenhower readily fell in with the Republican tradition of interfering little with the country's economy and the lives of its citizens. He had no plans for ambitious reform, social upheaval or dramatic foreign initiatives. His administration was benign and, on the whole, unexciting.

John F. Kennedy, who won the Democratic nomination for the election of 1960 and went on narrowly to defeat the Republican Richard Nixon, offered a style of Presidency different from Eisenhower's. At 43, he was the USA's youngest President. Furthermore, he was a Roman Catholic of Irish descent in an America usually dominated by white Anglo-Saxon Protestants (WASPs). He was known to sympathize with minority groups and the underprivileged, and he favoured active leadership, confident in the power of government to make beneficial changes. On taking office in January 1961, he called not only on Americans but on people everywhere:

> Man holds in his mortal hands the power to abolish all forms of human poverty and all threats to human life. . . . The trumpet summons us [to] . . . a struggle against the common enemies of man: tyranny, poverty, disease, and war itself. . . . And so, my fellow Americans: ask not what your country can do for you – ask what you can do for your country. My fellow citizens of the world: ask not what America will do for you, but what together we can do for the freedom of man.

At home, Kennedy outlined the challenge of crossing what he termed the 'New Frontier' to a more just society. Abroad, he offered the Alliance for Progress – signed in 1961 to help develop other countries in the Americas – and the Peace Corps of skilled volunteers to assist developing nations in general. At the same time, however, US involvement in Vietnam increased and there was a tense confrontation with the Soviet Union over missiles in Cuba (see sections 13.2.1 and 13.2.2). Handicapped by the 'checks' of the US constitution, Kennedy also found it difficult to pass his planned laws for reform (see section 2.3).

In November 1963 the President visited Dallas, Texas. While driving through the city streets he was shot and killed. Kennedy was the fourth US President to be murdered in office, and his death illustrated the violence which preyed on American society. Many citizens now carried arms, taking advantage of the easy availability of weapons and lax gun laws. Lee Harvey Oswald was arrested in connection with Kennedy's death but he too was assassinated before coming to trial, and the mysteries about the President's assassination have persisted. In the same decade Robert Kennedy, the President's younger brother and his Attorney-General, was murdered when campaigning for the Presidency in 1968. Only two months earlier, Martin Luther King, a moderate black leader, had been killed when campaigning for civil liberties in Tennessee. During the presidential election campaign of 1972, George Wallace was shot and left paralysed. In 1981, a gunman wounded Ronald Reagan almost as soon as he was declared President. Such violence disfigured US politics. In the case of John Kennedy it cut short the Presidency of a leader who had promised much but whose brief term in office produced not much more than rhetoric and inspiration. As in 1945, the Presidency now passed to the Vice-President, and Kennedy was succeeded by Lyndon B. Johnson.

Johnson inherited a mixed legacy. The USA was growing increasingly violent, as urban outbreaks and race riots were soon to demonstrate. The unrest was partly due to the USA's involvement in Vietnam, where Johnson tried desperately to win the war. He also tried with some success to pilot Kennedy's planned reforms through Congress, and to keep up the attack on inequality and injustice with his own programme for a 'Great Society'. By 1968, however, he was a broken man, and he declined to stand for re-election. He had easily won the election of 1964, defeating a Republican candidate who was far too right-wing even by the standards of conservative America, but in 1968 many voters were bitter and disillusioned. The New Frontier and the Great Society had not cured the USA's social problems; civil liberties had not ended racial problems nor prevented upheaval, arson and violence in the centres of urban decay. The continuing bloody stalemate in Vietnam caused American liberals anxiety and moral anguish and frustrated American conservatives since an anti-communist victory seemed out of reach. Compared with 1964, the Democrats lost twelve million votes and their candidate, Hubert Humphrey, was defeated by the Republican Richard Nixon, while Wallace, the Independent, made an unusual impact as a third candidate. The Democrats nevertheless kept control of the House of Representatives.

Nixon aimed to lead Americans into quieter waters than those of the 1960s. With skill rather than honour he withdrew the US from Vietnam, and he made impressive progress towards improving international relations (see sections 13.4.2 and 18.4.2). At home, society became less turbulent, though there was now a background of economic difficulties. Earlier political failures and doubts about Nixon's personal qualities seemed to have been overcome when he won a massive victory and re-election in 1972.

Almost at once the President's triumph began to turn sour. A scandal grew up which became known as the Watergate Affair, taking its name from the Watergate buildings in Washington which housed the Democrats' campaign headquarters. These headquarters had been illegally entered by Nixon's supporters, members of CREEP (the Campaign to Re-elect the President), who planted 'bugs' (microphones) and rifled through files. When the evidence began to come to light, Nixon tried to protect his staff by claiming 'executive privilege'. That failed to save them from prosecution and eventual imprisonment but in the meantime, in summer 1973, attention began to focus on the President himself. Nixon was pressed to release tapes of White House conversations which might have cleared up the question of his own knowledge of CREEP's activities. When he resisted, there were allegations of a cover-up, and when tapes eventually reached the Senate they seemed incomplete. There had been further embarrassment for Nixon in October 1973 when his Vice-President, Spiro Agnew, was forced to resign, enmeshed in scandals about corruption and tax evasion. Nixon himself was now under close scrutiny. Under threat of impeachment[G], he chose to resign in August 1974, to avoid legal action and further disgrace. He was America's first President to resign office.

Vice-President Gerald R. Ford thus took over from Nixon, less than a year after taking over from Agnew. Ford had to wrestle with economic crisis (see sections 2.4.2 and 21.1) as well as the aftermath of the Watergate Affair, and when he tried to win re-election in 1976 he faced an electorate tired of national politicians who so often brought disappointing results. Ford had not added to his popularity when he had granted Nixon a full pardon, and he had not shown great abilities as President. The Republicans nevertheless stood by him though the Democrats had won sweeping victories in the mid-term elections in 1974 and further Republican disasters seemed inevitable. In fact Ford did well, losing only narrowly to James (Jimmy) Carter.

Carter had a political background, but in Georgia – where he became Governor in 1971 – rather than in Washington. He made the most of his homely career as peanut farmer as well as politician. As President, he took a lively interest in human rights, fiercely criticizing the Marxist powers. But his Presidency coincided with many economic difficulties and, though expressing sympathy with the underprivileged, his domestic achievements disappointed Democrat voters. He also appeared accident-prone, humiliated over affairs in Iran (see section 20.2) and seemingly involved in a new Cold War with the Soviet Union (see section 21.2). Though he had some success in helping to bring together Egypt and Israel (see section 18.2.3), he looked in vain for some achievement which might help to bring his re-election in 1980. America's mood had by now changed again. The voters rejected another period of Carter's administration. Though they still returned a Democrat House of Representatives, they responded decisively to the appeal of the Republican Ronald Reagan.

Reagan was a staunch conservative, like many Republicans a strong believer in non-interference in economic and social affairs. He argued that the powers of government were overrated, and that not much could or should be done by government to try to cure the USA of its economic ills, apart from deregulation and tax-cutting (see section 2.4). Reagan was already 69 when he sought the Presidency, but he retained some of the glamour of his former career as a film star. He was also – like Carter – a man formerly remote from Washington, having been a successful Governor of California. Democrats such as Edward Kennedy, younger brother of the former President, alleged that Reagan's economic ideas ('Reaganomics') were naïve, and there were charges that his outlook on international affairs was also too simplistic, that he was ready to see only the light world of American freedoms and the dark world of communism. The margin of Reagan's victory over Carter was certainly decisive, but the lack of enthusiasm shown by many voters during the campaign suggested that Carter had perhaps done more to lose the election than Reagan had done to win it. Reagan was nevertheless re-elected in 1984 with massive popular support, helped by his folksy image at home and tough-talking abroad. Except for the unemployed and those dependent on state welfare, Reagan's Presidency seemed to have brought some renewed prosperity. Americans chose to disregard the President's age and to ignore an alarming deficit in the balance of payments, though in 1986 the White House was shaken by conflicts with Congress and scandals involving the sale of arms to Iran, murky deals over US hostages in Lebanon and even murkier payments to anti-communist rebels in Nicaragua (see section 21.2). It was perhaps little comfort to Reagan that Nixon came forward to praise his honesty and morality.

2.3 United States society

2.3.1 The land of freedom and opportunity

The population of the USA rose from about 150 million at the end of the Second World War to over 230 million in the early 1980s. Part of the increase was due to continuing immigration. Immigration was by no means uncontrolled by 1945, but it was the boast of Americans that theirs was the land of opportunity and of the free. Millions of Americans were of recent foreign origin. In 1960, for example, almost one American in five had been born outside the USA, or had at least one parent who had been. Among Europeans, a million and a quarter US citizens had been born in Italy, almost a million in Germany and nearly 700 000 in Russia. Half a million had been born in Asia, and more than that in Mexico.

An increasing proportion of Americans lived in towns and cities, growing prosperity going hand in hand with urbanization. The cities always housed vast numbers of low-paid industrial workers in crowded tenement-houses, but the problems of such areas multiplied in the second half of the twentieth century. After 1945, the movement of blacks from South to North speeded up. Many were descended from the slaves who had worked the plantations, and they went northwards in search of work, opportunity and greater equality. But cities such as New York, overcrowded and under-financed, were beginning to decay, their poorer areas turning into black ghettos. Here lack of purchasing power forced millions to live in atrocious slum conditions. Unemployment and low incomes, a social-security system very limited by most European standards, and a fiercely competitive society meant that in the richest country in the world millions lived in need and squalor. Such conditions bred resentment, turning the 1960s into a particularly turbulent decade.

The freedoms which most Americans enjoyed and cherished, however, included those of speech, association, occupation and movement. There were few restraints on US citizens and, with money, they were able to enjoy greater liberties and a standard of living in advance of most peoples elsewhere. Their own success and comfortable living testified to millions the advantages of American citizenship. Shortly after the Second World War, the USA was consuming about 40 per cent of the world's energy and far more than its share of almost all the world's resources.

The freedoms of some Americans were much restricted, however. There had long been a streak of intolerance in US society, liable to show itself in vindictive and sometimes violent action against those regarded as 'un-American'. The Ku Klux Klan, a racist organization, was formed in 1865 in protest against the ending of the American's liberty to own slaves. The Klan was revived in the 1920s to do battle with every alleged threat to 'pure Americanism', not only blacks and Jews but also, according to members in Kansas:

> every criminal, every gambler, every thug, every libertine, every girl-ruiner, every home-wrecker, every wife-beater, every dope-peddler, every crooked politician, every pagan papist priest . . . every Roman-controlled newspaper, every hyphenated American, every lawless alien.

The Klan claimed a membership of well over four million – mainly WASPs – among whom were extremists not above lynching their victims. Other WASPs condemned the Klan but many still feared and disliked what they thought un-American. This bred a hatred not only of communism but also of trade unions, strikes and many forms of co-operation. At the end of the Second

World War, the narrow-mindedness of many Americans was at odds with the pride they took in the freedom of the individual and, to many observers, America's seemed a harsh society.

2.3.2 A streak of intolerance

Truman's Presidency witnessed the sort of anxieties which increased WASP intolerance. Fear of communism was uppermost, partly encouraged by the government itself in order to gain support for its strong policies towards the Soviet Union (see section 4.1). Every alleged success for the communists thus added to the fears of US citizens. The result was a period of anti-communist witch-hunting which reached its peak in McCarthyism - named after Joseph McCarthy, Senator for Wisconsin, who began in February 1950 to make damaging allegations about communists in important offices. In 1949 the Soviet Union had begun successfully to make atomic bombs and China had installed a Communist government, so that US anxieties were now acute. The Korean War began in June 1950 and this added fuel to McCarthy's flames.

Loyalty tests had helped prepare the way for McCarthy within the USA. A Soviet spy-ring had been found in Canada in 1946 and Truman sought to secure himself against Republican charges of being 'soft on communists' by setting up machinery to review the loyalty of government employees. In 1948 Alger Hiss - who had worked in the US diplomatic service and accompanied Roosevelt to the summit meeting at Yalta - was accused of handing state papers to a communist. He was eventually tried for perjury, Richard Nixon being one of his prosecutors, and sent to prison. By that time, 1950, the loyalty tests had resulted in the dismissal of about two hundred government employees and the resignation of another two thousand, though nearly three million had been cleared.

Truman was having some problems in curbing illiberal opinion. Congress insisted on passing the Taft–Hartley Act in 1947 and the McCarran Act in 1950, both overruling the President's opposition. The Taft-Hartley Act came when the Republicans won control of both houses of Congress and seized their opportunity to reverse some of Roosevelt's legislation concerning trade unions. The Act forbade certain sorts of strikes (for example, by government employees) and required a pause (a 'cooling-off period') before strikes began. It outlawed closed shops (where workpeople were forced to join a trade union), limited what unions could spend on political campaigning and laid them open to legal actions. Both Roosevelt and Truman had hoped to encourage trade unionism to help the less privileged, but Truman himself used the Taft–Hartley Act against the miners in 1950 and the restrictions on American unions were still in force in the 1980s. The McCarran Act dealt with internal security and imposed restrictions on known communists, eleven of whom had been jailed in 1949 for conspiracy. Truman objected to the sweeping provisions of the Act, protesting to the House of Representatives that:

> the great bulk of them are not directed toward the real and present dangers that exist from communism. Instead of striking blows at communism, they would strike blows

at our own liberties and at our position in the forefront of those working for freedom in the world.

McCarthy rather than Truman, however, was now making the running, inflaming the American public's fears of communism. Early in 1950 the British made public the betrayal of atomic secrets to the Russians by Klaus Fuchs, a leading scientist. Three years later the Americans sent to the electric chair Julius and Ethel Rosenberg, a married couple alleged to have passed similar secrets to the Soviets during the wartime alliance between the US and the USSR. Not everyone was convinced of the case against the Rosenbergs, whose deaths perhaps owed a good deal to the hysteria McCarthy had aroused. McCarthy's tactics were to accuse and smear without much concern for evidence. He seized attention in February 1950 by suggesting there were communists in the State Department – 57 Party members and another 205 non-Party members. The precise charge was unclear but investigation found no communists whatsoever. McCarthy meanwhile rushed on to further scares, smearing leading

Fig. 2.2 Senator Joseph McCarthy found no difficulty in looking at himself in the mirror, though his anti-communist witch-hunt threatened the careers of thousands of innocent Americans and besmirched the good name of the USA.

Democrats such as George Marshall and Dean Acheson; military men such as Robert Stevens, Secretary of the Army; intellectuals McCarthy called 'twisted-thinking eggheads'; and people in all walks of life. The anxieties he encouraged helped Eisenhower and the Republicans to win the election of 1952, and in 1953 McCarthy became chairman of investigations on behalf of the Senate.

Bullying and humiliating those he accused before television cameras, McCarthy began to arouse a new unease, since his witch-hunting was obviously undermining human rights. When he began to make charges about the army, he alienated the new President. In December 1954 the Senate itself censured McCarthy for conduct which 'tended to bring the Senate into dishonour and disrepute'. By that time the Korean War was over and international relations seemed a little less tense. Stalin had died in March 1953 and the Soviet Union appeared busy with its own internal problems. There therefore seemed less need for McCarthy. His career ended abruptly and he died in 1957. Americans felt some sense of shame about what one critic called McCarthy's 'reckless cruelty', and some sympathy with his innocent victims, but opposition to communism and distrust of trade unions remained widespread, together with hostility easily redirected to whatever seemed un-American. Like the Ku Klux Klan, intolerance continued to surface from time to time in American society.

2.3.3 Black Americans and civil rights

Low pay, poor housing, bleak job prospects and limited opportunities made it obvious that even after the Second World War black Americans were generally much worse off than white Americans. As well as material disadvantages, most of the USA's fifteen million blacks faced racial discrimination. Many Southern whites openly treated blacks as inferior human beings, the descendants of the slaves their ancestors had brought from Africa. By 1945 several million blacks had moved to the North in search of work and dignity. Only too often, however, they found dead-end jobs, or none at all, and ended up in city slums.

From Roosevelt onwards, US Presidents tried with varying degrees of enthusiasm and success to improve the lot of the nation's blacks and of other deprived minorities, such as Indians and Puerto Ricans. It was mainly a struggle for civil rights – to ensure that the minorities had the equal rights laid down for all Americans in the constitution. There were limits to what could be achieved by new laws. Indeed, part of the problem lay in actually enforcing existing laws, or clarifying them where they had become clouded in arguments about state rights as compared with federal authority. Most of all, however, what needed to be changed was the attitude of prejudiced whites, something which was likely to happen only slowly but an area in which the authorities could at least provide an example. But blacks too needed to change, to throw off feelings of inferiority and to raise their expectations. The National Association for the Advancement of Colored People (NAACP), founded as early as 1909, soon became a mainly black movement. In the 1950s and 1960s it was a powerful force in the hands of Martin Luther King – a Baptist minister from Alabama – educating both blacks and whites as to what was at issue in the movement towards civil rights.

Truman achieved less in his sphere than he hoped for, but he did set up a Committee on Civil Rights which highlighted the extent of the problem. In the South, blacks were often robbed of their rights, for example being prevented from voting by the imposition of literacy tests and legalistic arguments about nationality. In a sort of American 'apartheid'[G], blacks were often segregated from whites, for example in separate schools and separate areas of buses and cafés. In the North, discrimination was less organized, but almost everywhere blacks ended up with poorer opportunities and facilities. For instance, living in the most deprived neighbourhoods in the North, the blacks usually attended the poorest schools and seemed trapped in a circle of poverty and pessimism. Congress blocked whatever Truman might have hoped to achieve by new laws, but he put his weight behind the employment and promotion of blacks in government service. His main achievement was the beginning of the desegregation of the armed forces (over which the President had direct authority): servicemen would no longer be separated into units on the basis of colour.

Eisenhower went on with Truman's work, but there was now growing interest in civil rights for the minorities and the pace quickened. In 1954 the Supreme Court issued an important judgement in the case of *Brown* v. *The Board of Education of Topeka*, ruling that segregated schools were illegal since black schools were inferior to white:

> In the field of public education, the doctrine of 'separate but equal' has no place. Separate educational facilities are inherently unequal.

Almost at once, Martin Luther King organized a boycott of buses in Montgomery, Alabama. His protest was against segregated seating and more specifically the arrest of Rosa Parks, who had refused to give up her seat to a white passenger. King favoured the non-violent tactics with which Mohandas Gandhi had protested against injustice in South Africa and British India and, by depriving the bus company of revenue when they walked instead of riding, his supporters won a major victory for blacks.

Eisenhower took the campaign a little further by securing Civil Rights Acts in 1957 and 1960. The first set up a Commission on Civil Rights, to watch over and try to enforce minority rights. The second aimed to protect black voting rights and to curb the activities of racists. Such Acts were very mild. It was Eisenhower's difficulty that many conservative Democrats and Republicans in the South, whom he had no wish to offend, staunchly supported white superiority. Authorities in the South were also slow to carry out the desegregation of schools, and matters came to a head at Little Rock, Arkansas, in 1957. Nine black children were kept out of a 'white' school by a mob of bigoted whites and by state troops. Eisenhower sent federal troops to ensure that the children were admitted but the troops seemed not to have been sent as crusaders for civil rights. Eisenhower explained rather uneasily:

> Mob rule cannot be allowed to override the decisions of our courts. Now let me make it very clear that federal troops are not being used to relieve local and state authorities of their primary duty to preserve . . . peace and order . . . .

The episode at Little Rock was only one of many struggles to get rid of segregation. Kennedy in 1962 had to send troops to secure the admission of James Meredith, a black student, to the University of Mississippi. In 1963 he had to take similar action at the University of Alabama where Governor Wallace was still trying to resist federal authority and racial equality. Meanwhile, the NAACP fought further court cases and, in 1960, the year of Kennedy's election, King and his followers launched new campaigns of popular action. They held sit-ins in places from which blacks were allegedly barred, for example cafés, and 'freedom rides' in which blacks and white sympathizers ignored rules about seating on buses. King insisted on non-violence but confrontations nevertheless occurred. In 1963 King's supporters marched on Washington, holding a rally a quarter of a million strong. Kennedy was sympathetic. It had always been part of his New Frontier policy to extend the liberties of blacks. He had forbidden discrimination in government-aided housing, and comprehensive civil-rights legislation was now before Congress. Congress was reluctant to accept it, however, with Republicans and Southern Democrats obstructing Kennedy's proposals. In November 1963 Kennedy was assassinated (see section 2.2).

Johnson kept up the momentum, driving through Congress the Civil Rights Act (1964) and a new Voting Act (1965). These were the most thorough laws to date, outlawing discrimination in areas such as education and employment, forbidding segregation in places such as hotels, withholding federal money where the law was flouted, and creating community-relations machinery to promote racial harmony. The office of US Attorney-General (held until 1964 by Robert Kennedy) was used to deal with officials who were reluctant to enforce the new laws. At last effective steps were taken to register black voters and safeguard their rights. It would still take decades to overcome deep prejudices, but the lot of blacks in the South began gradually to improve, and they began to make progress in gaining public appointments and public acceptance.

Economic deprivation remained severe, especially in US cities. Some blacks also suffered from white reprisals as a result of the civil-rights movement. Four black girls were killed in the bombing of a church in Birmingham, Alabama, and when King led a march to Montgomery in 1965 the demonstrators were ambushed and attacked with sticks and stones, tear gas and savage dogs. King himself never abandoned the path of non-violence, continuing to preach moderation, brotherhood and humanity, but new black leaders like Stokeley Carmichael and Malcolm X were emerging. They encouraged black nationalism and pursued 'Black Power', rejecting King's voice of moderate compromise in favour of confrontation and more vigorous protest. Some went as far as to demand a separate state for blacks. In 1964 there was rioting in Harlem, New York, and Johnson faced turbulent summers when he was re-elected. King continued to struggle for peaceful reform but his assassination in 1968 was a savage blow to his people and to civilized campaigning (see section 2.2).

An official enquiry into this violence in the cities, especially in the black ghettos, blamed it on 'white racism'. In 1968 a further Civil Rights Act tried to tackle housing problems by forbidding discrimination in the renting and selling of accommodation. The ghettos with their poverty, crime, squalor and despair were now explosive. The Watts district of Los Angeles erupted in 1965 and violent outbreaks occurred across the country in summer after summer. The unrest merged with protest against the war in Vietnam – to the dismay of Lyndon Johnson, who had done more than any President to try to improve the lot of blacks by legislation.

Violent confrontation lessened during the 1970s. Nixon dealt sternly with law-breakers, and perhaps earlier reforms were now beginning to take effect. The worsening economic climate may have led to a greater concentration on the struggle to make a living, while there were also splits in the ranks of the hard-line black leadership. By 1970 the USA's 25 million blacks were winning office as members of Congress, judges, diplomats, federal and state officials and mayors. Nixon himself appointed black ministers and ambassadors. A black middle class was developing and black incomes were rising. The vast majority still had a long way to go to achieve complete equality, however, and many struggles remained.

A new issue sprang up, resulting from the black migration to the North. The children of the black communities in the cities attended neigbourhood schools, many of which became predominantly black, with educational standards often alleged to be low. One solution to the problem was 'bussing' the children to other schools to try to achieve racial balance. This sometimes created more racial conflict – whites who had moved to the city outskirts objecting to black children being brought to their children's schools. For a time in the mid-1970s there was more rioting and strife in Boston and other cities. Worsening economic problems which affected the USA and much of the world in the later 1970s produced additional difficulties (see section 2.4.2). Blacks were especially vulnerable to unemployment, though Carter, and to a lesser extent Reagan, sought to use public money to keep up the level of jobs for the minorities.

About half a million Indians, original inhabitants of North America, were less successful than the blacks in winning civil rights in the USA. Many remained on reservations, 'protected' against intruders but otherwise neglected by the US government. Many were also involved in claims for lands the Indian tribes argued had been stolen from them in years past. Others drifted to the cities, often ending up rootless and impoverished, demoralized in an alien culture. Truman set up machinery in 1946 to deal with the Indians' claims against the US government, but Eisenhower preferred to reduce the government's responsibilities for the Indians, hoping they would merge unobtrusively into American society. Not much was achieved by either and Kennedy adopted a new approach, to 'give Indians proper development and growth on their own lands'. Even so, neglect continued to dog the affairs of the Indians, though there was increased lobbying on their behalf in the 1960s and 1970s by Indians themselves and by celebrities such as film star Marlon Brando. No President up to the late 1980s had yet made a sustained attempt to provide the Indians with all the amenities and opportunities which most whites took for granted and which blacks were struggling to attain.

2.3.4 Social reform and welfare

The Depression in the 1930s broke down some of the resistance of Americans to state systems of social security to care for society's casualties - the sick, the old, the unemployed and the impoverished. The Democrats under Roosevelt began to build what became in the second half of the century an extensive system of social security and welfare, with insurance against old age and unemployment, and various sorts of additional assistance to those in need. But the USA still lagged behind many European states: there was no National Health Service such as that operating in Britain, for example. Only with difficulty did the Democrats eventually make progress towards 'Medicare', to provide hospital and other treatment for the elderly, and the WASP establishment was always likely to prefer private to state insurance and private services to those set up by cities, states and the federal government. There were, of course, exceptions. Education, for example, took place to a large extent in public schools and universities, and was only supplemented by the private sector.

Truman hoped to extend Roosevelt's reforms, though he had to devote much of his time immediately after the war to economic management and the adjustment to peace. His ideas for reform were put forward in 1945 in a programme of 'Twenty-one Points', but not much of it was accepted by Congress. The Employment Act was passed in 1946, requiring the administration to aim for full employment, and Truman showed skill in promoting the resettlement of ex-servicemen. The G.I. Bill allocated jobs and provided financial help for their further education, retraining and setting up in businesses. This was more active government than Americans had been used to before the Depression. Truman also showed vigour when, faced with strikes, he seized coal-mines and threatened to draft railwaymen into the forces. But like the rest of his Twenty-one Points, more positive plans for winning the co-operation of trade unions came up against opposition in Congress. Congress found too radical his proposals for improved working conditions, racial equality in employment, more public-aided house-building and more extensive social security. Instead, Congress insisted on the Taft–Hartley Act to weaken trade unions and strengthen employers (see section 2.3.2).

The votes of trade unionists helped Truman to win re-election in 1948, and he now offered his 'Fair Deal'. Rather like his earlier Twenty-one Points, this was a programme for reform in employment, housing and social security, with proposals for higher minimum wages and better prices for farmers. There was a little more building of subsidized housing, and the Social Security Act of 1950 slightly extended the numbers covered by old-age insurance, but little else. Congress was now more interested in uncovering communist agents, and hopes for introducing Medicare were set back until the 1960s.

Eisenhower did not give priority to social reform. Indeed, he vetoed plans put forward by Congress which might have introduced parts of Truman's Fair

Deal. He nevertheless created a new Department of Health, Education and Welfare in 1953 to carry out more effectively the laws which had been passed, firmly asserting that 'there should be an unremitting effort to improve those health, education and social-security programmes which have proved their value'. But neither the President nor his Vice-President, Richard Nixon, saw any need for major additions to the reform programme, satisfied on the whole simply to respond to problems as they arose. Eisenhower therefore made a modest contribution to civil rights (see section 2.3.3), allowed private enterprise to flourish (even blocking anti-pollution laws), forced steel-workers back to work when they went on strike in 1959 and, alleging corruption among their leaders, introduced legislation to make trade unions more democratic. The drive towards further reform had to wait until the Democrats under Kennedy won the election of 1960.

Kennedy set a new style of youthful activity in government. He was ambitious for social improvement, not only in civil rights but also in cutting taxes, reducing unemployment and wiping out poverty. What he managed to achieve before his assassination in 1963 was very limited, however. Minimum wages were raised again; there was a further small improvement in the social-security and welfare systems – especially in help for the mentally handicapped – and an attack was begun on water pollution. Taxes were little changed. Perhaps the most useful law which Kennedy persuaded Congress to accept was the Trade Expansion Act of 1962, which cut tariffs, encouraging international trade and providing work.

Johnson was able to realize many of Kennedy's ambitions. Kennedy had not always been popular, and conservatives in Congress, some Democrats among them, had steadfastly resisted change. But Kennedy's death changed the mood for a time. Johnson swept to victory in the presidential election of 1964 and extended Kennedy's reform programme in his own vision of the 'Great Society'. A stream of proposals included laws for civil rights, the tax cuts Kennedy had wanted, numerous social reforms and a war on poverty. The Economic Opportunity Act of 1964 extended vocational training for the young, gave financial help to small farmers, businesses and local projects in areas of poverty, and set up a Jobs Corps. Tax cuts helped to increase the individual's purchasing power.

This programme continued when Johnson was re-elected but one of his main aims was the Medicare Act, to provide hospital and health care for those over 65. In 1965, as well as accepting Medicare, Congress agreed to finance improvements in public-aided housing and education. The Development Act of 1966 financed an attack on slums in many US cities. The Clean Waters Act provided funds for a major extension of sewage-treatment plants. New federal departments were set up to oversee the USA's urban problems and transport. Like earlier Presidents, Johnson continued to raise the minimum wage and social-security benefits; like other Democrats, he continued to use federal power to try to increase jobs. There were limits to what he could persuade Congress to accept, however. He could not secure any softening of the anti-union Taft–Hartley Act, and after 1966 Congress became generally less reform-

The Train Robbery

Fig. 2.3 Already in January 1967, this *Punch* cartoon by Mansbridge commented on the damaging effects of the war in Vietnam on President Johnson's reforming ambitions for the 'Great Society'. LBJ himself wields the axe, sacrificing reform to stoking up the war effort.

minded. Johnson's liberal image was somewhat tarnished when the Immigration Act of 1965 imposed the first barriers against immigration from northern Europe and produced a new immigration code based on would-be immigrants' special skills and relationship to US citizens.

What most checked the drive for reform, however, was the war in Vietnam (see section 18.4). Its cost strained the federal budget, its unpopularity with many US citizens added to the riots and uproar of the later 1960s, and the worry of it demoralized the President himself. The war also dominated the early years of Nixon's Presidency. Nixon too faced economic problems and he ran into storms over his choice of nominees for new appointments to the Supreme Court, though the succession to Chief Justice Earl Warren took place smoothly in 1969. (Warren had been appointed by Eisenhower in 1953 and had been influential in handing down many liberal judgments during his years in office, many of them safeguarding the liberties of US citizens.) Nixon showed a preference for conservative judges and, in his policies, for continuity rather than reform. A measure of stability returned to the USA's cities (see section 2.3.3), partly helped by Nixon's new Council for Urban Affairs, soon changed into his Domestic Council. Rising unemployment began to undermine what progress there had been towards Johnson's Great Society, however, and Nixon's ambitions for reform did not go much further than to set up machinery for curbing the pollution of the environment, a policy not likely to annoy the Republicans' WASP supporters. In his foreign policy Nixon had many successes (see sections 13.4.2 and 18.4.2). At home what was perhaps most distinctive about his Presidency was that, along with Ford, he acted as a bridge between the expectations and turbulence of the 1960s and the more sober, less forceful administrations of the later 1970s and 1980s.

Carter expressed the new mood when he took office in January 1977. In contrast to Kennedy, he announced that he had 'no new dream to set forth today', and admitted that 'we can neither answer all questions nor solve all problems' but 'must simply do our best'. Yet Carter was still a Democrat and he also asserted:

> Our commitment to human rights must be absolute, our laws fair, our natural beauty preserved; the powerful must not persecute the weak and human dignity must be enhanced.

In a Presidency beset with difficulties, not least economic (see section 2.4), Carter did his best to safeguard the social-security and welfare system but could undertake no dramatic new initiatives. Reagan, who followed him as President in 1981, believed strongly in self-help rather than state help, and once again many Americans looked with some suspicion at the apparatus they had built for the protection and aid of their fellow-citizens in distress.

2.4 The economic giant

2.4.1 The economic miracle

The United States economy grew dramatically for about thirty years after the Second World War. Between 1945 and 1975 the country's gross national product almost doubled. The number of Americans in work rose from about 42 million in the mid-1930s to about 72 million in the mid-1960s, by which time the Depression seemed to have been left far behind. Earnings ran ahead of increases in the cost of living, so that most Americans had money to spend. Consumer goods were plentiful: by 1975 there were almost 110 million cars in the USA. No earlier generation could match such wealth, and few peoples outside the USA could compete with the Americans.

Roosevelt had tried to lead the US out of the Depression in the 1930s by 'priming the pump' – spending federal funds to stimulate economic activity and to help provide work. In every year from 1932 to the Second World War, the USA ran substantial budget deficits: that is, the government spent more than it received from taxes, making good the shortfall by borrowing. The methods Roosevelt used to try to shape the economy were those set out in 1936 by John Maynard Keynes, a British economist, in his *General Theory of Employment, Interest and Money*. Keynes argued that, by public investment, public works and public controls (for example, of interest rates), governments could combat depression and provide work. Such work would provide more purchasing power, thus priming the pump and producing more work. Keynesian economics influenced much government thinking in the West during the next half century, though in the USA Democrats showed more enthusiasm than Republicans for Keynes's ideas. The Republicans eventually found their own economic guru in Milton Friedman.

Truman intended to continue with Roosevelt's economic policy as well as with his social policy, anxious that the end of the war in 1945 should not bring a return of unemployment. Economic controls had increased during the war and Truman wanted to keep many of these controls, at least during the transition to peace. He soon clashed with Congress: the price controls it would accept were too weak in Truman's view and he vetoed them. As a result, controls lapsed. Prices soared and anger over this helped the Republicans in the mid-term elections of 1946. Truman succeeded in keeping up the level of employment, which eventually helped to curb inflation when the supply of goods began to match demand, but he faced difficult years, especially when post-war labour unrest led to strikes and some large wage rises. When Truman retired, however, the USA was on a peacetime footing: GNP was higher than in 1945, and almost ten million more Americans had by 1953 found peacetime employment compared with the 1945 work-force.

All US Presidents after 1945 had to find money for the country's defence services and global interests, a burden far greater than in the 1920s and 1930s, and one which affected America's economy. In 1946 Truman set up the Atomic Energy Commission to continue costly research and the development of nuclear power. He also reorganized national security, setting up the Defense Department in 1949. Two years earlier, he had committed the USA to overseas involvement when he set out the Truman Doctrine. This led on to the Korean War even while Truman was still President (see Unit 4). The expense was further increased by the Marshall Plan of 1947 (see section 4.3), which cost the USA twelve billion dollars in its first three years. The Plan aimed to help the economic recovery of western Europe and to safeguard the area from communism. It also had another, more specifically American aim, however. Truman had been alarmed by the loss of markets in eastern Europe, closed to the West by the Soviet Union. He feared a return to unemployment and the Depression years if the USA could not sell its goods overseas. By providing money for the recovery of western Europe, the USA would be priming the pump – increasing purchasing power, stimulating trade and guaranteeing future markets and areas of profitable investment for US traders and financiers. In 1949 Truman extended the ideas of the Marshall Plan to friendly areas outside Europe, making a considerable contribution to economic recovery after the Second World War. Many of the ideas behind the Marshall Plan, including those of self-interest, were later given global application in the Brandt Report of 1980 (see section 21.3.2).

Eisenhower was fortunate to be President at a time of economic boom, for which Truman had laid many of the foundations. Eisenhower did little to interfere with the economy, and he preferred balanced budgets to overspending and deficits. The end of the Korean War helped reduce spending, and Eisenhower resisted Democrat demands for government action to counter periods of recession and increased unemployment in 1953 and 1957. He left the economy to businessmen and 'experts', assuming that market forces would overcome problems. In the 1950s, with the West recovering from wartime upheaval, there was greater affluence generally. Eisenhower believed that it was enough to encourage private enterprise and to reduce federal spending and taxes, to allow the 'economic miracle' to continue.

Steady economic growth continued during the 1960s, both Kennedy and Johnson pursuing mildly Keynesian policies. Each year the USA produced more and Americans grew richer. There was slight uneasiness, however. Automation and advancing technology took away jobs, making it more difficult to achieve full employment, though Kennedy and Johnson tried to secure it by federal spending and measures to promote international trade. At the same time, prices rose; the inflation rate during the 1960s averaged about three per cent a year, though the government tried to keep it down with controls. Ambitiously, Presidents at this time also tried to combine lower taxes with higher spending on social reform, but by 1968 taxes were rising, partly because of the growing cost of the war in Vietnam. Heavy government spending and fears of rising unemployment and inflation were therefore among the difficulties which Republicans inherited at the end of the decade, and defence spending continued to be a serious burden.

On top of defence costs, there was the expense of the USA's space programme. The Soviet Union had launched *Sputnik I* in 1957, the first man-made satellite to orbit the earth in space, and competition was then fierce (see section 13.1). When Kennedy called for a new US space programme in 1961, a series of *Apollo* flights followed, aimed at landing a man on the moon by the end of the decade. The costs of such ventures were enormous – Congress voted 24 billion dollars for *Apollo* – and the *Apollo* programme was eventually wound up in favour of the development of a space shuttle which could travel in space and return to earth. The shuttle could be used time and again, unlike earlier spacecraft which burned up on re-entering the earth's atmosphere. But that too was costly, and there was a major setback when the shuttle *Challenger* exploded on launching in January 1986, killing its crew.

Such programmes were not without military implications, and in the 1970s they added to the vast spending on missiles and arms by the US and other governments which was one of the factors that contributed to serious international economic disorder.

2.4.2 Crises after 1970

The USA's economic problems quickly worsened under Nixon. Unemployment rose to four million and prices rose even more sharply. Nixon was more vigorous than many earlier Republicans, trying to freeze wages and prices, imposing a surcharge on imports when the USA ran into problems with its balance of payments, and then devaluing the dollar by the end of 1971. More dollars were now needed to buy West German marks or Japanese yen, for example, but two years later the dollar was again in trouble, evidence of a general lack of confidence in the currency and in the US government - mainly because of the vast spending to which the administration was committed in many parts of the world. America's withdrawal from Vietnam helped, but Nixon's struggle with the economy was overtaken by the Watergate Affair (see section 2.2). Ford then had the misfortune to be plunged into new problems alongside those he had inherited.

Sudden large increases in the price of oil in the mid-1970s upset a world economy already out of balance. The resulting shocks brought widespread inflation, trading crises, recession and unemployment (see section 21.1). Even the USA was not immune from the disasters. The USA was the world's biggest user of energy, and higher oil prices damaged the country's balance of payments and weakened the dollar which Nixon had freed from a fixed relationship to the price of gold, allowing it to float downwards in value when under pressure. Fears that oil reserves might soon be exhausted caused anxiety about the extent to which America's economy and way of life were dependent on oil and petrol. Rising unemployment brought fears of a return to the 1930s, while inflation brought financial worries, especially since rises in interest rates made borrowing and mortgages more expensive. There was a general loss of confidence: it seemed as if the US economic miracle might be coming to an end.

Carter did what he could, while warning his supporters that problems could not be solved overnight. He had some limited success during the first couple of years of his Presidency, but things then worsened again. In 1979 the prices of goods and services rose by over thirteen per cent and by the end of the year interest rates were around fifteen per cent. In 1980 almost eight per cent of the labour force was unemployed, getting on for double the figure under Nixon. Meanwhile, the President launched a campaign to reduce the USA's use of energy, especially oil, though some of his measures were resisted in Congress. There was yet another anxiety when an accident occurred at the nuclear power plant at Three Mile Island, Harrisburg, in Pennsylvania. Arguments were reopened about the safety of such plant and about the development of nuclear energy. There was some argument too about Carter's attempts to use trade as a way of putting pressure on the Soviet Union. Nixon had tried to expand trade with both the Soviet Union and China, but in 1980 grain sales to the Soviets fell sharply when Carter began to impose restrictions in protest against the Soviet invasion of Afghanistan. US producers complained of their loss of profits, dampening the President's enthusiasm for the boycott.

Reagan alleged that the events of the 1970s showed that Keynesian policies had failed. He intended to follow the doctrines of Milton Friedman. By the

1970s Friedman was arguing that government attempts to regulate the economy did more harm than good, upsetting delicate market forces; governments should therefore abandon controls on the economy and cease to interfere except for pursuing a policy of *monetarism*. This meant tightly controlling the money supply which would in turn check inflation, always a likely product of deficit budgeting. President Reagan eagerly took up Friedman's ideas in the 1980s, turning away from the interventionist policies of the Democrats. But, not for the first time, circumstances played havoc with theory. Unemployment went up, reaching almost eleven per cent at the end of 1982 with almost twelve million Americans registered in search of work and perhaps two million more not officially listed. Interest rates and bankruptcies also went up. But by 1983 inflation seemed to have been cut back in spite of a large and persisting budget deficit, which was due mainly to the President's fierce anti-communism and heavy spending on defence. This deficit helped to revive the economy as Keynes might have forecast: the GNP began to grow rapidly and 1983 saw a drop in unemployment, which settled in the mid-1980s at around seven per cent. Reagan cut taxes, and the average income of Americans rose, leading to a sense that prosperity was returning.

The President sometimes appeared to make up policy as he went along. Even his anti-communism seemed flexible at times. At first he withheld grain and imposed other economic boycotts to embarrass the Soviet Union, but when other countries such as Canada and Argentina increased grain sales to the Soviets, Reagan reversed direction – in 1983 he signed a five-year grain deal with the Kremlin. This was popular with US farmers who would profit from supplying the USSR with grain. But Reagan asserted that the USA would not supply advanced technology – what really mattered, he claimed. He also tried to block supplies being used to build a pipeline which would bring Soviet natural gas to western Europe, leading to a storm of protest in Europe, if not in the USA.

There was unrest in the USA nevertheless. In the summer of 1983 a quarter of a million Americans assembled in Washington on the twentieth anniversary of Martin Luther King's rally in support of civil rights. They complained of the higher-than-average unemployment among minorities and roundly condemned Reagan's economic and social priorities. Complete equality was still a distant goal in which the President showed little interest. Many observers now hailed Jesse Jackson as the rising black leader who was destined to take on the mantle of Martin Luther King – perhaps even a future Democrat candidate for the Presidency. For the moment, however, Reagan seemed in tune with the WASPs and the aspirations of those who thought it right that the USA should be both the richest and the most influential power in the world, strongly aligned against communism, socialism and all forms of collectivism. In re-electing Reagan in 1984, voters ignored those in poverty, whom the administration itself ignored, and turned a blind eye to the vast deficits in US trade and in the federal government's budget. Reagan himself was no theorist and now seemed unworried as to whether this was anything like pure Friedmanism, since Reaganomics seemed to deliver both prosperity and votes.

Problems multiplied for Reagan in the mid-1980s, however. Irangate[G] and doubts about his attachment to military developments in space and his involvements overseas brought criticism and stiffening opposition in Congress. The US economy was coming to rely on loans, especially from Japan whose trading position was far healthier than that of the USA. The President stubbornly refused to cut arms spending and to raise taxes, and confidence in his administration sagged. In autumn 1987 there was a dramatic fall in prices on the New York stock exchange which revived memories of the Wall Street Crash of 1929 which preceded the Great Depression. Other countries were caught up in the crisis. Stock-exchange prices fell across the world and fears of an imminent recession grew, with the threat of reduced trade, production cuts and higher unemployment. Reaganomics now seemed a fragile basis on which to rest the US economy and with it the economies of the capitalist countries in Europe and elsewhere (see section 21.1).

2.5 United States foreign policy

One of the most important decisions taken when Truman was President was that the USA would not again withdraw into the neutralism and isolationism of past years. The Truman Doctrine, membership of NATO and intervention in the Korean War clearly signalled that the USA was now concerned not just about the Americas but also about Europe and the Far East. In 1950 Dean Acheson, Truman's Secretary of State, summarized what had by then become US policy:

> The six elements of the Strategy of Freedom - support of the United Nations, development of regional organisations, the rapid building up of our strength in partnership with our allies, economic co-operation, readiness to negotiate, and a firm adherence to the fundamental purposes and principles of our society - constitute a national policy, not a party policy. They have emerged from a long process of discussion and consideration as the practical requirements of a policy adequate to the problems which confront us. They are rooted in our traditions.

'Fundamental purposes and principles' and 'traditions' left room for some flexibility, but broadly all US governments now saw it as their role to defend capitalism and democracy and to resist the further spread of communism. Table 2.2 shows that US interests were now global and very few international 'problems' of importance did not involve the American President. Many of the pages which follow - and especially Units 4, 13 and 21 - will deal at greater length with US foreign policy after 1945.

Table 2.2 United States foreign policy

President	Secretary of State (notable appointments)	Principal themes in US policy	Specific events	Section references (see also Index)
Truman 1945–53	Byrnes, 1945–7	Post-war resettlement		4.3
	Marshall, 1947–9	Cold War and containment – Truman Doctrine, 1947		4.4
	Acheson, 1949–53			
			End of Second World War, 1945	1.2
			Setting up of United Nations, 1945	1.4
			Occupation of Germany, 1945–55	4.2
			Berlin Airlift, 1948–9	4.2.2
			Occupation of Japan, 1945–52	12.1
			Setting up of OAS, 1948	9.4
			Setting up of NATO, 1949	4.4
			Communists in power in China, 1949	11.1
			Korean War, 1950–3	4.5.2
Eisenhower 1953–61	Dulles, 1953–9	Cold War continued – 'brinkmanship', 'massive retaliation'		4.5
		Summit meetings, some thaw, 'peaceful coexistence'		13.1
			Korean War ended, 1953	4.5.2
			Geneva Conference on South-East Asia, 1954	11.4.3
			Setting up of SEATO, 1954	4.5.2
			Baghdad Pact, 1955	4.5.2
			Austrian State Treaty, 1955	4.6
			Suez War, 1956	14.2.5
			Hungary invaded, 1956	8.2.3
			Castro in power in Cuba, 1959	10.1
			Beginning of crisis in the Congo, 1960	13.2

Kennedy 1961–3	Rusk, 1961–9	Cold War – crisis and uncertain thaw		13.1
		Vietnam War developing		11.4.3
			Berlin Wall built, 1961	13.1
			Missiles Crisis, Cuba, 1962	13.2.2
			Setting-up of hot-line, and Test Ban Treaty, 1963	13.3.2
Johnson 1963–9	Rusk, 1961–9	Vietnam War – escalation		18.4.1
			US intervention in Dominican Republic, 1965	9.3.5
			Six-Day War in Middle East, 1967	18.2.1
			Non-Proliferation Treaty, 1968	13.3.2
			Czechoslovakia invaded, 1968	8.2.4
Nixon 1969–74	Kissinger, 1973–7	Pursuit of détente – improved relations with both Soviet Union and China		13.4
		Vietnam War – Vietnamization and withdrawal begun		18.4.2
			SALT talks begun, 1969	13.4.2
			Communist China admitted to UN, 1971	11.2.3(c)
			Allende overthrown in Chile, 1973	10.2.2
			East and West Germany admitted to UN, 1973	6.2.3
			Yom Kippur War, 1973, followed by oil crisis	18.2.1
Ford 1974–7	Kissinger, 1973–7	Détente, continuing		13.4
		Vietnam War – withdrawal completed, 1975		18.4.2
			CSCE agreement in Helsinki, 1975	13.4.3
			End of SEATO, 1975 (effective 1977)	18.5.2
			Crisis in Angola, 1975–6	15.4

Table 2.2 United States foreign policy *(continued)*

President	Secretary of State (notable appointments)	Principal themes in US policy	Specific events	Section references (see also Index)
Carter 1977–81	Vance, 1977–80	Conflict over human rights in communist states – a 'new' Cold War		21.2
		Confrontation with Iran		20.2
			Panama Treaties signed, 1977	9.4
			Mediation in Middle East: Camp David meeting, 1978	18.2.3
			Sandinistas in power in Nicaragua, 1979	10.4
			US citizens taken hostage in Iran, 1979	20.2
			Soviet occupation of Afghanistan, 1979	20.5
Reagan 1981–8	Haig, 1981–2 Shultz, 1982–8	Hard line towards Soviet Union, but summits held, 1987–8		21.2
		Crises in central America		10.4
		Anti-terrorism campaign		20.3.2
		Peacemaking efforts in Africa and the Middle East, 1988		17.5.2, 18.2.4
			Support for Contras in Nicaragua, 1981–8	10.4
			Peace-keeping force in Lebanon, 1982	18.2.4
			US invasion of Grenada, 1983	10.3
			Famine in Ethiopia and elsewhere in Africa, 1984–8	22.2
			US bombing of Libya, 1986	20.3.2
			Soviet withdrawal from Afghanistan, 1988–9	20.5

UNIT 3

The superpowers: 2 – the Soviet Union, the first Marxist power

3.1 The Soviet Union at the end of the Second World War

The 'Great Patriotic War' which the Soviet people fought against Nazi Germany ended in victory for the Soviets, but it left the Soviet Union itself grievously wounded (see section 1.2). The Red Army had overrun most of eastern Europe, carrying Soviet influence westwards beyond Berlin and Vienna, but within the Soviet Union in 1945 the tasks of reconstruction were immense. Joseph Stalin, the Soviet leader, was as determined as in the 1930s that Soviet output should match the best in the West. For the Soviet people, however, that could only mean further massive suffering on top of their earlier ordeals and sacrifices.

West of a line linking Leningrad, Moscow and Stalingrad (roughly the limit of the German advance), the devastation was almost total. In this area before 1941 the Soviet Union had produced almost half of its grain and about 60 per cent of its coal, aluminium, iron and steel. Now the achievements of the 1930s had been wiped out. In addition to restoring the industries destroyed in the German invasion, the Soviets needed to restore about 100 000 collective farms, some five million homes and about 65 000 kilometres of railway track. The economy had also to be restored to a peacetime footing. Wartime development in the comparative security of areas east of the Urals had been remarkably successful in making good much of the USSR's industrial output, but it was production geared to war while the Soviet people endured desperate shortages, including inadequate food, clothing and shelter. Post-war Soviet Russia would not offer its people luxuries; priority would need to be given to their basic well-being.

Reconstruction would also need to include vast programmes of resettlement. Well over ten per cent of the Soviet population died during the war, and many millions of people were uprooted and moved eastwards. Some fled from the Germans; some were moved by the government to carry on the war effort; and some were moved for security reasons – Crimean Tatars and Volga Germans, for example, were moved to eastern Siberia in case they collaborated with the

Fig. 3.1 Following the liberation of Belorussia, families return to their villages after hiding in the forests from the Germans.

Nazis. Not all of these people were allowed to return to their homelands when the war ended, but such resettlement as did take place nevertheless required massive organization. During elections in 1946, Communist Party spokesmen put the number of homeless at the end of the war at 25 million.

The system of government in the Soviet Union at the end of the war was that laid down in the constitution of 1936 (fig 3.2). This defined the Communist Party, the USSR's only political party, as:

> the vanguard of the working people in their struggle to build a communist society and the leading core of all organisations of the working people, both governmental and non-governmental.

The Party provided the members of local soviets (now, in effect, local governments) and of the Soviet parliament – the Supreme Soviet. This was made up of two houses – the Soviet of the Union, representing the people in proportion to population, and the Soviet of Nationalities, representing the many states which made up the Union of Soviet Socialist Republics. The Party also provided the members of the country's executive Council of Ministers (Sovnarcom) and of the various state governments. All Soviet citizens could vote by secret ballot at the age of eighteen, and the constitution guaranteed them such civil liberties as freedom of speech, of expression, of assembly and of religion. Individual states were guaranteed the right to leave the Soviet Union if

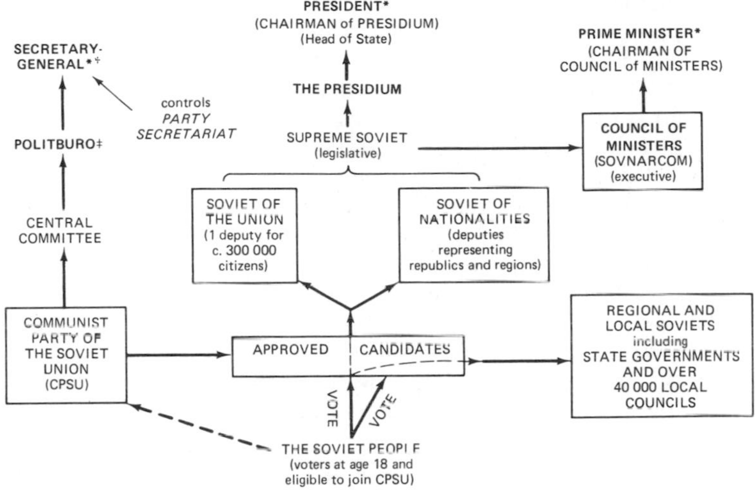

Fig. 3.2 The Soviet system of government after the constitution of 1936

they so wished. Voters could only elect the Communist Party members put before them, however, and none of the guaranteed rights could be exercised to the detriment of the Soviet system. The census of 1939 showed that the USSR then had a population of 170.5 million. Of these about 2.5 million were members of the Communist Party, with additional numbers in Komsomol, the Party's youth section. Party membership grew during the war and by 1952 stood at about seven million. Members were better able than others to influence Soviet affairs, but membership also carried with it the duty of loyalty and the acceptance of discipline. Indeed, loyalty and discipline were keynotes in Soviet society as a whole. The judicial system was designed to enforce them, and there existed a powerful state police and security service (known in 1945 as the NKVD), which from 1938 to Stalin's death in 1953 was controlled by Lavrenti Beria, Commissar for Internal Affairs.

Stalin's grip on the Soviet Union was even stronger in 1945 than it had been before the war, his prestige seemingly increased by leading his people to victory. After Lenin's death in 1924, Stalin had competed for power against rivals such as Leon Trotsky, but, from his entrenched position as Secretary-General of the Communist Party, he had overcome them by 1928. In the 1930s he conducted vicious purges against all those he suspected of being critics and opponents and he imposed a 'Terror' on the Soviet Union to bend even the humblest peasant to his will. He drove the USSR forward towards his economic goals with a ruthlessness that matched that of Hitler and the Nazis, and so deep were his fears and suspicions that even surviving Bolsheviks who had worked with Lenin in the Revolution of 1917 were condemned and put to death for alleged treachery. In 1941 Stalin added to his offices that of Prime Minister (Chairman of Sovnarcom). At the end of the war he also dominated the Politburo (the inner group of the Communist Party Central Committee) and the Presidium (which represented the Supreme Soviet when the latter was not in session). After 1945 Stalin remained as ruthless and suspicious as in the years before the war, and few dared even think of opposing him. His suspicions now extended to all those who had come into contact with the USSR's Western Allies and even to those the Nazis had taken prisoner, some of whom, on their return to the Soviet Union, were imprisoned or sent to work in remote areas in case they should spread Western propaganda. It was Stalin's intention that the Soviet Union should pursue post-war reconstruction with relentless fury, and that no dissenting voices should obstruct the country's recovery.

3.2 Stalin's last years

3.2.1 Reconstruction: industrial achievement

Gosplan, the state planning commission which had been responsible for the Soviet Union's pre-war economic plans, launched the Fourth Five-Year Plan in 1946. Within its allotted five years the Plan aimed not only completely to restore the USSR to its pre-war condition but also to surpass the output of 1940 in both heavy industry and agriculture. A much lower priority was given to consumer goods, but substantial resources were allocated to improving education and health services and to building homes. For the Soviet people, reconstruction meant more back-breaking labour, continued shortages and further burdens such as the Reconstruction Loans imposed on them from 1946.

Labour was a particular problem. The war had left an imbalance in the Soviet population – 55 per cent of which was now female – and much reliance was now placed on the labour of women. By 1948 the Red Army had been reduced from over eleven million to less than three million, the demobilized soldiers increasing the manpower available for reconstruction. (Manpower began to be diverted back to the Army as the Cold War developed after 1948.) This was further supplemented by 'volunteer labour', imported from eastern Europe, and by the use of 'forced labour'. At the end of the war there were three million or more prisoners in forced-labour camps; there were also large numbers of prisoners of war – mostly Germans – many of whom were forced to work towards the rebuilding of the USSR for some years after 1945.

Resources other than human were also in short supply. After the war the Soviet Union insisted on its right to reparations (see section 1.3.2). Plant, machinery and livestock were taken from Germany and other defeated Axis powers to equip factories and mines, to provide transport and to stock farms. In the absence of assistance from the USSR's wartime Allies, this went some way towards making good some of the Soviet losses. It took several years for Soviet output to begin to rise significantly, but by 1950 most industrial production was much in excess of pre-war levels, and the Fourth Plan had been largely fulfilled. Steel production, for example, was some 50 per cent higher than in 1940. Much of Soviet industry had been re-equipped with up-to-date technology, and towns and homes had been rebuilt where Nazi armies had ravaged. The industries east of the Urals, developed during the war, continued to be an important source of production. Before the Fourth Five-Year Plan was completed in 1950, the Soviets had also matched the USA in establishing a nuclear industry and, in 1949, by producing an atomic bomb. By the time the Council for Mutual Economic Assistance (Comecon) was founded in the same year, they had already begun consolidating a trading alliance in eastern Europe. In 1947 monetary reform had been carried out along with the abolition of rationing and, for the first time for many years, the Soviet people felt some real improvement in their standard of living.

A Fifth Plan was launched in 1951, again placing the main emphasis on heavy industry, though slightly less ambitious than the Plan of 1946. At the end of the war the Soviet Union's GNP had been less than a third of that of the USA; before Stalin died in 1953 the gap had narrowed a little, mainly as the result of the Soviet post-war 'industrial miracle'.

3.2.2 Reconstruction: agricultural disappointment

The First Five-Year Plan (1928) had begun the collectivization of Soviet agriculture. At that time the Soviet Union had about 25 million smallholdings, owned by a peasantry of whom only a minority – the *kulaks* – were rich enough to employ labour and to farm efficiently. The kulaks, like many of the peasantry, preferred private profit to Marxist ideology and to theories about their duty to supply cheap foodstuffs to their urban comrades and grain to assist the country's exports. In 1928 Stalin wanted 'to destroy the kulaks as a class', to end their bourgeois opposition to the Soviet state; he also wanted to bring together the smallholdings into large farming units where capital, expertise and technology could revolutionize outdated farming methods.

About 250 000 large farming units came into existence before the Second World War. They were of two sorts: one was the government-owned state farm (*sovkhoz*) where the workers received a guaranteed wage; the other was a co-operative (*kolkhoz*) where the peasants lived rent-free on state land, pooled their resources, hired expertise and equipment from Machine Tractor Stations (MTSs) set up by the government, and shared the profits on produce sold to the state. The basis of this system of collectivization was that the peasants' smallholdings were nationalized (transferred to the state). Stalin would have preferred most of the new farms to be sovkhozes, but the peasants preferred kolkhozes, especially those known as *artels* which left them with private homes and private plots and livestock from which they could make private profit to supplement their shared earnings. Of the 100 000 collectives subsequently ravaged by the Nazi invasion, 98 000 were kolkhozes and only 2000 sovkhozes.

The transformation of Soviet agriculture in the 1930s was not achieved easily. At times the authorities used methods which were brutal and bloody. At times too there was famine. As many as ten million peasants may have died before the kulaks were removed and the new farms were operating. A further 25 million had by then been diverted into industry. Many peasants had resisted collectivization, destroying property and slaughtering livestock rather than yield them to the authorities, and hostility to the new system remained widespread.

Life on the new collective farms was hardly less harsh than it had been under the old system. About 90 per cent of the produce was sold at fixed prices to the authorities, but selling private produce at market did something to lift incomes above the bare minimum. By 1937 almost all Soviet farming had been collectivized. Livestock totals had to a large extent recovered, and production was beginning to expand.

The war which began for the Soviets in 1941 had effects beyond the destruction of buildings, livestock and machinery, and the poisoning of farmland in the areas reached by the Germans. Elsewhere, private plots flourished and expanded and discipline weakened since the authorities, faced with shortages of labour and the desperate demand for output, grew more flexible. When the war ended, however, reconstruction had to include the rebuilding of the system. In 1946 the authorities began a drive to restore to the kolkhozes lands and animals which had been privatized, as well as to improve the efficiency of the farms with good management, and to re-equip them with labour and with machinery from the MTSs. Even so the agricultural sector fell short of its targets in the Fourth Five-Year Plan, and in 1950 it had not quite returned to the grain production levels of 1940.

Compared with industry, agriculture was still of secondary importance in Soviet planning. In 1948, grappling with the grave difficulties imposed on agriculture by the Russian climate, Stalin produced his own Plan for the Transformation of Nature, which included huge schemes for planting trees and for irrigation systems, mainly in the European part of the USSR. These, it was hoped, would increase crop yield, though the results were disappointing. Meanwhile, collectivization was introduced into those areas which had already been made part of the Soviet Union, such as the Baltic Provinces (Estonia, Latvia and Lithuania).

When Nikita Khrushchev was put in charge of Soviet agriculture by Stalin in 1949, his job was not to change the system but simply to make it more productive, as cheaply as possible. One trend which Khrushchev encouraged was the creation of even larger units by merging the collective farms. By 1953 the 250 000 units had been reduced to around 100 000, each with some 1200 hectares or more of arable land farmed by around 200 families. The movement to prefer sovkhozes to kolkhozes progressed only slowly: state farms still worked only ten per cent of arable land in 1953, while the authorities were still struggling at the time of Stalin's death to increase the national agricultural output and to wean Soviet peasants from their enthusiasm for private plots.

3.2.3 Soviet society

Soviet citizens continued to live in fear after 1945. Their lives were tightly controlled in order to preserve the system, though Stalin himself was respected

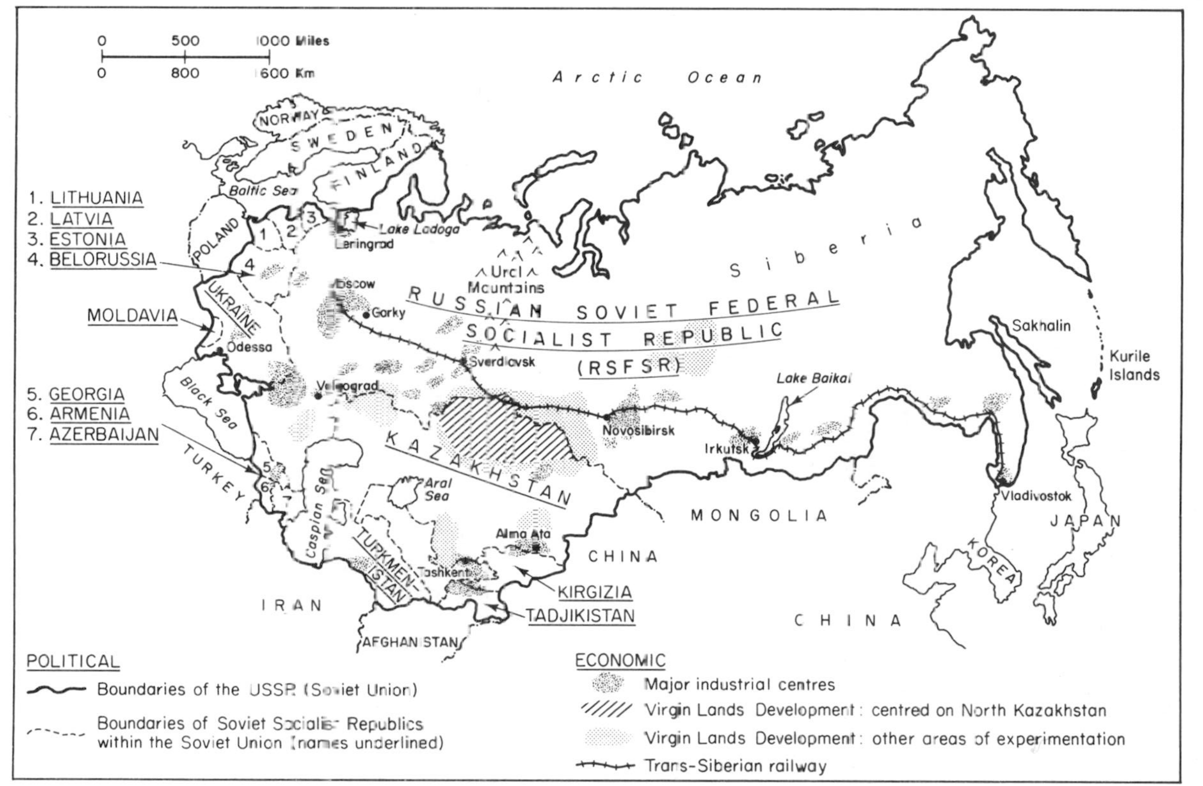

Fig. 3.3 The Union of Soviet Socialist Republics (USSR)

and to some extent even popular. Like the USA at this time, the USSR experienced a great fear of spies and foreign subversion, which led in 1948–9 to a new 'Little Stalin Terror' to root out enemies of the system. Beria and his police remained ever watchful. Equally watchful until his death in 1948 was First Deputy Prime Minister Andrei Zdhanov, who organized the tight, though often clumsy, censorship and 'thought control'. While a huge personality cult was built around Stalin, glorifying his every action, artists and scientists were subjected to a blundering regimentation, among the results of which were the disgrace of Sergei Eisenstein - one of the USSR's foremost film-makers - and vigorous attacks on the country's leading composers such as Prokofiev and Shostakovich. The authorities believed that the arts should be 'optimistic and heroic' and supportive of 'socialist realism'; those artists falling short were likely to be ridiculed as 'bourgeois' and 'decadent'. Intellectuals found such regimentation painful and destructive; Shostakovich, for example, tried to please the authorities by writing music in praise of Stalin's tree plantations, but there was a notable gap from 1945 to 1953 in his writing of symphonies.

Regimentation went further, however. National minorities complained of 'russification', the attempt to impose on them Russian values, hence denying them the respect for national differences guaranteed in the Soviet constitution. Religious groups were also persecuted, especially those like Catholics and Jews who had allegiances beyond the Soviet Union, to the Pope and the Zionist movement, for example. On the other hand, the Orthodox Church was widely tolerated as long as it did not oppose the authorities, even though the Soviet state was atheist and gave no official encouragement to religion.

Though real wages rose in the late 1940s and there was a small improvement in the supply of consumer goods in the early 1950s, Soviet workers remained poor by Western standards. However, they enjoyed an important social wage. A social-security system had been built up since the Revolution of 1917, and the state ensured that there was full employment - though some in the West scoffed at overmanning and inefficiency. Health services were free. Housing, heating, lighting and transport were kept relatively cheap, and basic education was free, though by 1953 the USSR was still struggling to provide a ten-year education for all. Some fees had been introduced in higher education in 1940 and were only abolished by Khrushchev nearly twenty years later. In spite of the vast post-war problems, however, positive efforts were made to increase the people's social wage. Moreover, taxation was light, especially direct taxation. Soviet society was very different from that in the capitalist world, its institutions moulded under close central direction to serve the system. Trade unions, for example, were concerned not only with improving working conditions but also with co-operative effort to boost output, encourage education and administer social services.

Stalin grew ever more secretive in his last years, even preferring to work at night rather than in daylight. When Zdhanov died in 1948, there was a purge of the minister's former colleagues and supporters, one of the upheavals which occurred from time to time in the Soviet leadership under Stalin. The Nineteenth Congress of the Communist Party, the first since 1939, met in 1952.

Stalin had planned to present sweeping changes to the Congress, including the abolition of the Politburo and the enlargement of many Party bodies such as the Central Committee – probably to entrench his own power even more deeply. He was in poor health, however, and Georgi Malenkov delivered the main address to the Congress, leading to speculation that he was Stalin's likely heir. The Congress was followed at the end of 1952 by a new purge, developing from the uncovering of an alleged 'Doctors' Plot', in which a group of leading doctors, mostly Jewish, were said to have murdered Zdhanov and other Party officials. Before Stalin's death from a stroke on 5 March 1953, the purge led to the arrest of 8000 alleged saboteurs and foreign agents, many of them Jews. But with Stalin dead the Soviet leadership was quick to declare the whole affair unfounded, and in 1954 a junior minister was executed for inventing it.

Pravda, the Soviet Communist Party newspaper, heaped praise on the dead Stalin:

> The heart of Lenin's comrade-in-arms, the standard bearer of his genius and his cause, the wise leader and teacher of the Communist Party of the Soviet Union, has ceased to beat.

For the last 25 of his 73 years, Stalin had been in almost total control of the USSR, an awesome and brutal dictator. But he had also been the leader of a people who had never known government which was not authoritarian. During his time in power the Soviet Union had fought off a savage and dangerous enemy in the Great Patriotic War, had developed unprecedented strength with which to resist the USA and hostile capitalists, and had even achieved a measure of prosperity. His death left a void and brought new anxieties for the Soviet people.

3.3 Soviet politics since 1953

3.3.1 The leadership in ferment, 1953–8

It is clear with the benefit of hindsight that the vital moves in determining the succession to Stalin were made within a fortnight of his death. Malenkov chose the office of Prime Minister, and Khrushchev took that of First Secretary (formerly Secretary-General) of the Communist Party. Malenkov's colleagues had persuaded him to hold only one office, hoping the USSR might then have a collective leadership and not a personal dictatorship, but Malenkov chose unwisely, undervaluing the power of the Secretaryship. At this time, Stalin's reforms of the Party in 1952 were reversed and an amnesty was granted to many short-term prisoners in his jails and labour camps. Khrushchev brought about the downfall of Beria, who was put to death for his misuse of power and crimes against the Soviet people, and in 1954 the KGB became the new Soviet Committee for State Security.

Khrushchev was aged 59 when Stalin died. Born the son of a miner, he had a long history of service to the Communist Party and the Soviet Union, one of his main achievements being the building of the Moscow Metro (underground railway). Malenkov was younger, had assisted Stalin in collectivizing agriculture and, after Zdhanov's death, had become the favourite to succeed Stalin. Malenkov now urged radical changes in policy – a greater emphasis on agriculture and consumer goods, and a relaxation of international tension which might reduce the need for high military spending. Khrushchev attacked such ideas as 'revisionist' (departing from the true path of Marxism–Leninism), and in February 1955 Malenkov was forced to resign, conceding that he lacked sufficient experience for the post and that he had acted wrongly in developing agriculture and neglecting heavy industry, errors which Khrushchev had criticized. Nikolai Bulganin, a former 'mayor' of Moscow and friend of Khrushchev, replaced Malenkov as Prime Minister, and Marshal Zhukov – hero of the Great Patriotic War and another Khrushchev supporter – became Defence Minister.

The Twentieth Congress of the Communist Party in January 1956 carried the First Secretary yet higher in his pursuit of supremacy. Taking a risk, though with a good deal of pre-arranged support and in a secret session, Khrushchev attacked Stalin's record and called for changes ('destalinization'). He attacked Stalin for his cruelty and the viciousness of his rule, for numerous errors of judgement in both war and peace, and for building a personality cult of grotesque proportions. Khrushchev is said to have described the dramatic impact of his 'secret speech':

> It was so quiet in the huge hall you could hear a fly buzzing. . . . This was the first most [delegates] had heard of the human tragedy which our Party had undergone – a tragedy stemming from the sickness of Stalin's character [of] which Lenin had warned us – and which Stalin had confirmed in his confession to Mikoyan and me: 'I trust no one, not even myself.'

Changes were already well under way towards 'peaceful coexistence' with the West (see section 4.6) and towards a less harsh environment within the Soviet Union; they now speeded up. More prisoners were set free, few new political arrests were made, and censorship was further relaxed. Khrushchev was also steadily taking up Malenkov's economic policies for agricultural expansion and more consumer goods, just as Stalin had taken up many of Trotsky's policies after the latter had been ridiculed for them and disgraced.

There were many Party members who disapproved of Khrushchev's secret (but leaked) speech, however. They drew together around Malenkov in what became known as 'the anti-Party group' for advocating more emphasis on good management than on ideology. Molotov, Soviet Foreign Minister from 1939 to 1949 and from 1953 to 1956, supported the group, and Bulganin flirted with it. But Khrushchev resisted demands for his resignation and, loyally supported by Zhukov, in 1957 outmanoeuvred his critics. Malenkov was sent to manage a hydroelectric plant far from Moscow; Molotov spent three years as ambassador to the Mongolian People's Republic; and Bulganin lasted as Prime Minister only until March 1958, when he was replaced by Khrushchev himself and became Chairman of the Soviet Bank. In the meantime, late in 1957, Zhukov too was forced into retirement, perhaps for pressing the interests of the army more strongly than those of the Communist Party. His place as Defence Minister was taken by Marshal Malinovsky.

By the end of 1958, Khrushchev's authority seemed secure in the two posts of Party Secretary and Prime Minister. But his success was most of all a triumph for the Party. The changes in policy, both foreign and internal, were changes with which most by 1958 were in agreement. The time was ripe to abandon the excesses of Stalinism without abandoning the basic goals of Marxism–Leninism. In 1961 Stalin's body was removed from Lenin's mausoleum and reburied by the wall of the Kremlin (the seat of the Soviet government), and Stalingrad was renamed Volgograd in the same year. Yet it appeared that the seemingly jovial and tubby Khrushchev had inherited something of Stalin's personal authority, albeit on a less grandiose scale. His power was never as completely unchallenged as Stalin's, and his opponents were disgraced rather than killed, but the system had again submerged collective leadership beneath the personality of the Party's First Secretary.

3.3.2 The Khrushchev years to 1964

Khrushchev's leadership proved erratic. Though he improved understanding with the West, there were nevertheless severe crises in East–West relations while, at the same time, relations between the Soviet Union and Communist China became strained. In marked contrast to Stalin, Khrushchev travelled extensively outside the USSR, but he was not always a dignified representative of the Soviets: he startled the United Nations and embarrassed his colleagues in 1960, for example, when he interrupted a debate by banging his shoe on his desk. But the strength of the Soviet Union continued to grow, perhaps briefly gaining the edge on the USA. The USSR launched the first man-made satellite in space, *Sputnik I*, in 1957, five months ahead of the American *Vanguard I*, while in 1961 Yuri Gagarin in *Vostok I* became the first man to orbit the earth in space, almost a year before the American John Glenn. Khrushchev's propaganda made the most of these successes, but he remained acutely aware of the dangers of nuclear conflict and was careful to withhold nuclear secrets from the Chinese, who assumed that success in space meant military superiority.

Khrushchev was aware too of the burden of military spending. He hoped that improved international relations might lead to some reduction in this, but admitted in 1963:

> It would be desirable to build more enterprises that make products for satisfying man's requirements . . . to invest more in agriculture, and to expand housing construction. [But] life dictates the necessity of spending enormous funds on maintaining our military power . . . This reduces and cannot help but reduce the people's possibilities for obtaining direct benefit.

Sections 3.4 and 3.5 will show that Khrushchev aimed to extend Soviet agriculture into the Virgin Lands and to improve output by decentralizing control and setting up regional economic councils. He also tried to bring about a more liberal society. But he was not without opposition. Decentralization was not successful and, in 1962, he alarmed the Communist Party with new ideas for dividing it into agricultural and industrial sections, which might improve economic management but could weaken the Party by undermining its unity. Those hostile to his plans, which might also lead to the weakening of the armed forces, rallied round Frol Koslov, once a close ally of Khrushchev, and Defence Minister Malinovsky. Already uneasy about Khrushchev's policies towards the West, in 1963 they bitterly attacked his apparent goodwill towards President Tito's independent-minded Yugoslavia.

Khrushchev survived the various power struggles, including that of 1963, but his colleagues were now tiring of his unpredictability, his incurable optimism which led to rash promises, and his growing tendency to act without consulting them. They found him proud and conceited. In July 1964 when Koslov's health had failed, Leonid Brezhnev replaced him as the Communist Party's First Deputy Secretary and Khrushchev's likely heir. In October, Khrushchev's colleagues voted to strip him of his offices and *Pravda* announced:

> The Central Committee satisfied the request of N.S. Khrushchev to relieve him of the duties of First Secretary of the Central Committee, member of the Presidium of the Central Committee and Chairman of the Council of Ministers USSR in connection with advanced age and poor health.

Two years later Khrushchev was also removed from the Central Committee itself. He spent his last years living on a pension in quiet retirement outside Moscow, until his death in 1971.

3.3.3 The Brezhnev years, 1964–82

Brezhnev immediately succeeded Khrushchev as First Secretary, a post again termed Secretary-General two years later. A renewed effort to avoid one-man domination led to the appointment of Alexei Kosygin as Prime Minister. Anastas Mikoyan, a Bolshevik of long standing, became Chairman of the Supreme Soviet but retired in 1965 in favour of Nikolai Podgorny. In effect Podgorny was Head of State, the USSR's President. The triumvirate of Brezhnev, Kosygin and Podgorny gave the Soviet Union government by veterans in the service of Party and country. Brezhnev was always the key figure, however. Aged 58 in 1964, his background was in land management and engineering. In the Party he had reached the Politburo in 1957. Like Kosygin, who came from a background of textiles and economic planning, Brezhnev was a moderate conservative who abhorred the excesses of Stalinism but was likely to avoid the erratic excursions of Khrushchevism. The triumvirate was cautious, in favour of stability and continuity, but it wasted no time in dismantling most of Khrushchev's recent administrative changes. The Party scrapped the divisions made by Khrushchev and, in the next year, 1965, the regional economic councils were also abolished in favour of a return to centralized control. Brezhnev personally condemned much of Khrushchev's reorganization as stemming from 'parochialism'; at the same time he encouraged Kosygin to make the old system less bureaucratic and more flexible – what Khrushchev had in fact aimed at – by giving to the managers of certain industrial enterprises greater freedom to pursue their own initiatives.

The Party remained supreme. The membership of about seven million in 1956 grew to over twelve million ten years later and to over seventeen million in the late 1970s. These were by no means passive members; those who joined the

Party simply to advance their careers were likely quickly to be removed from it. A higher proportion of the Soviet population (about 270 million in the early 1980s) was engaged in active politics than in most countries in the West, supporting the Soviet claim to be 'a people's democracy' in a one-party state. Brezhnev nevertheless achieved great personal stature, and this was confirmed when he replaced Podgorny in 1977, combining the Presidency with his role as First Secretary.

This was also the year in which the USSR adopted a new constitution. It declared the Soviet Union a 'socialist state of the whole nation' – still working towards true communism – and the Communist Party:

> the leading and guiding force in Soviet society and nucleus of all state and public organisations, [existing] for the people and [serving] the people.

Civil liberties were again guaranteed, in so far as they did not injure the interests of society, and this time the rights included those of peasants to private plots. There were no fundamental changes, however, though 'the dictatorship of the proletariat' was now officially consigned to the past.

By the time Kosygin resigned as Prime Minister shortly before his death in 1980, aged 76, the Brezhnev administration had begun to appear a government of old men. Brezhnev's power had lasted longer than any but Stalin's. He had certainly provided stability but by 1980 his health was failing, giving rise to speculation about the future. In some ways, the administration seemed to be drifting, in spite of the continuity provided by men such as Andrei Gromyko – Foreign Minister since 1957 and still vigorous at 71. Nikolai Tikhonov, only a year younger than Kosygin, succeeded him as Prime Minister. Brezhnev's successor seemed more likely to come from within the Party Secretariat, however.

While Kosygin's interests had been mainly economic and managerial, Brezhnev had been much concerned with foreign policy and international relations. He gave his name to the Brezhnev Doctrine of 1968, which was put forward to justify the Soviet bloc's intervention in Czechoslovakia, to overthrow an administration which was trying to liberalize the system (see section 8.2.4). The Brezhnev Doctrine held that any internal threat to an existing socialist system was automatically 'the concern of all socialist countries'. Brezhnev believed it his duty to preserve the Soviet system, including Soviet influence in eastern Europe. To the West, his regime seemed stern and unsmiling, ever careful of its 'security'. In the late 1970s President Carter of the USA was bitterly critical of the Soviet Union's record on human rights and of its alleged expansionist ambitions in Afghanistan and parts of Africa. Nor was Brezhnev able to do much to repair Soviet relations with China. There was genuine sorrow among many of the Soviet people, nevertheless, when Brezhnev died in November 1982; and it was not until some four years later, when Gorbachev was aiming to speed modernization in the Soviet Union, that Brezhnev's reputation came under sharp attack with developing criticism of the inefficiency and corruption over which he had presided.

3.3.4 A new generation

The average age of the Politburo in 1982 was 69. With Brezhnev's death, an era was ending, however. So far the Soviet Union had been ruled by men with personal memories of the Revolutions of 1917, who vividly remembered the horrors of Stalinism and of the Great Patriotic War, and the colossal struggles to build a prosperous USSR. It seemed unavoidable that the Soviet Union would soon pass into the hands of a younger generation of leaders, some of whom might be less awed by history than their elders, and perhaps less cautious. But there was no instant change. Two days after Brezhnev's death Yuri Andropov became Secretary-General by unanimous vote. A Deputy Secretary since 1962, head of the KGB since 1967 and full member of the Politburo since 1973, Andropov was already 68 years old and almost at once speculation began about his health. Meanwhile, the offices of President and Prime Minister remained in other hands – those of Vasily Kuznetsov and Tikhonov respectively. Andropov took over the Presidency only shortly before his death in February 1984. He was succeeded as Secretary-General and then as President by Konstantin Chernenko, though Chernenko was already over 70. For the moment, the older generation was holding on to power, though Andropov would have preferred the younger Mikhail Gorbachev as his successor. Sooner or later the Soviet Union would need to be reformed, probably along the lines urged first by Khrushchev, then by Kosygin and Andropov himself: less centralized control with the scope for more local initiatives. When Chernenko too died in March 1985, the way was clear for Gorbachev to become Secretary-General. The veteran Andrei Gromyko, the former Foreign Minister, took over the Presidency and Nikolai Ryzkhov, a Gorbachev supporter, became Prime Minister shortly afterwards.

Gorbachev had been born in 1931 of peasant stock and joined the Communist Party in 1952. He soon impressed foreign observers by an outgoing attitude different from that of many earlier Soviet leaders. By Soviet standards, many of his ideas seemed liberal and, university-educated in law, he seemed to encourage expectations that he might pursue administrative modernization, as well as scientific advancement and technological innovation on a scale unprecedented in the USSR. He had nevertheless to work within the Soviet system; Khrushchev's example remained as a warning to all of the perils of being too unorthodox, and in 1987 conservatives in the Party were stiffening their resistance to change. However, Gorbachev displayed more subtle political skills than Krushchev, steadily and skilfully isolating and moving opponents to *perestroika*[G] (restructuring) and *glasnost*[G] (openness) to less important positions in the party. In 1988 he was carefully building a broader base of support for reform than Krushchev had managed to do, though much remained to be done.

3.4 The Soviet economy since 1953

Economic planning and official control continued to be the central features of the Soviet Union's command economy[G] after the death of Stalin. Gosplan continued to regulate investment and output, fixing targets, prices and wages – the scale of its undertakings was massive – but there were changes from time to time in detailed organization, and politics sometimes dictated changes of emphasis. Khrushchev was quick to take over Malenkov's policy of diverting resources from heavy to light industry, aware of the need to raise the living standards of the Soviet people. He aimed to achieve 'goulash communism' – meaning that the people would have meat dishes and consumer comforts, not merely cabbage soup and bare necessities. He hoped the 1980s would see universal plenty and the attainment of full communism with its freedoms and universal prosperity. But there were other pressures, including those of the military, and heavy industry continued to dominate the economy.

When Khrushchev fell from power in 1964, the growth rate of the Soviet GNP was only 7.4 per cent, four per cent below what was usual in the late 1950s and the lowest peacetime rate since the 1920s. This was partly because reconstruction after the Great Patriotic War was now virtually complete and, as the Soviet Union grew richer, growth rates were bound to fall. (From 1951 to 1976, the USA averaged only an annual 3.1 per cent growth.) At the same time, it needed constant struggle and adaptation to make the Soviet planning machine more efficient and, in spite of Khrushchev's ambitions, the production of consumer goods was far behind that of the West. In the years 1961–5 the Soviet output of capital goods grew by 58 per cent, that of consumer goods by only 36 per cent.

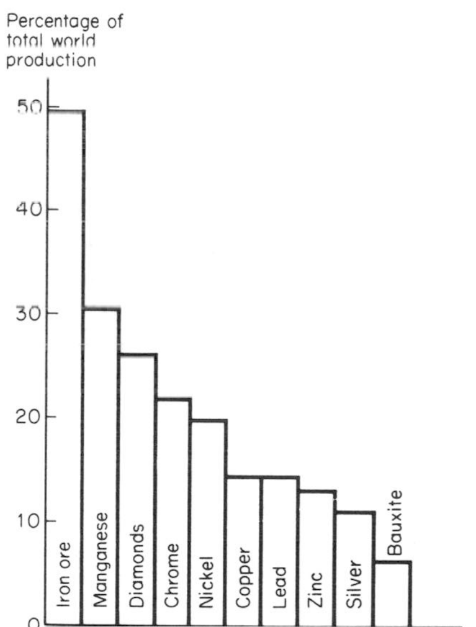

Adapted from M. Kidron and R. Segal, *The State of the World Atlas* (Pluto Press and Pan Books, 1981)

Fig. 3.4 Soviet resources: the Soviet Union's production of minerals, 1976

Khrushchev was also disappointed by the development of Soviet agriculture. Little came of his ideas for *agrogorods*, agricultural cities where farm workers might live and share more advanced amenities, but he continued to favour large-scale farming units (see section 3.2.2). In 1958 he abolished the Machine Tractor Stations, expecting that the kolkhozes would now be big enough to buy their own machinery, but the change was premature and output suffered. Khrushchev's largest enterprise, however, was the Virgin Lands Project, which aimed to increase Soviet grain-growing lands by more than 30 per cent by ploughing infertile and unproductive areas, mainly in northern Kazakhstan, a thousand miles east and south-east of Moscow. The work began in 1954 and, by 1962, 58 million hectares had been brought into production. Khrushchev demanded a great increase in the provision of fertilizers and farm machinery. In a vast resettlement programme hundreds of thousands of workers were taken to the new areas and encouraged by financial incentives and concessions to man what were for the most part new sovkhozes. Impressive early crop yields soon gave way to worse harvests, due largely to poor soil and a hostile climate. In 1963 the harvest failed both in the Virgin Lands and in the Ukraine, requiring grain to be imported from the USA and damaging Khrushchev's reputation. Brezhnev persevered with the project and, with improving technology, the new lands contributed usefully, if modestly, to the USSR's grain supplies.

Grain harvests as a whole continued to fluctuate, yielding 140 million tonnes in 1975, 237 million in 1978 and 179 million in 1979. The weather accounted for much of the variation, but the system too had its weaknesses. Though the state regularly put about a quarter of its investment into agriculture, the results were often disappointing and sometimes made worse by problems of storage and transport. The peasants for their part remained devoted to their private plots, which both Khrushchev and Brezhnev accepted; though they accounted for only a tiny part of the lands farmed, the private plots produced around a quarter of the USSR's total farm output in the late 1970s. Output overall tended to do little more than keep pace with rising population and in bad years the Soviets had to import grain from the USA and elsewhere. This occurred in 1972, though the Ninth Five-Year Plan in 1971 had promised 'a significant increase' in the standard of living, envisaging agricultural expansion and priority for consumer goods over heavy industry. Grain was again imported in 1975, when a contract was signed for annual US deliveries to the Soviet Union, mainly to ensure food for Soviet livestock to keep up the supply of meat to the people. President Carter, however, found withholding grain shipments a tempting diplomatic weapon to use against the Soviet authorities (see section 2.4.2).

The Ninth Five-Year Plan missed many of its targets and it was clear that Soviet industrial growth was slowing down. In the late 1970s, the annual growth in GNP was below four per cent, falling to three per cent and less in the early 1980s. During the 1970s the Soviet Union had extended its trading links with the West, especially with West Germany. It had stepped up oil production, prompted by the energy crisis in the mid-1970s though, at the same time, the

Soviets were less affected than most capitalist states by the international economic crisis (see section 21.1). The Soviets went on developing Siberia with its vast material resources, agreeing in 1981 to supply natural gas from Siberia to western Europe. In 1983 a United Nations economic survey predicted that, by reason both of resources and of policy, the Soviet Union was far better placed to achieve new economic growth than most countries in western Europe.

Although unemployment was widespread elsewhere, Soviet citizens still had work when Brezhnev died in 1982. They undoubtedly experienced improvements in their economic well-being during the Khrushchev and Brezhnev years, benefiting not only from the Soviet Union's social wage but also from social reforms made after 1953. Khrushchev made certain social security benefits more generous and gave some minimum-wage protection to the low-paid. Brezhnev too tried to raise the incomes of the poor, and succeeded in narrowing the gap between them and the higher-paid. A five-day working week was adopted in the late 1960s and by 1971 the average hours worked per week in industry were just under 41, almost ten fewer than when Stalin died. A special effort was made to assist farm workers, previously neglected. By giving them old-age pensions in 1964, Khrushchev began the move to bring the peasantry into line with industrial workers. Brezhnev slowly but steadily extended their entitlement to welfare benefits and education, and in the late 1970s also granted them the right to the passes necessary for travel within the USSR. When Brezhnev died, the gap between the incomes and rights of peasants and those of urban workers had been greatly reduced.

There was little evidence to suggest that this would produce immediate improvement in agricultural output. The Eleventh Five-Year Plan in 1981 aimed yet again to improve the lot of the Soviet consumer, but in the Plan's first year – and even on private plots – agriculture was so disappointing that an ambitious new agricultural programme was announced for 1982–90. The imbalance which persisted in the Soviet economy was starkly shown by growth in the period 1965–80, when industrial output grew by 270 per cent and that of agriculture by only 35 per cent.

It was clear, however, that even in industry the Soviet economy now lagged behind the West in many respects and, in quantity and quality, the production of consumer goods in particular was still disappointing for many Soviet citizens. Gorbachev wanted better management and higher standards of workmanship. He was ready to make use of examples in the West, offering rewards to encourage managerial enterprise and effort, reducing the people's suspicion of computers and more open information systems, and encouraging high technology which, while reducing traditional back-breaking labour, might also threaten jobs. Such revolutionary change inevitably challenged the conservative elements in the Soviet leadership who were suspicious of even limited amounts of private enterprise and shocked by Gorbachev's suggestions for reintroducing some measures of self-employment among professionals. These were changes that many Soviet citizens were now demanding, but Gorbachev's leadership would be tested in the struggle to effect such 'liberalization'.

3.5 Soviet society since 1953

3.5.1 Continuity and change

Compared with that of most other states, Soviet society has remained remarkably stable and docile since 1953. The outbreak of nationalist demonstrations in Azerbaijan and the Baltic republics in 1988 was the first large-scale and visible disturbance of this pattern. Given the system's foundations in co-operation rather than competition, Soviet citizens have been generally obedient and undemanding. Nevertheless, expectations have risen, and since 1953 the authorities have made considerable efforts to raise the people's living standards. Khrushchev's efforts included an attack on housing problems, though his large blocks of publicly owned flats put quantity before quality. He also encouraged building co-operatives to add to the stock of homes in private ownership, a policy which was continued by Brezhnev: by the 1980s the private sector owned about twenty per cent of urban homes (mainly flats) in the RSFSR (the Russian Soviet Federative Socialist Republic – see fig. 3.3). Two million homes a year were regularly built in the public sector after the death of Stalin, but housing still remained a major stumbling block in improving the quality of life of the Soviet people. The supply of household durables meanwhile increased. By the end of the 1970s about three in four Soviet homes had a television set, about three in five a washing-machine and refrigerator. Economic Plans were by now more ambitious about colour televisions and cars. In diet too there was slow but steady improvement after 1953, food prices being held down by substantial state subsidies, as were the prices of many essentials.

One problem facing the Soviet leadership was to raise standards not only in Moscow, where housing, for example, was generally better than in other cities, but also across the vast expanse of the Soviet Union. Another was to reconsider the scale of the USSR's free and subsidized services as the country grew more prosperous. Housing development suffered from a shortage of capital, most of it coming from rents and property taxes, which were kept artificially low. Free or very cheap fuel for heating and cooking had great social advantages but could lead to waste. Anti-socialists alleged that the massive social services consumed too many resources and stifled initiative; socialist themselves debated what might be the role of the authorities in a socialist society in the closing years of the twentieth century, in case order and co-operation gave way to disorder and discontent.

It had already become much more difficult to isolate the Soviet Union from outside influences, though the authorities still tried to keep contact between foreigners and Soviet citizens to the barest minimum when the Olympic Games were held in Moscow in 1980. Khrushchev's cautious relaxation of controls had allowed some travel, and cultural exchanges with the West were now encouraged and visitors were admitted into the USSR. One result was an embarrassing trickle of defections, with some Soviet citizens declining to return home after visits abroad – to the delight of Western propagandists. Another result was the access to the USSR of Western fashions and pop music – jeans and pop records even becoming a sort of underground 'currency' – and to traditional Russian problems such as alcoholism were now added spasms of hooliganism and vandalism, in spite of a disapproving society and a stern code of law. Stern laws – the formal introduction of the death penalty in 1962 – were also invoked to deal with the re-emergence of bribery, an old Russian problem which the Bolsheviks had tried to wipe out. Soviet authorities took a hard line against offences involving 'capitalist-type' crime, and it was therefore especially disturbing that Brezhnev's last years were clouded by what seemed like an increase in corruption, illegal private transactions and the misuse of public resources. Andropov, and then Gorbachev, gave priority to attacking such abuses with renewed vigour; they identified specific targets in corruption, drunkenness and inefficiency.

3.5.2 Minorities and dissidents

The census of 1979 showed a Soviet population of 262 million. Just over a half were Russians, the rest a mixture of well over a hundred nationalities with various languages and cultures (see fig. 3.3). The dominance of Russians and russification (the policy of imposing Russian values and practices) were resented as they had been in the time of the tsars, and nationalist protest against Russian arrogance – by Uzbeks, Ukrainians and the peoples of the Baltic Republics, for example – was probably the most widespread form of organized protest in the USSR. Such protest was sometimes linked with protest against religious intolerance and centralization, for example by Jews, by Muslims in Uzbekistan and other parts of Soviet Central Asia, and by Baptists, who had vigorously resisted the attack on their churches by Khrushchev. But active protest by all these national and religious groups within the Soviet Union was on a small scale, involving in the 1970s hardly more than a quarter of a million campaigners – a tiny percentage of the Soviet population. The diversities within the Soviet Union nevertheless brought Gorbachev a serious problem in 1987–8 when the Christian minority in the Republic of Azerbaijan protested against discrimination by the Muslim Azerbaijani majority, and demanded that the area in which it enjoys a local majority should be transferred to the neighbouring Republic of Armenia. The liberalization of the Soviet Union under Gorbachev also re-awakened national and ethnic grievances elsewhere, notably in the economically advanced Baltic Republics. The populations in these areas resented the russification of their lands and sought greater political as well as economic autonomy. These problems of ethnic management in conditions of greater political freedom seemed likely to cause major headaches for the Soviet leadership in the late 1980s and early 1990s.

Khrushchev had clumsily launched a campaign to reduce the number of churches of various denominations which still existed in the 1950s, asserting that the time had now come to end religious practices in the USSR. Many churches, synagogues and mosques were closed, but religious belief was not diminished. Brezhnev adopted a softer approach, advocating tolerance not only of the Orthodox Church with its 40 million or so members but also of many others which were unlikely to present political opposition to the Communist

Party. The state still tried to undermine religious belief in the hope that it would eventually die out. But among peoples of all faiths, belief persisted - publicly in registered places of worship, less openly in communities not registered with the authorities.

After the death of Stalin there was a general problem in defining and extending civil liberties. Khrushchev introduced a comparatively liberal phase (see section 3.3). Censorship was relaxed though not always consistent. Boris Pasternak's *Doctor Zhivago* was not officially available in the Soviet Union, for example, and Pasternak was denied travel rights to collect his Nobel Prize for Literature in 1958. On the other hand, Khrushchev in 1962 approved Alexander Solzhenitsyn's *One Day in the Life of Ivan Denisovich* - perhaps welcoming the first-hand evidence it provided of the barbarities of Stalin's prison camps, which Khrushchev was then emptying. Writers and artists generally were by no means free from criticism and obstruction, but they no longer lived in terror and many ideas were now allowed to surface. The poet Yevgeny Yevtushenko, for example, protested against anti-Semitism in *Babi Yar* (1961). In the next year, Shostakovich set this poem to music along with others in his Thirteenth Symphony. The authorities hesitated and expressed displeasure with both Yevtushenko and Shostakovich, and under Brezhnev the Symphony ceased to be performed in the USSR. Khrushchev responded unfavourably to abstract and modern art, to jazz and to non-traditional music. More importantly, his personal taste continued to influence how much freedom was available to Soviet writers, musicians and artists. They found it was rather more under Khrushchev than Brezhnev was later willing to allow.

Some tightening up began during 1965. In 1966 writers Andrei Sinyavsky and Yuli Daniel were imprisoned for publishing anti-Soviet opinions abroad. Thus began the history of Soviet *dissidents*, intellectuals who from a variety of differing standpoints criticized the Soviet system. By the 1980s they numbered perhaps 20 000, some in exile in the West or beyond the Urals, some in prisons or mental hospitals, some still at liberty. They had no mass support among the Soviet people, were rootless and isolated, and were therefore easily derided by Yuri Andropov of the KGB in 1977 as the product of:

> political or ideological aberrations, religious fanaticism, nationalist quirks, personality failures and resentments and, in many cases, psychological instability.

Yet they included eminent Soviet citizens such as Andrei Sakharov, scientist and peace campaigner, who, like Pasternak, was unable to collect his Nobel Prize (for Peace, in 1975) and in the early 1980s was to be found in internal exile in Gorky. Others like Alexander Solzhenitsyn, writer and mystic in a distinctively Russian tradition, had by then taken refuge in the West, where propagandists rushed to exploit any anti-Soviet opportunity and focused much attention on dissidents generally. In 1975 the Soviets had signed the Helsinki Agreement which included a guarantee of human rights (see section 13.4.3), and it was not only the West which turned the spotlight on the USSR's honouring of this guarantee. Yuri Orlov, a Soviet physicist, set up a group in Moscow to monitor the Soviet record, but Orlov was arrested in 1977 and his fellow dissidents struggled to keep the group in existence.

Little or nothing came from an attempt in 1978 to set up within the USSR free trade unions with the negotiating rights common in the West. Such political actions, like the activities of the dissidents, were a nuisance to the Soviet authorities but not a great threat. Brezhnev sought to preserve discipline with a population in prisons and labour camps of perhaps around two million, but of these the dissidents and political activists were a very tiny minority – like other 'criminals', unsupported by the Soviet people. The people as a whole were told only what the Communist Party wished them to hear and it appeared that, after the comparative liberalism of Khrushchev, Brezhnev had restored quiet uniformity. The attacks on Stalin's rule, for example, became more muted though his image was not much restored.

The West keeps alive the issue of the dissidents which tarnishes the Soviet reputation. Here again, Gorbachev moved towards more liberal policies. In 1986, for example, he allowed Anatoly Shcharansky, a Jewish physicist and campaigner for human rights imprisoned as early as 1977, to emigrate to Israel, while Andrei Sakharov was allowed to return to Moscow from exile in Gorky. Gorbachev wanted to improve the Soviet government's reputation, relaxing its secrecy, meeting the people personally on walkabouts and lessening the persecution of those critical of the Soviet system and especially of its record on human rights. He advocated policies of *glasnost* (for more openness and freer discussion in Soviet society) and *perestroika* (for more initiative and greater efficiency in the restructured economy). But at the same time, he naturally wished to preserve some of the stability and continuity which had been a feature of Soviet society since the death of Stalin.

3.6 Soviet foreign policy

There was continuity too in Soviet foreign policy. As early as February 1946 Zdhanov spoke of the need to be 'extremely vigilant' in a world full of 'reactionary elements . . . hostile to the Soviet Union'. From the outset in 1945 Soviet policy gave priority to the country's security and it continued to do so. Stalin's successors might differ from him on points of detail, becoming a little more outward-looking, for example, but they all put Soviet security first, adhering to the post-war thinking Malenkov had summarized:

> There [are] cases in history when the fruits of victory slipped out of the victor's hands. This must not happen to us. . . . We must, in the first place, consolidate and strengthen still further our Soviet socialist state. . . . And we must remember that our friends will respect us only so long as we are strong. . . . There is no respect for the weak ones, and the weak ones get beaten.

The pursuit of strength meant a furious arms race with the USA and heavy military spending which burdened the Soviet economy. It also meant a neurotic anxiety about Soviet frontiers, which manifested itself in a determination to create and preserve friendly 'buffer' states. This was most evident in eastern Europe – where the West was to call states such as Poland 'Soviet satellites' – but also in Mongolia and Afghanistan. Unlike the USA, the USSR had vast and

Fig. 3.5 Nikita Khrushchev (*centre*), with Walther Ulbricht on his left, during a visit to a collective farm at Hakeborn in East Germany, September 1957. Himself an 'expert' in agriculture, Krushchev showed a professional interest in the maize crop.

vulnerable land frontiers. After a brief period of friendship with Communist China in the 1950s, concern mounted over the long Sino–Soviet frontier which divided China's hundreds of millions from the often sparsely populated Asiatic lands of the USSR.

Ideological differences sharpened suspicions between the Soviet Union and other powers, especially the USA. What one saw as defensive, the other was likely to see as offensive – perhaps part of some deep-laid plan to extend ideology and influence by means of a mixture of subversion and ruthless aggression. Like the USA, the USSR became involved in international affairs far beyond its own borders (see Table 2.2). Neither superpower was willing to be left behind by the other, as will be seen in the units which follow, especially Units 4, 13 and 21. Both superpowers were guilty not only of hard-nosed meddling in the affairs of others in pursuit of their own interests, but also of the belief that a show of strength was an essential element of diplomacy.

For ten years after 1945 tension mounted in the highly charged outpourings of Cold War rhetoric. Khrushchev tried to put on the brakes, urging a policy of 'peaceful coexistence' (a phrase borrowed from Malenkov) in his speech to the Party Congress in 1956. Three years later, he expressed the alternatives simply:

> In our day there are only two ways, peaceful coexistence or the most destructive war in history. There is no third way.

Even so, Khrushchev plunged into dangerous diplomatic confrontation with President Kennedy over the placing of missiles in Cuba. This crisis in 1962 alarmed many of Khrushchev's colleagues since it coincided with worsening relations with China, thus exposing the Soviet Union to dangers in both the West and the East. Brezhnev, by contrast, pursued Soviet security through *détente* (the West's preferred term for peaceful coexistence) along rather quieter paths in the late 1960s and 1970s, achieving worthwhile results with President Nixon, but he could do little to heal the rift with China. In the late 1970s, arguments about human rights, Soviet policy in Afghanistan, and US policy in central America and numerous international trouble-spots brought what seemed to be a new East–West Cold War, occurring as they did at a time of growing anxiety almost everywhere about the relentless development of the nuclear arsenals of the superpowers. Andropov's administration began unhappily when in 1983 a South Korean airliner, trespassing in Soviet airspace, was shot down with the loss of 269 lives. The Soviets had seemed to confuse the airliner with enemy spy-planes, responding savagely to a flight in a sensitive military area not very far from Japan. Such concern for Soviet security was little removed from the concern Stalin had shown after the Second World War, and it continued to preoccupy the Soviet leadership.

UNIT 4

The East–West Cold War to 1955: the Ice Age

4.1 Post-war divisions

The Grand Alliance which defeated the Axis powers quickly crumbled with the coming of peace in 1945. Within four years of peace, the West created the North Atlantic Treaty Organization (NATO), claiming it was necessary for protection against the Soviet Union. In Europe and Asia, and on the world stage at the United Nations, the superpowers were competing vigorously, each in defence of its own interests (see sections 1.3, 1.4 and 1.5), and terms such as 'Iron Curtain' and 'Cold War' now became commonplace in the vocabulary of the media.

One result of post-war rivalries was the division of Europe into areas of US and Soviet influence, which were separated by a frontier the Soviets eventually equipped with wire, watch-towers, control posts and a guarded strip of bare no man's land. 'Iron Curtain' was not a new phrase but it was Churchill, speaking at Fulton in the USA in March 1946, who popularized it when he applied it to this frontier:

> From Stettin [more accurately, near Lübeck – see fig. 4.1], in the Baltic, to Trieste, in the Adriatic, an iron curtain has descended across the continent. Behind that line lie all the capitals of the ancient states of Central and Eastern Europe – Warsaw, Berlin, Prague, Vienna, Budapest, Belgrade, Bucharest and Sofia. All these famous cities . . . lie in the Soviet sphere.

At the end of 1955 the Curtain remained, though fig. 4.1 shows that by this time it took a rather different line, since Yugoslavia (defying direction from Moscow) and eastern Austria (evacuated by the Soviets) were then no longer 'in the Soviet sphere'.

Units 1, 2 and 3 have shown that Soviet influence over eastern Europe was one of several reasons for the East–West bitterness after 1945 which gave rise to talk of a 'Cold War'. The term was first used in April 1947 by Bernard Baruch, a US presidential adviser, and was symptomatic of the approach adopted by the US towards the Soviets at this time. As early as January 1946 President Truman had declared:

Fig. 4.1 Divided Europe: the Iron Curtain

> Unless Russia is faced with an iron fist and strong language, war is in the making. Only one language do they understand – 'How many divisions have you?' . . . I'm tired of babying the Soviets.

This reinforced the hard line Truman had adopted even in 1945 (see section 1.2). Now in 1947 he determined to 'contain' the Soviet Union; the Truman Doctrine was under lively consideration (see section 4.4), and the international temperature was getting rapidly more icy. The Cold War signified a war of words with the Soviet Union, a massive propaganda conflict. It also meant an ideological struggle, a weapons race, competition in espionage, economic conflict and a manoeuvring for position in Europe and elsewhere by almost all means short of armed confrontation. While Truman was US President and while Stalin lived, the Cold War was at its height, the frost most severe.

This unit traces some of the main developments which contributed to the Cold War during the ten years to 1955. Much of the hostility centred on Germany (see section 4.2), but Europe as a whole was also divided between East and West (see section 4.3). International relations grew worse with successive crises until the two sides confronted one another in armed camps (section 4.4). The crises spread to Asia (section 4.5), and only when new leaders came to the fore in and after 1953 were there signs of a thaw (section 4.6).

4.2 Two Germanies and two Berlins

4.2.1 Four-power occupation

Agreements at Yalta and Potsdam in 1945 provided a basis for the post-war treatment of Germany. West of the Oder–Neisse Line, the country was divided into three zones of occupation, to be administered by the USA, the USSR and Britain. A fourth zone was added when the French insisted on equal treatment. Berlin, deep inside the Soviet Zone, was similarly divided into four sectors (see section 1.3 and fig. 1.4). The Allies agreed that the Germans should be demilitarized, denazified and democratized ('the three Ds'), and the Allied Control Council – appointed to tackle the immediate post-war problems of hunger, disease, devastation, and enormous numbers of displaced persons – achieved healthy East–West co-operation. It soon became clear, however, that there was little detailed agreement on longer-term aims.

The US authorities had toyed with the idea of turning Germany into a mainly agricultural country, the Morgenthau Plan of 1944 proposing de-industrialization (a fourth 'D'). The idea was never practicable and, when the war ended, American attitudes became less vindictive. The Soviets, however, insisted on reparations to help Soviet rebuilding (see sections 1.3.2, 3.1 and 3.2). The USA and Britain came to think it essential to give aid to devastated German communities and thus, when the Soviets collected their agreed reparations from the West's zones of Germany, the USA and Britain began to fear that it was they who were helping to fund the USSR's revival. In May 1946, therefore, the Americans halted reparations from the US Zone.

It had been widely believed that US interest in Europe might not long outlast the Second World War and that US troops would be withdrawn. In September 1946 James Byrnes, US Secretary of State, made a speech in Stuttgart, clarifying his government's policy:

> We will not shirk our duty. We are not withdrawing. We are staying here. As long as there is an occupation army in Germany, American forces will be part of that occupation army.

This was an important departure from traditional US isolationism, and perhaps the point at which the Truman administration made up its mind to consolidate the West's position in West Germany.

The USA and Britain agreed to merge their zones of occupation to form Bizonia, a single economic unit which came into being in January 1947. They had already begun rebuilding the economy in their own parts of Germany, a policy about which the French as well as the Soviets had misgivings, in case Germany should again be in a position to threaten its neighbours. The French Zone was therefore not linked to Bizonia until 1948.

Germans in Bizonia were encouraged to take part in local and regional government and to launch new economic enterprises, in keeping with Western ideas of democracy and capitalism and with the announcement by Byrnes at Stuttgart that there should be preparations for 'the setting up of a democratic German government'. The USSR feared that West Germany would be hostile to the Soviet system, and grew even less co-operative, though the West alleged that it was the Soviets who first refused to treat Germany as a single economic unit, as agreed at Potsdam. About 6.5 million Germans, resettled west of the Oder–Neisse Line and mainly in West Germany, helped the economy of Bizonia to develop. There was also a westward flow of other refugees, many of them skilled, who preferred the traditionally more prosperous western Europe to its eastern counterpart. In due course the West German economy was boosted with Marshall Aid (see section 4.3), and the rift between the two Germanies grew wider.

The rift owed a good deal to the differing economic aims of the superpowers and the East–West dispute about the meaning of 'democracy' and 'democratization' (see section 1.2). Neither the Soviet Union nor the USA was willing to accept a reunited Germany which supported the ideology of the other, but for a time they could broadly agree on demilitarization (disarming the Germans) and denazification. Prominent Nazis who had so far survived were put on trial for war crimes in Nuremberg, all the Allies providing judges. Twenty-five Nazis were sentenced to death and twenty to life imprisonment. Rudolf Hess, once Hitler's deputy, was the longest-serving prisoner, remaining under four-power guard in Berlin's Spandau Prison until his death in 1987. Many local trials dealt with lesser Nazis, but many others escaped, some to South America, and the West especially continued for decades to be embarrassed by revelations of how Nazis had avoided arrest because of Allied 'errors'. The scale of the assistance and sympathies which allowed even death-camp officials to escape came to light only gradually, many years later. Even the Soviets were not blameless, though many of the sympathizers were strong anti-communists (see M. Elkins, *Forged in Fury* (Judy Piatkus, 1981)). Both East and West had a lively awareness of the usefulness to their arms programmes of German scientists, Nazi or not. But they agreed on the general need to remove former Nazis and their supporters from positions of authority and to cleanse Germany of the literature and trappings of the Nazi regime.

The Soviets promoted socialists and communists, especially those trained in Moscow, soon setting up in Berlin and East Germany in April 1946 the Socialist Unity Party or SED which became dominant. In West Germany, it was claimed that the use of Nazi sympathizers in official positions was sometimes necessary for efficient administration immediately after the war, though anti-Nazis such as Konrad Adenauer were given every encouragement. Western-type parties eventually emerged.

East–West suspicions persisted, with almost everything that occurred in the management of the German occupation giving rise to differing, all too often sinister, interpretations.

4.2.2 Disputes and crises, 1947–9

The American decision to stay in Germany was followed early in 1947 by the Truman Doctrine and the Marshall Plan, while the same year saw a general worsening in East–West relations in Europe as a whole (see sections 4.3 and 4.4). US forces also stayed in Berlin – an outpost of the West behind the Iron Curtain – which Stalin found worrying. When Ernst Reuter, once a communist but anti-Soviet, was elected Mayor of Berlin in June 1947, the Soviet Union protested, denying him authority in the city's Soviet Sector. The West's encouragement of political activity which was not only anti-Nazi but also at times anti-communist caused further disquiet, as did its determination to revive the economy in West Germany and West Berlin. When the USA, Britain and France discussed German affairs at a conference in London in February 1948, the Soviets protested at the secrecy of their meeting by withdrawing from the Allied Control Council: there was now even less co-operation among the occupying powers in Germany.

Currency reform proved the issue which launched a major crisis. The West wanted a new Deutschmark to replace the discredited and almost worthless Reichsmark, the new currency being badly needed to provide work incentives and to overcome the widespread post-war corruption. The Soviets feared the effects of admitting the new currency to East Germany and eastern Europe, where currencies were more rigidly controlled than in the West. (The Soviet rouble, for example, was not allowed to circulate on international markets, partly to safeguard the Soviet economy against speculators and bourgeois manipulation.) In April 1948 Stalin began in a small way to disrupt road and rail communications between Berlin and the West, as an expression of his resentment. The West persisted with its plans. In the seven days from 18 to 25 June, the West adopted the new currency for West Germany, the Soviets announced a different new currency for the Soviet Zone and the Soviet Sector of Berlin, the West declared that both currencies would be legal tender in West Berlin, and Stalin hit back by stepping up his interference with communications to West Berlin.

By early August 1948 the land blockade of West Berlin was complete, with all traffic from West Germany halted by road, rail and canal. West Berlin's 2.5 million inhabitants seemed likely to starve, and the lack of fuel and energy seemed likely to bring economic ruin as well as great discomfort. Stalin hoped the West would abandon the city, but 1948 was presidential election year in the USA, and Truman could expect to benefit from standing firm and engaging in confrontation with the USSR. A close colleague had reassured him:

> There is considerable political advantage to the Administration in its battle with the Kremlin. . . . In times of crisis the American citizen tends to back up his President.

The USA mounted a massive supply operation by air, countering the Berlin Blockade with the Berlin Airlift. British, but not French, planes helped the Americans and for eleven months transport aircraft ferried a total of over two million tonnes of food, coal, petrol and other supplies; by the end, planes were landing in Berlin at intervals of less than two minutes. The Airlift was not free from accidents and 29 lives were lost, but the Soviet response was limited to harassment, stopping short of a direct attack on the Allied aircraft.

While the Blockade continued, the city assembly met in West Berlin, leaving seats vacant for East Berliners. In December 1948 local-government elections took place in West Berlin, returning Reuter as Mayor with a Social Democrat majority. Like Germany as a whole, Berlin was now deeply divided. When Stalin lifted the Blockade in May 1949 the Western sectors were still in the hands of the American, British and French. The Blockade and Airlift had been a trial of strength, an episode in the Cold War which hardened attitudes on both sides. There was no guarantee that the Blockade would not be reimposed, but the West now made every effort to increase West Berlin's prosperity, to make it a shop window for capitalism, a tantalizing display of consumer goods and apparent affluence in a still devastated and drab eastern Europe.

4.2.3 Independent republics

The year 1949 was a decisive one. The USA prepared to commit itself more firmly to the defence of western Europe, joining NATO in April 1949 (see section 4.4). At the same time, preparations were under way to make West Germany and East Germany independent countries. The Federal Republic of Germany (West Germany) was subsequently set up on 23 May, the German Democratic Republic (East Germany) on 7 October.

The Federal Republic of Germany (FRG) had a system of government similar to that in Britain. It was founded on the Basic Law which had been worked out by a German council sitting in Bonn in 1948 under the chairmanship of Konrad Adenauer. This Basic Law, in effect, defined West Germany's constitution. When elections were held in August 1949, Adenauer became the West German Chancellor (chief minister) as the leader of the Christian Democrats, the largest single party – though, without an overall majority, forced to rule in coalition. Ludwig Erhard – who had already won acclaim for his expertise at Munich University, in the industrial reconstruction of Bavaria and in the economic development of Bizonia – had charge of economic affairs. Adenauer and Erhard held their federal offices until 1963, providing continuity during the

Republic's early years. The Basic Law provided an effective constitutional system, one reason being the exclusion from the Bundestag (the lower house of parliament) of minor parties which got less than five per cent of the total vote. In the first election, to the delight of the Republic's Western backers, only fifteen communists were elected to a Bundestag of 400 members.

Although the Federal Republic now had an independent government, the amended Occupation Statute remained in force, reserving to the USA, Britain and France control of German foreign policy, defence and certain matters such as reparations. Adenauer wanted more authority, and his anti-Soviet stance gained Allied confidence. In 1951 a West German Foreign Office was allowed, Adenauer himself taking charge of it until 1955, and in 1952 West Germany helped to found the European Coal and Steel Community (see section 4.3). But occupation forces remained and West Germany still had no military forces of its own. The rearming of Germany was a very sensitive issue: the Soviets would protest furiously, and France too was uneasy. By 1952, however, the West wanted West Germany to share the burden of Western defence, and the Bundestag showed itself willing to contribute.

It took several more years to find an acceptable way of rearming West Germany, given the fears of the French and other neighbours. A plan for a European Defence Community (EDC), in which Germany, France, Britain and others would pool their military forces, collapsed when Britain chose not to join and the French took fright. Success came in the shape of the Western European Union (WEU), set up by the Western powers. This later expanded to include West Germany, replacing the Brussels Treaty Organization (see section 4.4). Within the WEU, West German rearmament would be supervised by France, Britain and other members, while it was also agreed that German forces would be limited in number and would be put at the service of NATO. Adenauer agreed to these conditions, and the Federal Republic thus gained full sovereignty[G] on the day the WEU came into being: 5 May 1955. Adenauer still hoped that Germany would one day be reunited, but that was now even less likely – West Germany as a member of NATO was firmly in the Western camp.

The German Democratic Republic (GDR) had developed from the Soviet Zone. It was much smaller than the Federal Republic but firmly in the Eastern camp. A People's Congress in the Soviet Zone had in 1948 elected a People's Council. The Council had 400 members, the same as the West German Bundestag, but executive power lay with its Presidium of 29 members, all of them members of the Socialist Unity Party (SED). When the Democratic Republic became independent in October 1949, it was easy to develop its new constitution from this system. Elections returned a People's Chamber of SED members, with government in the hands of Walther Ulbricht, the SED leader, and Otto Grotewohl, who became Prime Minister. By dismantling the regional governments of the *Länder* (individual states, for example Saxony), East Germany was made more centralized than West Germany where the federal system still allowed for a state government in each of the Länder (such as Bavaria). Unlike Adenauer's Germany, East Germany in 1950 agreed that former German lands east of the Oder–Neisse Line were now permanently Polish.

Continuing economic hardship and war reparations to the USSR brought rioting in June 1953 in both East Berlin and East Germany, at a time when Soviet supervision was being reduced after the death of Stalin. Order was restored with the help of Soviet troops, and further concessions followed. Reparations were abandoned from the end of 1953, and East Germany was granted sovereignty by the USSR during 1954, allowing it to become a founder-member of the Warsaw Pact in 1955 (see section 4.4). Adenauer refused to recognize East Germany. There were nevertheless two Germanies by 1955, each with its own sovereignty, and while no peace treaty had been acceptable to the USSR and the West for both East and West Germany, the division seemed likely to be a long-lasting product of the East–West Cold War.

4.2.4 Divided Berlin

Ernst Reuter remained Mayor of West Berlin until his death in 1953. The city was not made part of the Federal Republic, but it continued to be guarded by US, British and French forces; East Berlin, on the other hand, was regarded by the East as part of the Democratic Republic, indeed its capital. When the Democratic Republic achieved its sovereignty, the East claimed that access to West Berlin was now a matter for the East Germans, but this only led to more wrangling since the West maintained that the Soviets were still responsible. The view of the USA, Britain and France in 1954 was that they could 'not recognize the sovereignty of the East German regime which is not based on free elections'. Soon afterwards in October 1954 the West reasserted that:

> The security and welfare of Berlin and the maintenance of the three Powers there are regarded by the three Powers as essential elements of the peace of the free world.

Here too stalemate had been reached. West Germany and East Germany were divided by a frontier which the East made highly dangerous to try to cross without permission. West Berlin and East Berlin were becoming similarly separated, though it was not until 1961 that a concrete wall partitioned the city (see section 13.1).

4.3 Two Europes

The West maintained that the Soviet Union had failed to abide by the Declaration on Liberated Europe agreed at Yalta (see section 1.3.1). In Poland and elsewhere in eastern Europe, pro-Soviet regimes came to power, emerging during 1945–7 in ways the West found inconsistent with the people's 'own choice' through 'free elections' (see section 8.1.1). The Soviet view was that these countries became 'people's democracies' from which their authorities tried to exclude bourgeois influences – which included Western economic interests. The states of eastern Europe thus became clients of the Soviet Union, acting as a buffer against the West and shielding the USSR not only in military terms but also economically and ideologically. The Soviet hold over eastern Europe probably owed more to Stalin's fears of dissent than to his desire to expand the frontiers of Marxism. Nevertheless, the policy of 'Socialism in One Country' that Stalin had practised in the USSR in the 1930s gave way after 1945 to that of 'Socialism in One Zone' – Soviet interests now strongly influencing the satellites east of the Iron Curtain.

Western Europe after the Second World War rebuilt its societies, economies and political systems to British and US patterns. It was soon argued that the economic health of the West generally would be improved by the rapid recovery not only of West Germany but also of western Europe as a whole. However, only the USA was strong enough after 1945 to support such rapid recovery. Truman's administration in Washington saw the issue as another aspect of the Cold War: prosperity, it believed, would make western Europe less sympathetic to communism. Large Communist Parties already existed in France and Italy, and fears of Soviet military expansion west of the Iron Curtain led to the policy of containment expressed in the Truman Doctrine in March 1947 (see section 4.4).

The Marshall Plan, which Truman himself called the twin half (with the Truman Doctrine) of 'the same walnut', developed from a proposal made in June 1947 by the US Secretary of State, George Marshall. Marshall reasoned that:

> Europe's requirements . . . of foreign food and other essential products – principally from America – are so much greater than her present ability to pay that she must have substantial additional help or face economic, social and political deterioration of a very grave character.

He proposed massive US financial support for European recovery – once Europeans could agree on a common programme. In theory, Marshall Aid would be available to the Soviet Union and to eastern as well as western Europe. Although the Soviet Foreign Minister Molotov attended discussions in Paris at the end of June 1947, it was never likely in practice that Marshall Aid would be extended so widely: the Soviets could not be expected either to open their economic affairs to US scrutiny or to link their economy to those of the capitalists. After the meeting in Paris, the Soviet Union refused to be involved in the Marshall Plan and put pressure on eastern-European states such as Poland and Czechoslovakia similarly to reject it (see section 8.1.1). Instead, the Soviets followed up the peace treaties of 1947 (see section 1.5.2) with bilateral trade pacts with the states of eastern Europe, condemning the Marshall Plan as a US plot to gain economic advantage. By offering the Plan to the Soviets, almost certain that it would be rejected, the USA had won a propaganda victory in the Cold War.

Ernest Bevin, British Foreign Secretary, was quick to respond constructively to Marshall's proposal. He took the lead in organizing sixteen European nations into the Committee on European Economic Co-operation which drew up the European Recovery Programme (ERP) in September 1947. In April 1948 the sixteen supporters of the ERP founded the Organization for European Economic Co-operation (OEEC) (see Table 4.1). The OEEC worked closely with the US Economic Co-operation Administration, which was to provide the Europeans with aid to the value of 17 billion dollars by 1952. Western Europe's remarkable economic revival after wartime dislocation was one result of this aid; another was that western-European markets and investments helped the USA itself to prosper, the American GNP rising (at current prices) from about 285 billion dollars in 1950 to over 500 billion dollars in 1960.

Belgium, the Netherlands and Luxemburg had recognized the value of economic co-operation as early as 1944, and made preparations in London during the war to set up the Benelux Customs Union, which came into being in 1948. On this base the three countries aimed to create a more far-reaching community, within which goods, capital, traffic and people could move freely and governments would pursue many common policies. These aims were realized in 1960 when the Benelux Economic Union was set up.

The Benelux countries also helped to found the European Coal and Steel Community (ECSC) in 1952, joining France, Italy and West Germany to create the first of the European Communities (see Table 4.1 and section 7.1.1). The ECSC owed a good deal to Robert Schuman, French Foreign Minister from 1948 to 1953, who looked forward to 'the pooling of the production of coal and steel . . . [to] establish a common basis for economic development'. Schuman saw this too as a contribution to peace between West Germany and its western neighbours, initiating:

> common interests which are essential for establishing an economic community between countries long opposed by bloody conflict . . . the basis for a European federation essential for the safeguarding of peace.

To supervise and organize the coal and steel industries, the ECSC had a High Authority to which the members surrendered some of their sovereign powers, a sacrifice the British refused to consider. Britain therefore stood aside from the Community as it also stood aside from the European Defence Community (see section 4.2.3).

These developments in western Europe were to some extent matched in eastern Europe. As the Americans had feared, they were shut out from eastern-European markets. The USSR's separate commercial treaties with countries such as Bulgaria and Poland were followed by the setting up of the Council for Mutual Economic Assistance (Comecon) in January 1949 (see Table 4.2). As its own economy began to recover from wartime devastation, the Soviet Union turned its attention to organizing recovery in eastern Europe, where Comecon co-ordinated the various national economies (though there was sometimes disquiet among its members over the extensive influence of the Soviets over their trade).

The Communist Information Bureau (Cominform) had been set up in 1947 to co-ordinate the activities of European Communist Parties. Its first headquarters were in Belgrade, Yugoslavia. Yugoslavia under President Tito defied direction by Stalin, however, preferring its own brand of Marxism. In 1948 Yugoslavia was expelled from the Cominform for its unorthodoxy, and the Cominform moved its headquarters to Bucharest, Romania. It was dissolved in 1956 as a gesture of goodwill by the new Soviet leadership. Yugoslavia meanwhile hovered between the two Europes (see fig. 4.1), a socialist state but not a Soviet satellite, not receiving Marshall Aid but also not a

Table 4.1 Associations of European capitalist states and their Allies

	Economic co-operation		Towards unity		Defence		
	OEEC, 1948/ OECD, 1961	EFTA, 1960	Council of Europe, 1949	ECSC, 1952/ European Community, 1967	Brussels Treaty Organization 1948	WEU, 1955	NATO, 1949
Austria	*	*	†1956				
Benelux							
Belgium	*		*	*	*	*	*
Netherlands	*		*	*	*	*	*
Luxemburg	*		*	*	*	*	*
Britain	*	*§	*	†1973	*	*	*
Cyprus			†1961				
Denmark	*	*§	*	†1973			*
Finland	†1968	‡					
France	*		*	*	*	*	*‖
Greece	*		†1949	†1981			†1952
Iceland	*	†1970	†1949				*
Irish Republic	*		*	†1973			
Italy	*		*	*		*	*

Malta			†1965			
Norway	*	*	*			*
Portugal	*	*		†1986		*
Spain	†1959			†1986		†1982
Sweden	*	*	*			
Switzerland	*	*	†1963			
Turkey	*		†1949	#		†1952
West Germany	†1955		†1951	*	*	†1955
Yugoslavia	‡					
Australia	‡					
Canada	‡(*1961)					*
Japan	†1963					
New Zealand	‡					
USA	‡(*1961)					*

* Founder-member
† Became a member at the later date
‡ Associate member
§ Left 1972
‖ Withdrew from military commitments, 1966
\# Applied for membership, 1988

The OEEC became the OECD, open to non-Europeans, in 1961.
The ECSC, EEC and Euratom became part of the European Community in 1967.

Table 4.2 Associations of communist states

	Cominform, 1947 (Dissolved 1956)	Comecon, 1949	Warsaw Pact, 1955
Soviet Union	*	*	*
Albania		*§	*§
Bulgaria	*	*	*
Czechoslovakia	*	*	*
East Germany		†1950	†1956
Hungary	*	*	*
Poland	*	*	*
Romania	*	*	*
Yugoslavia	*‖	‡	
Communist Parties in the West	*		
Mongolia		†1962	
Cuba		†1972	
Vietnam		†1978	

* Founder-member
† Became a member at the later date
‡ Associate member
§ Left Comecon and the Warsaw Pact in 1961 (the latter formally in 1968)
‖ Expelled 1948

The following non-members sent observers to Comecon's fortieth session in Warsaw in 1985: Afghanistan; Angola; Ethiopa; Laos; Mozambique; Nicaragua; South Yemen. (Yugoslavia was still represented as an associated power.)

full member of Comecon, beginning to develop under Tito as a leader of the world's non-aligned movement (see section 21.4).

4.4 Two alliances

Whatever the anxieties of the Americans, the French after 1945 seemed to fear renewed German aggression more than any Soviet threat. Before the Second World War they had long (but in vain) pressed the British for a binding alliance and guaranteed support; after the war they pressed again, this time successfully. In March 1947 Bevin agreed to the Treaty of Dunkirk:

> with the object of preventing Germany from becoming again a menace to peace.

Britain and France jointly promised 'all the military and other support and assistance' each could give the other in the event of 'hostilities with Germany'. This was a significant new commitment on Britain's part, departing from the general tradition of avoiding binding commitments in Europe.

A year later, in March 1948, Bevin committed Britain further, agreeing to the Brussels Treaty with France and the Benelux countries. Article 6 provided that:

> if any of the High Contracting Parties should be the object of an armed attack in Europe, the other High Contracting Parties will . . . afford the Party so attacked all the military and other aid and assistance within their power.

The Treaty still mentioned Germany as a possible enemy, but it expressed a firm belief in 'democracy, personal freedom and political liberty, . . . constitutional traditions and the rule of law'. It therefore seemed partly designed for defence against the Soviet Union if it were needed.

United States policy was already sharply anti-Soviet. Communists in the resistance movement to the Nazi occupation of Greece resented the restoration there of the monarchy and of the old capitalist order when the Second World War ended. Civil war broke out, with the British actively supporting the royalists, partly because of traditional ties. But it was a campaign Britain could ill afford and in February 1947 Prime Minister Clement Attlee warned the USA that Britain's withdrawal was imminent. The Greek communists had support from Yugoslavia, Albania and Bulgaria, and seemed likely to win. In Truman's view this must be part of a plot hatched in Moscow, proof of Soviet ambitions to overrun as much of Europe as possible. He linked the problem with Soviet pressures on Turkey: in 1946 US warships had been sent to Turkey to warn off the Soviets from any attempt to get control of the straits between the Black Sea and the Mediterranean, which Stalin alleged were in unfriendly hands.

Taking into account events in Germany and eastern Europe and those in Iran (see section 1.5.1), and under pressure from political rivals at home, Truman decided that US policy must be to 'contain' the Soviets within existing boundaries. He outlined his policy to Congress in March 1947 in what became known as the Truman Doctrine. Contrasting two ways of life 'at the present moment in world history' – the free and the unfree – Truman declared:

> I believe that it must be the policy of the United States to support free peoples who are resisting attempted subjugation by armed minorities or by outside pressures. I believe we must assist free peoples to work out their own destinies in their own way.

At the same time Truman and his advisers presented Congress with an alarmist picture of the Soviet threat, the more surely to obtain the 400 million dollars needed for military and other aid to Greece and Turkey. Both countries remained in the Western camp; indeed, both later joined NATO. The civil war in Greece ended in defeat for the communists in 1949.

Perhaps deliberately, Truman left unclear how widely his Doctrine and the policy of containment would be applied, rather uneasily combining general principles with the crises of the moment in Greece and Turkey. The President was supported enthusiastically by Dean Acheson, later Secretary of State from 1949 to 1953. He had less whole-hearted support from George Kennan, whose diplomatic experience in the Soviet Union made him the USA's leading adviser on Soviet affairs. Kennan believed the Marshall Plan was necessary and statesmanlike (see section 4.3), but he had doubts about the wisdom of the Truman Doctrine – based as it was on confrontation and the image of the Soviet Union as a potential aggressor, a view he thought ill-founded, since he believed Stalin's main concern was for Soviet security. Kennan nevertheless wavered: in 1948 he seemed to share many of Acheson's anti-Soviet fears, but his doubts about US policy re-emerged in 1949 and in 1950 he left the State Department.

Kennan's doubts were increased when 'the two halves of the same walnut' seemed to grow unequal: the Truman Doctrine led to more US emphasis on military aspects, overshadowing the Marshall Plan. East–West negotiations tended to take second place to confrontation. Some observers argued that the Truman Doctrine was the real beginning of the Cold War and Czechoslovakia one of the early victims. The Czechoslovak elections in 1946 had returned 114 Communists, the largest party in a parliament of 300, and government was by coalition of left-wing parties led by Klement Gottwald, a veteran of the Czechoslovak Communist Party. In February 1948 Gottwald staged a coup, instituting one-party government; he himself became the nation's President. The change put Czechoslovakia more firmly in the Soviet camp and emphasized the division between East and West still more clearly. Jan Masaryk, Czechoslovakia's Foreign Minister, who favoured friendship with the West, fell from a window in the Foreign Office in March 1948, the mystery of how he came to fall remaining unsolved. The harder communist line in Czechoslovakia seemed to owe at least something to communist anxieties about the Truman Doctrine.

The Truman Doctrine and further confrontations with Stalin during 1948 (see section 4.2.2) led the US administration to an even more revolutionary policy. For the first time the USA undertook binding peacetime commitments to Europe with the signing of the North Atlantic Treaty in April 1949. Canada also became a member of the North Atlantic Treaty Organization (NATO), the other founder-members being European (see Table 4.1). The new Treaty bound its members to mutual military support in case of attack slightly less tightly than did the Brussels Treaty. Nevertheless, Article 5 stated that:

> The parties agree that an armed attack against one or more of them in Europe or North America shall be considered an attack against them all; and . . . each . . . will assist the party or parties attacked by taking forthwith . . . such action as it deems necessary, including the use of armed force, to restore and maintain the security of the North Atlantic area.

In effect, the USA was now pledged to the defence of western Europe. NATO came into being in August 1949 and its machinery and strategy developed quickly. At the end of 1950 members agreed to set up Supreme Headquarters Allied Powers Europe (SHAPE) in Paris, and Dwight D. Eisenhower, a successful US general in the Second World War, was chosen as Supreme Commander of the NATO forces.

The East's counter to the North Atlantic Treaty was the Eastern European Mutual Assistance Treaty, commonly known as the Warsaw Pact after the city where the Treaty was signed in May 1955 by the Soviet Union and seven east-European states including East Germany (see Table 4.2). The immediate occasion of the signing was the rearming and admission to NATO of West Germany. The Warsaw Pact pledged its members to mutual support against attack in terms which echoed those in Article 5 of the North Atlantic Treaty and, like NATO, members of the Pact set up a unified military command (at first under the Soviet Marshal Ivan Konev) with headquarters in Moscow. East German troops were accepted into the Warsaw Pact forces in January 1956.

Meanwhile, the Soviet Union had begun to compete with the USA in the development of nuclear weapons (see section 1.1). The first Soviet atomic bomb was tested in July 1949. The USA went on to test a more powerful hydrogen bomb in 1952, which the Soviets matched in 1953. Britain developed its own atomic and hydrogen bombs in 1952 and 1957, and France and China later joined 'the nuclear club'. The Cold War thus took place against the background of a nuclear arms race which some regarded as a help to peace – providing a 'deterrent' to war, a 'balance of terror'. Others, including Kennan, saw the nuclear race in different terms – dangerous, expensive, and the product of Cold War rhetoric and mismanagement rather than of cool and persevering diplomacy between former Allies, who too swiftly after 1945 lined up in opposing alliances, NATO and the Warsaw Pact.

4.5 Divisions and conflict in Asia

4.5.1 The road to NSC-68

The USA and the USSR both bordered the Pacific Ocean and competition between them in the Far East and the Pacific seemed as unavoidable as in Europe. Communism was often intertwined with nationalism at the end of the Second World War, complicating the issues for the West in places such as Indonesia and Indo-China where struggles for independence took place (see sections 15.1 and 15.2.2). Communist rebels also tried to gain control in Malaya, where the British were preparing to grant independence (see section 14.2.4), and in the Philippines, to which the USA granted independence in 1946 (see section 12.4). Both superpowers favoured independence movements and the breaking down of the old colonial empires, but the Americans were again hostile to what they suspected were Kremlin-inspired plots to make the new nations Marxist.

The Americans were determined to keep down communism in Japan, and the Soviets were allowed no part in the post-war occupation there which lasted until 1952. Control of the occupation lay with the US General Douglas MacArthur and much was done to impose American institutions on Japan (see section 12.1). Communists won about ten per cent of the votes in the elections of 1949, but when the Korean War began in 1950 and until after occupation had ended, they were in effect banned from Japanese politics. The Treaty of San Francisco which most of the Allies signed in 1951 to make peace with Japan was not acceptable to the Soviet Union (see section 1.5.3). Japan gained economic benefit from the Korean War, however, and was firmly linked to the USA by the US–Japanese Security Treaty. When, a year later, the occupation of Japan ended, the USA kept Okinawa as a base from which to keep watch on its enemies.

The post-war development of Japan satisfied the Truman administration but that of China proved worrying. The Kuomintang government of Chiang Kai-shek, 'democratic' only in theory, grew increasingly unpopular with the Chinese people, and seemed unlikely to be able to survive the civil war with the peasant-backed communists that broke out anew at the end of 1945. Truman sent George Marshall to mediate, but Marshall tried in vain to persuade Chiang to compromise with the Communist leader, Mao Tse-tung. Compromise, like reform, was not to be part of Kuomintang politics, it seemed, and Marshall – now US Secretary of State – gave up the struggle and turned his attention to Europe.

US aid to Chiang continued, but it was half-hearted and much of it in any case found its way to the communists because of corruption and desertions among the Kuomintang forces. The Soviets, on the other hand, gave hardly any support to Mao and his followers: Stalin did not believe that a Marxist revolution could be brought about by peasants. The Soviets did, however, help Mao's forces to become established in Manchuria, having previously supported its liberation from the Japanese. After that the Chinese largely settled their own affairs. Chiang was defeated and forced to flee to the offshore island of Taiwan (Formosa), and in October 1949 the People's Republic of China was proclaimed in Peking under the leadership of Mao Tse-tung and the Chinese Communist Party (see section 11.1.2). The USA quickly took the view that Chiang Kai-shek nevertheless remained the rightful ruler of China and that, from Taiwan, he should continue to occupy China's seat at the United Nations and to exercise China's right of veto. The rights of 550 million mainland Chinese were ignored.

The USSR and China seemed to confirm US fears of a united communist bloc when Andrei Vyshinsky and Chou En-lai, on behalf of Stalin and Mao, signed the Sino-Soviet Treaty of Friendship and Alliance in February 1950. The Treaty, valid for 30 years, pledged its signatories to co-operation and mutual economic assistance. It also included the proviso that if:

> one of the Contracting Parties [be] attacked by Japan or any State allied with her and thus [be] involved in a state of war, the other Contracting Party shall immediately render military and other assistance by all means at its disposal.

But Russia and China had a history of uneasy relationships and shared a long and troublesome frontier. It was by no means certain that their new-found friendship would be strong enough to survive underlying Sino-Soviet problems (see section 11.2.3).

Korea had from 1910 been in the possession of Japan but was freed in 1945 at the end of the Second World War. As agreed at Yalta, Soviet forces temporarily occupied Korea north of the 38th Parallel (38° north latitude), US forces south of the Parallel. A united and democratic Korea was expected in the future but problems developed as in Germany. In August 1948 South Koreans and Americans announced the creation of a Republic of Korea under the Presidency of Syngman Rhee, an anti-communist nationalist. In the assembly of 303 members at Seoul 100 seats were left vacant for members from the North, proportions which were roughly in line with the respective populations. But when Soviet forces withdrew in September 1948, North Korea declared itself a People's Republic under the leadership of the Marxist Kim Il-sung. The North refused to take part in common elections with the South or to accept the constitution approved by the Americans. US forces nevertheless left the South in June 1949, leaving the two Koreas to argue bitterly about the future, with a good deal of provocation on both sides. Each Korea was armed by its supporting superpower, the North having the larger forces.

Acheson, the US Secretary of State, began 1950 by defining the areas of the Pacific that the USA – in keeping with a wide application of the Truman Doctrine – was committed to defending: the 'defense perimeter'. By accident or design he failed to mention Korea. The US National Security Council, prompted by Acheson and the President, also began work on a new definition of policy in a document which became known as NSC–68. The document was savagely hostile to the Soviet Union, going further than Kennan thought reasonable. The Kremlin, it asserted, was 'animated by a new fanatic faith', so that Soviet leaders required:

> the dynamic extension of their authority and the ultimate elimination of any effective opposition to their authority . . . . To that end Soviet efforts are now directed toward the domination of the Eurasian land mass.

The recommended US response would therefore be based on more military strength, diplomatic alliances, subversion of the Soviet system and little or no negotiations with Moscow. In Walter LaFeber's view (*America, Russia and the Cold War* (John Wiley, 1976)), 'Truman and Acheson were no longer satisfied with containment. They wanted Soviet withdrawal and an absolute victory.' But it was by no means certain in spring 1950 that the US people were prepared to support and pay for the whole of this programme. However, war in Korea reinforced their anti-communism.

4.5.2 The Korean War, 1950–3

North Korean forces invaded South Korea on 25 June 1950. Attacking with Soviet-built tanks, they hoped to rid the whole of Korea of US influence, and perhaps even to weaken US influence in Japan. Truman promptly sent supplies to South Korea, at the same time increasing US aid to anti-communists in Indo-China and the Philippines. He also sent the US Seventh Fleet to patrol the waters off Taiwan, giving obvious protection to Chiang Kai-shek. The North Korean attack was referred to the United Nations Security Council, which branded North Korea as an aggressor, with only the Yugoslav delegate abstaining from the vote. If, as the Americans believed, Kim Il-sung had acted on the orders of Stalin, the Soviets had bungled their schemes – the USSR's delegate was at that time boycotting the Security Council in protest at the exclusion from the UN of Communist China and there was therefore no Soviet veto to block Security Council decisions. On 27 June the Council went on to recommend military support for South Korea, only Yugoslavia voting against the proposal though India and Egypt abstained. US forces under the command of MacArthur arrived in South Korea almost at once. British troops were the first to arrive in support, and fourteen other countries eventually followed, though some sent hardly more than token forces. From the outset UN resistance to aggression had a striking resemblance to US resistance to communism.

Seoul had fallen within days of the invasion by the North Koreans, and most

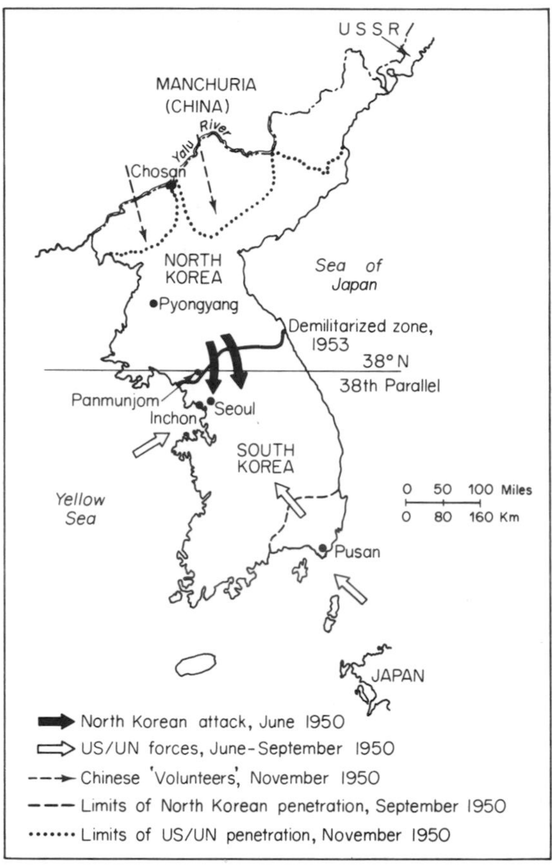

Fig. 4.2 The Korean War, 1950–3

of the South was quickly overrun: the first objective of the UN and the USA was simply the liberation and defence of South Korea. From his base at Pusan and with the help of a landing at Inchon, MacArthur drove the North Koreans back to the 38th Parallel. US aims then seemed to become more ambitious: to clear the communists from North Korea too, in keeping with NSC–68. MacArthur's rapid advance continued, and by mid-October his troops neared the Yalu River, which formed North Korea's border with China. Chou En-lai's warnings to the USA not to invade North Korea had been ignored, and some 200 000 Chinese 'volunteers' now joined the war; more than 100 000 others were held in reserve. North Korea was freed from US/UN forces and the tide of conflict again flowed into South Korea, Seoul being retaken by the communists in January 1951.

Further fierce fighting brought the US/UN troops back to the 38th Parallel where the conflict became static, nearing stalemate. Peace talks began in July 1951, dragging on in the village of Panmunjom until a ceasefire was at last agreed in July 1953 – when Eisenhower replaced Truman as US President and Stalin was dead. Korea remained divided, North and South separated by a demilitarized zone near the 38th Parallel. Negotiations for a peace settlement made little headway during the next 30 years. For the Koreans the Korean War had settled nothing, though it left more than four million of them dead – more than 80 per cent of those killed being from the North and the great majority of them civilians. The North remained under the tight control of Kim Il-sung, while the South remained under Syngman Rhee until he was overthrown in 1960 for corruption and oppression.

The USA suffered over 30 000 dead in the war, US allies about 4500. Some four times as many were wounded. Americans could rightly claim they had frustrated another communist takeover. It could also be argued that the United Nations had successfully resisted aggression, thus improving on the record of the League of Nations. The Soviets returned to the UN Security Council, but in the meantime the USA and other powers had taken the opportunity in autumn 1950 to pass the 'Uniting for Peace' Resolution, which claimed for the UN General Assembly the power to recommend action in support of collective security if the Security Council should be paralysed by a veto in a future crisis.

US policy had not been wholly successful, however. The change of aim, from defending South Korea to overthrowing North Korea's government and uniting Korea by force, had caused unease among American's allies. When MacArthur showed even greater ambitions – to carry the war into China, destroy communist bases there and perhaps even discourage communism by using nuclear weapons – there were protests within the USA as well as from its allies. Attlee hastily flew to Washington to urge restraint and demand reassurance. In April 1951 Truman dismissed MacArthur in favour of General Matthew Ridgway. MacArthur returned to the USA to a hero's welcome from a people now whipped up by Joseph McCarthy and violently anti-communist (see section 2.3.2). Even so, MacArthur failed to win nomination as a candidate for the Presidency in 1952. Truman stoutly defended his decision to dismiss MacArthur, now apparently reasserting the original aims of the war:

> I want to be clear about our military objective. We are fighting to resist an outrageous aggression in Korea. We are trying to keep the Korean conflict from spreading to other areas. But . . . we must . . . insure the security of our forces . . . if they are to continue the fight until the enemy abandons its ruthless attempt to destroy the Republic of Korea. That is our military objective – to repel attack and to restore peace.

In this Truman clearly succeeded.

The policy of containment was also strengthened elsewhere during the Korean War. US protection for Japan and for Chiang Kai-shek's Taiwan was emphasized, and the USA showed growing concern for the problems of the French in Vietnam and the rest of Indo-China (see section 15.2.2).

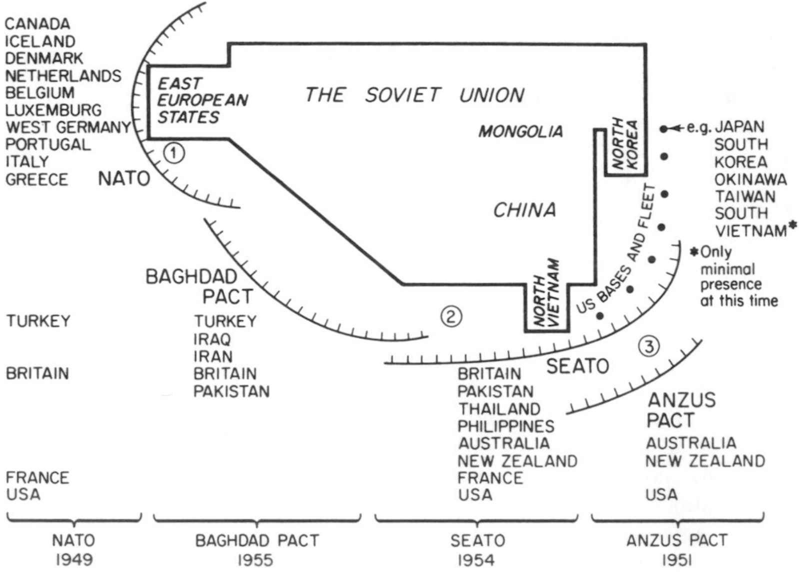

Fig. 4.3 The containment of communism by 1955

Truman built further defensive alliances against communism. In September 1951 Australia and New Zealand joined the USA in the ANZUS Pact, a security treaty for mutual support against an attack on any one of them. At the same time, in addition to its Security Treaty with Japan, the USA signed another with the Philippines. In September 1954, during Eisenhower's Presidency, the ANZUS powers together with Britain, France, Pakistan, the Philippines and Thailand set up the South-East Asia Treaty Organization (SEATO) for the promotion of free institutions and collective action against aggression and subversion. The South-East Asia Treaty was not very specific about how its signatories would 'act to meet the common danger' in the event of 'armed attack' or other threat, while the USA wrote into it a distinction between 'communist aggression' and 'other aggression'. SEATO was never quite so well defined and firmly supported as NATO.

In 1955 President Eisenhower also encouraged the Baghdad Pact which loosely bound Iraq, Turkey, Pakistan, Iran and Britain to 'co-operate for their security and defence'. From this the Central Treaty Organization (CENTO) developed in 1959, though Iraq then dropped out and the USA still declined to become a formal member. This alliance too seemed concerned to contain communism, completing the ring which the West and its sympathizers drew around the Soviet Union and other Marxist states (see fig. 4.3).

4.6 One Austria: cracks in the ice

The Nazi takeover of Austria in 1938 made the country part of Hitler's Great German Empire and an enemy of the Allies in the Second World War. When the war ended, Austria, like Germany, was subjected to occupation and divided into four Allied zones, with four Allied sectors of Vienna inside the Soviet Zone (see fig. 1.4). But with a population of a mere seven million Austria could never threaten its neighbours in the same way that Germany could, and from the outset the Allies allowed a civilian Austrian government to operate. The Soviet Union accepted, even encouraged, a provisional administration under Karl Renner, a veteran Social Democrat, who organized a general election in 1945. As a result Leopold Figl, leader of the People's Party, became Chancellor, while Renner was President of the Austrian Republic until his death in 1950. Only four Communists were elected to the Austrian parliament.

The occupying powers had made certain that Nazis played no part in the election of 1945, but in spite of a programme of denazification some former Nazis returned to political life at the next election in 1949. The Soviets were critical of this, and they were also distrustful of the injection into Austria of Marshall Aid. In 1950 Stalin backed an attempt by Austrian Communists to gain influence through strikes and industrial disruption, but the Communists remained only a small minority. For the present the Soviet Union appeared content to take its reparations, especially from the oil industry in the Soviet Zone, seeming almost to accept that Austria would prefer the West to the East, as had been indicated when Austria became a founder-member of the OEEC in 1948. When Stalin died in 1953 Austria was beginning to achieve economic success and post-war recovery.

Political changes in Austria in 1953 coincided with political changes in Moscow (see section 3.3.1). Julius Raab became Chancellor in Austria, with Figl as Foreign Minister, assisted by Bruno Kreisky, a Socialist and future Chancellor. These three set to work to persuade the occupying powers to leave their country and grant full sovereignty. Though the West had reservations about bargaining with the Kremlin, the Austrians wooed the Soviets with

Fig. 4.4 An Austrian Freedom stamp of 1955: in this year the Austrian State Treaty gave the Republic its freedom after ten years of four-power occupation. The stamp shows the Austrian Parliament on the Ringstrasse, Vienna, symbol of the Republic's commitment to Western democracy.

promises, offering to stand aside from all military alliances such as NATO. When Raab, Figl and Kreisky visited Moscow in February 1955, they promised a neutrality such as that maintained by Switzerland.

The Soviet leaders proved willing to withdraw from Austria in return for detaching the country from the Cold War and from NATO. All the occupying powers therefore agreed in May 1955 to the Austrian State Treaty, which restored to Austria full sovereignty and independence under a single democratic government in its ancient capital, Vienna, and within its boundaries of early 1938. Certain conditions were imposed, however. The Treaty had clauses for restraining Nazis and limiting armaments, and Article 4 insisted that Austria should:

> not enter into political or economic unity with Germany in any form whatsoever.

The Soviet Union also secured a share in the profits of Austrian oilfields for a further 30 years as part of the ending of reparations. Honouring its promises, the Austrian government then passed laws to ensure Austrian neutrality in international affairs.

The Austrian State Treaty and a cautiously constructive East–West summit meeting at Geneva in July 1955 provided glimpses of a thaw in the Cold War, though elsewhere - over the two Germanies, for example - attitudes hardened yet again during 1955. The readjustment of the Iron Curtain at least raised doubts about the Soviet Union's alleged intention to expand over all Europe (see fig. 4.1), though observers noted that the neutralization of Austria as well as Switzerland prevented a direct NATO link between West Germany and Italy. At Geneva, Eisenhower declared that 'the American people want to be friends with the Soviet peoples'. McCarthy had now been discredited, and the Soviets were already talking of 'peaceful coexistence' (see section 3.6). Even so, there was no progress towards East–West disarmament at Geneva, the Soviets firmly rejecting Eisenhower's proposal for 'open skies', with mutual rights to inspect weapons sites from the air. Nevertheless, the international outlook seemed slightly less bleak as the occupation forces completed their withdrawal from Austria at the end of 1955.

UNIT 5

The Western democracies: 1 – Britain

5.1 Post-war issues: the general election of 1945

A general election was long overdue in Britain when the Second World War ended in 1945. The last had been held in 1935, returning a National government (a coalition, but almost wholly Conservative) with a large majority in the House of Commons, enough to ensure that the government would remain in office for its full five-year term. But five years later, in 1940, Britain was at war and a general election was not possible. There was nevertheless a new Prime Minister: Winston Churchill took over from Neville Chamberlain, setting up a War Cabinet which included not only Conservatives and their allies but also Clement Attlee, leader of the Labour Party and the parliamentary opposition. A few months later Ernest Bevin, prominent in the Transport and General Workers' Union and the Trades Union Congress, entered the Cabinet as Minister of Labour. The war effort required total commitment to defeat the Axis powers, and party-political conflict was largely suspended while the war lasted. The defeat of Germany brought its speedy renewal, however. A general election was arranged for July 1945 and, to prepare for it, the Labour members withdrew from Churchill's Cabinet in May.

Britain could return to competitive politics more quickly than countries on the Continent, where Nazi occupation had caused more disruption. France, for example, needed to create a new constitution, and Italy had still to find a new way forward after the overthrow of Mussolini and to decide whether or not to keep its monarchy. Britain had no codified constitution, but its political system was firmly established on the basis of general elections, in which all adults (from the age of 21) were by now entitled to vote. At the beginning of the twentieth century British electors had, in the main, voted either Conservative or Liberal. In 1906, for example, they had preferred the Liberals, returning a Liberal government and thus a Conservative opposition. But after the First World War the Labour Party made progress and the Liberals' popularity declined: in 1935, 158 Labour MPs were elected but only 20 Liberals. Labour was by now providing the regular official opposition to the Conservatives, though the Labour governments led by Ramsay MacDonald between the two World Wars had been brief (1924 and 1929–31), without an overall majority in the Commons.

A choice of parties meant at least some choice of policies, though within a broadly capitalist framework. This was a common characteristic of the Western democracies, and in direct contrast to the one-party states modelled on the Soviet Union. After the Second World War, right-wing (conservative) parties continued to believe in conserving much of the existing order, introducing reform 'where necessary' and emphasizing individual freedoms. Left-wing parties were more inclined towards change – liberals tending to emphasize the individual and preferring liberty to equality; socialists emphasizing co-operation and collective action, perhaps preferring equality to liberty. The precise form taken by parties and their policies was influenced by various factors, including regional ones. On the Continent, for example in Italy, the Catholic Church helped to shape conservatism and the Christian Democrats. Both Italy and France had strong Communist Parties, whereas the British Communist Party remained outside the political mainstream, able to win only two parliamentary seats in 1945.

The Second World War had heightened political interest, in Britain as on the Continent. The pre-war Depression with its widespread unemployment and inequality was remembered with anger, while wartime organization and co-operation against the enemy seemed to have boosted the hope that peacetime organization and co-operation might conquer old economic and social problems. The Beveridge Report of 1942 had given the British people a vision of a much-expanded *welfare state*[G], organized by government for the well-being of all its people. Beveridge himself was a Liberal, but it seemed to many that it was the Labour Party that was most enthusiastic for such organization, and for active government generally – planning and intervening as it did to prevent unemployment, to take key industries into public ownership (nationalization) and to secure the needs of the sick, the old and the homeless. The Labour Party agreed that these were socialist aims and in the election of 1945 declared itself 'a socialist party and proud of it'. Churchill responded vigorously:

> There can be no doubt that Socialism is irreparably interwoven with totalitarianism and the abject worship of the state. . . . Socialism is in its essence an attack not only on British enterprise, but upon the right of the ordinary man and woman to breathe freely without having a harsh, clammy, clumsy, tyrannical hand clapped across their mouth and nostrils.

Thus were drawn the battle lines of many of the political controversies of the post-war world, in Britain as elsewhere: between 'socialist planning' and 'conservative freedom'.

During the election campaign of 1945, the Conservatives relied heavily on Churchill's personal prestige as the man who had led the nation to victory against Nazi Germany, but the election results showed that many voters wanted more than this. Nor was Churchill's rhetoric always to his advantage: he startled many voters by suggesting that Labour 'would have to fall back on some form of Gestapo', seemingly casting the mild Attlee in the role of a militant Nazi. In the election, some twelve million voters opted for Attlee and Labour and ten million for Churchill and the Conservatives, the two-party battle squeezing out most other candidates. The Liberals got just over two million votes. However, the British 'first-past-the-post' voting system (in which the candidate with the highest number of votes becomes the MP for the relevant constituency - even if his or her total vote is less than 50 per cent of the votes cast) exaggerated the scale of their defeat. Labour won 393 seats, the Conservatives 213, the Liberals only 12. Attlee formed the new government, with Hugh Dalton becoming Chancellor of the Exchequer and Bevin, the trade unionist, Foreign Secretary. It was the first time the Labour Party had taken office with an overall Commons majority.

5.2 Labour government, 1945–51

5.2.1 The economy

In common with other European states, Britain faced many economic difficulties after the Second World War. The country was near to bankruptcy, its debts to foreign creditors amounting to over £3.3 billion and its currency reserves low. Economic policy had to be shaped against a background of debt, limited resources and problems with the balance of payments (balancing the country's overseas earnings against overseas spending). Increased output would bring more wealth - and the British shared the almost universal belief in 1945 in the pursuit of economic growth - but the war had left handicaps. Plant was largely worn out; capital for investment was limited; and prices and wages had risen (prices by about 70 per cent since 1935), so exports threatened to be expensive to foreign customers. It was also essential to import foodstuffs and raw materials, but Britain's traditional method of paying for them - not only with its 'visible' exports (goods) but also with 'invisible' exports (services such as banking and shipping, and income from overseas assets) - was further handicapped by wartime shipping losses and the reduction of foreign assets. Britain's income from the latter was only half what it had been in 1938, many assets having been sold to pay for wartime supplies. There had been signs before the war that Britain was heading into balance-of-payments problems; after 1945 the problems became severe in a Europe where most countries lacked purchasing power and were struggling for economic survival. Attlee's government nevertheless intended to achieve full employment while grappling with its many difficulties.

Like the West generally, Britain looked for help to the USA. Already in 1944 President Roosevelt had called a conference at Bretton Woods, New Hampshire, where almost thirty nations agreed to set up the World Bank and the International Monetary Fund (IMF) to assist countries with balance-of-payments problems. But US Lend-Lease ended with the defeat of Japan in August 1945, and Dalton had to look urgently for new loans. The USA and Canada provided almost £1.5 billion. Tight controls kept Britain's imports

Fig. 5.1 Post-war Britain became used to financial crisis. In 1947, when this photograph was taken in Trafalgar Square, London, the USA was already preparing the Marshall Plan to help war-torn Europe.

down and encouraged exports by restricting the home market, for example in motor cars. Trade unions were persuaded to restrain wage claims to help keep down the costs of production. Wartime rationing continued, and after the severe winter of 1946–7 with its acute fuel shortages the British people had to endure the extension of rationing to potatoes. Even so it was difficult to find overseas markets, and a stubborn 'dollar gap' persisted: Britain could not earn enough to pay for all its imports and, after trade deficits in 1946–7, reserves of gold and dollars again fell perilously low.

Stafford Cripps replaced Dalton as Chancellor of the Exchequer in November 1947. At the Board of Trade Cripps had already played a part in organizing a tightly run economy. He now imposed the policy of 'Austerity', designed to increase production while further curbing costs and the demands of the home market. A small surplus on the balance of payments was won in 1948–9, but Cripps felt that devaluation of the pound was essential in order to make the country's exports cheaper. The government acted in September 1949, reducing the value of one pound in international exchange from 4.03 dollars to 2.80 dollars. In 1950 the surplus on the balance of payments rose dramatically. At the same time Marshall Aid was beginning to help European economies, and Britain was among those to benefit from the setting up of the OEEC (see section 4.3). British exports almost trebled during the years 1946–51, but Cripps retired in 1950, his health broken by the struggle. His successor, Hugh Gaitskell, faced a new balance-of-payments crisis in 1951 when the Korean War drove up the price of commodities on world markets and Britain's imports bill soared.

The government meanwhile pursued a policy of nationalization. The Labour Party had since 1918 been pledged to:

> secure for the producers by hand and brain the full fruits of their industry, and the most equitable distribution thereof that may be possible on the basis of the common ownership of the means of production and the best obtainable system of popular administration and control of each industry and service.

In taking industries into 'common ownership', Attlee's government bought out private shareholders with government stock (in effect, interest-bearing loans which the government would eventually repay) and set up public corporations to run the nationalized enterprises, loosely supervised by parliament. The Bank of England and the coal industry were nationalized in 1946, followed in 1947–8 by the cable and wireless, electricity, and gas industries. The British Transport Commission, set up in 1948, had authority over railways, inland waterways, docks and many of the country's road transport services (other than those run by local councils). Civil aviation came under two corporations – British European Airways (BEA) and the British Overseas Airways Corporation (BOAC), the latter dating from Conservative legislation before the Second World War. (BEA and BOAC became British Airways in 1973.) The Iron and Steel Act of 1949 brought together about a hundred companies as the British Iron and Steel Corporation, though this was fiercely resisted by the Conservatives.

The new Boards like the National Coal Board (NCB) were handicapped by debts arising from the compensation paid to the previous owners. But they were able to draw on public money for modernization and (often much-needed) new technology, and were able to consider social as well as purely economic interests. The Boards were intended to ensure good working conditions for their employees – conditions in some industries (the coal industry, for example) having been notoriously bad in the past. Nationalization was controversial, however, in a capitalist society. State monopolies reduced competition, and were alleged by their critics to lead to inefficiency. When the Conservatives returned to power in the 1951 election, they quickly denationalized iron and steel and returned some transport services to private owners. There followed renationalization and denationalization with successive changes of government. (Some nationalized Boards found that changing technology and overseas competition forced them in later years to reduce the scale of their industries, resulting in painful cuts in the labour force. By the end of 1987, only 51 000 worked in the steel industry. The NCB had about 700 000 mineworkers in the late 1940s; 40 years later, the figure was below 90 000, with further cuts threatening.)

Attlee's government, before it fell in 1951, kept its promise to maintain full employment: unemployment remained below 400 000, affecting almost exclusively only those in the process of changing jobs. The government also kept up its wartime practice of intervening with regulations and subsidies to try to manage the economy – restraining prices, wages, rents and interest rates, for example. In the election of 1951 there was fierce debate about the government's record. The heated charges and counter-charges which ensued became a feature of British elections and party conduct – more markedly so with the extension of the media after the Second World War to television as well as radio.

5.2.2 The welfare state

The Committee on Social Insurance and Allied Services, headed by William Beveridge, reported to the government in 1942 with a Plan for Social Security whose post-war aim was to:

> abolish want by ensuring that every citizen willing to serve according to his powers has at all times an income sufficient to meet his responsibilities.

Beveridge identified 'five giants' to be attacked – Want, Disease, Ignorance, Squalor and Idleness – and proposed a co-operative effort by government and citizens to overcome them. The country as a whole would need to increase wealth by more production; government would need to avoid Idleness by ensuring full employment; and the nation would need to build a more comprehensive system than had so far existed to insure its citizens against social hazards, to provide health care for all and to develop other services such as education and housing. The more Britain looked forward to peace, the greater grew interest in and enthusiasm for the Beveridge Report.

Two measures were enacted even before the election of 1945. The (Butler) Education Act of 1944 (named after R.A. Butler, the Conservative President of the Board of Education) set up a new Ministry of Education, guaranteed free secondary education for all, reorganizing those schools with pupils beyond the age of eleven, and proposed to raise the school-leaving age as soon as possible. (It rose to fifteen in 1947 and to sixteen in 1972.) The Family Allowances Act was passed in 1945 to help with the cost of parenthood, each child after the first qualifying for five shillings (25p) a week from the state.

The outcome of the election was influenced by Labour's warm support for the Beveridge Report, and busy legislation followed to build on existing insurance and relief schemes and to set up a more far-reaching welfare state. The National Insurance Act of 1946 allowed no exemptions from an extended insurance system based on principles introduced as early as 1911: regular contributions from workers, employers and government (from taxation) were collected into a single Insurance Fund, from which benefits would be paid out.

Benefits went to those qualifying by reason of sickness, maternity, widowhood, unemployment or old age, and were also allocated to help with the cost of funerals and (by another act) to compensate those suffering injury at work. *The Times* agreed with Attlee that this new social-security system was 'the most comprehensive of its kind ever introduced in any country', and it was welcomed in parliament and by the nation at large. Even so, the complex rules governing benefits (they were earned by contributions and sometimes limited in duration) left some cases of need outside the system. The National Assistance Act of 1948 therefore aimed to provide, from income from taxation, a safety net for those in Want and with no other means of support.

Squalor was tackled by the New Towns Act (1946), the Town and Country Planning Act (1947) and a campaign of house-building by local authorities directed by Aneurin Bevan as Minister of Health. Bevan was a radical ex-miner from South Wales, regarded as being on the left of the Labour Party. It was he who made the introduction of Britain's National Health Service (NHS) something of a crusade. The National Health Service Act was passed in 1946. attacking Disease and opening to all British citizens, without charge, almost all forms of health care, in and out of hospital. The costs, like those of education and defence, were met out of general taxation. When the NHS began to operate in 1948 there was a rush for treatment, medicines, glasses and dental repairs. In its first year, the costs of the NHS were around £200 million but advances in medicine and technology and increases in wages meant that 30 years later annual costs were almost 30 times higher. Costs led to arguments about the principle Bevan held sacred – that the sick should not be required to pay for their treatment. When Gaitskell imposed some trivial charges in 1951, Bevan was furious, rightly seeing that this would be a precedent for future governments, especially Conservative ones. Bevan was already unhappy that Attlee had moved him from Health to the Ministry of Labour in 1951, and he resigned ministerial office before the 1951 general election, complaining that the government was losing its fire.

A thorough-going welfare state had been built, however. Though often amended in detail, it remained largely intact for more than 30 years. Until the new Conservatism of the Thatcher governments after 1979, all parties broadly agreed with Beveridge that it was right in principle to use the power of the state to try to protect its citizens 'from the cradle to the grave'. From the outset, however, some observers were uneasy that such protection might stifle initiative.

British governments after 1945 were generally more active than those before the war. In the years to 1950, Attlee's government introduced many other acts, for example to protect deprived children, to provide legal aid for the poor, to encourage investment in important industries, and to restrict business monopolies. Attlee also made changes to the constitution, abolishing the right of some subjects (such as graduates) to more than one vote and extending voting rights in local government to others besides ratepayers (Representation of the People Act, 1948). The power of the House of Lords to delay legislation approved by the Commons was limited to only one year by the Parliament Act of 1949.

Labour also reversed Conservative legislation which had followed the General Strike of 1926: the Trade Disputes Act of 1946 widened trade-union rights to take industrial action and to collect a political levy on behalf of the Labour Party. (This restored the right given in 1913 to collect a levy from all members of a union with the exception of those who chose to contract 'out', a system the Conservatives had changed in 1927 by requiring those who wished to pay actively to contract 'in'.) The Labour Party had from birth had close links with trade unionism, differing in this from most European socialist parties, and trade-union rights were to provide another bone of contention in post-war British politics. Attlee gave the unions a new importance, inviting them to advise and in some cases to assist the government, a role which proved generally useful from 1945 to 1951 when strikes and disruption were much less common than they later became.

5.2.3 Britain and the outside world

There were other ways in which Attlee's government set Britain's course in the post-war world. As Foreign Secretary, Bevin firmly committed Britain to the side of the West in the Cold War and to the Atlantic alliance with the USA. Before his resignation in March 1951, only weeks before his death, Bevin had organized Europe's response to the Marshall Plan, co-operated in the Berlin Airlift, made Britain a member of NATO and sent troops to fight in the Korean War (see Units 1 and 4). His English-speaking alliance with the Americans was to be the central pillar of the foreign policy of all British governments after 1945, though there were some issues on which London and Washington did not fully agree – Bevin, for example, did not support the US refusal to recognize the new government of Mao Tse-tung in 1949.

At the end of the Second World War Britain still had a vast overseas empire, though the Labour Party saw that colonial empires were unlikely to survive long in the new age. Demands from the colonies for independence were growing more insistent, and were supported by both the USA and the USSR, who argued that colonies were out of date and morally wrong. A painful period of readjustment lay ahead for the European colonizing powers. The British showed more readiness than others to give way and, while the French and Dutch fought wars to try to regain their lands in Asia, Attlee's government delayed as little as possible the granting of freedom to India, Pakistan, Burma and Ceylon, the independent states which in 1947–8 took the place of Britain's Indian Empire (see section 14.2.2). At about the same time, Britain also withdrew from Palestine, though Bevin was in this case accused both of hostility to Zionism and of turning away from Britain's responsibilities (see section 14.2.3).

The decolonization of the rest of the Empire took place over many years. Most former colonies became members of the Commonwealth (see sections 14.2.4 and 14.4). Here too Bevin gave a lead, supporting India's Prime Minister, Jawaharlal Nehru, and others in beginning to change the British

Commonwealth of Nations from a club for the white Dominions[G] such as Canada into a multiracial association. One of Bevin's last initiatives was to push forward the Colombo Plan by which Britain and the Dominions, supported by the USA, set up aid machinery for helping the development of poor Asian nations – some (such as India and Ceylon) in the Commonwealth, others (such as Indonesia and the Philippines) outside it. Bevin's concerns were economic and humanitarian but, like the Marshall Plan, the Colombo Plan also aimed to safeguard its beneficiaries from communism.

Ties to the Empire, the Commonwealth and the USA left Bevin with less enthusiasm for closer links with Europe. Membership of the Council of Europe was acceptable, for debate and protecting human rights, but the Foreign Secretary took no steps to join the European Coal and Steel Community (ECSC), leaving successive Conservative governments similarly to stand aside from European Communities to which sovereignty would need to be yielded (see section 4.3). Concern for Britain's traditional international importance also led Attlee's government into the decision, secret in 1947, to develop Britain's own nuclear weapons, independently of the USA. The first British atomic bombs were not tested until 1952, by which time many members of the Labour Party had been deeply disturbed to learn of their leader's decision to equip the country with its own nuclear arsenal, in competition with the superpowers.

5.3 Government, opposition and issues from 1951

5.3.1 Butskellism and consensus

Table 5.1 shows how the political pendulum swung between Conservative and Labour governments. Though Labour was re-elected in 1950, the Conservatives were in office from 1951 to 1964, years of growing affluence for most of the British people as Britain – and Europe generally – recovered from wartime dislocation and used new technology to create more wealth. But they were also years of persistent economic problems, eventually dubbed by Labour the 'Thirteen Wasted Years', when investment, modernization and growth were less than they might have been.

Attlee's successor as leader of the Labour Party from 1955 was Gaitskell, whose outlook was less radical than that of Bevan whom he defeated in the battle for leadership and who eventually became his deputy. Indeed, so similar were the views on economic policy of Gaitskell and the Conservative Chancellor, Butler, that the term 'Butskellism' came into fashion to describe the consensus, middle-of-the-road politics often practised in the 1950s and to some extent in the 1960s too. Such compromising policies were fiercely attacked by more radical members of the Labour Party, and Labour's internal divisions helped the Conservatives to win the general election of 1959. Even Bevan seemed to lose some of his fire, disappointing many of his followers when in the late 1950s he accepted that Britain should keep its nuclear weaponry. Bevan

Table 5.1 British general elections and ministries from 1951

Date of general election	Seats in House of Commons*				Prime Minister	Chancellor of the Exchequer	Foreign Secretary
	Conservatives	Labour	Liberals	Others			
1951	**321**	295	6	3	Churchill	Butler	Eden
					Eden, 1955	Butler	Macmillan
1955	**344**	277	6	3	Eden	Butler	Macmillan
						Macmillan	Lloyd
					Macmillan, 1957	Thorneycroft	Lloyd
						Heathcote-Amory	
1959	**365**	258	6	1	Macmillan	Heathcote-Amory	Lloyd
						Lloyd	Douglas-Home
						Maudling	
					Douglas-Home, 1963	Maudling	Butler
1964	304	**317**	9	0	Wilson	Callaghan	Gordon Walker
							Stewart
1966	253	**363**	12	2	Wilson	Callaghan	Brown
						Jenkins	Stewart
1970	**330**	287	6	7	Heath	Macleod	Douglas-Home
						Barber	

1974 (Feb)	297	**301**	14	23	Wilson	Healey	Callaghan
1974 (Oct)	277	**319**	13	26†	Wilson	Healey	Callaghan
					Callaghan, 1976	Healey	Crosland
							Owen
1979	**339**	269	11	16	Thatcher	Howe	Carrington
							Pym
1983	**397**	209	23‡	21	Thatcher	Lawson	Howe
1987	**375**	229	22§	24	Thatcher	Lawson	Howe

Bold The party winning the general election and forming the government.

* The number of seats in the House of Commons increased to 630 in 1955, 635 in 1974 and 650 in 1983.

† Including 11 Scottish Nationalists (SNP) and 2 Welsh Nationalists (Plaid Cymru) – the best results Nationalists have ever obtained in a British general election.

‡ The 23 Alliance seats were won by Liberals (17) and the Social Democrats (SDP) (6).

§ The 22 Alliance seats were won by Liberals (16) and the Social Democrats (SDP) (6).

died in 1960 and Gaitskell in 1963, leaving the way clear for a new leader to restore Labour unity.

The task fell to Harold Wilson and he showed skill in tackling it, though he was fortunate to come to the fore when the Conservatives were faltering. In spite of considerable prosperity, Britain had not achieved an economic miracle such as that in West Germany, and Conservative Chancellors had seemed to move from one economic crisis to another (see section 5.4). Moreover, ill health forced the Conservative leader, Harold Macmillan, into retirement at the end of a long and distinguished career as a humane and sometimes progressive politician and statesman. The new Prime Minister, Alec Douglas-Home, could not match him in stature and popular appeal, but even so Wilson and Labour won the 1964 election by only a narrow margin, going to the polls again in 1966 to increase their majority when a favourable economic tide had begun to flow.

Wilson seemed to be in tune with the 'swinging' and colourful '60s, possessing an easy informality and coming from a background which suggested both intellectual ability and close links with the people. But economic frustrations persisted: to what seemed unending anxiety about Britain's balance of trade were added disquiet about growing industrial unrest and alarm at rising prices. It nevertheless seemed likely that Wilson would win the next general election. The Conservatives had dropped Douglas-Home after defeat in 1964 and now for the first time elected their leader - like other parties - instead of allowing him to 'emerge' in the traditional way from rather mysterious lobbying and discussion, a method which had usually favoured the well-connected from the public schools. Election made Edward Heath party leader, a former grammar-school boy and a talented musician as well as politician. Concentrating his attack on high prices, trade-union influence and the alleged need to liberate individualism, Heath pulled off a modest victory in 1970, confounding opinion polls which had suggested that Wilson's popularity would bring him further success.

5.3.2 Confrontation and disaffection

The 1970 election seemed to be a nail in the coffin of consensus politics. The Conservatives were now eager for a new balance, and aimed to reduce the role of the state with its economic and welfare machinery, regulations and subsidies, while renewing the emphasis on individual enterprise, competition and private profit. Economic 'lame ducks' were likely to be left to perish, procedures for regulating prices and incomes were to be abolished, and trade unions were to be curbed by new legislation. In practice, the government found itself rescuing lame ducks such as Rolls Royce and Upper Clyde Shipbuilders to prevent now-rising unemployment from rising further. Heath had also to restore prices-and-incomes machinery, using different names for it. The government moreover actually added to the apparatus of the welfare state by introducing Family Income Supplements and extending help to those unable to meet certain payments, for example of rent. The Industrial Relations Act of 1971 meanwhile brought confrontation rather than harmony. Government–union relations grew so sour that Heath called a general election in February 1974, vainly seeking firmer popular backing to deal with a coal strike which, combining with a world energy crisis (see section 21.1), had reduced the country to a three-day working week and a state of emergency.

Labour's policy in 1974 was to emphasize the need for co-operation and consent, 'to restore the sense of national unity', as Denis Healey put it when victory at the polls made him Chancellor of the Exchequer. A second election in 1974 made the Labour government more secure (see Table 5.1). But problems seemed to be multiplying in the 1970s. Inflation, rising unemployment, fuel shortages, trade difficulties and struggling enterprises confronted economic ministers throughout the capitalist world. Labour still relied heavily on state involvement in the economy: nationalization was extended to the aircraft and shipbuilding industries, the government was closely involved in developing Britain's new North Sea oil industry, and the National Enterprise Board was set up to steer industries towards new technology and profitability. Trade-union support for technological change and incomes restraint (to keep down labour costs) was to depend on a 'social contract' between unions and government, an informal understanding which did not in fact work well.

Wilson retired in 1976, leaving James Callaghan and Healey (as Prime Minister and Chancellor respectively), to continue along Labour's chosen road. They ran into new difficulties towards the end of 1978. Efforts to hold down wages – made partly under pressure from the IMF as the price of financial help to Britain – angered workers, especially the low-paid in the public services, and led to industrial unrest which in turn angered other members of society. Against this background and doubts about Labour's supposed expertise in dealing with the unions, the general election of 1979 became due.

Most government economic policy in Britain since 1945 had owed a good deal to Keynesian[G] ideas. By the end of the 1970s, right-wing opinion was impressed more by Milton Friedman than by Keynes, rejecting policies of government involvement since they put up a barrier to the competitive instincts of individuals on which it would be better to rely for prosperity (see section 2.4.2). Few took to Friedmanism more eagerly than Margaret Thatcher, the Conservative choice for leader in 1975 after Heath's electoral failures in 1974.

Thatcher's message in the election of 1979 bore some similarities to that of Heath in 1970. She went further in her zeal, however, upholding monetarism (the tight control of the money supply and tight limits on public spending 'to squeeze inflation out of the economy') and condemning support for economic lame ducks as a burden similar to that of government involvement generally. She also promised a vigorous attack on trade unions and a reversal of nationalization with policies of privatization (putting industries and services into the hands of private owners). She fully intended to start a new era in British politics, 'sweeping back' the state and liberating individual enterprise, seemingly placing efficiency above compassion. Victory in the election made Mrs Thatcher Britain's first woman Prime Minister, indeed the first in the Western world, though women had already held similar office in Sri Lanka,

India and Israel and were soon to do so in Yugoslavia and, in 1987, in the Transkei, South Africa.

The Conservatives retained power in the election of 1983, as Table 5.1 shows. This was in spite of massive unemployment and fierce controversy about Thatcherism, with its policies the Prime Minister called 'realistic' but critics found 'harsh', and an abrasive style of leadership which had caused the Soviets to dub Thatcher the 'Iron Lady'. There were even ripples of dissent among Conservatives, with criticism of the Prime Minister coming from former leaders such as Macmillan and Heath. In 1983, however, the Labour alternative seemed unattractive.

The Labour Party at this time fell to a new post-war electoral low. After defeat in 1979 it had again fallen into internal disputes with bitter arguments between 'left' and 'right', constitutional changes, resignations and the eventual expulsion of alleged 'extremist' members. Callaghan was criticized over the election campaign of 1979 and a new leader was elected – Michael Foot, veteran anti-nuclear campaigner, biographer and heir to Aneurin Bevan's Ebbw Vale constituency. Foot's inability to make much impact on the electorate in 1983 led to further change, the younger Neil Kinnock taking over the leadership with the hope of restoring calm and purpose – much as Wilson had done in the 1960s.

Kinnock's task was far from easy. The Labour Party seemed to be somehow trapped between Thatcherites determined to alter the direction of British politics and those on the left intent on 'breaking the mould' of the British political system. For some time Labour had suffered defections – mainly by right-wing members dissatisfied with the activities of radicals or uneasy about Labour's links with the trade unions. A group of these dissidents, including former Labour ministers Roy Jenkins and David Owen, in 1981 set up the Council for Social Democracy, intending to break the pattern of alternating Conservative and Labour governments and:

> to rally all those who are committed to the values, principles and policies of social democracy.

From the Council grew the Social Democratic Party (SDP), preaching moderation and condemning as extremist both Thatcher's Conservatism and left-wing influences on the Labour Party. On his return to British politics from the Presidency of the European Commission, Jenkins became the first SDP leader and he now found much common ground with the Liberals. The latter had persevered since 1945 in offering a moderate alternative to the larger parties, prizing freedom and supportive of reform, individualism and capitalism. A succession of leaders had been unable to save the Party from generally disappointing election results. The leader since 1976 had been David Steel, who now led the Liberals into the Alliance with the SDP, the better to erode the power of Conservatives and Labour (though the support of Steel and the Liberals had helped in the late 1970s to keep Callaghan in office when Labour's majority had been eaten away in by-elections).

In 1983 the Alliance won few seats. It claimed, nevertheless, that the mould had begun to break, Liberal and SDP votes being substantial. The Liberals had long complained of the unfairness of the British electoral system, where seats in the Commons failed to reflect the total votes cast for the competing parties. In 1951 and February 1974 governments were formed by parties who won fewer votes than their opponents but, more consistently, the system placed minority parties at a disadvantage. The Liberals in 1959 won nearly 6 per cent of the total votes but only 6 of the 630 seats in the House of Commons, and in 1964 over 11 per cent of the total vote but only 9 of the seats. The SDP agreed with them that the system ought to be changed to some form of proportional representation[G] which would better match seats to votes. In 1983 the minorities' sense of injustice was underlined: Labour won 28.3 per cent of the total votes and collected 209 seats; the Alliance won 26 per cent of the votes but only 23 seats. As was usual in British politics the government was formed by a party with less than half of the total votes of the people – in this case, only 43.5 per cent, fewer votes in fact than in 1979 in spite of the large Conservative majority in the Commons. Steel and Owen, who took over the SDP leadership from Jenkins, gave a high priority to the Alliance's intention to change the electoral system, but they received no encouragement from the larger parties who found the existing system convenient – as the Liberals themselves had when a major party at the beginning of the century.

The electoral tide still flowed strongly with the Conservatives when the next general election took place in 1987. They remained in power with a secure majority in the House of Commons (see Table 5.1). Their share of the vote was just over 42 per cent, almost identical to that in 1983. Explanations of the result were to be found in the feeling of prosperity among those in work, especially in southern England – where wages were still rising much faster than prices. There were also continuing doubts about the unity of the Labour Party and unease about quite what the Liberal–SDP Alliance stood for. Soon after the election the SDP became divided. In 1988 a majority of its members chose to merge with the Liberals to form a new party which eventually decided to be known as the Social and Liberal Democrats (later abbreviated to the Democrats) under the leadership of Paddy Ashdown. David Owen resisted the change and continued as leader of the now smaller SDP, which had three MPs including himself. There was therefore another new 'mould' in British politics. Anti-Thatcherites writhed in frustration at the inability of the left to overthrow her government at the ballot box.

5.4 Economic management since 1951

5.4.1 The 1950s and 1960s

Though Britain after 1951 seemed to be plagued with economic problems, they were the problems of a comparatively rich country. Like Europe generally, Britain was developed and prosperous in contrast to much of the world, especially the southern hemisphere. Economic difficulties nevertheless seemed unending, and voters were often swayed by whichever politicians seemed to offer the better hope of coping with them. Early optimism that the problems might actually be solved gave way to frustration in the 1960s and 1970s as Britain slipped down the production league table. In 1961, among members of the Organization for Economic Co-operation and Development (OECD), Britain came ninth in GDP per head of population. Fifteen years later it had fallen to eighteenth.

Growth in the production of wealth was slower than that of many competitors, usually around two or three per cent a year, only about half that of West Germany. While West Germany also had a healthy balance of trade, Britain had constantly to struggle to earn enough to pay for imports. It was often alleged that British goods were over-priced in foreign markets, and various reasons for this were put forward and argued about – complacent management, out-of-date machinery, shoddy workmanship, disruptive trade unions and too high wages among them.

Government seemed to be locked in a constant struggle to boost exports, curb imports and avoid balance-of-payments crises. Yet government could only seek to influence economic developments: it could seldom control them completely. In the 1950s the Conservatives alternated between 'Stop' and 'Go' – either trying to *stop* the economy becoming too active (overheated) and driving up prices and sucking in imports as the British people pursued goods too eagerly and then looked for higher incomes and greater purchasing power, or trying to *go* on to more production and full employment (and more votes) with the prospect of long-term rewards and affluence. Periods of 'Go' led almost inevitably to periods of 'Stop', when credit controls, higher taxes and income restraints were imposed. Thus, Butler's 'Go' from 1953 to 1955 was followed by a 'Stop' when the balance of payments plunged into deficit, and the pattern was repeated when Heathcote-Amory's 'Go' led to a larger deficit (about £260 million) in 1960. By 1964 Chancellor Reginald Maudling's attempt at 'Go' had led to a deficit of over £400 million. One underlying problem was that Britain was slow to take a long-term view and to invest substantially in industrial modernization. In the election of 1964 Wilson benefited from public exasperation that the Conservative 'age of affluence' had not solved economic problems. The electorate was attracted by the prospect he held out of catching up with 'the roaring prosperity of other Western powers' by embracing technological change.

Balance-of-payments problems continued. James Callaghan, Chancellor of the Exchequer in 1964, tided Britain over its immediate problems by borrowing from the IMF, imposing another 'Stop' with a squeeze on spending and on incomes and then, in 1967, again devaluing the pound, this time from 2.80 to 2.40 dollars. Roy Jenkins maintained the tight controls in the late 1960s. Meanwhile, Wilson's government had set up a National Board for Prices and Incomes, though George Brown, Minister of Economic Affairs, struggled in vain to bring in a National Plan for the whole economy. The Plan, based on a weak imitation of French experiments with 'indicative planning'[G], rather than on the 'command planning'[G] systems of eastern Europe, proposed a way of organizing longer-run strategic planning for the economy. However, it lacked critical political support, notably from Harold Wilson.

By 1970 Britain's balance of trade was much healthier. There were new worries, however. Retail prices had risen by about 40 per cent during the 1960s, and the pace was quickening. Unemployment was about double what it had been in 1960 though still around only 600 000. In addition, there were more days lost in industrial disputes in 1969 than in any post-war year so far – with the exception of 1957. From the mid-1960s, Britain ceased to be less strike prone than competitors such as Japan. After outlining some ideas in a discussion document, *In Place of Strife*, Wilson's government did not proceed with legislation on industrial relations. The voters' disquiet was enough to tip the scales in favour of the Conservatives in 1970.

5.4.2 The 1970s and 1980s

Four years later, in 1974, the balance of payments showed an alarming new deficit of about £3500 million, even though Heath's government had in 1972 allowed the pound to float downwards on the exchanges, a flexible method of changing its value henceforward preferred to formal devaluation. Prices had risen sharply and in 1974 were more than twice as high as in 1960. Unemployment was much the same as it had been in 1970, but industrial unrest had exploded in frustration over 'Stop–Go' policies – which seemed to continue though the jargon itself was less in fashion. In 1974 the voters switched back from Conservative to Labour.

It was now Healey's turn to wrestle with the economy, the problems made more grave by a worldwide upsurge in the price of oil, an energy crisis and a quickly developing recession (see section 21.1). Britain was very fortunate in finding oil supplies under the North Sea and the first oil came ashore in 1975; in the 1980s Britain became virtually self-sufficient in oil, to the great benefit of its balance of payments and the government's revenue from taxes on oil production. But other difficulties remained severe. Prices raced ahead, doubling again before the annual rate of increase was once more brought below ten per cent in 1978. Unemployment rose to 1.5 million before being checked for a time after 1977. The country struggled to maintain even the rather sluggish growth rates of the last 25 years. More days were lost in industrial disputes in 1979 than even in 1972 – the worst year Heath had to face – and the voters now switched from Callaghan to Thatcher.

Thatcher's government could claim two significant successes in its first term in office to 1983. Inflation[G] was again brought below ten per cent, having soared soon after the election; by 1986 it was running at around only three per cent. Meanwhile, the balance of payments moved into a large surplus by 1981, thanks mainly to North Sea oil. The surplus reached £3.5 billion in 1985 but, ominously, there was again a deficit in 1986. However, Thatcher's policies extracted a price for these improvements: Britain endured a recession deeper

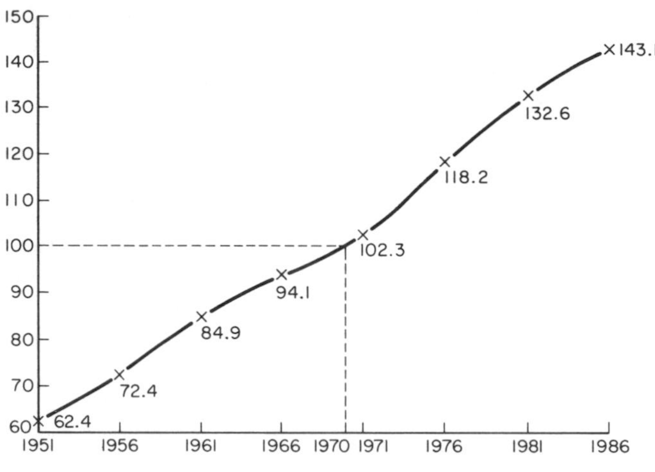

Fig. 5.2 Index of real personal disposable income per head of population (Britain)

than that affecting most of the Western world at this time. Unemployment rose above three million early in 1982 and bankruptcies ran at a record rate. The pound floated down to new lows, from about 1.80 dollars in 1982 to around 1.40 dollars in 1984. In 1983–4 the recession began to lift at last, but with little prospect that jobs would be recovered and unemployment substantially reduced. Unemployment was still above three million at the start of 1987 but several hundred thousand less by the end of that year. It continued to fall in 1988, although the reliability of the figures was constantly challenged in the light of the eighteen different administrative changes in the way unemployment had been measured since 1979.

Technological change usually substituted machines for people and Britain, like other countries, was now plunging into the electronics revolution, with computers and automated production bringing great 'savings' in costs and labour. The social consequences were immense. Old industries such as coal, textiles, steel and the railways had for decades been under growing pressure to shed employees – damaging and even destroying communities in the process – while the new high-technology industries and small businesses favoured by the Thatcher government had hardly yet begun to absorb the country's surplus labour. Moreover, industrial growth ceased altogether in the early 1980s, North Sea oil apart, and grew only slowly in the mid-1980s. Controversy raged. Thatcher persisted with her aim to bring about more enterprising attitudes on the part of workers and management. There was still general concern about too little investment for the future and the wasting of North Sea oil revenue, while in the mid-1980s doubts were raised as to whether, for all its new technology, Britain was actually keeping pace with its competitors in the application of micro-electronics. Lower wage settlements and fewer industrial disputes could again prove only temporary, this time the result as much of the fear of unemployment as of Thatcher's new industrial-relations laws.

Figure 5.2 shows that, in spite of the country's economic difficulties, average incomes of the British people grew steadily from 1951 to 1981 (though they were very unevenly distributed). Most governments in this period had seen improvements in overall production, exports and productivity (output per worker per hour), only to find problems persisting. Time and again it was pointed out that the British people paid themselves increased incomes in excess of the increases in output, which led to inflation, reduced competitiveness, difficulties in finding markets, and unemployment. Against this background there were regular elections, voters looking for what seemed the better economic managers, while governments shied away from pursuing unpopular policies for any length of time. In 1979 Mrs Thatcher claimed to offer a new choice between Labour's continuing attempts to manage the economy and her own intention to stand aloof from it. In practice, the Thatcher government busied itself continuously, privatizing, cutting back government spending and running down official machinery such as the Civil Service. Opponents claimed that this 'cure' for Britain's economic ills was more disastrous than the disease itself, threatening as it did to destroy the country's industrial base. Only in 1987–8 did British industry, except in oil production, begin to get back to the output levels of the 1970s. In 1983 and 1987 the voters nevertheless renewed Thatcher's period in office.

5.5 Society since 1951

5.5.1 The welfare state and social security

The detailed regulations of Britain's welfare state and system of social security (the term which came to be preferred to National Insurance and Assistance, especially when a Ministry of Social Security was set up in 1966) changed at a pace that was sometimes bewildering; the essentials, however, were preserved by all governments in the 1950s, 1960s and 1970s. Spending on social security began to run ahead of that on defence in the early 1960s, and with an increasing proportion of elderly in the population, rising costs of health care, and the return of massive unemployment, governments faced problems in finding enough resources for the state services that the people now took for granted. All western-European countries developed similar social-security systems after the Second World War, and by 1980 most were in fact spending a bigger percentage of their GDP on them than Britain's 21 per cent. The Netherlands, for example, spent 30 per cent. Thatcher's government set up an inquiry in 1984 to bring the Beveridge Report up to date, but the International Labour Organization (ILO), reporting at that time, did not prevaricate about the need for welfare provisions:

> It is beyond doubt that there has been no period since the aftermath of the Second World War when the need for effective social security policies has been greater.

Economic recession had simply underlined the importance of such policies.

The existence of organizations such as the Child Poverty Action Group (founded in 1965) bore witness to continuing inequalities in Britain. Ensuring that the needy received the benefits to which they were entitled from a system which seemed to grow ever more complicated remained a major problem. Party politicians argued furiously about matters of funding – prescription charges, levels of benefit and qualification requirements, for example. The general context of these arguments was almost always the same: the Conservative inclination was to encourage individual enterprise, for example in home purchase, private medicine and private schooling, and to prefer selective benefits, while Labour's inclination was to emphasize public-funded institutions such as council-built housing, the NHS and state schools, and to prefer universal benefits (funding for which could be taken back from the well-to-do in taxation). There was a typical tug-of-war over the Rent Acts: the Conservatives in 1957 removed the controls on rents which had been a device for protecting poor tenants but which had handicapped landlords; Wilson reimposed them in 1965. The parties continually manoeuvred to achieve the ideal balance between state services and private provision, but the differences between the parties on such issues became much sharper when Thatcher came to power.

5.5.2 Legislative snowstorms

Governments and parliament after 1951 kept up the post-war momentum, filling parliamentary sessions with the making of new laws far too numerous to consider in detail here. Many acts were to do with the economy: some, like the Aircraft and Shipbuilding Act of 1977, brought about nationalization, others, like the Transport Acts of 1953 and 1962, the Gas Act of 1986 and other Thatcher legislation, brought denationalization and privatization. Many changed the details of the welfare system – like the Social Security Pensions Act of 1975, relating the size of pensions to earnings. Other acts made administrative changes, among them the setting up of the Greater London Council in 1963, its abolition in 1986, and frequent alterations to the pattern of government ministries. But not all changes needed new acts of parliament. In the 1960s and 1970s most English secondary schools were reorganized, the separate grammar and secondary modern schools which were common after 1945 and defended by the Conservatives being replaced by comprehensive schools, a move much urged by Labour.

Conservative legislation before 1964 included the first Clean Air Act (1955) to curb pollution, and the Homicide Act (1957), the first step towards abolishing the death penalty. The Television Act (1954) created the Independent Television Authority (ITA) to compete with the British Broadcasting Corporation (BBC); this was matched by Heath's government in 1972 with the Sound Broadcasting Act, legalizing commercial radio under the supervision of the Independent Broadcasting Authority (IBA), to compete with BBC radio. The first measure was also brought in to check immigration from the

Commonwealth – Macmillan's Commonwealth Immigrants Act of 1962, which was followed by further immigration and nationality laws in 1968, 1971 and 1981 during the ministries of Wilson, Heath and Thatcher (see section 19.4.2).

Wilson's government in effect confirmed the abolition of the death penalty in the Murder Act (1965). In the same year came the Redundancy Payments Act, to help those losing their jobs through the economic change which was starting to accelerate, and the first of Labour's Race Relations Acts (others following in 1968 and 1976) which – taking account of changes in British society – aimed to shield ethnic minorities from discrimination and injustice. Labour applied similar ideas of equality to the sexes in the Sex Discrimination Act of 1975.

Much of the legislation still concerned administrative and economic organization. Wilson's government before 1970 dealt with docks and harbours, renationalized steel and produced another Transport Act (1968). Heath decimalized the coinage in 1971, thoroughly reorganized local government in 1972 (under the Local Government Act) and water authorities a year later (the Water Act), and legislated for 'fair trading'. Labour followed with the Trade Union and Labour Relations Act (1974), which began to dismantle Heath's Industrial Relations Act, and sweeping legislation for health and safety at work. A year later, in 1975, the Employment Protection Act was passed. Thatcher's government returned to the issue of industrial-relations law with several Employment Acts in the early 1980s. These had similarities to Heath's Act of 1971, but an attack on his system for local government led to new upheavals in conurbations such as London, Merseyside and Greater Manchester a mere dozen years later. As part of ongoing Thatcherite legislation, these local authorities were abolished, because the government claimed they were unnecessary, inefficient, and abused by left-wing councillors.

5.5.3 Property and affluence

Growing numbers of the British people prospered as the Second World War was left further behind. But wealth in Britain was redistributed from the rich to the less well-off much less rapidly than many imagined; the return of large-scale unemployment added to the want and misery from which a substantial minority always found it difficult to escape, even with the help of the welfare state. Housing was still a serious problem for many families, though the number of owner-occupiers grew steadily, most buying their homes with mortgages from building societies. By 1980 over half the country's dwellings were privately owned, a trend Thatcher's government was eager to encourage by forcing local authorities to sell properties to tenants who wished to buy. Public-authority house-building was always a likely issue for conflict between the parties. Under Thatcher it came almost to a standstill, to the fury of the opposition. Meanwhile, owner-occupiers improved and extended their homes, boosting new service industries supplying bathrooms, kitchens and windows and bringing great popularity to the DIY (do-it-yourself) industry.

In 1982 the British people spent on average 22 per cent of their incomes on housing, fuel and light, with a further seven per cent going on consumer durables and other household goods. Television had grown rapidly since 1945, becoming almost universal in the 1960s and well before that damaging attendances at cinemas. Many abandoned cinemas became bingo halls. In the early 1980s almost all homes had a television set, more than 80 per cent a washing machine and almost as many a refrigerator and telephone. Video machines and home computers were now being added to the list of goods which began as luxuries but quickly became commonplace.

Motor vehicles enjoyed a similar boom, making the population more mobile than ever before but creating problems for public transport services, many of which struggled for survival. In 1965, 40 per cent of households had the use of a car, in 1985 almost 63 per cent. In 1961 Britain had only 209 kilometres of motorway but still over 29 000 kilometres of railway. In 1981 the figures were respectively 2833 and 17 800. By then the country had some fifteen million cars – an explosion in numbers which first became marked in the late 1950s as the years of post-war austerity faded. In 1982 some fourteen per cent of personal income was spent on vehicles and travel, more than double the spending on

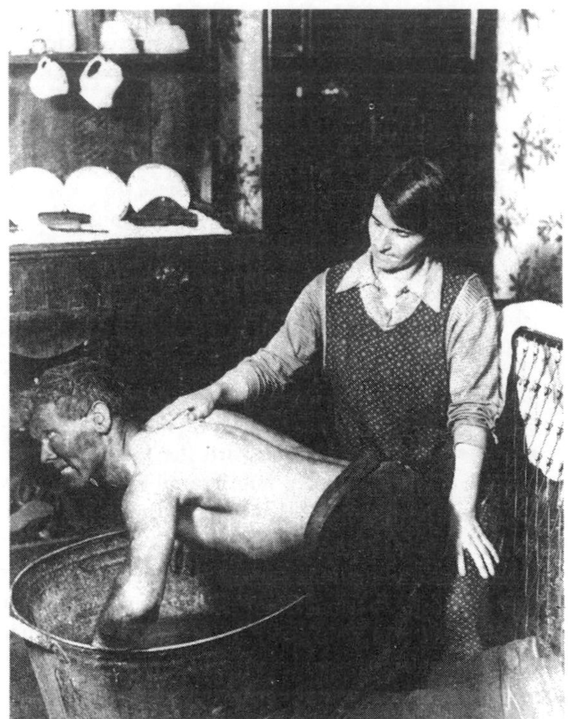

Fig. 5.3 A pitman's living room (bathroom and bedroom) in pre-war Britain: Britain's coal industry was nationalized in 1947, and the post-war years saw extensive changes in the housing and living standards of British workers in spite of persistent economic crises.

clothing and four times that on books, newspapers and various sorts of entertainment.

Advertising, not least on television, fuelled the wants of the British people and helped produce a society which sometimes seemed obsessed with acquiring material possessions. But a quarter of all spending was still on food, drink and tobacco.

5.5.4 Stress and conflict

Wealth did not automatically make British society a happier one. Admittedly, after a marked decline in religious observance, the churches began to recover support, and vast amounts of voluntary work and commitment by caring professionals showed that much survived in British society beyond mere greed for possessions. Twice as many students received a university education at the end of the 1970s compared with twenty years earlier. Yet it could not be denied that society grew more stressful, with many people bewildered by the pace of change and the complications of post-war living. Life expectancy grew slowly, reaching 70 years for men and 76 for women by 1980, but heart disease and cancer continued as major killer diseases and the extent of mental illness was a cause for real concern. By the late 1970s, one in three marriages ended in divorce, a rate which the British had once derided in the Soviet Union. In the late 1960s and early 1970s there were anxieties about drug abuse, especially among the young, a substantial minority of whom seemed alienated from a society apparently so committed to the pursuit of material wealth. Ten years later there was even greater alarm about heroin addiction in conurbations and areas of economic despair such as Merseyside.

Rebellious youth was not a new phenomenon after the Second World War, but television and other media now created greater awareness of things that were happening. Hooliganism and vandalism seemed to increase. In the 1970s public property such as telephone kiosks and bus shelters was often vandalized and the environment grew more shabby through damage, decay and graffiti. Public squalor existed alongside private affluence, at least some of it apparently due to disaffection. Political grievances were sometimes obvious, and violence lurked only a little below the surface in many confrontations. Deep social problems in Britain's inner cities erupted into riots and arson in 1980 in Bristol and a year later in Brixton (London), Toxteth (Merseyside) and other depressed areas. Moreover, trouble in Northern Ireland – which was far from new – escalated from the end of the 1960s to involve political terrorism, brutal attacks and much bloodshed (see section 19.4), providing a violent background to events in Britain. In fact political violence in Northern Ireland pushed the United Kingdom into an unenviable first place in the 1970s and 1980s: top of the European Community league table for politically motivated deaths and assassinations. Strong political beliefs created support for causes to which others objected, and society began to seem less tolerant. The National Front and the British Movement expressed extreme and racist views about ethnic minorities and British superiority, producing a backlash of left-wing opinion.

The Campaign for Nuclear Disarmament (CND) antagonized many on the right, who feared that the country might somehow be weakened against its 'enemies'. In the 1970s there seemed to be growing interest in direct action and politics in the streets rather than in parliament, which led to many clashes between interest groups and the authorities. Britain's was a traditionally mild police force – its members were only rarely armed – but disquiet concerning its role in the face of public disorder was another development of this period and led the Labour government in the 1970s to set up a Police Complaints Board.

Industrial disputes were sometimes bitter, the new mobility of the population giving rise to 'flying pickets' (who moved from one strike picket-line to another) and noisy conflicts such as that between thousands of striking miners and the authorities in 1972 at Saltley coke depot. Most industrial disputes were conducted at least as peacefully as in earlier times, but smouldering anger and sporadic outbreaks of violence always attracted the media: it became difficult to assess how far television, radio and the press distorted the true extent of hooliganism. A bitter coal dispute in 1984–5 nevertheless distressed much of the nation with its savagery (on the part of both striking miners and the police) and the deep hatred it stirred up.

Football hooliganism seemed a new phenomenon, at least in scale. Again, increased mobility contributed to it, just as in the 1960s rival factions of 'Mods' and 'Rockers' had arrived in force by scooter and motor cycle at holiday resorts such as Brighton, fighting seafront battles and leaving a trail of damage to property. Sporting occasions were now turned into brutal trials of strength between minorities of football 'supporters', and public property – including railway stock – again suffered extensive damage. By the end of the 1970s major football clubs were fencing off spectators both from the field of play and from rival spectators. A few years later, British football hooligans had become notorious throughout Europe and English clubs were banned from the Continent after 39 lives were lost at the Heysel Stadium, Brussels, in 1985.

It was much disputed to what extent British society as a whole had lost its traditional capacity for tolerance and compromise. But by the 1980s there were undoubtedly elements in society which reflected a modern world brutalized by wars, ever more hideous weaponry and political intolerance. 'Men of violence' were now to be found in numbers in almost all societies, and Britain's was no exception; it was certainly not only affairs in Northern Ireland which led political violence to spill over on to the streets of London and other cities. In 1971 members of the self-proclaimed 'Angry Brigade' were arrested following a series of explosions and machine-gun attacks against people in authority. Thereafter, like their counterparts in other countries, British cities experienced not infrequent bomb explosions and other acts of violence, some of which were connected with feuds among the nationals of other countries (see section 22.4).

5.6 Britain and the outside world from 1951

For many years after 1951 governments generally adhered to the external policy which took shape while Attlee was Prime Minister and Bevin Foreign Secretary (see section 5.2.3). The first of four elements in this policy was the Atlantic alliance, maintaining close ties with the USA. The second was the continued dismantling of the British Empire while building in its place the Commonwealth, a second English-speaking association but one which (generally) stopped short of binding commitments among its members. Thirdly, Britain was geographically part of Europe and part of the Western alliance there, but had yet to decide how close other links should be. Even in the 1980s Britain seemed hesitant, as if groping for a clear policy with regard to the Continent.

Writing in 1960, Anthony Eden, Foreign Secretary in 1935–8, 1940–45 and 1951–5, then Prime Minister in 1955–7, recorded the wider interests which seemed to obstruct closer ties with Europe:

> Britain's story and her interests lie beyond the continent of Europe. Our thoughts move across the seas to the many communities in which our people play their part, in every corner of the world. These are our family ties. That is our life: without it we should be no more than some millions of people living in an island off the coast of Europe in which nobody wants to take any particular interest.

This passage hinted at the fourth element in British policy – the national desire to be not only 'in the First XI' but also 'one of the opening batsmen', as Douglas-Home put it in 1963. Britain remembered its own pre-eminence in the days before the superpowers and, from time to time, aimed to pursue an independent line, defending the national interest. Eden briefly went to war with Egypt in 1956 – the Suez War (see section 14.2.5) – and Thatcher went to war with Argentina in 1982, when the Argentines invaded the Falkland Islands (see section 14.3.6), in just this spirit. But British initiatives could also be non-belligerent, for example in standing apart from the US war in Indo-China and in exerting pressure on the USA to end it. Britain nevertheless kept up its independent nuclear arsenal, governments arguing that the country's prestige and security demanded it. There was some drawing back from global commitments, however. Denis Healey, Defence Secretary from 1964 to 1970, committed Britain to withdrawal from all military bases 'east of Suez', excepting Hong Kong and the Persian Gulf.

Prime Ministers such as Macmillan and Wilson regularly aspired to making a British contribution to the settlement of superpower disputes. The British were still important enough to be present at summit meetings such as those at Geneva in 1955 and Paris in 1960, and British Prime Ministers made frequent visits not only to Washington but also to Moscow and, eventually, Peking. But Britain joined SEATO in 1954 and the Baghdad Pact a year later (see section 4.5.2) and Moscow regarded British Prime Ministers as clients of the USA. Washington, on the other hand, did not always closely consult with London when American interests were at stake: the Cuban Missiles Crisis in 1962 (see section 13.2.2) and the US invasion of Grenada in 1983 (see section 10.3) were just two occasions when the USA seemed to act first and consult later. Even so, Britain claimed to be the USA's foremost ally, relations sometimes being influenced by the personal bonds between Prime Ministers and US Presidents. Churchill and Eisenhower and Macmillan and Kennedy produced cordial partnerships, though Wilson probably got on better with Johnson than with Nixon, while Thatcher, welcoming the election of Reagan as a fellow Friedmanite, was sometimes less enthusiastic about the policies he adopted.

The decolonizing of the British Empire meanwhile went on steadily once Churchill had retired. Ghana and Malaya became independent in 1957, followed during the next 25 years by about 40 other former colonies. Rhodesia's independence was delayed until 1980 because of a well-entrenched white minority there, but this delay was exceptional (see section 14.3). Equality between the races and colours became an ever more sensitive issue in the post-war world and nowhere more so than in southern Africa. In 1961 South Africa resigned from the Commonwealth, the South African policy of apartheid[G] being out of place in a fundamentally multiracial association (see section 14.4). With the independence of Nigeria in 1960 and of Sierra Leone and Tanganyika in 1961, non-white states in the Commonwealth had begun to outnumber white states. Macmillan in 1960 acknowledged the nationalist 'wind of change' blowing through Africa towards independence, warning South Africa that the preservation of white privilege was out of tune with the times. Even so, Macmillan seemed a little hesitant about the wind towards a multiracial Commonwealth; at the conference at which South Africa resigned he seemed unwilling to condemn the South African government too fiercely. In fact, South Africa remained a problem for British governments, though Labour and the Liberals were more hostile towards it than the Conservatives. Investments, trade, and South Africa's important geographical position and rigid anti-communism helped to explain why Britain's attitude sometimes seemed equivocal – shielding South Africa from hostile votes at the United Nations, for example, while continuing to profess as much dislike of apartheid as states who preferred more active opposition. Heath provoked fury at the Commonwealth conference in Singapore in 1971 with his proposal to resume the sale of certain arms to South Africa that Wilson had banned.

Some British leaders at times seemed disenchanted with the Commonwealth. One such was Heath, who reminded members of the Commonwealth that Britain too had rights and interests. In his view it was in Britain's interest to join the European Communities (which at the time included the ECSC, the European Economic Community (EEC) and the European Atomic Energy Community (Euratom)). His first parliamentary speech in 1950 had been in support of European unity, and in 1961 he expressed Macmillan's and his own aim to make Britain:

> a full, wholehearted and active member of the European Community in the widest sense . . . [taking part] in the building of a new Europe.

When he tried to negotiate Britain's entry to Europe in 1963, however, that entry was prevented by the veto of the French President, Charles de Gaulle. Wilson met the same obstacle in 1967.

Many Conservatives and a section of the Labour Party had now come round to the Liberals' view that Britain ought to be in the European Communities: if not for reasons of idealism, then because it might after all be of economic advantage. De Gaulle retired in 1969 and when Heath became Prime Minister a year later he was at last able to negotiate membership. In 1973 Britain joined the European Community (the ECSC, the EEC and Euratom had merged in 1967) (see section 7.1.3). The Labour government after 1974 showed only limited enthusiasm for the venture and tried to renegotiate the transitional terms of entry before holding a national referendum in which the voters confirmed British membership. But when direct elections to the European Parliament were held in 1979, British electors were the most apathetic in Europe and most did not vote at all. The Thatcher government spent years haggling about the British contribution to the Community's funds, reinforcing the many doubts that existed about how seriously Britain had yet committed itself to Europe – doubts given further credence in 1988 by Mrs Thatcher's publicly expressed hostility to European integration.

UNIT 6

The Western democracies: 2 – Europe: the Six

6.1 Parliamentary democracy

Members of the Liberal–SDP Alliance in Britain liked to argue that political systems in western Europe, unlike Britain's, were based on co-operation and constructiveness rather than simple two-party confrontation. Even the seating in European parliaments – based on a semicircle – differed from the adversarial benches of the House of Commons where government and opposition sat in confrontation. It is true that proportional systems of election on the Continent tended to produce more parliamentary parties and often led to coalition governments (made up of several parties) but the extent of co-operation could be exaggerated. Similar divisions existed between left and right, with differing views about how society should be organized, and the number of parties at times produced not so much constructiveness as paralysis. Italy in 1980 formed its fortieth government since 1945. During the lifetime of the Fourth Republic, from 1946 to 1958, France had 24 governments, an average of two a year. The French then made changes, creating the Fifth Republic, the main characteristics of which were the reduced influence of parliament and, until he retired in 1969, the personal authority and presidential power of Charles de Gaulle. West Germany achieved more political stability than both Italy and the French Fourth Republic, partly due to that section of the Basic Law which excluded from the Bundestag all parties winning less than five per cent of the vote (see section 4.2.3).

Figure 6.1 shows the parties represented in several European parliaments in 1970. At that time Britain had a Conservative government. France still had a Gaullist President, directly elected by the people, with a Gaullist Prime Minister and Cabinet supported in the Assembly. West Germany had a coalition government of Social Democrats and Free Democrats, led by Chancellor Willy Brandt. One Italian government resigned in February 1970, unable to keep support in parliament. It took a month to put together a workable coalition but that too fell in July, another government being formed in August. As in France, but not Britain and West Germany, elections in Italy usually took place at fixed intervals, not when governments fell.

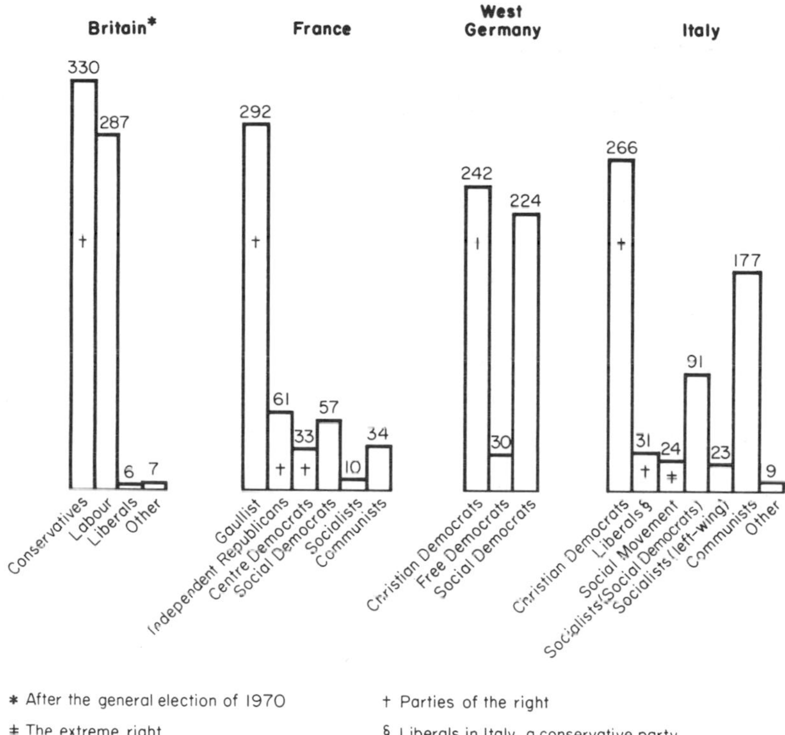

Fig. 6.1 Parliaments in 1970: a comparison

Figure 6.1 shows also that both Italy and France had Communist representation in parliament. Communist Parties in western Europe generally dated from about the beginning of the 1920s. In 1945 they still looked for leadership to Moscow, the Italians and French joining the Cominform (the Communist Information Bureau) when Stalin set it up in 1947. In that year in France, Paul Ramadier removed the Communists from his coalition government, and from then onwards other political groupings denied them access to power. The Italian Communist Party won strong support in the cities and industrial centres, gaining control of several city governments in the 1970s. On a national scale, it was usually second in popularity only to the Christian Democrats, with about a third of the national vote, but national office continued to elude it, to the relief of Italy's NATO allies.

Western Communist Parties had in fact turned away from Moscow towards a new 'Eurocommunism', seeking power through democratic elections and asserting the need for national variations in the form communism took, which did not have to include the overnight destruction of capitalism. Pietro Togliatti, head of the Italian CP in 1956 (the year the Cominform was dissolved), gave the lead, arguing in favour of independence and less rigid doctrine. The move away from Stalinism and the Kremlin continued after Togliatti's death in 1964, quickening when Enrico Berlinguer replaced Luigi Longo as the Party's Secretary-General in 1972. Waldeck Rochet (Secretary-General 1964–8) and then Georges Marchais, his successor, steered the French CP towards independence, achieving a new vigour by the early 1980s. In Spain, the Communist Party Franco had banned from 1939 was reborn after his death in 1975, winning ten per cent of the votes and 23 parliamentary seats in 1979. In that year the Portuguese CP, which had been banned for many years by Salazar, won nineteen per cent of the votes and 44 seats. In other parts of western Europe, Communist Parties like that in Britain had little electoral success, though there were about a dozen Communists in the Greek parliament when that country joined the European Community in 1981.

Franco and Salazar represented the survival in post-war Europe of pre-war regimes with similarities to that of Mussolini and the Italian Fascists. Italy still had neo-fascist groups such as the Social Movement (see fig. 6.1) and they were less easily kept out of parliament than were neo-Nazis in West Germany. Like extremists on the left, extreme right-wing movements also made their mark outside parliament with political violence throughout western Europe. Troubles escalated in the later 1960s, and were often linked with radical student unrest such as Johnson encountered in the USA and de Gaulle encountered in France. Student demonstrators had various grievances, ranging from the war in Indo-China to overcrowding on university campuses. Many were influenced by the criticisms of Western society made by the philosopher Herbert Marcuse, whose *One Dimensional Man* was published in 1964. Rudi Dutschke in West Germany and Daniel Cohn-Bendit in France were among the leaders of articulate student protest.

The majority – even among the student population – took no part in protests and demonstrations, which were in any case rarely more than noisy and obstructive. Some agitators, however, were at war with capitalist society. West Germany in 1968 experienced the activities of the Baader–Meinhof group of urban guerillas, named after Andreas Baader and Ulrike Meinhof, both of whom later died in prison. Bombing, murdering and kidnapping were part of a plague of political anger which went much further than most students and striking workers ever dreamed of going. It was sometimes a rather indiscriminate assault on existing systems. At other times, for example at the Olympic Games in Munich in 1972 when eighteen people died, it was the result of specific grievances – in this case an extension of the Palestinians' war against the Israelis.

Violence in West Germany brought a vigorous response from the authorities, the police gaining a reputation for determination, thoroughness and brutality against terror and disorder. Elsewhere, for example in France and Belgium as well as in Britain, anti-terrorist and riot squads were intermittently accused of savagery, and confrontations between the authorities and the discontented became more embittered. Italy's record of unrest was one of Europe's worst: not only were industrial relations turbulent, but the extreme right was matched by the left's 'Red Brigades'. In 1978 the latter kidnapped and then killed Aldo Moro, a veteran Christian Democrat and several times Prime Minister. In 1980 the bombing of the railway station in Bologna, seemingly a right-wing protest at the Communist city government, claimed 76 lives, outstripping even the sixteen deaths in a bombing in Milan in 1969. Like the British with regard to Northern Ireland, where the bombing of an inn at Ballykelly at the end of 1982 claimed sixteen further lives, Europeans became almost resigned to the continuing outrages, killing and maiming.

Once the dictatorships of Salazar and Franco had ended in Portugal and Spain, all western-European countries had broadly similar democratic systems, their governments changing in response to the wishes of the voters. Most had mixed economies[G] and societies similar to Britain's and shared too the almost universal disorders which, within about twenty years after the Second World War, had become a worldwide sickness.

6.2 The Federal Republic of Germany (West Germany)

6.2.1 Political alternatives

Konrad Adenauer, the former Mayor of Cologne who had been dismissed for opposing the Nazis, was Chancellor of the Federal Republic of Germany for fourteen years from its birth in 1949 (see section 4.2.3). The CDU (Christian Democrats), the party he had helped to found, remained in office for a further six years. Government was usually in coalition with minor parties, though from 1961 only four parties gained seats in the Bundestag – the CDU (with its south-German allies, the CSU (Christian Socialists)), the FDP (Free Democrats) and the SPD (Social Democrats). Adenauer was always inclined to a certain inflexibility, which in his later years led to the charge that his government was 'Chancellor dictatorship', and it was this vein of intolerance which led him to secure the outlawing from 1956 of the KPD (Communist Party). The ban lasted until 1968, five years after Adenauer had retired. In his last years in office, the Chancellor had lost much of his earlier popularity; as *der Alte*, the 'Old Man', he seemed reluctant to make way for younger politicians and antagonistic towards Ludwig Erhard, his Minister of Economic Affairs. When Adenauer at last stepped down at the age of 87, however, the CDU was the weaker for his loss. As Chancellor from 1963 to 1966, Erhard showed less ability than he had in his ministerial role (which he had held from 1949). Kurt Kiesinger followed Erhard as leader of the CDU. Though cleared in post-war denazification inquests, he was perhaps handicapped by his brief connection with the Nazis in the 1930s, and he was also hindered by the necessity of coalition with the CDU's main rivals, the SPD.

For the SPD, partnership in Kiesinger's government was of tactical advantage, Kiesinger offering them bargaining power and respectability. The SPD had gained 29 per cent of the votes in the first West German election in 1949, only two per cent below the CDU. But Kurt Schumacher, leader of the SPD, was less skilful than Adenauer in bargaining with the lesser parties, and the SPD aroused suspicion with its strong commitment to Marxism and less hostile attitude towards the Soviets. Schumacher died in 1952, but the SPD continued to show distrust of NATO, to condemn nuclear weapons and, when Adenauer created a new federal army, to oppose the conscription of young Germans. New ideas were adopted at the Social Democrat conference in Bad Godesberg in 1959, however, and in 1964 Willy Brandt was elected SPD leader. Brandt had already won distinction for his opposition to Nazism and, as Mayor of West Berlin since 1957, to communism too. He gave up office in Berlin to become Foreign Minister in Kiesinger's coalition government in 1966. By this time the SPD had much softened its Marxist image, appealing more to middle-class voters with a policy of 'as much freedom as possible and as much planning as necessary'. Like the British Labour Party under Wilson, the Social Democrats began to appeal to the middle ground of the electorate, especially when Brandt was able to show the fitness for national office of the SPD leaders. The election of 1969 revealed how far he had succeeded. The SPD won 22 more seats and Brandt became Chancellor, governing in coalition with the Free Democrats and ending the long period of conservative ascendancy.

The Social Democrats remained in office, with the CDU in opposition, for thirteen years. Brandt made substantial changes in West German foreign policy, but social and economic policies were not greatly changed from those of Adenauer and the CDU years. Consensus existed on the broad lines of what Erhard called the 'social market economy', combining considerable economic freedom with extensive social services. There were nevertheless those like Franz-Josef Strauss of the CSU and, on the left, members of the Socialist German Students' League who would have liked to move further from the centre. Brandt resigned in 1974, perhaps needlessly surrendering office after one of his secretaries was discovered to be an East German spy, but satisfied that he had already achieved his main ambitions in German politics.

The new Chancellor was Helmut Schmidt, whose background lay in regional politics in Hamburg and then several national offices under Brandt. Compared to Brandt, Schmidt seemed less radical though no less willing to adapt theories to circumstances. He was unfortunate in that his Chancellorship coincided with the energy and economic crises and social unrest of the late 1970s. He dealt firmly with disorders and, though the West German economy was now faltering, was confirmed in power in the election of 1980 in preference to a CDU government influenced by Strauss. Like the British Labour Party, however, the SPD was divided about how to deal with the recession and about the way ahead. Schmidt encountered further difficulties in appeasing the Free Democrats, still coalition partners in government. Tiring of the struggle, Schmidt resigned in 1982. The Free Democrats switched sides and backed Helmut Kohl of the CDU for Chancellor. Kohl remained in power after the federal election of 1983 and swung German politics back to the right.

6.2.2 The social market economy and the West German 'economic miracle'

West Germany's recovery from the Second World War to develop the strongest economy in western Europe was remarkable. Yet it was only in the late 1960s that West Germany's GDP and exports per head of population caught up with and then raced ahead of Britain's. Before then West Germany had more impressive growth rates than Britain (starting from a lower base), a strong currency and an apparently dedicated labour force which seldom resorted to strike action. So favourable was West Germany's balance of trade and so strong its currency that in 1969 the mark had to be revalued upwards, soon after the British pound had been devalued. In the crises of the 1970s, West Germany was slower than most Western countries to experience inflation and unemployment. At the end of the 1970s the West German GDP per head of population matched that of the USA and, with Denmark's, was the highest in the European Community, but the early 1980s saw the Federal Republic too running into serious economic problems. With them came uncharacteristic industrial unrest.

Credit for the 'economic miracle' which produced West Germany's post-war wealth was given almost universally to Ludwig Erhard (see section 4.2.3). From 1949 to 1963 he watched over the German economy, developing the 'social market economy': an economy left almost free from government interference so that it could respond to market forces, within a society supported by government measures for social security and for the provision of social services. There was nationalization of certain industries such as the railways; tax and fiscal policies (those concerning public revenue) encouraged enterprise and investment in industries of national importance; and, even after 1955 when Germany was rearmed, the country avoided spending on defence at anything like the British level. Co-operation in founding the European Communities further helped the West German economy, enlarging the market for German goods. Co-determination Laws in 1951–2 provided for works' councils and encouraged worker participation in the running of industries. The Laws were extended in 1976. With the co-determination policies and the organization of a limited number of large, modern trade unions (which had been banned under the Nazis), industrial relations were much less disorderly than in Britain.

The constant theme in post-war Germany was expansion. So successfully were the unemployed and the refugees from the East absorbed during the 1950s that foreign labour had to be imported in the form of Gastarbeiter (guest workers). Many were from Turkey and the poorer regions of southern Europe, such as Italy and Greece. In 1974 they did about twenty per cent of the country's manual work, though numbering less than three million in a population of around 60 million. But unemployment was then beginning to rise. It affected less than 200 000 in 1971 but some 900 000 in 1976, then reaching two million in 1982. Many Gastarbeiter were dismissed, but other workers could not be shielded from the loss of work and near industrial stagnation which seemed out of tune with the 'economic miracle' that Europe had envied.

The SPD had tended to argue in favour of more spending on health, housing and other social services and had criticized Erhard's rather aloof attitude to the inequalities which were a part of the competitive system he favoured. But once in office, the policies of different parties were often similar; like those in Britain, governments in West Germany had to take account of economic realities and world trends. Though, comparatively, the Federal Republic still

NEIGHBOURS

"Come on, Sam! It's up to us again."

Fig. 6.2 E.H. Shepard's cartoon in *Punch* comments on the Marshall Plan of 1947: the American Secretary of State aimed to reinforce the self-help of Europeans themselves in restoring the fabric of western Europe, and he insisted that Europeans should draw up the European Recovery Programme before Uncle Sam came to their aid.

raced ahead in the 1960s and early 1970s, the economic boom of earlier times gave way to less settled conditions, the temporary problems of the 1960s leading into more severe problems in the 1970s and worse still in the early 1980s. The 'economic miracle' had nevertheless contributed greatly to stability in West Germany. Political extremists could not get a foothold in the Bundestag. (The NPD (Nationalist Democrats), with its echoes of Nazism, almost reached the necessary five per cent of the vote in 1969 but then fell back.) On the other hand, prosperity did not save West Germany from the violence in the streets common to much of Europe (see section 6.1). Though the majority of the population seemed well satisfied with post-war development, contentment was by no means universal.

West Germany nevertheless weathered the economic storms better than many industrialized countries. Inflation and unemployment fell in the mid-1980s, and exports became buoyant again. Many West Germans approached the elections of 1987 with something not far removed from apathy, strengthening Kohl's expectations that he would be re-elected and perhaps even no longer dependent on the support of the Free Democrats (whose switch from the SPD to the CDU in 1982 had helped bring him to power in the first place). Under the new leadership of Johannes Rau, the SPD could make little headway and the opposition to the CDU was split by the Green Party whose campaign to protect the environment had minority appeal and won eight per cent of the vote. Kohl's conservative government had not been free from scandal, though otherwise unexciting, but his success in the polls of 1987 owed a good deal to the satisfaction of the majority with West Germany's economic recovery and material prosperity.

6.2.3 External relations

The division of Germany into East and West lay at the heart of superpower relations in the years 1945–55 (see section 4.2), but it dominated West German policy for far longer. Adenauer was staunchly anti-communist and pursued a hard line towards the Soviet Union and the East throughout his Chancellorship. He did, however, develop normal diplomatic contacts with Moscow, negotiating in 1955 for the release of some of the German troops still held in the Soviet Union and remaining coolly restrained at times of crisis, such as when the Berlin Wall was built in 1961. On the other hand, he insisted on the Hallstein Doctrine, named after an official in his Foreign Office, which proclaimed that any state other than the Soviet Union which recognized the government of East Germany could have no diplomatic relations with West Germany. This was a general handicap for East–West relations and Brandt set himself to remove it, beginning when a member of Kiesinger's government and continuing when Chancellor.

Brandt's *Ostpolitik* (Eastern policy) achieved near normal relations between West Germany and eastern Europe. He accepted the division of Germany into two states intent on:

> good neighbourly relations . . . on the basis of equal rights . . . [affirming] the inviolability of the existing frontiers between them now and in the future, and [respecting] . . . each other's territorial integrity.

Brandt also accepted the frontier between East Germany and Poland on the Oder–Neisse Line which Adenauer had always bitterly condemned. Brandt's concessions led to a hopeful period in East–West relations in Europe during the 1970s, and both West and East Germany were admitted to the United Nations in 1973. Little could be achieved with regard to Berlin, however: the city remained divided, located uneasily within East Germany and from time to time rocked by crisis. Situated in the middle of Europe, Germany and Berlin were bound to remain central to East–West relations, the two Germanies being the front-line members of NATO and the Warsaw Pact (see section 13.4).

While Brandt's main achievement in external policy was his Ostpolitik, for which he won the Nobel Prize for Peace in 1971, Adenauer's lay perhaps in the new bonds he forged between West Germany and the West, especially France. Economic partnership in the European Communities contributed to the developing goodwill (see section 7.1.1). In 1957 the French agreed that the Saar region – since the Second World War under French supervision – should be restored to West Germany. A personal bond then developed between Adenauer and de Gaulle, both of advanced years, conservative views and rather inflexible attitudes. On the eve of Adenauer's retirement in 1963, they agreed on an ambitious Treaty of Co-operation. Not all their respective electorates welcomed it, but it was a further firm step away from long-standing Franco-German antagonisms and fulfilled one of Adenauer's main aims.

6.3 France

6.3.1 Liberation and its aftermath

When patriots paraded to celebrate the liberation of Paris from the Nazis in 1944, General Charles de Gaulle strode at their head, the leader and symbol of the Free French who had refused to surrender in 1940 but had fought on in exile. In October 1944 the Allies recognized de Gaulle as head of the French provisional government, and the French people confirmed him in presidential office in November. De Gaulle had a passionate belief in the destiny of France:

> France is only herself when in the front rank . . . our country . . . must, under peril of mortal danger, aim high and hold herself upright. In brief, in my view, France cannot be France without grandeur.

Many found such views, often repeated, irksome. The General's relations with his wartime Allies had sometimes been prickly – President Roosevelt said of him, 'that man thinks he is Joan of Arc' – and de Gaulle was now disappointed that France was in 1945 invited neither to Yalta nor to Potsdam.

Believing his own destiny to be interwoven with that of France, de Gaulle was personally frustrated too. The assembly that the French elected to frame a new constitution leaned towards the left and included Communists, who had been strong in the resistance to the German occupation. The assembly showed little sympathy with the General's view that much greater power should be given to the President than had been the case during the Third Republic, and it showed him less respect than he thought was his due.

In de Gaulle's view the assembly was simply building a Fourth Republic likely to perpetuate the weaknesses of the Third, which the Germans had defeated in 1940. The National Assembly, to be elected only at five-year intervals, seemed likely to include the same variety of parties producing similar intrigue and short-lived coalition governments. De Gaulle feared the influence of the left would curb military spending, while the President – chosen by the National Assembly and the Council (the second parliamentary chamber, with little power) – would be little more than a figure-head. Unwilling to take part in a system so at variance with his visions of French 'grandeur', de Gaulle resigned early in 1946. A year later he founded the RPF (Rally of the French People) to keep Gaullist ideas before the public while working to frustrate communism and socialism. De Gaulle himself preferred to remain aloof, awaiting the emergency which might lead to a nationalist call to bring him from semi-retirement in Colombey-les-deux-Églises.

The new constitution gave women a voice in French politics but changed little else. The people greeted it without enthusiasm, and a third failed to vote at all on whether it should be adopted. The others accepted it by just over nine million votes to just under eight million. The Fourth Republic thus came into being in 1946 and was to survive until 1958.

6.3.2 The Fourth Republic

Léon Blum's Socialist government from December 1946 to January 1947 was the only government in the Fourth Republic to be formed by a single party. Its successors were all coalitions, and only three lasted for as long as a whole year. Since the voters were consulted only every fifth year (in 1947, 1951 and 1956), the intervals were filled with political haggling, which the RPF saw as discrediting France and putting political careers before the interests of the nation.

Until 1951 broadly left-wing (but non-communist) governments were usually in office, Socialists and the MRP (Popular Republican Movement) being prominent. From 1951 to 1954 there was a swing to conservatism. The RPF was dissolved as a parliamentary force, partly to free its supporters to make other alliances to strengthen the right, and perhaps also to emphasize Gaullist aloofness from the parliamentary musical chairs. In this period France was quite deeply divided between a large conservative peasantry and left wing industrial workers. In the later 1950s some lower-middle-class resentments such as had helped to fuel pre-war Fascism and Nazism were harnessed for a time by Pierre Poujade. The Poujadist movement won 52 seats in the National Assembly in 1956, despite its demands for fascist-like solutions to the problems of a parliamentary system its members despised. By this time governments were swinging back to the centre-left as represented by Radical Socialists such as Pierre Mendès-France (Prime Minister 1954–5) and the Socialists led by Guy Mollet (Prime Minister 1956–7). The Fourth Republic faced too many crises, however, and Pierre Pflimlin of the MRP, elected in May 1958, turned out to be its last Prime Minister.

Despite political instability, the economic record of the Fourth Republic was by no means one of failure. The Marshall Plan (see section 4.3) brought help in achieving post-war recovery, and successive governments achieved industrial expansion by adhering to the five-year Monnet Plan (devised by Jean Monnet, an economist) for investment, modernization and growth. Certain industries such as coal were nationalized, adding to those nationalized earlier, like French railways. Robert Schuman of the MRP, Prime Minister in 1947–8 and then Foreign Minister from 1948 to 1953, helped to launch the European Coal and Steel Community in 1952, and Mollet's government signed the Treaties of Rome in 1957, forming new Communities.

A new Plan was launched in 1954, maintaining economic growth which was at times quite substantial. Unemployment was low and foreign workers were needed to boost the labour force. But the French balance of trade was much less healthy than West Germany's. Like the British, the French tended to increase their standard of living faster than their output; as a result they sucked in imports, increased inflation and so weakened the franc that it had to be devalued in 1958.

France had had more limited social-security provision in pre-war years than had Germany, and when the war ended an effort was made to expand it. Insurance was compulsory after 1946. Emphasis was put on family allowances, partly to encourage growth in population; old-age pensions, on the other hand, began at very modest levels in 1945 and caught up only slowly with those of other European states. State provision, including that of health care, nevertheless grew during both the Fourth and the Fifth Republics. In areas such as education and housing, and in the general extent of benefits, however, it was the Fifth Republic which saw the more marked advances.

6.3.3 From the Fourth to the Fifth Republic: the Algerian crisis

The crisis which brought the Fourth Republic to an end began in Algeria. Governments of the Fourth Republic had faced a trying time, persistently seeking to preserve the French Empire overseas (see section 15.2.2). A messy struggle in Indo-China ended in humiliation at Dien Bien Phu and French withdrawal in 1954. There was further humiliation in the Suez War of 1956, when French and British troops were ordered out of the area around the Suez Canal by the United Nations (see section 14.2.5). At about that time, the French retreated from their protectorates in Tunisia and Morocco, leaving Algeria starkly exposed as the now most pressing problem. There was a large white minority in Algeria: French settlers (*colons*) who regarded the country as part of France and who would never concede independence to its Arab majority. The latter had nevertheless begun a war of independence in 1954 when the French were defeated in Indo-China. Fought between Arab nationalists and the French military supporting the *colons*, it was a war which grew increasingly savage (see section 15.2.3).

By 1958 the *colons* and the military lost confidence in the politicians in Paris. Fearful of a sell-out to Arab nationalism, they seemed to threaten an invasion of France itself and a political coup to stiffen French resolve. Neither President René Coty nor his Prime Minister Pflimlin had the confidence or will to risk the possibility of a civil war in France: people were quick to recall that the Spanish Civil War (1936–9) had begun with Spanish troops invading Spain from Morocco. The crisis called for someone with the authority to control the military and to win national confidence; the name which came most readily to the minds of the French was that of de Gaulle, who had written in his memoirs that his countrymen after 1946 still regarded him as 'a last recourse in time of stress'. He came back to Paris from Colombey to become chief minister, with full powers to govern and to produce the new constitution he thought France should have had twelve years earlier. The Fourth Republic was dead; the Fifth was about to be born. De Gaulle spelt out no policy for Algeria at this stage, though the *colons* and the military assumed that, as a former soldier and a patriot, he would suppress the Arabs and keep the country French.

6.3.4 The Fifth Republic under President de Gaulle

De Gaulle's first concern was to entrench in the new Republic a powerful Presidency. The President was to hold office for seven years. He would nominate the Prime Minister and could order new elections to the Assembly if the Prime Minister lost support there, thus stopping squabbling politicians being shielded from the voters. The President could also exercise emergency powers when necessary, and could put specific issues to the people's vote in referenda. The French people gave a clear vote of approval to the new constitution and de Gaulle became President when the Fifth Republic came into being in January 1959. In 1962 de Gaulle broke the spirit of the new constitution and through a successful referendum, moved to establish direct election of the President by universal suffrage. He was the first winner under this new system, defeating François Mitterrand in the Presidential election of 1965. The French President thus acquired very great authority, and, provided he had the support of a majority of the members of the National Assembly, became comparatively more powerful than a British Prime Minister or indeed an American President.

The UNR (Union for the New Republic), a new Gaullist grouping to support the President, did not have enough support to dominate the first Assembly of the Fifth Republic, and de Gaulle appointed Michel Debré as Prime Minister of a mainly UNR–MRP coalition. Debré gave way to Georges Pompidou in 1962 and Pompidou, a Gaullist, remained Prime Minister until 1968. Party names changed confusingly during the 1960s but three things were clear: de Gaulle, as President, exercised great authority; Gaullists in the Assembly commanded considerable support if not an outright majority; and the Gaullists were usually helped by divisions among the left-wing groups who opposed them. Figure 6.3 shows the composition of the Assembly after the elections of 1967. In new elections in 1968 the Gaullists increased their standing, though the downfall of de Gaulle himself was by that time close at hand.

De Gaulle had shocked a good many of his supporters when in 1962 he granted independence to Algeria under the nationalist leadership of Ben Bella (see section 15.2.4). The *colons* protested at what they saw as betrayal. Already suspicious of the President's policy, General Raoul Salan had helped them set up the OAS (*Organisation de l'Armée Secrète*) in 1961. Salan tried in vain to seize control of Algeria and was eventually caught and imprisoned until de Gaulle pardoned him in 1968. The OAS meanwhile made several attempts to assassinate the President but by 1963 it was a spent force. The majority of French opinion had quickly rallied behind de Gaulle, who freed not only Algeria but most of what was left of the French Empire, including vast areas of Africa (see section 15.2.4). In this field de Gaulle was a realist, seeing that reluctant overseas territories could now be no more than a burden on France, though the constitution of the Fifth Republic made provision for linking them in a new French Community. France's destiny in de Gaulle's eyes was to be pre-

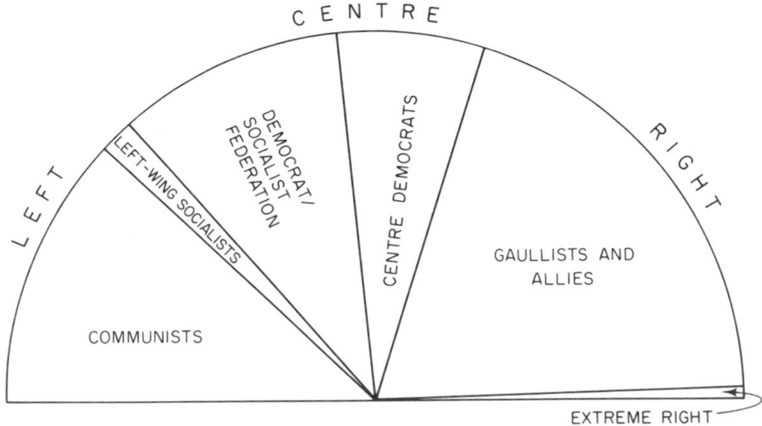

Fig. 6.3 The French National Assembly, 1967

eminent in Europe and a major force among the great powers (see section 6.3.6).

These international ambitions divided the French people. Among those on the left de Gaulle was always unpopular for his conservatism and his nationalism. Others were disturbed by what seemed like his arrogance and desire to dominate. But with more political stability the Fifth Republic was able to build on the economic foundations laid by the Fourth. For a time exports benefited from the devaluation of the franc in 1958 and, with continued planning, production grew and incomes rose. There were misgivings about Gaullist policies nevertheless. De Gaulle's determination that France should have its own nuclear weapons brought a great financial burden, and there were questions as to whether the building of the supersonic airliner Concorde was not also a costly and unwise effort aimed mainly at prestige. The Concorde project began in 1962 in partnership with Britain. As costs began to double and redouble the British might have pulled out of it but for French insistence on going on. De Gaulle meanwhile pursued a policy of accumulating gold reserves which some thought old-fashioned and which could not disguise the downturn in the country's economic fortunes. By 1969 a further devaluation of the franc was almost inescapable, but that seemed inconsistent with French grandeur, and the President refused to permit it.

Unemployment approached one million in 1968 and there was widespread discontent, industrial wages lagging behind those in much of western Europe. It was part of Gaullist policy to try to hold down prices by holding down wages but by 1968 there was dissatisfaction with the balance, coinciding with unrest in the educational system and protest against ungenerous social-security benefits. Demonstrations began in May 1968 among students, rallying behind agitators such as Cohn-Bendit, and quickly spread to French workers, with massive strikes, occupations and the erection of barricades. Ferocious police action led to escalating violence. The protests were strident but varied, and only hatred of de Gaulle and of the authorities seemed to unite the dissidents. De Gaulle briefly and mysteriously withdrew to West Germany but came back to declare his determination to continue in power, and to announce new elections to the Assembly. These showed strengthened support for the Gaullists as conservative opinion rallied against what was feared as revolutionary disorder.

By the end of June the rioting had been contained with the help of promises of better pay and more consultation with the workers in industry, and of reforms to modernize educational institutions. In July 1968 the President made Maurice Couve de Murville Prime Minister in place of Pompidou, calling on the latter to:

> remain in readiness to carry out any mission and to take up any office which the nation may one day call on you to assume.

De Gaulle perhaps had resignation in mind, and was here earmarking Pompidou as the likely Gaullist successor to the Presidency. Couve de Murville now launched a new programme of austerity, again stopping short of devaluation. In April 1969, however, de Gaulle made yet another appeal to the French people, the majority of whom seemed to have rallied to him in 1968. A referendum on minor constitutional reform became, in effect, a vote of confidence in his leadership – and he lost by some 12 million votes to about 10.5 million. He resigned at once, retiring to Colombey where he died the following year at the age of 79.

6.3.5 The Fifth Republic since de Gaulle

After de Gaulle's resignation, Pompidou became President of the Republic, defeating Poher in the second ballot of the Presidential election. The Gaullists remained dominant but, without the General himself, Gaullism seemed bound to change, its attitudes to soften. The devaluation of the franc was now carried out with some benefit to the country's balance of trade, and Pompidou no longer resisted the admission of Britain to the European Community. When Pompidou died in office in 1974, he was succeeded by Valéry Giscard d'Estaing, Minister of Finance in successive governments since 1962. Giscard narrowly defeated François Mitterrand by a half percentage point in the second ballot. He was a Republican rather than a Gaullist, but he continued with generally conservative policies in the face of the divisions of the left. But his coming to the Presidency coincided with economic crisis: in 1974 France had a serious trade deficit. During the rest of the 1970s, French governments like those elsewhere had to wrestle with fuel shortages, inflation, unemployment and recession, and France's recently impressive growth rate slowed markedly. Paris, like other capitals, also became prey to bombings and other acts of terrorism.

In spite of the problems, many French citizens still prospered under the Fifth Republic. Spending on social security, as a percentage of GDP, was now higher in France than in most of western Europe and, except in housing, the French matched the social amenities and comfortable standards of living characteristic of the West. Yet there were still deep divisions and tensions in French society, which were always likely to flare into open discontent, not least in industry. Sectional interests were stoutly defended, farmers and fishermen being among those who were quick to protest publicly at what they saw as injustices.

Scandals and economic setbacks brought Giscard unpopularity. But it was still possible that conservative influences and the weaknesses of the left would ensure his re-election as President in 1981, even though Gaullists complained that he was too much of a compromiser. Rival candidates included Georges Marchais (Communist) and Jacques Chirac (Gaullist) but at the second round of voting to arrive at an overall majority, the contest, as it had been in 1974, was between the two front runners – Giscard and François Mitterrand, the Socialist leader. The left this time united more effectively than the right, and Mitterrand reversed the narrow decision of 1974 to become President at his third attempt (he had also stood against de Gaulle in 1965). The left showed further unity in securing the election of a left-wing Assembly later in 1981: it included 269 Socialists and 44 Communists, but only 83 Gaullists and 64 Giscard supporters. For the first time the Fifth Republic had a left-wing government, and – for two years – the Communists shared government offices for the first time since 1947.

Mitterrand looked for Keynesian[G] rather than Friedmanite[G] and Thatcherite solutions to economic problems. There was a new round of nationalization, and Mitterrand steered successive Prime Ministers towards energetic programmes of reform, in the course of which the death penalty was abolished in 1981. But unemployment rose to two million during that year and inflation ran above the European average. A serious trade deficit brought a new wave of austerity, and efforts to restrain wages brought industrial turbulence once again, though the balance of trade showed improvement in 1983.

The unity of the left weakened again after the elections of 1981, and there were fierce arguments about Mitterrand's policies and leadership. In a western Europe at that time largely conservative, Mitterrand's position was exposed. Criticism, external as well as internal, helped the right to gain a small majority when elections to the French assembly were held in 1986. Mitterrand had to replace his Socialist Prime Minister, Laurent Fabius, with the Gaullist Jacques Chirac at the head of a right-wing cabinet. Thus, for the first time, the Fifth Republic now had a President and a Prime Minister whose political philosophies were antagonistic. Late in 1986 there was unrest in France which seemed to have similarities with that of 1968: demonstrations by students and street clashes led to industrial confrontations which by the end of the year had paralysed the railway system and other public transport and threatened to spread. Chirac's election had weakened President Mitterrand, but Chirac had already had to make concessions to protesting farmers and the credibility of his government was now in danger. With a weakened Presidency and a tottering Prime Minister, the Fifth Republic was beginning like the Fourth to seem vulnerable to France's traditional instabilities.

Mitterrand and Chirac lined up as rival candidates in the presidential elections of 1988. Mitterrand stood higher than Chirac in public-opinion polls and Chirac declared he would not continue as Prime Minister if Mitterrand won. Mitterrand had shown himself moderate in most of his policies and seemed likely to retain the Presidency, not least because many French voters were now worried by the recent popular appeal of Jean-Marie Le Pen whose platform was racist and anti-immigrant, and seemed not far short of neo-Nazi. That could only revive deep divisions in French society. Mitterrand was duly re-elected in 1988, by a decisive margin, becoming the first President of the Fifth Republic to be elected twice by universal suffrage. He dismissed Chirac as Prime Minister and called for fresh elections to the National Assembly. Despite a much less conclusive result than in the presidential contest the Socialists consolidated their position as the largest party in France, and Mitterrand appointed the moderate Michel Rocard as Prime Minister, entrusting him with the task of building a moderate centre-left coalition.

6.3.6 The foreign policy of the Fifth Republic

While dismantling the French Empire, de Gaulle pursued a foreign policy that was always distinctive. Working with Adenauer he continued the rebuilding of Franco–German relations, culminating in the Treaty of Co-operation in 1963 (see section 6.2.3). Developing independent French nuclear weapons, he refused in that year to sign the international Test Ban Treaty in case the ban on tests above ground hindered French research. He similarly refused to sign the Non-Proliferation Treaty of 1968. De Gaulle also pursued other policy independently of the USA, recognizing Communist China, seeking understandings with the Soviet Union, and in 1966 withdrawing France from military obligations to NATO. NATO headquarters were subsequently moved from Paris to Brussels. The French President was often critical of US policy, for example in Indo China and Latin America; he wanted to create a Europe less influenced by Washington and its English-speaking ally, Britain.

Building this Europe was part of his design. As early as 1950 he had asserted:

> Europe will not be made unless France takes the lead.

He therefore welcomed the European Communities, worked to shape them to French leadership and refused to accept Britain's admission to them (see section 7.1.3). Opinion polls suggested that he had the support of most of the French for his foreign policy: many on the right admired his nationalism, and many on the left endorsed his anti-Americanism. But sometimes his enthusiasm for things French overcame his better judgment, and he aroused storms of protest with his cry of *'Vive le Québec libre'* on a visit to Montreal in 1967 – it was no business of the French President to add to the problems of the Canadian government by encouraging the separatist ambitions of French Canadians in Quebec. Many found his vision of a united Europe stretching 'from the Atlantic to the Urals' equally lacking in grasp.

Again, after de Gaulle's resignation his successors softened his policies. Pompidou accepted Britain into the European Community; Giscard was less anti-American; Mitterrand was less hostile to NATO, rather more anti-Soviet, and in 1984 seemingly ready to develop the European Community towards closer political integration with less concern for French self-interest. But unlike West Germany, France refused to boycott the Olympic Games in Moscow in 1980, as President Carter had requested of Giscard, and, though French Presidents tailored their policies to circumstances, all preserved a lively awareness of France's independent identity and interests.

6.4 Italy

6.4.1 Parliamentary democracy

In 1981 Giovanni Spadolini, a Republican, became the first post-war Prime Minister in Italy who was not a Christian Democrat. He formed Italy's forty-fifth government since the overthrow of Mussolini in 1943 - yet another coalition in which, as usual, the Christian Democrats were prominent. Spadolini lasted longer than many Prime Ministers, surviving for more than a year. In 1983 Bettino Craxi became the first post-war Socialist Prime Minister, and he too led a coalition which included most of the parties in the Chamber of Deputies except the extreme right and the Communists. The severe, worldwide economic pressures of the 1970s and 1980s were now imposing even more strains on a political system which had often staggered from crisis to crisis, in a country which had more than its share (among west-European countries) of natural disasters, crime (much of it organized by the Mafia and the Naples-based Camorra), violence, terrorism (albeit on a considerably smaller scale than in Northern Ireland), scandals and various sorts of social unrest. It needed luck as well as skill for Italian governments to survive, and in 1985, even with a five-party coalition, Craxi had little more than a bare parliamentary majority.

Figures 6.1 and 6.4 show something of how representation in the Italian parliament was fragmented. The Christian Democrat Party was the largest in a country much of which was strongly Catholic and conservative, especially the rural areas. The cities and industrial centres were much more influenced by socialism, returning the Communist Party as the chief rivals to the Christian Democrats. Neither could win an overall majority, and coalition governments were usual, the Christian Democrats being driven into broader coalitions - even with parties on the left - when more turbulent decades followed the 1950s.

Alcide de Gasperi, an opponent and victim of Mussolini's Fascist regime and one of the founders of the Christian Democrat Party, headed various governments as Prime Minister from 1945 to 1953. He provided continuity and did much to rehabilitate Italy after the 'Fascist Era'. During his first two years in office, the Italian people in a referendum voted by the narrow margin of only two million for the abolition of the monarchy and the setting up of a Republic. De Gasperi at first sought as much agreement as possible by including Communists in government office. But the Communists were then dropped and de Gasperi's anti-communism was duly rewarded by the favour and assistance of the USA.

The Allies signed a peace treaty with Italy in 1947, confirming the loss of Italy's overseas empire, and of Istria and the port of Fiume to Yugoslavia, but

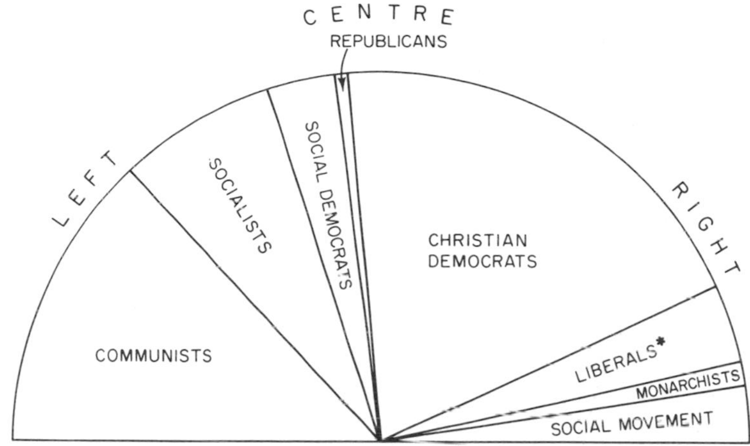

Fig. 6.4 The Italian Chamber of Deputies, 1963

allowing Italy to keep the South Tyrol. German-speaking inhabitants of this area had resented Italian government since it began there in 1919, and they now campaigned against it, eventually with violent protest in both Italy and Austria. They were quietened only when the Italians made concessions to the Tyroleans at the start of the 1970s, guaranteeing minority rights. The vexed question of Trieste was also left unsettled in 1947; after Allied occupation, the city and its surrounding area were in 1954 awarded, respectively, to Italy and Yugoslavia. De Gasperi died in that year. His governments had secured Marshall Aid to help Italy's economic recovery, had pledged Italy to NATO and had made it one of the Six who founded the European Coal and Steel Community. There had also been useful reforms, easing Italy through the transition from Fascism to democracy and encouraging its progress towards the social-security systems growing throughout western Europe.

The Christian Democrat Party had the advantage not only of encouragement from Western Allies but also of its own flexibility. It covered a wide spectrum of political opinion, not merely conservative but, in various ways, liberal too. Its religious connections were also useful, though public opinion in Italy was changing and laws were passed in the 1970s legalizing divorce and abortion. Changing attitudes were to be seen even more clearly in 1984, when the Italian government agreed to change the Lateran Treaties of 1929: Roman Catholicism would shortly cease to be Italy's official religion and religious education in state schools would be ended.

No later Christian Democrat leader quite achieved de Gasperi's authority, although Aldo Moro approached it in his role as Prime Minister from 1963 to

1968 and from 1974 to 1976. Elections produced chaotic parliaments in which the politicians spent their energies stitching together deals and coalitions but, as in France during the Gaullist years of the Fifth Republic, the right was able to profit from the divisions of the left, the Social Democrats and Socialists hesitating to draw close to the Communists. In the 1960s the Socialists preferred to join intermittently with the Christian Democrats. Figure 6.4 shows the composition of the Chamber of Deputies after the election of 1963; when Pietro Nenni then led the Socialists into coalition with Moro's Christian Democrats it was helpful to stability but the alliance was a rather unnatural one which led to revolt and breaking away by a section of the Socialist Party. Yet in 1976 even the Communists agreed to co-operate with the Christian Democrats, sharing power to tackle urgent problems, though they withdrew support from Giulio Andreotti in 1979 when they became dissatisfied with the pace of social reform. Unable to win a majority themselves, the Communists returned to opposition while new non-communist coalitions were patched together in the 1980s.

6.4.2 Society and the economy

The turbulence of Italian affairs contributed to the fact that in the 1970s Italy was the poorest of the Six who founded the European Communities; even among subsequent members it was for a long time poorer than any but the Irish Republic. Italy was not well endowed with natural resources, and the historic divisions between the industrial north and agricultural south had not yet been effectively bridged. The south was still one of the least developed areas of the European Community. The north, though richer, was one of the most stormy in industrial relations, and vulnerable to the plague of unemployment. It was evidence of Italy's problems that citizens from the south tended to migrate northwards in search of prosperity, and some Italians looked for work and wealth in other countries of the European Community. Dependent on imported oil, struggling to support a population rising above 55 million, with an economy that was fragile in spite of often impressive rates of growth, Italy encountered serious difficulties in the 1970s and 1980s when unemployment, inflation, and trade and currency problems mounted.

The Social Movement showed the persisting support for fascist ideas, securing about seven per cent of the vote and 42 seats in the election of 1983, almost matching its 56 seats in 1972. But like the Red Brigades on the left, other right-wing groups preferred violence in the streets to parliamentary haggling (see section 6.1). In 1980, for example, 122 deaths resulted from terrorist activities in Italy, and Italian courts were now among the most active in Europe with large-scale trials of kidnappers and murderers, political and non-political.

The country had nevertheless made progress since 1945, developing state insurance schemes, expanding social services (though the north was better covered than the south) and increasing private prosperity. The Italian gross national product surpassed that of Britain in the early 1980s, and under the reforming administrations led by Craxi the country seemed on track for full-scale modernization. Italy's weaknesses should be seen in the context of west-European affluence rather than the poverty of some nations of the world. Even so, it was sometimes asserted that southern Italy still had similarities, social and economic, to north Africa and countries across the Mediterranean.

6.5 The Benelux states

West Germany, France and Italy were the largest founder-members of the European Communities. The other members of the Six were the Netherlands, Belgium and Luxemburg, whose populations at the end of the Second World War were, respectively, 9.5 million, 8.5 million and 250 000. After liberation from the Nazis, the Netherlands and Belgium retained their monarchies, while Luxemburg had a Grand Duke. These were constitutional monarchies, however, like that in Britain, power resting with the parliamentary representatives of the people. As was common in western Europe, there were many parties in the three countries' parliaments, so coalition governments were usual. Each country had a small Communist Party representation, but the main political arguments were between the conservative right and the moderately socialist or liberal left. This balance was reflected in the countries' economies, with extensive private enterprise and a reliance on the markets, and in their societies, with extensive personal freedoms and state-organized welfare systems.

The post-war histories of the Netherlands, Belgium and Luxemburg therefore had many similarities, not only to one another but also to western Europe generally. Belgium and Luxemburg were more industrialized than the Netherlands, but the latter was efficient in agriculture and developed great commercial importance. In spite of similar economic problems all three prospered, achieving a GDP per head of population in the 1970s close to that of the French, below West Germany's but well ahead of that of Britain and Italy. All made marked progress in the development of welfare systems as well as of private wealth, but experienced social unrest from time to time, especially during the economic storms of the 1970s and 1980s. Meanwhile, they all three joined NATO and were firm partners in the Western alliance as well as in the movement towards European co-operation (see Table 4.1). The Netherlands lost almost all the large Dutch overseas empire after yielding, reluctantly, in 1949 to the nationalist movement in Indonesia (see section 15.1). Belgium's overseas empire was located mainly in the Congo, and that too was surrendered in 1960 (see section 15.3), at the time when de Gaulle was effecting great changes in the French Empire in Africa.

Post-imperial problems contributed to the outbreaks of violence in the Netherlands in the mid-1970s when, for example, South Moluccan exiles, protesting at their treatment by the government of Indonesia, took hostages and hijacked a train, a variant on the now commonplace hijacking of aircraft. They blamed the Dutch for allowing their islands to become part of Indonesia in 1949, but the issue was no longer one that the Netherlands had the power to resolve. Belgium meanwhile had communal problems arising from its own awkwardly balanced population. Over 40 per cent of Belgians were Walloon and French-speaking; the majority, living further from the border with France, were Flemings and Flemish-speaking. Gradually, by the 1970s, Belgian governments relaxed tensions by building into the constitution safeguards of the rights not only of Walloons and Flemings but of other minorities too, though language remained a sensitive issue.

Even before the Second World War had ended, the Netherlands, Belgium and Luxemburg saw the advantages to be gained from economic co-operation. They agreed in 1944 to set up a customs union known as Benelux, and when this came into being in 1948 it was made the basis for further integration between the three states. An Interparliamentary Consultative Council was set up in 1955 to discuss ways of achieving closer union.

One of the most active founders of Benelux had been the socialist Paul-Henri Spaak, Belgian Prime Minister 1938–9 and 1947–9 and Foreign Minister 1954–7 and 1961–6. Spaak's outlook was that of an internationalist whose strong support was given to the UN, the Council of Europe, NATO and the European Communities. The Benelux states were founder-members of the latter, starting with the Treaty of Paris (1951) which set up the European Coal and Steel Community (ECSC). They were therefore part of a movement towards a wider west-European integration, extending beyond that of just three small countries. Spaak saw the Communities as 'a stage on the way to political union', and he urged Europeans to 'work steadily and urgently' to make that happen. But the comprehensive Benelux Economic Union of 1960 proved easier to achieve than Benelux political union: even among the small Benelux states, national identities clearly remained. National interests sometimes differed and were jealously guarded, for example in the fixing of exchange rates in 1971 in response to currency problems.

By the 1980s, 40 years of co-operation had boosted prosperity and made Brussels an important international centre, the headquarters of both NATO and the European Commission. But the Benelux states, like western Europe as a whole, were still some distance from the broader integration at which Spaak and other pioneers had aimed.

UNIT 7

The Western democracies: 3 – Europe: the European Community and the lesser states

7.1 The European Community

7.1.1 From the Coal and Steel Community to the Treaties of Rome

The European Coal and Steel Community (ECSC) paved the way for further economic co-operation among its members, beyond that already achieved by the OEEC (see section 4.3 and Table 4.1). Steel production increased, and so too did coal production before competition from oil and other fuels brought cuts in Europe's output after the mid-1950s. Co-operation quickly proved useful in managing the industries and their associated social problems, and the foreign ministers of the six founder member states met in Messina as early as 1955 to discuss further joint action. Spaak, at the Belgian Foreign Office, provided leadership and enthusiasm, and in March 1957 the Six signed two Treaties of Rome.

One treaty set up the European Atomic Energy Community (Euratom) with a High Authority like that of the ECSC to develop the peaceful application of nuclear power. The other set up the European Economic Community (EEC), whose importance was such that its popular name, the Common Market, was often used for the European Community as a whole after the executive bodies of the ECSC, EEC and Euratom were merged to form the European Community in 1967. The EEC did more than create a 'common market', with a common tariff on exports from outside the Community but no internal customs barriers to impede trade between the Six themselves: it also set out to encourage the free movement of labour and capital between members, and aimed eventually to bring about common economic and financial policies. The EEC had a population slightly larger than that of the Soviet Union, though it was smaller in area, and its supporters hoped that – at least in economic strength – the Community might match the superpowers.

No other European state sought to join the Six when the EEC was set up in 1958. Britain remained suspicious of any loss of national sovereignty, preferring to counter the creation of the EEC with the less demanding European Free Trade Association (EFTA) which came into being in 1960. EFTA's members agreed to reduce tariffs between themselves to promote trade but they had few further ambitions. Journalists referred to the founders of EFTA as 'the Outer Seven', one of which was Portugal (see Table 4.1). It was partly to keep Portugal, as well as Spain, out of the EEC that the Treaties of Rome granted members of the Six the right to veto the admission of new members. Portugal and Spain in the 1950s, led by Salazar and Franco respectively, were considered undemocratic, and their membership was therefore unwanted. But it was a belated application for membership of the EEC by the British in the 1960s which actually brought the veto into use, British membership being blocked by President de Gaulle of France.

7.1.2 Institutions and policy

The EEC made swift progress in some spheres. The target dates were easily met by which customs duties between members were to be abolished and the free flow of labour and capital allowed. Output grew impressively during the early years, boosted by the enlarged internal market and the protection which the external tariff gave against competition from outside. Job opportunities in other parts of the EEC became available to those in the poorer areas such as southern Italy. The ECSC, meanwhile, continued to co-ordinate western Europe's coal and steel industries, while wrestling with the painful problems that resulted from modernization and technological change, and Euratom promoted joint research and the nuclear generation of electricity, chiefly to provide power for industry.

These activities were not without their critics, however. To the arguments that the EEC was a rich man's club, too little concerned with poorer nations outside, and a capitalist club, helping to deepen divisions between West and East, was added disquiet about its institutions. The European Commission, based in Brussels, was from the outset the Community's nerve centre. Made up of civil servants and paid officials, the Commission was deliberately given extensive powers in 1957, to enable it to withstand the pressure of member governments and other vested interests. But the bureaucracy grew rapidly and was expensive and sometimes irritating, producing a bewildering forest of EEC rules and regulations. The Council of Ministers, representing member governments, exercised only limited control over the Commission, and the European Parliament – whose members were until 1979 nominated by national parliaments, was no more effective. In 1974 the European Council was added for summit meetings between heads of government, though early meetings produced more talk than action.

The European Court of Justice, like the European Parliament, had been set up initially in 1952 as part of the ECSC, and this achieved something of a human face for the EEC, while the Economic and Social Committee also tried to relate the Community's work to the hopes and interests of the people of its member states. The European Investment Bank, set up in 1958, helped to finance development projects especially in the less privileged areas of the Community, bringing work and visible evidence of Community action. But even in the 1980s the feeling remained widespread in certain member states that

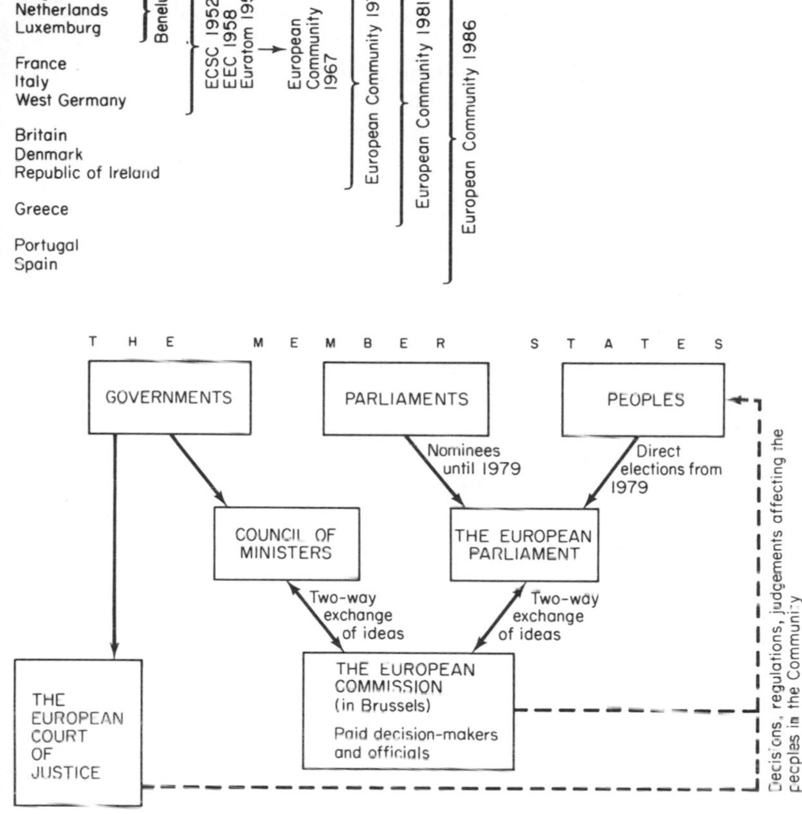

Fig. 7.1 The European Community: membership and main institutions

the EEC and its institutions were remote from the people who lived in it.

The policies of the EEC also attracted criticism, especially the Common Agricultural Policy (CAP). Agriculture was declining in western Europe both as a percentage of gross product and in terms of the percentage of population it employed. But member governments wanted to preserve the Community's agriculture, ensuring the prosperity of farmers as well as the supply of their produce to the consumers at reasonable prices. Subsidies encouraged the farmers to produce, even when surpluses could only be stockpiled in embarrassing 'lakes' of wine and 'mountains' of butter, grain and other produce. Peasant farmers in France and West Germany found the CAP especially helpful, and powerful farm lobbies defended it against those critical of its costs and inequalities. The CAP in the late 1970s cost about three-quarters of the EEC budget, much of the money being used in the payment of guaranteed prices to the farmers. By 1984, cutbacks seemed unavoidable, especially of dairy herds, though fierce arguments raged as to the extent of these cuts and where they should fall.

There was much wrangling too about other policy. The EEC was slow to work out a fisheries policy, to do justice to competing national claims in European waters and to prevent overfishing. Progress towards a common currency was similarly slow, though member currencies were controlled by common exchange rates in the early 1970s, leading to further regulation in the European Monetary System of 1979.

Meanwhile, the Yaoundé Convention had been signed in 1963, giving EEC commercial and technical assistance to former French states in Africa. The Community continued to give such modest help to poorer nations and the Lomé Convention in 1975 granted free access to the Community for the products of 46 developing countries in Africa, the Caribbean and the Pacific, a total which soon grew. These were mainly former European colonies, and the EEC also promised aid and guaranteed some minimum commodity prices. Critics argued that this assistance was still far from lavish, but it did something to improve the Community's image among liberals.

7.1.3 The Six, the Nine, the Ten: new members, 1973–81

Total production in the EEC grew by more than 25 per cent from 1958 to 1963, twice as fast as that in Britain where the government began to have second thoughts about staying out of the European Communities. In 1960 Britain had a balance-of-payments deficit of over £270 million and Macmillan appointed Edward Heath to negotiate for admission to the EEC. The prospect of membership aroused no great enthusiasm in Britain, however; the Liberal Party continued to show the support for membership it had shown from the beginning, but generally British opinion remained hostile. Britain had long-standing links with the Commonwealth, which often proved advantageous in trade. EFTA showed that the British preferred looser ties with Europe than the Communities demanded, and the French in particular doubted whether the British would be good Europeans. Fearing that British membership might rival his own leadership of the Communities, President de Gaulle also distrusted the close English-speaking links between Britain and the USA, and he forecast that Britain's admission would be followed by others, changing the nature of what the Six had created:

> It is foreseeable that the cohesion of all its members, who would be very numerous and very diverse, would not hold for long and that in the end there would appear a colossal Atlantic Community under American dependence and leadership which would soon swallow up the European Community.

Thus, Heath's negotiations came to nothing when de Gaulle in 1963 vetoed Britain's application. In the same year de Gaulle cemented Franco-German friendship in a new treaty with Adenauer (see section 6.2.3).

Most members of the EEC continued to do better than Britain in surmounting economic problems, trade with the outside world in the years

Fig. 7.2 A comment by Cummings in the *Daily Express* in September 1962: Macmillan's charge towards the EEC might be valiant, but de Gaulle's big gun was his power of veto. Macmillan had little support (other than Edward Heath's) for his application for membership, and Adenauer (extreme right) went along with de Gaulle.

1958–73 increasing by over 300 per cent, with exports growing more than imports. The Labour Party in Britain followed the Conservatives in knocking on the EEC's door, though Wilson fared no better than Macmillan when his application was in turn vetoed by de Gaulle in 1967. The French now expressed doubts about the health of the British economy, and it was perhaps no coincidence that in 1967 the pound had to be devalued.

De Gaulle's retirement gave new hope to those in Britain still seeking membership of the EEC – which had by then merged with the ECSC and Euratom to form the European Community (EC). When the Conservatives won the general election of 1970 and Heath became Prime Minister, the knocking on the door grew more insistent and Pompidou, de Gaulle's successor, was not inclined to resist further. He had had to devalue the franc and found it difficult to retain de Gaulle's lofty view of Europe's affairs.

There were other applicants at this time, too, including Denmark, one of the richest states in Europe, and the Republic of Ireland, one of the poorest. The Irish and British economies had grown more slowly during the last decade than those of any members of the European Community – indeed at only half the rate of most. Denmark shared a frontier with West Germany and the Danes had begun to feel a natural affinity with their Continental neighbours which they wished to develop. Another applicant, Norway, was separated by sea from the Community and maintained a certain sense of distance: when the terms of entry were made known to them, the Norwegians voted in a referendum not to take up membership. On 1 January 1973, therefore, the Six grew to Nine when Britain, the Irish Republic and Denmark joined the European Community. Along with Denmark came Greenland, a Danish dependency, but in 1982 a growing movement towards independence led the people of Greenland to vote

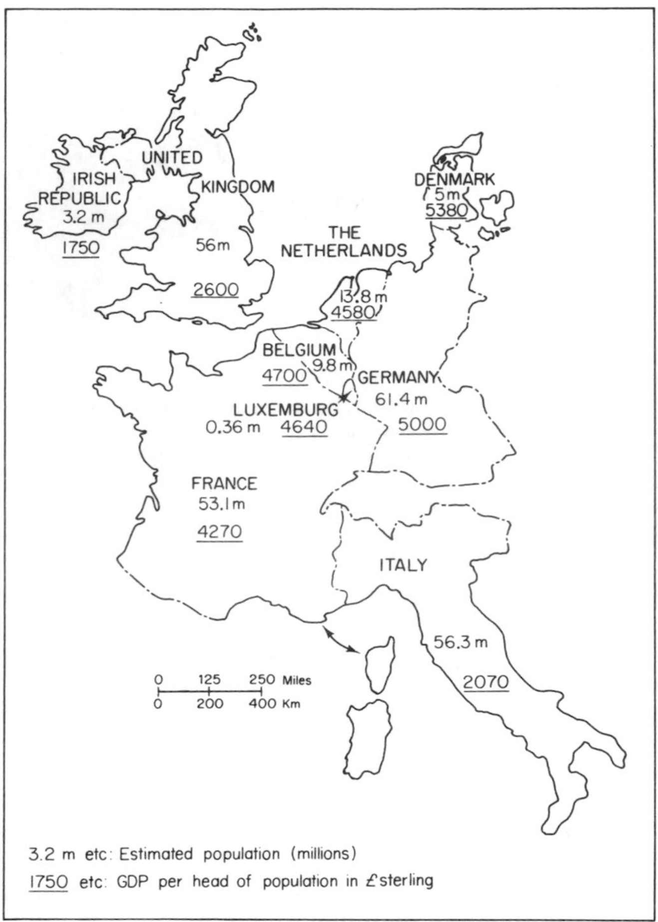

Fig. 7.3 The Nine: the European Community, 1977

to withdraw from the Community, a move which was effected during the following few years.

Britain and Denmark left EFTA when they joined the EC, and the Association – which since 1970 had included Iceland – now sought to improve its future by arranging free trade with the Community in industrial products.

The Nine of the Community became Ten when Greece secured membership at the beginning of 1981. For poorer countries such as Greece and the Irish Republic, the EC held considerable economic promise, offering a market for farm produce, allowing free movement to those in search of work, and providing assistance ranging from investment to regional aid. All new members had to accept the rules laid down in the Treaties of Rome, but each was granted a transitional period during which adjustment could be made to the new arrangements. Britain found the transitional period trying, and there was impatience that membership of the European Community produced few immediate benefits such as the Irish, and later the Greeks, seemed to find. In 1975 only Italy and the Irish Republic among the Nine had a lower GDP than Britain's, and there were already signs that, rather than encouraging British exports to Europe, membership of the Community was encouraging European imports into Britain.

The Heath government which had made Britain a member of the Community lost power to Labour in 1974. Wilson now tried to renegotiate some of the terms of the transitional period, winning some small improvement in help for the Third World, in the market in the Community for West Indies sugar and New Zealand dairy produce, and in Britain's freedom to pursue regional and other economic policies. Even so, the Labour Party and much of Britain remained deeply divided about Britain's role in the Community, so that a referendum was held in 1975 to give the British people a choice of remaining (a *Yes* vote) or withdrawing (*No*). 65 per cent of the electorate voted, two-thirds – over 17 million – voting *Yes*, and about 8.5 million *No*.

This did not entirely quieten British misgivings, however. Though Wilson had slightly improved the terms under which Britain contributed to the Community budget, such contributions by the early 1980s seemed out of proportion to Britain's lowly standing in the Community league tables of output. The CAP seemed to work to Britain's disadvantage, and disputes continued over fishing rights and the many detailed regulations issued from Brussels. Disquiet persisted about the effects of membership on Britain's trade. Meanwhile, Continental partners criticized Britain for not more readily sharing its wealth from North Sea oil, for refusing to join the European Monetary System and for general national self-interest. That was a charge to which most members remained vulnerable, however, though Thatcher and other British politicians seemed in the early 1980s more tenaciously obstructive than most. Being obstructive paid off, however, when Mrs Thatcher successfully negotiated improved terms for British contributions to the Community budget. By 1988 fierce arguments raged about the cost and inefficiency of the CAP, which seemed for years now to have feather-bedded Continental farmers.

However, attention on agricultural issues was increasingly deflected as member states focused on the year 1992, when remaining barriers to a truly common market were to be removed. The passage of the Single European Act by all member states between 1985 and 1987 eased the prospects for this aspiration. The Act replaced the power of each state to veto any proposal not in its national interests by a system of majority rule for many important EC decisions. Nonetheless it remained to be seen whether 1992 would prove a turning point in European integration or a damp squib.

7.1.4 New developments

Before 1979 the European Parliament, sitting at Strasbourg, had 198 nominated members. They grouped themselves not according to country but

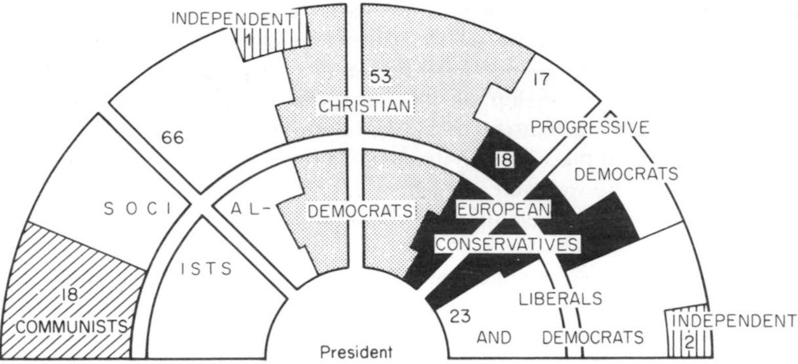

Source: The London Information Office of the European Parliament.

Fig. 7.4 The European Parliament: political groups before 1979 (seating plan)

according to political sympathies (see fig. 7.4). Thus eighteen Labour representatives from Britain sat with Socialists from the other states of the Nine; British and Danish Conservatives joined forces as European Conservatives; and there were Christian Democrats from the other seven states. Truly European-wide political groupings would take time to develop, but foundations had been laid on which it would now be possible to build.

Direct elections to the European Parliament were intended to bring the Community closer to the 260 million people who lived in it. The first elections were arranged for June 1979. It was hoped that as well as stimulating enthusiasm for the Community the elected Parliament would begin to exercise real democratic authority over the bureaucracy of the European Commission, and provision had been made in 1975 to extend the Parliament's powers. The Office of Official Publications of the European Communities now put the general issues before the voters:

> In the past, the development of the Community was largely at a technical level – abolishing customs barriers, creating a common agricultural policy, etc. Today, the issues are bigger. For example:
>
> What sort of society do we want for ourselves and our children?
>
> How can we best narrow the gap between the poor and prosperous areas of the Community?
>
> How much help are we ready to give the Third World?
>
> How far and how fast do we want to go on the road towards a more united Europe?

The new Parliament of 410 members (434 after the admission of Greece) meant that, on average, one member must represent well over 600 000 people. The United Kingdom, for example, was allowed 81 Euro-MPs, the same total as for each of France, Italy and West Germany. Of the 81 UK members, Wales had 4 and Scotland 8, for constituencies most of which were vast in area. Close links between Euro-MPs and the voters seemed unlikely, though each member state held elections under its own system of voting and candidates generally represented parties familiar to the voters in their national politics. The British elected 60 Conservative Euro-MPs, 16 Labour, a Social Democrat, a Scottish Nationalist and 3 other Euro-MPs from Northern Ireland. West Germany returned 42 CDU–CSU members, 35 Social Democrats and 4 Free Democrats. The 81 French Euro-MPs included 23 Socialists, 19 Communists, 9 Christian Democrats and various Liberals and Progressives. Figure 7.5 shows the main groups which formed in the European Parliament, the centre-right having a majority over the left-wing groups.

The turn-out of voters attracted almost as much attention as the results, however. In Britain it was dismal, less than a third of the electorate bothering to vote (except in Northern Ireland where 57 per cent voted in an election held under proportional representation[G]). In Denmark too the turn-out was below 50 per cent, though people elsewhere showed more interest – above 80 per cent voted in Belgium, Italy and Luxemburg.

The achievements of the elected Parliament during the next five years were not sufficient to increase the enthusiasm. The early 1980s were years of recession and high unemployment, and members of the European Community could not escape the general problems of the West. During 1983 unemployment climbed higher still – almost five per cent in that year alone – to stand at almost twelve per cent of the work-force in the Community as a whole. Unemployment was highest in the Irish Republic, at over fifteen per cent, but it was also over twelve per cent in the Netherlands, Belgium, Italy and the United Kingdom.

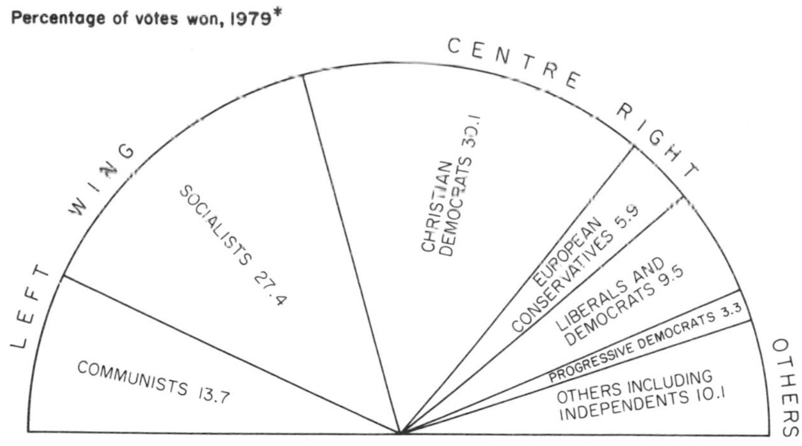

* Including elections in Greece, 1981

Source: The European Parliament's own 'best estimate' of its membership, reconciling the various national political affiliations of the Euro-MPs.

Fig. 7.5 The European Parliament: political groups after direct elections, 1979

There were still few signs of any common Community policy to deal with unemployment and with the problems which produced it. When the next Euro-elections were held in 1984, more than two-thirds of British electors again failed to vote, and turn-out in most states was lower than in 1979.

Voters in 1984 also tended to move towards political groups not previously represented at Strasbourg. Eleven 'Greens' were elected, seven of them in West Germany – members of Ecology Parties concerned about the environment, who questioned conventional ideas of the integration and nuclear defence of western Europe and the desirability of industrial growth. Older ideas of pre-war fascism were stirred when sixteen extreme right-wing Euro-MPs were returned, most of them French. It seemed on the whole that electors voted less for European causes than to express their views on their national governments. Thus Labour won fifteen seats from the Conservatives in Britain, and there was marked movement away from Chancellor Kohl's coalition of Christian Democrats and Free Democrats in West Germany. The political groups of the centre-right nevertheless kept a majority in the European Parliament, though the new Parliament was even more fragmented than the old, and perhaps less likely to make the forceful impact on the running of the Community which might promote the people's confidence in the Community's democracy.

Meanwhile, negotiations went on towards enlarging the Community from ten to twelve members, with Portugal and Spain seeking admission to take effect in 1986. Democratic institutions had been revived in both countries in recent years (see section 7.3), but farmers and fishermen in the Community had misgivings about accepting yet more competition into the common market. Doubts lingered in Portugal and Spain, too, as to whether membership of the Community was in their best interests. The Treaty of Accession was nevertheless signed by the Portugese and Spanish Prime Ministers during 1985.

One side-effect of the increasing contacts across the Pyrenees was that Britain and Spain came nearer to solving the problem of Gibraltar. Franco had disputed Britain's colonial presence there which dated from 1704, and in 1969 the border between Spain and Gibraltar had been closed in an effort to force the British out. The majority of Gibraltar's 25 000 people nevertheless voted to remain British, and Britain insisted on retaining sovereignty over the colony. The democratic government which followed Franco's death in Spain similarly insisted that Gibraltar was rightly Spanish and the border remained closed to most traffic even after Anglo-Spanish negotiations in 1980. But in 1984, in the Brussels Agreement, the two governments arranged to reopen the frontier and to establish more normal relations, while leaving the question of sovereignty over Gibraltar for further discussions. The Spanish Foreign Minister perhaps indicated further developments when he said:

> For Spain the end of the Gibraltar problem means reintegration of Gibraltar with Spain. This does not imply any pressure on Gibraltarians to change their life style or nationality. It is consistent with a special status for Gibraltar.

The Agreement of 1984 meanwhile was made in the spirit of the European Community, to promote Anglo-Spanish co-operation over Gibraltar:

on a mutually beneficial basis on economic, cultural, touristic, aviation, military and environmental matters.

Gilbraltarians were still suspicious of Spanish designs on the colony, however, and many of them protested in 1987 when Spain was granted rights at Gibraltar's airport.

7.2 The new members, 1973–81

7.2.1 Admissions in 1973

Britain was by far the largest of the Community's new members in 1973 (see Unit 5 and Table 7.1). Denmark, though much smaller, prospered following its admission and displaced West Germany as the richest member of the association in terms of GDP per head of population. Danish history was comparatively tranquil: constitutional monarchy was deeply rooted – as it was in Britain – and, after the Second World War, governments from time to time changed between moderately left and moderately right coalitions, in response to the wishes of the voters in general elections. There was a tradition of progressive reform which brought extensive social services and an advanced welfare state. Yet Denmark was no more isolated from economic difficulties in the 1970s and 1980s than the rest of the European Community, and this brought worries about unemployment and the country's balance of payments.

The Republic of Ireland had a population even smaller than Denmark's. It was also much poorer, and looked to Community membership both for economic advantage and for some increase in its international contacts. Until 1922 Ireland had been under British rule and, even then, Northern Ireland remained part of the United Kingdom. From 1922 to 1949 the Irish Free State was a Dominion within the British Commonwealth of Nations, though reluctant to continue acknowledging the British Crown and conspicuously neutral in the Second World War. In 1949 the Free State became the Republic of Ireland, at the same time withdrawing from the Commonwealth.

Membership of the United Nations, where the Irish Republic had an honourable record of support for peace-keeping operations in the Middle East and elsewhere, helped to establish the country's international identity. But the Irish declined to join NATO, partly because Britain was one of its chief members and British rule continued in Northern Ireland, preventing the reunification of the whole of Ireland (see section 19.4.1). It was the Republic's dilemma, however, that commercial links with the United Kingdom remained important: in 1970, 65 per cent of Ireland's exports went to the UK and more than half of Ireland's imports came from there. Moreover, a special relationship allowed the movement of Irish people into the UK on terms more favourable than were commonly open to other peoples, and this was a valuable aid to a country still comparatively poor. Admission to the European Community seemed attractive, not only economically, but perhaps in the long term as a key to solving the difficult problem of Northern Ireland, all parts of Ireland now being within the EC.

Table 7.1 States in western Europe: some comparative statistics

State	Population		Income per head, 1983 (US dollars)*	Number of people per doctor, c. 1980	Percentage of population literate over age 15, c. 1980†
	Estimated, 1985 (million)	Annual growth, 1980–5 (%)			
Austria	7.6	0.1	8 450	441	99
Belgium	9.9	0.1	8 240	385	99
Britain	56.5	0.5	8 948‡	618	100
Denmark	5.1	−0.3	10 680	462	99
France	55.2	0.5	10 400	516	99
Greece	10.0	0.6	3 624	394	93
Irish Republic	3.6	1.2	4 810	774	99
Italy	57.1	0.3	6 170	1 334	94
Netherlands	14.5	0.5	9 460	498	100
Norway	4.2	0.3	12 930‡	493	100
Portugal	10.2	1.1	2 247	473	80
Spain	38.8	0.7	4 780	390	93
Sweden	8.3	0.1	10 745	454	100
Switzerland	6.5	0.4	16 340	379	100
West Germany	61.0	−0.1	10 672	442	100

* At current market prices.

† Definitions of literacy differ and these statistics, like most which relate to national performance, should be treated with caution.

‡ Gross national product boosted by oil output.

Comparisons between this table and others of a similar nature in this book (such as 10.1 and 17.1) will show that most countries in western Europe are among the world's wealthiest and most developed.

Statistics from *Encyclopaedia Britannica*

The Republic had the necessary democratic qualifications for joining the Community: elections (held under proportional representation[G] to the Dáil Éireann (parliament) at Dublin determined the Irish government. But Irish politics were much coloured by the country's history and unique circumstances. Fianna Fáil ('Warriors of Destiny') was the republican party once led by the veteran nationalist Eamonn de Valera, who was Ireland's *Taoiseach* (Prime Minister) for many years (1932–48, 1951–4 and 1957–9) and President of the Republic from 1959 to 1973 when he retired, aged 90. Fine Gael ('United Ireland') was the chief opposition to Fianna Fáil, yet both were broadly conservative, the left being represented mainly by the smaller Irish Labour Party which in the post-war years often governed in coalition with Fine Gael. In the 1979 elections to the Parliament at Strasbourg, Fianna Fáil won five seats, its members joining the Progressive Democrats; four Fine Gael Euro-MPs sat with the Christian Democrats, and four Irish Labour members with the Socialists.

Membership of the European Community fostered rapid growth in Irish prosperity, especially in agriculture, but could not shield the Irish economy from the economic troubles of the 1970s and 1980s and unemployment soared. Ireland was on the fringe of the Community geographically, and it seemed clear that, for all its efforts to implement regional aid, the Community was still much more prosperous at its centre than in the areas at its edges, such as Ireland and southern Italy. Even in Britain, it seemed that ties with Europe prospered the south-east of England much more than the north, Wales and Scotland.

7.2.2 Greece

In 1981 another poor country at some distance from the heart of the European Community gained admission. Greece had a population of 9.7 million and a GDP per head of population (£1480 in 1977) lower than Ireland's. Greece had to struggle not only for economic development, however, but for democracy too. The defeat of Nazi Germany and the liberation of Greece at the end of the Second World War left the Greeks with a struggle for power between royalists and communists which degenerated into civil war from 1946 to 1949. Foreign interference in this meant that Greece was also caught up in the Cold War.

Britain was the first to interfere, having helped in liberating Greece. The British supported the Greek monarchy, but Greek communists had not resisted the Germans from 1942 to 1945 in order to have George II back – a king deposed in the years 1924–35 but who, before the Nazi occupation, reinstated himself and installed the right-wing dictatorship of General John Metaxas. George was again reinstated with British help and as the result of a plebiscite[G] in 1946, but Greek communists set up the Democratic Army to fight for control. They were assisted by Yugoslavs, Albanians and Bulgarians, and the expense quickly weakened Britain's determination to persevere with economic and military aid to the royalists. In effect, however, Attlee and Bevin handed the problem to the USA, where the Truman administration all too readily assumed that events in Greece were part of a Soviet master plan, hatched by Stalin. Acheson painted an alarmist picture of a Soviet breakthrough because, like

> apples in a barrel infected by the corruption of one rotten one, the corruption of Greece would infect Iran and all to the East . . . Africa . . . Italy and France.

The President responded with the Truman Doctrine (see section 4.4), and 300 million dollars were thrown into the support of the Greek monarchy, with US equipment and advice helping to ensure the defeat of the Democratic Army in 1949.

The Greek civil war left deep wounds, especially when, after it, the royalists executed over a thousand communists. George II had died in 1947 and his brother Paul reigned until 1964 with some democratic institutions but hardly a secure democracy. Alexander Papagos, the military victor over the Democratic Army, set up the Greek Rally, a right-wing political grouping which commanded the enthusiastic support of the USA. In 1952, the year Greece joined NATO, the Rally won electoral support, making Papagos Prime Minister until his death in 1955. Constantine Karamanlis succeeded him, leading conservative governments for the next eight years with further US backing.

Greek politics were now caught up in the problems of Cyprus, where the EOKA movement turned to terrorism in the 1950s in an attempt to drive out the British and in support of *enosis*, the union of the island with Greece (see section 18.3). The Cyprus problem caused tension in Greek relations with Britain and with Turkey, Turkish Cypriots fiercely resisting enosis. It also further undermined democracy in Greece. When Karamanlis resigned in 1963, going into exile some years later, George Papandreou came to power. His moderately left-wing Centre Union Party won support in elections in 1964 but alarmed vested interests. Army leaders distrusted Papandreou's interest in reform and wanted to back enosis. Papandreou also came into conflict with the new king, Constantine II, successor to Paul in 1964. In 1965 Papandreou was forced to resign, but the military wanted more and in 1967 'the Colonels' seized power. Constantine was sent into exile, but the monarchy was not abolished until six years later when the Colonels declared Greece a republic, the change being confirmed in a plebiscite in 1974 after the downfall of the military regime. Meanwhile, the Colonels, headed by George Papadopoulos, imposed such a narrow-minded and brutal authority that they were charged before the European Commission of Human Rights (Greece having been an associate member of the EEC since 1962). Papadopoulos and his colleagues also proved incompetent, offering the people few constructive ideas for improving the Greek economy or solving the problems of Cyprus. They meddled in the latter, however, giving ill-judged support to the overthrow of Archbishop Makarios in 1974. This brought Greece itself near to revolution, and the military stood down, opening the way for a new effort to make democracy work in Greece. Karamanlis returned from exile to become Prime Minister, winning massive support in elections before the end of 1974. Papadopoulos was jailed for life.

Karamanlis had long hoped to make Greece a full member of the European Community. His ambition was fulfilled in 1981, by which time Karamanlis himself was President of the Greek Republic. In the same year, however, elections returned a socialist government in Greece, when Pasok (the Panhellenic Socialist Movement) won a clear majority in parliament. Andreas Papandreou became Prime Minister. He was son of the former left-wing leader, who died in 1968. Pasok had ambitious plans for social reform but was sceptical about the advantages of Community membership and hostile to NATO and to US bases in Greece. Elections to the European Parliament nevertheless took place, returning ten members of Pasok, eight members of New Democracy – now the Greek opposition, and at Strasbourg grouped with the Christian Democrats – four Communists and two others.

Papandreou's government was generally more cautious in its relations with the outside world than electoral rhetoric had suggested it might be. Greece had pressing domestic problems, with a serious balance-of-payments deficit and persistent inflation, and a five-year plan was started in 1983 to try to increase output and to bring Greeks nearer to the standard of living of others in the European Community. Papandreou and Pasok were confirmed in power in general elections in 1985.

7.3 The newest members, 1986: Portugal and Spain – from fascism to democracy

For some time after 1945 Spain and Portugal continued to remain separate from the mainstream of western-European development. This was partly due to their geographical location – beyond the Pyrenees – but their authoritarian right-wing regimes also kept Spain and Portugal in isolation. Both had been neutral in the Second World War, though, with Salazar in Portugal and Franco in Spain sharing some of the characteristics of the fascists, they had been closer in spirit to the Axis than to the Allies.

7.3.1 Portugal

Antonio Salazar had led Portugal as Prime Minister since 1932. He ruled virtually as a dictator, leading the Portuguese National Union with the support of the army in a one-party republic. Some effort was made to develop the Portuguese economy and to advance the people's welfare, but the results still left the Portuguese standard of living far below even that of Greece. Salazar took Portugal into NATO but he had few overseas ambitions other than to preserve what remained of the Portuguese Empire. He resolutely frustrated the aspirations of nationalists in Angola and Mozambique and in smaller Portuguese territories elsewhere in Africa and in the Far East, but the costs of maintaining the increasingly restless Empire mounted. Salazar's principal instinct was nevertheless to stand firm, even to stand still.

At home he protected the vested interests of the Catholic Church, the property-owners and the military, just as he aimed to preserve the system in the Empire. His rule was distinctively Portuguese though he borrowed some ideas from Mussolini's corporate state[G] and, in pale imitation of Mussolini, pandered to his own reputation by naming Europe's largest bridge, across the

Tagus at Lisbon, the Salazar Bridge. His long rule came to an end in 1968 when he suffered a stroke, though to his death in 1970 he remained unaware that he had been replaced as Portugal's leader.

Marcello Caetano, the new Prime Minister, had long been close to Salazar: he too had few thoughts of changing the system. But exiles like Mario Soares were already working to liberate Portugal from authoritarian rule, just as nationalist groups, like FRELIMO in Mozambique, were already trying to free Portugal's overseas territories (see section 15.4), and Caetano was forced to spend 40 per cent of government income on the armed forces. The bitter struggles in Mozambique and Angola helped bring a revolt by the Portuguese military in 1974, 'to save the nation from the government'. Caetano was overthrown in spite of his recent, more spirited, attempts to improve Portugal's economy. One of the leaders of the coup was General Antonio de Spinola, author of *Portugal and the Future* which argued that the 'wind of change' in Africa could not be deflected merely by military means. Spinola and his colleagues roused popular enthusiasm in Portugal by promising free elections at home and self-determination for the colonies. Exiles were welcomed back and Soares became Foreign Minister in a broad provisional government, led by Spinola as President.

The dissolution of the long period of authoritarian rule by Salazar and Caetano led almost inevitably to confusion, and before the end of 1974 there were further political upheavals. Spinola stood down, and General Francisco Gomes, chief-of-staff of the armed forces, became President, hoping for a sustained term of office which would enable him not only to contain pressing economic problems but also to secure a successful transition to democracy. Much of the Empire was given independence in 1974–5, Portugal willingly shedding what had become a burden. In Portugal itself, extremists on both left and right were resisted and a new constitution was hammered out in line with Western democratic practices and with a socialist emphasis on nationalization and 'the rights of workers, workers' committees and trade unions'. The first free elections for half a century were held in 1976 and Soares, leader of the Socialists who won a third of the votes, became Prime Minister in a minority government.

Soares survived in office until 1978. There were then new elections in 1979, when voters gave a majority to the Democratic Alliance of five moderate parties including Social Democrats and the centre-right. Socialists and Communists formed the opposition, their position confirmed in yet another election in 1980. Not without difficulty, and arousing unrest among the electorate, the Alliance government amended the constitution, diluting its emphasis on the workers and nationalization. But Portugal continued to face grave economic difficulties and the income per head of population (about ten million people in 1980) was still little more than a third that of the British. The Alliance broke up amid the strains of deepening crisis – inflation, unemployment and a vast balance-of-payments deficit. New elections in 1983 returned a coalition of Socialists and Social Democrats, with Soares again Prime Minister.

The struggle for democracy in Portugal won sympathy from the European

Community, not only benefiting the negotiations for admission but also bringing loans and other economic help. The USA also aided its fellow-member of NATO, and Portugal got further help from the International Monetary Fund[G]. Gradually Portugal was moving into the more turbulent mainstream of western-European development, leaving behind the stable but outdated era of Salazar. It was Soares who negotiated Portugal's admission to the European Community, though elections late in 1985 produced a Social Democratic government under Cavaço Silva. In 1986 Soares was elected President of Portugal.

7.3.2 Spain

The turning-point in Spain's post-war history came in 1975 with the death of Francisco Franco. Franco had ruled since 1939 when he emerged victorious from the vicious and bloody Spanish Civil War as Spain's 'Caudillo [leader] of the Realm and Chief of State'. His victory had been helped by Hitler and Mussolini and he was backed by the Falange, a fascist party. He ruled virtually as a dictator, developing a corporate state similar to that led by Mussolini in Italy and not unlike Salazar's in Portugal. The Falange was expanded into the National Union, making Spain a one-party state, supported by a brutal police force and the army.

The Civil War left a bitter legacy. The army, the Catholic Church, the propertied, and right-wing forces in general had brought Franco to power and theirs were the interests which, together with his own, he tried to protect. But the forces of the left were hostile – among them students and workers, as far as they were able to organize, and, eventually, Church leaders too. Franco needed to be watchful against his political enemies but he also faced regional discontents. Other countries in western Europe, such as Belgium, uneasily combined different peoples within one state, while France faced demands for secession from Corsica and the United Kingdom faced similar demands within Northern Ireland, but regional problems plagued no country more than Spain. Foremost among those resentful of rule from Madrid were the Basques, a distinctive people in the western Pyrenees of whom half a million lived in Spain and 100 000 in France. Some Basques wanted an independent state, *Euzkadi*; most wanted at the least self-government. The Basques had fiercely resisted Franco and the Nationalists in the Civil War when the Basque town of Guernica had been singled out for devastation from the air by German bombers. Franco then ruled them with an iron hand, though ETA (*Euzkadi ta Azkatasuna*, an organization for Basque liberation and for secession) grew bolder during his later years, using terrorist methods similar to those of the IRA in Northern Ireland. Spain had other restless areas too, such as Catalonia in the north-east and Andalusia in the south, where a strong regional identity persisted. But Franco gave them little room for active protest.

The legacy of the Civil War also included international difficulties for Franco. He was seen in western Europe as the associate of Hitler and Mussolini, though he had not openly joined them in the Second World War. Spain was kept out of NATO, though the USA signed a defence pact with Franco in 1953. Entry into the United Nations was not granted until 1955, and Spanish demands for Gibraltar won little sympathy in Europe while it was Franco who made them. Nor could entry into the European Communities be considered while Franco ruled. In 1947, however, he had been proclaimed Caudillo for life.

Franco's rule was not entirely unproductive. The economy made some progress and some welfare reforms were introduced, for example for insurance against sickness and old age. Spain did not receive Marshall Aid but some US aid was granted in the 1960s, helping towards industrialization. When Franco died, Spain's income per head of population was similar to that of the Republic of Ireland and well ahead of that of Portugal. But Spain at that time had a population of over 35 million, large enough to make it one of the major states of western Europe. Its geography and history had first to be overcome, however. Franco himself saw some need to make arrangements for the future, at least in restoring the Spanish monarchy, which had been abolished in 1931. The Law of Succession in 1947 provided for its restoration in succession to Franco, and Juan Carlos, grandson of Spain's last king, Alfonso XIII, was groomed for the inheritance from 1954 onwards. Nearing death in 1975, Franco allowed new political parties to form, though not communist ones. Thus, when Franco died later that year, Juan Carlos was on hand to guide Spain through the difficult years of transition from dictatorship to democracy.

Juan Carlos moved cautiously. The restoration of the monarchy in the 1970s, when monarchy was generally out of fashion, suggested that conservative opinion still ran deep in Spain, especially in the rural areas: liberal reform was steady but not hasty. A Communist Party was now legalized and work began on a new democratic constitution, but at the same time law and order were sternly upheld, and regional and other dissidents were contained. Elections in 1977 and 1979 gave a majority to the UCD (Democratic Centre Party), a centre-right alliance led by Adolfo Suarez, on whom Juan Carlos had come to rely. Once a member of Franco's National Union, Suarez was cautious enough to be dubbed by critics, 'the Snail'. At this time, however, lines of development were drawn for social reform and economic progress, for self-government in restless regions, starting with the Basques and Catalonia and then extending to others, and for alliances beyond Spain's frontiers. Spain joined NATO in 1982 and negotiated for entry into the European Community.

Suarez resigned as Prime Minister in 1981. It had not been easy to hold the UCD together: economic difficulties festered; ETA actively campaigned using terror to demand Basque independence rather than self-government; and there was unrest about various policies from joining NATO to liberalizing divorce laws. Suarez hoped that democracy would survive and not prove yet again 'a parenthesis in the history of Spain', but his resignation was followed by an attempted military coup which it took skill and determination on the part of Juan Carlos and supporters of the constitution to overcome.

In new elections in 1982 there was a decisive swing to the left, bringing to power a Socialist government led by Felipe Gonzales Marquez. It was a government reluctant at first to play much part in NATO, but it pursued entry to the

European Community. Like Portugal, Spain was persevering in the struggle to become part of democratic western Europe. On the day that Gonzales signed the Treaty of Accession to the European Community, however, there were fatal casualties caused by ETA bombings in Madrid, a reminder of problems Spain had still to solve. In 1986, the year that Spain's entry into the EC took effect to the general satisfaction of the Spanish people, a referendum on continued membership of NATO won only a bare majority with 52 per cent of the vote. Gonzales himself, after earlier opposition to NATO, had recommended continued membership, and he had further success in June 1986 when the voters confirmed him in power with a majority almost as large as in 1982.

7.4 Western Europe outside the Community

Prosperity in western Europe was not confined to members of the European Community. Sweden and Norway enjoyed the advanced living standards and political stability common throughout Scandinavia. The Swedes after 1945 showed a long attachment to government by the Social Democrats, strongly committed to the people's welfare and to the United Nations and international co-operation generally. Sweden had been neutral in the Second World War and continued after it to remain apart from alliances such as NATO. Norway, a constitutional monarchy like Sweden, pursued a rather less distinctive course: a founder-member of NATO, there were more frequent changes of fortune between its various political parties, much as in other parts of western Europe.

Switzerland had agreed to 'perpetual neutrality' as long ago as 1815, soon gaining benefit as a centre for international activities which added wealth to the country's tranquillity. The Swiss parliament included an unusually large number of parties but, with a population in 1980 of only about six million, the republic was small enough to base its democracy not just on electing a central government but also on regional decision-making and the frequent consultation of the people on specific issues.

Austria, Switzerland's neighbour, arrived at its international neutrality in 1955 as part of its post-war settlement with the Allies (see section 4.6). From a precarious economic position between the World Wars, it then advanced quite markedly. Austria's population was not a lot larger than Switzerland's, but almost a quarter of the Austrian people lived in Vienna, the capital, whose size remained more suited to the vast Habsburg Empire it had commanded up to the First World War. One problem for governments of the Austrian Republic was to reconcile Viennese radicalism with the conservatism of the country's rural areas. But change came quickly after 1955: industrialization was rapid, welfare services expanded, and Vienna competed successfully with other cities such as Geneva to become a centre for international agencies, conferences and exchanges. Kurt Waldheim, born near Vienna, became the UN Secretary-General in 1972. Waldheim became President of Austria in 1986, though by that time there were rumours and controversy concerning the part he had played in the Second World War in support of the Nazis. By 1988 he was a very lame President indeed.

The first governments of post-war Austria were cautious coalitions and not until 1966, when the People's Party won control, was any party strong enough to rule alone. These early governments, led by Chancellors such as Figl and Raab, laid firm foundations for economic success. Their policies for encouraging initiative were similar to those of Erhard in West Germany, but they also placed a strong emphasis on a mixed economy[G], combining private enterprise with a large public sector. Many industries were nationalized, and from 1956 they were administered centrally by the Austrian Board of Industry and Mining.

Since helping to negotiate Austria's freedom in 1955, Bruno Kreisky had served as Foreign Minister. In 1970 he led a coalition government as the Republic's first Socialist Chancellor. Elections in 1971 enabled him to lead a Socialist government and he and the Socialists then remained in power for twelve years. Compared with other west-European countries, Austria weathered the economic storms of the 1970s very successfully, with lower inflation, less unemployment and fewer strikes. Growth rates ran ahead even of West Germany's and welfare services were maintained. But in spite of Kreisky's vigorous leadership Austria was not entirely unaffected by the economic blizzards of the 1970s, and when Kreisky grew older and sick the electors chose in 1983 to return to coalition government.

Since the collapse of the Habsburg Empire in 1918, the takeover by the Nazis in 1938, and their defeat and the Allies' occupation in 1945, Austria's transformation had been remarkable, achieving much of what was best in western-European society. Austrians enjoyed a comfortable standard of living combined with the protection of human liberties and with cultural excellence, especially in music. Though in the heartland of Europe, Austria also enjoyed cordial and peaceful relations with its neighbours. Even Austro-Italian tension over Italy's continued possession of the South Tyrol (dating from 1919 and confirmed in the peace settlement of 1947) was defused by negotiation and compromise and diverted into a rivalry which merely added spice to Austro-Italian football matches. The conditions under which freedom had been won in 1955 kept Austria out of the European Community, but in also keeping the republic out of alliances such as NATO the Allies allowed Austria to commit very little of its resources to costly competition in the arms race. The result for the Austrian people was increased prosperity, sometimes envied by its neighbours in the Eastern bloc.

UNIT 8

The people's democracies of eastern Europe

8.1 People's democracy: communist government

8.1.1 Communist government established 1945–9: the satellites

When the Second World War ended in 1945, eastern Europe had had little experience of Western democracy, except in Czechoslovakia during the twenty years before the German conquest in 1938–9. The Declaration on Liberated Europe, agreed at Yalta in 1945, seemed too readily to assume that parliamentary government would spring up once Nazi influence was removed (see section 1.3.1). But eastern Europe was a patchwork of liberated states such as Poland and Czechoslovakia and defeated Nazi collaborators such as Hungary and Bulgaria, almost all with a variety of peoples whose traditions differed from those in the West. The war had taken a heavy toll on their economies which, for the most part, had been less developed before the war than those in western Europe, and much of eastern Europe now faced vast problems of reconstruction.

Moreover, most of eastern Europe had been overrun by the Soviet Red Army by the time Nazi Germany surrendered, and Stalin was determined to use this to ensure that neighbours of the Soviet Union should henceforth be friendly and help to protect the USSR. Speaking at Yalta, Stalin himself summed up the Soviet interest and intention:

> Throughout history Poland has been the corridor for attack on Russia. . . . During the last thirty years Germany has twice passed through this corridor. The reason for this was that Poland was weak. Russia wants a strong, independent and democratic Poland. . . . It is not only a question of honour for Russia, but one of life and death.

By 'independent' and 'democratic' Stalin meant independent of anti-Soviet influence and democratic within pro-Soviet influences. Averell Harriman, US ambassador in Moscow, spoke of a 'barbarian invasion of Europe' by the Soviets as early as April 1945 – while the USSR and USA were allies against Nazi Germany – and attitudes quickly hardened with the onset of the Cold War. As suspicious of the West as the West was of him, Stalin extended his ambitions for Soviet security to the whole of eastern Europe, encouraging the setting-up of pro-Soviet people's democracies. He used the pressure of the Red Army, Soviet advisers and local communists, many of them Moscow-trained, and the West saw these states as 'satellites', part of a Soviet 'empire' (see section 4.3).

Communist domination in Poland was secured by the end of 1948. The Government of National Unity, set up after the Yalta Conference, combined the Lublin Poles and the London Poles. The former were part of a Democratic bloc, favourable to socialism and to the Soviet Union, while Stanislaw Mikolajczyk returned from London to lead the Peasant Party and other groups more favourable to the West. It was an uneasy alliance, however, and when elections returned strong support for the Democratic bloc in 1947 Mikolajczyk's role, now in opposition, grew more difficult. Fearing arrest for alleged illegal activities, he fled to the West.

There was further in-fighting among groups in the Democratic bloc. Wladyslaw Gomulka, organizer of wartime resistance against the Nazis and communist leader of the Polish Workers' Party, seemed to Stalin too much of a Polish nationalist, and Boleslaw Bierut was therefore preferred as the leader of the reorganized and now dominant Polish United Workers' Party in December 1948. No other political group now had much influence over Poland's affairs and even Gomulka was eclipsed for the time being. The Soviet Marshal Rokossovsky was made War Minister in 1949, and in 1952 a new constitution established Poland as a people's democracy with a Soviet-style system of government. There was a single official list of parliamentary candidates, and the key figure in Polish politics until his death in 1956 was Bierut, the leader of the communist United Workers' Party.

Similar paths to people's democracy were trodden in other east-European states. Bulgaria became a people's democracy with a Soviet-style constitution as early as 1947. At the end of the war the left-wing Fatherland Front had deposed the monarchy and won a general election. The Front had then been purged of non-communists such as some members of the Agrarian Party, whose leader, Nikola Petkov, was hanged, and later of most Social Democrats. Here too the communist Party Secretary, Georgi Dimitrov, was the chief political force, until his death in 1949.

Romania ran an almost parallel course. The constitution was approved in 1948, power resting with the Popular Democratic Front and Communists led by their Secretary, Gheorghiu-Dej. By this time the Front had twice won post-war elections, had been purged of anti-communists and had abolished the Romanian monarchy.

Hungary too had become a republic, its Soviet-style constitution established in 1949. By then control lay with the United Workers' Party and especially with veteran communist Secretary, Mátyás Rákosi, who had held office when Bela Kun set up a brief communist regime in Hungary in 1919. The first post-war elections in 1945 had given the Hungarian Communist Party less than twenty per cent of the vote, the electorate much preferring the Smallholders' Party, but four years later the latter had been outmanoeuvred in spite of support from the Catholic Church, which was almost as strong in Hungary as in Poland.

Walther Ulbricht was the key figure as leader of the Socialist Unity Party when the German Democratic Republic (East Germany) was set up in 1949 (see section 4.2). Here too there was now a Soviet-style constitution, with a prescribed list of candidates at the election of 1950. Ulbricht, who had fled Nazi Germany for the Soviet Union in the 1930s and was now a fervent Stalinist, remained in office until 1971.

Czechoslovakia, on the other hand, seemed likely after 1945 to return to Western-style democracy. Soviet troops left Czechoslovakia by the end of 1945 and free elections in 1946 gave the Communist Party almost 38 per cent of the vote and a dominant voice in the coalition government led by Klement Gottwald. Before new elections in 1948, however, the Cold War exerted its pressures in Czechoslovakia. The Truman Doctrine quickened Stalin's anxieties, while the rejection of Marshall Aid, on which Stalin insisted, undermined support for the Communist Party among Czechoslovak electors. Czech communists carried out a coup in February 1948, purging the government of non-communists. Jan Masaryk, the Foreign Minister, fell to his death from a window (perhaps suicide) and Eduard Beneš resigned as President of Czechoslovakia, dying soon afterwards. Both were respected in the West for their attachment to democracy, and their passing was deeply regretted.

Gottwald, succeeding Beneš as President, consolidated communist authority in Czechoslovakia, ruling with an iron hand. Even Rudolf Slansky, Secretary of the Communist Party until replaced by Gottwald in 1951, was not secure. He was tried for various offences involving treason and, with ten collaborators, was hanged in 1952, only a short time before Gottwald himself died from pneumonia contracted at Stalin's funeral in Moscow.

8.1.2 Independent communists

Many east-European communists had won a reputation during the Second World War for their work in the resistance to Nazi Germany. None was more successful than Josip Broz, Secretary of the Yugoslav Communist Party since 1937. Using the name Tito, Broz led the Yugoslav Partisans who provided more effective national resistance to the German invaders than that of the country's anti-communist *Chetniks*. General Mihailović, leader of the Chetniks, was outmanoeuvred by Tito when the war ended. Soviet influence was now stronger in the Balkans than that of the West but Tito had no need to rely on the help of the Red Army: he was the obvious choice to lead the new government of Yugoslavia and, as President of the country from 1953 (the monarchy was abolished in 1945), he continued to rule until his death in 1980. Some attempt was made to appease the strongly Serbian interests of the Chetniks (Serbs and Croats being Yugoslavia's main racial groups) by devising a federal constitution for Yugoslavia, within which Serbia was one of the country's six socialist republics with a good deal of regional authority. Mihailović was executed in 1946, however, for resisting the new government, having also been charged with collaborating with the Germans.

Though the Soviets played no part in these developments in Yugoslavia, the pattern was similar to that in other countries of eastern Europe, leading from a

Government of National Unity to a Soviet-style system of government dominated by Tito's Communists and the purge of rivals. But Tito did not intend to be a Soviet puppet in the way of some other east-European leaders. He had fought on the side of the Bolsheviks in Russia's civil war after 1917 but he was a Croat and above all a Yugoslav patriot. As a result he quarrelled with Stalin and in 1948 Yugoslavia was expelled from the Cominform (see section 4.3). As the guardian of Yugoslav independence and the champion of non-alignment, Tito then nurtured his own brand of Marxism, dealing with both East and West and avoiding deep involvement in their Cold War.

Albania, like Yugoslavia, did not have a common border with the USSR and here too a measure of independence was preserved. Enver Hoxha emerged to lead Albania as a wartime guerilla leader and Secretary of the communist Workers' Party. He led Albania's first post-war government, soon achieving dictatorial powers while resisting Yugoslav influence over the country. Tito after 1945 showed that he had his own ambitions to spread communist and Yugoslav authority, and was more involved than was Stalin in the affairs of Greece which led to the Truman Doctrine. Rivalry with Tito caused Hoxha in 1948 to prefer diplomatic adherence to the Soviet Union, but after 1956 Hoxha stubbornly followed his own course. He resented Khrushchev's criticisms of Stalin and, while Mao Tse-tung was alive, preferred to support the Marxism of the Chinese rather than that of the Soviets. The result was near-isolation, but Albania under Hoxha saw no reason to belong to any great power bloc. When Hoxha died in 1985, the Albanians rebuffed Soviet messages of condolence.

8.2 The Communist Bloc: organization and dissent

8.2.1 Co-operation

The Communist Information Bureau (Cominform), set up in 1947, may seem at first sight to have been a device for securing communist takeovers and imposing the authority of Moscow on its European members. Admittedly, the expulsion of Tito's Yugoslavia clearly showed the need for members to toe the common line (see section 4.3 and Table 4.2), but it is likely that the West overestimated the importance to the Soviets of Cominform. It gave expression to communist solidarity but was not much involved with detailed policy nor even with doctrine. Andrei Zdhanov, when Cominform was founded, suggested that Stalin, whom he represented, was still thinking mainly of defence against 'US imperialism'. Cominform members were advised to:

> support all the really patriotic elements who do not want their countries to be imposed upon, who want to resist enthralment of their countries to foreign capital. and to uphold national sovereignty.

Communists in the West were also warned against trying to start revolutions and when, in 1956, Cominform was dissolved, the Soviets seemed not to regret its loss.

The Council for Mutual Economic Assistance (Comecon), founded in 1949, and the Warsaw Pact (1955) were of greater and more lasting importance (see section 4.3 and Table 4.2). Stalin at first perhaps intended Comecon simply as a tool for the economic boycott of Yugoslavia, but it soon developed into a major association, aiming to organize trade and promote economic harmony among its members, most of them the communist states of eastern Europe. At the end of the Second World War, the Soviet Union had ruthlessly used eastern Europe to help repair the Soviet economy, before showing much concern for eastern Europe itself. But the Molotov Plan was launched as a counter-stroke to the Marshall Plan, to boost east-European development, and Soviet credits to fellow-members of Comecon continued to be important to their economies. Suspicion of Soviet motives nevertheless lingered, combining with national pride to produce resistance when Khrushchev tried to give the Council supranational powers, proposing that it should organize eastern Europe as a whole, with Czechoslovakia and East Germany concentrating on industry, Bulgaria, Hungary and Romania on agriculture and Poland on both. Like the EEC in the West, Comecon found it difficult to overcome the vested interests of individual members, and Khrushchev's plan had to be diluted.

Comecon machinery nevertheless evolved. When Khrushchev retired in 1964, representatives of member governments were meeting annually to review overall strategy and there existed an executive committee, a secretariat, many standing commissions for special areas such as finance, coal and scientific research, and a Bank for Socialist Countries, part of whose work was to promote investment. At that time, Comecon members exported about half as much as EEC members. East Europeans sold about a third of their exports to the Soviet Union and another third to fellow members of Comecon. In the following years growth rates tended to match those in western Europe, but as Comecon became more involved in trade with the outside world some members, like Poland, fell heavily into debt to the West. World energy crises, on the other hand, increased the importance to eastern Europe of the cheap oil supplies it obtained from the Soviet Union.

The Warsaw Pact developed out of the network of post-war defence pacts with states in eastern Europe made by Molotov, Stalin's Foreign Minister from 1939 to 1949 (see section 4.3 and Table 4.2). Molotov was Foreign Minister again from 1953 to 1956, before he was eclipsed for opposing Khrushchev. In creating the Warsaw Pact in 1955, Molotov was responding to the adjustments in European alignments at the time of the Austrian State Treaty and of West Germany's admission to NATO. The essence of the Pact was that it set up a unified military command, effectively under Soviet direction, and obliged members to defend one another in the event of outside attack. With a Soviet military adviser attached to each member state, the structure of the alliance was such that it could at times become an instrument for the control of dissent within the satellite states.

8.2.2 Patterns of dissent

The convulsions which from time to time shook post-war Europe, both West and East, arose from many varied grievances. While anti-Americanism was not uncommon in western Europe, most grievances there tended to come from general economic and social problems – such as those that inflamed workers and students in France in 1968 – though specific causes produced unrest and terrorist activity in places as far apart as Spain, Italy and Northern Ireland. In eastern Europe, there was unrest in East Germany in 1953, soon after the death of Stalin. Disturbances followed in 1956 in Poland and then, more seriously, in Hungary, where an unsuccessful attempt was made to leave the Warsaw Pact. Czechoslovakia exploded in 1968, at a time of considerable discontent in the West, but while Czechoslovakia then subsided under the crushing impact of a Soviet invasion, Poland grew more restless, crises erupting there in 1970, 1976 and 1980.

Tight control of movement in eastern Europe led to many attempts to escape across the Iron Curtain to the West, and protest movements developed against generally restrictive government throughout eastern Europe. Various groups of dissidents – such as Charter '77 in Czechoslovakia – persisted in demanding human rights and greater freedom, defying persecution. Such dissent and outbreaks of protest stemmed from economic and social discontent and dissatisfaction with national governments, as in the West, but Soviet supervision of eastern Europe added nationalist, and sometimes religious, anti-Sovietism to the unrest, potentially involving the USSR in every crisis.

The West tended to classify these outbreaks of protest as popular rebellions by the satellites against Moscow. This view, though an incomplete one, had some support from events. At the time of the Czechoslovak outbreak in 1968, Brezhnev asserted the right of socialist states to intervene in any state where a threat was offered to an existing socialist system; this Brezhnev Doctrine thus emphasized the unity of eastern Europe and its interdependence with the Soviets. But the actual governments in the satellites could also sometimes be anti-Soviet. Nicolae Ceausescu, General-Secretary of the Romanian Communist Party and the country's leader in succession to Gheorgiu-Dej in 1965, successfully insisted on a strong measure of national independence, especially in foreign policy. Nor could the Soviet Union take for granted the unfailing obedience to Soviet wishes of fellow-members of Comecon. The influence of the Soviet Union over eastern Europe was more direct than that of the USA in western Europe, but eastern Europeans nevertheless retained their own identities and interests, from time to time reminding the Soviets that their fellow socialists were not just subservient members of a Soviet 'empire'.

8.2.3 Unrest in the 1950s

Stalin demanded the same sacrifices and obedience from eastern Europe as from the citizens of the Soviet Union, but only Yugoslavia, with the advantage of Tito's determined and secure leadership, dared to offer defiance. When Gomulka showed signs of claiming similar independence for Poland, he was removed from office as part of a general weeding out of Titoists throughout eastern Europe. But Stalin's death quickened hopes for change and for the end of post-war austerity. Disturbances broke out in 1953 in Plzeň, Czechoslovakia, then in East Berlin and East Germany. Soviet troops were needed to put down the East Germans whose protests were directed against the collectivization of agriculture and continuing low standards of living. The new leadership in Moscow then turned to reform. German war reparations ended and the authorities throughout eastern Europe were encouraged to try to raise the living standards of workers in industry while slowing down, or even suspending, agricultural collectivization (which many peasant farmers resented) and relaxing Stalinist repression.

The easing of controls in both eastern Europe and the Soviet Union encouraged new ambitions, however. They surfaced in 1956 when Khrushchev

Fig. 8.1 Illingworth's cartoon in *Punch* in 1956 carried on the long tradition of British cartoonists who had portrayed Russia as a bear. Here, Krushchev has become the trainer of bears, some of the satellite states of eastern Europe. But by 1956, Yugoslavia had long been disobedient, and both Poland and Hungary now threatened to follow Yugoslavia's wayward example.

denounced Stalin's excesses and cruelties. Taking advantage of the death of Bierut, the Poles demanded more of the freedom Khrushchev seemed to be advocating. Serious rioting broke out in Poznan, resulting in more than 50 deaths. Gomulka had been released from custody in 1955 and now became the focus of hopes for a Polish, rather than Soviet, socialism. Soviet forces backed off from confrontation with the rioters, leaving the Poles to install Gomulka as First Secretary of the Party, and in effect the country's leader, in October 1956. Rokossovsky returned to Moscow and Gomulka released Cardinal Wyszyński, whose detention in 1953 had added to the disaffection of Poland's millions of Roman Catholics. Collectivization was all but abandoned, leaving some 80 per cent of Polish farming in the hands of small private producers. The Soviet Union cancelled Poland's debts and Gomulka cautiously undertook to try to increase the access of the Polish people to consumer goods. Stability was thus restored in Poland, and Gomulka remained in power until 1970. He was never a radical leader and his liberalism probably owed more to expediency than to conviction. In any case, he grew even less liberal in the 1960s, anxious to preserve his authority when Polish unrest resurfaced.

The unrest in Poland in 1956 triggered unrest in Hungary, where the detention since 1948 of another Catholic prelate, Cardinal Mindszenty, had also caused resentment among the devout, and where dissatisfaction with the harsh rule of Rákosi ran deep. Not without pressure from Moscow, Rákosi resigned in July 1956, but the Hungarian government could not halt the demands for greater freedom and better living standards. In October, János Kádár became Communist Party Secretary, while Imre Nagy became Prime Minister. Kádár and Nagy shared a history of opposition to Rákosi: Kádár had been imprisoned by him, and Nagy had in 1955 been expelled from the Communist Party for urging change. Nagy now embarked on an even more dangerous path, appointing a Cabinet which included a few non-communists, legalizing non-communist political groups, setting free Mindszenty and proposing a neutral Hungary, with a status similar to that won by Austria, Hungary's neighbour, in 1955. With this in mind, Nagy announced that Hungary would leave the Warsaw Pact.

The Soviet Union might have left Hungary, like Poland, to sort out its own problems had the Warsaw Pact not been involved. But even Kádár was alarmed now. Nagy seemed set on widening debate about policy and on winning popular favour, yet he seemed unable to control the turbulence sweeping the country. Radio Free Europe, the voice of the USA, urged the Hungarians on towards 'liberty'. Kádár however alleged that Hungary was moving back towards fascism, and Khrushchev later claimed that Nagy was 'the leader of a *putsch*', lacking legal authority:

> Although he was a Communist, Nagy no longer spoke for the Hungarian Communist Party. He spoke only for himself and a small circle of *émigrés* who had returned to help the counter-revolution.

Soviet troops were therefore sent to enter Budapest to ensure control for the Kádár faction. Over 150 000 Hungarians fled to the West and perhaps as many as 30 000 were killed before the support for Nagy was crushed and the disorders were put down. But world concern was distracted when Britain and France launched a simultaneous attack on Egypt, pursuing a quarrel of their own; though the West had encouraged the Hungarians, active support for them was never likely and was not forthcoming.

Mindszenty took refuge in the US legation in Budapest, leaving only in 1971 when allowed to go into exile. Nagy was arrested and eventually executed in 1958. Meanwhile, government authority was reimposed by Kádár who long remained Party Secretary and who, after 1958, encouraged the cautious introduction of many of the domestic reforms the Hungarians wanted. Hungary grew more liberal. The state achieved a compromise with the Papacy and the Catholic Church, starting in 1964, though Mindzenty could not accept it. Kádár had insisted on completing the collectivization of agriculture by 1961, but in general he set great store by reconciliation. Contacts grew with the West and living standards rose as the Hungarian economy grew more flexible and in some ways less centralized.

Hungary under Kádár made no further move to leave the Warsaw Pact but the events of 1956 were remembered with bitterness, and all Kádár's skill as well as time were needed to bring genuine reconciliation between Hungarians and their government and between Hungarians and the Soviets. Kádár's pre-eminence lasted until 1988 when the Hungarian Communist Party overthrew him and voted in a younger reforming technocrat, Károly Grósz, as his successor. Grósz seemed more open to the idea of further political as well as economic liberalization.

8.2.4 The 1960s and crisis in Czechoslovakia

The changes Khrushchev was trying to effect within the Soviet Union and in East–West relations had further repercussions. Communist China grew ever more critical of the Soviet Union, until soured relations led the Soviets to withdraw their technical aid from China in 1960 (see section 11.2.3(a)). In the Sino-Soviet wrangling which became common, most of eastern Europe sided with Moscow. Albania, however, took a different line. Hoxha had not approved of Khrushchev's condemnation of Stalin in 1956, and he supported Mao Tse-tung's view that the new Soviet leadership was 'revisionist', moving away from Marxism–Leninism. Khrushchev fiercely denounced the Albanians as 'afraid of democratization' and attacked Hoxha for baring:

> his fangs at us even more menacingly than the Chinese themselves . . . like a dog who bites the hand that feeds it.

But Hoxha seemed unconcerned when in 1961 Albania was excluded from Comecon and suspended from the Warsaw Pact, which it left formally in 1968.

The 1960s were a restless decade. Students across the world brimmed with idealist visions for improving it and much was beginning to be questioned anew. The superpowers moved hesitantly towards *détente*, encouraged by Brandt's Ostpolitik which improved East–West relations in Europe (see section 13.4.1). But President Kennedy in the USA was assassinated and Secretary

Khrushchev in the USSR was forced into retirement. Sino–Soviet relations remained bleak. Among the many uncertainties, the Kremlin least of all wanted new unrest in eastern Europe. Romania showed signs of seeking some of the independence achieved by Yugoslavia and Albania, but it was Czechoslovakia in 1968 which presented Moscow with its biggest test.

Antonin Novotný, who succeeded Gottwald in 1953, had maintained the tight Stalinist control of Czechoslovakia, growing increasingly unpopular as had similar hard-liners in Poland and Hungary. Novotný had concentrated on industrial development and economic performance had been uneven, especially in recent years. Nor could Novotný do much to reconcile rivalries between the country's main racial groups – the Czechs and the Slovaks. It was time for new leadership and, aware of Novotný's declining authority (especially over the peasantry, with whom he had little sympathy), the Soviet leaders were not sorry to see him retire.

In January 1968 he was replaced as Secretary of the Czechoslovak Communist Party by Alexander Dubček, a Slovak, and as President of Czechoslovakia in March by General Ludvik Svoboda, a hero on the Russian front in the Second World War as the leader of the Free Czechs. Oldrich Černík became Prime Minister and the new leaders were welcomed by Brezhnev. Their programme was 'The Czechoslovak Road to Socialism', their aim 'Socialism with a Human Face', liberalizing the regime Novotný had established. But they differed as to how far to go. Dubček himself had no thoughts of relaxing Communist Party control, though in favour of greater freedom, less rigid economic regulation and more contact with the West. He encouraged free expression, though he was less ready than Černík to abandon censorship completely. None of the leaders intended to leave the Warsaw Pact as Hungary had planned in 1956. The Czechoslovaks were nevertheless allowed unusual liberties during the so-called Prague Spring of 1968, and they responded excitedly with public assemblies and lively debate.

Such ferment alarmed Czechoslovakia's neighbours. Ulbricht in East Germany was especially worried, already feeling threatened by increasing contacts with West Germany. Brezhnev reminded Dubček of the need for discipline and uniformity, concerned that changes in Czechoslovakia might endanger the security of all eastern Europe. The Czechoslovaks tried to assert their loyalty to the USSR while arguing in support of liberties, but by July other Warsaw Pact countries (though not Romania) were alarmed enough to send a formal warning:

> The development of events in your country evokes deep anxiety. . . . We cannot agree to let hostile forces push your country off the road to socialism. . . . Anti-socialist and revisionist forces have laid hands on the press, radio and television . . . [and] a situation has thus arisen which is entirely unacceptable for a socialist country.

A month later, Warsaw Pact (but mainly Soviet) forces entered Czechoslovakia though condemned not only by Yugoslavia and Albania but also by Romania. UN censure was vetoed by the Soviets. It took time, however, to persuade the Czechoslovaks to come into line, though bloody confrontation was generally avoided. The Brezhnev Doctrine was asserted to justify the intervention, which the Soviet leader saw as an 'international duty' to preserve 'socialist solidarity' against counter-revolution engineered by the West. Many liberties were withdrawn but a new federal constitution was introduced to try to solve Czech–Slovak rivalries and buy goodwill. The Czechoslovak Communist Party, on the other hand, resisted changes in its leadership, as Dubček himself had often resisted Moscow's pressures upon him.

Early in 1969, however, Jan Palach, a student, publicly burned himself to death in protest at the intervention and, soon afterwards, Prague riotously celebrated a national ice-hockey victory over the Soviet Union. The Soviets could tolerate Dubček no longer and he was replaced as Secretary by Gustav Husák in April 1969. This was the key to Czechoslovakia's normalization, though Černik remained in office until 1970 and Svoboda, never much more than a figurehead, until 1975. Dubček was steadily downgraded, sent as ambassador to Turkey for a time and expelled from the Party in 1970. A series of political trials in 1972 combed out surviving 'right-wing opportunists' and removed the last traces of the liberal experiment.

Like Gomulka in Poland and Kádár in Hungary, Husák worked to combine conformity with reconciliation, gaining some advantage from his own past sufferings as a victim of Stalinist repression. Modest reform was introduced from time to time, for example in decentralizing economic management, but Husák's chief function was successfully to restore Czechoslovakia to stability. He retired at the end of 1987, aged 74. It is likely that Gorbachev regarded him as a leader in the Brezhnev mould who was unsympathetic to glasnost and perestroika and to the liberalization now wanted by younger members of the Czechoslovak Communist Party. The new Secretary was Milos Jakes whose age (65) suggested that his appointment would give the Party time to reconsider the way ahead but was not likely to be long-lasting. Jakes nevertheless echoed Gorbachev in criticizing corruption and inefficiency, though Dubček was not yet allowed to return to favour.

8.2.5 Persistent restlessness: Poland

The crises in East Germany, Hungary and Czechoslovakia were all followed by long periods of the stability and order that the Soviets most wanted in eastern Europe. Bulgaria remained loyal and orderly throughout, while Romania's ambitions for limited independence in foreign policy and economic development could be tolerated since Romania was geographically isolated from the West and no danger to Soviet security. Polish restlessness persistently worried the Soviets, however.

Gomulka's waning authority came to an end in 1970. When rioting broke out in the shipyards and other industrial centres against increases in food prices, workers were shot in Gdansk and Gdynia, martyrs well remembered in later outbreaks of unrest. Gomulka could not survive, and he was replaced by Edward Gierek who managed, with Soviet help, to hold prices down while presiding over impressive economic growth during the early 1970s, when annual growth rates ran ahead of those of most of Europe. But the Poles remained dissatisfied with the supply of consumer goods in spite of efforts to increase them. In 1976 Gierek faced renewed rioting, forcing him to abandon proposals to raise prices to take some account of the inflation now affecting much of the world. Artificially sustained by controls and subsidies, the Polish economy grew more unhealthy. Growth fell. Debts, owed mainly to the West, mounted and exports to help pay them led to shortages within Poland, including serious shortages of food.

To economic discontent was added a growing clamour for liberties, and the election in 1978 of a Polish cardinal as Pope John Paul II, the first non-Italian Pope for over 450 years, fired Polish nationalism as well as religious fervour. In 1979 John Paul added to the excitement with a visit to Poland, the first Pope to cross the Iron Curtain. Gierek could not contain the mounting criticisms of his government. Workers demanded trade unions free to bargain for higher wages and independent of government in the way of the capitalist world. Farmers demanded higher prices for their produce, though consumers did not want to pay them. A free trade-union movement, *Solidarność* ('Solidarity'), was founded in centres such as Gdansk and Szczecin, served by folk-heroes such as Lech Walesa, an electrician who combined religious devotion with industrial leadership and developing ambitions for political liberalization. Solidarity's membership grew to about ten million before it was banned, but not crushed, in 1982 and Walesa imprisoned. Rural Solidarity recruited half a million small farmers before it too was banned.

Gierek could not withstand the pressure: after a heart attack, he gave way to Stanislaw Kania in 1980. Events were now moving quickly, however, and in 1981 Kania was replaced by General Wojciech Jaruzelski who introduced martial law to curb the continuing strikes and demonstrations. Such dependence on the military rather than the Party was irregular, as well as extremely unusual, in the socialist world, but Poland had become a special case – of special concern to the Soviet Union because of its geographical position. Jaruzelski, with Polish military support, was preferred to active Soviet intervention, but the new leadership had to tread with great care when the time came in 1983 to begin to relax some of the emergency controls.

The Poles seemed to want to combine both the socialist and capitalist systems; they were optimistic but not entirely clear about how they might obtain the best of both worlds – such as prosperity and freedom without unemployment and deep social divisions. They showed no obvious intention of leaving the Warsaw Pact, though traditional hostility towards Russians linked up with fierce support for Roman Catholicism in the strong assertion of Poland's national identity. Cardinal Wyszyński died in a Warsaw hospital in 1981, to the end a symbol of resistance and inspiration. Lech Walesa, released from detention, was awarded the Nobel Peace Prize in 1983, adding to the embarrassment of the Polish authorities, who hoped support for Solidarity would wither away. Walesa's prize was for his services to human rights and efforts:

> to solve his country's problems through negotiations and co-operation without resorting to violence.

There had been comparatively little bloodshed during the many disturbances and, when he paid another visit to Poland in 1983, Pope John Paul urged reconciliation among Poles. Jaruzelski had already launched the Patriotic Movement for National Revival. Reconciliation and revival could not be expected without prolonged struggle, but there seemed on all sides a desire to restrain extremists and to avoid bloody confrontation. There were nevertheless further embarrassments for the authorities when in 1984 members of the security forces kidnapped and then murdered Father Jerzy Popieluszko, a popular priest and an outspoken supporter of Solidarity, in what seemed like some confusion over orders. By 1988 Jaruzelski's regime had become as precarious as those of his predecessors: Poland's foreign debt and declining economy had created insurmountable barriers to a reform programme which might win the backing of a resurgent Solidarity.

8.3 Different roads to socialism

8.3.1 Economic aspects

In 1955 Khrushchev visited Yugoslavia, beginning a process of reconciliation with Tito, whom he later described as 'always . . . a good Communist and a man of principle'. But Khrushchev was not much impressed by the less centralized planning Tito preferred to the Soviet system. Nevertheless, he cautiously agreed that there could be 'different roads to socialism' and that, in certain ways, the states of eastern Europe might differ from the USSR. Khrushchev, in fact, later came round to supporting decentralized planning, though he could not accept the Yugoslav workers' councils, a localized form of management he thought inefficient and mere 'window-dressing'. He also found merit in the tourist industry that Yugoslavia was encouraging and, gradually, almost all the states of eastern Europe turned to tourism as a means of earning foreign currency, though not all as readily as Yugoslavia and Romania.

The states of eastern Europe continued to have much in common, including not only close supervision by their respective communist parties under the system of people's democracy but also extensive economic planning and a high priority for social welfare. But they found increasing scope for differences in detail. Most states collectivized agriculture – Romania rather slowly, taking until 1962 to complete it; Bulgaria following the Soviet pattern eagerly; Poland making little headway at all before 1970 and only slow progress thereafter; and Yugoslavia turning back from collectives in favour of private smallholdings. At the same time, cautious experiment went on over the years as to how best to run regulated economies, matching similar debates in the Soviet Union. Tito leaned more towards centralized planning later in life, after economic difficulties had forced Yugoslavia to seek IMF help in the 1970s. Hungary at that time was travelling in the opposite direction, away from strict centralization. Kádár in the 1970s encouraged not only decentralization, but also bonuses, incentives and even profit-making. Workers had a say in the running of factories, and even trade unions had some similarities with those in the West.

Figure 8.2 and Table 8.1 show the relative wealth achieved by the states of

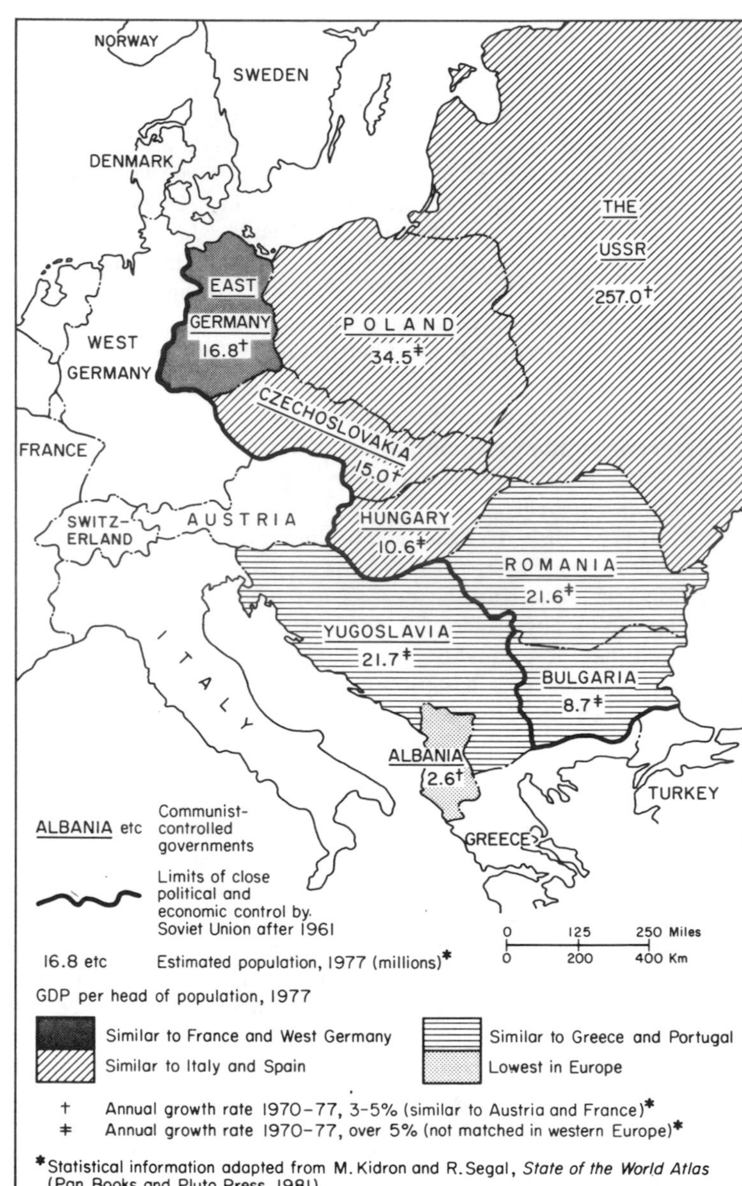

Fig. 8.2 Eastern Europe in the 1970s

Table 8.1 States in eastern Europe: some comparative statistics

State	Population		Income per head, 1983 (US dollars)*	Number of people per doctor, c. 1980	Percentage of population literate over age 15, c. 1980
	Estimated, 1985 (millions)	Annual growth, 1980–5 (%)			
Albania	3.0	2.1	930†	890	71
Bulgaria	9.0	0.3	2 920†	402	94
Czechoslovakia	15.6	0.3	5 690	293	99
East Germany	16.7	−0.3	5 300	494	100
Hungary	10.7	0.0	1 750	329	99
Poland	37.2	0.9	3 860	555	98
Romania	22.7	0.6	2 000	652	96
Soviet Union	277.5	1.0	2 590	258	100
Yugoslavia	23.3	0.8	1 710	673	84

* At current market prices † 1982

Statistics from *Encyclopaedia Britannica*

eastern Europe by the late 1970s and early 1980s. Except for Yugoslavia, they had at first been isolated from the economic upheavals in the rest of the world, but increased contacts with the West were part of the liberalization which followed the death of Stalin. In the 1970s general problems began to be felt in eastern Europe: Hungary began to feel the effects of inflation; Romania, once an oil producer, ran into fuel shortages and rationed petrol for tourists. Instances of unemployment began to occur in societies which had taken pride in avoiding it, even if this involved the uneconomic use of labour. Even East Germany incurred debts which led it to cut back on imports, though members of Comecon as a whole thirsted for Western technology which might increase their output, and for Western consumer goods which would increase their comfort. Romania had joined the World Bank and the IMF for these reasons even while remaining in Comecon.

In the difficult years of 1975 to 1983, however, all eastern-European states continued to increase their industrial production in spite of world recession, most of them steadily, though production stuttered in Hungary and faltered even more in Poland. This marginal progress could not be sustained, however; and by the late 1980s all the east-European economies, with the exception of East Germany, were either stagnant or experiencing falling levels of prosperity.

8.3.2 Political aspects

All the states of eastern Europe remained regulated societies. Ceausescu's independence from Moscow did not mean that the authorities within Romania were any less vigilant for signs of dissent, while Hoxha in Albania ruled even more fiercely. Even Tito took care to preserve his authority, the more difficult in Yugoslavia because of rivalries between the country's nationalities. A quarter of the Yugoslav people were Croats, generally more prosperous than the more numerous Serbs from whom they hoped to secede. From time to time the desire for secession led to active disturbances. Disorder was hated throughout eastern Europe so the authorities, while often seeking to avoid it by concessions, were ever ready with regular and irregular police forces to suppress it. Religious activity, though frowned on, was widely tolerated in the interests of peace, especially in Poland and Hungary, where Western books and other influences also circulated. But the champions of human rights who, like members of Charter '77 in Czechoslovakia, dared to speak out – especially after the Helsinki agreements of 1975 – were carefully isolated from the masses by a mixture of suppression and ridicule.

The systems of eastern Europe, like most systems in the world, were self-preserving. Propaganda, censorship and punishment were thorough when it mattered, and dissidents could make little headway within or outside the ranks of the authorities. Changes in leadership, notable for their infrequency, were usually smooth. In East Germany Ulbricht at last gave way in 1971 to Erich Honecker, only the second Party Secretary since independence, and in the way not uncommon in the people's democracies Honecker also became Head of State in 1976. Todor Zhivkov became Party Secretary in Bulgaria in 1954, remaining in office for the next 30 years to become (save for Hoxha) eastern

Table 8.2 The people's democracies: one-party states, 1986

	Ruling party or group	Voting strength in most recent election (%)
Soviet Union	Communist Party	99.9
Bulgaria	Fatherland Front (Communist Party; Agrarian Union; others)	99.9
Czechoslovakia	National Front	99.4
German Democratic Republic	National Front (Socialist Unity; others)	99.7
Hungary	Patriotic People's Front	97.6*
Poland	National Unity Front (United Workers Party; Peasants Party; Democrats; others)	99.0
Romania	Social Democracy and Unity Front	99.9
Albania	Communist (Labour) Party	99.9
Yugoslavia	League of Communists, and supporters	—

* There is a small Independent Party in Hungary.

Europe's eldest statesman, a man devoted to the Soviet Union. Under Zhivkov, Bulgaria developed major engineering industry and was no longer predominantly agricultural. Other long-serving statesmen preserved tranquillity in Hungary (Kádár) and Czechoslovakia (Husák) after the upheavals of 1956 and 1968 respectively, though the situation in Poland after Gierek remained uncertain in the 1980s. Jaruzelski remained, however, entering his seventh year in authority in 1988.

There was some uncertainty in Yugoslavia when Tito died in 1980. He had planned for collective leadership to pilot Yugoslavia through the probably difficult years after his death – leadership of the Party and the country's Presidency to be held separately by members of a nominated panel for yearly terms. The system worked during the first half of the 1980s, preserving the essentials of Titoism in spite of inflation, unemployment and separatist agitation. In 1982 the leadership appointed Milka Planinc to be Prime Minister. She was a Croat whose appointment might pacify a restless minority, though at that time and again in 1983 there was Serb unrest and a Muslim demand, backed by Albania, for the independence from Yugoslavia of Kosovo Province. Mrs Planinc survived in office until 1986 in spite of grave economic problems, unemployment topping a million and inflation reaching 80 per cent in 1985. However, Yugoslavia's ability to preserve itself came under increasing pressure in 1988, when renewed ethnic tensions culminated in a mass seizure of the state parliament by aggrieved Serbs.

Planinc was the first woman Prime Minister in socialist eastern Europe, where strong theoretical emphasis on equality between the sexes had done little to break the political stranglehold of men. As in the Soviet Union by the 1980s, it was also in the main a political stranglehold of old men with memories of the Second World War. They still dominated eastern Europe with a conservative anxiety to avoid reckless change and the violent disorders which seemed to affect so much of the world. Systems were unlikely to change quickly unless obliged to do so. Succeeding Hoxha as Secretary of the Albanian Communist Party, Ramiz Alia hastened to assert that there would be continuity and that nothing fundamental would be altered. Alia (aged 60), and two years later in Czechoslovakia Jakes, seemed still to represent the older generation of conservative leaders who would preserve existing systems as long as they could. But change, however cautious, seemed inevitable when the time came for younger men to take control. With the advancement of Gorbachev, the process seemed already to have begun in the Soviet Union, whose influence in eastern Europe remained strong. Change was in the air and Gorbachev in 1988 visited Yugoslavia in another effort to increase goodwill, and to confirm the possibility of 'different roads to socialism'.

UNIT 9

The USA's special bloc

9.1 The Americas

Geography provided the USA with a measure of isolation which was never available to the Soviet Union. The Atlantic and Pacific Oceans cushioned civilian Americans against the close involvement in two World Wars which the peoples of Europe and Asia could not escape. Further to preserve its security, the USA jealously guarded the American continent as a whole against what it considered alien and undesirable forces. Most citizens of the United States had long been convinced that the Americas were their very own special sphere of influence, important not only strategically but also as a vast area in which US economic interests could flourish almost unchallenged.

It was not unusual for governments in Washington to protest loudly about the abuse of human rights in the Soviet Union, eastern Europe and other parts of the communist world. They said far less about the denial of human rights to millions in the Americas, and far less too about the gross inequalities resulting from capitalist enterprise in much of Central and South America, where large-scale poverty persisted. In general, Washington used its influence to ensure that political regimes in Latin America remained anti-communist, and it interfered hardly at all where they were merely anti-humanitarian or downright corrupt, provided that US business interests were secure.

North of the USA, Canada struggled to preserve an individual identity based on its history, its membership of the Commonwealth and its own liberal international policies, though the unrelenting march of the Coca-Cola cans and other pressures from across the long border made it difficult to retain genuine economic independence from the USA. Canada, however, preserved the essentials of Western democratic government, many features of its constitution having been worked out when it was still a Dominion within the British Commonwealth of Nations. In practising democracy and respecting the rights of its minorities, from those of French descent (about a quarter of the population) to much smaller groups of Indians and Canadian Eskimo, Canada's record was at least equal to that of the USA. Canadians as a whole, moreover, were almost as wealthy as the people of the USA.

To the south of the USA, almost all the mainland American republics had once been in the Spanish Empire (Brazil had been part of the Portuguese Empire) before winning independence in the early nineteenth century. Spain and Portugal had left them with a firmly rooted Roman Catholic Church, deep social divisions and widespread poverty, but with no strong traditions of representative government or progressive thinking. By 1945 democracy had, in almost all cases, made even less progress than had industrialization, and most states continued to protect such vested interests as those of landlords, businesses, the military and perhaps the Church, more zealously than the interests of the masses.

The Caribbean islands are much smaller than most of the mainland states. In 1945 some of them - along with British Honduras, British Guiana, French Guiana and Dutch Guiana on the mainland - had still to gain their independence from old European colonial empires (see sections 14.3, 15.1 and 15.2). Most others had been Spanish but, like Cuba and the Dominican Republic, were now independent. The USA had taken Puerto Rico from Spain in 1898 and later bought the Virgin Islands from Denmark. Haiti, formerly Spanish, then French, then independent in 1804, had achieved the reputation of being one of the poorest and least progressive countries in the world.

As early as the Monroe Doctrine of 1823, when the Spanish Empire was crumbling, the USA had warned Europeans not to attempt further colonization in the Americas. After that the USA grew more ambitious, claiming policing rights to keep Latin America in order, receptive to US business and financial activity, and sometimes intervening openly to set in authority what Woodrow Wilson, US President from 1913 to 1919, called 'good men'. Early twentieth-century Presidents were ready enough to use the 'Big Stick' (a display of force) to bring about compliance with the wishes of Washington: Wilson himself sent troops to the Dominican Republic and Haiti as well as chastizing Mexico. US governments also practised 'Dollar Diplomacy', using their wealth to shape events, though Presidents Hoover and F.D. Roosevelt in the 1930s preferred to act as 'Good Neighbors', seeking more willing agreement. The influence of the USA nevertheless remained strong. All the republics quickly rallied to the USA in the Second World War, except Argentina and Chile, and they too came into line before it ended.

After the war most of the republics continued to endure formidable economic and social problems, made worse by population growth faster than elsewhere in the world. The well-to-do tended to look to rule by the military to protect their interests; the poor and downtrodden were often tempted by thoughts of revolution. Ernesto 'Che' Guevara, an Argentinian, became a revolutionary when he saw how Eisenhower's government in 1954 protected the interests of the United Fruit Company in Guatemala. Americans through the CIA (Central Intelligence Agency[G]) helped to overthrow Guatemala's reforming socialist government, an elected one, in favour of a right-wing regime willing to preserve the status quo, whatever its injustices. Guevara helped Fidel Castro seize power in Cuba, to establish a socialist state there (see section 10.1), but he was then drawn to the desperately underprivileged masses

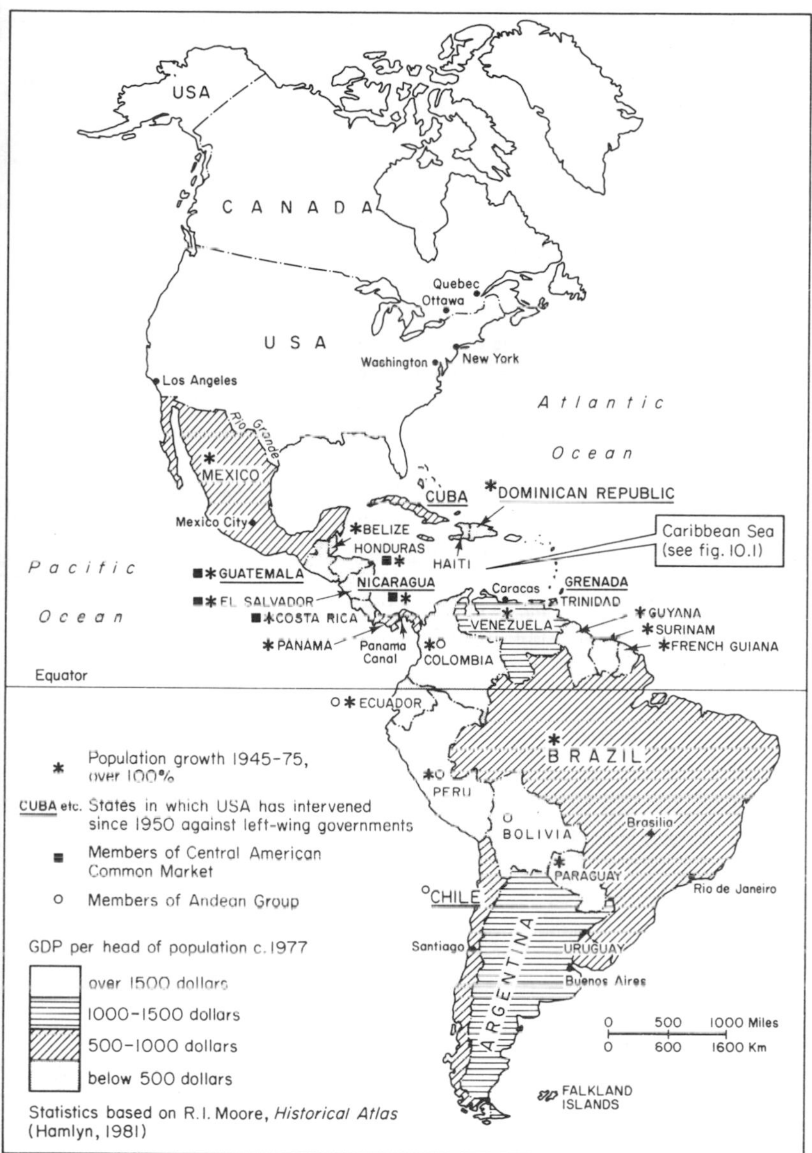

Fig. 9.1 The Americas since 1950

of the mainland, hoping for a Maoist peasant revolution like that in China to liberate them. He went to Bolivia to fight for the poverty-stricken tin-miners but in 1967 was captured and killed by the Bolivian army, at that time the tool of the country's dictator, General Barrientos, one of South America's many military rulers.

Such governments were seldom disturbed by the USA, which gained the reputation of preferring the status quo to social justice, and hard-line authoritarianism to democracy - at least when US interests, economic and strategic, were involved. There was no lack of would-be dictators in Latin America in the 40 years after the Second World War. Trujillo in the Dominican Republic, Batistá in Cuba and Duvalier in Haiti disfigured the Caribbean. Perón in Argentina, Jiménez in Venezuela, Somoza in Nicaragua and Pinochet in Chile were some of the many who imposed strong-arm rule on the mainland.

It was by no means only US businesses, looking for commercial privileges, cheap raw materials, cheap labour and healthy profits, which created the problems of Latin America. The republics themselves lacked the capital, the expertise and often the stability to make rapid headway. Their geographical position was a further handicap, denying them complete freedom to work out their own problems. The USA built well-meaning alliances with them and from time to time promoted generous aid programmes (see section 9.4), but every step forward in liberal terms was matched by heavy-handed intervention by the US government and the ubiquitous CIA. John F. Kennedy in 1958 asserted:

> The objective of our aid programme in Latin America should not be to purchase allies, but to consolidate a free and democratic Western Hemisphere, alleviating those conditions which might foster opportunities for communistic infiltration and uniting our peoples on the basis of . . . constantly increasing living standards.

Aid assisted many in Latin America, but there were millions who saw speeches such as Kennedy's as little more than the rhetoric of Washington politicians serving US interests.

9.2 The USA's immediate neighbours: Canada and Mexico compared

9.2.1 Economies and societies

Mexico's gross domestic product (GDP) per head of the population in the 1970s was still less than a quarter of Canada's and less than a fifth of the USA's. Mexico was nevertheless more prosperous than many of the states to the south and east of it, in Central and South America and in the Caribbean. Industrialization and urbanization had grown dramatically during the Second World War, but Mexico still lagged well behind North America, lacking the capital and expertise for the economic and social development which might begin to close the wealth gap. Though much smaller in area then Canada, Mexico had a population three times larger (over 70 million by the early 1980s): in common with that of much of Latin America, it had risen rapidly since 1945, increasing at an annual rate of about 3.5 per cent in the 1950s and not falling below three per cent until the 1980s. Illiteracy was also a problem: when a new education campaign was launched in 1944 half the population was illiterate, and almost one in five adult Mexicans were still illiterate in the early 1980s – though by then the country had fifteen million children in primary schools, nearly four million in secondary schools and about a million in higher education.

Oil reserves helped finance such social expansion, lifting Mexico, like Venezuela, above the poorest American states. But like other oil-producers, Mexico tended to rely too heavily on oil exports to have a balanced economy. Moreover, the country received only some of the benefits of an oil-based economy. Private capital tended to be drawn northwards into the United States, especially when US interest rates were attractive. Like many less developed countries, Mexico borrowed heavily to finance what development there was, becoming deeply enmeshed in debt by the 1980s and heavily burdened with interest payments. Social reform to lessen inequalities and to raise living standards for the poor came only slowly. Mexico spent an even smaller proportion of its GDP on welfare schemes than the USA, in contrast to Canada, which soon surpassed its southern neighbour. Wide differences in wealth persisted between Mexican citizens.

Canada's economy was well developed, in line with that of the USA and much of Europe. By the 1950s Canada had become a major industrial country. It too was an oil-producer, but oil was not allowed to distort the national economy. Canada suffered its share of booms and slumps, of course, in common with the rest of the capitalist world, running into the persistent inflation and high unemployment of the 1970s and 1980s (see section 21.1). Unemployment affected over ten per cent of the working population in the depths of the recession, but Canada – with a much lower birth rate – did not have Mexico's population pressures.

Both Canada and Mexico were bound to be acutely aware of their powerful neighbour. For many Mexicans, the wealth of the USA was a standing temptation to try to move northwards. The USA fought a long campaign against the illegal immigration of the 'wetbacks', who swam into the USA across the Rio Grande. But there were US citizens with a vested interest in the cheap labour they could extract from illegal immigrants hoping to avoid detection who, having experienced poverty in Mexico, were even less likely to complain of exploitation.

For the Canadian and Mexican authorities there was a shared problem of resisting the dominance of US business interests. The majority, and the most powerful, of the world's transnational companies were US-based, and as early as 1938 Mexico had taken the precaution of nationalizing its oil industry – to the frustration of US companies. Even so, US investment in Mexico had much increased during the Second World War, and it soared in Canada after about 1950. As Table 9.1 shows, the economies of North America were bound to be intertwined with the USA – it was the main supplier and customer of both Canada and Mexico, and for the latter also especially important as a financier.

Table 9.1 Trade in the Americas, 1980

Country *(Estimated population, millions)	Main exports (% of total)	Main export market (% of total)	Main supplier (imports) (% of total)
North and Central America			
Canada† (23.9)	Vehicles 17 Machinery 10	USA 68	USA 73
USA (226.5)	Machinery 25 Chemicals 15	Canada 18	Canada 18
Mexico (67.4)	Crude oil 60	USA 63	USA 66
Guatemala (7.3)	Coffee 30	USA 27	USA 35
Honduras (3.7)	Bananas 27 Coffee 25	USA 52	USA 42
El Salvador§ (4.8)	Coffee 58	West Germany 22	USA 25 Guatemala 25
Nicaragua (2.7)	Coffee 42	USA 39	USA 27
Costa Rica	Bananas 24 Coffee 23	USA 33	USA 33
Panama (1.8)	Bananas 22	USA 49	USA 34
The Caribbean			
Cuba (9.7)	Sugar 84	Soviet Union 64	Soviet Union 58
Jamaica† (2.2)	Alumina and bauxite 78	USA 37	USA 32
Haiti‖ (5.0)	Coffee 39	USA 59	USA 45
Dominican Republic (5.4)	Sugar 45	USA 46	USA 45
Puerto Rico‡ (3.2)	Chemicals 32	USA 82	USA 61
Trinidad and Tobago† (1.1)	Petroleum and crude oil 92	USA 57	Saudi Arabia 31 USA 26
South America			
Colombia§ (27.3)	Coffee 49	USA 23	USA 34
Venezuela (14.0)	Petroleum and crude oil 96	USA 28	USA 48
Ecuador (8.4)	Crude oil 52	USA 31	USA 38
Peru (17.8)	Petroleum products 21	USA 34	USA 37
Brazil (123.0)	Coffee 14 Soya 12	USA 17	USA 19 Iraq 16
Bolivia§ (5.6)	Natural gas 46 Tin 33	Argentina 36	USA 28
Chile (11.1)	Copper 46	USA 15 Japan 11	USA 21
Paraguay (3.1)	Cotton 34	Argentina 24	Brazil 24 Argentina 22
Uruguay (2.9)	Wool and meat 28	Brazil 18 Argentina 13	Brazil 17
Argentina (27.9)	Meat 12 Wheat 10	Soviet Union 20	USA 23

* One million inhabitants and over
† Member of the Commonwealth
‡ Dependency of the USA
§ Trade figures, 1981
‖ Trade figures, 1978

Source: *Encyclopaedia Britannica*

Canadians spent more of their annual GDP on welfare than their North American neighbours, and social inequalities were generally less marked than in Mexico. However, Canada had an awkward minority problem. Twenty-five per cent of Canadians were French-speaking, living mainly around Quebec, and some of them were bitterly resentful of what seemed like English-speaking dominance. A French separatist movement under René Levesque attracted fluctuating support, achieving great publicity in 1967 when de Gaulle, the visiting French President, uttered the ill-judged cry of '*Québec libre*'. A free and independent Quebec would be a French-speaking and largely Roman Catholic island in a predominantly English-speaking, Protestant northern part of the continent. It would weaken Canada, perhaps undermining its ability to remain separate from the USA. Successive Canadian governments struggled to pacify the separatist Quebec Party, though economic difficulties in the 1970s seemed only to increase its appeal. Prime Minister Pierre Trudeau, himself of French descent, granted safeguards concerning language and culture, with increased political influence for French Canadians at both federal and provincial levels. This helped to stem the tide, preserving national unity into the 1980s. One further result of the agitation of French Canadians was a more general awareness of, and an attempt to improve, minority rights - including those of the aboriginal American Indian and Innuit (Eskimo) people, who together formed less than two per cent of Canada's population.

Mexico's population was nearly one third Amerindian, the majority of Mexicans being *mestizo* - of mixed Spanish and Amerindian descent. In rural areas, the people remained deeply conservative; elsewhere, the slowness of social change led to student unrest, which joined hands in the 1960s with that in the USA and much of Europe, winning publicity with some violent confrontations during the Olympic Games in Mexico City in 1968. Afterwards, student unrest continued in Mexico, expressing disapproval both of the generally slow reduction of inequalities and of recurring corruption in high places.

9.2.2 Politics and policy

Student unrest in Mexico was increased by the awareness that the Institutional Revolutionary Party (PRI), while dominating the country's politics, promised far more revolutionary change than it delivered. The Mexican constitution gave the elected President strong powers, stronger than those of the US President. The PRI regularly won the Presidency and dominated Congress. There were liberal and conservative factions within the PRI, providing some political debate, but the impact of opposition parties was very limited. The system provided a stability which many other developing countries might envy, but most governments proved cautious and rather authoritarian.

One of their chief concerns was economic development, where Miguel Alemán (President 1946–52) set the pattern, combining it with very modest social reform. His successor, Adolfo Cortines (1952–8), granted the vote to Mexican women and launched an attack on corruption - a recurring theme to which President Miguel de la Madrid Hurtado found it necessary to return when elected as late as 1982. López Mateos (1958–62) moved more to the left than was usual for Mexican Presidents, responding to unrest in impoverished rural areas by reviving pre-war policies for redistributing land to the benefit of smallholders. Diaz Órdaz (1964–70) made some effort to continue the reform but met the student unrest of 1968 with vigorous police action. Echeverria Álvarez (1970–76) and López Portillo (1976–82) continued the tradition of firm government with a concern for the economy; public investment and state action were not unusual, partly to deter US involvement. Mexican railways were nationalized in 1970, for example. Echeverria also made efforts to transfer more land to the poor.

Mexico nevertheless had its share of the unrest, and even of the terrorism, which grew widespread in the world. The policy of successive Mexican Presidents to crack down on disorders met with approval in the United States. The Presidents also tried to please Washington by implementing the cutbacks in spending demanded from time to time by the IMF, running - as far as was possible amidst the economic crises which affected the West - an orderly house. In spite of the difficulties common to developing nations, Mexico therefore remained comparatively tranquil, and the USA saw no reason to attempt here the more dramatic interventions it undertook elsewhere (see Unit 10).

Canada practised a more genuine democracy than that of Mexico, but even so, the Liberal Party dominated government for long periods, only briefly interrupted by Conservative rule. Canada was a federal state like the USA, but its parliamentary system was like Britain's - the Prime Minister leading the elected government. The British monarch continued to act as the Canadian head of state, though it was a role with little effective power.

The Liberals held power in Canada from 1935 to 1957, regularly re-elected, first under Mackenzie King, veteran statesman of the British Commonwealth of Nations, and then under Louis St Laurent. John Diefenbaker led Conservative governments from 1957 to 1963, but the Liberals returned in 1963 under Lester Pearson, continuing from 1968 under Pierre Trudeau. Save for a brief Conservative interlude in 1979–80, Trudeau remained in power until he retired in 1984. The socialist New Democratic Party failed to break the Liberal–Conservative alternation in power, although by the late 1980s its performance in opinion polls presaged a possible realignment in Canadian politics. However, socialists in Canada, in common with their counterparts in the USA, remained a minority, but most Canadian politicians were moderates who sought to combine a mainly capitalist economy with a socially just society. Voters tended to be influenced by their leaders' skills in management, though they were sometimes influenced by personalities and, at least in turning to Diefenbaker in 1957, by anti-Americanism. They hoped that the Conservatives could reduce US influence on Canada and strengthen the country's Commonwealth ties with Britain.

Americanization was a matter on which Canadians remained sensitive. All Canada's Prime Ministers aimed to pursue distinctive Canadian policies at home and abroad. But even Diefenbaker could not reduce Canada's reliance on the USA for trade, though he did actively promote Commonwealth developments such as the introduction of Commonwealth Assistance Loans and scholarships. Like other Canadian leaders, he encouraged the Commonwealth to grow into a multiracial association. He condemned apartheid in South Africa and was not sorry to see the latter leave the Commonwealth. St Laurent had already pledged Canada to backing the Colombo Plan for development in south and south-east Asia, and subsequent Canadian Prime Ministers continued to support both the Commonwealth and its poorer members in the Caribbean, India, Pakistan and Africa. Canada won a reputation for being liberal and forward-looking in its international relations. Cynics sometimes suggested that Canadians saw the Commonwealth as a refuge from the USA which was not entitled to join it (see sections 14.2 and 14.4). It was not surprising that the first Secretary-General of the Commonwealth, Arnold Smith, was a Canadian. But membership of NATO was just one of the many ways in which Canada inevitably had to follow its neighbour's lead, whatever misgivings the Canadians might have.

Lester Pearson's interest in international affairs centred on the United Nations. Before becoming Prime Minister in 1963 he had been a diplomat and had helped set up the UN. When he stepped down from Canadian politics he went on serving the UN, and campaigned for assistance for the world's poorer nations.

Perhaps the most colourful of Canada's Prime Ministers, however, was Pierre Trudeau. His long period in office ended in a sharp decline in popularity, though he had retained much of the athleticism and vigour which had kept him in the public eye. He gave Canada generous social-security provision, especially for the unemployed, and he bridged the gap between the French community and the rest of Canada with his policy of 'one Canada with two official languages'. Constitutional changes brought guarantees of wide-ranging human rights; they also loosened the ties with Britain, though Canada stopped short of becoming a republic. Trudeau led Canada in difficult years, however. Like many other national leaders he had to remind his people that, while they grew richer, they must also be prepared to face economic problems, unpalatable realities and periods of austerity. In the crisis of 1975 he said:

> We must accomplish nothing less than a wrenching adjustment of our expectations – an adjustment of our national lifestyle to our means.

Inflation, unemployment and growing national debt combined with personality clashes to weaken Trudeau's appeal. The Conservatives were too weak in 1979 to take a firm grip, but when Trudeau retired in his mid-60s six years later the Liberal Party seemed much less secure than it had for many years. Canada seemed to be nearing the end of an era. The Progressive Conservative Party convincingly won the general election in September 1984, barely two months after Trudeau stepped down, winning 211 out of 282 seats in the Canadian House of Commons. Brian Mulroney became Canada's Conservative Prime Minister, though scandals and economic disappointments soon began to undermine the popularity of what some Canadians had called 'new beginnings' after the Trudeau years. However, the Liberals were not able to capitalize upon the mid-term unpopularity of the Mulroney administration, and by 1988

Canadian party politics was more unpredictable than at any time since 1945. Later that year Mulroney won a second term of office for the Conservatives, albeit with a considerably reduced majority, having been aided by divisions in the ranks of the opposition. The key issue in the election was a free-trade agreement recently signed between Canada and the USA. Despite Mulroney's victory, most Canadians remained worried that the treaty had left Canada wide open to American cultural and economic domination.

9.3 The house in order: Latin American republics

9.3.1 Brazil

Brazil is the largest Latin American republic both in area and in population, the latter having doubled between 1920 and 1955 from 30 million to 60 million, and doubled again by 1980 to 120 million. Industrial development went on quite successfully in the post-war period, though Brazil – like Mexico and other developing countries – was handicapped by lack of capital. Only in the early 1980s did machinery and vehicles begin to rival coffee and other agricultural produce among the country's main exports. Governments actively promoted economic development, seeking to exploit Brazil's rich deposits of industrial minerals, such as iron and manganese, and to diversify the economy. United States help proved valuable and, especially in the 1970s, Brazil had rates of growth far above the world average. Brazilian governments were nevertheless wary of outside investment: many industries were nationalized – oil in 1953, for example – but even so US businesses invested heavily in the country. By the mid-1980s Brazil had the largest external debt (total debts to foreign creditors) of any country in the world (see section 21.1).

The constitution of 1946 restricted the electorate by excluding the many illiterate, but it granted Brazil the trappings of Western democracy. Political parties existed, including at times a Communist Party. The size and regional differences of Brazil also required that its organization should be federal, a 'United States of Brazil', but federalism like democracy itself worked only fitfully. Central government, and particularly the President, wielded great power, which in the case of the President sometimes bordered on dictatorship. Meanwhile, powerful groups such as the army, the guarantor of the constitution, readily interfered to protect their own interests. Post-war political parties were divided and fragmented, too, and the election of Presidents often owed more to personality and sectional interests than to party loyalties. It was therefore difficult to set up a stable democracy.

Democratic freedoms existed precariously, when they existed at all, and the living conditions and well-being of the Brazilian people varied widely. In cities such as Rio de Janeiro great wealth coexisted with shanty-town squalor, while in many rural areas the masses lived in poverty though landlords prospered. Illiteracy remained a serious obstacle to an effective social and economic programme, in spite of marked progress in higher education and the introduction into Brazil of advanced industrial technology including, as in Mexico and Argentina, nuclear power stations. Programmes of social improvement tended to benefit urban workers more than peasants. Some changes were spectacular, President Kubitschek for example founding the futuristic city of Brasilia, Brazil's capital from 1960. But like many developing countries and much of Latin America, Brazil was a land of contrasts, renowned for its colourful extravaganzas like Carnival and its prowess in football, while behind them lurked murky areas of tyranny and poverty.

Getúlio Vargas, ruling as a fascist-like dictator from 1937 to his overthrow in 1945, took many of his ideas from Salazar. (Portuguese-speaking, Brazil still owed some of its characteristics to Portugal itself.) The next President, General Dutra, achieved a measure of democracy to go with the new constitution, though he outlawed the Communist Party. Partly because of economic difficulties, Vargas was restored in 1951 but he was now less forceful and committed suicide in 1954, amid widespread complaints of corruption. Juscelino Kubitschek won the election of 1955. Brasilia was not his only ambitious project and some rapid development was achieved at the cost of inflation, external debt and further charges of corruption. Conservative forces secured the election of Jânio Quadro as President from 1961 but he resigned within the year, protesting at intrigue which made effective rule impossible.

In an effort to stabilize the system, changes were made to increase parliamentary power and to raise the office of Prime Minister above that of President. But when that produced a new deadlock presidential power was restored in the hands of João Goulart. Inflation continued to soar while divisions almost paralysed government. Perhaps in an attempt to counter conservative and military influences, Goulart leaned towards the urban workers and trade unions and even seemed to encourage communist activity. Plot and counter-plot brought civil war nearer. The military intervened decisively and Goulart fled in April 1964.

Brazil thus began a long period of military rule, the army leaders undertaking a programme for national revival which involved purging the corrupt and the left-wing, especially communists, and seeking to steady the economy by austerity. The constitution was modified and Kubitschek, Quadro and Goulart were deprived of their political rights. Political parties were reorganized and reduced to only two: the right-wing ARENA (the Alliance for National Renewal) was favoured by the Generals over a selected moderate opposition party. For the next twenty years Brazil was ruled by a narrow élite, sponsored by the military. The system was even more centralized than under Vargas and during the 1970s it grew harsh and authoritarian. The Catholic Church, once a support of the establishment, was now developing as the country's social conscience, criticizing the military for its neglect of Brazil's inequalities and of welfare and human rights.

In 1979 the new President was General João Baptista da Figuerido whose intention was to bring Brazil to 'genuine democracy'. He granted an amnesty to exiles, and elections were held in 1982 at which five parties won seats in parliament. The Social Democrats, a centre party sponsored by da Figuerido's military government, won most seats though not an overall majority. Economic crises and demands from the IMF for further austerity in debt-ridden

Brazil led to unrest, creating a difficult climate in which to return to civilian rule and democracy. Military rule had not got rid of corruption, either, and there was now open hatred of its repressiveness and the resultant social stagnation. The army nevertheless began to relax its hold.

In 1985 an electoral college chose Tancredo Neves as the new civilian President, a popular Social Democrat with an honourable record of opposition to the military. Neves quickly came to embody the people's hopes for the future but there was a further setback. Before he could even take up office Neves underwent several severe operations, the last of which he did not survive. Rumours circulated that he had been murdered and his deputy, Jose Sarney, was left to carry on in even more difficult circumstances, grappling with annual inflation of over 200 per cent and massive debt. Sarney was helped by a steady growth in output, but his Presidency was turbulent. Parliament shortened his term in office to four years and decided there would be new elections towards the end of 1988.

9.3.2 Argentina

Population pressures in Argentina were less acute than in Brazil. From 16 million in 1947, the population grew to 20 million in 1960 and 30 million in 1984. More than was usual in Latin America, Argentinians tended to live in towns and cities but, even so, the main exports in the 1980s were still meat, grain and other agricultural produce from Argentina's large, rich farmlands. Living standards generally compared favourably with Brazil's, partly because of one of the highest literacy levels in Latin America and partly because of the extensive social programmes of the Perón government soon after the Second World War. With a health and hospitals programme, Perón also helped Argentina towards one of the highest levels of life expectancy in the Americas, not far behind that of Canada. Fascist sympathies meant that Argentina had joined the USA and the Allies only very late in the Second World War, and neutrality had given the country advantages, allowing it to reap commercial benefits as well as building its industries.

What Argentina lacked, however, was a strong democratic base. The federal constitution was modelled on that of the USA and the wide electorate from 1947 included women. But in practice, political life after 1945 seemed to revolve mainly around military interventions and dictatorships and the strongly personal rule of Juan Domingo Perón and his wives.

Perón himself was an army officer who took part in a coup in 1943 and became Minister of Labour, then rising within governing circles to become Argentina's elected President in 1946. Washington tried to discredit him by publicizing his wartime sympathies with the Axis powers, but the results were counter-productive: Argentinians supported him all the more in defiance of US meddling. Perón was a populist and a nationalist. His ideas were a mixture of fascist and socialist, and his wife Eva ('Evita') helped him to consolidate his reputation as a champion of the underprivileged – Argentina's *descamisados* or 'shirtless ones'. For a time, Argentina seemed to prosper in their hands. Social reform with some redistribution of wealth (though conspicuously few transfers of land to smallholders), strong economic management with an active state sector and nationalization, and the goodwill of trade unions and the Catholic Church helped towards Perón's re-election in 1951. When he met with resistance, however, he was always ready to use force, including the army, and the elections of 1951 were marred by the harassment of opponents.

A new constitution in 1949 formally laid down that:

> the state may intervene in the economy and monopolize any given activity to safeguard the general interest.

Perón used this authority to control Argentina's trade through the Argentine Trade Promotion Institute, and he used that control to buy cheaply from Argentina's farmers to sell expensively in export markets. The profits helped to finance industrialization and reform for the benefit of the urban poor. Eva Perón developed ambitious programmes to improve housing, expand education and health services, and to maintain high levels of employment while entrenching her own popularity as head of the Perónista feminist wing. When she died in 1952, Argentina was developing advanced social-security provision, with benefits and pensions on the lines of those in Britain. But Perón's effects on agriculture and the rural communities was damaging. The economy deteriorated in the 1950s, undermined in part by inflated wages in industry.

Part of Perón's appeal lay in his strong nationalism. Argentinian independence was stressed, and foreign-owned enterprises such as the largely British-owned railways were taken over, though they were usually bought out rather than merely seized by Perón's government. When Eva died, however, Perón seemed to lose his way, and began to be accused of favouring business and capitalism, and even of pandering to Washington. The halting of wage increases angered the shirtless ones, while the Church was angered by moves towards legalizing divorce and prostitution. Corruption and repression seemed suddenly more irksome, and there was dismay when the nationalist Perón allowed Standard Oil, of California, privileges to exploit Argentinian oil.

A military coup 'in defence of Catholic Christianity' in 1955 forced Perón into exile. After a brief military dictatorship, civilian rule was restored in 1958 when Arturo Frondizi and the Radicals won the elections with promises of vigorous left-wing government. But they brought in foreign oil companies, imposed restrictive economic policies to please the IMF and lost the goodwill of many Argentinians, especially the Perónistas whose hope was to bring back Perón himself. Revolution lurked below the surface, and in 1962 the army seized power again. An attempt at civilian rule was made a year later, however, lasting under Arturo Illia until 1966. Illia won popularity by removing US oil companies but there were too many economic problems and too much social tension for comfort. The army stepped in yet again, to administer a further dose of discipline to the Argentinian people, especially to students, trade unionists and the shirtless ones.

Perón was at last allowed back into Argentina in 1973. The poor had suffered greatly during the economic crises of the last twenty years and, when the military allowed his election, they looked to Perón as a saviour. He won more than 60 per cent of the vote in a turbulent election, taking office as President with Maria ('Isabelita'), his third wife, as Vice-President. The redistribution of wealth in favour of the poor was one of Perón's priorities, though a purge of Marxists was one of his first actions. He was now 78 years old, however, and he died within a year of taking office. Maria took over the Presidency but could do little to avert mounting economic crises or to curb widespread violence. Among other problems she faced a left-wing guerilla campaign by the *Montoneros*, who were well aware that she was no Evita. Inflation rose above an annual rate of 600 per cent and even the trade unions, strong Perón supporters, began to desert the President. The pattern which by now seemed inevitable was repeated: the army ousted Maria Perón in March 1976. Since the death of her husband 21 months earlier, 1700 Argentinians had been killed in political violence.

Now led by Lieutenant General Jorge Videla, the military aimed to restore order and – with the help of the IMF and the USA – economic stability, cutting back debt and inflation. Their rule was harsh, and Argentina's record became scandalous for the number of 'disappeared ones', the victims of right-wing death squads operating with or without official approval. President Carter of the USA was among those who protested at the disregard of human rights, though his successor Reagan commended the Generals' anti-communism. The military now ruled Argentina for seven years, Videla giving way to General Roberto Viola who, in turn, was overthrown in 1981 by General Leopoldo Galtieri. It was Galtieri who, carried away by nationalist enthusiasm, launched the ill-judged invasion of the Falkland Islands (which Argentina called the Malvinas) in 1982, provoking armed confrontation with Britain (see section 14.3.6). Disaster there led to Galtieri's replacement by Major General Reynaldo Bignone, and it was Bignone who in 1983 at last returned Argentina to civilian government.

Elections in 1983 made Raúl Alfonsín President at the head of a Radical administration in preference to the Perónistas, partly because Maria Perón remained in Spain. Alfonsin had to continue the struggle with the Argentinian economy, negotiating with the IMF and banks in the USA and elsewhere to reschedule debts. Inflation still ran at over 300 per cent during 1983 and output was still faltering. By 1985, inflation reached 1000 per cent and the President imposed a dramatic freeze on prices and wages. Economic results could well have threatened the success of Argentina's return to democracy, but Alfonsin himself was committed to maintaining civilized government. He meant to pursue the issue of human rights, investigating the 'dirty war' the military had waged against dissidents. Nine military leaders were brought to trial, including Generals Videla and Viola who were found guilty and imprisoned. Galtieri was acquitted of responsibility for the dirty war but sentenced to twelve years in jail for starting, and losing, the Falklands War. Alfonsin's success in institutionalizing democracy would be tested in the next Presidential contest. Carlos Saul Menem, a Perónist was widely expected to defeat Eduardo Angeloz of the Radicals, and was not a pleasing prospect for the military.

9.3.3 Peru

The population of Peru, like that of its neighbours, almost doubled in the period 1961–86, from ten to twenty million. Almost half of the population was of Amerindian descent, and in the 1970s Quechua became an official language alongside Spanish. Peru's parliamentary constitution dated from 1856 but power rested with the landed, the military, the rich and the white who used it to preserve a rather narrow oligarchy[G]. After 1945, as Peru's economy expanded and the pace of change began to quicken, the middle and labouring classes looked for a share in power and the benefits it might bring, such as better education, higher standards of living and greater opportunity. APRA (the Popular Revolutionary Alliance) won some electoral success, but a period of political confusion ended in a military coup in 1948 when General Manuel Odria became Peru's President.

Odria's regime brought economic development, aided by the USA, and his dictatorial rule was eventually relaxed with the holding of new presidential elections in 1956. Odria gave way to Manuel Prado y Ugarteche, a representative of Peru's traditional élite but a President enlightened enough to re-legalize APRA which had widespread support among the masses. Tension continued, however, since the left wanted fundamental reforms that Prado had no wish to concede. The army intervened again to preserve Peru's stability, and not until elections in 1963 was a Popular Action (AP) Party government under President Fernando Belaúnde allowed into power, staunchly Catholic and committed to reform. The army intervened again in 1968, however, setting up the military rule of General Juan Velasco to slow the pace of change and preserve privilege. It was Velasco's government, nevertheless, which nationalized the oilfields that were now vital to Peru's economy – though this angered US oil-financiers in the former International Petroleum Company and moved Peru to the left.

General Morales Bermúdez replaced Velasco in 1975 and began cautiously to restore Peruvian democracy. When elections in 1980 showed firm support for Belaúnde and the AP, Bermúdez handed over the Presidency. APRA provided the main parliamentary Opposition, and Peru now enjoyed a further period of constitutional rule under a government considerably more reformist than most of its predecessors.

The country's zest for democracy had survived the repeated interventions of the military, while, as Table 10.1 shows, Peru had since 1945 held its own in the economic and social development of Latin America. Like most Latin Americans, however, Peruvians struggled to finance the modernization so greatly needed, and difficulties in marketing exports increased Peru's burden of debt in the 1970s and 1980s. Frustration fuelled non-democratic forces, and Belaúnde had also to struggle with the problem of Maoist guerillas whose revolutionary Shining Path movement threatened to undermine his government and to provoke the military into further political intervention. But Belaúnde survived to fight elections in 1985, and power was handed over democratically to Peru's new President, Alan Garcia Pérez, and to APRA. For the moment, at least, constitutional rule continued.

9.3.4 Contrasts: Bolivia and Venezuela

Bolivia and Venezuela represented, respectively, one of the poorest states in Latin America and one of the richest. Venezuela's wealth lay in its oil: not only was it a founder-member of the Organization of Petroleum Exporting Countries (OPEC), but OPEC was in fact born at a meeting in 1960 in Caracas, Venezuela's capital. Oil wealth was slow to reach many of the country's people but they were better off than those in Bolivia. Bolivia too had its resources, large deposits of tin and natural gas, but industrial development other than mineral extraction remained low. About half of Bolivia's six million people in the early 1980s were Amerindian, a group traditionally amongst the poorest in Latin America, many living in almost feudal conditions and few speaking the official language, Spanish. Of some fifteen million in Venezuela, on the other hand, only about 50 000 were Amerindian. Moreover, Venezuela's geographical position, fronting the Caribbean, compared favourably with that of landlocked Bolivia.

Differing levels of development were reflected in the countries' politics. Bolivia was ill-favoured - one of the reasons 'Che' Guevara chose it for his attempted revolution in the 1960s. The military, landlords and tin-mine owners (both of which had vested interests) and the National Revolutionary Movement (MNR) jostled for power. Not much room was left for democratic practices, though elections were held from time to time. Violence was not unusual. The fascist sympathizer Major Gualberto Villaroel was deposed and lynched in 1946, but not until 1952 was there a genuinely reforming President, the MNR then installing Victor Paz Estenssoro, partly by vote and partly by revolt.

Paz made some sweeping changes, nationalizing the tin mines, transferring land from the great *haciendas* (estates) to smallholders, granting civil rights to the Amerindians, expanding education, and extending the vote to all adults. Much of this reform was encouraged by the USA. Paz was President until 1956 and again from 1960 to 1964, and the MNR remained dominant throughout the years 1952–64. It was a much divided movement, however, some sections being more extreme than others, and it kept power by means that were often undemocratic. When Paz eventually sought partnership with General René Barrientos, he found himself deposed in a coup by Barrientos and a military junta. Barrientos went on to secure election, defeat Guevara and preserve some of the MNR reforms, before he was killed in an air accident in 1969.

Confusion followed, with a succession of coups leading to the dictatorship of General Banzer Suarez from 1971 to 1978. He too fell in a coup, the first of several more. Elections took place in 1980 but the army stepped in to set them aside in a new coup. The new junta's contempt for human rights provoked protest from the Catholic Church and boycotts by the USA and other governments. Trade unionists and political opponents were savagely attacked and yet another coup in 1981 brought only limited relief. Defaulting on its debts, Bolivia's economy was now tottering and crisis deepened.

In 1982 the military agreed to accept the election results of 1980 when Paz and the MNR had been defeated by moderate United Democrats. Siles Zuazo, their leader, thus returned from exile to become President, one of his first tasks being to agree terms with the IMF and to stabilize Bolivia's finances. He had also to try to contain the strong-arm tactics to which so many in Latin America seemed so readily to turn. It was hardly surprising that Latin America, where fascist sympathies were widespread, gave shelter to many Nazis who escaped from Europe in 1945, and it was perhaps evidence of his intentions that Siles allowed Klaus Barbie, the 'Butcher of Lyons', to be winkled out of Bolivia in 1983 to face trial in France for his war crimes. Elections in 1985 again produced parliamentary confusion, but in indirect elections Paz was again preferred to Siles as President.

Venezuela had meanwhile been rather better served by its politicians, though the early years after 1945 were not promising. The army set aside the election of 1947, Marcos Jiméniz emerging from the military junta in 1952 to rule as dictator. Little economic and social progress was achieved and the armed forces overthrew Jiméniz in 1958, restoring elected government a year later. Rómulo Betancourt became President as leader of the moderately socialist Democratic Action Party (AD). He survived a good many plots to depose and even to assassinate him, and Venezuela gained useful reforms. The constitution did not allow a second term and so, when the AD won elections in 1963, Betancourt handed on the Presidency to Raúl Leoni.

The Christian Socials won the next election in 1968, continuing moderate reform. They legalized the Venezuelan Communist Party in 1969, though its appeal was limited. Office continued to swing between the Christian Socials and the AD, much as in the USA it swung between Democrats and Republicans, though Venezuelan politics were rather less conservative. The military accepted successive election results and Venezuela seemed sophisticated enough to pursue a comparatively tranquil course. It was not free from political violence and terrorism, and the authorities were not entirely untarnished, but Venezuela featured less in the reports of Amnesty International, who watched over human rights, than did most of the states of Latin America.

By 1973, Venezuela's GDP per head of population was higher than those of Mexico and Portugal, and not far short of Spain's. The State Development Corporation steadily promoted new industries and the oil industry and central bank were nationalized in 1976. Social programmes based on state assistance and self-help brought some well-being. The level of illiteracy had been much reduced as early as the mid-1960s.

But prosperity did not spread to all Venezuela's citizens. In some respects – for example in the standards of urban housing, slum clearance and hospital provision – Venezuela had still to match Argentina, and the gap between rich and poor remained almost as wide as in Brazil. Like the whole of Latin America, Venezuela had to wrestle with acute economic problems in the 1970s and 1980s, accumulating foreign debt and struggling against unemployment. Oil could not answer all problems and Venezuela too had to adopt austerity measures.

9.3.5 Parallels: Haiti and the Dominican Republic

Haiti and the Dominican Republic shared the Caribbean island Columbus had known as Española (Hispaniola) (see fig. 10.1). The Spaniards had lost the west of the island to the French, and the French had lost it to a slave uprising led by Toussaint L'Ouverture who created independent Haiti. The larger, eastern part of Hispaniola gained independence from Spain in 1821, eighteen years after Toussaint's death, but it was not free from claims upon it by Haiti until a settlement in 1844. Neither state prospered, however. Haiti was plagued by conflict between blacks – some 95 per cent of the population and mostly former slaves – and the mulatto minority (of mixed descent, mainly Spanish and Afro-Caribbean). Dictatorship, corruption and disorder retarded almost all forms of development, and for almost twenty years, before Roosevelt withdrew them in 1934, Haiti was occupied by United States troops. Its finances were controlled by US experts who remained until 1947.

What became known as the Dominican Republic had a population about three-quarters mulatto, with whites outnumbering blacks among the rest. Here too the USA intervened in the early twentieth century, financially to protect investments and militarily to impose order. Washington also encouraged some material progress, but it did little to establish democracy or to secure human rights. In 1930 the Dominican Republic came under the dictatorial rule of Rafael Trujillo who made good use of the US-trained constabulary against his opponents. Trujillo was still in power in 1945. Haiti at that time was under the progressive Presidency of Elie Lescot, a mulatto, but in 1946 the army ousted him in favour of the black Dumarsais Estiḿe. In 1950 the army ousted Estiḿe, this time in favour of Paul Magloire, another black.

The Dominican Republic endured Trujillo until 1961, sometimes as President and sometimes as the force behind puppet leaders. His rule was vicious and corrupt, and there was only rejoicing when he was finally ambushed and killed by machine-gunners. Just as he had named the country's capital Trujillo City, Trujillo had given himself the title 'Benefactor'. Admittedly, he carried out some public works and provided the stability the Republic had lacked from 1844 to 1930, when there had been more than 50 revolutions, but few thought him a real benefactor and his people commemorated the anniversary of his assassination with a special stamp, depicting the breaking of their chains (fig. 9.2).

Elections made Juan Bosch the new President, with a programme of 'Land and Dignity' to diversify the economy and implement social reform within a democratic framework. The army, supported by men with money, found this much too progressive and Bosch was overthrown in 1963. Two years later there was civil war against the military junta. Those seeking to restore Bosch were smeared as 'communists', to the alarm of Washington, already smarting from its setbacks in nearby Cuba where Castro was now in power (see section 10.1.2). President Johnson rushed to intervene with a massive military presence in the Dominican Republic which he eventually tried to make respectable within an Inter-American Peace Force of some Central Americans and Brazilians. The Americans were sent, he said, to protect American lives; but he then added that

Fig. 9.2 This Dominican Republic stamp of 1962 gleefully remembered the end of the rule of Trujillo on 30 May 1961.

they were to thwart communism, be neutral and restore democracy. He met a good deal of criticism within the Americas and beyond. In the Dominican Republic a new military junta was set up and order gradually restored.

The USA resisted arguments that Bosch should be allowed to complete his presidential term. There were new elections in 1966 when Bosch was defeated and Joaquin Balaguer, an anti-socialist, became President. The Inter-American Peace Force withdrew, but not before the Caribbean had echoed to slogans such as 'Yankee, Go Home', showing the unease of those who saw that the USA was always likely to bring pressure to keep the Latin American house in order – order as the USA saw it.

The Dominican Republic now settled down, however. Balaguer remained in office until 1978 and US aid helped the country make some delayed economic and social progress. GDP per head of population was still barely a tenth of that in the USA and industries were yet few. Economic dependence on sugar was gradually reduced but the extraction of metals grew more than manufacturing, the USA remaining, not unnaturally, the country's main trading partner. The military had remained at Balaguer's elbow, however, and they interfered in the elections of 1978 at which he lost power to Antonio Guzmán Fernández. Guzmán committed suicide in 1982 and the new elections made Jorge Blanco President with a moderately reforming government. Unemployment was then running at almost 30 per cent of the labour force and the Republic still faced acute problems, but democracy had begun to take root and the military was rather less prominent. Balaguer was re-elected President in 1986.

Haiti meanwhile stagnated. Magloire's Presidency lasted from 1950 to 1956, during which time he showed some ability to govern and US aid helped finance some development, including the building of the Peligre Dam to improve irrigation. Rumours that Magloire intended to extend his years in power led to his forced resignation. When the army then allowed elections in 1957, François Duvalier became President. He was to rule as a dictator, using an iron fist against the mulattos. He relied on the appeal of voodooism to keep a good deal of genuine support, but opponents were dealt with ruthlessly by the Tonton Macoute, a sinister private army of thugs. Magloire and others failed to depose

Fig. 9.3 A US cartoon by Dennis Renault on the presidential election in the Dominican Republic in December 1978, and on the sinister role of the military which provoked an international outcry.

the President, and able and educated Haitians often felt they had little choice but to emigrate. Even army leaders, if troublesome, were liable to be shot, and the Catholic Church excommunicated Duvalier.

Dictatorial rule was extended further when constitutional changes in 1964 allowed the former doctor Duvalier, 'Papadoc', to become President for Life and gave him the power to nominate his successor. Hero worship was carried to absurd lengths: a prayer circulated among the largely illiterate people which began:

> Our Doc, who art in the National Palace of Life, hallowed be thy name . . .

The economy was moribund and, barely touched by Western civilization. Haiti developed hardly any industries. Its GDP per head of population was less than a quarter that of the Dominican Republic, and only a fiftieth of that of the USA. The latter gave little aid after 1962, embarrassed by Duvalier's viciousness and corruption, though he had seemed at first a useful bulwark against communism.

Papadoc gave way to Babydoc: when Duvalier died in 1971 his son, Jean-Claude, became another President for Life. One person, it was claimed, voted against this arrangement in a national referendum, while two abstained and 2 391 916 allegedly gave support. Jean-Claude talked about liberalizing and developing Haiti and reducing corruption, and some economic progress did take place, for example in mining bauxite and attracting tourists. The outside world remained generally unenthusiastic, however, though loans from the USA, France, the IMF and foreign banks helped to keep the economy afloat. The Tonton Macoute declined in importance, but a force of anti-communist 'Leopards' developed to make good the gaps in the regime's defences. When in 1983 municipal elections were allowed, the first since 1957, opposition leaders were arrested and the powers of town mayors severely curbed. Meanwhile Babydoc had given himself power such as his father had had to nominate his successor, offsetting occasional talk of further elections.

A sudden upheaval in February 1986 removed Babydoc and ended the Duvalier tyranny. At last it seemed possible to begin making Haiti into a modern state. An important part of the process would be to persuade a million or so Haitians, now educated and skilled, to return from exile, mainly in the USA. During 1986–7 order was maintained by military rule as was so often the case in Latin America. Elections were nevertheless arranged for November 1987: they proved disastrous. Haiti's death squads made election day a day of murder, driving voters from the polling stations and killing about 150 people. Most of the killers seemed to be Duvalier supporters intent on frustrating democracy, but the army did little to restrain them. George Shultz, the US Secretary of State who had encouraged Haiti's movement towards democracy, commented:

> It is a shame that the democratic process was not allowed to go on. People want to vote. People want to express themselves. People want freedom, and we will continue to work for that.

Some of the Haitian people, however, recalled that it was Washington which had helped to put General Henri Namphy and the military into power when Babydoc fled. They also noted that not only were members of the Tonton Macoute still active in Haiti terrorizing liberals, socialists and trade unionists, but also that Namphy remained in power. He staged another election early in 1988 which convinced hardly anyone. Candidates for reform boycotted the election since voting was not secret and they feared for their own and their supporters' safety. The election made Gregoire Eugene, a right-wing lawyer, Haiti's President, but he was widely regarded as no more than a front for the military, who in any case soon deposed him.

9.4 The regional institutions

The USA had sponsored organizations to hold together the Americas since the International Bureau of American Republics was set up in 1890. In 1948 the latest such association, the Organization of American States (OAS), was set up in Bogotá, Colombia, by 21 American republics. One of the aims of the OAS was to provide for the collective security of the Americas in accordance with the

Treaty of Rio de Janeiro (1947), which pledged its signatories to regard an outside attack on any one of them as an attack on all. The OAS also built on the foundations of the Rio Treaty, providing for the peaceful settlement of disputes within the Americas, and for the monitoring not only of human rights but also of doctrines and propaganda. Central to the OAS were a Council to supervise it and the Pan-American Union, a permanent body with headquarters in Washington, which co-ordinated policy. Special agencies were developed for the economic and social advancement of Latin America.

Such advancement inevitably depended on help from the USA. Brazil wanted a Marshall Plan for Latin America, but had to be satisfied with the Inter-American Development Bank which Eisenhower set up in the late 1950s. The USA supplied half its funds. There was always likely to be a distrust of US money, however, since it was difficult to divorce it from political influence in Latin America. President Kennedy tried to overcome suspicion with his Alliance for Progress (1961), originally a ten-year plan to effect:

> a peaceful revolution on the hemispheric scale . . . a vast co-operative effort, unparalleled in magnitude and nobility of purpose, to satisfy the basic needs of the American people for homes, work and land, health and schools.

But members of the Alliance were expected to resist the spread of communism: again, generous US aid had its price. Much useful work was done, however, organizing economic activity, increasing output, promoting trade, and improving standards of housing, medicine and education – benefits Kennedy and Johnson were eager to spread. By 1974 the Inter-American Development Bank could report Latin American growth rates averaging over seven per cent a year.

The Latin states also organized among themselves: the Organization of Central American States (OCAS) was set up in 1951, its aims economic and social. Guatemala opposed a political proposal that communism be resisted, and subsequently left OCAS in 1953. It returned a year later, after the USA had helped to overthrow its left-wing government, the leader of which – Arbenz Guzmán – had made land available to the peasants and tolerated communist political activity. His fall brought back the right-wing military rule the USA obviously preferred in Guatemala, and OCAS then added orthodox political and defence aims to its Charter.

The OAS too revised its constitution in the mid-1960s, making the meetings of its General Assembly annual and adopting additional cultural aims, including the welfare of Amerindians. The Pan-American Union became the General Secretariat. By now, however, there was an emphasis on economic unions among the Latin Americans, seeking to advance their own well-being. In 1960 the members of OCAS created the Central American Common Market with a Central American Bank and plans for extensive integration between members. Trade between them grew rapidly during the 1960s. The Latin American Free Trade Association (LAFTA) dated from 1961, with a membership stretching from Mexico to Argentina, but it was less successful in increasing unfettered trade and in 1980 became the Latin American Integration

Association (LAIA), seeking closer co-operation. The Andean Group, set up in 1969, brought together Bolivia with some of its neighbours, their co-operation leading in 1975 to some co-ordination of their petrochemical industries. The Latin American Economic System (SELA) was born in that year with an initial membership of 25 states.

States in the Caribbean also sought partnerships. The British-sponsored Federation of the West Indies collapsed in 1962 (see section 14.3.1), but English-speaking islands went on to set up the Caribbean Free Trade Association (Carifta) in 1968 and, five years later, the Caribbean Community and Common Market (Caricom) into which Carifta was merged. Caricom aimed at economic integration and a more general co-operation, including the co-ordination of foreign policies. Though situated on the mainland of South America, Guyana (formerly British Guiana) joined both SELA and Caricom.

Of all these associations only the OAS formally included the USA. Most Latin American republics, like developing nations generally, had to rely for financial assistance on the International Monetary Fund (IMF). After 1974 the Latin American economies faltered, increasing the pressures from the IMF. A UN Commission reported that in 1982 Latin America's economic performance was one of the worst since 1945. Output fell during the year; foreign debt stood at 247 billion dollars; inflation averaged around 80 per cent; and unemployment or severe underemployment was around 30 per cent. Only in balancing its visible trade did Latin America hold its own.

The OAS meanwhile grew as more newly-independent Caribbean states joined, for example Trinidad & Tobago in 1967 and Barbados a year later. But Canada, the largest American state in the Commonwealth, did not join; nor had it signed the Treaty of Rio de Janeiro, preferring to join NATO which involved western Europe and was not just a predominantly US bloc.

Unit 10 will give further examples of how Washington used the OAS as an anti-communist watchdog, especially with regard to Cuba. The OAS could also promote accord, however. From the Panama Canal's beginnings at the start of the twentieth century, the USA had insisted on leasing the Canal Zone with land on both sides of the waterway. Frustrated by this continuing occupation, Panama broke off diplomatic relations with Washington in 1963–4 but not until President Carter came to office, willing to compromise, could the OAS promote agreement. Carter agreed that the land should be restored to Panama in January 2000. Not all Panamanians thought the deal a good one with over twenty years to wait, but few Latin Americans were any match for the USA when it came to a clash of interests.

UNIT 10

Latin America and the Caribbean: dissent

The Second World War had important effects in Latin America. The demands of the Allies for raw materials and foodstuffs boosted Latin American economies, bringing fuller employment and quickening expectations of higher standards of living. Latin Americans became more directly involved in European ideological conflicts and there was a marked increase in Marxist influence – in labour movements and even, for a time, in government where a few communists won office, for example in Ecuador and Chile. But the Cold War weakened communism again, linking it with the 'threat' from the Soviet Union. To US intelligence authorities, US businesses and US-based transnational companies, it seemed right to keep the American house in order, manipulating when useful, undermining when advisable, and involving Washington in even grosser interference when necessary. There have been examples in Sections 9.1 and 9.3.5 of that grosser interference in Guatemala in 1954 and in the Dominican Republic in 1965, but between 1954 and 1965 Washington was horrified by developments in Cuba.

10.1 Cuba: the revolution

10.1.1 Cuba under Batistá

For years after helping to free Cuba from Spain in 1898, the US government reserved the right to intervene there and, in addition, forced the Cubans to grant the USA a military base at Guantánamo. In 1934 Roosevelt cancelled the Platt Amendment which had enshrined the rights of intervention but, like all later Presidents, he kept Guantánamo. Fulgencio Batistá was then in power in Cuba following a military coup. Batistá was a sergeant, self-promoted to colonel, and an admirer of Italian Fascism. The key to his power was his control of the army, though he also won elections in 1940. From 1944 to 1952 he surrendered power and went into exile, allowing Grau San Martin and then Prio Socarrás to govern, but he came back in another coup. From 1952, now a general, he presided over a dictatorship, given some legal veneer by an unopposed election in 1954.

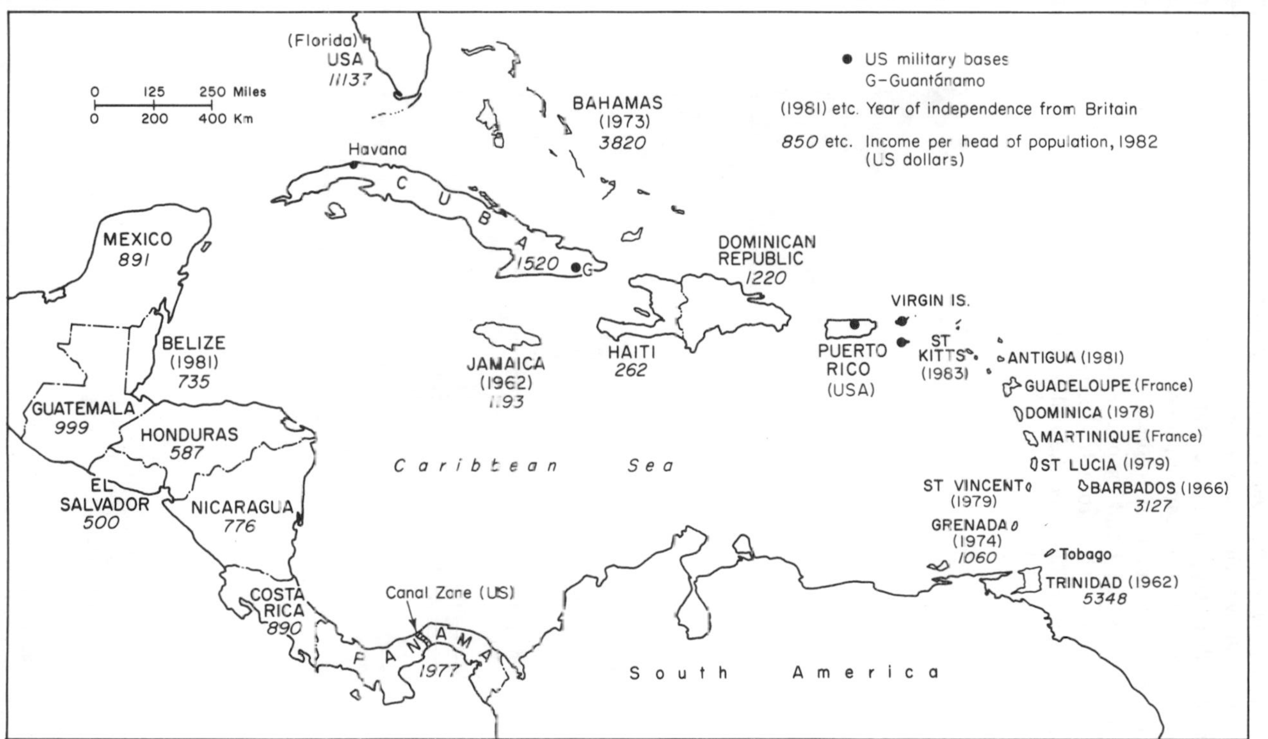

Fig. 10.1 Central America and the Caribbean

At that time Cuba had a fast-growing population of some six million, divided almost equally between urban and rural dwellers and three-quarters white. Batistá made show of caring for the welfare of urban workers with faint echoes of Perónist rule in Argentina. The Cuban economy remained heavily dependent on sugar and on foreign capital, however. US business interests dominated many enterprises, from sugar production and other agricultural activities to the railways and electricity and telephone services, while Havana, the capital – replete with casinos and brothels – provided a playground for US tourists. Batistá's government favoured the well-to-do and largely neglected the masses,

Fig. 10.2 Fidel Castro, second in line behind 'Che' Guevara, with his handful of anti-Batistá guerillas in Cuba's Sierra Maestra in the late 1950s: Batistá fled and in January 1959 Castro entered Havana to become Cuba's Prime Minister. Guevara lost his life in Bolivia in 1967 in a vain struggle to help Bolivia's impoverished tin-miners.

to the great disadvantage of blacks, mulattos, women and the poor generally. Illiteracy remained high, and other social problems such as poor housing and a shortage of land for smallholdings were acute. Even the sugar industry began to decline, and unemployment increased. The regime grew so repressive, so callous and corrupt, that even Batistá's allies, including the military and the US government, began to drift away from him.

Among Batistá's errors of judgment was the release of Fidel Castro under an amnesty in 1955. Castro had been imprisoned for opposition to the government and an attack on the Moncada barracks in 1953. He was now exiled but was back in Cuba by the end of 1956, making a base in the Sierra Maestra mountains with 'Che' Guevara, to wage a guerilla war against Batistá. In 1957, as civil war gathered pace, Castro was 30 years old. Of prosperous Spanish descent and a lawyer by training, he was a convinced enemy of exploitation and a champion of the underprivileged. He described his typical follower as one who could say:

> I have lived all my life without fuel, without electric light, without transport, without medicines, without everything.

Castro was also coming to detest US imperialism, though at that time there were sympathies for him in the United States and Eisenhower even stopped US supplies of arms to Batistá. At the end of 1958 Batistá fled to the Dominican Republic, his support having almost vanished. Castro's guerillas entered Havana on 8 January 1959.

10.1.2 Cuba under Castro

(a) The Marxist revolution: Castroism Exactly when Castro became a Marxist is uncertain, though he claimed in 1961 that it was as a student. His views hardened in conflict with the USA and a distinctive 'Castroism' evolved. Its basic ingredients were a Caribbean nationalism and fierce anti-imperialism, in protest at the influence of the USA which so distorted the economies of its neighbours. Combined with this was a passionate reform programme aimed at the socialist transformation of Cuban society. There was also the authoritarianism which put off elections until 1976, and which was to turn Cuba into a one-party state. From 1965 this party was the Cuban Communist Party (CCP). Critics alleged that Castro was merely a puppet of the Soviet Union – an allegation Castroists vigorously denied, asserting that Castroism was as individual as Leninism, Stalinism and Maoism.

The destiny of Cuba was shaped not only by Castro's revolution against Batistá but also by the events which quickly followed. On taking office as Prime Minister, Castro began rounding up those unsympathetic to the revolution, purging speculators and corrupt officials, and evicting sources of US influence. Cuban exiles were subsequently welcomed in the USA and by President Trujillo in the Dominican Republic. Castro also made a start on nationalizing key industries: by the end of 1960 a billion dollars' worth of US assets had been seized, at first in exchange for Cuban government bonds. In reply, during 1960 the USA boycotted Cuba's sugar exports and banned all supplies to Cuba except medicines and a few foodstuffs. Washington most likely assumed that the boycotts would bring Cuba to heel, but Castro instead turned to the Soviet Union. Khrushchev seized his opportunity, undertaking to supply Cuba with oil and other requirements and to buy Cuba's sugar, though the Soviets themselves had no need of it. Cuba now depended heavily on the Soviet Union for trade (see Table 9.1) and in 1972 it became a member of Comecon. Cuban–US relations deteriorated further when Kennedy became President in 1961, immediately lending US support to an attempted invasion of Cuba, which foundered at the Bay of Pigs (see section 10.1.2(b) below).

The Popular Socialist Party, Castro's initial supporters, provided strong centralized government. Raoul Castro, Fidel's brother, took charge of the military while 'Che' Guevara became President of the National Bank and, in 1961, Minister for Industries. Guevara visited China and the Soviet Union in 1960 and Castro went to Moscow a year later, after the Bay of Pigs episode. In 1962 the ruling party changed its name to the United Party of Socialist Revolution; in 1965 it became the Cuban Communist Party (CCP). A new constitution in 1976 led at last to the holding of indirect elections, resulting in the National Assembly based on a system resembling that of people's democracies in eastern Europe. Castro himself, elected by the National Assembly, now added the Cuban Presidency to his office of Prime Minister.

One priority in 1959 had been to nationalize all large-scale enterprises. Guevara played his part in this before he left for Bolivia in 1965, and he also supervised land transfers which enabled Cuban peasants to set up farming co-operatives. In the later 1960s many smaller enterprises were also nationalized and the farming co-operatives were encouraged to become collectives. Cuba thus developed an economy in which the public utilities and most businesses were run by the state, agriculture included state farms and collectives, and a small private sector supplied 'extras' on a small scale. Businessmen, especially foreign ones, had been deprived of the power they exercised in most of the Americas. On the other hand, the CCP made only limited progress towards another Castroist goal – that of diversifying the economy and reducing the dominance of sugar. Even in the 1980s sugar made up more than 80 per cent of Cuba's exports, annual production being around eight million tonnes. But Cuba's first Five-Year Plan had been launched in 1976 and metal extraction, especially of nickel ore, manufacturing and the traditional tobacco industry were all developing.

Controversy raged about the success of the Cuban economy, with the capitalist world seldom hesitating to belittle it. Nevertheless, Cuban growth rates were sometimes impressive (over ten per cent in 1973–4), and growth rates on a small scale continued during the world recession of the late 1970s and early 1980s. Like the communist world in general, the Cubans in any case stressed the social aspects of economic policy, for example curbing unemployment.

The social revolution was vital to Castro's aims. In some respects, Cuba practised austerity: consumer goods had a low priority and even essentials were sometimes rationed to ensure a fair share for all, controls keeping prices low. The CCP meanwhile devoted its energies to developing one of the world's finest health services, also greatly reducing illiteracy, improving housing, transport and social services generally, and ensuring the supply of clean piped water. In the mid-1970s Cuba had a much reduced level of infant mortality, and life expectancy began to match that in the USA. The poor benefited extensively, and the status of women and of blacks was now much improved. But Cuba's average income per head was still only about an eighth of that in the USA.

However, there was a price to be paid for Cuba's revolution: certain civil liberties and the freedom of debate and expression the West prized were lacking. The Catholic Church had to struggle to keep its hold on the people. Thousands of Cubans went into exile when Castro first took power, and again at the end of the 1970s when he encouraged 'undesirables' to leave. In 1981 Amnesty International reported about 250 long-term political prisoners on the island. At the same time, the regime was more honest than most Cuba had known, genuinely seeking the welfare of the people and the avoidance of corruption. It was also more independent than previous regimes – economically dependent on the Soviets, but far from subservient. But it was not always efficient, tireless though Castro himself might be. Technical training developed only slowly and some of the complete factories imported from the USSR failed for lack of expertise among the Cubans. Like other developing countries, Cuba had still to struggle for prosperity.

(b) Cuba's external relations Cubans had to bear another burden: the government maintained a costly military force, which was put to the test after Kennedy became US President in 1961. Cuban–US relations had deteriorated to such an extent that Kennedy severed diplomatic ties. He inherited from Eisenhower a plan to depose Castro, hatched by the CIA and Cuban exiles led by Jose Cardona, and unwisely he allowed it to proceed, withholding US troops and air cover, but not US ships. Cardona's force (about 1500 men) invaded Cuba at the Bay of Pigs in April 1961, but other Cubans failed to rally to them and Cardona's men were easily routed. Washington increased the USA's humiliation by denying for some time that it had anything to do with the fiasco. Castro's prestige soared and the prisoners he took were eventually returned to the USA for the equivalent of around 50 million dollars, mainly in the form of medical supplies.

The Cuban military force was not only for defence, however. In 1962 US spy-planes detected Soviet missile sites in Cuba, and in the resulting international crisis Khrushchev was forced to back down and to withdraw the missiles he and Castro had agreed to install there (see section 13.2.2). But Khrushchev insisted he had won something from the affair. He wrote to Castro:

> The main point about the Caribbean crisis is that it has guaranteed the existence of a Socialist Cuba. If Cuba had not undergone this ordeal, it is very likely the Americans would have organized an invasion to liquidate Cuba's Socialist way of life.

Kennedy had now pledged the USA not to mount such an invasion, no doubt still mindful of the fiasco at the Bay of Pigs. Castro was nevertheless disappointed when the missiles were returned to the Soviet Union, but he

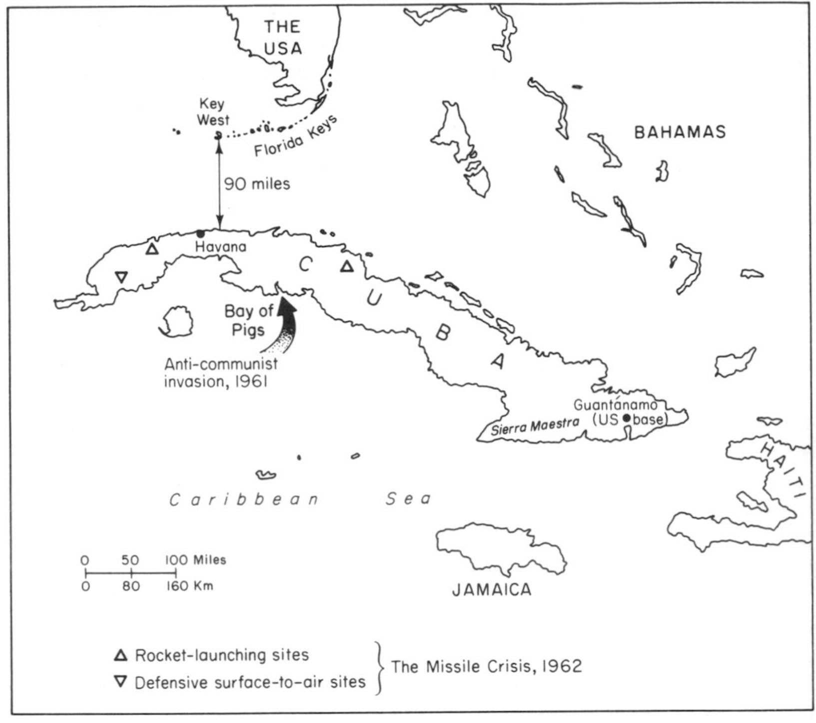

Fig. 10.3 Uneasy neighbours: Cuba and the USA

rapidly developed his ambitions to continue harassing the USA. In 1963 Cuba introduced male conscription from the age of seventeen.

The Organization of American States (OAS) could not expel members but it barred Cuba from participation at the start of 1962. With the exception of Mexico, other American states gradually followed the USA in breaking diplomatic relations with Cuba, though what angered them most was Castro's attempt to meddle in the internal affairs of Venezuela, encouraging left-wing opposition there. A trade boycott was also organized. Castro's reply was to set up the Latin American Solidarity Organization in 1966. Its members were revolutionaries from all parts of Latin America, pledged to guerilla action against the USA and the capitalism it fostered. US intervention in the Dominican Republic had increased their fury, and Cuba was now a symbol for all who were hostile to 'Yankee imperialism'. In the late 1960s, when hijacking became a fashionable form of protest, the island was often the terminus for hijacked aircraft.

But neither Washington nor the CCP could win outright victory. Cuba's influence on its neighbours was limited. Jamaica under Michael Manley in the

1970s was one of several to benefit from the social improvements Castro was eager to spread, assisted for example in an urgent housing programme. Marxist ideas took root in the island of Grenada and on the mainland in Nicaragua, but both Castro and his enemies were inclined to overstate Cuba's connection with this fact – many American states had good reasons of their own for seeking revolutionary change. Inevitably, however, Castro was seen as the guru of American Marxists, just as Guevara was their martyr, and when Marxists gained power in Grenada and Nicaragua in 1979, Cuban advisers, civilian and military, soon arrived. As in Jamaica, much of their work was towards social improvement: Cuba became renowned, in fact, for its generous provision of teachers and work-teams. The vast majority of American states were still capitalists, however, and the USA under Reagan was eager to reverse the recent developments in Grenada and Nicaragua, just as Nixon had earlier helped to do in Chile when it turned to Marxism (see section 10.2.2).

In 1972 the boycott of Cuba began to weaken. The English-speaking states – Guyana and Trinidad, then Jamaica and Barbados – resumed diplomatic and trading links. In 1975 the OAS ended its trade ban, and Venezuela began shipping oil to Cuba in 1976. The USA continued its own trade ban but even in US–Cuban relations there was movement. For a time there was even an anti-hijacking pact, but Castro cancelled it in 1976, accusing the CIA of involvement in planting a bomb which destroyed a Cuban airliner and killed 73 people. There was a partial normalizing of relations in 1977 when US tourists began cautiously to return to a Havana they found much changed from their earlier playground. The situation remained uneasy, however, especially when Reagan took over from Carter as US President.

Castro had not confined his activities to the Americas. Cuban troops were sent to Angola in Africa in 1975 to help consolidate Marxists in power there against rivals backed by the USA, the West, South Africa and even China. From Angola, the Cubans seemed to threaten not only South Africa's hold on Namibia but also white supremacy in southern Africa as a whole (see sections 17.5.2 and 19.2.3). Cubans also arrived in Ethiopia to support the government of Mengistu (see section 22.2). In 1983 Castro was also chairman of the non-aligned movement where he created controversy by arguing that for developing countries non-alignment must mean support for socialism against capitalism, if not exactly support for the Soviets against the USA. He won much approval in Latin America, however, when he condemned 'the colonialist aggression of Great Britain against Argentina' during the dispute over the Falkland Islands. An over-simplified perspective was that Castro acted merely as the agent of Moscow – 'Soviet-backed, Cuban-managed' as Reagan put it. This view did less than justice to Castroism with its own blend of Marxism and nationalism, anti-imperialism and giant-killing romanticism, and less than justice to the accessible, talkative and bearded Fidel who had made Cuba much more than simply the largest island in the Caribbean.

10.2 Chile: democracy frustrated

10.2.1 Democracy in action

Chile had come nearer to democracy than most Latin American republics in the years before 1945. The army interfered less than elsewhere and a wide range of political opinion, from fascist to Marxist, was usually, though not always, tolerated. The constitution of 1925 provided for the direct election of Presidents and by 1945 there was extensive welfare provision as part of active social reform. Over half of Chile's population of about five million already lived in towns and cities, and most were literate, but many problems remained. Improved sanitation and other reforms having cut the death rate, population was growing quickly. Land was still distributed very unequally. Copper extraction, in which much foreign capital had been invested, dominated the economy, and inflation was already persistent.

Collectivist and capitalist ideas competed to solve Chile's difficulties. The broad division between left and right tended to run on class lines, dividing the working classes from the middle and upper classes with their land and business interests. Within the broad divisions, however, political groupings were often confusing. González Videla became President in 1946 as the leader of a left-wing Popular Front, but he turned against the Communist Party, banning it in 1948, and alienated many of his own supporters. His successor, Carlos Ibáñez, tried to straddle left and right without much success at all. In 1958, the year the Communist Party was legalized again, the right-wing candidate Jorge Alessandri won the elections. Alessandri was supported financially by the USA and he did little to reduce the grip of large landowners on 90 per cent of Chile's soil. With the growing population, Chileans found themselves becoming worse off. Opinion shifted to the left.

Eduardo Frei won the Presidency in 1964, with the strong support of the middle classes, defeating Salvador Allende of the Popular Action Front. Frei was a Christian Democrat, though more left-wing than most of that name in Europe. Christian Democrats also did well in elections to the Chilean Congress in 1965 and Frei was able to begin modestly to transfer land from the rich to the poor, encouraging peasant co-operatives. Social problems were not overcome by his cautious reform, however, and inflation rose to an annual 30 per cent in 1969. Unrest developed, even some soldiers going on strike for better pay. Frei secured extra government revenue from the copper mines and began to buy a share of their ownership. In 1970 he also acquired control of Chile's electricity industry at a price to US investors of 81 million dollars, but the left argued that the pace needed to be faster and that nationalizing all key industries, especially copper, was essential to proper economic management and fair rewards for the country's workers.

Allende fought his fourth presidential election in 1970, this time clearly winning it though without an overall majority against Alessandri and a third candidate. Allende was a doctor and a Marxist who inclined towards Castroism, but he had a long history of democratic participation in politics through the Chilean Socialist Party. As in 1964, he was backed in 1970 by a left-wing coalition, his government including Socialists, Communists, Radicals, Social Democrats and others – even an Independent Marxist. During the election he had given the middle classes firm guarantees of the civil liberties Chileans were used to, but his radical economic programme proved too much for the supporters of private enterprise and their US backers, who were furious when Allende's government quickly nationalized the banks, copper, iron, textiles and some fisheries. Most owners, Chilean and foreign, were bought out (received payment for their assets), but in some cases, some US copper interests for example, there was no compensation. Transfers of land to the peasants continued. It seemed likely that the organization of Chile's economy would become like Cuba's, and Castro visited Chile in 1971.

10.2.2 The intervention

From the start Allende had to face obstruction. Business firms were not co-operative, copper exports were boycotted in some markets and unrest was stirred up by anti-Marxists. The government made early progress in curbing inflation and reducing unemployment but conditions worsened during 1972, the year the powerful transnational ITT (International Telegraph and Telephone Company) was dispossessed and reported to the UN for allegedly plotting Allende's overthrow. Allende was also handicapped by the lack of majority support in the Chilean Congress. His rule was nevertheless democratic and respected human rights.

From the beginning Washington aimed to destabilize his regime. When Allende was elected, Henry Kissinger, Nixon's Secretary of State, had at once required to know:

> the pros and cons and problems and prospects involved should a Chilean military coup be organized now with US assistance.

The Nixon government devised a secret 'Policy Towards Chile', a programme to stop all loans to Chile and to ruin its economy as fast as possible. The CIA admitted to spending eight million dollars on its Chilean activities while Allende was in office. It was, of course, true that the costs of nationalizing industries, raising wages and carrying out urgent reforms had severely strained Chile's economy, and inflation had soared to around an annual 300 per cent during 1973. But enemies on the right, aided and abetted by the USA, wasted no opportunity to create the chaos which might 'save Chile from communism'.

Chaos there was. Truck-owners, objecting to nationalization, did their best to paralyse transport during 1972–3. An attempt to freeze prices led to bankruptcies, and shopkeepers and professional people like dentists went on strike. Yet Allende's government was not rejected in congressional elections in 1973 and Allende himself, and many opponents like Frei, remained loyal to democratic practices. It was the army that intervened with the first military coup in Chile since 1925. The presidential palace in Santiago was stormed in September 1973 and Allende died during the attack – by suicide, the military claimed. Allende's supporters were rounded up, his ministers sent to prison in

Table 10.1 The Americas: some comparative statistics

State*	Population		Income per head, 1983 (US dollars)†	Number of people per doctor, c. 1980	Percentage of population literate over age 15‡, c. 1980
	Estimated, 1985 (millions)	Annual growth, 1980–5 (%)			
North and Central America					
Canada	25.4	1.1	12 060	547	99 (14+)
USA	238.8	0.9	14 070	526	95
Mexico	78.0	2.6	2 240	1 773	82
Guatemala	7.7	2.3	1 120	2 543	46
Honduras	4.4	3.5	670	3 180	59 (10+)
El Salvador	5.2	2.7	710	3 145	64
Nicaragua	3.0	3.8	900	2 228	87
Costa Rica	2.5	2.3	1 020	1 502	93
Panama	2.2	2.1	2 070	1 127	87
The Caribbean					
Cuba	10.1	1.0	1 590	637	95
Jamaica	2.3	1.1	1 290	3 061	96
Haiti	5.3	1.9	330	5 994	35
Dominican Republic	6.2	2.7	1 370	2 624	67
Trinidad and Tobago	1.2	1.9	6 850§	1 450	92

South America					
Colombia	28.8	2.0	1 410	2 004	86
Venezuela	17.3	3.0	4 110§	880	76
Ecuador	8.6	2.9	1 430	1 604	85 (10+)
Peru	19.7	2.6	1 040	1 430	72
Brazil	135.6	2.3	1 890	1 149	77
Bolivia	6.4	2.6	510	1 963	63
Chile	12.0	1.7	1 870	1 616	95 (12+)
Paraguay	3.4	2.6	1 410	1 802	80
Uruguay	3.0	0.8	2 490	506	90
Argentina	30.6	1.6	2 030	470	95

* One million inhabitants and over

† At current market prices

‡ Except where indicated

§ Gross national product boosted by oil output. Other countries like Canada, USA and Mexico also produced oil.

Statistics from *Encyclopaedia Britannica*

the far south, and many thousands more to the National Stadium in Santiago for 'processing' for beatings, jail and execution. The coup was led by General Augusto Pinochet, who promptly disbanded Congress, suspended the constitution and began a purge not only of communists and socialists but also of liberals. He also promised the 'restoration' of the Chilean economy and the compensation the USA wanted for its business interests. US denials of complicity in Allende's overthrow rang hollow. The Nixon administration had placed the destabilization of an elected Marxist government well ahead of respect for democracy or human rights.

Pinochet imposed a brutal dictatorship and only similar right-wing tyrannies regarded him kindly, though the USA gave economic co-operation. This did not prevent inflation rising even higher before it fell to around 25 per cent at the end of the 1970s and then rose yet again. By then Pinochet claimed that he was pursuing monetarist policies similar to Margaret Thatcher's in Britain. But the results were disastrous: in 1983 inflation was about 30 per cent, output was down, unemployment up, and debts were pressing. In the mid-1980s the regime could not even claim proven economic success to justify its viciousness.

Pinochet nevertheless imposed a new constitution in 1980, extending his own period in power for at least eight more years and legalizing harsh repressive powers:

> The measures adopted by virtue of this provision are not subject to any kind of appeal, except reconsideration by the authority that ordered them.

The limited concessions made to trade unions in 1979 were virtually cancelled out. Few organizations concerned with human rights – the UN and the OAS among them – had not by now repeatedly condemned the Pinochet regime, though Pinochet promised elections in 1989 and spoke of the restoration of real democracy in about 1997. Many countries boycotted Chilean trade, especially the sale of arms to Chile. Those selling such arms, like Britain's Thatcher government, raised storms of protest. During the Falklands War, however, Thatcher found Chile's generals more attractive than Argentina's and commended Chile's propaganda against Argentina. The Chilean people hardly shared her enthusiasm. Opposition to the military began to grow within Chile and civil disturbances in 1986 were met with further fierce repression. Reagan now found Pinochet an embarrassment, and the USA sponsored a UN resolution condemning his abuses of human rights.

In October 1988 Pinochet held a referendum in an attempt to bolster his position. Voters were asked whether his period in office should continue after 1990. Over 56 per cent of the population voted loudly and clearly *No* in the first relatively free vote since 1973. Nevertheless Pinochet claimed that he had won the vote – on the spurious grounds that he would have more support in the next presidential election than anyone else (given the existence of 16 opposition parties)! He declared he would remain in office until 1990, when his 'legal' term would expire, and showed no willingness to concede to opposition demands for early elections. However, with the armed forces openly divided and his last shreds of legitimacy in tatters, Pinochet's position looked increasingly precarious, and the prospects for the eventual restoration of Chilean democracy at their best since his coup.

10.3 Grenada: 'The Ant and the Elephant'

Grenada was a British colony until 1974 when it became independent, one of the smallest members of the Commonwealth with a population of around 100 000. Other Commonwealth leaders boycotted the independence ceremony, objecting to the rule in the island of Eric Gairy, Prime Minister since 1962. Gairy had support in Grenada from landowners, businesses and some farmworkers he had undoubtedly helped, but he was anti-communist and fiercely authoritarian, deploying his Mongoose Squad like a mini-version of Haiti's Tonton Macoute against opponents he belittled as 'stupid, mentally premature, wicked people who cannot smile'. They had little to smile about: the Mongoose Squad was reinforced by the Night Ambush Squad, while the economy – heavily dependent on cocoa, nutmegs and tourists – sagged towards bankruptcy. Gairy nevertheless 'won' the elections of 1976 against an opposition at the heart of which was the New Jewel Movement (NJM), which aimed at a social revolution through economic planning and the massive improvement in health, housing, education and living standards the people needed. Gairy seemed to prefer to pursue his interest in flying-saucers. While away from the island in 1979 he was overthrown by an NJM coup which made Maurice Bishop Prime Minister in his place.

Gairy at once set out to win support for the rescue of Grenada 'from communism'. The CIA was not inactive but President Carter was cautious and most of Grenada's neighbours came round to recognizing Bishop and the NJM as the legitimate government. There was some uneasiness, however. Bishop had

Fig. 10.4 Eric Gairy, a Grenada independence stamp in 1974. The people of Grenada were proud of their independence but less enthusiastic about Gairy's Mongoose and Night Ambush Squads. Gairy was deposed in 1979.

high ideals. His priorities were economic and social reform, and he told a conference of the non-aligned movement in Delhi:

> Half the resources at present allocated to military expenditure in one day will finance a programme for the total worldwide eradication of malaria.

He admired and was admired by Castro, and a good many Caribbean leaders feared the effects of NJM influence on their own subjects. Cubans arrived to help develop Grenada and by 1981 social and economic progress, with honest administration, were already significant. Land reform was under way and literacy was already rising. In 1981, however, Reagan became President in Washington and US policy hardened. In Bishop's terms, 'the elephant' set out to crush 'the ant'. Washington obsessively saw a communist plot in almost everything that happened. It assumed that Castro (and the Soviets) were involved with Bishop in a conspiracy. That was not the view taken by Europeans in the EEC, who had begun to build Grenada an airport to help its development – to Reagan, a threat to the USA – and in 1982, moreover, even the IMF approved the good management of Grenada by NJM. The USA wanted to destabilize Bishop's government.

But Bishop's popularity seemed to grow throughout the Caribbean, with the people if not necessarily with governments. Bishop claimed to be aware of the danger in which he stood from Reagan's determination to regard Grenada as part of the 'geo-political game'. In October 1983, however, he was put under house arrest by some of his own more radical colleagues, freed by popular demonstration, but then taken and murdered by the military in a single day when perhaps 60 lives were lost in Grenada. A military council took power. The circumstances of this upheaval were mysterious but Bishop's overthrow angered the Cubans and stunned his admirers throughout the world. It was the NJM's enemies who were quickest to react. Responding, it was said, to an appeal by some of Grenada's conservative neighbours like Tom Adams of Barbados and Eugenia Charles of the tiny island of Dominica, the USA invaded Grenada within a week. *Time* magazine had already reported a Washington official as saying that the Reagan government was:

> looking for any opportunity that came along where we could take a direct punch at the other side's nose with . . . minimum risk of entangling with the Soviets themselves.

Here apparently was the opportunity. By the end of October 'the elephant' had put more than 7000 men into Grenada and the Grenadian army officers were overthrown.

The invasion too was shrouded in mystery and propaganda. Washington exaggerated the Cuban presence in Grenada (in fact, fewer than 800 and most of them construction workers), underplayed Grenadian opposition to the invasion, and understated US casualties. Though the USA got many expressions of support from sitting Caribbean governments, governments further afield – Britain's included – were critical. Reagan claimed the invasion was actually a 'rescue mission', 'to restore order and democracy'. Mourning '24 Cubans who died in Grenada', Castro saw it as an outstanding example of 'the dirty, perfidious and aggressive nature of imperialism', designed to safeguard US influence, economic and strategic, throughout the Caribbean. The Soviets called the invasion 'international banditry'.

US forces remained in Grenada until 1985, even after a Caribbean peacekeeping force had taken over from the US army. US 'security specialists' remained even longer. Elections were held in 1984 for fifteen parliamentary seats. With the support of US and other business leaders and, less directly, of the Reagan government, Herbert Blaize and the New National Party won fourteen. Gairy, back in Grenada from exile, won little support, and the left was in disarray. The elephant at last seemed well satisfied with the behaviour of the ant, especially when the murderers of Bishop were found guilty and sentenced. There were other developments in Central America, however, which Washington found far more alarming than events in tiny Grenada.

10.4 Nicaragua, the Sandinistas and Central America

Mexico irritated the USA by befriending Castro, but south of Mexico, in Central America, lay smaller and more troublesome republics. Since US intervention in 1954 Guatemala had been kept in line mainly by its generals, such as Romeo Garcia (1974–82). Carter found the methods of their death squads so hideous, however, that US military aid was suspended for a time from 1977. Honduras swung between constitutional rule and military coups. In 1969 it went to war with El Salvador, superficially over defeat in a football match but in fact as the result of deep anxieties about low standards of living, economic competition and illegal migration from heavily populated El Salvador into thinly populated Honduras. Discontent and violence were marked in Honduras, while the democratic intervals seemed to grow briefer, the military more prominent. El Salvador was in a similar ferment. Here too Carter for a time suspended aid, affronted by right-wing death squads and political terrorization. Carter also tried to curb the CIA's activities in Central America, but under Reagan it took on a new lease of life. It was Reagan's view that there was crisis in the region and that Nicaragua was at the centre of it.

Nicaragua was comparatively large but thinly populated. It had a history of US occupation but from 1936 the Somoza family had kept it on a right-wing path generally acceptable to business interests and to Washington. Anastasio Somoza Garcia was assassinated in 1956 but the family, now very wealthy unlike most of their subjects, kept control. In 1967 Somoza's second son, General Anastasio Somoza Debayle, became President. A Somoza majority in parliament hardly disguised his government's brutality, corruption and self-interest. The official response to a major earthquake in Nicaragua exposed the corruption and venality of Somoza's regime and fortified opposition to his rule. Somoza had to flee in 1979 from the Sandinista National Liberation Front – a resistance movement founded in 1961 and named after Augusto Sandino, a freedom-fighter of the 1930s. Forces supporting the Sandinistas ranged from Marxists to the Catholic Church and included not only workers but also many of the middle classes. President Carter had also abandoned Somoza, outraged

Fig. 10.5 The Soviet view (in *Pravda*, the Party newspaper of the CPSU) in 1979 of the destabilizing ambitions of the American CIA towards governments that inclined to socialism. Allende in Chile had been a victim; and forked tongues and propaganda were the stock in trade of the intelligence agencies of the major powers.

by his disregard of human rights. The military defended him, however, and before he fled the war was bloody, claiming about 30 000 lives. In 1980 Somoza was murdered in exile in Paraguay.

A five-member Sandinista committee now ruled Nicaragua. It quickly seized Somoza's personal properties, welcomed the friendship of Cuba, nationalized metals and some banks, and set up some state farms and co-operatives. Nicaragua faced acute social problems as well as economic ones which included inflation and a heavy national debt. The civil war had left half a million homeless, adding to the widespread poverty. By 1981 some economic and social progress had been made but when Reagan became US President Nicaragua met with fiercer antagonism from its neighbours. From the start its enemies had called the Sandinista movement communist and, since elections were delayed, undemocratic. The USA now accused the Sandinistas of a military build-up and of support, in alliance with Cuba and the Soviets, for the Farabundo Martí Liberation Front in El Salvador, where civil war had begun in 1979. The USA imposed trade sanctions against Nicaragua and supplied weapons and advisers to the *Contras*, the anti-Sandinista forces which grew up in Nicaragua, many of them based and trained in Honduras. Laying mines in Nicaraguan waters seemed to be another American way of showing disapproval of the Sandinistas.

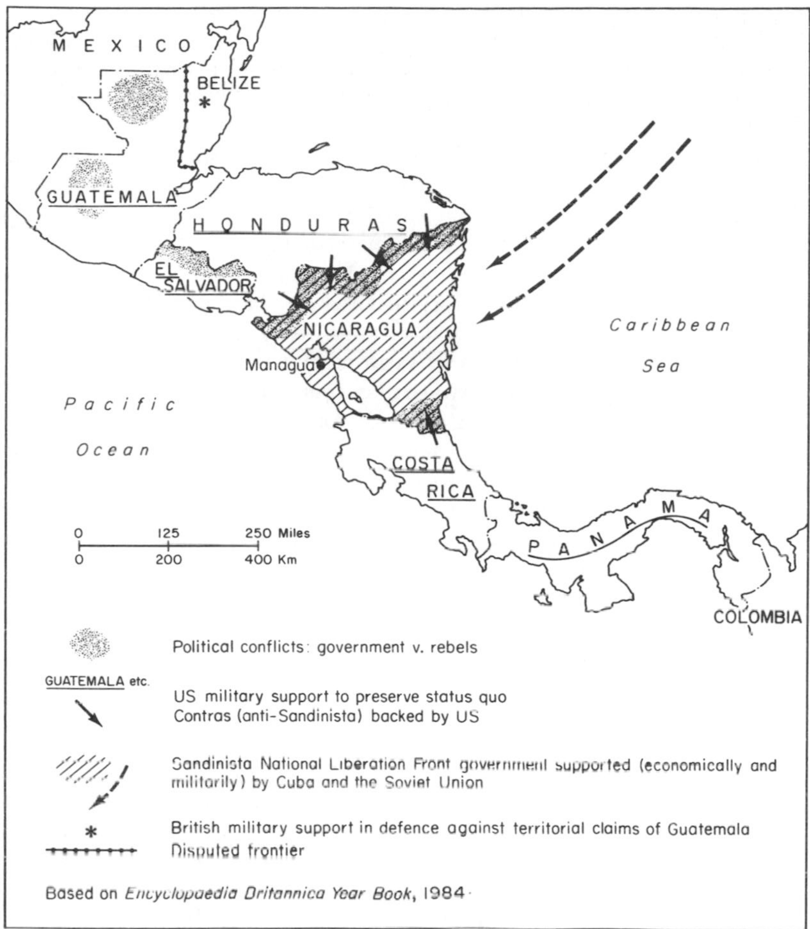

Fig. 10.6 Conflicts in Central America in the mid-1980s

Daniel Ortega emerged as the leader of the Sandinistas. He certainly aimed at a social revolution, asserting that:

> The enemies of the revolution have not yet realized that neither bullets nor ballots will be able to overthrow the power of the people, the Sandinista power, the revolutionary power.

But the government was far less vicious and bloody than those in El Salvador and other neighbouring states at that time. It even tolerated a comparatively free press. It nevertheless alienated many of the middle classes and some Church leaders, though its stated aims were an economy and society neither

Soviet nor Cuban: a mixed economy, a strong private sector, social justice and equality, and elections. Many landed estates were left untouched, peasant co-operatives grew very slowly and there was no extensive nationalization. There was, however, an influx of Cuban doctors, teachers, workers and military advisers.

As the threat of war grew, Latin American states such as Mexico and Venezuela in 1983 founded the Contadora Group to try to mediate in Central America's tangled affairs. Nicaragua and Honduras with its strong right-wing military influences became bitter enemies; so too did Nicaragua and El Salvador. Meanwhile, there were fears that Reagan might intervene even more directly, especially after his victory in Grenada. He had to contend with obstruction in the US Congress and warnings from across the world, but he seemed convinced that America had a new mission.

The Sandinistas increased Nicaraguan output, eliminated polio, improved literacy and housing, and won a good deal of economic support from governments in western Europe. They also at last held multi-party elections in 1984 which left them in power under President Ortega and which many neutral observers declared acceptably democratic and fairer than many in Central America. Washington refused to accept such a verdict.

The struggle meanwhile continued in El Salvador. Elections were held in 1982 but were boycotted by the left because of what it regarded as a hostile climate. They were won by the extreme right whose death squads and abuse of human rights embarrassed the USA. Washington preferred less extreme conservatives such as José Napoleon Duarte, a right-wing Christian Democrat who had been President by agreement with the military junta[G] from 1980 to 1982. Duarte's election as President in 1984 brought some relief to the Americans, his promises of land reform holding out some hope of progress for El Salvador's people. But his election did not end the civil war. Too much blood had been shed for rapid reconciliation – the resistance movement demanded more radical change. Duarte's success seemed to encourage Reagan, however. In May 1985 he announced a total trade boycott of Nicaragua, though his European partners at the economic summit that month were openly uncooperative.

Information about Central America at this time was always likely to be distorted in the fierce propaganda war. What the USA thought the Sandinistas might do seemed more important to Washington than what they in fact did. When Ortega visited Moscow in 1985 Reagan took it as confirmation that he was right to support the Contras. He insisted on believing in a Cuban–Soviet conspiracy. Yet international observers put the number of Cuban workers in Nicaragua at about 6000 and of Cuban military advisers at fewer than 1000. 'Communists' in Latin America were by now much divided in any case – united in a desire for social revolution and in a general anti-Americanism but not necessarily pro-Soviet, pro-Chinese nor even pro-Castro. The Soviets for their part seemed to accept that Central America was as firmly within the US bloc as eastern Europe was within the Soviet bloc. So cool was their support for Nicaragua that Castro stayed away from Chernenko's funeral in 1985 in protest, sending his brother Raoul to represent Cuba. The friends of the USA and many Democrats within it meanwhile continued to argue that for the elephant to go on trying to trample those it saw as communists in small republics with severe social and economic difficulties would more likely increase than reduce anti-Americanism.

US support for the Contras certainly increased Nicaragua's economic difficulties. The annual growth rate fell below two per cent in 1985 and 1986. The trade boycott reduced export earnings and in spite of austerity measures inflation in Nicaragua rose to 300 per cent in 1986. The Sandinistas found it difficult to meet the costs of the war. They also became more authoritarian, curbing press freedom and suppressing *La Prensa*, the main opposition newspaper. They kept a good deal of peasant support, however, and gained favour when many of the state farms of 1979 were divided into private smallholdings. The Contras seemed to be nearing defeat in 1986. The US Congress blocked the funds Reagan wished to send them, though new sources of finance for the Contras were found by the President's aides when they illicitly sold American arms to Iran, an aspect of the scandal journalists called Irangate (see section 21.2).

By 1987 the Contadora Group had made little headway in bringing peace to Central America and a new peace initiative was launched by President Oscar Arias Sãnchez of Costa Rica (see fig. 10.5). The Presidents of the Central American states joined him in the Arias Peace Plan to bring a ceasefire and reconciliation in Nicaragua. In an angry confrontation with President Reagan, Arias argued:

> The Contras are not the solution [to Nicaragua's difficulties]. They are the problem.

Since being elected President of Costa Rica in 1986, Arias had already forbidden the Contras and their US supporters the bases they had established in his country. He was awarded the Nobel Peace Prize for his efforts to quieten the conflicts in Central America but Duarte in El Salvador and President José Azcona Hoyo of Honduras were less ready to condemn US interference. Arias denied that he had ideological sympathies with the Sandinistas and he condemned Nicaraguan support for rebels in other parts of Central America – each country should be left to work out its own future, he argued. Political changes early in 1988 seemed unhelpful to the Arias Peace Plan. Panama fell into the hands of the military who were less sympathetic to negotiations over Central America's problems than the government they overthrew. El Salvador soon afterwards lurched to the far right when Duarte lost elections to the fiercely anti-communist National Republican Alliance led by Roberto D'Aubuisson, who had a reputation for backing neo-Nazi death squads. Neither change was welcomed in Washington, but Reagan rushed 3200 US troops to Honduras when the Sandinistas chased Contra rebels out of Nicaragua across the Nicaragua–Honduras border. The US President raged about the invasion by the Sandinistas of an independent state, while Ortega spoke bitterly of 'US Superman':

> Superman was defeated in Vietnam . . . and Superman will be defeated again if he disembarks in Nicaraguan territory.

President Gromyko of the Soviet Union warned:

> We resolutely denounce the forces carrying out a policy of institutionalised terrorism with regard to Nicaragua.

The Arias initiative seemed to be near collapse.

But almost at once it recovered. The Nicaraguan government and the Contras suddenly agreed a two months' truce on 25 March 1988 and their representatives together sang the Nicaraguan national anthem. Detailed arrangements were set in motion for separating rival forces into zones, freeing prisoners and allowing the Contras a part in Nicaragua's political life. National elections would be held in 1990 if the new-found goodwill continued. Reagan announced the withdrawal of his 3200 troops from Honduras to speed the process of reconciliation. The Sandinistas went even further than Arias had recommended in agreeing that humanitarian aid to the Contras from the USA would not be obstructed. Expectations for peace had now been raised. Although fulfilling them would still be difficult, the outlook was marginally brighter now than it had been for many years.

UNIT 11

Contrasts in Asia: 1 – China and the communist East

Note The Chinese government in 1979 requested standardized (Pinyin) spellings of Chinese names in roman lettering. These have been adopted in many cases in this unit, for example Liu Shaoqi and Deng Xiaoping (instead of Liu Shao-chi and Teng Hsiao-ping). In a few cases, traditional spellings have been retained since these are still widely encountered. Pinyin equivalents are as follows: Chou En-lai (Pinyin, Zhou Enlai); Mao Tse-tung (Mao Zedong); Chu Teh (Zhu De); Peking (Beijing); Hong Kong (Xianggang).

11.1 Nationalist China

11.1.1 Chiang Kai-shek and the Kuomintang

President Chiang Kai-shek had led China for twenty years by 1945. He was the successor to Sun Yat-sen, the founder of the Kuomintang (National Party) who died in 1925. But though Chiang led the Kuomintang he had already, within three years of Sun's death, moved away from the latter's 'Three Principles of the People': Nationalism, Democracy and Livelihood (Socialism). Chiang's rule became a dictatorship rather than a democracy, and his idea of nationalism seemed to be to try to purge the socialists in the Kuomintang, to create a Chinese nation obedient to himself.

The Japanese seized Manchuria from China in 1931 and in 1937 launched an all-out war against China which merged into the Second World War and lasted until 1945. But Chiang seemed to regard the Japanese as something of a distraction from his main business of hunting down Chinese Marxists. He had set out to purge the Kuomintang of Marxism in 1927 but his success was limited. Under leaders such as Mao Tse-tung, Chou En-lai and Chu Teh, the Marxists built the Chinese Communist Party (CCP), put down strong roots among the millions of peasants Chiang neglected, and developed an effective guerilla force, the Red Army. In their Long March, retreating northwards to Yenan in 1934–5 to escape the butchery of Chiang's army, the Communists won prestige and support. From 1937 Chiang was forced into an uneasy alliance with them against the Japanese invaders. When the Japanese were defeated in 1945 by the USA and China's other allies, however, Chiang was hoping to use the US weapons that he had stockpiled rather than use against the Japanese, to settle with the Communists once and for all.

Chiang's main weakness was that he had neglected to build support for his own government. The Communists on the other hand had taken pains to cultivate the peasants who made up over 90 per cent of China's huge population. In 1943 Mao Tse-tung wrote:

> We should go to the masses and learn from them . . . then do propaganda among the masses, and call upon them to put [our joint] principles and methods into practice so as to solve their problems and help them achieve liberation and happiness.

In thousands of villages, spreading in the north of China from Yenan, the Communists were redistributing the land from the landlords to the masses, teaching better ways of farming it, and promoting equality based on discipline and justice. At the same time Red Army guerillas often seemed more patriotic than Chiang's Nationalists, readier to do battle with the Japanese. But when the Japanese withdrew, Chiang was quick to seize the railways and reoccupy the cities, his power base. It was a narrow power base, resting mainly in businessmen, financiers, landlords and the minority middle classes, and in the Nationalists' army which respected Chiang's own military background.

11.1.2 The power struggle, 1945–9

Both Nationalists and Communists rushed into Manchuria, as did the Soviets, when Stalin declared war on Japan in August 1945. The Soviets dismantled industrial plant for use in the Soviet Union but were more likely to return other captured supplies and weapons to the Kuomintang than to the Chinese Communists: Stalin did not expect much of Communists who were backed by peasants rather than industrial workers, and he had never given more than token support to the CCP. The USA had strongly favoured the Kuomintang, China's official government. When rivalry in Manchuria triggered a renewal of the Nationalist–Communist civil war in China at the end of 1945, Truman sent General Marshall to mediate. Marshall tried for a year but failed. Chiang Kai-shek rejected all advice that he should make concessions to his old enemies, and the civil war went on.

Chiang was hopelessly defeated in the propaganda war. He could show little evidence of any concern for China's 500 million peasants or for the far fewer urban workers. He was criticized for his links with the USA and for encouraging foreigners to profit from China's economy and, far worse, condemned for protecting landlords in their exploitation of the people. The poverty of the masses, precarious food supplies and outdated social conventions Chiang failed to challenge underlined the failures of Kuomintang government. China's backward economy, the civil war, poor management, the withdrawal of foreign capital and the foolish printing of money created roaring inflation. Like Marshall, the moderate Democratic League could do little to persuade Chiang towards less authoritarian rule. Indeed, Wen I-to, one of its leaders, was murdered and the League broken up in 1946. Corruption was rife too. Chiang, his family and supporters found government profitable, but the system demoralized the Kuomintang as a whole and its army. Inflation, corruption and repressive rule alienated many in the middle classes. Chiang seemed too inflexible and traditionalist to see what changes were needed: to him and his circle, members of the CCP were simply 'bandits'. Having lost huge rural areas where the Communists 'swam' like 'fishes' in the 'sea of peasants', Chiang began also to lose the towns.

The Nationalists had had some early military successes and it was to them that the Soviets restored Manchuria when the USSR withdrew in 1946. For a time the Kuomintang even occupied Yenan. But support for Chiang crumbled everywhere. The United States ceased to pour in supplies – many of which were carried to the Communists by deserters from the Kuomintang anyway. Guerilla warfare wore the Nationalists down until in 1948 the Communists began larger-scale operations. They won Manchuria and freed most of northern China, and a massive and decisive battle was fought at the end of 1948 when Suchow was taken. Peking fell to the Communists in January 1949, and Nanking and Shanghai a few months later. Other CCP forces drove southwards deep into the interior of China towards Chungking, Chiang's capital during the war with Japan. Defeats destroyed Nationalist morale, just as victories now brought the CCP Soviet support and supplies. Too late, Chiang called a national assembly.

In October 1949 the Communists proclaimed the People's Republic of China (PRC). Mao Tse-tung, Chairman of the CCP, now aged 56, summed up how it had come about:

> Chiang Kai-shek betrayed Sun Yat-sen and used the dictatorship of the bureaucrat, bourgeoisie and landlord class as an instrument for suppressing the common people of China. This counter-revolutionary leadership . . . has only now been overthrown by the common people under our leadership.

Chiang, now aged 62, retired to the island of Taiwan (Formosa), there – in exile from the mainland – to keep Nationalist rule alive.

11.2 The People's Republic of China: Chairman Mao

11.2.1 Politics and the economy

(a) The opening years and the Soviet model The Communist system of government in the PRC had similarities to that in the Soviet Union. It began as a 'People's Democratic Dictatorship', which meant that the CCP, which in 1949 had some three million members, ruled on behalf of the people both before and after the first PRC constitution of 1954. As Chairman of the CCP, Mao Tse-tung remained a key figure until his death. From 1949 to 1959 he was also Chairman of the Republic, effectively the head of state. Chou En-lai, as leader of the State Council (the executive) until his death, was effectively Prime Minister. In 1949 Mao and Chou were already CCP veterans. Mao once a librarian, Chou once a factory worker, they had devoted their lives to advancing the CCP and to ousting Chiang Kai-shek. Victory in 1949, to which Chu Teh also greatly contributed as founder of the Red Army, now enabled them to lead the Chinese people to the better life they foresaw.

The people for their part played a greater role in the politics of the PRC than they had in past governments. They voted for the National People's Congress, which the constitution of 1954 made China's parliament though its work in practice was mostly carried on by a Standing Committee. It was the Communist Party which controlled the system, however, and to it all members of Congress had to belong – just as in the USSR. The politically concerned and ambitious had to join the CCP and conduct their arguments within it. Aware of the pressing need to unite a massive population in a vast country with as yet poor communications, the PRC was meanwhile kept as a unitary, not federal, country: it therefore differed from the United States, and from the Soviet Union with its individual republics.

It soon became clear that divisions over policy were likely within the CCP. These could well be between moderates and radicals, though that is much to over-simplify. Divisions became clear in the late 1950s when Mao engineered the 'Great Leap Forward', a more radical programme for change than anything the PRC had undertaken up to that point, and a programme which seemed to turn away from the Soviet model more moderate Party members seemed to prefer.

The PRC had not surprisingly looked to the USSR for support in 1949, perhaps hoping to find there a model for communist development. Stalin responded, and the Sino–Soviet Treaty of Friendship was signed in February 1950 when Mao made his first visit to Moscow. Soviet aid and expertise flowed into China to assist its reconstruction, and much was achieved, including the speedy elimination of inflation. The roots of the CCP were among the peasants, however, the section of society with which the Soviet government seemed to have its greatest problems, and some in the CCP were uneasy about trying to reproduce in China the Soviet emphasis on industrialization. But while Stalin lived, they, like Mao, bowed to his greater experience. A Chinese Planning Commission was set up in 1951, and the PRC's first Five-Year Plan (1953–7) echoed Soviet ambitions for expanding heavy industry and imposing economic controls through nationalization. China was also busily building railways and roads and expanding power supplies in the 1950s, and the GNP rose markedly.

Agriculture prospered too. One of the first priorities in 1949 had been land redistribution, promoting equality by dividing the land of four million or so landlords between almost a hundred times that number of peasants. 'Speak Bitterness' campaigns encouraged the identification of the worst landlords for trial in the People's Courts, along with corrupt officials and others who had exploited the people. Chiang Kai-shek claimed that some nine million were executed, though this is probably a considerable exaggeration. Others were 're-educated', but the CCP moved with caution against private business in the PRC, needing help in repairing the ravages of the years before 1949.

Under the Agrarian Law of 1950 the peasants shared the land in private holdings, helped towards better farming by mutual-aid teams and CCP advisers

Fig. 11.1 An agricultural commune in Kwantung Province, China, after the Great Leap Forward. Small-scale industry was encouraged in the communes, such as in the manufacturing of agricultural equipment seen here. The emphasis in Mao's China was more on busy hands and human labour than on advanced technology.

and then (during the mid-1950s) organized into farming co-operatives, sharing equipment and livestock. The next stage was to pool the land in large collective farms, similar to collectives in the Soviet Union: better equipped, more modern and allegedly more efficient even than co-operatives, these did away with all private ownership except that of the small private plots members of a collective could retain. By 1958, starting in Honan, collectives began to be put together in communes, even larger units of several thousand families.

These changes in agriculture were broadly those which Mao Tse-tung wanted. He grew more uneasy about industrialization, however, especially about expanding towns, costly technology, powerful 'experts' and foreign influence. In 1945 he had written:

> We stand for self-reliance. We hope for foreign aid but cannot be dependent on it; we depend on our own efforts, on the creative power of the whole army and the entire people.

With other CCP radicals, Mao wanted a great national team effort to make a society fit for 'socialist man'. The death of Stalin left the USSR in the hands of leaders he respected less, and the episode of 'the Hundred Flowers' in China itself persuaded him that China's revolution needed new methods. The customary censorship had been lifted in 1957 when the CCP suggested:

> Let a hundred flowers bloom, let diverse schools of thought contend.

The thoughts expressed were 'diverse' enough to cause alarm: some intellectuals and experts showed a preference for capitalism, private profit and Western democracy, and a lack of sympathy with Maoist aims. The result was a new clamp-down on such bourgeois ideas and more intensive re-education of the 'timorous greybeards' who seemed unable to grasp Mao's vision. Mao wanted 'permanent revolution' to keep alive ideas of radical change, and in an urgent shift away from Soviet-style policies a second and distinctively Chinese Five-Year Plan was launched in 1958 under the slogan 'the Great Leap Forward'.

(b) The Great Leap Forward and steps back The Great Leap was intended to result from the energy and commitment of China's masses. The plan was to extend the system of communes throughout the country, attaching to them small industries – not only light industries but also backyard iron and steel furnaces and small-scale coal extraction. The gulf between industry and agriculture, between urban and rural communities, would thus be narrowed in a new wave of egalitarianism, while the dedicated labour of hundreds of millions of Chinese would bring astonishing increases in output within a few brief years. Cadres[G] of CCP enthusiasts rushed hither and thither as project after project began for factories, dams, roads, power lines and new crops.

Observers were impressed by the vast scale of the operations and the apparent enthusiasm of the response to Mao's leadership. But those more closely involved, like the Soviet technicians in China, had serious doubts. The upheaval was too vast, much of the labour too amateur. The change overwhelmed those trying to organize it, and even the goals began to seem confused. There were fears for the future of family life and personal possessions and, though millions found a new prosperity, others found their betterment halted or even destroyed. In 1960 Khrushchev withdrew aid and recalled Soviet technicians, some even taking away the blueprints of the projects on which they had been at work.

By then the Great Leap Forward was badly off course. It was later alleged that famine caused the deaths of twenty million Chinese by the end of 1962, half of them during 1960. In 1962 Liu Shaoqi, then Chairman of the PRC, judged that the disaster was:

> seventy per cent man-made, and thirty per cent due to natural causes.

China had suffered drought then floods and, instead of soaring, crop yields had fallen sharply. Industry too was dislocated and most of the production in backyard furnaces, in the 'Campaign for Little Steel', was useless. Some blame inevitably fell on Chairman Mao. In 1959 he had been succeeded as Chairman of the PRC by Vice-Chairman Liu Shaoqi, another hero of the Long March. But Mao remained Chairman of the CCP and he was even able to increase his authority over the army by making Lin Biao, a strong Maoist, Minister of Defence.

Criticism of Mao was therefore muted. With the help of Deng Xiaoping as General Secretary of the CCP, Liu restored some respect for technicians and expertise, and in the new, more realistic Plan of 1962 he brought back some private incentives to help recovery. But the communes remained: in 1964 there were some 74 000, each with about 2000 families – rather smaller than they had been at the height of the Great Leap Forward. As Mao intended, they continued to provide units in which to organize local government, welfare services and education. Mao was influential enough to insist on further re-education in 1963–4 when the Socialist Education Movement and the campaign for 'Four Clean-ups' brought about vigorous new purges of the ideologically suspect. Relations with the Soviet Union remained bad even when Khrushchev fell from power in 1964. Mao and China's radicals still preferred that 'politics' should be 'in command'. Liu and the moderates made only limited headway in pursuit of 'economics in command' and, like Chou En-lai, believed it was still a time for caution.

(c) The Cultural Revolution In September 1965 Lin Biao urged China's students to protect the revolution against bourgeois liberalism and Soviet revisionism (see section 11.2.3) below). Early in 1966 revolutionary squads of Red Guards began to clamour for adherence to the teachings of Chairman Mao. Mao himself returned to the centre of the stage with his Great Swim (for nine miles) in the Yangtse in July 1966, demonstrating his personal fitness at the age of 73.

China was now involved in a new upheaval: a power struggle and a clash of ideas known as the Cultural Revolution. As Mao had written in 1940:

> revolutionary culture is a powerful revolutionary weapon for the broad masses of the people.

He wanted now to make sure that the revolutionary culture was secure and that the momentum of change would continue. In May 1966, writing to Lin Biao, he again asserted that it was vital to:

> promote the step-by-step narrowing of the gap between workers and peasants, town and countryside and mental and manual labour.

Mao deeply distrusted the policies of Liu Shaoqi with their centralization, incentives and other hints of élitism. He thought it time to shake up the Party and rescue it from the drift away from the revolutionary path. That meant ousting Liu and his supporters and curbing the influence of the moderates. Liu was derided as a 'Chinese Khrushchev' and downgraded, though not until 1968 was he stripped of all his offices. Like Khrushchev, Liu was then allowed to spend his last years in quiet retirement. Meanwhile, in 1969, the post of Chairman of the PRC was abolished.

This shaking out of Liu and his followers from the top ranks of the CCP had been comparatively bloodless and orderly when set against the background of the ferment in the country at large from 1966 to 1968. Gangs of Red Guards, most of them youthful, roamed China in search of 'revolutionary experiences'. They were armed with little red books of the *Thoughts of Chairman Mao Tse-tung* for frenzied chanting at frequent intervals. Their attack was on anything

Fig. 11.2 Chinese opera singers sing Mao's praises (with Lin Biao on his left and Chou En-lai on his extreme right) while brandishing copies of the little red book of his *Thoughts*.

Western and on Soviet-style revisionism[G] with its alleged emphasis on deals with capitalism, on consumer goods, on technicians and other élites, and on the promotion of industry at the expense of agriculture. Their cause was to bring revolutionary idealism to the young and to restore it to the old, to revive China's 'permanent revolution', brandishing Mao's *Thoughts* before all who might not know them. Schools and colleges were closed for a time in 1967–8 (universities until 1971) to rethink the aims and curriculum of Chinese education, and the economy was again disrupted as 'politics' took 'command' and town-dwellers and intellectuals were forced to experience life and work on the farms. Enemies of the revolution were rooted out, sometimes with physical violence, usually with chants and jeers. In their hero worship of Chairman Mao – and apparently with official backing – the gangs of Red Guards often became gangs of bigots and hooligans. Chou En-lai led the demands for a return to stability and in June 1967 the army was told to restore order. It took time to achieve this, even after Mao himself called a halt late in 1968. Ironically, many Red Guards who had come from the towns eventually ended up being sent to work in rural communes themselves. By 1970 China seemed quiet again, though some of the several million victims of the Cultural Revolution still remained in jails and labour camps.

The CCP had been submitted to a thorough spring-cleaning, and 'thought reform', it was assumed, had cleansed the whole country of backsliders. Mao was entrenched as a leader of almost superhuman stature, hero of a personality cult dwarfing even Stalin's. But he was of course ageing, and thoughts inevitably turned towards the succession.

(d) Mao's last years Lin Biao had been named Mao's heir in 1969, taking the place of Liu Shaoqi. The army had risen in significance too, for a time well represented alongside the Party in all important committees. But Lin died in 1971 – presumed killed in a mysterious accident when his plane ran out of fuel over Mongolia. The story emerged that he was on his way to Moscow and had been plotting against Mao and the CCP, to make the army even more powerful and to bring back pro-Soviet policies.

The Party now weakened the army's grip but within the CCP two major groups seemed to emerge from the confusion. On the one hand Chou En-lai achieved renewed popularity, securing the reappointment of a good many moderates including Deng Xiaoping. Deng became a Vice-Premier and a member of the Politburo, the CCP's inner circle. A rival faction was strongly influenced by Jiang Qing, a former actress and Mao's fourth wife. This group sought to revive radicalism with a new campaign against Confucianism – a philosophy based on the traditional teachings of Confucius which looked back to a long-gone golden age when everyone knew his place. In 1973 the campaign took a new name, 'Criticize Lin Biao and Confucius'; it became fiercely hostile to Western culture (except Beethoven's *Pastoral* Symphony which seemed properly rural) and in 1975 offered the sinister suggestion that there was in the CCP an:

> unrepentant top person in authority taking the capitalist road.

In this year, 1975, the new constitution was at last published. It declared Mao Head of State and Commander-in-Chief of the armed forces, as well as Chairman of the CCP. Citizens were entitled to certain rights such as free speech, personal religious beliefs and the right to strike, but the constitution also insisted that they 'must support the leadership of the Chinese Communist Party'. The CCP remained the system's nerve centre; the CCP veterans however, were dying out. The year 1976 saw the deaths first of Chou En-lai, then of Chu Teh and later of Mao Tse-tung himself. The radicals were able to prevent Deng Xiaoping (almost certainly the suspected 'top person') stepping into Chou's office as Prime Minister, a post filled instead by Hua Guofeng, Mao's favourite. Deng suffered a further setback when dismissed from other positions after there was rioting in Peking in April 1976. This seemed to have grown out of arguments about the qualities of the dead Chou En-lai, quickly turning into anti-radical demonstrations and, it was seen later, starting the April 5 Movement in favour of a more moderate road. Mao himself died in September 1976 at a time when a new struggle for power and policies seemed inevitable.

The upheavals since 1958 had slowed economic growth but the fourth Plan was completed successfully in 1975. The growing population (now about 900 million) remained in full employment, mostly on the land, and food production was usually adequate. Industrial complexes had grown in the 1960s and there had been marked progress in improving communications and power supplies. China was able to develop its own nuclear bomb in 1964, a symbol of technological progress. By 1976 manufactured goods made up more than a quarter of the country's exports. China had clearly survived the withdrawal of Soviet aid and, when Mao died, had extensive two-way trade with Japan, as well as some trade with the USA.

Economic statistics for China were scarce, however. The leaders up to 1976 had generally shown little interest in profit and Western methods of measuring efficiency; by Western standards the Chinese people were still poor. It is likely that their GDP per head was two or three times higher than it had been in 1949, but still hardly above the equivalent of 200 dollars a year, and consumer goods were still in short supply. But China's was a fairly stable economy, firmly rooted in the soil and with narrower wealth differences between town and country than in many poor states. A problem for Mao's successors was how China could catch up with the wealth of the developed world while preserving this underlying stability, which had survived even when 'politics' were in stormy 'command'. Meanwhile, China's population, already the largest in the world, continued to grow.

11.2.2 Society and social reform

From the start, Communist rule in China meant vigorous programmes for change. The goal was equality and the creation of 'socialist man'; the methods adopted were, when considered necessary, authoritarian. Critics deplored the regimentation involved - the drab uniform-like clothing worn by both sexes, the organized life and the labour teams of the communes, and the constant emphasis on serving the community and respecting the Party. Education and thought-training went hand in hand (as they do in most countries, though not usually so openly), seeking to change many old attitudes, such as those that had depressed the status of women and condemned the mass peasantry to ignorance and poverty.

The Marriage Law of 1950 fixed minimum ages for marriage: twenty for men and eighteen for women. The authorities went on to encourage marriages delayed well beyond that, and to advocate stern self-discipline in the form of celibacy and birth control to curb China's massive population. The state provided free birth-control support including abortions and vasectomies. An annual rate of population growth approaching three per cent was reduced to about one and a half per cent in the 1970s, with a target of not above one per cent. The Marriage Law had also extended women's rights and ended old practices such as forced and child marriages, bigamy and the killing of infant girls. Women were encouraged to play their full part in China's economic and organizational activities, and this brought equal pay and, especially through the communes, facilities for childcare and the provision of food, thus freeing women from many household tasks.

Much had to be organized almost from scratch, including a nationwide postal service. The CCP decided the objectives of the reform programme. In 1957 Mao described those for education:

> Not to have a correct political point of view is like having no soul. . . . Our educational policy must enable everyone who gets an education to develop morally, intellectually and physically and become a cultured, socialist-minded worker.

It was necessary to attack mass illiteracy as well as greatly to expand all kinds of educational provision. During the first decade of CCP rule, numbers in primary schools almost quadrupled, and those in universities expanded even more than that. Enormous gaps remained in this sphere, however, and the same was true of other services. Crash campaigns were needed for health. 'Barefoot doctors' (1.3 million by 1975) with minimal training were sent into rural areas where any doctor at all had previously been a luxury, while systems of health insurance and hospital care were developed and expanded. Newly formed trade unions as well as the communes were made agencies for promoting health care and welfare. By 1976 life expectancy in China was 60 for men and 63 for women, better than in Brazil though not as good as in Mexico. Much was achieved by the use of herbs and by acupuncture, about which there was often scepticism in the West.

When, during Mao's last years, Chou En-lai began to improve China's foreign contacts and to open the country to more outsiders, the West found much about China that seemed strange. Corruption and vice had been greatly reduced since 1949 and, in spite of some savage attacks on 'capitalist-roaders', China seemed quiet, law-abiding and hard-working. The cities had few of the slums and shanties of other countries, and the people seemed to avoid not only the crime and immorality of the West but also the alcoholism of the USSR. Many families had acquired bicycles and some useful possessions like a sewing-machine or perhaps a radio, but consumer goods were obviously scarce. Television sets were few, receivers estimated at only 30 000 in 1965. But there were also few people in want. Housing, food and utilitarian clothing were cheap and usually available. Health facilities, education (a basic five years in primary school and four years in middle school was usual after the Cultural Revolution), benefits and pensions were commonly provided by the authorities. At work, most decisions – even about wages – were reached by consultation and agreement, the gap narrow between managers and the work-force. The state services were paid for mainly from the profits of nationalized industries and a levy on the communes, and personal taxation of the sort common in the West was almost unknown.

Mao Tse-tung, China's Great Helmsman, had thus achieved many of his goals, though the West insisted that the cost was high in terms of bureaucracy, inefficiency and the control of opinion. The apparent happiness of many Chinese, even those too young to remember how different things were before 1949, seemed at odds with the misery that many in the West assumed such a system ought to produce. The Chinese still prized their private plots, however, and in spite of the absence of advertising were beginning in the 1970s to show interest in consumer goods, especially in colour televisions. Already not uncommon in cities like Shanghai, outside influences seemed certain to penetrate further in the late twentieth century. It had yet to be seen how deep were the roots of the Communist revolution in China. There were 28 million members of the CCP in 1973 but, when Mao died three years later, it was soon to become still clearer that not all of them were Maoists.

11.2.3 External relations

(a) China, the Soviet Union and the USA in the 1950s While the USA after 1949 blocked any change in China's representation at the United Nations, maintaining the pretensions of Chiang Kai-shek, the Soviets welcomed the PRC with the Sino-Soviet Treaty of Friendship and Alliance (see section 4.5.1). The Korean War and SEATO followed, widening the gulf between the PRC and the USA (see section 4.5.2). US administrations continued to insist that the Nationalist government in Taiwan was the legitimate Chinese government, entitled to China's seat and powers of veto in the UN Security Council, and Taiwan was put under the protection of the US Seventh Fleet and a Mutual Security Pact signed by Eisenhower and Chiang Kai-shek in 1954.

By then Stalin was dead. Mao Tse-tung tended to regard Stalin's successors as less senior Communists than himself and he was critical of their moves towards 'destalinization' and coexistence with the West. In 1955 Chou En-lai attended the Bandung Conference, seeking to identify China with the poorer

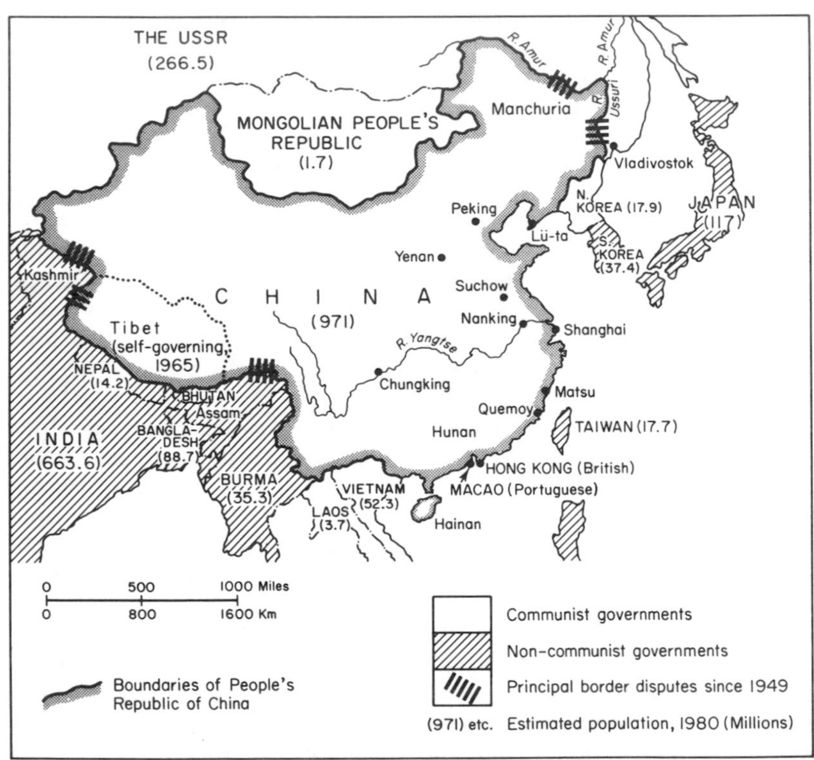

Fig. 11.3 China and its neighbours, 1980

nations of the Third World, though not necessarily with the non-alignment favoured by India (see section 21.4). Bandung gave China a glimpse of a world role very different from that which Washington assumed for it as a mere puppet of Moscow. Khrushchev's 'secret' speech of 1956 then alarmed the Maoists further (see section 3.3.1). In Mao's view, this was revisionism, taking the USSR away from the true path of Marxism–Leninism. Mao preferred 'permanent revolution' and no compromising at all with capitalism and the West. But that, to Khrushchev, seemed to be dogmatism, ideology dangerously rigid in the world of nuclear weapons.

When the Soviet satellite *Sputnik I* was launched in 1957, Mao saw it as the 'East wind prevailing over the West wind'. He seemed to want a much tougher line against the USA, based on an assumed Soviet superiority in technology. Khrushchev had growing doubts about Mao, however, and about his slogans, including that about a Hundred Flowers. Khrushchev later wrote:

> There was Mao's other famous slogan: 'Imperialism is a Paper Tiger'. I find it perfectly incredible that Mao could dismiss American imperialism as a paper tiger when in fact it is a dangerous predator.

Mao, he said, had also suggested that the nuclear bomb itself was a paper tiger, and such unworldly ideas led the Soviets to withhold the nuclear secrets the Chinese had been promised. This further angered Mao, as did Soviet silence when a new crisis blew up in 1958 over Quemoy and Matsu, tiny offshore islands held by Chiang Kai-shek and used for Nationalist raids on the mainland. The Chinese Communists bombarded them, but when the USA threatened retaliation Khrushchev stood aside and Peking had to back down.

The Great Leap Forward proved the last straw for Khrushchev. Convinced that a peasant-based revolution could not (or should not) succeed, and furious that Mao's contempt for the Soviet industrial model was now obvious, Moscow withdrew Soviet advisers from China in 1960. The Sino–Soviet quarrel emerged into the open with a bitter propaganda war between 'dogmatists' and 'revisionists' and competition for support among communists across the world. Enver Hoxha took Albania into the Chinese camp, but the rest of eastern Europe (and also Cuba) remained pro-Soviet.

Not only differences about Marxism–Leninism and about their respective economies divided the USSR and China. The Soviets were well aware of China's growing population and of their own temptingly under-populated Asiatic lands. Russia and China were old enemies and the long borders between them were not wholly agreed. China also thought the USSR had too much influence over the Mongolian People's Republic, part of the Soviet 'hegemony'[G] of which the Maoists grew noisily critical after 1960.

(b) China's frontiers As well as Taiwan, Quemoy and Matsu, still held by Chiang Kai-shek, 'Red' China also did not gain possession in 1949 of British Hong Kong or Portuguese Macao. In 1950 the Soviets had also insisted on the 'independence' of the Mongolian People's Republic, though it had once been part of China, while Port Arthur (Lü-ta) remained a Soviet base until 1954. In

1950–1, however, Red China took over Tibet, reclaiming ancient rights there. The Tibetans rebelled in 1959 when there was a fierce struggle and Tibet's Buddhist religious leader, the Dalai Lama, was forced to flee to India. Tibet remained within the PRC but in 1965 was given a good deal of regional independence.

The CCP had earlier tried to define China's south-western boundaries, agreeing its frontiers with Burma, Nepal and, eventually in 1963, Pakistan. There were problems with India, however. India's population, like China's, was vast but India was not a communist state and Indian–Chinese rivalry was perhaps to be expected. Events in Tibet increased Indian unease and there was concern about the ill-defined frontiers in remote Himalayan areas. It was India which seemed the more militant, eventually going to war in 1962 to drive the Chinese from disputed territories to the north of Assam and from the borders of Kashmir. India had support and supplies from the USA, ever ready to condemn communists. It also had similar support from the Soviet Union, which rushed to condemn Mao for aggression just as Mao was now condemning Khrushchev for weakness in the Cuban Missiles Crisis and, a year later, would condemn him for the (Partial) Test Ban Treaty (see sections 13.2.2 and 13.3.2). Indian troops had the worst of the fighting, but China refused to exploit its victory, declining to invade Assam and holding only what it considered its own territory. Indian–Chinese relations remained poor after 1962 and, in crises, China inclined towards Pakistan, India's chief regional enemy.

The Peking government now turned its attention to frontier problems to the north. Sino–Soviet boundaries were disputed along the Amur and Ussuri Rivers to the north of Manchuria, and Sino–Soviet relations grew more tense when the Chinese successfully tested an atomic bomb in 1964 and a hydrogen bomb in 1967, going on to launch a space satellite in 1970. Propaganda, often loaded with insults, increased the tension further. During the Cultural Revolution the Chinese *People's Daily* belaboured the Soviets as 'filthy Soviet revisionist swine', while *Pravda* was only a little less outspoken about Peking's 'unbalanced mad dogs'. Border clashes took place in 1969 and both Peking and Moscow rushed more troops to the frontiers. Between the Mongolian People's Republic and the Pacific the border was over 4000 miles long and there was plenty of room for conflict. Yet neither side wanted all-out confrontation, settling instead for propaganda and skirmishing. There were casualties nevertheless – probably 30 or more Soviet dead in the first fighting at Damansky Island in March 1969.

(c) About-turns and tripolar diplomacy It seemed unlikely that relations between the USA and Mao's China would improve. Mutual denunciation had continued since 1950 and China implacably opposed US activities in Vietnam and the rest of Indo-China (see section 18.4). The Sino–Soviet quarrel nevertheless changed things while, at the same time, it became more difficult for the USA to block Red China's admission to the United Nations as Third World states became more numerous there, each with a vote in the General Assembly. Other Western countries had, in any case, been much less hostile than the USA towards Peking. President Nixon changed US policy. Trade restrictions and other anti-Chinese policies were moderated during 1969. A US table-tennis team went to China in 1971 ('ping-pong diplomacy') and the new goodwill was enough for the USA to agree to China's membership of the UN later that year. Though Washington had misgivings, the Americans could not then prevent the expulsion of Taiwan and Red China's seating as a permanent member of the Security Council. In 1972 Nixon visited Peking. A remarkable change had taken place, suddenly increasing China's trade and all forms of contact with the West in the wake of the Cultural Revolution. The improved relations owed a good deal to Chou En-lai and perhaps showed that the ageing Mao in the 1970s was less a force than he had been. The US reversal was a grave disappointment to Chiang Kai-shek, however, clouding the last years before his death in 1975.

China's energies now seemed to be directed towards condemning the USSR's 'aggression' and pursuit of hegemony. Great-power diplomacy had become tripolar – no longer simply capitalist *v.* communist but now with the USA, the USSR and China at three separate corners. The USA could not immediately abandon Taiwan, however, and even when Mao died in 1976 vast ideological differences remained between China and the West. Meanwhile, China sought influence in the Third World. Peking gave aid to the poor, built people's palaces of culture, and seemed better equipped to win sympathy than either the USA or the Soviet Union. In 1945 Mao had written:

> We Communists are like seeds and the people like the soil. Wherever we go, we must unite with the people, take root and blossom among them.

But that was not always popular with other governments. The Chinese were often accused of subversion, of peddling their revolutionary principles, and were likely therefore to be expelled, for example from Cameroon in 1961 and Kenya in 1965. It was nevertheless China which, at the end of the 1960s, built the Tan-Zam Railway linking Zambia with the Tanzanian coast, one of many memorials to Mao Tse-tung's efforts in Africa (see section 14.3.4(b)). The CCP still denied there was any intention to make China a superpower, but Mao left it a much greater force in the world than it had been before 1949.

11.3 China since Mao

11.3.1 Inside China

A period of uncertainty followed the death of Mao Tse-tung, similar to that in the Soviet Union after the death of Stalin. The uncertainty was the greater in the eyes of observers since no single government office seemed clearly to reflect paramount influence in the CCP. The pre-eminence assumed for Hua Guofeng did not last. Having followed Chou En-lai as Prime Minister, Hua also succeeded Mao as CCP Chairman and he seemed at that time to be Mao's heir, but in 1980 he lost the office of Prime Minister to Zhao Ziyang and, a year later, the Chairmanship to Hu Yaobang. By then Hua had helped to destroy the radical 'Gang of Four' who might have led China into another Cultural

Revolution. Two of the Four, including Mao's widow, Jiang Qing, were in 1981 given suspended death-sentences for conspiracy, and the others received long imprisonment. But Hua himself had come under fire in the meantime. He had travelled, like Khrushchev, representing himself at home and abroad as China's new leader. But he was accused of building a new personality cult and of 'leftist errors', leaning towards radicalism when China's needs were for flexibility and modernization, for more freedom within China and more technology from the West.

The man behind the criticisms of Hua, and behind the appointment of his successors as Prime Minister and Chairman, was Deng Xiaoping, Vice-Chairman of the CCP. Despite his earlier setbacks, Deng seemed to have become the new force in China by the 1980s. In Chinese terms he was something of a liberal. China's new constitution in 1978 placed emphasis on individual freedoms and rights which were protected by law, while it also confirmed the leadership of the CCP and the importance of the thought of Marx, Lenin and Mao. Cautious changes were now taking place in the official view of the past, however. Deng led criticisms even of Mao himself which eventually revealed some of the suffering caused by the Great Leap Forward and some of the excesses of the Cultural Revolution. As early as 1978 Deng condemned the zealous adherents to Maoism:

> They make this a blind faith and do not allow people to use their brains, much less to discern truth from falsehood.

For the moment Mao's personal reputation survived and it was agreed that his 'merits were primary and his errors were secondary'. Nevertheless, the memory of Liu Shaoqi – discredited during the Cultural Revolution – was rehabilitated and policies were adopted that Mao would have resisted violently.

China had adopted a new Ten-Year Plan in 1976 but arguments had gone on about many details of the planning, for example between centralization, which Hua seemed to want, and decentralization, sometimes favoured by Deng. Competing pressures led to a new Five-Year Plan in 1981 when there was a general trend towards 'responsibility', allowing local and personal initiatives in both industry and agriculture. By the mid-1980s Deng was steering a course of 'modernization' which involved investment, technology and expertise from the West, incentives in the workplace and the dismantling of some communes. A rectification programme had begun to persuade CCP members against lingering admiration for the Cultural Revolution, and Maoist egalitarianism was denounced.

An agreement with Britain on Hong Kong in 1984 conceded that when the latter returned to China's possession in 1997 (when the lease of much of the colony expired), capitalism could continue there for 50 more years. Even so, when Hong Kong defeated China in a football match in 1985 there was violent rioting in Peking against foreigners, the worst since the Cultural Revolution itself. At the same time, however, Deng was worried by other factions in the CCP that seemed too ready to overturn Chinese socialism to embrace Western ways. Recent reform seemed too limited for some, especially among the young.

At the end of 1986 Chinese students protested vigorously, demanding, among other things, more free enterprise, more civil liberties, and even Western-style politics with opposition parties. The *Peking Daily* angrily condemned the students as being 'poisoned by bourgeois liberalism'. On the other hand, Deng, Prime Minister Zhao and Hu Yaobang, Chairman of the CCP and also from 1982 its General Secretary, by weakening the grip of the Maoists, had helped to destroy the socialist ideological certainties to which more conservative elements had clung. To them, China seemed now to be flirting dangerously with market forces, incentives and profit-making, undermining its communes, encouraging peasant industries, liberalizing state industries, and exposing its people to tourism and Western-style inequalities and values. The West had begun to speculate whether China was moving away from socialism altogether, as at least a handful of students seemed to want.

Economic growth in China in response to liberalization was impressive in the mid-1980s – almost 20 per cent in 1985 alone. As the communes were wound up, millions of peasants became smallholders and pursued private profit. Industry expanded and overseas trade increased. The part played in both by private enterprise grew. But such rapid change brought to China problems already familiar in the West. Prices rose steeply and the money supply threatened to get out of control; competition for markets brought the spectre of unemployment and with it spasmodic unrest; the demand for consumer goods grew with the rising expectations of the Chinese people, and a flood of imports threatened to increase external debt. Fearful of 'Western chaos' during 1986, the CCP reimposed controls and tried to reinvigorate centralized planning. Growth was curbed at around an annual eight per cent and the money supply was cut back.

China faced the problem of all Marxist states – to achieve a more enterprising economy and society while preserving stability, good order and socialist values. It needed to bring in Western technology without the Western consumer goods it could as yet ill afford. Even Deng, the force behind modernization and liberalization though officially still only Vice-Chairman, worried at the speed of change. More conservative Communists worried even more and in January 1987 they secured the resignation from office of Hu Yaobang, Deng's close associate. Deng was well over 80 in 1987, and debate began to focus not only on policy but also on a new generation of leaders. Deng himself began to play a less active role though his influence remained paramount. Though he was less than five feet in height the *People's Daily* wrote of him:

> He stands taller and sees further than we.

At the CCP Congress late in 1987, Zhao Ziyang criticized 'defects in our system of leadership':

> In the past few years there have been frequent cases among certain Party members of tax evasion, smuggling and trafficking in smuggled goods, bribery, extortion, embezzlement and theft [and] moral degradation.

Zhao had taken over from Hu as General Secretary while remaining Prime Minister. But Zhao was aged 69 in 1987, and he too seemed likely soon to give way to younger leaders, to carry on the political as well as economic and social reorganization he and Deng favoured. But while he remained, Zhao seemed to wish to bring to China some of the openness of Gorbachev's 'glasnost'. In 1988 some political prisoners were freed, though not yet Jiang Qing whose sentence had been long since been commuted to life imprisonment. Cautious debate about China's past, present and future became more public, but it was the CCP which still determined the limits of the debate.

11.3.2 External relations

The goodwill between China and the West which Chou En-lai had helped to build continued after his death. In 1978 China signed a peace treaty with Japan, more than 30 years after the end of the Sino-Japanese and Second World Wars. Japan gave up any lingering support for the Nationalists in Taiwan, and Sino-Japanese trade, already substantial, could now expand markedly. The Treaty expressed Sino-Japanese opposition to any attempt to win hegemony in 'the Asia-Pacific' region, almost certainly a slighting reference to the Soviet Union, whose activities in Afghanistan from 1979 China bitterly condemned (see section 20.5).

The end of US intervention in Indo-China meanwhile helped further to improve US-Chinese relations, though it also led to new regional problems. North Vietnam took over the whole of Vietnam, but it irritated the Chinese that North Vietnam preferred Moscow to Peking. China backed the communist Khmer Rouge government which took over Cambodia (Kampuchea), but that meant support for Pol Pot with his policies of extremism and genocide (see section 18.5). When Vietnam invaded Kampuchea at the end of 1978, China chose to see it simply as Vietnamese aggression, perhaps on behalf of Moscow. In retaliation China attacked Vietnam in 1979, fighting a brief war that went less well for the Chinese than they might have expected, as the Vietnamese once more successfully repulsed the invaders of their country. Sino-Vietnamese relations remained bad. They seemed unlikely to improve while the Vietnamese remained in Kampuchea, but there were other bones of contention. China was angered by the Vietnamese persecution of Chinese minorities in Vietnam. There were border disputes too. In 1988 there were renewed armed clashes over ownership of the Paracel Islands, south of Hainan, about which there had been earlier conflict in 1974. China refused to negotiate until the Vietnamese left Kampuchea, but in 1988 that remained to be done.

Taiwan was another outstanding problem for Peking. The Chinese were dismayed when Reagan renewed military support for the Kuomintang (KMT) regime there in 1982, but China's need for Western technology was too great to renew an open quarrel with the USA. In any case, Sino-Soviet hostility persisted and this was a greater problem for Peking. The Soviets and the Chinese both made cautious overtures from time to time, but even new leaders in both Moscow and Peking in the late 1970s and 1980s could only moderate rather than remove antagonisms (see section 21.2). However, tentative diplomatic moves in 1988 presaged better Soviet-Chinese relations.

11.4 North Korea and North Vietnam

11.4.1 Liberation

Outer Mongolia became independent from China in 1911 and was turned into the Marxist Mongolian People's Republic thirteen years later. Chiang Kai-shek recognized its independence in 1946 though, distrusted by the West for its close links with the USSR, it was not admitted to the United Nations until 1961. Communists elsewhere in Asia had made slow progress before the Second World War. The colonial empires of the Western powers still dominated much of Asia, and Japan too had built an empire, for example annexing Korea in 1910. Here as in other colonies nationalist movements grew, their goal independence. Not uncommonly, Marxists were among the most active nationalists.

The Second World War acted as a catalyst, so weakening the grip of occupying powers, even those victorious in the war, that major changes in the colonies were bound to follow the peace. The USA gave independence to the Philippines in 1946. For a time it seemed that the communist Hukbalahap movement might gain control of the new state. The 'Huks' had won influence as resistance fighters during the war, fighting against Japanese occupation and combining nationalist and Marxist aims. But after 1946 there was no colonizing power to fight against and Filipinos came to prefer non-Marxist government; moreover, the Huks had little or no outside help while the USA, still influential, gave every assistance to anti-Marxists to keep the Philippines capitalist. Communist movements were also unable to prevail in other emerging countries such as Indonesia (the Dutch East Indies until 1949) and Malaya (British until 1957) (see sections 16.6 and 14.2.4).

In two areas, however, Marxist governments did take power. In North Korea the Korean People's Republic was proclaimed in 1948. In North Vietnam the Democratic Republic of Vietnam was proclaimed in 1945, though not fully independent of the French, the colonial masters of Indo-China, until 1954. The upheavals caused by the Second World War helped to bring about these Marxist successes, but they also owed something to the fact that both North Korea and North Vietnam had direct cross-border links with China, while North Korea shared a border with the Soviet Union too.

11.4.2 The Korean People's Republic (North Korea)

With the retreat of the Japanese from Korea in 1945 came the division of the country between US and Soviet occupying forces. Occupation proved temporary but the division lasted, even after the Korean War of 1950–3 (see section 4.5).

From the start North Korea was led by Kim Il-sung. He tried to emphasize his roots as a Korean nationalist, but he had also been active with the Chinese Communists in Manchuria and by 1945 had joined up with the Soviets, who now helped him into power. He became Secretary of the communist (North) Korean Workers' Party in 1945 and then gradually consolidated his hold on the

Party and North Korea's government. Like other Marxist regimes North Korea became a one-party state, the people electing members of the Workers' Party to the Supreme People's Assembly, power resting with the leadership of the Party. While remaining Party Secretary, Kim for a time was also Prime Minister and became his country's President. A personality cult similar to Stalin's developed around him and the 'Song of General Kim Il-sung' became the North Korean national anthem. In the 1970s he began preparing his son Kim Chong Il to succeed him, a move unwelcome to the Soviets but - perhaps for that reason - encouraged by the Chinese. After the death of Albania's Enver Hoxha in 1985, however, Kim himself had been in power far longer than any other Marxist national leader.

By then, Marxist-style economic planning had long been under way in North Korea, with special programmes adopted from time to time, for example to recover from the Korean War and to speed industrialization. In 1946 large estates had been broken up for the benefit of about 750 000 smallholders. During the 1950s the land was collectivized and in 1958, influenced by China's Great Leap Forward, communes were introduced. There was a drive for mechanization and more scientific methods of farming, and large state farms took over much of the livestock farming, but the people were allowed to keep small private plots. At the same time there was progress in developing social services. Life expectancy in North Korea in the 1970s was similar to that in China, with which North Korea naturally had many similarities. But Soviet influences were perhaps even more apparent. Kim tried to keep out of Sino-Soviet quarrels but the USSR remained North Korea's most important trade partner well into the 1980s. Minerals helped the North Koreans achieve a higher GDP per head than that of the Chinese, though it remained below that of the Soviets.

Smaller in population, less industrialized and less favoured by foreign investment, North Korea still could not match the overall output of South Korea, but the wealth gap between them in the 1980s was not very wide. The regrets many Koreans felt over the way ideology had divided their country since 1945 began to be shown during the 1970s in moves towards co-operation between the two Koreas, as the painful memories of the Korean War grew less sharp. Little came of them, however, and by 1988 North Korea under Kim Il-sung seemed still to be less enterprising and further removed from outside influences than most states in the Communist world.

11.4.3 The Vietnamese Democratic Republic (North Vietnam)

Ho Chi Minh's record as a nationalist seemed more solid than Kim Il-sung's. When he returned to Vietnam in 1943 to fight the Japanese invaders, Ho had already spent over twenty years campaigning for a free Indo-China and the removal of the French. He was an eager member of the Vietnamese Nationalist Party, founded in 1925. He had also become a Marxist, receiving some training in Moscow and field experience with the Chinese Communists. Chiang Kai-shek imprisoned him in 1941 but when he got back to Indo-China he was soon leader of the Vietminh, a nationalist and radical organization wanting liberation and – like the CCP in China – change, especially for the peasants.

Victory over Japan allowed the Vietminh to proclaim the Vietnamese Democratic Republic in 1945. Ho's popularity and the Vietminh's authority were beyond challenge in Tonkin (northern Vietnam). Chiang Kai-shek's forces, the first into Tonkin as the Japanese withdrew, ignored the Vietminh, preferring looting to politics. But further south British liberation forces, the first to take over from the defeated Japanese, tried to curb the Vietminh in Saigon, preparing for the return of the French. The French for their part wanted simply to recover their pre-war empire with direct control of at least Cochin-China and sovereignty over the rest of Vietnam (Annam and Tonkin) and the rest of Indo-China (Laos and Cambodia). This was not acceptable to the Vietminh and a new war of liberation began in 1946.

It took eight more years to persuade the French that European rule was no longer possible in Indo-China (see section 15.2.2). During these years the Vietminh organized a successful communist state in North Vietnam. Ho Chi

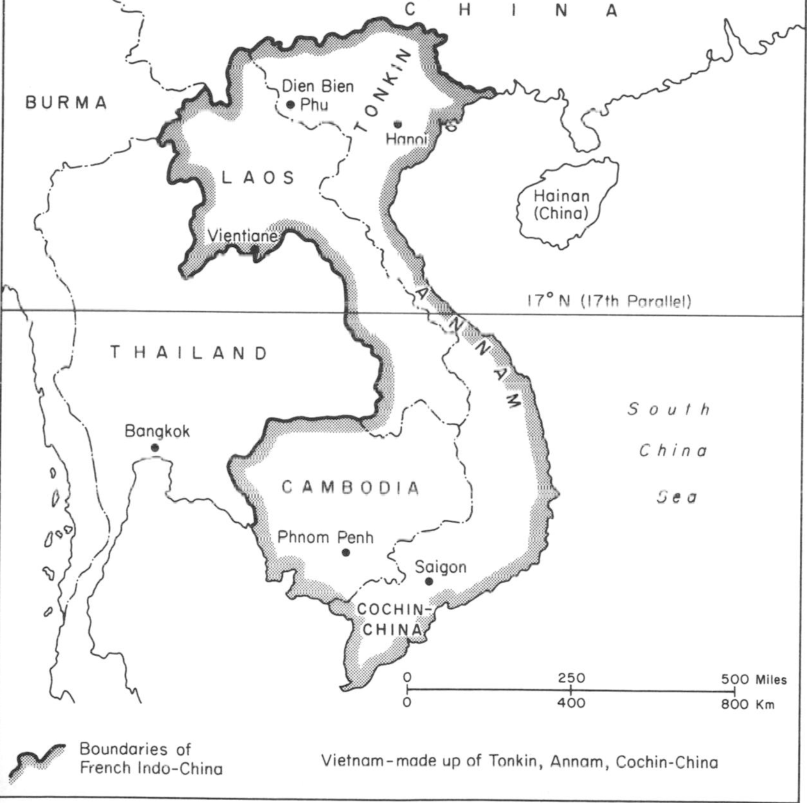

Fig. 11.4 French Indo-China before 1954

Minh was its President and, from 1951, it was governed from Hanoi by a left-wing coalition known as the Lien Viet ('Fatherland') Front grouped round the Communist Workers' Party. The USSR and Red China gave this Democratic Republic official recognition in 1950, and Chinese supplies helped ensure its survival. But it proved difficult to liberate the rest of Vietnam, since the French had US support in this further crusade against communism: by 1954 the USA was paying three-quarters of France's military costs in Indo-China – 1000 million dollars in 1954 alone.

Vietminh forces were led by General Vo Nguyen Giap, like Ho a veteran nationalist. His guerilla tactics, and his encouragement of a resistance in the south which came to be known as the Vietcong, cost the French 74 000 men by 1953. In 1954 Giap drew the French into a decisive engagement at Dien Bien Phu, besieging and bombarding them for two months during which time another 3000 French were killed, though Vietminh losses were several times that. When they surrendered another 10 000 French troops died of wounds, sickness and imprisonment before there was an armistice and the French agreed to leave Indo-China.

The Geneva Agreements of 1954 provided for the independence of three Indo-Chinese states: Vietnam, Laos and Cambodia. But for the moment Vietnam was left divided at the 17th Parallel – the North under Ho and the Fatherland Front, the South under Bao Dai, once the Emperor of Annam. Bao Dai could not command much support and in 1955 was deposed in favour of a republic of which Ngo Dinh Diem took charge.

Diem was a Catholic, an anti-communist and almost certainly manoeuvred into power as the choice of the French and Americans. It had been agreed at Geneva (though not by the USA) that free elections would be held throughout Vietnam in 1956. Since there was almost universal agreement that these would be won by Ho, Diem decided not to hold them in the South. He could rely on US backing. Washington committed itself bit by bit under Eisenhower and then under Kennedy to the all-out defence of a non-communist South Vietnam (with its useful supplies of rubber, tungsten and other minerals). The result was the 'Ten Thousand Day War' during which, at enormous cost to the people of Indo-China and its own reputation, the USA fought the Vietminh and Vietcong (see section 18.4).

Ho Chi Minh remained President of the Democratic Republic until he died in 1969, widely respected for his honesty, courage and sense of purpose. The US view of his rule was perhaps predictable. William Colby, a director of the CIA, wrote of the mid-1950s:

> The Communists had a full job organizing North Vietnam for the first two or three years. They went through land reform that managed to create an enormous famine. They killed a lot of landlords and things of that nature.

But too rapid land redistribution did produce crisis in 1956 and opponents (landlords and others unsympathetic to movement towards equality) were killed. The Communist Workers' Party ruled. Pham Van Dong was Prime Minister, Giap Minister of Defence and both gave long service, and much was done that was constructive.

The constitution of 1960 declared North Vietnam a:

> people's democratic state based on the alliance between the workers and peasants led by the working class . . . advancing step by step from people's democracy to socialism.

By the time of Ho's death, agriculture had been organized in co-operatives which were later grouped into larger units. Economic planning had been introduced, with some success in building a heavy industrial base and developing the mining of anthracite, coal and other minerals. There were social changes too, including a campaign against illiteracy and others to improve health and general living standards. But the struggle for South Vietnam against the world's richest country inevitably drained meagre resources, and worse followed in 1964 when the USA began the wholesale bombing of North Vietnam. Ten years later the standard of living in Vietnam, North and South, was still below not only that of Latin America but also that of China and indeed much of Africa.

By then the US government was accepting defeat and leaving Indo-China. In 1975 the Communists at last took over the whole of Vietnam, and Saigon, the capital of South Vietnam, was renamed Ho Chi Minh City. For Vietnam as a whole the name Socialist Republic of Vietnam was adopted in 1978. Giap retired in 1982 but Pham Van Dong continued as Prime Minister, providing continuity and preserving links with the pioneering days of Ho.

The problems of reconstruction were immense. Apart from the loss of life and the destruction, the war left the soil of Vietnam polluted by US chemical weapons. In South Vietnam's towns the people had been scarred by exposure to the seamiest aspects of American civilization with its drugs, prostitution and profusion of dollars. Now there was a flight of refugees from Vietnam: Chinese minorities fearful of ethnic discrimination, American collaborators fearful of revenge, and dissidents of all sorts seeking a non-communist way of life. It was estimated that the Vietnamese War had produced three or four million displaced persons and that by the end of the 1970s about one million had left the country, those fleeing by sea being known to the outside world as 'the boat people' (see section 18.5.1).

The struggle to achieve economic stability and social reorganization, with freedom from capitalism, required renewed effort. Vietnam joined Comecon in 1978 and received a lot of help from the Soviet Union, but the price of that help was the hostility of China as well as of the USA. Admission to the United Nations was won in 1977 after some US obstruction, but when Vietnam invaded Cambodia (Kampuchea) in 1978 China retaliated with war on Vietnam in 1979 (see section 11.3.2). The rest of Indo-China had turned communist when the USA withdrew in 1975, but the area's post-colonial problems were far from settled. It was estimated that in 1983 the Soviets were spending the equivalent of three million US dollars a day to support Vietnam, with further support being given to Laos. But that was only a fraction of the enormous cost to Indo-China of the area's great upheavals since the retreat of the Japanese in 1945 and, 40 years later, living standards were still severely retarded by the strife (see section 18.5).

UNIT 12

Contrasts in Asia: 2 – Japan and the capitalist East

12.1 Occupied Japan, 1945–52

12.1.1 Politics

The militarism and aggression the Japanese had practised in the 1930s and early 1940s ended in defeat, nuclear destruction and occupation. Unlike that of Germany, the occupation which lasted for seven years was almost exclusively American, save for some Commonwealth forces in western Japan. The Treaty of San Francisco which imposed peace terms on Japan in 1951 was also largely US-made (see sections 1.1 and 1.5.3). All the Allies had agreed at Potsdam that:

> there must be eliminated for all time the authority and influence of those who have deceived and misled the people of Japan into embarking on world conquest, for we insist that a new order of peace, security and justice will be impossible until irresponsible militarism is driven from the world.

But the problem as Washington saw it was not just to suppress Japanese militarism, but also to prevent the Soviet Union gaining much from its late entry into the Pacific war and from Japan's defeat.

General Douglas MacArthur, having led US and Allied forces to victory in the Pacific, quickly became the Supreme Commander of the occupation forces in Japan. Until dismissed in 1951 he impressed not only an American but also a personal stamp on Japan, his anti-communism all the stronger as a result of the birth of the Chinese People's Republic and of events in Korea (see section 4.5). There were grounds for arguing that MacArthur reconstructed Japan very largely in the American image, with a democratic constitution, Western reforms and a reinforced anti-Sovietism. But Japan was a country of some 85 million people, with a long and distinctive history; the comparatively brief occupation, even if the Americans so wished, could hardly eliminate Japan's deep-rooted traditions. Its achievements were nevertheless remarkable.

The Japanese, like the Austrians, were allowed their own government after their surrender in 1945, though MacArthur banned 'undemocratic' forces. This meant mainly the right-wing supporters of militarism but in 1950 MacArthur extended the ban to Communists who, a year earlier, had won 35 parliamentary seats quite democratically. A new constitution introduced in 1947 set Japan firmly on its new course. Emperor Hirohito remained Head of State. He had distanced himself from Japan's war criminals such as General Tojo and had won the goodwill of MacArthur himself, but the Emperor was no longer to be regarded as divine and had now to work within the constitution. This provided for adult suffrage in elections to the Diet of two Houses (Representatives and Councillors), a majority in the House of Representatives determining which party governed through the Prime Minister and his Cabinet.

The constitution also provided for basic civil liberties of the sort common in the USA but including also some Soviet-type rights, such as the rights to work and to equal educational opportunity. Trade unions were encouraged under an associated act of 1945, though MacArthur outlawed a general strike in 1947. A Supreme Court similar to that in the USA headed Japan's remodelled judicial system, and there was an overhaul too of the country's civil service and local government. The intention was clearly to shift Japan's public life away from the undemocratic practices of the past, and MacArthur recognized the importance of downgrading the country's warrior traditions. Article 9 of the constitution therefore required the rejection of a military role:

> The Japanese people forever renounce war as a sovereign right of the nation and the threat or use of force as a means of settling international disputes. . . . Land, sea and air forces . . . will never be maintained.

In 1950, however, in view of changes elsewhere in the Pacific, MacArthur agreed to what was later called a 'national defence force', starting as an armed police but growing into an army, navy and air force in all but name. The defence force remained small, however: the Japanese were now reluctant to waste money on armaments and they in any case had a guarantee of US protection in the Security Pact of 1951, renewed as the Security Treaty in 1960.

When the occupation ended in 1952, the Americans left Japan democratic and politically stable. Yoshida Shigeru, a Liberal, had been Prime Minister since 1948, co-operating closely with MacArthur. He was to keep office until the end of 1954 and already the pattern was emerging which would last for decades to come – a Liberal-Democratic (broadly conservative) government and a Socialist Opposition.

12.1.2 The economy and social reform

In 1945 the Americans were in no hurry to restore Japan's economy. It seemed more urgent to dismantle the old order including the *zaibatsu* – family combines such as Mitsubishi which monopolized capital and exercised great industrial and commercial power. The Deconcentration Act of 1946 aimed to break down such enterprises into smaller units. The results were not far-reaching (stopping short of banking, for example) but were nevertheless damaging to the Japanese economy and the US policy was subsequently halted. The zaibatsu re-emerged, though their family ties were weaker. They contributed to Japan's economic recovery, Mitsui, for example, becoming one of the world's major trading companies in the 1950s. Helped by US finance, technology and markets, by the Korean War which increased demand, and by the energy and enterprise of the Japanese themselves, industry regained pre-war levels of output and stood ready to make further advances by the time Yoshida stood down as Prime Minister in 1954.

More enduring than the attack on the zaibatsu was MacArthur's attack on the great estate owners, buying them out in order to resell the land in smallholdings to millions of peasants. As was usual, he worked through Japan's parliamentary system, and legislation in 1946 led to the transferring of about five million acres. There were improved farm prices, too, to raise living standards, while peasant ownership helped to give stability and a broader base to Japanese society, at the same time reinforcing the conservative element in Japanese politics.

The Americans also pressed for educational reform, broadening the curriculum and liberalizing, expanding and decentralizing the system. The new system was similar to that in the USA and children were to receive schooling for a minimum of nine years. But the Japanese were uneasy at the lack of central direction and what seemed a new classroom informality. When the Americans left there was movement back towards centralized control while, to the outside world, Japanese education seemed to become remarkable for its rigorous examinations and fierce competition for advancement. What was not restored, however, was the traditional emphasis on the Shinto religion with its nationalism, admiration of the military and emperor-worship.

This redirection of Japanese energies was probably the main achievement of the occupation. When the Americans left, Yoshida's government was already embarking on his 'reverse course' towards the restoration of centralized authority, for example in encouraging the zaibatsu and re-emphasizing national discipline, not only promoting discipline in schools but also restoring some of the police powers weakened by the occupation. But though this meant adjusting the balance between traditional Japanese and imported American values, Japan was now firmly set on a course different from that before the Second World War. In many ways it was a Westernized, capitalist democracy, accepted in 1964 as a natural member of the Organization for Economic Co-operation and Development (OECD) alongside most of western Europe, the USA and Canada. By 1952 abortion had been made legal in an effort to curb fast population growth, the emancipation of women had begun, Western labour codes had been adopted and some ideas had been imported for the improvement of housing and for the support of the unfortunate.

The Americans had quickly abandoned their intention to collect reparations from Japan and by 1952 living standards were climbing, with the population revealing a growing appetite for consumer goods and something of the American way of life. Yet Japan was by no means free from contradictions. Violence and anti-Americanism lurked not far from the surface and, even in the late 1950s and in spite of a strong industrial base, the majority of Japanese were hardly richer than the people of Jamaica, trailing far behind those of Britain and West Germany. In the thousands of small industrial companies which existed alongside the zaibatsu, wages were often low and conditions poor, and the state regulation of society often fell far short of what was common in western Europe.

12.2 Japan since 1952

12.2.1 Politics

After Yoshida, Japan had a succession of Liberal–Democratic governments and unexciting Prime Ministers, suggesting a generally satisfied electorate. The satisfaction rested on the remarkable economic progress of the country as a whole. But the Liberal–Democratic ascendancy was also based on in-built Japanese conservatism and the disunity of the opposition. The Communist Party had been savaged by the ban on many of its leaders in 1950, and its co-operation with the Socialists was only fitful. Both Communists and Socialists

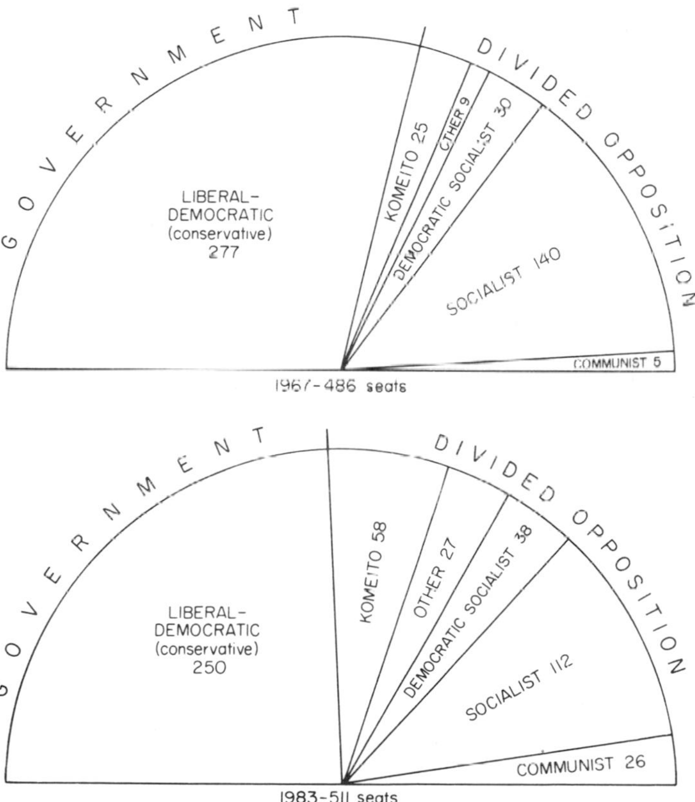

Fig. 12.1 Seats in the Japanese House of Representatives

were uncertain about how far to promote disobedience and opposition to the government outside parliament, and largely on this issue the Democratic Socialist Party broke away from the Socialist Party in 1959. A new centre party, Komeito ('Clean Government'), also emerged. Figure 12.1 shows how opposition to the Liberal–Democratic group was fragmented at the election of 1967 and remained divided sixteen years later in 1983. The Liberal–Democrats usually held power with less than 50 per cent of the vote, inevitably resulting in some frustration on the left.

Outside parliament, Japan often seemed turbulent, even violent. Anti-Americanism provided a focus for dissent, especially in 1954 when Japanese fishermen were exposed to fall-out from US nuclear tests at Bikini Atoll. There was violent protest when the Security Treaty was renewed in 1960, and brutal confrontations between angry demonstrators and baton-wielding police then erupted fairly frequently. Many of the protestors were young and critical of US influence, the continued US occupation of Okinawa (until 1972), Japan's fiercely competitive educational system and a society seemingly dominated by the pursuit of consumer goods. Japan had its share of the worldwide disturbances of 1968. Riot police were now much in evidence and in the 1970s a bitter but eventually unsuccessful campaign was fought against them as dissidents

Fig. 12.2 Japanese students in confrontation with the police, Tokyo, June 1960. Student demonstrations were not unusual in Japan: on this occasion, the students aimed in the wake of the U-2 incident to bring about the cancellation of President Eisenhower's visit to Japan and the end of the American–Japanese Security Treaty. Eisenhower stayed away but the Treaty remained.

tried to stop the building of a new Tokyo airport. Meanwhile a Japanese 'Red Army' carried terrorism abroad, at various times helping Palestinians and other freedom-fighters elsewhere.

Yasuhiro Nakasone took office in 1982 as Japan's sixteenth Prime Minister since 1945. Like his predecessors Nakasone had to adhere to the moderately conservative expectations of the various sections of the Liberal–Democratic group and of their financial supporters in the business world. Successive governments had aimed to provide a climate in which capitalism could flourish and individuals grow more prosperous, preserving most of the human rights encouraged during the occupation. A good deal was subordinated to these ends. Welfare legislation was for a long time less far-reaching than in most of Europe, and in non-economic international affairs Japan tended to keep a low profile. Japanese voters returned Nakasone and the Liberal–Democratic group to power in 1986, though the group still fell short of 50 per cent of the poll.

12.2.2 Japan's 'economic miracle'

The Japanese economy in the 1950s and 1960s created wealth on a scale which seemed to add up to an 'economic miracle'. Already equipped with skilled and disciplined workers and with a tradition of joint effort between management and labour, Japan overcame its shortages of raw materials with a hugely successful exports drive which earned it important foreign currency. Profits were commonly reinvested to fuel further enterprise: investment in the 1950s and 1960s grew at around 14 per cent a year. An Economic Planning Agency looked ahead and set targets from 1958 onwards for the growth of GDP. The targets were seldom below eight per cent a year and they were usually exceeded. As a result Japan quickly took the lead in world shipbuilding and went on to astonish competitors with the range of its successful products, from motor-cycles and vehicles to electronics and computer equipment, and from cameras to fertilizers. Agriculture prospered too, so that Japan became largely self-supporting in food and, with some exceptions such as oil, so independent of imports that rivals in the OECD in the 1970s and 1980s repeatedly complained of their trade imbalances with Japan. They alleged that, while selling vast quantities of their own goods abroad, the Japanese discriminated against foreign goods at home. Massive growth and trade surpluses quickly lifted Japan from being a comparatively poor country to being one of the wealthiest, by the mid-1970s ahead of Britain in GDP per head of population.

The success owed a good deal to hard work and to the imaginative development of up-to-date technology. Although mainly a private-enterprise society, there was little rigid dogma. Railways, telecommunications and broadcasting were nationalized from an early stage, while investment was handicapped neither by heavy spending on armaments nor by ambitious social programmes. Service in the zaibatsu provided security for some workers and protection against unemployment in a uniquely Japanese way, but for many the impressive economic development had a social cost. The mass of Japanese shared only modestly in the increased wealth, partly because population still grew steadily, reaching 120 million by the mid-1980s. Urbanization grew too, so that housing and environmental problems were often severe. Trade unionism was less effective than in much of Europe and incomes often low by Western standards, adding to the discontent of the dissenting minority.

The oil crisis which disrupted OECD economies in the mid-1970s seemed likely to have grave consequences for Japan. After their experiences in 1945 the Japanese had delayed developing nuclear energy and were vulnerable to interruptions in the supply of oil and increases in oil prices. Their response was an even more vigorous exports drive which enabled Japan to weather the storm quite successfully. After some wild fluctuations Japan returned to large trading surpluses – four million million yen in 1978 and in 1982, over ten million million in 1984. The surplus in 1982 was equivalent to about 5.5 billion dollars. Japan's GDP in 1982 (about 800 billion dollars) was still less than a third of that of the USA, however. Annual growth had fallen to about three per cent but unemployment was still below three per cent and Japan's economic performance during the recession of the 1970s and 1980s continued to be far superior to that of most of its rivals. In 1984 Japan's GDP was the equivalent of 1250 billion US dollars and now more than a third of that of the USA.

The increasing number of material possessions at home and of Japanese tourists abroad clearly showed the growing affluence of many Japanese citizens. Baseball, bingo, sex shows, pollution and squalor in the cities, as well as imported music and other arts, also showed that many influences in Japan were now Western. In some respects – for example in literacy, general education, telephone provision and hospital services – Japan was among the world's leaders, and life expectancy was the highest in Asia. Yet much of the old Japanese culture survived the coming of the new. In rural areas, the Japanese clung to the extended family and tried to preserve old social and religious values, especially Shinto and Buddhist. Even in the cities where East and West coexisted, the Japanese sought to retain their distinctive identity in spite of the imported American image. Many traditional attitudes lingered, for example in the reluctance to turn to the law and to pursue 'rights' in the Western fashion. At times Japan's seemed a strangely docile population in the turbulent modern world, enduring agonies such as those of vastly overcrowded commuter travel uncomplainingly; yet at other times fierce clashes between the police and demonstrators bore witness to the underlying conflicts which persisted in the new Japan.

12.2.3 Japan's international role

After defeat in 1945 Japan had to agree terms with its former enemies. Japanese governments now took care to cultivate good relations with the USA, the West and its own non-communist neighbours. A peace was formally signed at San Francisco in 1951 (see section 1.5.3). The Japanese renounced their empire in the Pacific but that did not entirely satisfy the Soviets, to whom it seemed that Japan was now becoming an American puppet. The USSR therefore rejected the Treaty, after which the Japanese refused to sign any separate agreement with Moscow until the Soviets restored to Japan four tiny islands to the south of the Kuriles. But though anti-communist, Japan was careful to avoid involvement in much that could be considered controversial. It therefore stayed outside SEATO, though signing a peace treaty with Chiang Kai-shek's Taiwan in 1952. The Soviets delayed Japan's admission to the United Nations until 1956 and, once there, the Japanese supported the USA in blocking the admission of Communist China. Prompted again by the USA, they made an

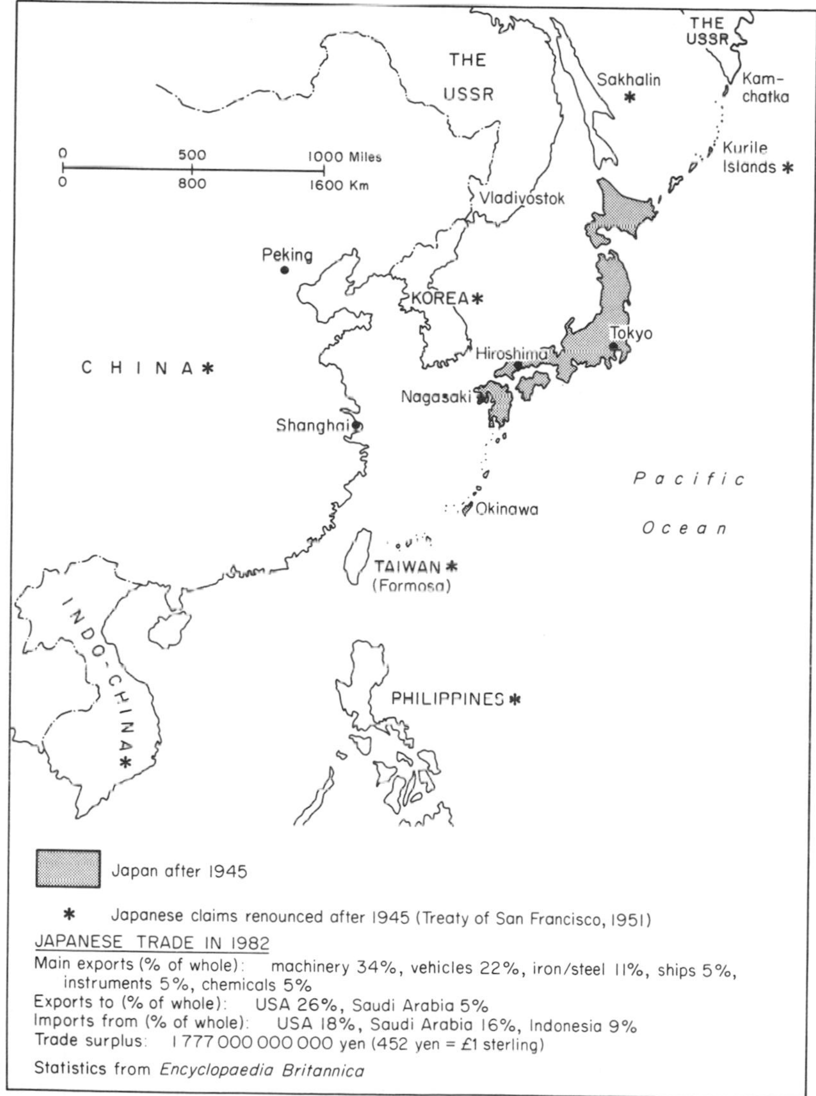

Fig. 12.3 Post-war Japan

agreement in 1965 with South Korea, at the same time refusing to recognize North Korea – but, significantly, they did not join the Americans in the war in Vietnam.

Trade was Japan's chief concern, however. After joining the OECD, Japan took a leading part in planning an Asian Development Bank in 1966 and staged the international trade fair, EXPO 70, four years later. In 1975 Prime Minister Takeo Miki went to France for the first economic summit meeting between the leaders of wealthy capitalist states, after which Japan was regularly invited to such meetings. By then the Japanese were making progress in the vast and tempting markets of mainland China. Prime Minister Kakuei Tanaka had visited Peking in 1972, recognizing China's Communist government and agreeing that:

> the Japanese side is keenly aware of Japan's responsibility for causing enormous damages in the past to the Chinese people through war, and deeply reproaches itself.

This paved the way for the Sino–Japanese peace treaty which was at last signed in 1978 when Deng Xiaoping visited Tokyo (see section 11.3.2). The price of these changes was the goodwill of Taiwan – but Taiwan was a very much smaller market.

Japan's international role steadily expanded. Shortly after 1951 it had signed friendship treaties with many countries in Asia, such as India and Indonesia, Vietnam and Cambodia. It had joined the Colombo Plan to assist the development of poorer nations, though it was seldom much to the fore in international aid until the mid-1980s. In 1978 it began showing goodwill towards the Association of South East Asian Nations (ASEAN). At Stockholm in 1972 Japanese statesmen also joined in expressing concern about the world's environmental problems, not least pollution – though in pursuit of profit Japan (like the Soviet Union at that time) persistently offended conservationists by its determination to continue killing whales, threatening their extinction (see section 22.4.1). In this respect, the 'merchant's diplomacy' which the Japanese preferred to more political involvement in international affairs seemed less skilful than usual. That the Japanese could be stubborn, however, was shown by their continuing refusal to come to terms with the Soviets. Japanese–Soviet relations remained strained, likely to become inflamed at times of crisis such as that in 1983 over the shooting down of a Korean airliner (see section 3.6). Within Japan there were sometimes nationalist pressures for a return to a more forward stance in foreign affairs, but when Nakasone attended the economic summit of 1985 it was still business rather than prestige which most concerned post-war Japan.

12.3 South Korea and Taiwan

In the years after 1945 United States support and protection were also given to the Republic of Korea (South Korea) and Taiwan (see section 4.5). It was support for capitalism if not necessarily for democracy: South Korea could only stagger towards democracy through corruption and authoritarianism, despite the constitution of 1948 fashioned under US supervision, while Chiang

Kai-shek's government in Taiwan was that which had been rejected in mainland China.

Over the years, and with US encouragement, both South Korea and Taiwan began to follow Japan's example, expanding industry and trade and successfully winning markets, but they moved less impressively towards liberal democracy. Even in the 1980s the Nationalists (Kuomintang) operated a one-party state in Taiwan, and in South Korea coups and military Presidencies had retarded the growth of healthy democracy, though the assembly included several political parties. Both could claim, of course, that tight internal security was vital in resisting external pressures. The People's Republic of China (PRC) remained tolerant towards Taiwan even when the USA began to run down its presence there after 1972, but Peking did not abandon its claims on the island. South Korea and North Korea still clashed from time to time along their border, even though they were also involved in long discussions about the possible reunification of Korea into a single state.

Syngman Rhee was the right-wing President of South Korea from his election in 1948 to his overthrow in 1960. His government was authoritarian and corrupt and no advertisement for Western democracy, though backed by the USA for its anti-communism. Though Rhee was re-elected as late as March 1960, there were many demonstrations against him and he fled before the year was out amid accusations of ballot-rigging. Then aged 85, he retired to Hawaii.

Hopes of more genuine democracy were dashed by a military coup through which Park Chung Hee became President. President Park was confirmed in office by elections in 1963 and 1967, but there were still allegations of fraud concerning the Republic's parliamentary elections, and Park's government sought vigorously to suppress discontent. There were protests when he normalized relations with Japan in 1965, and political frustration joined hands with social discontent brought on by rapid industrialization and urbanization. Students were turbulent in the 1960s and were angered further when Park changed the rules to allow himself a third term as President. He won the elections of 1971 but he then made more changes, seeming to aim at being President for Life. There were periods of martial law, and Park also had the help of South Korea's own CIA, a Central Intelligence Agency on the US model. The flouting of human rights led in 1979 to further violent unrest and to strife among Park's advisers, which led to his assassination by the leader of Korea's CIA. The army took power again, fiercely suppressing disorders and the dissenting students, many of them armed, and in 1980 Chun Doo Hwan was made President.

Chun set himself to reduce the Western influences which, he felt, threatened traditional Korean values, but he also expressed liberal and democratic intentions and by the mid-1980s went some way towards implementing them. It was felt that multi-party democracy could well breed conflict, however, and in 1983 Chun summed up the dilemma felt by many developing nations in their pursuit of Western parliamentarianism:

> Dogmatic and blind confrontation between politicians, and between political parties, is a waste of the nation's resources.

Soon afterwards, on a visit to Burma, there was an attempt to assassinate Chun. He escaped but four cabinet ministers were among the 21 dead. Two North Koreans confessed to planting the bomb which killed them. Elections in 1985 left Chun's Democratic Justice Party with a reduced majority in the assembly. The issue of constitutional reform now became dominant and pressures increased on President Chun to allow the people more genuine choice concerning their government. When Seoul, South Korea's capital, was chosen to host the Olympic Games of 1988 – to the dismay of North Korea which resented this favouring of its rival – protesters increased their pressures. The world began to pay more attention to South Korea, anxious that the Games might be disrupted. Clashes between demonstrators and the security police occurred even more often in 1986 and many protests linked US influence with the authoritarian government of Chun that students especially resented.

Presidential elections in December 1987 brought hopes of peace and liberal reform. There had been no presidential election since 1971 but Chun had now given way to demands for change, though he hoped the Presidency would be won by his preferred right-wing candidate, Roh Tae Woo. Roh did in fact win, though there were some allegations of electoral fraud and of the manipulation of voters by the media on Roh's behalf. The left had fielded two candidates, however, splitting the vote against Roh and thus allowing him to win with about 36 per cent of the votes cast. The *Korean Times* angrily condemned the divisions among the left-wing politicians who had thus:

> overturned the feast table prepared by the people through their years of hard struggle.

Roh promised further movement towards democracy but by 1988 progress in that direction was still hesitant in South Korea. Meanwhile, South Korea's economy developed under the guidance of an Economic Planning Board similar to that in Japan. Technology and investment were attracted from the West and from Japan. Like Japan, South Korea made marked progress in shipbuilding, engineering and electronics as well as in textiles, lifting the living standards of its growing population. As many Asian states were beginning to do in the 1980s, South Korea began to imitate Japan in penetrating world markets, not just those of the USA, its protector. In spite of this unrest, GDP grew from 1985–6 at around twelve per cent for the next two years.

Taiwan was also achieving success now, busily industrializing and building its exports, in 1986 outstripping South Korea in the growth of GDP and reaching a GDP per head far in advance of mainland China's. This growing economic importance helped to offset Taiwan's more precarious political fortunes. When Chiang Kai-shek fled from mainland China in 1949 he found in Taiwan the higher standards of education and higher levels of economic activity left by the Japanese. Protected by the US navy and a Security Pact signed with Eisenhower in 1954, the Nationalists and about two million refugees from the mainland were able to build on these foundations. Technological help even extended to the nuclear-energy industry, and US and Japanese investment encouraged rapid progress.

Until he died in 1975 Chiang Kai-shek continued to claim to be President of the whole of China, but he suffered a setback when in 1971 the USA at last allowed the PRC to replace Taiwan at the United Nations (see section 11.2.3). Chiang had groomed his son Chiang Ching-kuo to succeed him as Chairman of the Kuomintang and, by 1975 the younger Chiang was already Prime Minister. There were therefore few changes in policy when Chiang Kai-shek died, and in 1978 Chiang Ching-kuo moved up to the Presidency.

The USA had been growing increasingly hostile, however, and 1978 was also the year in which President Carter recognized the PRC and set a time limit of only two more years for Washington's Security Pact with Taiwan. Taiwan was facing growing isolation but the election of Reagan in the USA offered some hope of a rescue: he cautiously extended US military support for the Nationalists. In 1987, however, the younger Chiang was already 77 and the political future of Taiwan was beginning to seem even more uncertain, especially when the Kuomintang allowed preliminary movement towards setting up an opposition party and took a less repressive view of hostile opinion and even of political demonstrations. The Kuomintang still held all the seats in Taiwan's parliament, but hopes were kindled that the elections due in 1989 might bring change. The sudden death of Chiang Ching-kuo in January 1988 brought further uncertainties, however. Though his will was alleged to include recommendations that Taiwan should pursue democratic reform and, when possible, reunification with China, he had not named a successor. A power struggle such as that which had followed the death of Mao Tse-tung in China now seemed likely in Taiwan.

12.4 The Philippines and post-colonial Asia

Korea and Taiwan had been Japanese-dominated before the Second World War, but further south the Philippines had been taken from Spain and held for half a century by the USA, and before 1939 almost all the other parts of southern Asia had at some time or other been added to the colonial empires of the Europeans. Australia and New Zealand had early achieved their independence within the British Commonwealth of Nations, but when the Second World War ended in 1945 nationalist movements elsewhere were now also lining up for the struggle for independence (see Units 14 and 15). The result was the birth of more than a dozen new nations during the next 30 years or so, each facing the problems of nation-building and of achieving stability with economic viability which later units in this book will discuss. Most of these emerging Asian nations set up capitalist, not communist, systems – a process encouraged by their former colonial masters, such as the Americans in the Philippines, which was the first to become independent.

The constitution of the Philippines was very similar to that of the USA, and Truman launched the country into independence with the help of a Rehabilitation Act and the US–Philippines Trade Act of 1946. Some 620 million dollars were given initially for rehabilitation and repairing war damage, and the Trade Act provided mutual trade preferences for almost 30 years. In 1947 Washington

Table 12.1 States in Asia: some comparative statistics

State	Population		Income per head, 1983 (US dollars)*	Number of people per doctor, c. 1980	Percentage of population literate over age 15†, c. 1980
	Estimated, 1985 (millions)	Annual growth, 1980–5 (%)			
Afghanistan	18.1	2.6	210‡	13 467	20
Australia	15.7	1.4	10 810	559	99
Bangladesh	98.7	3.1	130	8 908	26
Brunei	0.2	3.9	2 140‖	2 474	78
Burma	37.7	1.0	180	4 940	66
China	1 043.1	1.1	300	1 910	77 (12+)
Hong Kong	5.4	1.9	6 000	1 258	78
India	768.1	2.0	260	2 545	37
Indonesia	167.6	2.1	560‖	9 774	72 (10+)
Japan	120.8	0.6	10 100	761	100
Kampuchea	7.3	1.9	160§	15 905	48
Korea, North	20.1	2.3	790‡	429#	90
Korea, South	41.2	1.6	1 840	1 441	93
Laos	4.1	2.0	150	17 290	44
Malaysia	15.7	2.2	1 870	3 497	75
Nepal	16.5	2.3	170	28 768	24 (6+)

New Zealand	3.3	0.9	7 410	635	100
Pakistan	100.4	3.1	370	2 911	21
Papua New Guinea	3.3	2.8	790	16 052	43
Philippines	54.7	2.5	760	6 713	84
Singapore	2.5	1.1	6 500	1 101	85 (10+)
Sri Lanka	16.1	1.7	330	7 631	87
Taiwan	19.1	1.5	2 680	1 462	89
Thailand	51.3	2.0	810	6 870	82 (10+)
Vietnam	60.5	2.1	170	4 067	65

* At current market prices
† Except where indicated
‡ 1982
‖ Gross national product boosted by oil output
'Doctor' includes dentists
§ 1977

This table gives some indication of the widely differing stages of development in Asia in the 1980s. Comparatively wealthy developed states such as Australia and Japan had achieved a favourable provision of doctors in relation to population, and almost universal literacy, suggesting comparatively advanced health care and educational provision. In the poorest countries, such as Bangladesh and Nepal, these figures suggest a different picture and indicate the struggle facing many developing nations. The rate of population increase caused concern generally but especially in countries which already had a large population where such growth was not unrelated to continuing low incomes per head. Industrial development helped countries like South Korea, Singapore and Taiwan to begin to follow in the footsteps of Japan. Brunei's wealth owed much to oil.

Statistics from *Encyclopaedia Britannica*

made the first of a series of defence agreements, securing US bases in the Philippines.

Right-wing Nationalists soon dominated the Filipino Presidency and opponents of Ramon Magsaysay (President, 1953–7) considered him little more than a US puppet. It was during his Presidency that the Marxist Hukbalahap movement was finally defeated (see section 11.4.1). Though the Liberal Diosdado Macapagal was President from 1962 to 1965, the Nationalists continued to dominate Congress and in December 1965 Macapagal was defeated for the Presidency by Ferdinand Marcos. Partly through elections but also by strong-arm measures, Marcos was now to remain in office for more than twenty years. He several times introduced martial law in the early 1970s and amended the constitution. Martial law was continuously in force from 1972 to 1981 when Marcos was confirmed in the Presidency in an election boycotted by the main opposition groups.

By then a communist New People's Army had developed and taken root in the face of Marcos's prolonged grip on power and in succession to the 'Huks'. Marcos also faced a Muslim challenge, Muslim separatists aiming to create a breakaway state in the south. The Muslims were fewer than five per cent in a predominantly Roman Catholic country, however, and their threat was not great. Most of the population (around 48 million in 1980) lived on eleven main islands, but the Philippines as a whole consisted of more than 7000 islands, and there were many languages – Tagalog (a Malayan dialect) and English being the official ones, and Spanish one of the minority languages. Governments therefore faced a typical Third World problem in their need to try to build one nation out of diversities (see sections 16.1 and 17.1). They also faced the economic problems typical of developing countries, which mounted in the 1970s to combine serious balance-of-payments deficits with unemployment and inflation (see section 21.1).

Such problems were not infrequently put forward to explain the need for authoritarian rule, but the assassination of the Liberal Benigno Aquino in 1983 underlined the grave doubts many felt about the rule of President Marcos. Aquino was killed at Manila airport when he returned to the Philippines from exile and medical treatment in the USA. He had long been the leading Liberal opponent of the President and had spent eight years up to 1980 in Marcos's jails. He returned in order to campaign for freedom and democracy, but even a bullet-proof vest could not save his life. Murders, arrests, torturings and disappearances gave the Philippines an image similar to that of some of the countries of Latin America. At Aquino's funeral mass, the leader of the Catholic Church there described the country's:

> atmosphere of oppression, and corruption, the climate of fear and anguish.

Meanwhile, though literacy standards in the Philippines were high (and helped to trigger student unrest), standards in nutrition and health were only modest – well below Japan's – and welfare provision remained comparatively low. Textiles and electronics were nevertheless developing and the government made some reforms, for example in transferring large estates to smallholders. US bases and links remained, in spite of some anti-American demonstrations.

Most trade in the 1980s was still with the USA (though privileges had ceased with the repeal of the Trade Act in 1974) and Japan, but the GDP per head in the Philippines was still hardly more than that of the poorest states in Latin America. In this the Philippines were typical of much of non-communist Asia, though Filipinos were better off than the masses in the poorest states such as India and Pakistan. They had yet to break through to commercial prosperity in the way of Taiwan, Hong Kong and Singapore, and even less did they match the successes of Japan and the comfortable standards of Australia, but they had, in 1986, survived 40 years of independence in a harshly competitive environment. The cost in terms of hardship and loss of freedom was high, however, though by no means uncommon among the developing nations of the post-colonial world.

Marcos eventually fell from power in 1986 when Aquino's widow, Corazon, led a wave of popular denunciation. Marcos lost the backing of the USA and, in spite of claiming victory over Corazon Aquino in the new Presidential election, was forced to resign, his corruption and self-enrichment now too obvious. Like South Korea's Syngman Rhee before him, Marcos went to Hawaii, his move aided by the US government. Corazon Aquino was now installed as the Filipino President, inexperienced as yet, and uncomfortably sandwiched between right-wing pro-Marcos elements and communist guerillas on the left. But the Philippines had at least the chance of a new beginning, in spite of the formidable difficulties which stood in the way of the President's policy of 'national reconciliation'.

For the moment, though without marked enthusiasm for her government, the army gave its support to Mrs Aquino. She survived intrigue and attempted coups during 1987 and in spite of considerable disorder local elections were held in January 1988 in all but ten of the Philippines' 73 provinces. The elections claimed almost a hundred lives, however. Marcos claimed that many Filipinos wanted his return to keep the political left under tighter control, but he was given no encouragement by the USA. (Indeed in October 1988 Marcos and his wife faced multiple charges in US courts, relating to extortion, embezzlement and fraud.) The New People's Army continued its struggle, however. During 1986 its guerillas had set up bases in Manila, the capital of the Philippines, where they ambushed and wounded the mayor soon after the local elections in 1988. President Aquino renewed her appeal that 'democracy in our country' should be allowed to 'gain a foothold', but the violence of 40 years of independence would not disappear overnight. The opposition in Taiwan and South Korea nevertheless hoped that democracy would triumph in the Philippines and they looked forward to a 'domino phenomenon' which would spread democracy where it was so far absent in Asia.

UNIT 13

East–West coexistence and détente, 1955–75

13.1 Peaceful coexistence and summits

'Summit meeting' was the phrase used by Winston Churchill when he called in 1953 for a conference between Eisenhower and Stalin, leaders of the superpowers, to improve East–West relations. Churchill hoped they could meet without a rigid agenda, simply to seek better understanding. Stalin's death in that year brought to power in the Kremlin leaders more flexible than he had been, and only then did the ice of the Cold War begin to crack, making an eventual summit meeting more likely (see Unit 4). The Soviets in 1954 joined in the Geneva Agreements, seeking to settle the future of Indo-China when the French gave up colonial control there (see section 15.2.2). In May 1955 Moscow accepted the Austrian State Treaty (see section 4.6), and in July that year Khrushchev and Bulganin attended a summit meeting at Geneva with Eisenhower and, from Britain and France, Eden and Faure. The Soviet leaders were beginning a new era in which, unlike Stalin before them, they were ready to move outside the boundaries of the USSR to pursue their diplomatic objectives.

Among these objectives, Khrushchev in 1956 identified 'peaceful coexistence' between East and West. The idea was not entirely new: Lenin had spoken of East–West 'cohabitation', and Malenkov's 'New Course' in foreign policy since 1953 had already shown some movement away from Stalinist rigidity and from confrontation. Peaceful coexistence did not mean that there would be any abandonment of the Soviet Union's socialist principles, even though the Chinese derided it as 'a bourgeois pacifist notion': it would, however, reduce the risk of war for the sake of ideology or for supremacy, while allowing continuing competition with the West and with capitalism in peaceful pursuits.

Such competition inevitably extended to the development of technology and that inevitably included the development of weaponry (see section 4.4). In 1957 the Soviets launched *Sputnik I*, the world's first satellite to orbit the earth in space, and *Sputnik II* which took Laika, a husky, into orbit. Washington replied in 1958 with an American satellite, *Vanguard I*, but Moscow then put a cosmonaut, Yuri Gagarin, into space in 1961, a feat matched the following year by the Americans with John Glenn's orbit of the earth in *Mercury*. In 1962 the Soviets sent into space the first woman cosmonaut, Valentina Tereshkova. The United States gained greater satisfaction when Neil Armstrong in *Apollo II* landed on the moon in 1969, the Soviets having decided against human landings there in favour of unmanned probes. In 1975 the *Apollo-Soyuz* link-up (a brief union of spaceships in space) temporarily improved US-Soviet relations before the USA had a further morale-boosting success in 1981: a reusable space vehicle was launched, starting a new phase in travel in which passengers and freight could be piloted to and from space in the *Shuttle*. The development of rockets to launch satellites into space was, of course, inseparable from the development of missiles to carry nuclear warheads between countries (see section 13.3).

The Soviet leaders were aware of the enormous dangers ever present in the Cold War with such technological developments and with the growing stockpiles of nuclear weapons. They were also aware of the great cost of armaments, and Khrushchev especially wanted to direct more of the Soviet Union's resources to the well-being of its people (see Unit 3). Peaceful coexistence held out the hope of reduced tension and less spending on arms. But the German problem still dogged the superpowers in the 1950s, the Soviets still being anxious about a remilitarized West Germany. The Geneva summit of 1955 made little progress towards solving the problems of the two Germanies; Eisenhower and Khrushchev therefore tried to disguise their failure by instructing their Foreign Ministers to meet in order to:

> propose effective means for their solution, taking account of the close link between the reunification of Germany and the problem of European security.

All that the summit seemed to have achieved was to prepare the way for some East-West cultural exchanges, and the Foreign Ministers proved no more successful than their leaders.

Khrushchev himself continued to travel. In 1956 he and his Prime Minister Bulganin visited London but events in Hungary later that year again soured East-West relations (see section 8.2.3). Adam Rapacki, Poland's Foreign Minister, then proposed in 1957 a 'nuclear-free zone' in central Europe (including Germany), together with the banning of further tests of nuclear weapons. The West suspected this Rapacki Plan was a plot backed by Khrushchev to weaken western Europe against the non-nuclear forces of eastern Europe and, like all similar proposals, the Plan foundered on mutual distrust. Khrushchev nevertheless went to Camp David, Maryland, for another meeting with Eisenhower in 1959, to discuss Berlin and the continuing arms race. They spoke enthusiastically of 'the spirit of Camp David' and agreed:

> that negotiations would be reopened with a view to achieving a solution [concerning Berlin] . . . in accordance with the interests of all concerned.

A four-power summit, to include Britain and France who also had interests in Berlin, was arranged for 1960 in Paris.

To the dismay of Macmillan and de Gaulle, who were hoping to play a useful part in it, the Paris summit broke up almost as soon as it started. The powers had argued for many years about how they might keep a check on one another's arms stocks: the West insisted that 'open skies' – the rights to fly over each other's territory – were necessary in order to verify any agreement that might be reached, but the Soviets protested against US spy-planes which took illicit photographs of Soviet territory. Just before the summit, a Lockheed U-2 equipped with cameras was shot down near Sverdlovsk and its pilot, Gary Powers, was taken prisoner. At Paris, Khrushchev demanded an apology from Eisenhower for the U-2 mission and, when it was refused, stormed out from the summit in a blaze of publicity. The Soviets went on to cancel their earlier invitation to the American President to visit Moscow.

Tension was increased over the West's access to Berlin and, at the UN General Assembly, Khrushchev noisily demanded attention for his grievances by banging a shoe on his desk. He demanded that the West recognize East Germany and accept East German control of access to West Berlin, but seemed now to be reverting to policies of confrontation. Yet he reasserted the Soviet Union's belief in peaceful coexistence and, in spite of fierce criticism from China, got support for his policy before the end of 1960 from most of the world's Communist Parties. When John F. Kennedy won the US Presidency, Khrushchev quickly agreed to a new summit, which met in Vienna in June 1961.

Fig. 13.1 East Germans began building the Berlin Wall in August 1961. By the time of this photograph in December 1961 the wall and its fortifications were developing. A water-tanker cleans up after the latest work at the Friedrichstrasse crossing-point.

It later became the fashion to argue that the Vienna summit allowed Khrushchev to size up the comparatively young US President, that he mistakenly concluded that Kennedy was weak enough to be bullied, and that this led to a new adventurism in Soviet policy. That was hardly apparent in 1961. For the moment, Khrushchev backed down on his demands that West Germany should leave NATO and that the West should immediately recognize East Germany. In August the East Germans were encouraged to build the Berlin Wall, sealing the border between West Berlin and the rest of the city in an almost desperate attempt to stem the flow of defectors to the West: some three million had crossed into West Berlin since 1945. But there Khrushchev seemed content to leave the German question for the time being. Events were gathering pace elsewhere, the rivalry of the superpowers beginning increasingly to spill over into the emerging nations of the Third World.

13.2 Coexistence or confrontation?

13.2.1 Indo-China and the Congo

American anxieties about communist influence in countries newly independent of colonial control had not ended with the Korean War (see section 4.5). By 1961 it seemed that an East–West struggle for influence would threaten many emerging nations, despite their attempt to resist the danger by launching the non-aligned movement at an Afro–Asian conference hosted by Indonesia at Bandung in 1955 (see section 21.4).

Already when Kennedy became President, the USA was drifting into involvement in Indo-China, increasingly determined to prevent the unification of Vietnam agreed at Geneva in 1954 when the French withdrew (see section 11.4.3). In May 1961 US troops were sent to Thailand, ready to invade Laos to save it from communism. At Vienna, however, Kennedy and Khrushchev agreed to leave Laos to manage its own affairs. Returning from the Vienna summit, Kennedy met de Gaulle in Paris and the latter spoke plainly to him:

> You Americans wanted, yesterday, to take our place in Indo-China . . . to assume a succession to rekindle a war that we ended. I predict . . . you will, step by step, be sucked into a bottomless military and political quagmire.

Kennedy nevertheless stepped up US aid to Diem's anti-communist regime in South Vietnam, starting with a trickle of military help – in the form of helicopter units – at the end of 1961 (see section 18.4).

Events in the Congo quickened Soviet suspicions about the West's global interests. When Belgium, with too little preparation, granted Congolese independence in 1960, Patrice Lumumba, the left-wing leader of the Congolese National Movement, became Prime Minister, announcing to the Europeans:

> From today, we are no longer your monkeys.

But independence brought chaos (see section 15.3). The regions of Katanga and South Kasai attempted to secede from the Congo, apparently encouraged by the Belgians, European mining interests and mercenaries interested more in their own profits than in the well-being of Africans. Lumumba in his frustration called for outside help. The United Nations intervened, though this was more to keep the peace than to preserve Congolese unity, and Lumumba was criticized when he acquired military equipment and technical aid from the Soviet Union. In September 1960 Colonel Mobutu and the Congolese army seized control and Khrushchev protested to the UN that:

> the UN command is working in concert with the NATO powers to discredit the legal government of M. Lumumba.

When Lumumba was seized by Congolese soldiers, taken to Katanga and murdered at the beginning of 1961, he promptly became a martyr to the cause of socialism – a victim of Western imperialism and capitalist intrigue. Though it took till the mid-1960s to restore stability in the Congo, preserving its unity, it was the USA and the West that then had the dominant political and economic influence there. When Mobutu renamed the country Zaïre in 1971 it was firmly in the capitalist camp. Lumumba was nevertheless remembered in the communist and non-aligned blocs, and the Soviets gave his name to a university for Afro–Asian students in the USSR.

At the time of Lumumba's murder, Khrushchev laid part of the blame at the door of Dag Hammarskjöld, UN Secretary-General, and vainly demanded his dismissal. When Hammarskjöld was killed in an air disaster in the Congo, Moscow tried to replace the Secretary-Generalship with a 'troika' system, a three-man commission which would include a nominee from the communist powers. This proposal failed too and in November 1961 Hammarskjöld was succeeded by U Thant. Though U Thant served with impartiality as well as with distinction, the Kremlin took this to be yet another example – like the exclusion of Communist China from the UN and the UN intervention in the Korean War – of the power of the USA to manipulate the international organization in the interests of the West.

13.2.2 The Cuban Missiles Crisis

Developments in Cuba were also of great concern to the superpowers by the end of 1961 (see section 10.1.2). Kennedy had broken off relations with Castro and given some encouragement to the attempt to overthrow him which ended ignominiously at the Bay of Pigs. In economic conflict with Washington, Castro had turned for aid to Moscow. During 1962 the Cuban–Soviet bond grew stronger, and in October 1962 Washington announced dramatic news: photographs obtained by illicit U-2 flights over Cuba showed that the Soviets were building missile sites there from which nuclear attacks could be launched on any part of the United States (see fig. 10.3). Kennedy insisted that the sites be dismantled and the missiles removed and on 22 October he declared a naval blockade of Cuba, ready to intercept further missiles on their way from the Soviet Union. The President told his television audience:

> We will not prematurely or unnecessarily risk the costs to the world by a nuclear war in which even the fruits of victory would be ashes in our mouth, but neither will we shrink from that risk.

Khrushchev tried to bargain. He demanded the removal of US missiles from Turkey, as much on the doorstep of the Soviet Union as those in Cuba were on America's, and he again looked for some softening of the West's position regarding West Berlin and East Germany. The USA made no concessions, its President aware that Soviet ships carrying missiles had already been halted and were turning back. On 28 October Khrushchev agreed to dismantle the sites in Cuba and to remove the missiles that were already there. In exchange he was given a promise that the USA would make no further attempt to overthrow Castro, and this the Kremlin sought to present as a victory. Castro was not impressed. The Cuban leader sometimes claimed that the initiative for installing the missiles was Cuban, not Soviet, and, resenting the way the superpowers had excluded him from the negotiations, he refused to allow UN supervision of the removal of the Soviet equipment.

The equipment was nevertheless removed and the world stepped back from what had seemed the brink of nuclear war. In November, when Khrushchev further agreed to remove Soviet bombers from Cuba, the USA lifted its blockade. Though he tried to disguise it, Khrushchev had suffered a diplomatic defeat while Kennedy's prestige had soared. The Chinese criticized the Soviet leader for giving way, while his colleagues in the Kremlin were divided between those who would not have installed the missiles in Cuba at all and others who might have risked defying Kennedy's threats. Khrushchev's authority was undermined and he was force to retire in 1964.

13.3 Arms and agreements

13.3.1 A balance of terror

Since the Austrian State Treaty of 1955 there had been few formal East–West agreements in spite of the pursuit of peaceful coexistence. An initiative by Eisenhower had led to the Antarctic Treaty of 1959 in which the USA, the USSR, Britain, France and other interested parties such as Argentina accepted the status quo in Antarctica for the next 30 years, outlawed nuclear test explosions there and promised scientific co-operation. Elsewhere, however, the development of weaponry caused growing alarm. By 1959 the types of atomic bomb used in 1945 had begun to look puny alongside the hydrogen bombs being stockpiled by the superpowers. Britain had become the third nuclear power in 1952 and, in spite of the resistance of peace movements such as the Campaign for Nuclear Disarmament (CND) in Britain, other states were expected soon to join 'the nuclear club'. The debate about nuclear weapons was already heated, those in favour of them asserting that they created a 'balance of terror', helping to keep the peace by making war too frightful to contemplate. Technology did not stand still, however, and the superpowers inevitably dreamed of 'systems' which might make it possible to win almost instant victory without the certainty of a devastating response.

There was growing awareness, however, that along with the enormous destructive power of nuclear bombs went lethal radioactivity. Though the Americans talked of NATO using 'tactical' nuclear weapons as part of conventional warfare in Europe, as if the bombs could be scaled down, even test explosions now caused anxiety and protest – especially when in 1954 fall-out from US tests in the Pacific showered Japanese fishermen.

The United Nations had in 1946 set up an Atomic Energy Commission and in 1947 a Conventional Armaments Commission, but neither made much progress towards disarmament, or even arms limitation, and the Soviets withdrew from them in 1950. A new, unified Disarmaments Commission was set up in 1952, and its machinery revised in 1959 and again in 1962, but it still met with little success. The superpowers argued about how the honouring of agreements could be verified, and endlessly disputed which of the powers was the more menacing. Bernard Montgomery, a British field marshal in the Second World War, defended nuclear weapons, claiming:

> when both sides have nuclear sufficiency, the deterrent will merely serve to deter each side from using it as a weapon.

But 'sufficiency' was undefined, and the stockpiles soon passed the point at which the USA and USSR could destroy one another (and much of the world besides) several times over. Meanwhile, Britain's insistence on having its 'own independent nuclear deterrent' established the dangerous precedent that not only the superpowers should have nuclear stockpiles. The weapons were deployed in the air in bombers and at sea in submarines, as well as at land-based missiles sites. Nuclear war needed little more than the touch of a button.

13.3.2 The (Partial) Test Ban and other agreements

Delegates from seventeen nations assembled in Geneva in March 1962 for a new Disarmament Conference. The Cuban Missiles Crisis gave the Conference a new urgency and the discussions helped to bring about a telex link, a 'hotline', between Washington and Moscow which could be used in future emergencies and might help to avoid 'accidental war'. The nuclear powers also agreed in August 1963 on a (Partial) Test Ban Treaty. The USA, the USSR and Britain undertook to cut down 'radioactive debris' by outlawing nuclear explosions in the atmosphere, in space and under water. Over 400 test explosions had occurred by this time (259 American, 126 Soviet, 23 British and 7 French). After the Treaty, the tests would have to take place underground; their number rapidly passed the previous 400, however. Other countries were invited to sign the Test Ban Treaty and about a hundred did so during the next decade, but they did not include France and China. De Gaulle believed the honour of France demanded French nuclear weapons, and French atmospheric tests went on in the Pacific from 1960 to the 1980s, remote from France itself and causing growing anger. In Peking, Chen Yi a government minister, asserted in 1963 that:

> China will have to manufacture the most modern weapons within a few years or be relegated to the status of a second or third-class power.

Thus China exploded its first nuclear bomb in 1964 at Lop Nor, ignoring the Test Ban Treaty and joining the nuclear race.

The superpowers moved on to other agreements in the wake of the Cuban Missiles Crisis, especially after the USA withdrew its plan to create a NATO nuclear force, which had alarmed the Soviets who feared that the West Germans might have access to nuclear weapons. Summit meetings began again when Kosygin, the Soviet Prime Minister, met President Johnson in 1967 at Glassborough, New Jersey. They could not agree a joint policy towards the crisis in the Middle East (see section 18.2.1), nor could Kosygin persuade Johnson to abandon the US campaign in Vietnam, but they were less divided about the need for more arms controls. The United Nations had meanwhile brought about the Outer Space Treaty of 1967, forbidding nuclear weapons in orbit around the earth. But the Treaty did nothing to restrict the use of missiles and it did not prevent the superpowers launching 'spy satellites' to listen to and photograph each other (incidentally reducing the need for arguments about verification).

A stronger agreement was signed in 1968 when, in the Non-Proliferation Treaty, the USA, the USSR and Britain promised to ban the transfer of nuclear weaponry and associated technology to non-nuclear powers. With this they hoped to stop the dangerous spreading of nuclear arms. More than a hundred other states soon signed the Treaty, with France and China again the notable absentees. For a time the Treaty seemed to work well, but by the end of the 1970s there was speculation that the capacity for weapons manufacturing was being developed in countries such as Brazil, Israel and South Africa. India exploded a nuclear device in 1974 but did not immediately produce a stock of bombs, though keeping a watchful eye on Pakistan in case its neighbour should also become a nuclear power (see section 22.6.3).

New treaties brought further, though minimal, self-imposed limitations by the superpowers. The Sea-Bed Treaty of 1971 forbade the siting of nuclear weapons on the sea-bed except in one's own territorial waters. Biological, but not chemical, weapons were outlawed a year later. In 1974 the USA and the Soviet Union agreed a maximum size for their underground test explosions in the Threshold Test Ban Treaty, but conservative opinion in the US Senate prevented its approval and implementation.

13.4 East–West détente gathers pace

13.4.1 Brandt's Ostpolitik

The early 1970s were a time of optimism when it seemed that the superpowers were at last beginning to build détente on the foundations of peaceful coexistence. By 'détente', the West seemed to mean a more positive relationship in which tensions would be relaxed further and friendly agreements advanced. At the same time, international relations had been complicated by the emergence of China, not only fully independent of the Soviet Union but also hostile to it (see section 11.2.3). Unease over China, especially when it relaxed its hostility towards the USA, perhaps made Brezhnev and the Soviet Union more open to friendly approaches from the West. The initiative for such approaches owed a good deal to Willy Brandt, the Social Democrat Chancellor of West Germany in 1969. Brandt's Ostpolitik softened West Germany's previous policies towards the East and did much to take the heat out of the German problem. By the time Brandt retired in 1974, the two Germanies seemed likely to coexist indefinitely and, divided by the Wall, Berlin too had achieved comparative stability (see section 6.2.3).

The specific achievements of Brandt's Ostpolitik lay in the treaties he brought about. He was not put off by the East–West ill-feeling which resulted from the Soviet suppression of the Czechs in 1968 (see section 8.2.4). In 1970 he signed a non-aggression pact with Brezhnev (the Treaty of Moscow) and an agreement with Poland to respect existing central European frontiers (the Treaty of Warsaw). Further goodwill treaties followed with other members of the Warsaw Pact, but at the heart of the Ostpolitik lay the Basic Treaty between the two Germanies, signed at the end of 1972. The two states stopped short of full recognition of each other's sovereignty, both believing there was really only one German nation, but the Treaty laid down that:

> the Federal Republic of Germany and the German Democratic Republic shall develop normal good-neighbourly relations with each other on the basis of equal rights.

In Brandt's view, this fulfilled his aim to:

> prevent any further alienation of the two parts of the German nation [and to] arrive at a regular *modus vivendi* and from that to proceed to co-operation.

Encouraged by the new flexibility in international relations, the East – including the Soviets and East Germany – had made concessions on Berlin. The Four-Power Pact of June 1972 had left the West with garrisons in and access to West Berlin, while preventing West Berlin becoming part of West Germany. Brandt had thus helped to bring about an increase in goodwill which at last brought within reach the agreement on European frontiers and the East–West security pact so often and so fruitlessly discussed in the past. The Americans and Soviets were already working towards this.

13.4.2 SALT and the Nixon–Brezhnev summits

The Non-Proliferation Treaty of 1968 had led to renewed efforts to limit the armaments of the superpowers. Strategic Arms Limitation Talks (SALT) opened in November 1969 in the hope that the further growth of nuclear stockpiles, with their staggering costs, might be curbed. By that time Nixon was President of the USA. He employed Henry Kissinger as his National Security Adviser before promoting him in 1973 to Secretary of State. Kissinger served as a sort of roving ambassador and master of 'shuttle diplomacy', shuttling from capital to capital in pursuit of deals and agreements. Nixon and Kissinger were professional politicians, hardly idealists and none too scrupulous in their methods, and with the co-operation of Peking and Moscow they achieved a remarkable measure of détente in the early 1970s. The improvement in international relations owed a good deal to Nixon's determination to end the USA's involvement in Vietnam and the rest of Indo-China, an involvement which had overshadowed Johnson's Presidency and cost the Democrats dearly in the election of 1968 (see section 2.2). It took Nixon some years to effect withdrawal (see section 18.4.2) but, with the end of US involvement in sight, relations grew warmer with both Peking and Moscow.

There were three strands to the peace-building process: US–Chinese, US–Soviet and SALT. Relations improved between the USA and Communist China and between the USA and the Soviet Union, Nixon himself following in Kissinger's footsteps to visit Peking in February 1972 and Moscow three months later. This latter visit was the first of three summit meetings between Nixon and Brezhnev. Also in 1972 the arms talks ended in SALT 1, the first agreement to put limits on the numbers and locations of the missiles of the superpowers. SALT 1 fell short of actual disarmament but it slowed down the arms race, and a new round of talks began in Vladivostok later in 1974.

An important milestone on the way to less frosty US–Chinese relations was the ending of Washington's obstruction of the admission of Communist China to the United Nations (see section 11.2.3(c)). At the Peking summit with Mao Tse-tung, Nixon had to tread carefully on the issue of Taiwan, where Chiang Kai-shek was still under US protection (see section 12.3). The US President agreed that this protection would have to be withdrawn, though gradually:

> The United States acknowledges that all Chinese on either side of the Taiwan Strait maintain that there is but one China and that Taiwan is part of China. . . . It will progressively reduce its forces and military installations on Taiwan as the tension in the area reduces.

The USA did not give full recognition to Communist China until 1979 but in the meantime trade and contacts of various sorts grew between China and the West, and a procession of visitors followed Kissinger and Nixon to the People's Republic.

Nixon's meeting with Brezhnev in Moscow in May 1972 had speeded up the signing of SALT 1 and affirmed the joint belief of the superpowers in 'peaceful coexistence'. Brandt had provided the example and Kissinger had prepared with thoroughness, while Nixon himself set the tone of the summit:

> We should recognize that great nuclear powers have a solemn responsibility to exercise restraint in any crisis, and to take positive action to avert direct confrontation. . . . We should recognize further that it is the responsibility of the great powers to influence other nations in conflict or crisis to moderate their behaviour.

1972 was an election year for Nixon, and the agreements – suitably embellished with propaganda – became part of his campaign as a distinguished statesman, though the Pentagon[G] worried whether too much was being conceded. In 1973 Brezhnev visited Washington and in 1974 Nixon was again in Moscow. The new summits aimed at advances in trade, in controlling pollution and in co-operating in space research. Nixon and Brezhnev, but not the US Senate, had agreed on the Threshold Test Ban Treaty. After Nixon's downfall over the Watergate Affair, Brezhnev attended a second summit in 1974, meeting President Ford at Vladivostok, but progress was now more difficult. The hesitant start on talks aimed at SALT 2 was nevertheless followed in 1975 by the *Apollo–Soyuz* space link-up as a token of superpower co-operation (see section 13.1).

13.4.3 The Conference on Security and Co-operation in Europe

Nixon's recognition of East Germany in 1974 cleared the way for a long-awaited European security treaty. The 'age of negotiation', as Nixon had called the early 1970s, culminated in 1975 at Helsinki where the USA, Canada and 33 European states signed wide-ranging agreements in the Final Act of the Conference on Security and Co-operation in Europe (CSCE). Existing European frontiers were accepted by all. 'Confidence-building measures' were agreed,

Table 13.1 Stockpiles of nuclear weapons, 1982

	USA*	Britain	USSR†	France	China
Main delivery systems of missiles‡					
Land-based					
Inter-continental ballistic missiles – ICBMs (IBMs)	1 050	—	1 300	—	4
Intermediate-range ballistic missiles – IRBMs (INFs)	172	—	1 300	18	150
Short-range ballistic missiles – SRBMs	158	36	700	42	—
Airborne					
Strategic and medium-range bombers	850	100	650	69	90
Underwater-based					
Submarine-launched missiles	500	64	950	80	—
Strategic warheads§	10 000	—	8 000	—	—
Total number of warheads	c.30 000	c.1000	c.22 000	Below 1000	Below 1000

* Including weapons based in western Europe and Turkey but not those under British control

† Including weapons based in eastern Europe

‡ Other missiles include surface-to-air, air-to-air, and anti-submarine

§ Other nuclear weapons include torpedoes, depth bombs and tank-borne weapons

Based on M. Kidron and D. Smith, *The War Atlas* (Pluto Press and Pan Books, 1983)

further designed to prevent 'war by accident' between East and West – for example, each would now give the other notice of military exercises. The states looked forward to more economic and technological co-operation, and the Final Act also included Article VII:

> The participating States will respect human rights and fundamental freedoms of thought, conscience, religion or belief, for all without distinctions as to race, sex, language or religion. . . . [They] recognize the universal significance of human rights and fundamental freedoms, respect for which is an essential factor for peace, justice and well-being necessary to ensure the development of friendly relations and co-operation among themselves and among all States.

In 1974 Nixon had pressed Brezhnev to allow the Soviet people greater freedom of movement, especially Jews wishing to emigrate, and East and West still had differing understandings of 'human rights and fundamental freedoms'. Article VII now began rapidly to divide the superpowers, though both had signed it.

There were few further agreements when the CSCE assembled again at Belgrade in 1977–8 and at Madrid in 1980–3. Wrangling about rights and freedoms quickly eroded goodwill. The West savagely attacked the abuse of human rights east of the Iron Curtain, especially the denial of freedom of expression, of religion and of movement. Table 13.1 shows how the superpowers reassured themselves with nuclear stockpiles. The great powers were now deep in what *Pravda*, the newspaper of the Soviet Communist Party, called 'a long and still frosty winter'. The movement towards coexistence and détente begun in 1955 had reached its peak in 1975 at Helsinki before the impetus was lost and a new East–West Cold War began (see section 21.2).

UNIT 14

Decolonization: 1 – Britain

14.1 Old assumptions; post-war realities

The upsurge of new thinking at the time of the American and French Revolutions in the late eighteenth century all but ended colonial empires in the Americas, where the main losers were Spain and Portugal. But much of Asia remained in the hands of European colonizing powers, the 'mother countries' as they liked to think of themselves, while most of Africa was colonized during the nineteenth century. When the Second World War ended in 1945, therefore, Europeans still claimed possession of empires more than a dozen times larger than Europe itself. But the end of these empires could already be foreseen. Both the USSR and the USA condemned colonies as an outdated form of imperialism, at the same time condemning each other for practising modern imperialism in spreading their own ideology, influence and economic control. The difficulty of resisting US influence in any part of the Americas had already shown how the removal of a colonial 'mother' readily opened the way to a 'neo-colonialism', a sort of informal imperialism (see Units 9 and 10). As the colonizing powers retreated, superpower influence was therefore often close at hand, as parts of Asia witnessed (see sections 11.4, 12.3 and 12.4).

Nationalist movements for independence from colonial rule grew steadily in the early twentieth century, especially in the Indian subcontinent and other parts of Asia. They were also growing, but less advanced, in Africa and the Caribbean. The Second World War gave them a boost, having destroyed the myths of the moral superiority and physical invincibility of the Europeans. The Japanese overran many European possessions in Asia, including Burma, Malaya, Singapore and Hong Kong (all British), the Dutch East Indies, French Indo-China, and the US Philippines. In Europe, it seemed that only Britain survived the Nazi onslaught, and then only with extensive outside support from the British Commonwealth of Nations and the USA, while it took the combined weight of the Grand Alliance finally to defeat the Axis powers. When European mother countries sought to regain their colonial properties in Asia, they were

Fig. 14.1 In a flourish of the grandeur which was a hallmark of the British Empire, this stamp of 1920 reminded Jamaicans that their island was a Crown Colony and that King George V was their 'Supreme Lord'. Such imperialist concepts could not long survive the Second World War.

therefore given little encouragement either by their former subjects or by the superpowers.

The war had widened the horizons of colonial subjects. Many served in the armed forces of the Grand Alliance, where they were told that the war was for freedom and equality, and they were able to contrast the comparative wealth of the developed world, even in wartime, with the deprivation and squalor of the colonies, as described for example in the Meyne Report on the British West Indies (which was suppressed during the war). Ndabaningi Sithole, a Zimbabwean nationalist, summed up another effect of the war:

> African soldiers saw white soldiers wounded, dying and dead. The bullet had the same effect on black and white alike. After spending four years hunting white enemy soldiers, the African never again regarded them as gods.

The mother countries now faced a difficult period during which they had to come to terms with the ending of their colonial empires. Whether they struggled to resist like the Dutch and the French, tried to ignore the problem like the Belgians and Portuguese, or made at least some attempt to withdraw gracefully and by agreement like the British, the result was the same for all. Within 30 years of 1945, almost all the colonies were independent; empires, some of which had taken centuries to build, had collapsed. In the process, scores of new nations were born, most of them poor and inexperienced, all of them hopeful.

These nations broadly made up the South in the North–South divide between the developed nations and those of the Third World, and they varied in size from the vastness of India to mere specks on the map like Antigua and Tonga. For most of them the East–West Cold War was almost irrelevant beside the urgent problems of nation-building and economic survival. Many tried to steer clear of superpower rivalries by following the path of non-alignment but, in practice, ideological conflict, superpower meddling and exploitation were difficult to avoid. The rights and interests of the Third World were recognized only slowly in the North, though awareness grew, prodded by the pioneering work of those like the authors of the Brandt Report (1980) (see sections 21.3 and 21.4).

This unit and Unit 15 will consider how the colonial empires ended; the units that follow will examine some of the many problems that the passing of those empires left behind and will consider how the world began to come to grips with the aftermath of one of the greatest and most rapid upheavals it has ever known. It was not surprising that the turbulence was extensive; that it was not even more extensive was remarkable. Colonial empires had been built on master–servant relationships, on assumptions about the superiority of whites and about 'the white man's burden' and his duty to 'civilize' the non-Europeans. Such assumptions are quaintly old-fashioned in the late twentieth-century world, though the realities of political and economic power mean that for many of the weak and unfortunate the climate is still a hostile one.

14.2 The British Empire and the Commonwealth of Nations

14.2.1 The Dominions

Before the Second World War, Britain had granted independence to five Dominions, sometimes called the white Dominions. Australia and New Zealand had strong similarities to Britain itself, practising its constitutional democracy and sharing most of its values and its passion for cricket. Canada, the oldest Dominion, had a large French minority and was much influenced by the USA, but it too retained much that was British (see sections 9.1 and 9.2). South Africa had become independent in 1910 and was a white Dominion only in the fact that power and privilege rested with the country's white minority. The Irish Free State (Eire) had become the youngest Dominion in 1922, but was an unwilling one, fretful that the independence of the Dominions was not quite total.

Arthur Balfour, a former British Prime Minister, defined Dominion status in 1926. Dominions were, he said:

> autonomous communities within the British Empire, equal in status, in no way subordinate one to another in any aspect of their domestic or external affairs, though united by a common allegiance to the Crown and freely associated as members of the British Commonwealth of Nations.

Balfour's definition was given the force of law in 1931 in the Statute of Westminster. Each of the Dominions at that time regarded George V as its head of state, but this constitutional arrangement did not mean any British control over policy, a fact which became clear in 1939 when at the outbreak of war each Dominion decided for itself whether to support Britain against Nazism. South Africa did so by only a narrow majority in its parliament, while Eire was the odd one out, choosing to stay neutral. In the ferment of change which followed the war, Eire elected to become a republic (relinquishing its allegiance to the Crown) and to leave the British Commonwealth of Nations, which it did in 1949. The Irish Republic was the product of prolonged nationalist resistance to British imperialism. The struggle left too little goodwill for membership of the Commonwealth, and the continuing allegiance of Northern Ireland to the United Kingdom carried with it continuing bitterness (see section 19.4.1).

The other white Dominions gave valuable support to the Grand Alliance, and in 1945 they were willing enough to remain linked both to the British Crown and to the Commonwealth. The more urgent question now for the British was how soon there should be new, and non-white, Dominions, one effect of which would be to change the Commonwealth of Nations from the 'white man's club' it had so far been. The Indian subcontinent demanded immediate attention from Attlee's Labour government (see section 5.2.3).

14.2.2 The independence of the Indian subcontinent

After years of nationalist pressure, mainly from the Indian Nationalist Congress, the British were ready in 1945 to honour wartime promises and to give way to Mahatma Gandhi's demand that they 'quit India'. The British Empire in India was a vast and awesome responsibility, and after the Second World War Britain had neither the resources nor the will to prolong it. The electoral defeat of Churchill, who might have tried to do so, was decisive.

The Indian National Congress had matured since its foundation in 1885. It was now ready to take power under Jawaharlal Nehru, an English-educated barrister and veteran of the campaign for Indian independence. But India's population of more than 400 million was diverse and divided, Muslims especially fearing domination by the Hindu majority. When the British made Nehru Prime Minister in 1946 as a prelude to independence, the Muslim League objected, naming 16 August 1946 Direct Action Day in support of a separate Muslim state under Mohammed Ali Jinnah. Jinnah condemned the Indian National Congress as a mainly Hindu organization, and he gave his followers the slogan 'Pakistan or Perish'.

The British were ready to treat Burma and Ceylon separately from the rest of their Indian territories, but they hoped to make the subcontinent a single independent Dominion. That was also the ambition of Nehru and Gandhi, but Jinnah was immovable. Lord Wavell, Viceroy of India since 1943, could not bring them to agreement. Even the saintly and much respected Gandhi had to struggle to stop bloody atrocities and reprisals developing into civil war. British forces helped to police the strife-ridden areas, while Attlee's government sent a new commission to India and summoned Indian leaders to London for talks, both without success.

Lord Mountbatten arrived in Delhi in March 1947 to replace Wavell. It began to seem unavoidable that the Indian subcontinent would be partitioned between Hindus and Muslims, though the British were still reluctant. In separating Pakistan from India in the west and in the east it would be necessary to divide up two large provinces, the Punjab and Bengal, and that was sure to involve bloodshed. The killing soon began there, not just between Hindus and Muslims but in the Punjab also involving the Sikhs, anxious about their own interests. A commission under Cyril Radcliffe, a British lawyer, worked amid the chaos to draw up new boundaries. Suddenly, Mountbatten and the politicians in London were in a hurry: 15 August 1947 was appointed for the ending of British rule in the subcontinent. India and Pakistan became independent, each a Dominion within the British Commonwealth of Nations. In India, Mountbatten stayed on as Governor-General, representing George VI, though Nehru, whom Mountbatten called 'a world-renowned leader of courage and vision', held the real power as Prime Minister. In Pakistan, Jinnah insisted on being the Governor-General and Liaqat Ali Khan became Prime Minister.

This was the first major step in the post-war decolonization of overseas empires. Nehru caught something of the drama, addressing the Indian parliament:

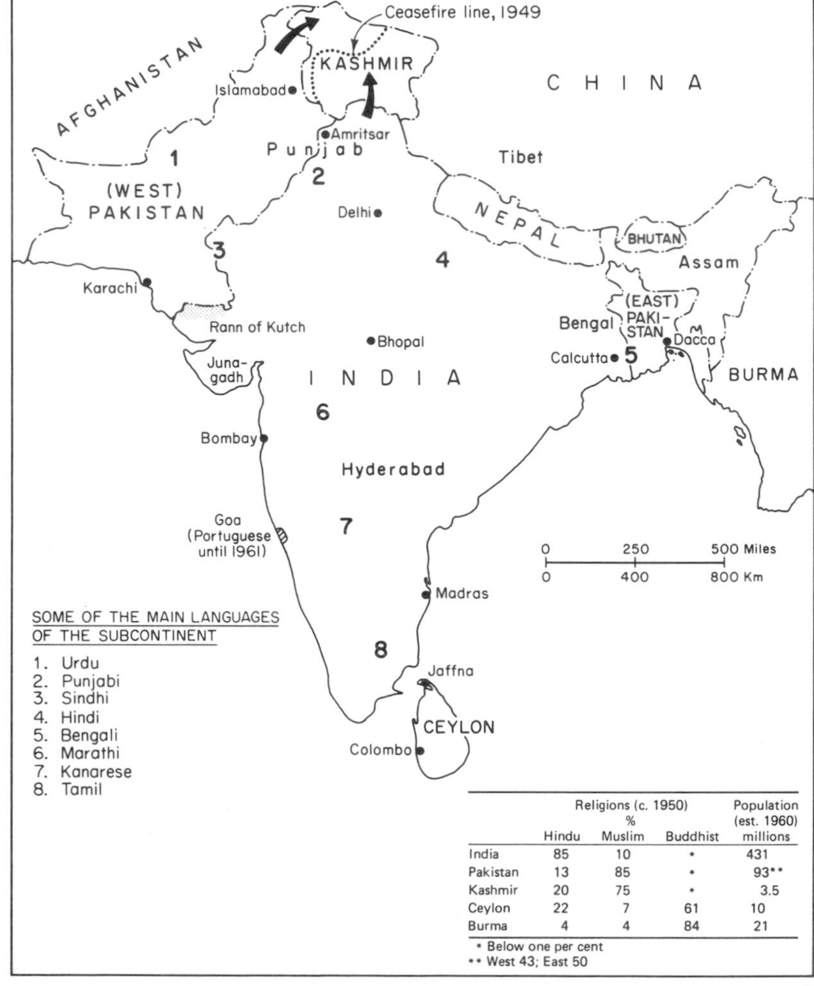

	Religions (c. 1950) %			Population (est. 1960)
	Hindu	Muslim	Buddhist	millions
India	85	10	*	431
Pakistan	13	85	*	93**
Kashmir	20	75	*	3.5
Ceylon	22	7	61	10
Burma	4	4	84	21

* Below one per cent
** West 43; East 50

Fig. 14.2 The Indian subcontinent after independence

> At the stroke of the midnight hour, while the world sleeps, India will awake to life and freedom. A moment comes, which comes but rarely in history, when we step from the old to the new, when an age ends.

An Indian journalist later recalled the feelings of the 'enormous crowd' outside parliament as Nehru spoke:

> Somehow one had forgotten all about what we'd been through and the killings and the riots. One felt very elated: at long last the country was free and we could manage our own affairs.

But further violence followed. At least a quarter of a million people died in the bitter religious (and now national) feuding in the Punjab alone, half a million in all during partition, and nearly fourteen million became refugees, fleeing into or out of Pakistan.

The politicians struggled to curb the passion that had been unleashed, none to better effect than Gandhi, always the apostle of tolerance and non-violence. But Gandhi himself was assassinated in January 1948, killed by a fellow Hindu with a fanatical blood-lust. The death of so respected a campaigner, who campaigned not only for India's freedom but also for the dignity even of the poorest, caused a sense of shock which helped at last to curb the bloodshed.

Jinnah too died in 1948, leaving Pakistan in considerable difficulties. The new nation existed in two parts, divided by more than a thousand miles of Indian territory. Pakistan's Muslim League was less united than the Indian National Congress so that, while India enjoyed a long and comparatively stable period of democratic rule by Nehru and the Congress, Pakistan fell into disarray, especially after Liaqat was assassinated in 1951. It took until 1956 to work out a new republican Islamic constitution, and democracy was then suspended when Ayub Khan took control in 1958. India in the meantime produced a new constitution in 1950, confirming a parliamentary system similar to Britain's but ending India's allegiance to the British Crown, the mark of Dominion status. The Commonwealth of Nations, however, saw no reason why India should not remain one of its members as Nehru wished, even though he now led a republic.

Partition left many problems in the Indian subcontinent. Not all the subcontinent had been under direct British rule and native princes, such as those of Hyderabad, Junagadh and Kashmir, had to come to terms to merge their states into the new nations. This was often decided more by geography than by religion, but Kashmir was an exceptional problem. It bordered both West Pakistan and India. Its Maharajah was Hindu, most of its people were Muslim, and conflict over the future of Kashmir could not be avoided (see section 16.3). Indo-Pakistani problems had also to be settled concerning shared rivers, the resources left by the British (not just financial but also including skilled civil servants and trained soldiers), and the millions of refugees. Both new nations faced daunting economic and social problems, and their tasks in nation-building were enormous (see sections 16.2 and 16.4).

Attlee's government meanwhile quickly promoted the Ceylon Independence Act and Ceylon became a Dominion within the Commonwealth in 1947, remaining in the association when it became the Republic of Sri Lanka in 1972 (see section 16.5). Burma received independence in 1948 but chose not to join the Commonwealth, following instead its own course towards becoming a Socialist Republic and avoiding heavy Westernization (see section 16.6).

14.2.3 Withdrawal from Palestine

The peace settlement at the end of the First World War left Britain and France in charge of mandated territories in the Middle East which had belonged before the war to the Turkish Empire: Britain held Iraq, Transjordan and Palestine; France held Syria and Lebanon. Subject to the supervision of the League of Nations Mandates Commission, Britain and France – like all mandated powers elsewhere – had the duty to prepare the territories for independence while regarding the 'well-being and development' of the people living there as 'a sacred trust of civilization'. Britain found little difficulty in discharging this duty in Iraq and Transjordan, which became independent in 1932 and 1946 respectively. The mandate in Palestine ended far more controversially in 1948.

Palestine was mainly an Arab land when Britain took control of it in 1920. There were fewer than 100 000 Jews, outnumbered more than six to one by Arabs, but both races – for historical, religious and national reasons – aspired to possess Palestine as an independent state. For twenty years British policy was hesitant, seeking to keep the peace, but erratic regarding Jewish immigration. When the Second World War began, the Jewish population of 460 000 was almost half that of the Arabs, and the Nazi persecution of the Jews was increasing the pressures to admit far more Jewish refugees. The end of the Second World War made the problem urgent. *Irgun Zvai Leumi* and the Stern Gang, Jewish terrorist organizations, fought Arabs and British alike to make Palestine a Zionist[G] state. The world had a guilty conscience about the Jews now clamouring for admission to their promised land, and a strong Jewish lobby in the USA pushed Truman into putting pressure on the British to admit them.

Bevin, the British Foreign Secretary, tried in vain to bring about a compromise in the shape of a joint Arab–Jewish state. He insisted that the terrorist organizations should be disbanded before further immigration was allowed, but Britain was not able to achieve that. The blowing-up of the King David Hotel, used by the British administration in Jerusalem, caused nearly a hundred deaths in July 1946 in one of the more spectacular outrages. Ill-feeling mounted, and there were anti-Semitic riots in London and other British cities. Skilful Zionist propaganda pilloried the British government, never more successfully than over the much-publicized *Exodus*, the ship which carried 4500 Jews from America to Palestine in 1947. They were forbidden to land and, since refugee camps in nearby British Cyprus were full, were transferred to British transport vessels to be taken elsewhere – perhaps foolishly to the British Zone of Germany, though the refugees themselves turned down French hospitality. The Zionists falsely represented Bevin as anti-Semitic. He did, however, wish to be fair to the Arabs as well as the Jews, telling the House of Commons:

> I do not want the Arabs to be dismissed as if they were nobody.

The pressures were too strong for a British government heavily burdened with other problems. It decided to opt out, to surrender the mandate on 15 May 1948 and meanwhile to leave the United Nations to settle Palestine's future. The United Nations Special Commission on Palestine (UNSCOP) was already recommending partition, and the General Assembly accepted this by majority vote in November 1947. Partition satisfied neither the Jews nor the Arabs and they prepared for confrontation while the British forces steadily withdrew, reluctant to have any further involvement, even in peace-keeping.

When May 1948 arrived, Palestinian Arabs and their supporters refused to recognize the new Jewish state of Israel. Egypt, Iraq, Lebanon and Syria all fought the Jews and lost, and Israel took more than three-quarters of Palestine, instead of UNSCOP's allocation of just over half. Jordan's King Abdullah, however, seized the West Bank of the River Jordan and east Jerusalem – ostensibly for the Arabs but more especially for his own Kingdom of Jordan (formerly Transjordan) – thus leaving the Palestinian Arabs without any state at all. Some 750 000 of them fled from Israel to become stateless refugees, the victims of an injustice of which the world was constantly to be reminded in future years (see section 18.2).

14.2.4 The European–Asian Commonwealth

The return of Churchill as Prime Minister in 1951 slowed further granting of independence to Britain's colonies, though the queue was already forming. The British returned to Malaya after the expulsion of the Japanese and reorganized the administration there to form the Federation of Malaya in 1948. They also fought a jungle war against guerillas led by Chin Peng whose goal was an independent communist Malaya. Australia and New Zealand helped the British to resist the challenge but the 'Emergency' lasted from 1948 to 1960. It was partly to outmanoeuvre Chin Peng that Macmillan granted independence to Malaya in 1957. Much of the groundwork had been done by General Gerald Templer who from 1952 pursued the guerillas ruthlessly, using helicopters and trained jungle fighters. Templer also conducted a 'Hearts and Minds Campaign' to rally opinion against the communists. A resettlement programme, part of a strategy to starve the guerillas of support and supplies, led to 'new villages' with elected councils and running water and other amenities. This programme was particularly successful among Malaya's Chinese population, who might otherwise have been influenced by the Communist Party's success in China.

Independent Malaya's first Prime Minister was the Tunku Abdul Rahman, like Nehru an English-educated barrister. He had formed the nationalist Alliance only in 1952. The Tunku took pains to unite Malaya's races, and the Alliance brought together Malays, Chinese and Indians. In spite of the Emergency, Malaya's transition to independence was comparatively smooth and Abdul Rahman remained in office until he retired in 1970. By that time, Britain had put other territories under his government, extending it to the Federation of Malaysia in 1963 (see section 14.3.1). Both Malaya and Malaysia were ready members of the Commonwealth.

The Commonwealth in the 1950s was clearly changing. Even its name was growing simpler, from 'the British Commonwealth of Nations', to 'the British Commonwealth', and then to simply 'the Commonwealth'. It had become a partnership of whites (of mainly British descent) and Asians (whose leaders were mainly British-educated), but it was a partnership of equals, united by common bonds of language, trade, and values not always easy to define. John Strachey, a minister in Attlee's government, captured something of the bonds between members when he said:

> To know a no-ball from the googly and a point of order from a supplementary question is genuinely to have something in common.

14.2.5 The Suez War, 1956

New nations were not always welcomed in the old world, however. Britain had not resisted the independence of Egypt when the Turkish Empire was fragmented after the First World War, but had insisted on keeping British troops in the Canal Zone to protect the Suez Canal and British and French financial interests in it. The Anglo-Egyptian Treaty of 1954 allowed the British troops to remain but only until June 1956. By then, Egypt was under new management. A military coup led by General Mohammed Neguib overthrew King Farouk in 1952, and Neguib was replaced two years later by Colonel Gamal Abdel Nasser. Colonel Nasser, a fervent nationalist, intended to free Egypt of foreign forces. But he also intended to go further than this and, as Egypt's President, to effect social reform and an industrial revolution. His immediate plans focused on a High Dam at Aswan to use the waters of the Nile for electric power and irrigation.

One problem was to finance the building of the dam. Western aid was withdrawn because of disapproval of Nasser's policies. Egypt had recognized Communist China, criticized the Baghdad Pact, encouraged nationalist resistance to colonial rule in French North Africa, and begun to buy arms from Czechoslovakia and the Eastern bloc. The Soviet Union offered help with the dam but Nasser could see another source of capital: in July 1956 he nationalized the Suez Canal Company, compensating the shareholders at the current value of their shares but asserting that it was right to make the Canal the property of Egypt, where it was after all situated. This touched British nerves still raw from struggles with Mussadiq in Iran over the nationalization of oil (see section 1.5.1), and it raised fears of similar takeovers of profitable European enterprises in the Third World as colonial mastery faded.

With his love of rhetoric and his military associations, Nasser reminded Eden, Britain's Prime Minister, of pre-war European dictators. Eden's view was that it was necessary that Nasser be stopped, and he informed Eisenhower:

> My colleagues and I are convinced that we must be ready, in the last resort, to use force to bring Nasser to his senses. For our part, we are prepared to do so.

He soon found accomplices. Already humiliated in Indo-China and now angered by Arab nationalism in Algeria, the French were ready to strike, while

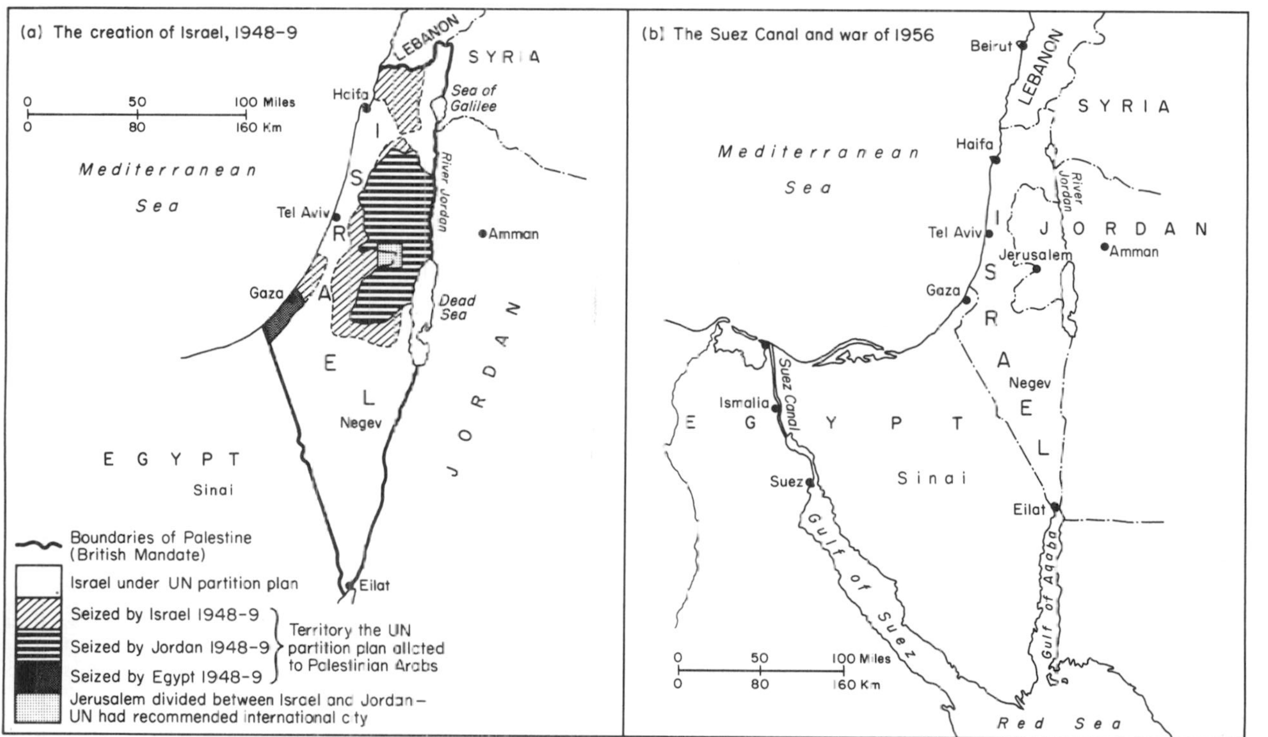

Fig. 14.3 Israel and the Suez War

Israel regarded Nasser as the ringleader of its Arab enemies. The Israelis could see advantages in an attack on Egypt, especially if European allies would destroy Nasser's air force. The Israeli attack was launched on 29 October 1956, its forces driving across Sinai. Britain and France demanded a ceasefire but, in addition, the withdrawal of:

> all Egyptian military forces to a distance of ten miles from the Canal . . . [and] the temporary occupation by Anglo-French forces of key positions at Port Said, Ismalia and Suez.

Nasser refused to consider such a surrender. Britain and France vetoed a UN Security Council condemnation of Israeli aggression and began military operations to seize the Canal, which the Egyptians promptly blocked with nearly 50 scuttled ships. Within two days of the landings at Port Said, however, Eden had to agree to a ceasefire on 7 November when the Anglo-French operations were condemned almost universally – by almost all the Commonwealth excepting Australia, by the Soviet Union who threatened to support Egypt with missiles, and by the USA where Eisenhower was busy winning re-election. A financial crisis for sterling added to Eden's embarrassment. Eisenhower had warned Eden of 'the unwisdom even of contemplating the use of military force at this moment', and events had proved him right. On the other hand, Eden could rightly complain that other Americans in the State Department had given him encouragement and US policy had not been so clear-cut.

UN troops took up station along the Canal to restore an uneasy peace between Israel and Egypt, and Anglo-French troops withdrew. Eden resigned soon afterwards, and the French Fourth Republic tottered still nearer to its end. Egypt kept control of the Suez Canal, soon to be reopened, and Nasser's prestige soared. Arab nationalism had not vanquished Israel but it had routed seemingly arrogant Europeans, reminding them that the colonial age was over. The Commonwealth endorsed that verdict and early in 1957, even before Malaya, Ghana won its independence from Britain, the first African state to become a member of the Commonwealth at the start of a new era for black Africa. In this age of change, the Suez War seemed almost bizarre.

14.3 The end of the British Empire

14.3.1 Federal solutions and non-solutions

Britain had begun to give serious attention to the future of its Empire during the 1950s. For a time it seemed that smaller or poorer colonies could be grouped together in federations whose eventual independence might give them a viable future. The first, the Federation of the Rhodesias and Nyasaland or the Central African Federation, was set up in 1953. The West Indies Federation followed in 1958 and the South Arabian Federation in 1959. None survived, but the Federation of Malaysia, formed in 1963, proved more successful. The British put Singapore and the colonies of Sabah and Sarawak in north Borneo into this Federation, in effect under the leadership of Abdul Rahman, the Prime Minister of Malaya. Oil-rich Brunei declined to join, and Singapore insisted on leaving in 1965 to become an independent republic under Lee Kwan Yew. Some 75 per cent of Singapore's population was Chinese, though in Malaysia as a whole Chinese were outnumbered by Malays. Malaysia also seemed to prefer protectionist policies to the free trade the port of Singapore demanded, while Lee had no wish to be overshadowed by Abdul Rahman. But the separation of Malaysia and Singapore seemed not greatly to handicap either.

The essence of federation was that each member state surrendered a good deal of authority to a central government (like the systems operating in the USA and the Soviet Union). In return they gained strength through unity and, usually, economic advantages. The Central African Federation (CAF) included Southern Rhodesia, Northern Rhodesia and Nyasaland. Northern Rhodesia had rich copper deposits but was underdeveloped and fairly thinly populated. Nyasaland was almost entirely agricultural and one of Africa's poorest states. Southern Rhodesia on the other hand had developed sufficiently to have been to some extent self-governing since 1923 and now stood on the threshold of independence. But power and privilege there lay with a white minority of about 200 000, who were greatly outnumbered by some three million blacks. The capital of the CAF was in Salisbury, Southern Rhodesia's capital, and its first Prime Minister was Godfrey Huggins, Southern Rhodesia's Prime Minister since 1934. Whatever the economic advantages of federation, Northern Rhodesians and Nyasalanders suspected that the CAF was a device to consolidate white rule to resemble that in neighbouring South Africa.

Neither Northern Rhodesia nor Nyasaland had many white settlers. Both set up African National Congresses, similar to India's Congress, to press for black independence. A similar African National Congress already existed in Southern Rhodesia, in opposition to white rule. But Huggins was not the man readily to share power with blacks in either Southern Rhodesia or the CAF. His successor in 1956, Roy Welensky, believed in the Federation, but he too was a white Rhodesian born in Salisbury but politically active in the North. Black Africans were allowed only twelve of the 59 seats in the federal parliament even after constitutional reform, and only four of the twelve were so elected as to be truly representative of black opinion. All the National Congresses were banned in 1959. Looking into the resulting unrest and disturbances, the Devlin Commission reported back to Macmillan that Nyasaland was like a 'police state'.

The imprisonment of black leaders, such as Kenneth Kaunda in Northern Rhodesia, Hastings Banda in Nyasaland and Joshua Nkomo in Southern Rhodesia, offered no long-term solution to the problems. Whites in the North's copper-belt expressed the prejudice that finally doomed the CAF when they rioted against Welensky's proposals to forbid racial discrimination in cafés and cinemas. Kaunda asserted the viewpoint of Northern Rhodesia's black opposition:

> We shall untiringly attack systems that for reasons of race alone deny about three million Africans the full enjoyment of democratic rights in this country. . . . We make no apologies for being in the forefront in the struggle for national independence and self-determination. Freedom is our birthright.

Table 14.1 The developing Commonwealth

Year	Admissions (Estimated population in millions, 1980)	Resignations	Total membership at end of year
The British Commonwealth of Nations (the white Dominions)			
Before 1945	**Britain** (56); **Canada** (24); **Australia** (15); New Zealand (3); South Africa (28); Irish Free State (3)		6
The British Commonwealth (mainly European Asian)			
1947	*India* (630); *Pakistan* (77)		8
1948	*Ceylon* (14)		9
1949		Irish Republic (former Irish Free State)	8
1957	*Ghana* (11); Malaya (Malaysia, 1963) (13)		10
The Commonwealth (multiracial)			
1960	*Nigeria* (80)		11
1961	Cyprus (0.8); *Sierra Leone* (3); *Tanganyika* (*Tanzania*, 1964) (17)	South Africa	13
1962	Jamaica (2); Trinidad and Tobago (1); *Uganda* (13)		16
1963	*Kenya* (15)		17
1964	*Malawi* (6); Malta (0.4); *Zambia* (6)		20
1965	*The Gambia* (0.6); Singapore (3)		22

1966	*Guyana* (1); *Botswana* (0.8); *Lesotho* (1); Barbados (0.3)		26
1968	Mauritius (1); *Swaziland* (0.6); **Nauru** (*)		29
1970	*Tonga* (0.1); Fiji (0.6); Western Samoa (0.2)		32
1972	*Bangladesh* (83)	*Pakistan*	32
1973	The Bahamas (0.3)		33
1974	*Grenada* (0.1)		34
1975	*Papua New Guinea* (3)		35
1976	The Seychelles (0.1)		36
1978	*The Solomon Islands* (0.2); Tuvalu (*); *Dominica* (0.1)		39
1979	*St Lucia* (0.1); *Kiribati* (*); *St Vincent* (0.1)		42
1980	*Zimbabwe* (7); *Vanuata* (0.1)		44
1981	*Belize* (0.2); Antigua (0.1)		46
1982	*The Maldives* (0.1)		47
1983	St Kitts and Nevis (*); **Brunei** (0.2)		49

* Below 70 000

Bold The richest members of the Commonwealth with per capita income p.a. in the early 1980s over 7 000 US dollars.

Italics The poorest members of the Commonwealth with per capita income p.a. in the early 1980s below 1 000 US dollars.

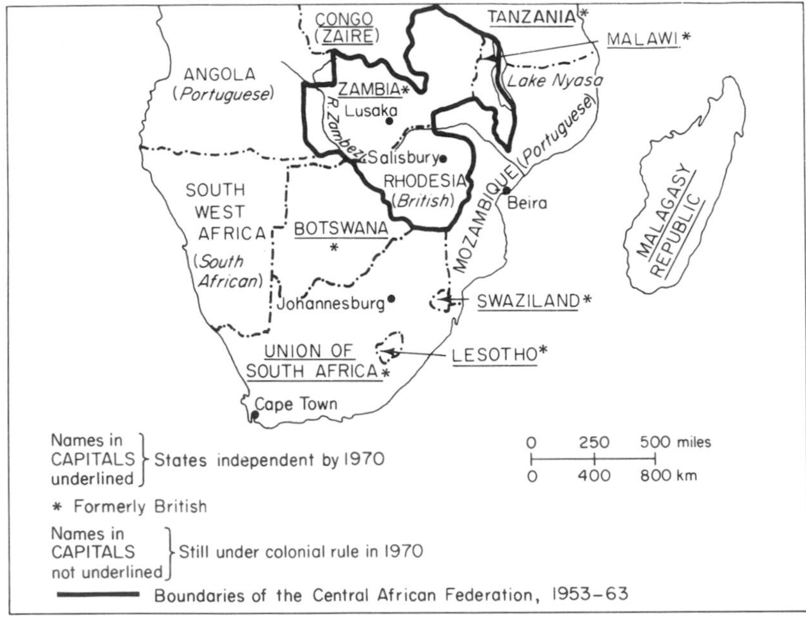

Fig. 14.4 The wind of change in southern Africa by 1970

Macmillan sent the Monckton Commission to investigate, which in 1960, while pleading for more African representation in the federal parliament and less racial discrimination, asserted that members of the CAF had the right to withdraw from the Federation. Welensky rightly saw this as sounding 'the death-knell' of the CAF. Efforts to save it were too little, too late, and it was dissolved at the end of 1963.

In July 1964 Nyasaland achieved independence under Banda's leadership, taking its African name, Malawi. Zambia (Northern Rhodesia) quickly followed under Kaunda, and both states became republics. Britain withheld independence from the more economically advanced Southern Rhodesia, however. British governments were now thoroughly embarrassed by the privileges of the white minority there (see section 14.3.4).

The West Indies Federation lasted only from 1958 to 1962. Britain's Caribbean Empire included mainland British Guiana and British Honduras, the comparatively large islands of Jamaica and Trinidad, and a host of smaller islands – some, like Anguilla and Montserrat, with a population of only a few thousand. Federation seemed to offer a way of uniting these scattered possessions, preparing the way for their independence. A conference at Montego Bay, Jamaica, launched the scheme in 1947. Guiana and Honduras refused to join, however, while Jamaica and Trinidad feared that Britain intended to burden them with responsibility for the small islands, many with rickety economies.

The Federation was set up despite these misgivings. When elections were won by the Federal Labour Party, Grantley Adams of Barbados became its Prime Minister, neither Norman Manley of Jamaica nor Eric Williams of Trinidad having enough confidence in the Federation to put it before their island politics. Jamaica, Trinidad and Barbados paid 91 per cent of federal revenues, the host of small islands in the Windwards and Leewards sharing the remaining nine per cent. Arguments soon raged about representation in the federal assembly, the constitution, inter-island migration, trade policies and taxes, and in 1961 Jamaica voted to withdraw, though the majority was far from convincing. Trinidad followed, and in May 1962 Britain wound up what was left of the Federation.

It remained to arrange for the independence of the individual colonies, Jamaica and Trinidad & Tobago leading the way in 1962, followed in 1966 by British Guiana (renamed Guyana) and Barbados. Guyana's independence came only after a delay, since neither Britain nor the watchful USA approved its voters' choice of government. The British tried to introduce Westminster-style democracy throughout their Caribbean territories, with a good deal of success, but Guiana used the system to elect Cheddi Jagan and a government of the People's Progressive Party (PPP). London and Washington feared the PPP's Marxist inclinations and made no scruples to obstruct Jagan. The 1960s were turbulent and the excuse was seized to postpone independence, granting it only when Forbes Burnham and the People's National Congress (PNC) won the electoral advantage. By that time, the racial divisions within Guyana had widened between the largely Afro–Caribbean supporters of the PNC and the largely Asian supporters of the PPP.

The smaller islands took their lead from Grenada which, with a population of barely 100 000, became independent in 1974 (see section 10.3). The islands which followed – some even smaller than Grenada – first achieved Associated Statehood with self-government under British protection, then complete independence and membership of the Commonwealth. St Lucia, St Vincent, Antigua and St Kitts took the plunge, and, on the mainland, British Honduras (renamed Belize) (see Table 14.1). Only the smallest and most isolated islands still hesitated in the 1980s.

With the founding of the Caribbean Free Trade Association (Carifta) in 1968, the English-speaking West Indies meanwhile began to remake some of the agreements that would have existed within the now-defunct West Indies Federation. Carifta led on to Caricom (the Caribbean Community and Common Market) in 1973, its membership including not only the former members of the Federation but also Guyana and Belize. Relations between members were not always harmonious; they were hindered by the great distances which separated the islands and by a parochialism that had become traditional. Members also had to wrestle with the economic difficulties which dogged all the world's poor. Like the Third World in general, however, the new states of the English-speaking Caribbean, having won their independence, eagerly sought to preserve it whatever the obstacles. Independence ideally meant freedom of choice, and, even under Burnham, Guyana defied the USA by becoming an associate member of Comecon in 1978.

The South Arabian Federation of 1959 was intended to consolidate British influence in South Yemen, south of Saudi Arabia, and to counter the influence there of Nasser and of Arab socialism in the wake of the Suez War. Britain gave economic and military support to the dozen friendly Arab rulers under its protection who joined the Federation and in 1963 attached its colony of Aden to the Federation as a step towards Aden's independence. By then Yemen had been deeply penetrated by Nasserite, republican and Marxist forces, and civil war spread to Aden itself in 1965. With casualties mounting, the British decided the struggle was a hopeless one. They withdrew in 1967, leaving Aden to join the former protectorates in the People's Republic of South Yemen, which was renamed the People's Democratic Republic of Yemen three years later. Far from joining the Commonwealth, the Republic turned towards Moscow. Even Nasser and the Egyptians had long since been left behind in Yemen's movement towards Marxism, and Aden in due course became a base for Soviet forces.

14.3.2 The shifting balance, 1957–61

Many colonies became independent without any involvement at all in federations though, especially in Africa, their boundaries were the rather artificial ones Europeans had drawn to suit themselves. The Gold Coast combined former slave-trading areas with later conquests from Ashanti, and the British mandate in what had been part of German Togoland. The colony was given experience of self-government after 1945 and it became independent in 1957 with the African name Ghana and a government of the Convention People's Party led by the Party's founder, Kwame Nkrumah.

Ghana became independent amid great hopes on all sides. Its government, civil service and judiciary had been trained and prepared. Its finances were sound and its economy fairly healthy though heavily dependent on cocoa exports. But Nkrumah was over-ambitious and the high hopes were not fulfilled (see section 17.2).

In 1960 Nigeria became independent. Nigeria had a population of more than 50 million, making it the largest British colony in Africa. It had valuable resources, which included oil, but its boundaries too were European-made, the state made up of Northern, Western and Eastern Regions. Tribal rivalries were always likely, especially between the Hausa (in the north), Yoruba (west) and Ibo (east), and successful government called for enormous tact and skill (see section 17.3).

Ghana and Nigeria began to change the Commonwealth yet again, broadening its racial composition. When Nigeria joined, the white Dominions were for the first time outnumbered by non-white members. In 1961 the balance shifted more sharply in favour of non-whites: Sierra Leone and Tanganyika increased the black African membership, while the accession of Cyprus was more than offset by the withdrawal of South Africa whose white government clung tenaciously to policies of apartheid[G]. South Africa's resignation confirmed that the Commonwealth was now a multiracial association in which privilege and discrimination on grounds of colour were not acceptable (see section 4.4). Once

South Africa had resigned, the end of the Central African Federation could be only a matter of time (see section 14.3.1).

14.3.3 The flood tide

Table 14.1 shows how the dismantling of the British Empire turned from a trickle into a flood. By the end of the 1960s most of the former Empire in Asia, Africa and the Caribbean was independent. British governments had long since ceased seriously to resist independence, though efforts to prepare for it and to time the change-over to the best all-round advantage sometimes brought criticism that the process was unduly protracted.

Kenya gained independence in 1963 only after bitter conflict during the 1950s. Kenya had a small but influential white minority, mainly farmers, whom the British wanted to safeguard. Kenyan nationalists found the delay vexing, and suspected that there might be some plot afoot to prolong white rule, as seemed to be the case with the CAF. Extremists in the dominant Kikuyu tribe set up a secret society known as the Mau Mau and in 1952 launched a campaign of atrocities to speed Britain's departure. Jomo Kenyatta, a Kikuyu and nationalist leader, was imprisoned from 1953 to 1961, blamed, without firm evidence, for instigating terrorism. Such victimization simply ensured that Kenyatta consolidated his authority as leader of the independence movement. The Mau Mau was not very effective after about 1954, though its barbarism continued to embitter relations with the British. In fact, the Mau Mau suffered far more casualties than they claimed victims, most of whom were fellow black Africans (nearly 2000) while fewer than a hundred were white. By contrast, 10 000 Mau Mau terrorists were killed by security forces and a further thousand hanged. In 1959 another thousand were being held in the Hola detention camp, where eleven died from beatings. This 'Hola massacre' persuaded Macmillan and his Colonial Secretary, Iain Macleod, of the folly of resisting independence movements. The Kenya African National Union won elections and, released from prison, Kenyatta became Kenya's Prime Minister. In the spirit of the new Commonwealth he promptly offered an olive-branch to Kenya's whites:

> I have suffered imprisonment and detention; but that is gone and I am not going to remember it. . . . Many of you are as Kenyan as myself. . . . Let us join hands and work for the benefit of Kenya, not for the benefit of one particular community.

Such goodwill was not unusual in the British Empire, even after the previously bitter confrontation. Most whites stayed in Kenya and it later became one of Africa's most prosperous countries (see section 17.4.3).

The flood of new nations and new admissions to the Commonwealth continued in the 1970s and 1980s, though few colonies now remained that were not merely small islands or sparsely populated. Where independence was held back it was because of special problems: Gibraltar wanted Britain's protection against a possible takeover by Spain; the Falkland Islands feared Argentina; Hong Kong had still to work out its future relations with China after 1997 when Britain's lease of the mainland territories would end. Southern Rhodesia, on the other hand, continued to embarrass the British government after the ending of the CAF in 1963, its white population determined to hold on to power and privilege. These were the remnants of a once vast empire, almost all of which had been decolonized within little more than 30 years.

14.3.4 From Southern Rhodesia to Zimbabwe

(a) UDI Southern Rhodesian whites bitterly resented the withholding of their independence when Malawi and Zambia became independent after the collapse of the CAF (see section 14.3.1). It was usual now to refer to Southern Rhodesia simply as Rhodesia. From 1962 the Rhodesian Front dominated white politics and therefore the government. Opinion seemed to have moved steadily to the right: though Huggins had been followed as Prime Minister by the comparatively liberal Garfield Todd, Todd had offended white opinion when he proposed that more blacks be allowed to vote and trade unions be legalized. Edgar Whitehead replaced him in 1958, but himself lost to the Rhodesian Front and Winston Field in 1962 when he publicly denounced racial discrimination. When Field failed to wrest independence from Britain, he had to step down in 1964 in favour of the even tougher Front leader, Ian Smith.

The blacks were allowed only fifteen of the 65 seats in the Rhodesian parliament and, like their African National Congress, effective political organizations were quickly banned. Nationalists like Nkomo and Sithole were always likely to be imprisoned, and Smith jailed Garfield Todd too when he spoke up for compromise. Smith's demands were simple: that Britain should grant independence and that Rhodesia's constitution should not be changed to give blacks any promise even of future control of the country (for which their name was not Rhodesia but Zimbabwe). Neither Douglas-Home's Conservative government nor Wilson's Labour government, elected in 1964, would agree to this. As a result, Rhodesia's whites seized independence illegally in November 1965 when Smith announced his unilateral declaration of independence (UDI) – a blow, he claimed, for 'justice, civilization and Christianity'. In effect, Smith was claiming that Rhodesia was a white Dominion and its 217 000 whites more entitled to rule than its four million blacks and 20 000 Asians.

(b) Economic sanctions and diplomatic negotiations Wilson had already outraged black opinion, but reassured the whites, by declaring that British troops would not be used against the Rhodesian Front unless there was a breakdown of law and order – unlikely as yet, given Rhodesia's vigorous security forces. With misplaced confidence, he asserted instead that economic sanctions would quickly bring the illegal UDI to an end. The United Nations gave support, and a British patrol off Beira did its best to stop the landing of oil which would flow to Rhodesia through the Mozambique–Rhodesia pipeline. Smith had powerful allies, however. Neighbouring South Africa had a vested interest in the well-being of white Rhodesians; the Portuguese rulers of Mozambique were also sympathetic; and there was no lack of freelance sanctions-busters, eager for quick profits. The British claimed that geography made the military defeat of Rhodesia wellnigh impossible, but it seemed that geography also hindered economic sanctions, the Bingham Report at the end of the 1970s revealing something of the extent to which sanctions were evaded, even by British companies.

Rhodesia's economy suffered some damage, especially to its tobacco exports, but the sanctions perhaps damaged Zambia more than Rhodesia. Zambia's economy relied on the oil pipeline from Mozambique and on rail links through Rhodesia. In 1970 China stepped in to finance and build the Tan–Zam Railway, to link Zambia with the coast of Tanzania (the country formed by the union of Tanganyika and Zanzibar in 1964), and use was made of such roads as there were from Zambia into friendly Tanzania. Zambia nevertheless suffered great hardships in its honest attempts to abide by the sanctions policy.

The British meanwhile negotiated with Rhodesia, making NIBMAR ('No Independence Before Majority African Rule') the basis of their case. Safeguards that this might come about in the future would have been enough for a settlement, since Britain was keen to relinquish its responsibility, but Smith would not concede even that to his black countrymen. He met Wilson in 1966 on *HMS Tiger* in the Mediterranean and in 1968 on *HMS Fearless* at Gibraltar, but whatever schemes for constitutional change they negotiated were rejected by the Rhodesian Front in Salisbury. Heath and Douglas-Home produced another constitutional formula in 1970 but, consulted by the Pearce Commission, black opinion found it too much of a surrender. The gulf between the Rhodesian Front and black Rhodesians was now too wide to be bridged by uncertain compromises. Land-apportionment laws in Rhodesia fiercely preserved white privilege, the white and black populations being allocated equal amounts of land in spite of their numerical differences. The scales were weighted against blacks socially and economically: job prospects and wages for blacks were inferior, their education separate and their primary schools organized by tribe to hinder unity. A 'Declaration of Rights' issued by the Smith government was less a guarantee of liberties than a charter for repressing them, and Rhodesia seemed to show growing similarities with apartheid South Africa.

But in spite of fierce external criticism Smith's government made no concessions. It made Rhodesia a republic in 1970 and completely revised the constitution to separate the races on the voting lists – a step closer to apartheid. Smith also boasted of an influx of white settlers, eager to share 'prosperity' and privilege in defiance of sanctions. It was one of Africa's misfortunes that it regularly attracted white mercenaries and fortune-hunters.

Arguments about sanctions dragged on amid growing cynicism. Nixon lifted the embargo on Rhodesian chrome because the USA 'needed' it and could get it more cheaply from Rhodesia than elsewhere. Non-white states tried to boycott those nations suspected of secret dealing with Rhodesia, while the morality of white supremacy in southern Africa was debated repeatedly. It was to the Rhodesian Front's advantage that white privilege was also entrenched in South Africa, in South Africa's mandated territory of South West Africa, and in

Portuguese Mozambique and Angola, a formidable bloc. This was about to change, however. In 1975 the Portuguese Empire collapsed and Mozambique and Angola suddenly had independent black governments (see section 15.4).

(c) The bubble bursts Rhodesia now faced hostile black governments on three sides – those of Botswana, Zambia and Mozambique. Only South Africa to the south remained supportive of the Rhodesian Front, and even South Africa began to recommend compromise as Smith's position was weakened by guerilla warfare. Rhodesia's veteran nationalist Nkomo, released from prison in 1974, directed the forces of the Zimbabwe African People's Union (ZAPU), mainly from Zambia. Robert Mugabe, also freed from detention in 1974, directed the Zimbabwe African National Union (ZANU) forces from Mozambique. The Soviet Union backed Nkomo, and China backed Mugabe. In 1976 ZAPU and ZANU agreed to co-operate in the Patriotic Front (PF). Kaunda explained their reliance on the Communist bloc:

> The people of the West have refused to help the freedom fighters. . . . This leaves these young men and women with no choice but to go to the only area where they will be supplied, namely the East. So they go there to train in the use of weapons.

In Rhodesia the death toll began to rise in what was now a war of liberation.

Diplomatic pressure on the Rhodesian whites increased. The USA boycotted chrome again and sent Kissinger to negotiate. In December 1975 Smith signed a Declaration of Intent along with Nkomo in which:

> both parties publicly expressed their commitment to work out immediately a constitutional settlement which will be acceptable to all the people of our country.

A conference at Geneva in 1976 made little progress towards such a constitutional settlement and the fighting intensified. Smith was evasive: he hoped he could make a deal with moderate black leaders who were still in Rhodesia, among them Bishop Abel Muzorewa, Sithole and Chief Chirau, and that between them they could outmanoeuvre the PF. An apprenticeship system was devised in 1978 to train approved black government ministers under white supervision. The PF rejected the system and so too did the now influential heads of state, the neighbouring 'front-line Presidents' of Angola, Botswana, Zambia, Tanzania and Mozambique, who were the black leaders nearest to southern Africa's remaining white regimes. Smith nevertheless persisted and elections were held, as a result of which, in 1979, Muzorewa became Prime Minister of what was now called Rhodesia–Zimbabwe.

(d) The settlement Britain still refused to grant Rhodesia–Zimbabwe legal independence, rejecting this last-ditch attempt at an 'internal settlement' to stop Nkomo, Mugabe and the PF. By now the war had claimed nearly 20 000 lives, black and white, and the pressure seemed irresistible. The Commonwealth Conference at Lusaka, Zambia, in 1979 prepared the way for the Lancaster House Conference in London where Lord Carrington, Thatcher's Foreign and Commonwealth Secretary, acted as Chairman to try to solve the

Fig. 14.5 A settlement signed at last – the Lancaster House Conference in London, December 1979, which determined the constitution and imminent independence of Zimbabwe. Lord Carrington, Britain's Foreign Secretary (at the microphone), chaired the Conference with Ian Gilmour, Lord Privy Seal, on his left. To the left of Gilmour were Joshua Nkomo and Robert Mugabe, leaders of the Zimbabwean Patriotic Front; to the right of Carrington Bishop Abel Muzorewa whose 'internal settlement' with Ian Smith had not survived and who had just resigned as Prime Minister of Rhodesia-Zimbabwe.

Rhodesian problem. Not without many difficulties, the parties eventually agreed: the PF would stop the war in exchange for a new Zimbabwean constitution. Muzorewa surrendered power to a British Governor, Lord Soames, who organized elections early in 1980, held under British and Commonwealth supervision to ensure their fairness.

The twenty seats reserved for whites in the Zimbabwean parliament were all won by the Rhodesian Front, but the new government was decided by the election of 80 black members. The black electorate, 94 per cent of whom voted, returned 57 ZANU(PF) supporters of Robert Mugabwe, 20 ZAPU(PF) supporters of Joshua Nkomo, and only 3 supporters of Bishop Muzorewa. This rout of supporters of the 'internal' settlement candidates meant that the black electorate had overwhelmingly endorsed the national liberation struggle fought by the guerrillas to obtain Zimbabwe's independence. Britain made haste to grant Zimbabwe legal independence as soon as Mugabe became Prime Minister.

The division of the voters between ZANU and ZAPU was to a large extent a tribal one, between the Shona and the Ndbele. 'Big Josh' Nkomo, the 'Father of Zimbabwe', who had given a lifetime's service to its struggle for independence, had won all the Ndbele seats in Matabeleland, but Mugabe was supreme elsewhere. Nkomo found it hard to believe the people's verdict was genuine, though the external observers of the election gave it their approval. A few years later Nkomo wrote of the election results:

> I could not believe it. . . . It was beyond belief. I was deeply distressed. . . . That my party should have won not a single seat in Salisbury and only twenty seats from Kariba right down to Beitbridge, I could not believe and still do not believe.

He nevertheless tried to co-operate. Mugabe became Prime Minister and Nkomo Minister of Home Affairs but it was an uneasy partnership, all the more tense because the guerilla armies were disbanded and resettled only slowly. Rhodesian Front whites feared Mugabe's Marxist inclinations and, though the Prime Minister, like Kenyatta, spoke persuasively of reconciliation, some white emigration occurred, especially to South Africa where the pastures still seemed green for whites. Zimbabwe became a republic on its independence, and it soon became evident that Mugabe also favoured a one-party state - by the 1980s a common device in new African countries since it helped to bridge tribal divisions. The partnership between Mugabe and Nkomo broke down in 1982 in the face of Zimbabwe's difficulties in nation-building (see section 17.5.1).

For Britain, however, 1980 had at last brought relief from its long-running 'Rhodesian problem'. For the Commonwealth too, 1980 brought success. As early as 1966, Lester Pearson of Canada had summarized what was at issue:

> The idea that a white minority regime might attain and retain independence on a minority racial basis - this is contrary not only to democratic principles and basic human rights but it violates the multiracial character of our Commonwealth and could destroy our association.

When Zimbabwe became independent under a majority government, NIBMAR had been achieved: the British Empire had lost its last large colony but one of the fundamental principles of the modern Commonwealth had been upheld, and Britain and the Commonwealth had avoided the creation of another South Africa.

14.3.5 Hong Kong

After Zimbabwe's independence, Hong Kong was easily Britain's largest remaining colony - its population reached five million early in the 1980s. Situated on the coast of Communist China, it bustled with economic vigour. Britain had seized the island colony by force in 1842 and had added the mainland 'New Territories' by lease from the Chinese government in 1898. Without these Territories the island could not survive economically, but the lease was due to expire in 1997.

China was prepared to wait, and relations between Peking and Hong Kong were largely amicable. Commercially and financially the colony was useful to the Chinese though it could also be a nuisance, for example as a haven for anti-communist dissidents. The British hardly needed to encourage Hong Kong's devotion to capitalism and, for its size, the colony's penetration into world markets was almost as impressive as Japan's. At the same time, the British tried to implant Western political values and hoped to prolong them.

It was difficult to see any long-term future for Hong Kong except as part of China, however. In the 1980s Britain and China negotiated on what should happen in 1997. An Anglo-Chinese Accord was signed late in 1984, with the best safeguards Mrs Thatcher could obtain for the people of Hong Kong when China should take over the whole of the colony. Peking agreed that Hong Kong's capitalist system and its unrestricted trading would survive for a further 50 years and that liberties would be protected by extensive self-government. The terms of the agreement were in keeping with the moderation China had shown towards Hong Kong since 1949, and with Deng Xiaoping's pragmatic approach to China's problems in the 1980s (see section 11.3). On the other hand, 1997 was still more than a decade away and it was unlikely that Britain would ever be in a position to enforce agreements on a reluctant China. For the present, however, the Accord tidily arranged for the transfer of Britain's last large colony when the time should come.

14.3.6 The Falklands War, 1982

Arrangements for the future of the Falkland Islands were less tidy. The Falklands had a population of about 1800, the English-speaking descendants of settlers from Britain some 8000 miles away. Argentina knew the islands as the Malvinas and, from a distance of about 300 miles, claimed that they were rightly Argentine property, denying that their conquest 150 years previously and subsequent settlement made them British. Tiring of fruitless diplomatic exchanges and taking advantage of weak defences, the Argentines seized the Falklands early in 1982.

Thatcher's government responded vigorously. A huge task force was assembled and despatched to uphold British sovereignty and 'the rule of law' and to punish the government of General Galtieri, now branded as a fascist and tyrant though he had recently been commended for his anti-communism and welcomed as a customer for British arms. In ten weeks, the Islands had been liberated, though at the cost of the lives of about 1800 Argentinians, 255 British troops and 3 Falkland Islanders. Some critics detected echoes of the Suez War in the enterprise, and many questioned whether there were not better ways to solve colonial disputes in the late twentieth century. But Thatcher's prestige soared while that of Galtieri plummeted: he lost power and was eventually jailed by his own people, while she went on to win her second term of office.

The United Nations had condemned the Argentine aggression which began the war, but the British action was not universally applauded. The Spanish-speaking world sympathized with Argentina, and Italy and the Irish Republic refused to apply EEC sanctions against the Argentinians. The USA was uneasy about European activity in the Americas, and moralists were outraged by the apparently unnecessary sinking of the *General Belgrano* in which over 350 Argentinians lost their lives. The strengthening of the Falklands defences (a 'Fortress Falklands' policy) followed the war, and Thatcher insisted that, whatever the cost, sovereignty would not be abandoned while the Falkland Islanders chose to remain British. With equal stubbornness, President Alfonsín and the Argentine people maintained that the Malvinas belonged to Argentina.

There was considerable outrage late in 1986 when Britain imposed a 150-mile fishing zone around the Islands to shut out aliens, and then defied a UN resolution urging negotiations with Argentina about the Islands' future, including the question of sovereignty. Only Belize, Oman and Sri Lanka now voted with Britain against the resolution: the USA and most Commonwealth and European countries voted for it, well aware that the original dispute still rankled and that war had not solved it.

14.4 The multiracial Commonwealth

14.4.1 The withdrawal of South Africa

For 50 years South Africa was a Dominion within the Commonwealth, though an increasingly uneasy one, especially after the Nationalists began to win elections in 1948 (see section 19.2). The apartheid they implemented ran contrary to ideas of racial equality, but South Africa's white governments resisted all pressures for reform. Matters came to a head in 1960–1 when the Commonwealth was at a crossroads, poised between its past as 'a white man's club' and its imminent enlargement with a host of new non-white members (see section 14.3.2). Harold Macmillan toured Africa and reached Cape Town early in 1960 where he spoke bluntly. The British found apartheid objectionable, and he went on:

> The most striking of all the impressions I have formed since I left London a month ago is of the strength of . . . African national consciousness. . . . It is happening everywhere. The wind of change is blowing through the continent. Whether we like it or not, this growth of national consciousness is a political fact. Our national policies must take account of it.

The warning that apartheid should be modified was plain but, so far, the 'wind of change' had only made South African governments more, rather than less, obstinate in their attachment to it.

Hendrik Verwoerd, the South African Prime Minister, was recovering from an attempt on his life when the Commonwealth Conference of 1960 met, and he sent Eric Louw to meet the criticisms South Africa expected there. Abdul Rahman of Malaya led the attack, while Louw denied that apartheid was any business of the Commonwealth. He defiantly gave notice that South Africa was to hold a referendum among whites as to whether it should become a republic. The Conference asserted in closing that 'the Commonwealth itself is a multiracial association' and that, while South Africa was free to choose to be a monarchy or a republic, its further membership of the Commonwealth as a republic would need the consent of fellow-members. The white referendum supported republicanism, and the stage was set for further debate at the Commonwealth Conference of 1961.

This time Verwoerd himself was present in London, making his first journey overseas for over 30 years. He would make no concessions on apartheid though he hoped to remain in the Commonwealth. Robert Menzies, Australia's Prime Minister, seemed supportive and Macmillan wriggled uncomfortably. Others were more openly critical though conciliatory, taking their cue from Nehru and Abdul Rahman. The Canadians and New Zealanders, however, firmly declared that apartheid was not consistent with Commonwealth membership, partly persuaded perhaps by a message from Julius Nyerere of Tanganyika whose independence was imminent. Tanganyika, he declared, could not join the Commonwealth if South Africa remained – 'a sacrifice,' Nyerere said:

> we must be prepared to make in our fight to preserve the dignity of man in Africa and wipe out racialism.

Verwoerd himself provided the solution, to the relief of everyone except perhaps Menzies. The Republic of South Africa withdrew its application to stay in the Commonwealth. For South Africa, the results were not immediately grave. Britain had second thoughts about allowing some remaining southern-African colonies to join South Africa in much the same way as Sarawak and Sabah were shortly to join Malaya and, in due course, each became independent in its own right – Botswana (formerly Bechuanaland), Lesotho (formerly Basutoland) and Swaziland. But trading and other links between South Africa and the outside world were for some time scarcely affected. South Africa's withdrawal from the Commonwealth was nevertheless a serious setback for the whites of southern Africa, and Welensky of the CAF complained of Britain's 'naked appeasement' of their critics.

For the Commonwealth, 1961 was an important milestone, its significance more immediately obvious. Tanganyika was the first in a flood of new members, all of them emerging nations eager to play a part in adapting the association to the late twentieth-century world.

14.4.2 The evolution of the Commonwealth

Adaptability was one of the Commonwealth's main characteristics. With the independence and admission of Brunei at the end of 1983, its membership reached 49 but even at this stage formal machinery was limited. Heads of government met in Commonwealth Conferences, usually at two yearly intervals. (After 1965 such meetings took place in other cities, not only London.) The Commonwealth Secretariat had been set up in 1965, its first Secretary-General the Canadian Arnold Smith, followed in 1975 by Shridath Ramphal who had been Foreign Minister of Guyana. Secretariat headquarters were in London, its staff multiracial, but the Commonwealth was still a voluntary – some thought even amateur – organization. It operated without formal votes or even formal debates, preferring what Attlee had called 'talk round a table between friends'. Among its few professional bodies were the Commonwealth Development Corporation (CDC), the Special Commonwealth African Assistance Plan (SCAAP) and the Commonwealth Fund for Technical Co-operation (CFTC). Their emphasis was on helping the developing nations, and in 1983 some three-quarters of Britain's overseas aid went to members of the Commonwealth, part of the complex web of assistance schemes whereby members helped one another. But the Commonwealth also achieved a great deal through voluntary bodies of doctors, teachers, journalists, lawyers, parliamentarians and other professionals. Such bodies promoted friendship and spread expertise, relying on common links in heritage, shared values and the English language.

It was sometimes suggested that Britain had invented the Commonwealth from its own reluctance to let go of past glories. No other overseas empire left behind any similarly successful organization. Commonwealth members no doubt had their own particular reasons for supporting it: Canada's enthusiasm, for example, owed something to the fact that in the Commonwealth it could not be overshadowed by the USA. But there was also genuine widespread support for the Commonwealth's ideals of co-operation and partnership, mutual respect and equality. New nations could gain confidence among members who were sympathetic to their problems. Like the United Nations, the Commonwealth gave their new-found independence official recognition, but its proceedings were much less formal and were little influenced by the superpower rivalries which dogged the larger association.

Though the Commonwealth grew, ties between its members were in some ways weakened over the years, however. Trade patterns changed, regional links outside the Commonwealth becoming stronger when, for example, Britain in 1973 joined the EEC. Yet Commonwealth markets and supplies still remained important to the association's members, both rich and poor. The Commonwealth also remained alive to the huge differences in wealth between countries such as Canada and others such as Malawi, and to the need to try to reduce this gap (see section 21.3). In 1950 the Commonwealth had helped to pioneer the Colombo Plan which grew into a major programme for the development of emerging nations in south and south-east Asia. Thirty years later, at the time of the Brandt Report, the Commonwealth could offer an unrivalled fund of understanding and expertise to those only just becoming aware of the seriousness of the North–South divide (see section 21.3).

It was not the aim of the Commonwealth to devise joint policy or even to undertake joint defence. The organization was seldom able to solve problems like that of Kashmir, and it was itself the victim of international feuds. Bangladesh joined the Commonwealth in 1972, having broken free from Pakistan, but when the Commonwealth admitted Bangladesh, Pakistan resigned its membership in protest the same year (see section 16.4.1). Commonwealth Conferences generally concerned themselves more with common attitudes. The meeting in 1961 took a common view of apartheid; that of 1975 in Kingston, Jamaica, formulated ideas for stabilizing commodity prices. Meanwhile, the 1971 Conference in Singapore discussed the sale of arms to South Africa. Heath found this Conference an uncomfortable one, since Britain was attacked for his pursuit of naval co-operation with the South Africans, a policy perhaps contrary to UN guide-lines. But the Conference ended in general agreement, steered towards it by the skills of Singapore's Lee Kwan Yew. The Declaration of Commonwealth Principles was agreed, affirming that members recognized:

> racial prejudice as a dangerous sickness threatening the healthy development of the human race and racial discrimination as an unmitigated evil of society. Each of us will vigorously combat this evil within our own nation.

The Conference of 1977 in Britain returned to the South African problem, arriving through informal talks at the Gleneagles Agreement to discourage sporting links with South Africa until apartheid was abandoned. Thus the multiracial basis of the Commonwealth was regularly reaffirmed and, in spite of critics who derided it as a sham or as a pressure group for the poor and the Third World, the Commonwealth lived on. Many members no longer practised Westminster-style parliamentary democracy, and trade patterns had been much diversified, so that by the late 1980s the Commonwealth was very different from the British Commonwealth of Nations half a century earlier. Its chief importance now lay in its multiracialism and in its systems of mutual aid, especially for those nations which had recently emerged from the age of British colonialism.

UNIT 15

Decolonization: 2 – the European empires

15.1 The Dutch Empire

When the Second World War began, the Dutch still held colonies in the East Indies and in the West Indies. Japan seized the Dutch East Indies in 1942, a blow from which the Dutch Empire could never recover. The nineteenth-century 'culture system' the Dutch had imposed on the East Indies left the economy geared to cash crops for sale and export rather than for local consumption, while twentieth-century reform to protect the land-owning rights of the East Indians and to improve social conditions had done little to raise standards of living, partly because of population growth. Nationalist movements, therefore, already threatened Dutch rule even before the Japanese arrived. Claiming their intent to liberate fellow Asians from the Europeans, the Japanese encouraged Indonesian (East Indies) nationalists like Achmed Sukarno, whom the Dutch had jailed as early as 1929. Yet Indonesians soon found the Japanese as eager as the Dutch to gain economic benefit – especially oil – from the occupation. On the verge of defeat in the Second World War, however, the Japanese declared Indonesia independent.

With Japan's surrender, British troops were the first into the main islands of Indonesia. They appeared to recognize the independent Republic of Indonesia and the leadership of Sukarno, whom the Indonesians made their President in December 1945. But the British were concerned more with urgent post-war administration than with constitutional legalities, and the Dutch took a different view. They were prepared to set up a partnership, making a United States of Indonesia part of a federal Netherlands–Indonesia Union, but they would not concede the sovereignty Indonesians demanded. Nor would they accept the leadership of Sukarno who they alleged had collaborated with the Japanese.

Conflict broke out during 1947 as the Dutch tried to reimpose their authority. In 1948 they stepped up their action, now intent not only on denying Indonesian independence but also on crushing an Indonesian communist movement. The Dutch had some success but the fighting was savage, alarming those like the Americans to whom colonialism was distasteful, and the Australians and

Indians to whom it was deeply offensive. The UN Security Council expressed disapproval, and external pressures persuaded the Dutch at the end of 1949 to accept a United States of Indonesia with full sovereignty. Cosmetic links with the Netherlands survived for five more years, soothing Dutch pride, but the huge East Indies empire, held since the seventeenth century, had been lost. Sukarno was free Indonesia's first President.

With the population of Indonesia scattered across some 3000 islands over a distance of several thousand miles and speaking some 25 languages, Sukarno faced daunting problems in building the Indonesian nation. In 1950 the Dutch-designed federation was replaced by the unitary state that Sukarno had always favoured, reinforcing the influence of Java, where more than three in five of the population lived, over the other islands. At the same time there were still frontiers in dispute. In 1949 the Dutch refused to let go of West Irian, part of New Guinea. To put pressure on the Netherlands, Sukarno in 1957 nationalized Dutch property in Indonesia and expelled Dutch citizens, but not until 1962 was West Irian handed over to the United Nations. It became part of Indonesia a year later. At that time, Sukarno was involved in the 'Confrontation' with Malaysia over the rights he claimed to the whole of Borneo. Sarawak and Sabah, in north Borneo and once British colonies, were now part of Malaysia. Sukarno distrusted the Malay leadership, seeing it as neo-colonialist, perpetuating British imperialist values, while the Malaysians accused Sukarno of fomenting rebellion in Brunei, a British protectorate in north Borneo. The Confrontation involved propaganda, economic warfare and even small-scale military action, including parachutist activity against Malaya. But Sukarno could not divide the Malaysian Federation. The Commonwealth, the USA and most of the members of the UN stood behind Malaysia, unmoved even by Indonesia's withdrawal from the United Nations in 1965. Indonesia's isolation, supported by few powers other than China, merely helped to bring about Sukarno's forced resignation from office in 1967.

General Suharto, who succeeded Sukarno, ended the Malaysian Confrontation and restored Indonesia to the UN, but his attention soon turned to Timor, an island divided until 1975 between Indonesia and Portugal. Portuguese (East) Timor seemed to want independence when the Portuguese Empire fell apart in the 1970s. But Suharto invaded in December 1975, proclaiming a union with Indonesia that FRETILIN, an East Timor resistance movement, continued to dispute. There were other secessionist movements too in Indonesia. South Moluccans turned to terrorist tactics in the Netherlands in the 1970s, in a hopeless attempt to persuade the Dutch to help their fight for independence from Indonesia. The Papuan Freedom Movement fought a guerilla action in the late 1980s, seeking to rid Irian Jaya (West Irian) from the Javanese who dominated Indonesia.

Settling the frontiers of Indonesia was only one of the new nation's problems, however. Like other new nations all over the world, Indonesia struggled to create unity and sensible boundaries in the wake of fallen colonial empires, while grappling with the formidable economic, social and political difficulties of independence (see Units 16 and 17). Sukarno finally fell from power when the army leaders turned against him. The background to his fall was one of economic disappointments made worse by the Malaysian Confrontation; 'guided democracy' which cloaked only thinly Sukarno's dictatorial methods in the 1960s; and upheaval and bloody reprisals against an attempted communist coup in 1965, of which it was suspected Sukarno had advance knowledge. Sukarno had helped bring Indonesia to independence and led it through the early years of independence, outwitting the Dutch. He had made Bandung an important centre, in 1955 hosting the meeting of Afro-Asian nations which favoured non-alignment. Suharto, on the other hand, gave a vigorous priority to economic development in the late 1960s and 1970s, and tried to curb the rising population which persistently handicapped advancement. Like other first-generation leaders in independence he was sometimes over-ambitious, however, spending extravagantly rather than prudently. At the same time, he too kept firm political control, ruthlessly when he thought it necessary (see section 16.6).

The Dutch meanwhile tried to avoid surrendering in the West as they had been forced to surrender in the East. In 1954 the Netherlands West Indies (islands like Curaçao and the mainland territory of Surinam) were made part of the Kingdom of the Netherlands with the right to control their own internal affairs. In 1975, however, independence was granted to the Republic of Surinam (later Suriname). The islands (the Netherlands Antilles), all of them tiny, with an overall population in the 1980s of less than a quarter of a million, kept their direct link with the Netherlands and, through the Netherlands, with the European Community.

15.2 The French Empire

15.2.1 The Middle East mandates

French collaborators with the Nazis might well have delivered Syria to Germany during the Second World War, enabling the Germans to strike at pro-British Iraq, had not British and Free French forces moved quickly, occupying Syria in 1941 to keep the Germans out of it. British and French forces also took control of Lebanon, with Syria part of the French mandate at the end of the First World War but since 1926 administered separately from Syria. In 1944 de Gaulle and the Free French gave Lebanon independence while the Syrians simultaneously claimed their independence. The French government thought of regaining Syria, however, when the war in Europe ended, but they were frustrated by British forces sent by Churchill, who no doubt hoped to promote British influence in the Middle East but recognized too that, like Iraq and Jordan, Syria and Lebanon had now outgrown colonial rule. French troops left Syria in 1946, a comparatively painless withdrawal when set alongside the traumas which were to follow in Indo-China and north Africa.

15.2.2 Conflict in Indo-China

The Japanese occupied Indo-China from 1941 to the end of the Second World War, declaring in 1945 the abolition of French authority there and the region's

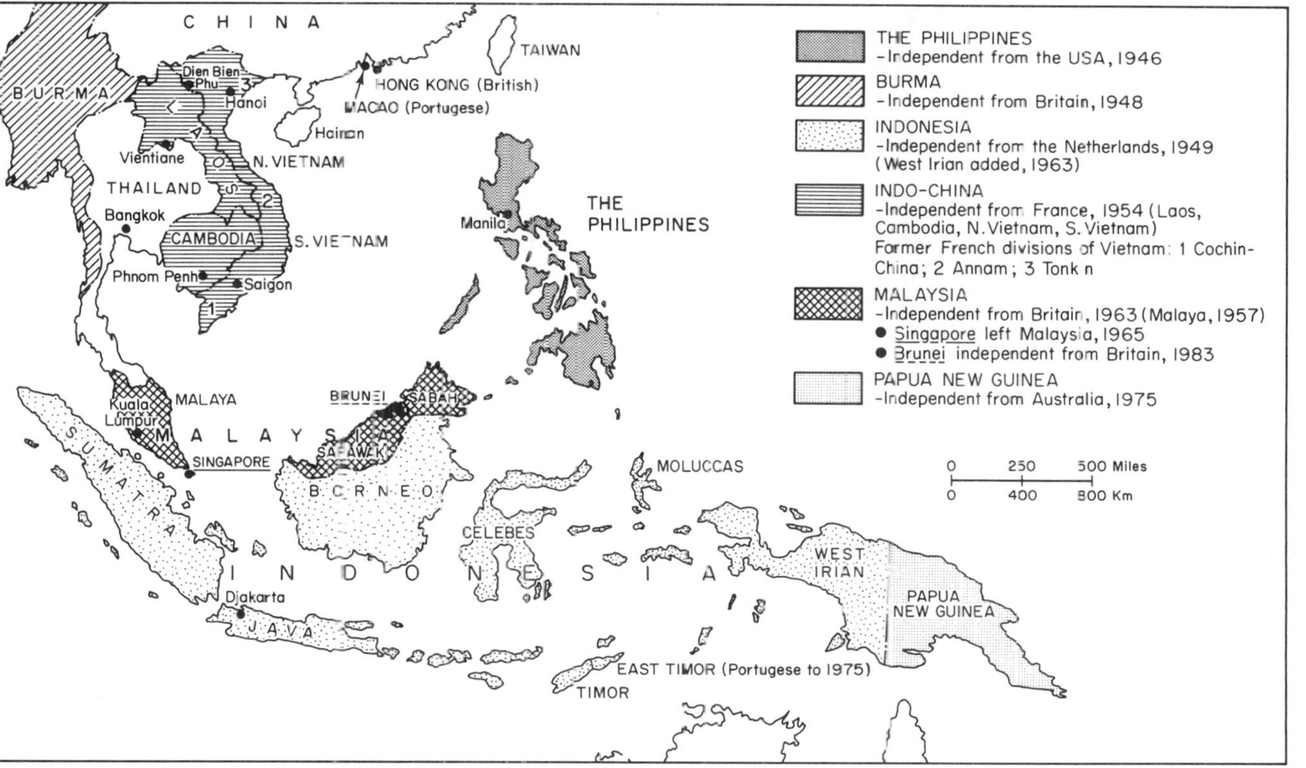

Fig. 15.1 The end of colonial empires in south-east Asia

independence. Following the Japanese surrender, British and Kuomintang Chinese arrived in Indo-China to remove the Japanese, but they ignored claims for independence and handed Indo-China back to the French in 1946.

France had ruled directly only in Cochin-China, the area around Saigon, while exercising authority elsewhere over the protectorates of Annam, Tonkin, Cambodia and Laos. This was the system the French would have liked to restore but, like the Dutch in Indonesia, they found conditions much changed. Nationalist Vietnamese had campaigned against the French as early as the 1920s, seeking freedom for a united Vietnam made up of Tonkin, Annam and Cochin-China. After 1941, the nationalists developed the Vietminh, a guerilla movement to resist the Japanese. The Vietminh was especially strong in Tonkin, around Hanoi, and under the leadership of Ho Chi Minh and Vo Nguyen Giap was well placed in 1946 to resist the return of the French. Ho was a Marxist as well as a nationalist and as early as 1920 had helped to found the French Communist Party. Giap was younger, a Marxist economist and historian turned soldier, soon to prove a match for France's top military men, including General Raoul Salan.

France would accept the Democratic Republic of Vietnam proclaimed by Ho only if it remained subject to French supervision within the French Union, an association set up in 1946 to prepare French colonies for self-government while preserving the final authority of France. This was unacceptable to the Vietminh. At the end of 1946, bombardment by French warships killed some 6000 Vietnamese at Haiphong in a mistaken show of strength which hardened opinion against France, and the Vietminh now fought a war of liberation.

French plans for Indo-China now focused on a federation of three self-governing states: Cambodia, Laos and Vietnam, the last under Emperor Bao Dai, a former puppet-ruler in Annam and in 1945 the Japanese nominee for rule in Vietnam. But the Vietminh demanded a totally independent Republic of Vietnam and gained support from the Soviet Union as well as supplies from China when the Communists came to power there in 1949. The French sent a succession of military leaders and some of their best troops. Unlike the Dutch in Indonesia, they also had American aid, which Eisenhower sought to justify in 1953:

> Let us assume we [the West] lost Indo-China. . . . The tin and tungsten that we so greatly value from that area would cease coming. . . . When the United States votes 400 million dollars to help [the French] . . . we are voting for the cheapest way to prevent . . . something that would be of a most terrible significance to the United States of America.

France was nevertheless defeated: over 16 000 French troops were surrounded, many killed and the rest forced to surrender in May 1954 after many weeks of fighting at Dien Bien Phu. In the following month, Mendès-France came to power in Paris, pledged to end the war.

At the Geneva Conference in July 1954, France gave up the whole of Indo-China, making Cambodia, Laos and Vietnam independent. Britain, the USA, the Soviet Union and Communist China also attended the Conference, and it was decided that Vietnam should be divided, temporarily, at the 17th Parallel – the Democratic Republic under the Vietminh to the north and the government of Bao Dai and his minister Ngo Dinh Diem to the south. Elections scheduled to be held within two years were optimistically expected to unite Vietnam under a single agreed government, though the division seemed at least as likely to lead to war between the two Vietnams, especially when Bao Dai and Diem refused to sign the Geneva Agreements. The Americans also refused to sign, asserting their:

> traditional position that peoples are entitled to determine their own future and that the United States will not join an arrangement which would hinder this.

It soon became ominously clear that this meant that, whatever efforts the French made to bring about reconciliation in Vietnam and whatever the people of Vietnam might want, the USA was not prepared to accept a united Vietnam under communist control (see section 18.4).

15.2.3 Crises in North Africa

The disaster in Indo-China gave a boost to nationalist agitation against French rule in north Africa. The French had little heart for continuing to resist the call for independence in the protectorates of Tunisia and Morocco. Mendès-France prepared the way for the independence of Tunisia, negotiating with the veteran nationalist leader Habib ibn Ali Bourguiba, who became Prime Minister when independence was granted in 1956 and President when Tunisia became a republic a year later. Edgar Faure meanwhile restored the monarchy in French Morocco in readiness for independence there in 1956, and, when Spanish Morocco was also given independence, the two Moroccos were reunited later the same year. But no government of the Fourth Republic could contemplate giving independence to Algeria where the *colons* (white settlers) considered the state a part of France itself and demanded French protection against the Arab nationalists. Arab rebellion, hinted at in the 1930s, was persistent from 1954 onwards, the conflict growing in scale and savagery.

The French blamed President Nasser of Egypt for encouraging Arab nationalism generally and the rebellion in Algeria in particular. Now under the premiership of Guy Mollet, and in a reckless attempt to deal with Nasser and to regain lost prestige, the French joined Britain and Israel in the Suez War of 1956 (see section 14.2.5). But that brought only a further humiliating defeat, while adding fuel to the war in Algeria which the Fourth Republic now seemed unable to control. The French had one success in 1956, however, when they captured Ahmed Ben Bella, the founder and leader of the Algerian FLN (National Liberation Front), when his airliner was diverted to Algiers while flying from Cairo to Tunis. Ben Bella was imprisoned and not released until 1962.

Europeans were heavily outnumbered in an Algerian population approaching ten million. Only about 400 000 Algerians were of French descent. They nevertheless confidently expected the French army to preserve their Christian French culture against the Muslim Arabs. The *colons* distrusted the politicians of the Fourth Republic, however, and the military feared a sell-out, especially when the government in Paris showed reluctance to allow action against FLN bases in neighbouring Tunisia. In 1958 the military put pressure on President Coty to recall to power General de Gaulle and when, playing for time, Coty made Pflimlin Prime Minister, a man unsympathetic to the French Algerian cause, General Salan roused the Gaullist clamour in Algiers to a new pitch. The Fourth Republic thus came to an end, unable to resolve the Algerian crisis. The destinies of France and Algeria now rested once more with de Gaulle who seemed to be the nation's loftiest patriot (see section 6.3.3).

15.2.4 A patriot but a realist: the end of the French Empire

Those who in 1958 assumed that de Gaulle would preserve *Algérie Française* and the rest of the French Empire were bewildered when, a few years later, almost nothing remained of that Empire in Africa, vast though it had been. When the Fifth Republic was set up in 1958, de Gaulle designed a French Community within which France's overseas territories would be linked in federation, each with its own internal government but subject to common French foreign and defence policies. This was a limited concession to nationalism compared with the French Union of 1946, but de Gaulle showed little desire to negotiate about it, offering black Africans a referendum but asserting his own position in true Gaullist style:

> The referendum will tell us whether secession [from the French Community] carries the day. But what is inconceivable is an independent state which France continues to help. If the choice is independence, the government will draw, with regret, the conclusions that follow from the expressions of that choice.

In effect, this was an ultimatum. Twelve French territories could become independent and face the harsh realities of independence alone, or they could remain under French patronage within de Gaulle's French Community. Eleven shrank from independence but Guinea under Sékou Touré overwhelmingly voted against the Community. Touré explained why:

> We do not have to be blackmailed by France. . . . We say 'No' unanimously and categorically to any project which does not cater for our aspirations.

The French took revenge, withdrawing all assistance from Guinea and even smashing furniture and crockery in the Governor's residence in its capital, Conakry. Far from intimidating other African states, however, Guinea's example inspired them, especially when Touré received other offers of aid and support.

Senegal and other French colonies now demanded independence and de Gaulle wasted no time in argument. He was as aware as Macmillan of the 'wind of change' blowing in black Africa, and in 1960 independence was granted to eleven French colonies still within the Community, and to Cameroon and Togo, UN trust territories which France had formerly held as mandates. Figure 15.2 shows the new nations which thus came into existence in West and Central Africa, along with the Malagasy Republic (the island of Madagascar). This

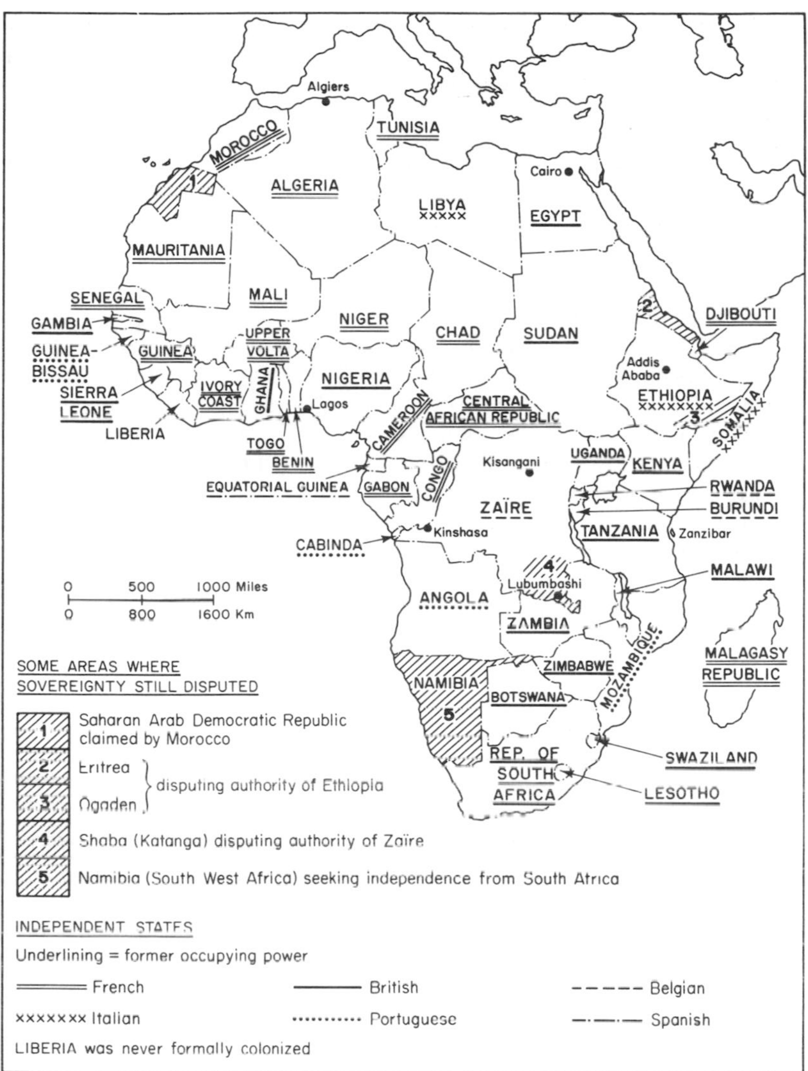

Fig. 15.2 Africa, 1985

upheaval in the rest of Africa in 1960 underlined de Gaulle's need to settle the still festering problem of Algeria.

The OAS (*Organisation de l'Armée Secrète*) was set up in 1961 by the *colons*, their sympathizers and the military led by Salan who now suspected that de Gaulle might also grant independence to Algeria under a government of the

FLN. The OAS tried to assassinate the President but lost popularity by threatening the Fifth Republic in this way. De Gaulle set up talks at Évian between Prime Minister Pompidou and Ben Bella, newly released from prison, and Algerian independence was conceded subject only to the referenda de Gaulle so favoured. In both France and Algeria there was firm support for the agreement, perhaps increased by the efforts of the OAS to disrupt the settlement through terrorist tactics. Ben Bella became Prime Minister then President of Algeria, though he was overthrown by a military coup led by his Defence Minister, Boumédienne, in 1965. General Salan was meanwhile arrested and imprisoned and the OAS quickly faded into insignificance.

De Gaulle remained the supreme French patriot but, in his view, the key to the greatness of France was not in Africa but in Europe (see section 6.3.4). He was realist enough to wind up one of the largest colonial empires within a mere two or three years. The French Community lost its meaning, but after the upheavals of 1960 de Gaulle saw the sense in being generous. Independence proved no barrier to French assistance after all, and France was able to keep considerable goodwill in its former African colonies and influence at almost all levels. A naval base and weapons-testing sites were retained in Algeria, and strong economic ties survived with almost all the former colonies in black Africa. Most of the latter went on to found the Africa and Malagasy Union in 1961, to promote their joint interests through their common French language. In 1963 they widened the movement, helping to found the Organization of African Unity (OAU), which aimed to rid all Africa of colonialism. France meanwhile kept an alert eye on French interests throughout the continent, sometimes interfering more blatantly than other Europeans dared. Granting independence in de Gaulle's view was far from being an abject withdrawal.

15.2.5 The rest of the French Empire

Guadeloupe and Martinique (islands in the West Indies) and French Guiana (on the South American mainland) had been made overseas *départements* of France when the Fourth Republic was set up in 1946. They were represented in the French Assembly and no longer considered colonies. In 1950 and 1954 the French smoothly transferred to India French possessions in the Indian subcontinent such as Pondicherry. French Somaliland in East Africa (from 1967 known as Afars and Issas) was denied independence until 1977, when it took the name Djibouti.

After that, some small territories in Antarctica and islands in the Pacific were all that was left of the French Empire. There was still nationalist agitation here and there in the West Indies and the Pacific in the 1980s. Yet where independence had long been granted, French influence often persisted. There were French troops in several black African states, and currencies in a Franc Zone, based on Dakar in Senegal, were still supervised from Paris. In 1986 President Mitterrand brought to Versailles the leaders of nearly 40 French-speaking nations, to promote their common heritage. He claimed that they were in effect 'a community' still, because they were:

> bearers of a culture which can have the ambition of being universal.

Observers suggested this was an attempt to begin to match the Commonwealth which had survived the passing of the British Empire (see section 14.4.2). At all events, it emphasized what a huge empire the French had once possessed and how deep-rooted French culture remained, especially in Africa.

15.3 The Italian and Belgian Empires in Africa: independence and secession

The price of Italy's Fascism and of defeat in the Second World War was that Italy forfeited its overseas empire (see section 6.4). The international community took its time in deciding the future of Italy's African colonies. Libya was administered by the British and French until the United Nations agreed to its independence in 1951 under the monarchy of King Idris. Italian East Africa had soon fallen apart when Italy joined the Second World War, and Ethiopia quickly regained its independence and Haile Selassie his throne, lost to the Italians only in 1936. The former Italian colony of Eritrea was made part of a federal Ethiopia in 1952 by the decision of the UN General Assembly, but it was from the start an uneasy union and became all the more so when Ethiopia in 1962 withdrew Eritrea's rights to self-government. Eritreans began a persistent war of liberation which, as it dragged on, demonstrated yet again the problems of achieving satisfying frontiers in post-colonial Africa. The British and then the UN meanwhile took over Italian Somaliland, to the south-east of Ethiopia, eventually in 1960 merging British and Italian Somaliland in a new independent state, the Republic of Somalia. By the 1970s Somalia laid claim to the Ogaden region of Ethiopia, encouraging a Somali secessionist movement there against the Ethiopian government in Addis Ababa (see section 22.2).

One way or another, most of Africa's frontiers in the late twentieth century had been determined by outsiders, especially Europeans. Independent African governments had to live with the results, and nowhere was the problem more acute than in the Congo, where secessionist movements and civil war erupted when Belgian rule there came to a rather sudden end in June 1960.

Unlike the French, who had carved out almost a dozen states from their colonies of French West and French Equatorial Africa, the Belgians in 1960 gave independence to the whole vast area of the Congo, a single country more than 70 times the size of Belgium itself though with a population of only about fifteen million. There was little thought given to the viability of this vast area as an independent nation, and perhaps even less preparation for its effective government. Not until 1957 were the Congolese allowed to elect even town councils, and the Belgians trained very few of their colonial subjects for jobs in administration and the professions. There were not even federal arrangements for the huge new republic with its 150 tribes and variety of languages. After nationalist rioting in 1959, Belgium held a round-table conference with Congolese leaders in January 1960, and granted independence just six months later. Belgium was eager to be rid of an embarrassing, and potentially costly, struggle with African nationalism at a time when other colonial empires were crumbling on almost all sides of the Congo.

The first President of the Congo was Joseph Kasavubu, leader of one nationalist group and well supported by the Bakongo tribe. Patrice Lumumba, leader of the Congolese National Movement and representing the Batatele tribe, became Prime Minister. Order broke down within a month. By the end of July 1960 the Belgians had sent in paratroopers, a UN peace-keeping force had arrived, and the region of Katanga, rich in mineral deposits and the stronghold of the Lunda tribe, had declared itself independent of the Congo under Moise Tshombe, an opportunist businessman. Tribal and regional differences also led to a secessionist movement in the west of the Congo where Albert Kalonji aimed at an independent state in Kasai. The Belgians soon concentrated their efforts, not on maintaining the Congo Republic they had created but on supporting Tshombe and Katanga, where the European company Union Minière wanted to preserve its profitable interests in copper-mining. These might be threatened by a government led by Lumumba, the associate of Nkrumah in Ghana and Nasser in Egypt who combined socialism with his nationalism (see section 13.2.1). For the United Nations, Dag Hammarskjöld asserted that UN troops were in the Congo 'to help restore law and order' but not to preserve Congolese unity:

> The United Nations cannot interfere in the internal conflict in the Congo . . . it cannot interfere in the political dispute between Katanga and the Central Government.

Such were the main ingredients of the Congolese tragedy, but worse followed. Lumumba sought Soviet support against the Belgian-backed Katangese and the less-than-helpful United Nations. This not only embroiled the Congo in the Cold War but it also angered Kasavubu and quickened a conflict in which each declared the other dismissed from office. Units of the Congolese army took sides, the Chief-of-Staff Mobutu backing the President against the Prime Minister. Lumumba left the capital, Léopoldville (later Kinshasa), to rally his supporters in the east of the Congo around Stanleyville (Kisangani), but he was handed over by disaffected troops to the Katangese, who murdered him in January 1961. In the eyes of the communist world, he was a 'victim of imperialism and the financial interests of capitalism'. Hammarskjöld also died, killed in an air crash later in 1961 while seeking a solution to the Congolese dilemma.

Gradually, UN opinion mobilized against Tshombe and Katanga and in favour of the Congolese Republic. Members were disturbed by the gangs of mercenaries who helped Tshombe, most of them whites motivated by greed, not principles. There were also fears about the effects the break-up of the Congo might have on the rest of Africa. Tshombe still had his supporters, however, for example in the British government. Spasmodic fighting began between Tshombe's troops and the UN peace-keeping forces, and this effectively ended the secessionist movement. Tshombe retired to Europe in 1963 and UN troops left the Congo in 1964. Tshombe remained popular in business circles, however, and in July 1964 Kasavubu invited him back to the Congo as Prime Minister. The country now faced open rebellion around Stanleyville where the People's Republic of the Congo was proclaimed in opposition to the government in Léopoldville. Tshombe hit back fiercely, and more brutal killing occurred: mercenaries arrived and regular Belgian troops were sent in, adding to the discontents until Kasavudu dismissed Tshombe little more than a year after his return.

Tshombe was now a marked man. In exile his aircraft was hijacked in 1967, and he died in 1969 in an Algerian jail. Kasavubu fell from power too, and before the end of 1965 Mobutu seized power in a military coup. He restored something like order by 1967 and continued to rule with the backing of the army though confirmed as President by election in 1970. His regime soon became a byword for corruption.

In 1971 the Congo adopted the name Zaïre and Africanized most of its place-names.

The Belgian Empire thus ended in chaos and bloodshed through the lack of adequate preparation for independence, great-power meddling even after independence, and tribal and regional jealousies. Ruanda-Urundi, a Belgian mandate since 1923, lying between the Congo and Tanganyika, meanwhile became independent in 1962 as the small states of Rwanda and Burundi. Even here, tribal conflicts in the 1970s brought savage fighting between the Tutsi and the Hutu, the latter suffering dreadful casualties, being the victims of genocidal attacks by their 'fellow nationals'.

The frontiers of the Belgian Congo were preserved, however, and Mobutu was able to resist renewed unrest when it broke out in Katanga. The Organization of African Unity (OAU) helped him at last to clear the country of white mercenaries in 1968, and nationalizing the copper mines reduced the level of European involvement. Mobutu nevertheless remained pro-West and, when Angola became independent, he interfered there to try to prevent successful government by the Marxist MPLA (see section 15.4). As a result, Angola supported a new uprising in Katanga (now Shaba) in 1977, where the National Liberation Front (NLF) was aiming to overthrow Mobutu's government. Some blamed the uprising on Soviet and Cuban intrigue and Mobutu suppressed it with help from right-wing Morocco and Sadat's Egypt. But a year later the NLF invaded again from bases in Angola. Whites were among those killed at Kolwezi, a mining centre, and Belgium and France now rushed in troops. They restored order and drove the rebels back, but the capital of Katanga was now renamed Lumumbashi in honour of the former Prime Minister whom the left had not forgotten.

Zaïre was therefore caught up in the East–West ideological struggle as well as in the usual social and economic problems facing new Third World[G] nations. Nor was it easy to escape the interference of the former colonizing powers. President Giscard of France, like the Gaullists, seemed to believe that the French had the right and duty to intervene not only in what had been French colonies but in Zaïre too, and he tried to organize a sort of military 'fire-brigade' ready to put out the slightest glimmer of socialist and anti-Western flames. Instability was not unusual in former French states such as Chad where neighbouring Libya interfered in support of the left and, urged on by the USA, the French became involved in the 1980s in spite of the reluctance of President Mitterrand to adopt Gaullist interventionist policies. What were perceived to be

European (and American) interests were still upheld in the developing nations long after they won formal independence.

15.4 The Spanish and Portuguese Empires: independence delayed

Spain and Portugal had already lost most of their once huge empires by the start of the twentieth century. Spain had little left at all, though Portugal still held large areas of Africa. Still backward by European standards after 1945, and governed by outdated dictatorships, neither Spain nor Portugal showed much awareness of the African 'wind of change' to which Macmillan referred. Portugal claimed that its possessions were Overseas Territories, not colonies but somehow part of Portugal itself, and both Salazar and Caetano therefore tried to ignore African nationalism during their successive terms of office. Franco in Spain had fewer territories with which to concern himself but also showed little thought for their future (see section 7.3). On the other hand, he did not struggle hard to keep what was left of Spain's Empire: Spanish Morocco was made independent with French Morocco in 1956, and the coastal province of Ifni was transferred to Morocco in 1969, while in 1968 independence was granted to Spanish (now Equatorial) Guinea. However, Franco held on to Spanish Sahara, a profitable source of phosphates on Africa's north-west coast, south of Morocco.

Saharan nationalists launched a campaign to free their country in 1972, grouping soon afterwards in the Polisario Front. When Franco died in 1975, the Spaniards agreed to give up the Sahara as part of Spain's movement into the modern world. But rather than granting independence they simply handed it over to be shared between Morocco and Mauritania, its neighbours. Polisario proclaimed the Saharan Arab Democratic Republic in 1976, and thus began a new war of liberation in the wake of yet another mismanaged European withdrawal.

Mauritania withdrew its claims in 1979, leaving Polisario to continue its bitter struggle against Morocco. The Saharans saw the Moroccans as aliens within their land, eager to exploit Saharan minerals and fisheries and careless of the Saharans' national and religious identity. The Democratic Republic had some help from Algeria, Libya and eventually Cuba, and was recognized by the OAU, the communist world and non-aligned countries such as India and Yugoslavia. But the West tended to see the Saharans' struggle as another ideological conflict and inclined towards the right-wing King Hassan II of Morocco. The Saharan war therefore dragged on, into the late 1980s, with the Moroccans taking the extraordinary step of building an enormous war throughout the Sahara, to quarantine and contain the threat posed by Polisario. Mohamed Abdelazia, leader of the Polisario and of the Saharan Arab Democratic Republic, in 1986 blamed the war's length on President Reagan:

> Just when we believed a political solution was possible, Mauritania signed a peace. . . . In a meeting with the Moroccans at Bakamo we felt they too were ready to make peace. The increased US aid put off that chance of peace.

In Portugal, Salazar and Caetano had put off concessions to nationalism until independence movements began to take a costly toll of Portuguese resources, especially in Angola and Mozambique, Portugal's largest African territories. Caetano had eventually to spend 40 per cent of his government's income on the armed forces. A bitter struggle began in Angola as early as 1961, inflamed by events in the neighbouring Congo. Portuguese Guinea rebelled in 1963, and the independence struggle in Mozambique began a year later.

From the outset, Marxists were prominent in organizing the freedom-fighters: in Angola the MPLA (Popular Movement for the Liberation of Angola) and in Mozambique FRELIMO (Front for the Liberation of Mozambique). They had outside assistance too, the MPLA's coming from Guinea and FRELIMO's from Tanzania and, eventually, from Zambia. Agostinho Neto, physician and poet, led the MPLA and Eduardo Mondlane, at one time a professor of sociology in the USA, led FRELIMO, until he was killed by a parcel bomb in 1969. He was succeeded by Samora Machel. The Portuguese sent in and recruited locally more and more forces, which were supported by white mercenaries from the West and from South Africa. About 150 000 Portuguese troops could contain the nationalists but it seemed impossible to suppress them, which not only burdened the Portuguese economy but also further handicapped the development of the colonies as the wars of independence persisted.

Angola and Mozambique were still primarily agricultural, with little industry, and both had populations even smaller than that of Portugal. For a time there was apparent stalemate, the Portuguese claiming that they ruled to the benefit, and with the support, of most of their overseas subjects. The claim was never convincing. Walter Rodney wrote in 1972:

> The Portuguese stand out because they boasted the most and did the least. Portugal boasted that Angola, Guinea and Mozambique have been their possessions for 500 years, during which time a 'civilising mission' has been going on. At the end of 500 years . . . the Portuguese had not managed to train a single African doctor in Mozambique and life expectancy in Eastern Angola was less than 30 years. As for [Portuguese] Guinea, some insight into the situation there is provided by the admission of the Portuguese themselves that Guinea was more neglected than Angola and Mozambique! [*How Europe Underdeveloped Africa*]

Portuguese rule was undemocratic and negative, and Caetano found that as the costs of the colonial wars increased their popularity diminished.

Guinea's unilateral declaration of independence (UDI) in 1973, combined with escalating violence in Mozambique, helped bring about Caetano's overthrow in Portugal in 1974 (see section 7.3.1). General Antonio de Spinola, who replaced him in the coup, had first-hand experience of the wars in Africa and recognized their futility. But his plans for some sort of Portuguese Federation within which the overseas territories would have home rule were also outdated, scarcely different from those which de Gaulle had abandoned in the French Empire more than a dozen years earlier. More radical elements in the Portuguese army demanded an immediate end to the empire in Africa. Guinea was set free as the Republic of Guinea-Bissau, while Mozambique gained independence in June 1975 under Machel's FRELIMO government, the predictable arrangement. São Tomé and the Cape Verde Republic, formerly small Portuguese territories, also became independent comparatively smoothly.

Angola's independence was arranged for November 1975 but the Portuguese withdrawal here was as mismanaged as that of the Belgians in the Congo. Political and tribal divisions among Angolan nationalists had deepened during the independence struggle. The MPLA was opposed by the FNLA (National Front for the Liberation of Angola) and UNITA (National Union for the Total Independence of Angola). The FNLA, led by Holden Roberto, was strong among the Bakongo and was now encouraged by the USA and Zaïre. UNITA was led by Jonas Savimbi and had support fom the Ovimbundu and eventually from the Republic of South Africa. The OAU helped to bring about a coalition of the three movements but there were clashes almost at once. Militarily weaker at the outset than the FNLA, the MPLA received supplies from the Soviets and advisers from Cuba, as well as manpower from the Katangese who had supported Tshombe in the Congo. The USA could not openly get involved after its disastrous record in Indo-China (see section 18.4); it nevertheless provided extensive funds and arms for the FNLA and encouraged Mobutu of Zaïre to send troops. A diplomatic initiative patched up a united front between the FNLA and UNITA, which was supported by South Africa and the anti-Soviet Chinese. Anti-Soviet propaganda made the most of the situation, and Kaunda of Zambia, supporting UNITA, referred to the MPLA support as that of 'a plundering tiger and its deadly cubs'.

South Africa's involvement, the use of white mercenaries and the intrigues of the American CIA weakened the FNLA-UNITA cause, however. The US Congress chose not to supply the funds the CIA wanted to keep the war going, and Soviet supplies and now Cuban troops resolved the issue. By early 1976, Neto's MPLA government of the Angolan People's Republic had won wide recognition and seemed to be in control, if not entirely unchallenged. When Neto died in 1979 following surgery in Moscow, the government still had to fight off its opponents, especially Savimbi's UNITA which continued guerilla warfare into the late 1980s, vigorously encouraged by South Africa (see sections 17.5.2 and 19.2.3).

The end of Portugal's African Empire had radically changed the situation in southern Africa. Rhodesian whites were now far more exposed, and an effective campaign was soon mounted to end their UDI and to bring about the legitimate independence of Zimbabwe (see section 14.3.4). This brought independent black Africa to press more severely on South Africa itself. Despite UN condemnation, South Africa continued to rule Namibia, which had a long border with Angola. At the same time, South Africa bitterly denounced the use of Angola as a base for SWAPO (the South West Africa People's Organization) guerillas fighting Namibia's war of liberation. South African raids into Angola and Mozambique were not uncommon as the struggle continued for the end of white supremacist regimes. (Indeed South Africa was widely held responsible for the death of Mozambique's President Samora Machel in a mysterious air-crash.) Portugal had delayed change by clinging to its empire in Africa when other Europeans had seen the outdatedness of colonialism. But with the Portuguese Empire and British rule in Zimbabwe at an end, South Africa now faced mounting difficulties (see section 19.2).

Meanwhile, the Portuguese also withdrew from their empire in Asia where, in any case, their possessions after 1945 were mere fragments. In 1961 Nehru tired of fruitless negotiation with Salazar over the freeing of Goa and other tiny Portuguese outposts in India. Force was used to rid the subcontinent of the Portuguese. In 1975, when the Portuguese Empire in Africa disintegrated, Portugal also gave up East Timor (see section 15.1), though it held on to Macao, a small province with 300 000 inhabitants on the coast of China, long overshadowed by nearby Hong Kong. The Chinese seemed more tolerant over this than the Indians had proved over Goa. It was nevertheless unlikely that Macao could remain Portuguese when Hong Kong ceased to be a British colony in 1997, and in 1988 Portugal agreed that Macao should be restored to China in 1999.

The tiny remnants of the great colonial empires were now merely reminders of an age that had passed. Even the reluctant Portuguese had been forced in the end to yield when the nationalist wind became a hurricane. The decolonization of overseas empires created the Third World, in which most of the emergent nations faced a long and hard struggle to achieve stability and prosperity. The units which follow will look at some of the main problems they inherited as legacies of the colonial empires.

UNIT 16

Legacies of empire: 1 – nation-building in Asia

16.1 The problems of nation-building

Opposition to the final years of colonial rule gave unity and strength to nationalist movements, but that unity seldom continued for long under self-government. Divided by political and factional differences, regionalism, tribalism, economic inequalities and sometimes religion, many countries besides Zaïre threatened to disintegrate in the initial years of independence. The struggle for independence tended to create unrealistic expectations of happiness and prosperity which the new rulers could not fulfil. Most former colonies inherited acute social and economic problems; incomes were low while demands were high. Shortages of capital and of expertise would handicap development for generations to come. Many of the new states were still utterly dependent on agricultural and other primary products. Many also suffered from a rapidly rising population, which all but cancelled out what little addition to GNP they were able to bring about. Moreover, the Third World suffered (and continues to suffer) more drought, flood, famine and other natural disasters than other parts of the world.

It was therefore not surprising that many new states were plagued by instability, enabling the superpowers and former European colonizing powers to continue meddling in their affairs. At the least the developed world wanted to go on organizing economic exchanges for its own benefit, buying cheap in the Third World but selling dear there its own manufactures (see sections 21.1 and 21.3 for further consideration of the world economic order). But the developed world also continued to nourish those ideas of racial superiority which had underpinned colonialism. West Europeans and Americans assumed that the new states ought to practise Western-style democracy, however weak the foundations laid for it during colonial rule. The new states seemed also to be expected to be free from the vices of the old world and were quickly condemned, especially in the popular press in Britain and elsewhere, for wasting money on armaments, squandering resources on domestic and international squabbles, and practising brutality and – more commonly – corruption in their politics.

Only slowly did understanding grow of the injustices of the divide between the prosperous northern hemisphere and the ex-colonial South, and with it came recognition both of the need to bridge the gap and of the interdependence of the two halves of the world. Sympathies grew slowly, and it would obviously take time to break down the racist and imperialist attitudes which had persuaded many in the North that the coloured peoples in the South were somehow inferior and unable to set their own houses in order. But setting the house in order had taken many centuries in Europe, and it was made more difficult in the Third World by the sometimes deliberate policies of destabilization pursued by the superpowers against their ideological opponents. The USA and USSR seemed to see the Third World as a vast arena in which each should strive to outwit the other, especially when the Iron Curtain had firmly divided their spheres of influence in Europe. The USA saw its activities as the containment of the Soviets – every new interest in Marxism outside the Soviet bloc was likely to be regarded as a communist plot to be put down by the CIA and the forces of Western 'civilization'. By the Soviets, the containment was seen as the onward march of monopoly capitalism, the perpetuation of imperialism for the economic and financial benefit of the West. By the Third World, such attitudes were seen as ritualistically rigid, based on greed, prejudice and self-interest, and harshly detrimental to new nations struggling to assert their own identities.

Even without outside meddling this struggle was difficult enough. To other handicaps was added the cultural confusion of the post-colonial years, blurring the identities of the emergent states. Some colonizing powers like Belgium and Portugal had made little provision for the future nations which would arise from their colonies. Some like France assumed that the future was simply to follow the example of the 'mother' nation. Britain, though it made some preparation for colonial viability and success in independence, usually left its colonies under Western-educated leaders, resulting, as a commentator on Ghana observed, in:

> the perpetuation of neo-colonial values and practices among a political élite which ostensibly rejects them. [P.J. Foster, *Education and Social Change in Ghana*, Routledge, 1965]

But neo-colonialism[G] always seemed likely to be rejected whole-heartedly by the more forward-looking in the new states, just as involvement in the East–West Cold War was rejected by the non-aligned movement. A new generation of nationalists would wish to unite their states behind national values, not those handed down from Europe.

The legacies of empire, therefore, hardly included tranquillity. When overseas empires collapsed, about half the world came under 'new management': how new such managements actually were, how well they would manage and how long they would last had still to be determined.

16.2 The Republic of India

16.2.1 The foundations: Jawaharlal Nehru

India's independence in 1947 was the result of a long struggle (see section 14.2.2). The country's vast size and diversity (in spite of the partition of the subcontinent), its rapidly growing population and one of the lowest incomes per head in the world did not augur well; nor did the lack of a common language other than English (see fig. 14.2). On the other hand, India had a distinguished pre-colonial history and civilization, and the Indian National Congress (a broad-based nationalist party) commanded widespread support. These factors inspired confidence and so too did Nehru, the close associate of Mohandas Gandhi and a leader of Congress since the 1920s. His English education combined with his respect for Soviet economic planning to make him an open-minded Prime Minister, strongly principled but also pragmatic enough to adapt his policies to India's needs. He remained Prime Minister until he died in 1964, by which time he had ensured a united India and firmly committed the country to parliamentary democracy at home and non-alignment abroad. These were no mean achievements. Inheriting something of the mantle of Gandhi (the revered Mahatma and religious leader) he also proclaimed high moral standards for his leadership, though they were tarnished in the eyes of his critics

Fig. 16.1 India's Prime Minister Jawaharlal Nehru with his daughter Indira Gandhi and grandson Rajiv Gandhi, October 1950. Indira and Rajiv were later Prime Ministers of India. The Nehru family steered India through more than forty years of independence, but critics complained of a Nehru dynasty in Indian politics.

when he used force in defence of India's interests in Kashmir and in Goa, and in the conflict with China in 1962. Moreover, progress under his government was sometimes disappointing, though his inability to achieve miracles in relation to India's social and economic problems should be viewed alongside the vastness of those problems.

The republican and federal constitution of 1950 provided a firm base for Indian democracy. Hundreds of princely estates had been incorporated in the new India since 1947, and the country now had a central government based on elections to parliament's lower house, the Lok Sabha, and elected state governments in seventeen provinces. The scale of nationwide elections was vast even by American standards. Illiteracy among electors was massive – around 80 per cent in the early 1950s – yet all adults were allowed to vote and the elections were comparatively free from corruption and extreme disorder. The province of Kerala fell to the Communists in 1959 but, while Nehru lived, Congress was dominant in central government and in most state governments. After the death of his rival, the conservative Vallabhbai Patel, in 1950, Nehru was almost unchallenged within the party. India's government was therefore stable, in some ways like a one-party state such as those often sought in Africa and elsewhere as a way to achieve unity, though in India Nehru and Congress achieved such unity while tolerating opposition parties.

Nehru's social and economic policies leaned towards socialism. He wanted to give special help to the poor and underprivileged, though little could be achieved overnight. The caste[G] system rigidly divided Hindu society, and religious traditions hindered modernization: a start had to be made on changing attitudes. The constitution aimed at the emancipation of women and new laws in 1955 gave them property rights. In the same year the government outlawed discrimination against *harijans*, the 'untouchables' outside the caste system whose traditional lot was social isolation and only menial employment. Nehru wanted to effect a social revolution, relaxing the marriage laws, promoting birth control and family planning, and asserting the rights of women and untouchables to equal treatment and opportunity. But nurturing new ideas took time. It also needed resources. The constitution set a target of free and compulsory education for all children to the age of fourteen, but India had not achieved this when Nehru died. Instead, even in the late 1970s over 60 per cent of adults were still illiterate and, though a majority of young people now had primary education, fewer than half went on to secondary schools.

Nehru's government sought growth through an Economic Planning Commission and Five-Year Plans. Industrial output wellnigh doubled – that of motor vehicles trebled – but industry still employed only one per cent of the population. The state took control of some basic industries, building the steel plant at Dargapur for example, but Nehru favoured a mixed economy in which private enterprise too had a major part to play. It was agriculture that mattered most to the masses, however, and Nehru looked for a 'green revolution' greatly to increase output. He wanted to protect the peasants from famine and also from their landlords: smallholdings were enlarged and rents limited. Millions more acres were put into cultivation with a rash of new irrigation schemes, often linked with hydroelectric plants. Village co-operatives were encouraged as Gandhi would have wished, and food production grew markedly, though not enough yet to make India self-sufficient.

The average income per head remained below the equivalent of £30 a year and had risen very little by the time Nehru died. It was the population which rose – to around 450 million – offsetting economic growth, while wealth was also syphoned off in the shape of interest on the loans India had been forced to take out to finance economic development and social improvement. It remained almost impossible to escape trading deficits with the developed world, exports of produce such as tea and jute far from matching the costs of industrial machinery and other expensive imports. Like many Third World nations, therefore, India found enormous difficulties in increasing medical provision and other social services, and cities like Calcutta remained notorious for their armies of homeless beggars.

In 1964 problems seemed to multiply rather than decrease. The cartoon in fig. 16.2 shows how attention now focused not only on economic difficulties but also on the corruption which Nehru was finding it a problem to control in a country so vast.

Yet the launching of Indian independence under Nehru was by no means unsuccessful even though prosperity was still far off. Nehru won acclaim after 1947 as an international statesman. He firmly believed in the multiracial Commonwealth whose members might:

Fig. 16.2 Taking as his theme the country's bed of nails, Laxman in *The Times of India* in July 1964 commented on the corruption alleged to be widespread in India and showed his impatience with those who seemed unable, or unwilling, to eradicate it.

> sometimes disagree . . . sometimes pull in different directions . . . [but always] meet as friends, try to understand each other and try, as far as possible, to find a common way of working.

He was nevertheless forthright in condemning Britain's part in the Suez War of 1956, and he caused exasperation in the West by refusing to join SEATO and by muting his criticisms of the USSR's suppression of the Hungarian uprising. His pursuit of non-alignment nevertheless brought economic aid from both East and West and Soviet sympathies when India was involved in a frontier war with China in 1962 (see section 11.2.3(b)). Partition in 1947 left tensions between Hindu India and Muslim Pakistan, however, and relations between the two were persistently uneasy (see section 16.3). But in the end Nehru was remembered as the statesman who readily sent Indian troops to help UN peace-keeping in Palestine, the Congo and Cyprus, who tried to mediate in the Korean War and in Indo-China in 1954, and who gave the Third World a voice in a world often dominated by the superpowers and Europe (see section 21.4).

16.2.2 The years of crisis: Indira Gandhi

(a) Political upheavals The stable foundations Nehru had laid and the persisting strength of Congress led to the smooth succession of Lal Bahadur Shastri as India's Prime Minister in 1964. Within two years, however, Shastri died of a heart attack while seeking to solve the problem of Kashmir at a meeting arranged by the Soviets at Tashkent (see section 16.3). The new Prime Minister was Indira Gandhi, Nehru's daughter and since 1960 a widow. She had defeated Morarji Desai in the election to the leadership of Congress, a victory for the party's younger and more radical elements but also a tribute to the lasting reputation of her father. Nehru himself had encountered difficulties with the 'Syndicate', a conservative group of Congress party bosses, and the split widened when Indira Gandhi outmanoeuvred them to get her own nominee, Venkata Giri, made President. Desai and other traditionalists therefore broke away from Congress in 1969, leaving Mrs Gandhi to win the elections of 1971, gaining over a hundred seats for what eventually became known as the Congress (Indira) Party.

Mrs Gandhi remained Prime Minister from 1966 to 1977 but the 1970s were years of further crises. She and her supporters were accused by Desai and others of electoral malpractice in the poll of 1971. In 1975 a court found her guilty and barred her from office. She replied with a wave of arrests and sweeping new powers to rule during the ensuing state of emergency. Her government's argument was that stern measures were needed to hold together a state which was threatening to disintegrate, especially as the mid-1970s were also a time of world-wide economic crisis. Her opponents accused her of dictatorship, corruption, brutality and nepotism, and maintained that she was trying to create a Nehru dynasty in which she herself would be succeeded by her son Sanjay. Sanjay Gandhi led the Congress Youth Wing but became especially unpopular for his efforts to control the ever-growing population by a campaign for sterilization, some of it forced and ruthless. In Delhi, his housing schemes also showed ruthlessness not matched with constructiveness. An Indian MP alleged:

> The travail of the people is indescribable. They are packed into trucks and carried miles away from their demolished houses. They are unpacked . . . in vacant lots with no amenities, not even drinking water; and . . . without alternate work in the areas to which they have been forcibly shifted.

Indians also remembered how government money had been used in 1970 to enable Sanjay to set up the unsuccessful Maruti car factory, and this fuelled their allegations of corruption. Thousands were detained during the crisis. Amnesty International listed some 60 parliamentarians in prison in March 1976, including not only Desai and members of the Syndicate but also socialists like Raj Narain who protested at the illegal activities of the government.

Nevertheless, after being delayed, elections were held in 1977 and, heavily defeated, Indira Gandhi resigned to make way for Desai and a Janata government, an uneasy coalition of Gandhi's opponents. Desai was over 80 when he came to office, and new judicial proceedings against Mrs Gandhi were not enough to unite his government. There was rioting, especially in Uttar Pradesh and Bihar, and the government proved so ineffective that Desai had to resign. New elections were held at the end of 1979. Congress (Indira) won a massive victory, taking as many seats as it had in 1971 and almost destroying the Opposition Congress with 351 seats to a mere 13. Among the other parties, two rival Communist Parties shared 45 seats. Indira Gandhi returned to office in January 1980, given a new mandate by India's vast electorate who once more hoped she might combine the progressive policies and political freedoms they associated with Nehru, her father.

The death of Sanjay Gandhi in an air accident later in 1980 was a bitter blow to Mrs Gandhi. Sanjay's elder brother, Rajiv, reluctantly entered politics, perhaps to try to fill the gap. India was still a difficult country to rule: the population explosion had led to a population approaching 700 million, and among its millions festered many antagonisms. Rioting and communal violence were not unusual, and the police themselves had a reputation for ferocity. Soon after her re-election, Gandhi had to take more repressive measures though she stopped short of the 'tyranny' of which she had been accused in 1976.

Several states were particularly unruly. An election campaign in Assam in 1983 was bloody, but it was in Punjab that the crisis deepened. Most of India's Sikhs, about two per cent of the nation's population, lived there and extremists among them demanded their own nation, Khalistan, separate from India. They threatened to withhold food from the rest of India and turned their Golden Temple at Amritsar into a fortress. They bitterly resented what they saw as the sacrilegious attack on it by the army in June 1984 when Gandhi's government tried to restore its authority. Sikh fanatics rejoiced when Sikh members of Gandhi's bodyguard shot and killed her on 31 October. Her murder led to a violent anti-Sikh reaction and more killing, especially in Delhi. More than 2000 Sikhs died before uneasy calm was restored. The Punjab remained in constant turmoil during the next four years as Sikh militants fought both Hindus and moderate Sikhs.

Rajiv Gandhi was persuaded that it was in India's interests that he should take over from his mother as Prime Minister, a decision that won decisive support in new elections late in 1984, which gave Congress (I) the biggest majority of any government since independence. Elections were deferred, however, in Assam and Punjab where ethnic disturbances continued. A united India had been preserved but at a cost, and the struggle persisted to make of it one nation.

(b) Indira Gandhi's achievement Disruption had taxed the resources of Indira Gandhi's government but she had nevertheless persisted in pursuing reforming policies, spurred on by pressures from the left. Communist-led coalitions regularly won elections in the regional states of Kerala, in the south, and in West Bengal and Tripura in the north, and a revolutionary communist insurgency, the Naxalite movement, briefly ignited passions in 1967. The right wing, led by traditionalist Hindus, was also powerful in certain regions, and highly critical of Indira Gandhi. Her quarrel with the Syndicate was partly due to her policy of nationalizing the banks and taking from the princes their privy purses (the guaranteed incomes which had compensated them for surrendering their estates to the Indian state under Nehru). Her main problem, however, was to achieve the dramatic conquest of poverty which might make India more contented. Meanwhile, she steadily pursued her father's policy of promoting unity through Hindi as a common language, making slow progress.

She also persisted with economic planning and by the late 1970s India was able to feed itself, developing production further in the 1980s. Industry developed too, and was advanced enough in 1974 to effect an atomic explosion, though the government denied any intention to stockpile nuclear weapons. Yet problems seemed to grow faster than achievements. India was plagued by natural disasters like the tidal wave which in 1971 killed thousands on the coast of Orissa. About that time, there was also the problem of the millions of refugees fleeing into Bengal from the butchery then going on in East Pakistan. In 1984 a disastrous leakage at the American-owned pesticide plant at Bhopal, capital of Madhya Pradesh, killed over two thousand and poisoned and blinded a great many more in the nearby shanties. Arguments about responsibility dragged on, and Union Carbide in 1986 provisionally agreed to pay 350 million dollars' compensation. The Indian government claimed three billion dollars on behalf of 526 000 claimants.

India suffered many economic setbacks too. It was hard hit when oil prices soared in the 1970s, the rising cost of living adding to the country's unrest. Unemployment rose too, made worse by the population explosion. Opponents complained that the government spent too much on defence, with a sharp increase in the national budget after the brief war with China. The figures were distorted by inflation, however, just as income per head, though the equivalent of nearly £200 a year by the mid-1980s, was in real terms not a great deal better than the pitiful £20 or so in 1947. With some truth Indira Gandhi asserted in 1976:

> The success achieved by India has been spectacular by any standard, either west or east, or developing or developed countries.

But about half of India's population remained desperately poor in spite of the country's economic growth, and the poverty simply added to the undercurrents of violence and instability.

India had nevertheless become an important world power as well as an influential member of the Commonwealth. Sheer size gave it some authority but Mrs Gandhi, like Nehru, achieved personal standing. Some 114 nations were represented at her cremation, most at the highest level. She had continued to support non-alignment, though the West was critical of the cordial links between Moscow and Delhi, one result of which was an Indian in space in 1984 as part of a Soviet mission. On the other hand, one reason for the increase in defence spending to around fifteen per cent of the government's budget at the time of her death was Gandhi's determination not to be bettered by Pakistan, India's neighbour and its main rival since independence (see section 16.3).

16.2.3 The continuing struggle

Informed opinion estimated that by the end of the century, unless in some way checked, India's population would reach around 960 million, prolonging the struggle for prosperity. Yet life expectancy had risen markedly since 1947 to stand at about 53 years in the early 1980s, and the provision of amenities such as hospitals showed that India had also advanced ahead of much of Africa and the very poorest nations. It remained a land of great diversities, though Rajiv Gandhi helped provide stability after his mother's assassination. Setbacks in a number of provincial elections showed that his position was not wholly secure, however. Government was still plagued by the problems of minorities within the subcontinent and before long the Indian Prime Minister was heavily involved in crises in Sri Lanka, where the minority Tamils looked for support against persecution to their fellow Tamils in southern India (see section 16.5).

The Punjab was an even graver problem. The clamour for independent Khalistan had only been fuelled by the furore surrounding Indira Gandhi's death, and the Golden Temple at Amritsar continued to be a warren for Sikh nationalists, ranting priests and heavily armed guerillas. Its storming in 1984 had cost the lives of hundreds of Indian soldiers but the Sikhs had soon reoccupied it. Rajiv Gandhi's forces stormed it again in 1986, and again the rebels returned. In 1987 the Prime Minister imposed direct rule on Punjab and introduced fierce emergency laws, but by early 1988 disturbances were taking around 200 lives a month. Not all those killed were involved in the struggle for Khalistan. Some so-called freedom-fighters were little more than bandits who took advantage of factional rivalry among the Sikhs and the general disorder to prey on their fellow Punjabis. Gandhi's security forces seemed unable to get a grip on their activities, and there was speculation that the Prime Minister might be content to tolerate the mayhem in the Punjab in the hope that moderate opinion might come to unite behind Congress in preference to the Khalistani separatist movement which had given rise to such violence and disruption.

That India had survived intact for more than 40 years since independence and had largely preserved its democratic fabric owed a good deal to the Nehru tradition. But for many millions of Indians life offered little but toil and poverty.

The great majority still worked on the land, like most Asians, and they knew little of the material possessions and systems of social security and welfare so widely taken for granted in the northern hemisphere. Poverty and sectional interests were a ready breeding-ground for religious fanatics and political agitators, and violence lurked only just below the surface. At best, Sikh and Hindu Punjabis coexisted uneasily, while the Punjab itself ominously bordered both Muslim Pakistan and troubled Kashmir. To the north-east of India lay China, from whence in the past had come the Maoist ideas which inflamed Naxalite agitators against Congress government in Delhi. In 1987–8 China had to deal with unrest in Tibet where many Buddhists still looked for spiritual leadership to the Dalai Lama, long since exiled to India. Indian subjects were always likely to be unsettled by events on their borders; religious and political controversies there might at any time reawaken deep divisions in Indian society. Assassination always threatened India's leaders. Rajiv Gandhi, moreover, seemed to lack the authority his grandfather had had in the early years of independence, and in 1988 it began to seem likely that he might seek an early national election whenever Congress showed signs of returning popularity, in the hope of strengthening his rule.

16.3 Kashmir and Indo–Pakistani relations

Religious divisions and national rivalries combined with geography to make it highly likely that India and Pakistan would quarrel over Kashmir – more accurately, Jammu and Kashmir – after independence (see section 14.2.2). Hari Singh, the Hindu Maharajah of Kashmir, declared his state part of India when Pakistani ambitions seemed to threaten Kashmiri independence in October 1947. Some three million of his Muslim subjects objected and only Kashmir's 800 000 Hindu approved. Armed struggle broke out and both Pakistan and India sent in troops. The United Nations arranged a ceasefire in 1949 and recommended a plebiscite[G]. But the ceasefire left most of the area in Indian hands and Nehru was well aware how Hindu Kashmiris would be outvoted by the Muslims; negotiations therefore made little headway. Sheikh Abdullah became Prime Minister of Kashmir but, when he claimed independence, Nehru imprisoned him, and in 1957 India declared Kashmir part of the Indian Republic.

Earlier pressure from Mohandas Gandhi, on the other hand, had brought concessions for Pakistan regarding the further £44 million the latter claimed from India as part of the independence settlement. India and Pakistan also eventually reached agreement about the disputed division of the Indus basin waters. A treaty in 1960, made with the help of the International Bank, paved the way for co-operation and the ambitious irrigation developments both states needed.

In 1962 the Chinese took Ladakh, that part of Kashmir they claimed was part of Tibet. The Kashimiri problem then flared again when the Pakistanis tested Shastri after Nehru's death. The Indo–Pakistani war there in 1965 spread to the swampy Rann of Kutch (see fig. 14.2). In Kashmir there were tank battles and air strikes before Kosygin, the Soviet Prime Minister, brought Shastri and Ayub Khan of Pakistan to Tashkent for talks. The talks brought a ceasefire but were then frustrated by the sudden death of the Indian Prime Minister. His successor, Indira Gandhi, released Sheikh Abdullah but gave no ground when he and his successors went on expressing the view that Kashmiris should decide their own future by plebiscite.

Kashmir was caught up in Indo–Pakistani warfare again in 1971 when India went to the help of East Pakistanis seeking independence from West Pakistan as the new nation of Bangladesh (see section 16.4.1). There was fighting not only in Kashmir but also on the frontier between West Pakistan and India, further south. When peace was restored between Pakistan and India at Simla in 1972, however, nothing could be agreed about Kashmir but to hold further talks at a later date. The problem remained unsolved and the temporary division of 1949 persisted: Pakistan held areas in the west and north-west; China had hived off the east and north-east; and India held the rest, rather more than half of what had been Jammu and Kashmir in 1947 and including Kashmir's minority Sikh community. India had invested heavily in the lands it held and no Indian leader was willing to give them up, just as no Pakistani leader would concede them. National prestige was involved and Kashmir therefore remained a symbol of the bitter rivalry which played a major part in determining the policies of both India and Pakistan. India's non-alignment contrasted with Pakistan's pro-West stance, and the two pursued very different policies towards both the USSR and China.

16.4 Pakistan and Bangladesh

16.4.1 Pakistan's struggle: from Jinnah to Yahya Khan

Whatever India's problems, Pakistan's seemed greater. The early years of independence were gravely disappointing. After Jinnah's early death in 1948 the nationalist dream quickly faded (see section 14.2.2). His successor Liaqat Ali Khan was murdered in 1951 for seeking coexistence with India, and Pakistan then had six Prime Ministers in five years. The Muslim League could offer no decisive leadership, and factionalism and corruption set in. The new Islamic constitution was at last worked out in 1956 but hopes for the Democratic Republic were again soon dashed. Within two years there were five more Prime Ministers. The gulf widened between West Pakistan, mainly Urdu-speaking and wheat-eating, and East Pakistan, Bengali-speaking, rice-eating, and the uneasy result of the division of the former Province of Bengal between Pakistan and India. East Pakistanis felt that their interests were neglected by the government in Karachi which was dominated by West Pakistan. Until the mid-1950s Islam was the bond between the two parts of Pakistan, but the East then turned against the Muslim League in favour of the more localized Awami League, and it was the army that came increasingly to stand between Pakistan and total disintegration. Major-General Iskander Mirza, Head of State, recognized as much when in 1958 he suspended the constitution and proclaimed martial law.

General Mohammed Ayub Khan, the Commander-in-Chief, became President and civilian politicians were driven into retirement while the military set out thoroughly to reorganize the Republic. This was a political role always denied to the military in India by the more stable rule of Nehru and Congress. For many states in Latin America, Africa and Asia, however, the military provided a centre of discipline and organization. It was the hope, by no means always fulfilled, that military rule might achieve what civilian rule had conspicuously failed to achieve – order, honesty and justice. Ayub had some undoubted successes but in the end, in 1969, he was forced to step down under bitter attack for his repressive practices and for encouraging hero-worship.

'Pakistan is my passion, my life,' Ayub declared, and added:

> History would never have forgiven us if the present chaotic conditions were allowed to go any further.

He intended to restore democracy in due course but would first prepare the way with 'basic democracy'[G]. The people therefore elected local councils in 1959, and the councils then voted in favour of Ayub's Presidency in 1960. The councils soon afterwards elected members to a parliament, though this had little but advisory powers. Ayub allowed some opposition, however, notably under Jinnah's sister, Fatima, who opposed Ayub when presidential elections were held again in 1965. Ayub nevertheless won majority support in West Pakistan and, rather less convincingly, in East Pakistan. Though opponents already complained of dictatorship, Ayub's methods seemed so far to have won approval. His policies too found favour. The attack on corruption removed civil servants as well as politicians; tax-dodgers and speculators were weeded out; price controls were imposed and standards of efficiency raised – even trains began to arrive on time. Above all, however, land was forcibly redistributed to the poor, the landlords being compensated. Co-operatives were encouraged and a loan scheme was set up to help improve output. Nehru's economic planning was copied to develop industry and expand exports. Social policy included rehousing schemes and an ambitious programme of educational expansion.

Ayub's reputation suffered, however, when war with India in 1965 failed to win either Kashmir or glory. His social reforms were resented by landlords and other vested interests, while the mullahs[G] complained that his government had too little regard for Islam and religious opinion. In spite of strict censorship and repression, left-wing agitators roused the ill-paid urban workers and, throughout, the people of East Pakistan nursed bitter resentment against West Pakistan. Ayub's repressiveness now attracted more attention than his reforms. It was recalled that even Mirza had been sent into exile when Ayub first established his authority, an authority that was now preserved not only sternly but also with a developing personality cult. The press and radio heaped praises on President Ayub. His son Gohar became a powerful industrialist, while the masses remained only too aware of their own continuing poverty, hardly alleviated by the reforms. This was especially true in East Pakistan. In 1968 the killing of a student in Rawalpindi led to student rioting and touched off almost open rebellion among the Bengalis. Ayub conceded that there must be a return to parliamentary government but, before he could organize it, the army replaced him in 1969 with General Yahya Khan, its Commander-in-Chief since 1966. Ayub soon afterwards went into retirement.

Yahya Khan reimposed martial law and severely repressed the disorders. But the demand for elections was still insistent and in 1970 he gave way. They were held in West Pakistan in December 1970, and in East Pakistan in January 1971 after delays caused by a cyclone and disastrous flooding. Zulfikar Ali Bhutto and the People's Party he had founded won a convincing victory in the West. Formerly Ayub's Foreign Minister until he resigned after the Tashkent Agreement of 1966, Bhutto was now committed to Islamic socialism. In East Pakistan, however, victory went to the Awami League and Sheikh Mujibur Rahman - so convincingly that the League had a majority in the Pakistani parliament with 167 seats to the People's Party's 86. Bhutto spoke for West Pakistan in refusing to accept government by the Awami League, though Mujibur Rahman was in any case more interested in autonomy for the East.

Faced with two governments rather than one, Yahya reverted to a soldier's solution. In March 1971 Rahman was arrested, the Awami League banned and an attempt made to subdue East Pakistan by force. A group of freedom-fighters, the Mukti Bahini, resisted, and their supporters proclaimed 'the Sovereign Independent People's Republic of Bangladesh'. Yahya's forces tried savagely to repress the uprising and millions of refugees fled into India from the fighting and the twin threats of cholera and starvation. Indo-Pakistani relations quickly deteriorated until the two countries were at war early in December 1971. Pakistan hoped for support from China, while India had recently signed a treaty of friendship with Moscow, but neither Communist power became actively involved and Yahya soon found the combined strength of the Bangladeshis and India much too great. 60 000 West Pakistanis were taken prisoner and in mid-December Yahya agreed to a ceasefire and, in effect, to Bangladeshi independence.

The President could not survive the humiliation. Bhutto took over the Presidency of (West) Pakistan and Yahya went into retirement. Mujibur Rahman was freed and became Prime Minister of Bangladesh, a new country of around 70 million people, among the poorest in the world. Jinnah's Pakistan had fallen apart. International recognition for Bangladesh was almost immediate, to the further humiliation of Bhutto and West Pakistan. It was admitted to the United Nations and to the Commonwealth, and Pakistan angrily resigned from the latter in protest in January 1972.

16.4.2 Pakistan since 1971

Bhutto, like Nehru, was an English-educated barrister. Like Nehru he now faced a major task of nation-building, restoring Pakistani pride and making the smaller state secure. There were threats of further secession on the north-west frontier and in Baluchistan, and the unity of what was left of Pakistan after the loss of Bangladesh could not be taken for granted. Bhutto preserved the frontiers, however. He amended the constitution, raising the status of the Prime Minister at the expense of the Presidency (more in line with Indian practice), and in 1973 he himself switched offices to lead Pakistan as its Prime Minister. He agreed terms with Indira Gandhi at Simla – for the return of Pakistani prisoners-of-war, for example – and there was hope of less strained relations in the future. Kashmir still rankled, however, and there was further tension there. Indo–Pakistani diplomatic relations (and rail services) were not restored until 1976 following new talks at Islamabad, Pakistan's new capital since 1967.

Within Pakistan, Bhutto aimed to encourage peasant farmers with land redistribution and tax concessions. He tried to stabilize prices and to promote economic growth as a basis for expanding the social services. The economy did begin to grow but disastrous floods in the Indus valley in 1976 again disrupted output. Meanwhile Bhutto's high-handed methods and the use of a Federal Security Force to guarantee his authority created opposition. When elections were held in 1977, opposition groups united against him in the National Alliance, only to be routed by his own People's Party. At once there were accusations of fraud. Riots broke out in many parts of Pakistan and lives were lost. More flooding added to the chaos and, with the economy tottering, the army stepped in again. General Zia-ul-Haq seized power in July 1977, imprisoning both Bhutto and his rivals. Bhutto was eventually accused of conspiracy to murder and, in spite of international protests, was executed in April 1979. Though driven underground, the People's Party lived on in the hands of his supporters and family – his sons and then his daughter Benazir.

General Zia meanwhile postponed the new elections he had promised and slipped easily into his role as an iron-fisted dictator and a firm devotee of Islam. He became President as well as Chief Martial-Law Administrator. A ban was imposed on political parties in 1979 and it persisted, though Zia from time to time toyed with ideas for constitutional change. The election of local councils in 1979 seemed to echo Ayub Khan's regime, but Zia was far more intent than Ayub on promoting Muslim orthodoxy. Savage punishments were decreed for crime, adultery and drinking alcohol, and it was suspected that Zia intended to remain in power with the backing not so much of the army as of Islamic fundamentalists such as those who came to power in Iran in 1979 (see section 20.2).

Zia kept on good terms with China and won the support of Reagan and the USA, especially when he adopted a fiercely anti-Soviet stance and backed Islamic and anti-Soviet forces in Afghanistan (see section 20.5). (Bhutto had earlier blamed the pro-Soviet government in Afghanistan for encouraging secessionist movements within Pakistan.) At the same time, Zia's relations with India were again far from cordial, and the tension heightened in the mid-1980s when Pakistan seemed near to becoming a nuclear power.

At home Zia faced growing unrest and in 1984 the opposition began to unite against him in the Movement for the Restoration of Democracy (MRD). Zia lifted martial law and outlined plans for an Islamic assembly which would operate without a genuine political opposition. A referendum on policy was taken as approval of his leadership and confirmation of his Presidency for another five years, until 1990. In France, however, Benazir Bhutto voiced the opposition opinion:

> General Zia has transformed his eight-year old unconstitutional martial-law regime into a presidential-cum-authoritarian political order. This new order is not sustained by the will of the people of Pakistan.

In 1986 Ms Bhutto returned to Pakistan to revive her father's People's Party and to lead the MRD in campaigning for free elections. Not surprisingly, she was hindered and then detained by the authorities.

Average incomes in Pakistan were by this time slightly higher than those in India, though Pakistan too faced rapid population growth – its population was already over 90 million in the mid-1980s and likely to be above 130 million by the end of the century. In many respects Pakistan shared India's social and economic difficulties, but Zia demonstrated two fundamental ways in which Pakistan's history since 1947 had differed from that of India – the frequent periods of authoritarian military rule and the pervasive influence on government of Islam. While Zia kept the support of the army and the security forces, and appeased the forces of Islam, Pakistan was unlikely to return to democracy. His determined support for Islamic fundamentalists in Afghanistan not only angered the USSR but also began to exasperate the USA, who saw it as an obstacle to a settlement there and the withdrawal of Soviet forces (see section 20.5).

Zia's sudden death in an air crash in 1988, when accompanied by senior Army commanders and the American ambassador, plunged Pakistan into renewed uncertainty. His death was almost certainly no accident but it paved the way for further progress in settling the conflict in Afghanistan and, just as importantly, improved the prospects for a restoration of democracy in Pakistan. Zia's passing was mourned by Islamic fundamentalists and Western powers who saw him as a bulwark of 'anti-communism' in the region, but democrats wept no tears over the departure of a brutal military dictator. In the general elections held under the auspices of a caretaker government, the Pakistan People's Party, led by Benazir Bhutto, emerged as the largest single party in the national assembly, but without an overall majority. Having formed a coalition with minor parties, Bhutto was appointed Prime Minister in November 1988, but it remained to be seen how willing the Pakistan army would be to relinquish its grip on the political direction of the country, and whether she would prove more law-abiding and democratic than her father had been.

16.4.3 Bangladesh

To build a successful new nation in Bangladesh was a daunting task. Its 75 million people were the poorest in the Indian subcontinent, their economic outlook bleak. US Secretary of State Kissinger, already highly critical of its secession and of India's support of it, referred to Bangladesh as 'an international basket case', destined to rely on foreign aid. In the mid-1980s the population grew to 90 million and the poverty of the people had not been much alleviated, yet some economic growth had by then been achieved in spite of recurring natural disasters and political upheaval.

It took some time to repair the ravages of the war of independence and to resettle the millions of refugees. The minority Biharis complained of persecution by the Bengalis, who resented the support they had given to united Pakistan, and many Biharis were sent to West Pakistan via refugee camps. The world economic crisis in the 1970s dealt Bangladesh a further blow. Mujibur Rahman and the Awami League were re-elected by an overwhelming majority in 1973, but even with generous American food aid the country hovered on the brink of starvation. Rahman could not cope and, in a desperate effort to save the deteriorating situation, he imposed martial law in 1974, making himself President again in 1975. He looked for 'a second revolution', to end:

> the old and rotten colonial system and usher in a new era to bring good to the exploited millions

But such a social revolution would take many years of struggle and before he could make a start Rahman was assassinated later in 1975. Opponents alleged

Fig. 16.3 A scene in Dacca, Bangladesh, and a glimpse of living conditions in one of the world's poorest nations. Dacca had an official population of over a million and a half in the mid-1970s, and like many Third World cities had shanty-town slums of awesome squalor.

that his government had degenerated into 'rampant favouritism and corruption'. It had, in fact, fallen victim to the effects of Bangladesh's grinding poverty and devastating floods.

There were more assassinations in the political confusion which followed Rahman's death. But it was the military who now dominated and Major-General Ziaur Rahman emerged as the new leader, becoming President of Bangladesh in 1977. Ziaur genuinely aimed to combine reform with a return to democracy. He held and won presidential elections in 1978 and set up the Nationalist Party which in 1979 promptly won the parliamentary elections, in which all adults could vote. This was a more rapid return to democracy than the Pakistani military had achieved. At the same time vigorous reform was introduced: a programme was mounted to check population growth through voluntary sterilization, and there was an effective drive to increase agricultural output which Arab oil-producers helped to finance. Ziaur also coped with an influx of Muslims from Burma, fleeing persecution by Buddhists and adding to Bangladesh's social problems. Though the President tried to purge the administration of corruption, his government was nevertheless accused of corrupt practices and its troubles grew as secessionist rebels became active along its borders. In 1981 Ziaur was assassinated at Chittagong where he was trying to deal with disaffection stirred up by a rival would-be President, Major-General Abdul Manzoor. Manzoor himself was killed only days later and power passed in 1982 to General Mohammed Ershad who brought back martial law.

Ershad made the usual declarations of intent about restoring democracy and wiping out corruption, but unrest and rioting meanwhile required strong-arm measures. Bangladesh nevertheless benefited from earlier economic reform, and food production rose to record heights in 1983. Ershad showed some preference for the private over the public sector, gaining approval in the USA and the West. Like Zia in Pakistan, however, he had to face a Movement for the Restoration of Democracy (MRD). The MRD did well when some local elections were held in 1984, but Ershad delayed further movement towards democracy, using the excuse of strikes, disorders and arguments about how free any elections might be. The Jatiya movement tried to group supporters of his rule, but in 1985 the President felt secure enough only to hold a referendum on his own leadership – the massive support registered was considered highly suspect by the MRD. Jatiya won parlimentary elections in 1986, defeating the Awami League led by Mujibur Rahman's daughter, Hasina, but accusations of fraud and intimidation were widespread. When Ershad organized another national election in March 1988, the opposition and the great majority of voters boycotted it. Sheikh Hasina called the election 'a total farce' though the government declared it 'successful, free and fair, and reasonably peaceful'. The results showed a massive victory for Jatiya, but independent observers estimated that only five per cent of voters had actually voted. Ershad himself, though still supported by the World Bank and governments in the West, lost further credibility among Bangladeshis.

The vast majority of Bangladeshis remained desperately poor despite outside aid of more than a billion US dollars a year. Industry and trade employed fewer than one in five of the working population and contributed only about 25 per cent to the country's GDP. Life expectancy in the mid-1980s was still below 50 years, well behind that of India though not far short of that of Pakistan. Ershad had presided over some economic progress but he had not united the country behind a programme of modernization. Opposition to his rule was itself disunited, however. Sheikh Hasina led the Awami League, while Begum Khaleda Zia, the widow of Ziaur Rahman, led the rival Nationalist Party. Western governments still regarded Ershad as the ruler who could best hold Bangladesh together, but the country remained a turbulent and unhappy emergent nation.

16.5 Sri Lanka

Ceylon (renamed Sri Lanka in 1972) was steered through the early years of independence by the United National Party (UNP), first under Don Stephen Senanayake and then under his son Dudley. The People's Front led by the Bandaranaike family offered a socialist alternative. At first there was stability and the elder Senanayake was compared with India's Nehru. Like India, however, Ceylon had ethnic and religious diversities. The majority of its ten million people were Sinhalese and Buddhist, but a million or so were Indians – Tamil-speaking and mainly Hindu. Smaller minorities were Muslim and Christian. The problem of reconciling minority Tamils – deprived of the vote for a time in the early years – and the majority Sinhalese was to prove Ceylon's biggest obstacle to nation-building. Many Tamils were labourers on the tea plantations and very poorly paid. The Tamils complained of discrimination against them by the majority Sinhalese, but in spite of the social inequalities prevalent under the UNP, Dudley Senanayake succeeded his father in 1952, though he stood down in 1953 because of poor health. UNP rule continued under John Kotelawala until the general election of 1956.

The People's Front won that election and Solomon Bandaranaike was Prime Minister until he was murdered by a Buddhist monk in 1959. His attempt to make Sinhalese the official language, in place of English, further angered the Tamils while other policies, such as getting the British to give up their military bases and working towards a republic, angered the right wing. His murder plunged Ceylon into disarray, out of which emerged the world's first woman Prime Minister when the Freedom Party won the elections of 1960. Sirimavo Bandaranaike, widow of the former Prime Minister, claimed only to want 'to get my husband's party on its feet again', but she remained in office until 1965, her policies vigorous and, to begin with, broadly conciliatory towards the Tamils. The election of 1965 returned another UNP government under Dudley Senanayake until in 1970 the pendulum swung and Mrs Bandaranaike became Prime Minister again, supported by a big majority.

The Westminster-style two-party system seemed to be working quite effectively in Ceylon in spite of undercurrents of unrest. Even the UNP was now mildly socialist and politics leaned towards the left. In 1972 Mrs Bandaranaike was able to set up the Democratic Socialist Republic of Sri Lanka, which remained within the Commonwealth. It was a turbulent republic, however, and for most of the 1970s Bandaranaike ruled with emergency powers. Soon after losing the elections of 1977 she was accused, like Indira Gandhi, of malpractice and the abuse of power, and in 1980 she was banned from political life.

The Freedom Party had forcibly repatriated about a quarter of a million Tamils to southern India. Indians had nevertheless grown as a percentage of Sri Lanka's population, from below ten per cent in 1948 to almost twenty per cent in the 1970s. When the UNP under Junius Jayewardene won the elections of 1977, he offered the Tamils the hope of a share in regional government and concessions on language. At the same time, in a constitutional change like that made by de Gaulle in France in 1958, he made himself President of the Republic. Since 1972, however, Tamil hard-liners had been demanding a division of the island and the setting up of the independent Tamil state of Eelam. The Tamil United Liberation Front now stepped up their campaign. The Front's freedom-fighters (terrorists in government eyes) demanded more than minor concessions and the conflict went on into the 1980s with lengthening lists of casualties and atrocities. In 1983 a group known as the Tamil Tigers killed thirteen Sri Lankan soldiers. Sinhalese supporters of the UNP struck back viciously, killing about 2500 Tamils and forcing thousands more to flee, many into India. Sri Lankans in general were a little better off than people further north: they were better fed, for example, and more educated, at least to secondary level. Sri Lankan industry and trade played a bigger part in the economy, but development was now gravely handicapped by the unrest and violence in a society which had not yet solved the problems of nationhood.

Jayewardene cancelled elections in 1982 and grew more autocratic. That did nothing to solve the Tamil problem and outrages by both Tamils and Sinhalese continued. Matters came to a head in 1987 when, after a series of bus massacres and bombings, the UNP launched the Sri Lankan army against Tamil areas in the east and north. Tamils in India erupted in protest, forcing Rajiv Gandhi to send supplies to the Sri Lankan Tamils beleaguered in the Jaffna peninsula. Open war between India and Sri Lanka was warded off when Jayewardene and Gandhi reached agreement in July 1987 that Sri Lankan Tamils should have self-government while remaining part of the Republic of Sri Lanka. Some 50 000 Indian troops were sent to Sri Lanka to help restore order and to oversee the introduction of the new system. They soon found themselves in conflict with the Tamil Tigers who wanted not self-government but an independent Eelam and seemed prepared to hold the Jaffna peninsula against all comers. By 1988 some 6000 lives had been lost in the Tamil–Sinhalese struggle, and the casualties now included Indian soldiers. In India there was bitter criticism of Rajiv Gandhi's policies. In Sri Lanka there was bitter criticism of Jayewardene and, escaping the ban on her political activity, Mrs Bandaranaike led the Freedom Party in angry denunciation of the presence of Indian troops in Sri Lanka. In the south of Sri Lanka, the extreme left organized a violent new confrontation with the UNP, demanding a social revolution. Forty years after independence, Sri Lankan hopes for unity and an enduringly prosperous economy were savagely blighted.

16.6 Burma

The assassination of U Aung San, president of the Anti-Fascist People's Freedom League, by a political rival during the negotiation of Burma's independence from Britain was a prelude to the brief civil war and continuing turbulence which plagued Burma after independence was granted in January 1948. The constitution left by the British, based on their own, was not well suited to an impoverished Asian state. From the outset, the military leader General U Ne Win became Burma's strong man, standing behind the politicians who struggled to contain the deep tribal and political differences which threatened stability and retarded development. There were also religious conflicts between the majority Buddhists and minorities such as the Muslims, some of whom were regarded as 'foreigners'. U Nu, a devout Buddhist, was Prime Minister from 1948 to 1958 and from 1960 to 1962 and Burma persevered in trying to practise democracy, carry out socialist reform and build a unified nation. Conflict rather than co-operation, and feuding even within the ruling party, exasperated the military, however – much as had happened in Pakistan during the 1950s. In 1962 General Ne Win seized power, temporarily imprisoned U Nu, and abolished the parliamentary system.

Burma was declared the Socialist Republic of the Union of Burma, an anti-communist but pro-socialist one-party state under the Burma Socialist Programme Party (BSPP) and the Chairmanship of Ne Win. The Party's aim was 'Burma for the Burmese', though the comprehensive programme of public ownership and social reorganization it carried out seemed to the West little different from communism. The Programme was nevertheless distinctively Burmese, and externally Burma sought neutrality and to maintain equally good relations with both East and West. Ne Win retired in 1981 and was succeeded by U San Yu, a former military officer whom he had groomed as his successor. The BSPP remained the only party during the 1980s, though communist resistance to it continued outside the one-party assembly.

In 1988 unexpected mass riots toppled the military government and, after a bewildering series of coups and demonstrations, free competitive elections were grudgingly promised by the authorities. Years of stagnation and falling output in agriculture, and the example of other popular movements in Asia (in the Philippines and South Korea), lay behind the insurgency. After decades of insular stability, Burma's political future had become dramatically uncertain.

16.7 Indonesia and other Asian states

Most post-colonial states included minorities like the Tamils in Sri Lanka. Indonesia faced the formidable problem of building a national identity in its many scattered islands (see section 15.1) and, like Malaya, was home to a substantial Chinese minority. In Singapore, Chinese were in the majority, Malays and Indians the minority. The Chinese were, in fact, widely spread, and were sometimes referred to as 'the Jews of the East'. Many had migrated as labourers but they often became successful in business, their prosperity breeding envy. In addition, they were sometimes suspected of being agents for Chinese communism. It was not unusual, therefore, for the Chinese to be involved in ethnic tensions and in political controversies of the sort which brought the downfall of Sukarno. 'The father of Indonesia', Sukarno had been one of the earliest rulers to turn to the 'guided democracy' or 'basic democracy' practised in Pakistan and other new nations. It was argued that the combination of father-figure control and popular participation in restricted elections helped a nation to become established. But father-figures such as Sukarno and Ayub Khan inevitably risked being accused of authoritarianism.

Prolonged rule by a leader such as Lee Kuan Yew, Prime Minister of Singapore for more than twenty years after independence, undoubtedly provided stability. Lee combined his authority with popularity, rather like Nehru, and regularly won sweeping victories in elections. Economic successes helped this popularity, industry, trade and finance making the Republic of Singapore wealthy, especially by Asian standards. The eradication of corruption was his most notable achievement. Even so, Lee was criticized for authoritarianism and for his rigid ideas about the sort of disciplined and thrusting society he wished to develop in the country.

Not all new states were as fortunate in their prolonged leadership as Singapore. The sort of corrupt dictatorships practised by the Duvaliers in Haiti and by Somoza in Nicaragua were all too common. In the Philippines, Ferdinand Marcos, abetted by his wife Imelda, presided over an increasingly unattractive regime until forced into exile in 1986 (see section 12.4). The fall of Marcos and the success against him of Corazon Aquino gave hope to others campaigning against authoritarian rule, especially Benazir Bhutto in Pakistan.

Malaysians meanwhile kept a firmer grip on democracy, helped by good foundations laid by the Tunku Abdul Rahman, as well as by modest economic development and cautious policies to try to preserve harmony between the Federation's ethnic communities. The Chinese community was sometimes uneasy but less of a 'problem' than it had been during the communist guerilla struggle of the 1950s (see section 14.2.4). There was new anxiety in the 1980s, however. More than half the people of Malaysia were Muslims and the growth of Islamic fundamentalism of the sort that had taken root in Iran alarmed the authorities. From Indonesia, where Muslims dominated, to the Philippines, where they were a rather small minority, militant Islam was beginning to cause concern, threatening perhaps to undermine the nation-building that had already taken place.

Suharto, who preferred to be known only by the one name, was trying in the 1980s to unite Indonesia behind the five principles of *pancasila*, combining democracy, social justice, humanitarianism and nationalism with belief in a supreme god. That was not entirely to the liking of Islamic fundamentalists who called for a *jihad* (holy war) in 1984 and went on to clash with the army. Indonesia remained markedly poorer than most of its neighbours outside the Indian subcontinent in spite of oil, minerals and Suharto's improvements to the economy through Five-Year Plans. But oil prices collapsed and in 1987–8 severe financial problems hindered further development and especially Suharto's resettlement schemes, whereby Indonesians were moved from over-populated to more thinly-populated islands.

Suharto had preserved Indonesia as one country in spite of the language differences and regional rivalries of its almost 170 million people. He had also kept communism at bay, one of his reasons for coming to power in 1967. Yet Indonesian 'democracy' was still guided. The people were allowed some say in the country's affairs with an elected parliament, but the system was controlled to prevent factions from destroying it and this gave rise to charges against the government of electoral irregularities and authoritarianism. When the People's Consultative Assembly re-elected Suharto to the Presidency in 1983, he gave notice of his intention to retire in 1988, when Indonesia would be challenged once again to make the difficult transition from an old leadership to the new. But Suharto then changed his mind and was re-elected President in 1988 for another five years, and the challenge was postponed.

UNIT 17

Legacies of empire: 2 – nation-building in Africa

17.1 Unity and democracy

The choice of political parties which was part of democracy in western Europe more often than not produced only chaos in Africa. The states which emerged from the colonial empires grouped regions and tribes in ways that sometimes made little sense. Yet in each of the states the people had shared a common colonial experience. The élites among them also shared a common European language - usually English, French or Portuguese - and, sometimes, common institutions. The task of holding the state together, however, was such that hardly any African state could long persevere with multi-party democracy. Many turned to the one-party system such as was found in communist countries, arguing that co-operation was needed more than competition, and that multiple parties too often represented only regions, tribes and self-interested factions and led inevitably to feuding and strife. Alternatively, as in Pakistan and Bangladesh, the army intervened to clear out squabbling or dictatorial politicians and to try to achieve that disciplined co-operation which was a necessary part of nation-building. But the quality of military rule could vary too, sometimes being efficient and constructive but at other times corrupt and bloody.

Within this general framework some three dozen black African states were, by the 1980s, struggling to find their identities and to make a success of independence. They ranged in size from tiny Gambia and Swaziland to heavily populated Nigeria and sprawling Zaïre, which covered more than twice Nigeria's area. Each was individual though they had many problems in common.

Zaïre's early troubles illustrated the difficulties commonly faced in achieving unity, democracy, freedom from outside interference and a sense of real nationhood (see section 15.3). By late 1965 General Joseph Mobutu and the army were firmly in charge. Twenty years later, Mobutu was elected President for a third term with over 99 per cent of the votes, but no other candidate stood in the election. Moreover, the National Legislative Council consisted only of members of the Popular Movement, united behind Mobutu. Zaïre was still important to the West for its copper, cobalt and uranium, and for Mobutu's anti-communist stance, and the West therefore gave its support both to Zaïre's fragile economy and to its President. Mobutu thus preserved his authority despite opposition movements which from time to time aimed to depose him, and he also preserved Zaïre's unity despite the country's size and tribal divisions. It remained one of the poorest and most corrupt countries in Africa, however, and rule was authoritarian rather than democratic.

Gambia, on the other hand, a fraction the size of Zaïre and with a population well below a million, was one of few African states in the 1980s still to preserve at least something of a multi-party democracy. This was partly due to the prestige of Dawda Jawara, the leader of the People's Progressive Party and now Gambia's President. The People's Progressive Party and Jawara had led Gambia into independence in 1965, their status similar to that of the Indian National Congress and Nehru in India, albeit on a smaller scale. As Prime Minister, Jawara accepted aid from both West and East and laid foundations of stability and tolerance unusual in a newly independent land. The state was English-speaking and largely Muslim, in contrast to French speaking, mainly Christian Zaïre. But though small, Gambia, like other African states, had a mixture of tribes, the largest, the Mandinkas, being less than 50 per cent of the population. Jawara maintained the state without entirely abandoning the political traditions the British had hoped to leave behind in all their former colonies but which, when Gambia won its independence, were already fading fast in Ghana.

17.2 Ghana, black Africa's pioneering state

17.2.1 Kwame Nkrumah, the 'Founder of the Nation'

The Gold Coast became independent in 1957, together with its Ashanti lands and what had been Britain's mandate in Togoland, and it seemed fitting that the first black African state to gain its freedom should revive an African name, Ghana. The preparation for independence had been quite thorough. Kwame Nkrumah, leader of the Convention People's Party (CPP), had been educated in the USA and Britain, imprisoned by the British for nationalist agitation, but then given experience of government as Prime Minister of the colonial Gold Coast. This was to prove a not unusual apprenticeship for leaders in the run-up to independence, but Ghana was also prepared with a trained civil service, useful communications and some sound educational and similar foundations. It depended too heavily on cocoa exports but had useful mineral deposits, including gold. The miscellaneous origins of Ghana, together with its tribal, linguistic and religious mixtures, already suggested that the new state might meet difficulties, but hopes were high. In the event, Nkrumah simply banned tribal and regional organizations, authorizing imprisonment without trial by the Preventive Detention Act only a year after independence.

Dr Nkrumah was a man in a hurry. He intended to make Ghana a show-case of what Africans could achieve, freed from colonial rule. He also intended to lead the whole of Africa towards independence; Ghana's role in 1957 was that of a pioneer. A few years later Nkrumah wrote:

> I at once made it clear that there would be no meaning to the national independence of Ghana unless it was linked with the total liberation of the African continent.

He supported Lumumba in the Congo. He then rushed into a union with neighbouring Mali and Sekou Touré's Guinea, and he played a major part in founding the Organization of African Unity (OAU). While claiming non-alignment, he bitterly condemned the neo-colonialism of the West and drew closer to the Soviet Union. The Ghana–Guinea–Mali Union collapsed in 1963 and Nkrumah was by then under criticism from fellow Africans such as the Nigerians and the Congolese for interfering in their affairs.

He also had problems within Ghana, where economic difficulties joined with his ambitious schemes and strong-arm tactics to arouse opposition. When Ghana became a republic in 1960, Nkrumah was elected President but he drifted towards dictatorship, imprisoning opponents such as Joseph Danquah who contested the presidential elections. Danquah died in jail, while hero-worship of Nkrumah spread. An unofficial creed circulated, which the President seemed not to discourage, which told how Nkrumah had:

> suffered under British rule, was imprisoned in Fort James, was released and rose again . . .

In 1964 Ghana became a one-party state under the CPP which Nkrumah already dominated. He went on not only to interfere with the courts but also to take personal charge of the army. The army was already restless, however, uneasy about growing Soviet influence, especially in the developing Guards Regiment which Nkrumah seemed to be grooming as a new élite close to the Presidency.

Nkrumah favoured economic planning and aimed at a socialist society mindful of the people's well-being. But his schemes often outstripped the reach of the economic plans and Ghana had to borrow heavily at uncomfortable rates of interest. Over-ambitious industrialization led to corruption rather than solid achievement; extravagant prestige projects increased debt but brought little benefit to the people. Africa's largest dry dock and the motorway from Accra to Tema were little used, and fine official buildings in Accra seemed premature when there was much else to be done. On the other hand, there was some benefit to Ghanaians. The government expanded the fishing, forestry and cattle-rearing industries, improved water supplies and other social services (universal primary education was introduced in 1961), and promoted village co-operative developments. Most ambitious of all, the Volta River Project aimed to provide irrigation, hydroelectric power and eventually an aluminium-smelting plant. Again, however, capital had to be borrowed. The reserves of 1957 had long been spent and there were now government debts of somewhere between £250 million and £400 million. Nkrumah tried to bring about a rise in cocoa prices to earn foreign currency, but the opposite happened: when cocoa prices collapsed in the mid-1960s, Ghana's economy was in deep trouble.

The elections of 1965 were cancelled, the President simply nominating the CPP members of parliament. In 1966 he went to China and North Vietnam, trying both to mediate in the war in Vietnam and to raise a further loan denied him in Washington and Moscow. In an almost bloodless coup, the army deposed him in his absence.

Nkrumah had worked for Ghana and for Africa but his career showed the impossibility of creating a new nation overnight and the folly of trying to force the pace too hard. It also showed how easy it was for popular leaders to fall prey to corruption and the abuse of power. Nkrumah spent some time in Guinea and died in 1972 in a Romanian hospital. Meanwhile, the 'Founder of the Nation' left Ghana deep in debt and in the hands of the military.

17.2.2 The military–civilian see-saw

Ghana after Nkrumah see-sawed between military rule and elected civilian governments. The National Liberation Council under Major-General Joseph Ankrah purged Nkrumah's supporters, outlawed the CPP and made a start on rooting out corruption and stabilizing the economy. Brigadier Akwasi Afrifa took over from Ankrah, speeding up the new constitution which prepared the way for elections in August 1969. The Progressive Party won 105 of the 140 parliamentary seats and Dr Kofi Busia, an academic with a reputation as a constitutionalist, became Prime Minister. The National Liberation Council was dissolved.

Theory was one thing, practice another, however, and the Busia government had little success. The constitution restricted it to prevent any further abuse of power, and it was soon in difficulty. Inflation, unemployment and labour troubles led to clashes, as a result of which the Ghanaian Trades Union Congress was abolished. Though the burden on the economy was lightened, Ghana's creditors would not cancel the country's crippling debts and servicing them was handicapped by another fall in cocoa prices. Ghana's currency was devalued twice but the country's economy showed little signs of recovery. In January 1972 Colonel Ignatius Acheampong restored military rule with a National Redemption Council.

Acheampong was less interested than Ankrah and Afrifa in restoring democracy. From the start he took a harder line than his predecessors, revaluing the currency, repudiating some of Ghana's debts and limiting foreign shareholding in Ghanaian businesses. Improving cocoa prices helped the economy, but soaring oil costs in 1974–5 dealt it another blow. Inflation could not be brought down. Unemployment persisted, and shortages brought a flourishing black market. The government delayed constitutional change and in 1978 Acheampong, by now a General, was removed by fellow-officers alleging that he was corrupt and despotic and that he dabbled in ju-ju.

His successor, General Fred Akuffo, freed prisoners and began to prepare for elections and renewed civilian rule, but events moved too fast for him. In June 1979 radical junior officers seized power, led by Flight-Lieutenant Jerry Rawlings of Ghanaian–Scottish descent. They protested at the country's leadership in the first generation after independence and at the wealth many had accumulated while the masses remained poor. In anticipation of the sweeping changes the officers intended, Afrifa, Acheampong and Akuffo were executed. People's courts dealt out swift 'justice' in a furious attack on profiteering and corruption. Rawlings won popular acclaim but in rushing to restore civilian government seemed to underestimate the scale of Ghana's problems. He stayed in power for only four months before handing over to the diplomat Hilla Limann, who became President when his People's National Party won 71 of the 140 seats in parliament.

Limann's government solved none of Ghana's problems. Cocoa prices fell yet again, and Ghana's plight became evident in public dissension (some of it tribal), shortages and general disrepair. The government dithered and in January 1982 Rawlings emerged from premature retirement to seize power again with a Provisional National Defence Council of which he became Chairman. Intent on restoring the economy, efficiency and honesty, Rawlings attacked Ghana's problems energetically but there seemed no prospect now of an early return to parliamentary democracy.

Afrifa had written that, in ousting Nkrumah, he found it:

> painful . . . to come to the conclusion that the coup was necessary to save our country and our people.

The history of Ghana since Nkrumah, however, showed that it was easier to agree on a coup than to achieve measures for the country's salvation. In 1982, 25 years after independence, Rawlings asked Ghanaians 'for nothing less than a revolution' – a measure of the task that still lay ahead to put Ghana firmly on the road to stability and prosperity. Even the country's overdependence on cocoa had changed little since 1957, and it still accounted for around three-quarters of Ghana's export earnings.

17.3 Nigeria, Africa's restless giant

17.3.1 From independence to civil war

From independence in 1960 Nigeria promised to become the leading state in black Africa. It was already the largest in population, and endowed with a variety of resources (see section 14.3.2), but there were weaknesses. The federal constitution divided authority between the central government and four regional governments in the North, East, West and Mid-West. It was designed in the hope of satisfying tribal interests jealously guarded by the Fulani and Hausa in the North, Ibo in the East and Yoruba in the West. The constitution also aimed to protect national unity from religious differences, Islam being strong especially in the North, and from differences of language. In 1961 part of the English-speaking Cameroon, a British mandate, was added to Nigeria in preference to joining the former French mandate of Cameroun.

Dr Nnamdi Azikiwe, an Ibo, was independent Nigeria's first Governor-General, becoming President when a republic was declared in 1963. Azikiwe had a standing among Nigerian nationalists which in some ways resembled that of Nkrumah in Ghana. But Nigeria also had a Prime Minister, Abubakar Balewa, a Hausa, whose Northern People's Congress (NPC) with Ibo support commanded a majority in the federal parliament. The Yorubas, however, felt that the federal government was a government of their rivals. Their representatives in parliament, the Action Group, had little influence and their resentment grew when Balewa in 1962–3 arrested their leaders, Chiefs Awolowo and Enaharo.

Balewa's difficulties mounted. There were allegations of corruption, favouritism and incompetence, especially after the turbulent elections of 1964. In the West, where disorders increased, the Action Group was outmaneouvred by forces led by Chief Akintola, a ruthless and unscrupulous ally of Balewa. But in 1966 both Balewa and Akintola were deposed and murdered in a coup by junior officers, one of whom identified their targets:

> Our enemies are the political profiteers, swindlers, the men in high and low places who seek bribes and demand ten per cent, those who seek to keep the country divided permanently so that they can remain in office as ministers and VIPs of waste, the tribalists, the nepotists.

It was senior army officers who took control, however, with Major-General Johnson Aguiyi-Ironsi at their head. Ironsi was an Ibo, and the Northerners increasingly saw the upheavals of 1966 as some sort of Ibo plot and takeover. Ironsi's plans for abolishing regional parliaments and suspending political activity led to a new outbreak of fury in the North. Ironsi was captured, flogged, then executed. Northern officers debated secession but rallied behind a new Nigerian government under Colonel Yakubu Gowon, a Northerner and a Christian from a minority tribe who was also acceptable to the West. It was now the Ibos who stood outside the revolution and who were falling victim to tribal killing, especially the Ibos living in the North. Thousands died as, throughout Nigeria, as many as a million Ibo struggled to make their way to the safety of the Eastern Region.

It was the Eastern Region which now sought to secede from Nigeria, its prospects for future prosperity brightened by the possession of oil deposits and seaports. Colonel Emeka Ojukwu, English-educated and wealthy, was ambitious to rule there and commanded military support. He made little response to Gowon's peacemaking overtures but instead built up stocks of arms. There were twelve million or more people in the Eastern Region, rather more than half of them Ibos, and in May 1967 Ojukwu declared them subjects of the new independent republic of Biafra. Gowon meanwhile announced a new federal twelve-state Nigeria, which might well have appealed to the minorities in Biafra had Ojukwu allowed them a choice. In fact, Ojukwu's forces began advancing westwards towards Lagos, which they bombed with a single elderly aircraft. By the end of 1967, federal forces had struck back and Biafra was surrounded.

It was soon clear that Biafra would be defeated but, fearful of genocide, the Ibos resisted fiercely and Ojukwu refused to surrender. France and Portugal gave them some support and arms, and Biafra was recognized by the Ivory Coast, Tanzania and Zambia. Otherwise, it had few friends. The OAU and most world powers, including Britain and the USSR, preferred Nigeria to remain united, partly to discourage other secessionist movements which might plague Africa. On the other hand, Ibo suffering aroused much public sympathy as the federal troops chipped away at Biafra. Western governments launched extensive relief operations and, for the United Nations, U Thant spoke of 'universal distress' caused by Nigeria's civil war.

Ibo resistance ended in January 1970, weakened when Azikiwe came out in support of federal Nigeria rather than Biafra. Ojukwu escaped into exile. Gowon imposed a federal military administration but, from the start, it was outstanding for its conciliatory policies. The genocide of which Ojukwu had always warned did not happen. Comparatively few were punished for rebellion and vigorous efforts were made to restore Ibos to their former jobs and, where possible, to their former properties - even in the North. Gowon's constitutional reforms and the new co-operation of the people in nation-building suggested that, ten years after independence, Nigeria might now be about to flourish. It was still under military rule, however, and the civil war left economic and social problems which included a disturbing level of crime.

17.3.2 Another military–civilian see-saw

The military coup which overthrew Balewa in January 1966 played its part in inspiring the military in Ghana to depose Nkrumah a month later. Both Nigeria and Ghana found it difficult, however, to set aside military rule once it had been introduced. But the Nigerian army was far from united. Most of its leaders saw military action as 'corrective', aiming to right the country's ills while remaining non-political in the way many had been trained to be in Britain. On the other hand internal jealousies arose and many suspected that influence in the army rested mainly with conservative Northerners.

Gowon began to outstay his welcome. Unemployment remained high, prices rose and while trying to hold down wages the government ran into labour conflicts. Gowon's rule was not oppressive, and its influence was often constructive, but it developed an over-large bureaucracy and often seemed slow-moving. Several specific issues weakened it. Chief Awolowo had co-operated at first but became hostile as Gowon's rule lengthened, Gowon eventually suggesting that 1976 would be too early to return to civilian government, as had first been envisaged. Students protested strongly when Gowon devised a compulsory National Youth Service Corps. The census of 1974 caused further dissension: it put Nigeria's population at almost 80 million but allegedly exaggerated the population of the North, perhaps to gain electoral and other regional advantage. Towns grew rapidly leading to overcrowding, poverty, disorder and traffic accidents, and the government seemed to be losing its grip. Many officials seemed concerned only to grow rich, and charges of corruption spread. While Gowon was at an OAU meeting in 1975, fellow officers deposed him, leaving him to study politics in exile in Britain until allowed back to Nigeria in 1983.

Nigeria's new leader, General Murtala Mohammed, promised elections in 1979 but was murdered in a mutiny in 1976. His successor, General Olusegun Obasanjo, developed the nineteen-state federal system Mohammed had introduced and stuck to the electoral timetable. Approved political parties had to be national, not regional. The National Party of Nigeria (NPN) led by Shehu Shagari gained 168 of the 455 parliamentary seats contested in 1979, ahead of Awolowo's United Party (111) and Azikiwe's People's Party (79). Shagari had strong support in the North, especially among his fellow-Fulanis. But the NPN had backing elsewhere too. Shagari defeated Awolowo for the Presidency and formed a minority government with support from the People's Party. Obasanjo now stood down. Among his other achievements, he had reduced the size of the military, expanded primary education and curbed waste and corruption. He had also made every effort to restore genuine democracy to a united federal Nigeria.

Shagari nevertheless faced an uphill task. The difficulties of nation-building were increased at the end of 1980 when Muslim fundamentalists rioted and killed 'infidels' in the North, the start of Islamic disturbances which were to continue during the 1980s. Oil revenues, industrialization and its large size nevertheless made Nigeria the corner-stone of the Economic Community of West African States (ECOWAS), founded in 1976, and a key member of the OAU. Yet dependence on oil also brought its problems, as later units will show. Agricultural and manufacturing output threatened to decline rather than to increase, and the balance of the economy and distribution of wealth gave little cause for satisfaction. The rising population undermined living standards. Controversy flared when, in 1983, Shagari began deporting around two million illegal immigrants, half of them Ghanaians, drawn to Nigeria and its cities by its oil economy. The NPN nevertheless won sweeping success in elections in 1983 and Shagari was re-elected President. He himself seemed above the corruption now widely alleged against his regime, but he was discredited when opponents complained of electoral fraud and more than 70 people were killed in rioting over the election results. Shagari had also to take responsibility for Nigeria's seriously ailing economy. He claimed:

> Our ultimate aim is to phase out food imports through self-sufficiency as quickly as possible.

But with more than half its people still working in agriculture, it seemed remarkable mismanagement (perhaps the result of the preference for cash crops) that Nigeria in the 1980s could not already feed itself.

At the end of 1983 another military coup occurred. Shagari was arrested and Major-General Mohammed Buhari took charge with a Supreme Military Council. The coup was almost bloodless and the new regime promptly embarked on a programme of economic belt-tightening . It also purged the army leadership and prepared charges of 'economic sabotage, corruption and unjust enrichment' against civilian ministers and officials. There was more upheaval in August 1985, however, when Buhari fell to a new military coup. Major-General Ibrahim Babangida became Nigeria's sixth military leader since independence. His first priority was not democracy but the repair of the economy. Already in 1986, however, there were riots in favour of more democratic rule and against Babangida's decision to make Nigeria a member of the international Organization of the Islamic Conference.

17.4 East Africa: stability and instability

17.4.1 Tanganyika/Tanzania

For 25 years after its independence in 1961, Tanganyika's course was charted by Julius Nyerere, one of 26 children of an African chief, a graduate of Edinburgh University and a former school-teacher. As leader of the popular Tanganyika African National Union (TANU), he was the natural choice for Prime Minister at independence, and later became President of the Tanganyikan Republic in 1962 and of Tanzania (united Tanganyika and Zanzibar) in 1964. He became Tanzania's, indeed Africa's, teacher (*mwalimu*).

Nyerere's contribution to leadership was distinctive, combining high moral standards with a positive philosophy for co-operative development, an 'African socialism' which proved controversial. He gave his country stability, avoiding the military coups common in Ghana and Nigeria, but he made it a one-party state almost from the start, discouraging opposition. Nyerere's system was authoritarian in spite of regular elections and public consent, and critics were also quick to point out that Tanzania and Tanzanians remained very poor in spite of all his fine words. Tanzania was a land with few resources, heavily dependent on agriculture and cash crops such as coffee, cotton and sisal.

At the heart of TANU's programme lay *ujamaa*. Nyerere wrote:

> Ujamaa, or 'Familyhood', describes our socialism. It is opposed to capitalism, which seeks to build a happy society on the basis of the exploitation of man by man; and it is equally opposed to doctrinaire socialism which seeks to build a happy society on a philosophy of inevitable conflict between man and man.

The Arusha Declaration of 1967 developed this view and TANU's programme. The policy was 'to build a socialist state' on the basis of self-reliance:

> Independence cannot be real if a nation depends on gifts and loans from another for its development.

TANU was said to be 'a Party of peasants and workers', its leaders being forbidden 'practices of capitalism or feudalism', two or more salaries, shares in companies, the fine cars and personal enrichment taken for granted elsewhere. The emphasis was on co-operation at village and peasant level, and industrialization, urbanization and arms-spending were not TANU ambitions.

Suspicious of this African socialism, the West and the IMF gave support rather grudgingly, critical of how Tanzania was governed and of how what aid there was (much of it Chinese and Swedish) was spent on the people's welfare rather than on industry. By the 1980s this brought universal primary education, levels of health care above the average in Africa, clean water for many villages and a much improved life expectancy. On the other hand, living standards were low and co-operative village projects with their shared services had achieved less than was hoped. 'Villagizing' in the 1970s moved millions of Tanzanians into new *ujamaa* villages to speed up co-operative development, but the disruption and its attendant bureaucracy brought confusion, hardly increasing output while undermining self-reliance. When Nyerere retired in 1985, the Tanzanian economy was far from healthy, crippled by expensive oil imports, beset with shortages and with output low, even food having to be imported. As usual, shortages were a breeding-ground for corruption. Supporters of TANU argued that their party's plight owed a good deal to the capitalist pressures of the USA:

> It is hard to come to any other conclusion than that the US under Reagan set out to force the collapse of Nyerere's regime.

The IMF demanded a change to more orthodox capitalist goals, as well as privatization, profit incentives and currency devaluation.

Nyerere had been a somewhat uncomfortable diplomatic neighbour, outspoken from the outset, for example about South African apartheid and the nature of the Commonwealth (see section 14.4). He helped FRELIMO win independence for Mozambique and black nationalists that of Zimbabwe. He was never slow to denounce racism and what he saw as moral wrong, and – what was worse, in the eyes of his detractors – he maintained links with China and the Soviets. The Chinese built the Tan–Zam Railway and Tanzania's Friendship Textile Mill, though Nyerere refused to sacrifice independence in exchange. In 1967 Tanzania joined its neighbours Kenya and Uganda in the East African Community, hoping to promote economic co-operation and regional development. But Kenya was strongly capitalist and the partnership was uneasy. Moreover, Uganda became unstable and the Community collapsed after Amin came to power there in 1971 (see section 17.4.2). Nyerere eventually helped in the overthrow of Amin's bloody dictatorship, in 1979, but at some further cost to Tanzania's ailing economy.

There was a smooth transfer of power when Nyerere stepped down. The new President, Hassan Ali Mwinyi, was a Muslim from Zanzibar who represented the religion of a third of Tanzania's people. TANU retained power and the principles set out in the Arusha Declaration were little changed, the merits of this distinctive sort of nation-building being much disputed between capitalists and socialists. Mwinyi made cautious efforts in 1986 to come to terms with the IMF, only too well aware that the World Bank counted Tanzania among the 25 least developed countries in the world.

17.4.2 Uganda

Uganda was less dramatically successful than Tanzania in avoiding tribal and religious dissension. It was granted independence from Britain in 1962 with a federal system, allowing the southern Kingdom of Buganda extensive self-government under its *Kabaka* (leader), Mutesa II. Mutesa became Uganda's President when a republic was set up in 1963. But real power rested with Prime Minister Dr Milton Obote who deposed the Kabaka in 1966 and reduced Buganda's privileges. Its people, mainly Baganda, were fiercely repressed and the Kabaka died in exile and in poverty in 1969.

One of Obote's main instruments in humbling the Baganda was Idi Amin, newly raised to the post of Colonel and then to that of Commander-in-Chief of Uganda's armed forces. With Amin's ruthless support, Obote consolidated his power as both President and Prime Minister. Uganda became virtually a one-party state under Obote's United People's Congress (UPC), as had been Obote's aim almost from Uganda's independence. He was a northerner of the Langi tribe. The Baganda were southerners, and many other Ugandans were Bantu of various tribes. It was no easy task to create unity among Uganda's eight million inhabitants, but Obote wanted power as well as unity. He said:

> Organized opposition against the government is a typically capitalist notion.

Having got power, Obote used it to crush opposition, and a new constitution in 1967 was followed not by elections but by more repression.

The armed forces grew in number but loyalties were divided between Obote and Amin, who was now building personal support among groups coming, like himself, from the north-west. When Obote went to the Commonwealth Conference in Singapore in 1971, Amin seized control of Uganda, bringing dancing crowds on to the streets of its capital, Kampala, and great relief in Buganda. Ugandans soon found they had exchanged one tyranny for another, more bloody one, however. Amin ruled as President in the interests of the north-west, of Islam (fewer than twenty per cent of Ugandans were Muslim), and of his own brand of nationalism which led quickly to attacks on Uganda's Asians, its foreign population and all who resisted the new regime. A fellow African observed of Amin, who began his military career as an NCO under the British:

> He was just the type that the British liked, the type of African that they used to refer to as from the 'warrior tribes': black, big, uncouth, uneducated and willing to obey orders.

Now Amin gave orders, to the embarrassment of more sophisticated Africans and the great hurt of the Ugandan people. It was alleged that ten thousand people were slaughtered within three months of his successful coup:

> Crocodiles basked beneath the Karume Falls Bridge, the Bridge of Blood, spanning the River Nile. They grew both fat and lazy. [J. Kamau and A. Cameron, *Lust to Kill*, Corgi, 1979]

Amin's regime lasted for eight years and was condemned almost everywhere, except among extreme anti-Israeli factions whose cause, along with Islam, Amin espoused. The overthrow of his vicious rule and of his blatant promotion of tribal self-interest was eagerly awaited.

It was Nyerere who acted, partly in reply to Amin's claims to, and brutal attacks on, parts of Tanzania. Nyerere seized the opportunity to back Ugandan rebels, invading Uganda in 1979 and putting Amin to flight. Tanzanians remained in Uganda until 1981, helping to reconstruct its shattered society and economy – an enterprise they could ill afford – and Nyerere's critics made pious complaints about interfering in another country's affairs. Few Ugandans, however, felt anything but relief to be rid of Amin, who took refuge first in Gadafy's Libya and then in Saudi Arabia.

Nyerere encouraged the coalition Uganda National Liberation Front (UNLF), and Ugandans hoped they might now achieve stability and personal liberties. The UNLF prepared for the first Ugandan elections since 1962 but its own interim Presidents, the academic Yusuf Lule and Godfrey Binaisa, a lawyer, were both overthrown as ineffective. Obote returned from exile in Tanzania to restore the UPC and its vote-winning machinery. Commonwealth observers declared the elections of 1980 acceptable and Obote again became Uganda's President.

Thatcher's Britain in particular gave Obote strong economic support, but it was soon alleged that he was again ruling in the interests of the northerners, and that the killings and cruelties of the regime threatened to exceed even those of Amin. Obote again had to rely on the military, and the Baganda and other unfavoured tribes suffered. Guerillas of the National Resistance Army (NRA) became active north and west of Kampala, seeking Obote's overthrow, and his regime seemed to grow more savage and more corrupt while Uganda's economy tottered. Obote himself claimed to want reconciliation, but problems overwhelmed him when there was a split in the army between the Langi and Acholi tribes. Another coup deposed him in favour of military rule by Basilio Okello, who had strong Acholi support.

The killing was not yet over. At the root of Uganda's problems lay differences between north and south: northerners and southerners competed for influence in the Ugandan army, and northerners demanded a share in Uganda's wealth, traditionally centred on Kampala. This division was further complicated by tribal conflict. In 1986 the NRA, many of its soldiers children, drove Okello from Kampala and set up Yoweri Musevini as President. Musevini had been a guerilla leader throughout the 1980s, angered by what he regarded as the fraudulent election which in 1980 restored Obote. Since he had once assisted FRELIMO in Mozambique, he had a reputation as a Marxist. His family had come to Uganda as refugees from Rwanda and Musevini was born in southern Uganda. Though to some extent standing aside from Ugandan tribal rivalries, he nevertheless attracted the hostility of the northerners, especially the pro-Obote factions. His moderate economic policies and his efforts to broaden the base of his government won him the support of Western governments, together with the help that Uganda's faltering economy desperately needed. Northern Uganda resisted his rule, however, and in 1987 he revived dictatorial presidential powers in yet another attempt to unite the country. Meanwhile, evidence mounted of the massacres and purges which had occurred under Musevini's predecessors and of wrongs to be avenged. Musevini faced guerilla actions not only from Obote supporters but also from followers of Amin and Okello. To these were added in 1987 the devotees of Holy Spirit who found a leader in prophetess Mama Alice Lakwena, whose faith moved her to try to overthrow President Musevini by rebellion. Lakwena was captured and jailed but the Holy Spirit rebellion went on, especially among the northern Acholi. Estimates put the dead in 1987 alone at 8000, including 1000 NRA soldiers. In early 1988 the MRA seemed to be nearing a peace with other resistance forces, but the Lakwenas went on hacking and burning to death their fellow Ugandans – in the name of the Father, Son and Holy Ghost. A Catholic priest tried to explain their movement as 'a mixture of superstition, religion and tribalism'.

Some academics saw it as 'a peasant rebellion'.

Internal conflicts had devastated Uganda's economy, and little repair work was possible while they continued. Average income per head in the mid-1980s was only a little higher than that of Tanzania and considerably lower than that of Nigeria (see Table 17.1).

17.4.3 Kenya

Jomo Kenyatta was already in his sixties when he became Prime Minister of independent Kenya. A year later, in 1964, he became President of the Kenyan Republic. His tribe was the Kikuyu, who made up about a fifth of Kenya's population and some of whose members had fought for independence through the Mau Mau (see section 14.3.3). But Kenyatta did not intend the Kenya African National Union (KANU) to be a tribal party: he worked closely with Tom Mboya, a Luo, who held several offices in government and who, until he was assassinated in 1969, seemed likely to succeed Kenyatta when the old man retired or died.

A Kikuyu, Isaac Njoroge, was hanged for Mboya's murder but it took skill to preserve Kenya from a tribal conflict such as was then brewing in Uganda. The Luo tribe had fewer numbers than the Kikuyu but rivalry was strong and Oginga Odinga threatened to exploit it in his left-wing challenge to the government of Kenyatta and KANU. Odinga was arrested, his socialist Kenya People's Union banned and thus, when elections were held at the end of 1969, Kenya was effectively a one-party state. Kenyatta maintained stability, dealing firmly with all opposition when he thought it necessary. Like Nyerere, he was criticized for authoritarianism, though repression in Kenya was very limited by standards elsewhere in the world. There was also criticism of the wealth of Kenya's élite, including some members of Kenyatta's family, and an outspoken critic, Joseph Kariuki, was mysteriously murdered in 1975.

Kenyatta's success owed more to policy than to crude repression, however. Africanization was one of the keys to his nation-building. Asians and others who preferred to retain British citizenship when Kenya became independent were deprived of privileges and jobs, and their property was transferred to black Africans and those who were Kenyan by birth or by choice. Many Asians had to leave Kenya in the late 1960s, victims of this Africanization, though Kenyatta never pursued the policy as ruthlessly as Amin did in Uganda in the 1970s. Africanization helped to create a new national bond among black Kenyans, regardless of tribe, and it also helped to raise the status of blacks in business and public services. At the same time, those who took Kenyan citizenship, including white farmers remaining after independence, were treated as equals regardless of colour.

The KANU government also adopted flexible policies which combined economic planning with a mainly capitalist system which won the approval and willing support of the West. Kenya became more industrialized than Tanzania and Uganda, though it still relied heavily on exporting coffee and tea even after an oil industry developed, and balancing the books was always a struggle.

Fig. 17.1 Prime Minister Jomo Kenyatta attended a preparatory conference in London in September 1963, shortly before Kenya's independence. To the left of Kenyatta sits Tom Mboya, to his right Oginga Odinga, members of his government. Kenyatta, himself of the powerful Kikuyu tribe, intended to avoid rivalries between Kenya's thirteen tribes, and Mboya and Odinga were of the Luo. Kenyatta and Odinga here wear the caps favoured by African nationalists – what Ian Smith in Rhodesia called 'unconstitutional hats' and banned.

Kenyans became more prosperous than their neighbours, though living standards were still low by non-African standards. As was often the case, population growth tended to slow down other advances: population more than doubled between independence and the mid-1980s, when it reached 20 million.

Kenyatta won a reputation for moderation and for statesmanship but unease persisted about the gulf between rich and poor in Kenya, and there were doubts whether stability could continue when Kenyatta died. In fact, when the old man died in August 1978, Vice-President Daniel arap Moi stepped smoothly into the Presidency. New elections in 1979 gave Moi a vote of confidence though, as was usual by now, the voters chose to turn out some KANU members in favour of others. In 1982 the President survived an attempted coup by members of the air force and students, a group Kenyatta had found troublesome at times. The economy was still far from secure in spite of American help, and shortages and inequalities caused unrest.

Moi renewed the restrictions on Odinga and kept a firm grip on likely opponents, continuing Kenya's one-party state. Students still protested from time to time, however, and in 1986 Kenyatta University was closed by the government for a couple of months. Later that year Moi increased his presidential powers and there was unease among Western supporters of his government at what seemed to be the increasing authoritarianism of his methods. But Kenya had survived more than twenty years of independence without the upheavals common in other parts of Africa. Its success as a new nation owed a good deal to the foundations laid by Jomo Kenyatta - *mzee* ('Old Father') to the Kikuyu and to many other Kenyans.

17.5 Central Africa

17.5.1 English-speaking states: the front line

Tribal divisions threatened national unity in Malawi, Zambia and Zimbabwe no less than in the rest of Africa. Malawi at independence had numerous tribes in its small population of under four million. Zambia, equally small in population though greater in area, had 73 tribes including the northern Bemba. Each country gained independence under national leaders whose popularity owed a good deal to the long struggle to be free from European rule and white privilege (see section 14.3.1). The Malawi Congress Party (MCP) monopolized power from the outset and Hastings Banda swept into office, first as Prime Minister, then as republican President in 1966, remaining as Malawi's President-for-Life from 1971. In Zambia, Kenneth Kaunda, leader of the United National Independence Party (UNIP), became republican President before the end of 1964, faster than Banda in Malawi. He persevered with multi-party democracy until 1972, before turning, like Banda, to what seemed the greater stability of the one-party state. Like Tanzania and Kenya, both states avoided military coups. Zimbabwean independence was delayed until 1980 but the elections which led to it showed the stark division within the country between the Shona and Ndebele tribes (see section 14.3.4(d)). There, too, a one-party state was advocated as the key to national unity, by Prime Minister Robert Mugabe.

Banda and Kaunda provided their countries with continuity during the first twenty years of independence, but they seemed to have little else in common. Banda was ruthless in his internal policy, cautious and conservative abroad, and especially careful not to provoke South Africa or to get involved in the struggle against racism which Nyerere and Kaunda thought it would be wrong to avoid. Malawi lacked resources and its people were among the poorest even in Africa. Improvement thus came very slowly. But Banda and the MCP preserved order, and on the whole the country remained tranquil amid the upheavals that took place around it.

Kaunda aimed higher. He was a Christian humanist who shared some of

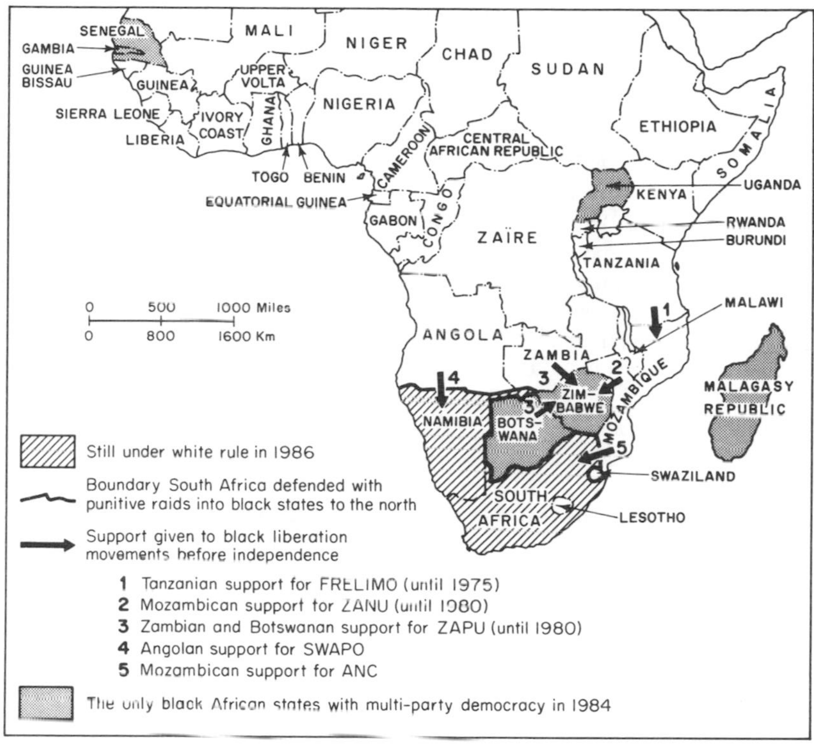

Fig. 17.2 Central and southern Africa in the mid-1980s

Nyerere's ideals, though the realities of office brought him some disillusionment. Like Nyerere and Kenyatta, he hoped the ruling party, UNIP, would rise above the sectional interests of tribalism. Kaunda and his Vice-President, Simon Kapwepwe, were of the Bemba tribe, and in 1969 relations between them became strained when it was alleged that Kapwepwe was promoting Bemba interests. Zambia had other factional problems: its vociferous Jehovah's Witnesses were hostile to earthly government and disruptive, while the racial problems of southern Africa still affected the Zambian copper-belt where white experts seemed to cling to special privileges, provoking labour unrest. Kaunda thought it necessary to crack the whip. At the end of the 1960s he took personal control of the UNIP machinery, and the state took control of the copper industry. Strikes were forbidden, and the elections of 1968 proved to be the last contested by any party other than UNIP. The African National Congress was accused of inciting violence. Kapwepwe left UNIP in 1971 to found a new opposition United Progress Party (UPP) 'to stamp out capitalism, tribalism and sectionalism', but all parties other than UNIP were banned in 1972 and Kapwepwe spent a brief period in detention. He made peace with UNIP in 1977 but did not hold office again.

Zambia's economy, meanwhile, depended rather unhealthily on copper. Whereas Malawi's exports were almost wholly agricultural, Zambia's were largely mineral, of which copper accounted for about 90 per cent. The fluctuating price of copper in world markets made planning difficult and the national income uncertain. The Zambian economy was also undermined by the turmoil surrounding neighbouring Rhodesia. Zambia's trade and communications were interdependent with Rhodesia's, and Zambia had to pay a price for its earnest efforts to apply the sanctions that the world demanded against Smith's Rhodesian Front regime. Detesting racism, Kaunda also supported Nkomo and the guerillas who fought against the Smith government. Zambia was therefore in the front line of the war of liberation until Zimbabwe's independence in 1980 eased its difficulties.

Zambia's dependence on copper was still a serious problem, however. Improved prices in the 1980s helped the country's balance of trade, but it was by now heavily in debt. Repeated droughts handicapped the production of maize, but the outside world was critical of Zambia's failure to diversify its economy and the IMF insisted on changes as the price of help. One effect of the subsequent removal of government subsidies was an increase in the cost of foodstuffs to the Zambian people. Extensive rioting resulted in 1986–7 and Kaunda restored the subsidies. He also cut back Zambia's payments to its foreign creditors, and Zambia was blacklisted by the IMF. Zambians argued that the efforts of the IMF to improve their economy by exposing it to market forces and demanding greater efficiency had only injured them. They pointed out that in 1987 the IMF took more money out of Africa than it injected, and Kaunda optimistically declared that Zambia would work out its own salvation to achieve growth 'from our own resources'. There were echoes here of the principles of Nyerere, Kaunda's long-time friend. Refusing to pay more than ten per cent of the country's export earnings to foreign creditors in any one year, Kaunda was challenging the world economic system (see section 21.1). But with rising unemployment in the copper-belt, goods in short supply and the threat of continuing unrest, Kaunda's defiance of the IMF seemed to involve an almost desperate risk.

Independent Zimbabwe inherited a stronger, more industrialized economy but one damaged by fifteen years of economic sanctions and civil war (see section 14.3.4). Civil war also left behind it hatreds, armed gangs, crime and violence; and tribal rivalry between Shona and Ndebele made the problem worse, especially when in 1982 there was open rift between Mugabe, whom the Shona supported, and Nkomo, backed by the Ndebele. Nkomo had remained Minister of Home Affairs for only two months after independence and in 1982 he left the government altogether, taking refuge in Britain for a time. In Prime Minister Mugabe's view, however, a one-party state was needed as soon as possible to create a climate of co-operation. When Nkomo returned home, repeated efforts were made to reach agreement on how to introduce a one-party system, especially when elections in 1985, while confirming Mugabe and ZANU (PF) in power, again starkly exposed Zimbabwe's tribal divisions. Ian Smith's party, now the Conservative Alliance, won fifteen of the twenty seats guaranteed to whites despite the fact that about a half of Rhodesia's 250 000 whites had now left the country. As a result of this apparent persistence of support for white sectional interests, Mugabe gave notice that reserved white seats would be abolished. Elections in October 1987 led to their replacement by twenty members of ZANU, eleven of them whites who now supported Mugabe. Further changes followed before the end of the year. Nkomo's ZAPU party merged with Mugabe's ZANU, the joint party retaining the name of the latter – the Zimbabwe African National Union (Patriotic Front). They took as their objective the building of 'a Socialist society in Zimbabwe on the basis of Marxist–Leninist principles', and looked forward to the end of the violence which since independence had plagued Matabeleland, the homeland of the Ndebele. On the last day of 1987, Mugabe became President of Zimbabwe for a six-year term, combining the roles of head of state and leader of the government. Zimbabwe was now a one-party state in all but name.

Meanwhile, Zimbabwe walked a tightrope between its hostility to apartheid and the need for coexistence with South Africa, its powerful neighbour and still an important factor in Zimbabwe's economy. The relationship was uneasy but, for the present, Mugabe's main interests were in building the new Zimbabwe, healing its tribal divisions, stopping the killings and restoring the nation's economic health. But the Mozambique National Resistance (MNR), resisting the rule of FRELIMO in Mozambique, had also declared war on the ZANU government of Zimbabwe in 1986 and it was impossible for Mugabe to stand aside from the continuing conflicts in southern Africa, even if he wished to (see sections 17.5.2 and 19.2). The success of Zimbabwe's Five-Year Plans, the second of which was launched in 1986 and included the aim of attracting foreign investment, might well depend on how successfully the country could cope with the armed turmoil surrounding it.

17.5.2 Angola and Mozambique

The former Portuguese states in central Africa were born out of turbulence, and turbulence continued after their independence (see section 15.4). Angola and Mozambique both had Marxist governments that were targets for anti-communist rivals encouraged by South Africa and, especially in Angola, by the USA. This was another factor with which new African nations had to cope – the sometimes very deliberate destabilizing of existing regimes by outside intrigue.

President Samora Machel maintained FRELIMO government and a one-party system in Mozambique for more than a decade after independence. Inside Mozambique, FRELIMO aimed to develop a Marxist collectivist system based on multiracialism and co-operation. The country's geographical location led to difficulties, however. Members of FRELIMO were aware of the help they had had in overthrowing the Portuguese, and they in turn backed Mugabe and the guerillas fighting to liberate Rhodesia, consequently suffering hundreds of Rhodesian reprisal raids. Mozambique also supported the African National

Congress in its aim to liberate blacks in South Africa, and this brought South African reprisals. South Africa and anti-communist interests supported the Mozambique National Resistance (MNR), which in turn exploited tribal and other divisions in its attempt to overthrow FRELIMO.

Mozambique's government had help from China, the USSR and North Korea, but Machel took care to preserve FRELIMO's independence from foreign control. But in 1984, as civil war, natural disasters and famine began to take their toll in Mozambique, he was reduced to dealing with South Africa and he signed a treaty of goodwill. It was another attempt to assert the country's independence but the move was not popular with all members of the FRELIMO government. Machel was a realist, however. At the beginning of the 1980s, Mozambique relied on the US market for a quarter of its exports and on South Africa for almost as much of its imports. South Africa also employed many migrant workers from Mozambique. Machel was well aware that his country was too poor, too underdeveloped and too insecure to play a dominant part in international affairs. Like other African leaders, his first priority was to build a united nation with rising living standards, and that could not be achieved while the MNR (commonly referred to as Renamo) tore at the fabric of the state. By 1986 almost half of his government's total spending went on resisting Renamo and its foreign supporters. The rebels grew more vicious, massacring and terrorizing Mozambican civilians and destroying plant and communications. South Africa also increased economic pressures against FRELIMO, disregarding the treaty of 1984, and ended the recruitment of Mozambicans to work in South African mines.

About the same time, in October 1986, Mozambique suffered another serious blow when Machel died in an air disaster. Recalling the earlier assassination of Eduardo Mondlane, Joaquim Chissanó, Machel's successor, declared:

> This is the second time that, under tragic circumstances, the Mozambique people have lost their top leader.

Mugabe repaid the help that FRELIMO had given him in coming to power in Zimbabwe, and Zimbabweans fought alongside Mozambicans against Renamo; but while the latter had the backing of South Africa, Mozambique seemed likely to remain a stricken country. Chissanó had worked closely with Machel and was Foreign Minister from 1975 to 1986. He now needed all his experience and prestige, however, simply to keep his government in power. The famine which afflicted countries to the north such as Ethiopia began also to afflict Mozambique as the civil war dragged on in 1987–8.

Though more prosperous at the outset than Mozambique, Angola had also lost its first President with the premature death of Agostinho Neto. Angola's difficulties were made worse not only by South African support for rebels opposing the MPLA government, but also by US interference. It was President Reagan's ambition 'to get back Angola'. A cartoon in *Soviet Weekly* in 1986 (see fig. 17.3) provided one view of the way in which US support for Savimbi's UNITA helped to keep alive the ideological and tribal civil war which hindered

Fig. 17.3 Yuri Ivanov's view of the influence of the USA behind UNITA in Angola's civil war: the cartoon was published in 1986 in *Trud* ('Labour'), the newspaper of the Soviet trade-union movement.

Angola's development. South Africa gave more active support to Savimbi, making air attacks and punitive raids into Angola.

Neto's successor in Angola was José Eduardo dos Santos who, like Machel in Mozambique, tried to negotiate with South Africa. Civil war was draining the resources of the Angolan government and damaging the country's economy. Drought added to the difficulties and in 1984 it was necessary for Angola to import food. Though oil for a time sustained a deceptively healthy balance of trade, Angola now had grave social and economic problems which were similar to those of Mozambique. The Soviet Union, Spain and others provided relief supplies, but the life expectancy of Angolans in the mid-1980s was hardly more than 40 years and little different from that of Mozambicans. Peace was desperately needed. South Africa seemed determined to prevent it, resolutely supporting Savimbi and UNITA. Though Botha protested at the presence of Cuban troops in Angola and the Cuban–Angolan encouragement of rebel forces who wanted to free Namibia from South African rule, his true intention seemed to be to destroy Angola's socialist MPLA government. Speaking at a conference of the non-aligned movement in Angola in 1985, Robert Mugabe bitterly condemned not only South Africa's apartheid but South Africa's:

> aggression, intervention, interference, discrimination, destabilization and racism . . . a threat to international peace and security of the same genre and origin as Nazism.

Table 17.1 States in Africa: some comparative statistics

State	Population: Estimated, 1985 (millions)	Population: Annual growth 1980–5 (%)	Income per head, 1983 (US dollars)*	Number of people per doctor, c. 1980	Percentage of population literate over age 15, c. 1980†
Angola	8.6	2.7	1 032§	13 958	15
Botswana	1.1	3.6	920	7 378	52
Cameroon	9.6	2.3	830	14 303	55
Chad	5.0	2.1	100	44 160	6
Gambia	0.7	2.6	290	5 910	20
Ghana	12.8	3.2	320	7 245	43
Guinea	5.4	2.3	300	8 100	19
Guinea-Bissau	0.9	2.1	180	7 306	19
Kenya	20.3	4.0	344	8 336	47
Malawi	7.1	3.3	210	52 645	50
Mozambique	14.1	2.9	358‡	33 883	33
Nigeria	96.0	3.0	780‖	9 591	34

Sierra Leone	2.9	2.6	363	18 284	15
South Africa	32.9**	2.9	2 450	786#	79
Swaziland	0.6	2.9	890	5 790	56
Tanzania	21.7	3.2	240	20 687	74 (10+)
Uganda	14.7	2.8	220	22 281	53
Zaïre	33.1	3.0	160	15 065	55
Zambia	6.7	3.0	580	7 261	69
Zimbabwe	8.1	2.8	750	6 411	71

* At current market prices
† Except where indicated
‡ 1981
§ 1982
‖ Gross national product boosted by oil
Excluding black homelands
** Includes 5.4 million in 'independent' black homelands

The generally low incomes per head (cf. USA in 1983, 14 070) reflect the lack of earning power of most African countries, the limited establishment of industry, and still widespread subsistence farming which produces no measurable income.

Statistics from *Encyclopaedia Britannica*

Cuba had some 35 000 troops in Angola during 1987 and dos Santos had supplies from the Soviet Union. UNITA nevertheless drove deep into Angola's central highlands at the end of the year when South African intervention moved into a higher gear. Botha demanded that the Cubans leave Angola and claimed that his forces were seeking to destroy the bases of SWAPO, the nationalist organization which aimed to liberate Namibia. Early in 1988 the Soviets urged dos Santos to open talks with Savimbi. Savimbi in turn was pressed by the USA to negotiate. Washington hoped that matters in Angola could somehow be separated from the problems in Namibia and the tangled affairs of southern Africa with its deep divisions on race, and that a settlement could be reached. Like Zimbabwe and Mozambique, however, Angola stood in the front line of the confrontation between black Africa and white South Africa (see section 19.2). Though dos Santos and Savimbi seemed to be edging towards reconciliation, encouraged by the superpowers and mediators from the Organization of African Unity, serious obstacles remained. With its forces inside Angola protecting Namibia's northern frontier with black Africa, South Africa seemed in no hurry to allow Angola the peace it needed. Nor did Castro intend quickly to withdraw the Cuban forces which defended the MPLA government. Angola's future seemed now more than ever to depend on international agreement, but South Africa already showed an ominous lack of concern for international opinion.

17.6 A stricken continent

Nkrumah's vision of a united Africa came little closer to realization during the 30 years after Ghana became independent. The Organization of African Unity (OAU) was founded in 1963 to end colonialism and to promote inter-African co-operation. The Organization's failure to resolve problems in Biafra seemed symptomatic of its apparent powerlessness to overcome even the policial problems of the continent, however. Nor was it to the OAU's credit that Amin of Uganda was its Chairman in 1975–6. The civil war in Angola was just one of the many issues on which members of the OAU were divided. Of course, Africa is vast, its many new nations varied and its problems enormous, and 25 years is only a very short time in which to begin to judge the effectiveness of the OAU. Though famine in the 1980s provoked horror and outrage at the scale of the continent's suffering and a huge response from peoples outside Africa, in general the very size of Africa's problems made them difficult to comprehend, let alone solve.

Many African states began to look to the non-aligned movement for support, linking up with non-African states such as India, Cuba and Yugoslavia (see section 21.4). In 1986 the Chairmanship of the movement was assigned to Zimbabwe where Mugabe was beginning to impress as an international statesman. He helped focus even more attention on the racism of the government of South Africa, and he also drew attention to Africa's other problems, many of them economic. Aid packages and economic unions merely scraped the surface of the continent's needs. Nkrumah's hopes for prosperity were unfulfilled and, like

Ghana, Africa's other nations incurred crippling debts in their struggle to develop. Mugabe declared in 1985:

> It is scandalous . . . to expect Africa, a continent fighting for its survival, to shoulder a debt burden of 59 per cent of its export earnings.

Export earnings were still largely from primary products and low in value, while in the developed world there were still many financiers and businesspeople eager to make a profit from transactions involving the impoverished Africans.

Table 17.1 shows how many African states struggled in the 1980s, remote not only from Nkrumah's goals but also from even the modest comforts of which millions of their subjects dreamed. For all its struggles, most of Africa still had few resources with which to finance social advancement, and nowhere was the vast gulf between North and South more clearly on view than in the African continent (see section 21.3).

UNIT 18

Legacies of empire: 3 – international conflicts

18.1 A legacy of conflict

Twentieth-century world wars brutalized whole generations and left a legacy of violence; colonial empires left a legacy of pressing problems. The two together helped to make the world after 1945 stormy and bloody, the more so since it seemed to be awash with weapons which the superpowers and others with access to their manufacture were only too ready to distribute to clients and customers. A United Nations study in 1984 estimated that about 21 million lives had been lost since 1945 in various conflicts, an average of almost 2000 lives a day, more than half of them civilian. Some were wars of liberation, such as were fought by Polisario, the Eritreans and the Namibians. Some were civil wars such as that which deposed Somoza in Nicaragua. Many involved armies which crossed frontiers: those of the superpowers when the USA fought in Indo-China and the USSR in Afghanistan, and those of lesser states such as Tanzania intervening in Uganda. Other conflicts were difficult even to classify, involving terrorism, civil war, counter-strikes and foreign interference in a succession of bewildering developments and a tangle of conflicting interests such as came together in Lebanon in the 1980s. The constant factor was the mounting toll of casualties, not only the maimed and dead, but the uprooted, the bereaved and the embittered whose thirst for revenge fuelled future conflict. UN officials recorded 40 separate conflicts going on in 1983 alone.

Few statesmen could point the way to higher standards of human behaviour. President Reagan of the USA was perhaps not untypical when in 1986 he ordered the bombing of cities in Libya in retaliation for the involvement of Libyans in terrorist acts against American citizens, allegedly on the orders of Colonel Gadafy. Americans bombers killed some 37 people, many of them civilian, an action that Gorbachev of the Soviet Union called 'state terrorism' and about which many could still feel outrage. The Soviets had themselves used naked force in Hungary in 1956 and in Czechoslovakia in 1968. And Pieter Botha, Prime Minister and then President of South Africa, did not hesitate to strike violently against the independent states on his borders.

This unit will consider three areas – the Middle East, Cyprus and Indo-China – where the aftermath of empire produced conflict which was noteworthy even by the violent standards of the second half of the twentieth century, and where the struggle to establish new nations was particularly difficult.

18.2 The Middle East

18.2.1 The set pieces, Arab–Israeli wars 1948–73

The proclamation of Israel in 1948, on land that the Arab world believed rightly belonged to Palestinian Arabs, marked the beginning of a new struggle in the Middle East (see section 14.2.3). Arab–Israeli wars occurred in 1948–9, 1956, 1967 and 1973, but the intervals between the wars were far from peaceful and, until 1977, no Arab state even contemplated recognizing the rightful existence of Israel. At the heart of the problem was the creation of the state of Israel through the repression and expulsion of Palestinian Arabs. Many of the refugees, forced to reside outside Israel, and their descendants, in all numbering some 750 000 people, fought as *fedayeen* (militants) to regain their homeland, first as followers of the *Mufti*, their traditional leader. In desperation, they later turned to Al Fatah, a relatively moderate guerilla group, and to terrorist organizations such as Black September. In 1964 the Palestine Liberation Organization (PLO) was founded in an effort to unify anti-Israeli activity, but this was not easy. The PLO was weakened by splits between sections such as the Al-Fatah followers of Yasser Arafat, more extreme left-wing groups, and right-wing groups more acceptable to conservatives such as King Hussein of Jordan. Hussein expelled both the fedayeen and the PLO from Jordan in 1971, after Palestinian in-fighting brought his country to civil war.

Israel's Arab neighbours were members of the Arab League, founded in 1945 by Saudi Arabia, Iraq, Egypt, Syria and Lebanon, and by Jordanians and Palestinians who expected early independence. Jordan won it, and other Arab states joined the League later. An appendix was added to the League Covenant to assert the League's aim of freeing Palestine which, from 1948, meant dispossessing the Jews who had taken control of Israel. The Arabs failed to achieve this in the war of 1948–9. Indeed, as a result of that war, Israel grew larger (see fig. 14.3). The Arabs refused to sign a peace treaty: it seemed clear that the end of the war was only a truce, with existing borders policed uneasily by a UN Commission. In 1950 Britain, France and the USA guaranteed to preserve existing frontiers in a Tripartite Declaration which was no solution at all to the Palestinian problem. The Arabs looked for a new champion and found one in Nasser, President of Egypt from 1954.

Nasser obtained arms from Czechoslovakia and, when he offended Britain and France as well as threatening Israel, the scene was set for the Second Arab–Israeli confrontation, the Suez War of 1956 (see section 14.2.5). Israel again proved stronger than its enemies, overrunning Sinai. But American pressure forced Britain and France to call off their war against Egypt, and Israel, their ally, was persuaded to surrender its conquests. An uneasy calm returned, with

UNEF (United Nations Emergency Force) policing of the Egyptian–Israeli frontier and with the reopening of the Suez Canal which Nasser had blocked.

One effect of the war of 1956 was to confirm Soviet support for Egypt, though Moscow had not originally opposed the creation of Israel. Other results were the enhanced reputation of President Nasser and a union of Egypt and Syria in the United Arab Republic (UAR). The UAR lasted only from 1958 to 1961, when Syria broke away, but the two states continued to share a hatred of Israel – kept alive by skirmishing – and a determination to honour their pledges to the Palestinians. In May 1967 Nasser repeated that the issue was:

> the aggression which took place in Palestine in 1948 with the collaboration of Britain and the United States. It is the expulsion of the Arabs from Palestine, the usurpation of their rights, and the plunder of their property. It is the disavowal of all the UN resolutions in favour of the Palestinian people.

Egyptian forces massed in Sinai and Nasser closed the Gulf of Aqaba to Israeli shipping and rashly demanded that U Thant withdraw UN peace-keeping forces. Syrians meanwhile shelled Israeli settlements from the Golan Heights and skirmishing on the Syrian–Israeli border led to clashes in the air.

The Israelis made Moshe Dayan, hero of the 1956 war, Minister of Defence and on 5 June he decided to strike the first blows in the war that seemed to be brewing. Within three days Israeli forces again reached the Suez Canal, destroying Nasser's air force and many of his land forces. The Israelis routed the Jordanians on the West Bank and the Syrians in the Golan Heights, and after only three days of war Hussein capitulated. The Israelis now advanced towards Damascus, Syria's capital. On 9 June Nasser declared:

> Whoever starts with Syria will finish with Egypt.

But the next day Syria and Egypt surrendered and Israel had 'finished with' both of them. Nasser offered to resign but 'bowed' to popular demand that he remain in office. The Israeli victory was nevertheless a shattering one and they not only reopened the Gulf of Aqaba but also kept possession of the Golan Heights, the West Bank, Gaza and Sinai. Blocked again, the Suez Canal this time remained closed until 1975. Indeed, it was now a frontier. UN Security Council Resolution 242 in November 1967 required the:

> withdrawal of Israel armed forces from territories occupied in the recent conflict.

But the Israelis took no notice, just as the Arabs ignored the further demand in the Resolution for the:

> acknowledgement of the sovereignty, territorial integrity and political independence of every State in the area [of the Middle East].

Border skirmishes recurred from time to time and the UN in 1970 again had to arrange a ceasefire. The UN's Count Folke Bernadotte, who lost his life in 1948 at the hands of Jewish terrorists, had been followed by a succession of UN mediators seeking to perform the thankless task which now fell to Gunnar Jarring. He could make little headway. The Palestinians meanwhile turned increasingly to terror to draw attention to their plight. They hijacked aircraft and destroyed three airliners that had been hijacked to Jordan in 1970. In 1972 a Japanese suicide squad in support of the Palestinians arrived at Lydda airport, Tel Aviv, and gunned down a hundred people, of whom some 30 died. Later that year eleven Israeli athletes were killed at the Olympic Games in Munich when five terrorists also died in a shoot-out with the West German police. Israel itself was never slow to hit back, or hit first, exacting heavy casualties in air strikes and raids on suspected guerilla bases and refugee camps. Like war and attempts at mediation, terror left the Israeli–Palestinian problem unsolved, and even the sudden death of President Nasser in 1970 seemed at first to make little difference to the bloody stalemate, though Anwar Sadat, his successor, in 1972 sent home from Egypt Soviet military advisers.

October 1973 brought another Arab–Israeli confrontation: the Yom Kippur War – so named because the Arabs began the conflict with a surprise attack on Israel on Yom Kippur, the Jewish Day of Atonement. The early Arab advantage failed to last. Within three weeks a truce was arranged, by which time the Israelis were advancing into both Egypt and Syria. The UN again began creating demilitarized zones to keep Arabs and Israelis apart. Ominously, however, an Arab summit at Algiers before the end of 1973 declared:

> the ceasefire is not a peace. Peace requires . . . (1) the withdrawal of Israel from all the Arab occupied territories, and first and foremost from Jerusalem; (2) the restoration to the Palestinian people of their established national rights.

Frustrated by its own military failure, the Arab world now sharply increased the price of oil and, in some cases, began withholding supplies. This was a new weapon, intended to unbalance Western economies and to undermine the support which the USA and other powers habitually gave to Israel, ensuring its superiority in armaments. Like terror, it was not a very discriminating weapon and the effects of the shock to the world's economic system were grave (see section 21.1). It did not, however, secure the rights of Palestinians.

18.2.2 Israel: building the nation

The main influences in Israel to begin with were those of the western Ashkenazis who built Israel on largely European lines. Generous immigration policies, however, admitted Jews from all over the world and the balance eventually began to shift towards the Sephardis with their oriental traditions. To create one nation was a major task. In the mid-1980s the population topped four million – more than 80 per cent were Jews of varying origins and fewer than 20 per cent were Palestinian Arabs, many living on the West Bank which had been taken into Israel in 1967. Hebrew was developed as a national language, though it was still far from universal in the 1980s. But what most united the Jews in Israel, perhaps even more than religion, was their fierce patriotism in the face of external dangers.

The need for heavy spending on defence (about a quarter of GNP) distorted the economy. Since Israelis also demanded of their governments a European standard of living the results were debt, inflation and a reliance on support

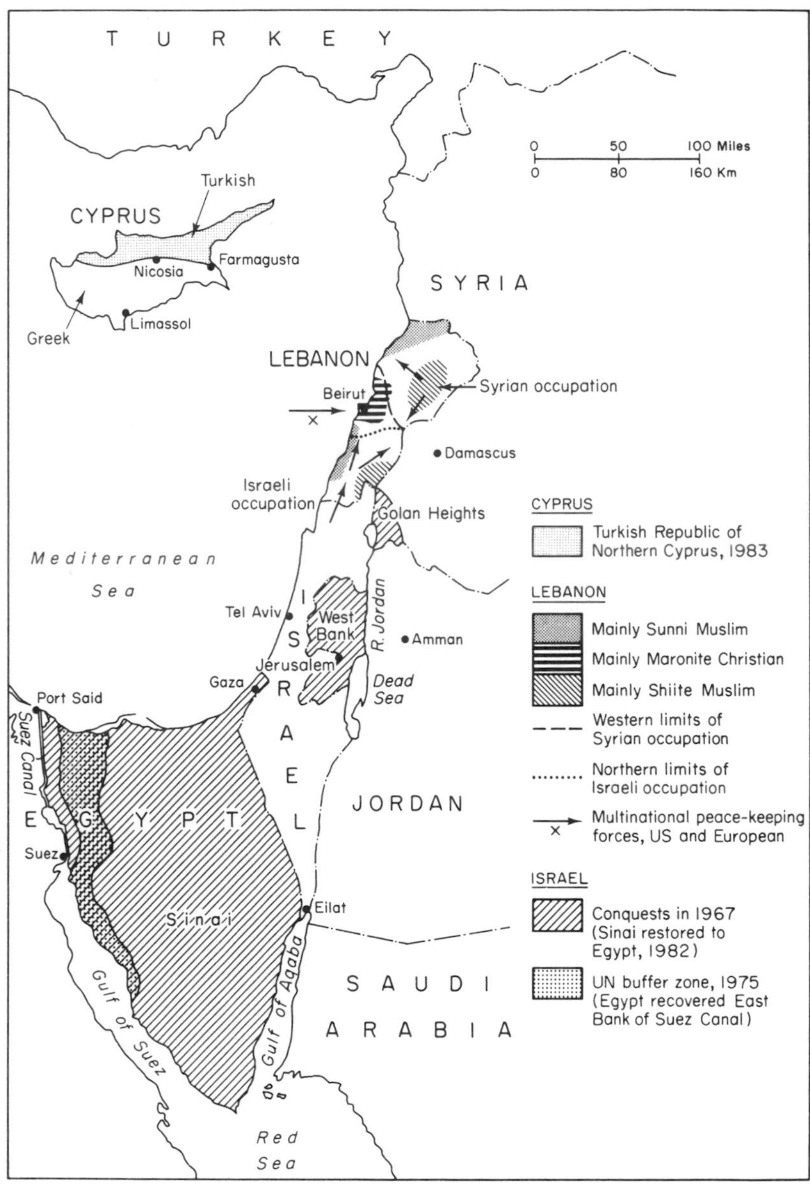

Fig. 18.1 The eastern Mediterranean from 1967

from the West. The external threat also brought hard-line attitudes which, especially after the end of the early dominance of the Labour Party, damaged Israel's reputation. In spite of the efforts of the peacemakers, these hard-liners (and profiteers) insisted in the 1980s on building Jewish settlements among the Palestinian people of the West Bank, and Israeli aggression in Lebanon at the same time did more to spread misery than to solve problems.

Israel's Labour Party (originally the Workers' Party, the *Mapai*) dominated Israeli politics from 1948 to 1977. Stable leadership which helped lay firm national foundations was provided by David Ben-Gurion. Born in Poland, Ben-Gurion was Prime Minister of Israel from 1948 to 1953 and from 1955 to his retirement in 1963. His policies were moderately socialist and he carried on the traditions of the Zionist movement, at first in partnership with Chaim Weizmann, President of Israel until his death in 1952. Foreign help was vital, much of it coming from the USA and until 1965 including an annual reparation of £14 million from West Germany. Ben-Gurion's vigorous economic and social policies promoted rapid development. About a thousand *kibbutzim* (co-operative villages) were founded and by the time of Ben-Gurion's retirement high capital investment had produced marked industrialization and impressive irrigation schemes 'to make the desert bloom'. On the other hand, there was already evidence that immigration was straining the economy – many Israelis, especially Sephardis, existed hardly above the poverty line. Moreover, though exports of diamonds, fruit and textiles were growing, Israel had a serious deficit in international trade.

Levi Eshkol took over as Prime Minister from 1963 to his death in 1969 when Golda Meir succeeded him. Both had come to Israel from the Soviet Union. Towards the end of the 1960s, however, Israel's Labour movement became faction-ridden. Even Ben-Gurion, in retirement, set up a breakaway group (the Rafi). Mrs Meir was criticized for doing little for the poor and the Sephardis. The Yom Kippur War united her supporters but after it she was criticized for inadequate preparations. She came into conflict with Dayan, her Defence Minister, and in 1974 she resigned. General Yitzhak Rabin became the last Labour Prime Minister before the elections of 1977 ended the Party's long tenure of power. Labour won only 32 seats in the Knesset (the Israeli Parliament) while Likud, a conservative alliance, had 43 seats and the support of other right-wing groups including some who were fearsomely orthodox and dogmatic in their religion. Menachem Begin became Prime Minister, a fervent Israeli nationalist born in Brest-Litovsk and, before independence, a leader of the terrorist organization Irgun Zvai Leumi. He narrowly survived the elections of 1981 and remained in office for six eventful years. He retired in 1983, leaving behind him controversial involvements in Lebanon which seemed to contradict his earlier role, with Sadat of Egypt, as peacemaker (see section 18.2.3). He left Israel in other difficulties too: inflation seemed to be out of control, and debts and the trading deficit had soared, making US aid even more essential. Moreover, the rapid Jewish settlement of the West Bank, often without regard for law or official policy, further embittered Israel's Arab population and stoked the fires of terrorism.

With Begin gone, national politics grew more confused and the nation more uncertain of itself. The elections of 1984 gave almost equal representation in the Knesset to Labour and to Likud, and returned many other small groups and parties. Israel seemed to be in crisis. A government of national unity seemed the best, perhaps the only, way forward. A Labour–Likud coalition was cobbled together, at first under the Prime Ministership of Labour's Shimon Peres, a defence expert in Ben-Gurion's governments and, like Ben-Gurion, Polish by birth. The coalition was to change its Prime Minister in mid-term, allowing Likud's Yitzhak Shamir to return to the office he had held briefly after Begin's retirement. Until the change-over in October 1986 Shamir was Foreign Minister. The coalition had constantly to paper over Labour–Likud differences. Visiting Israel in 1986, Britain's Shadow Foreign Secretary, Gerald Kaufman, found many problems unsolved, its people 'schizophrenic':

> They could not agree on answers to simple questions. Are we rich or poor? Do we want peace or war? Are we one nation of many kinds of Jews? Or are we many nations of Jews living in one land?

Yet Israel had survived for almost 40 difficult years, resisting all the efforts of its enemies to overthrow it. It had preserved its parliamentary system, achieved great economic advances with impressive progress in engineering, chemicals and mineral extraction as well as in agriculture, and provided a far from insignificant standard of living for most of its diverse population.

18.2.3 Egypt and Sadat's peace initiative: half a step forward

Though the United Arab Republic (UAR) had long ceased to exist, Nasser kept the title for Egypt as long as he lived. He ruled Egypt through the Arab Socialist Union, the only official party. Nasser had a genuine wish for the social and economic advancement of the Egyptian people and undertook useful land reform, irrigation schemes, agricultural development and industrialization, but, like Israel, Egypt was handicapped by heavy military spending. Nasser's ideas for uniting Egypt with Yemen and Iraq were even less successful than the short-lived UAR and, though he kept his standing as the outstanding leader of the Arab world, he seemed in the late 1960s to have become a prisoner of his own rhetoric. He might well have preferred a lower profile and greater concentration on domestic affairs, but he was trapped by his strong anti-Israeli image. Such was his standing, however, that he had comparatively little trouble with the strident Muslim Brotherhood of Islamic fundamentalists, and he was able to combine anti-communism at home with Soviet friendship abroad. It was even possible that, had he lived, he might have begun to achieve an Arab reconciliation with Israel.

Anwar Sadat, Egypt's Vice-President, was confirmed as President in 1970 with little opposition. The title 'UAR' was officially abolished in 1971 in favour of the name 'Arab Republic of Egypt', but Egypt remained a one-party state of the Arab Socialist Union, and Sadat, less radical than Nasser, moved cautiously. Eventually, however, he made major changes in the country's external relations. The treaty of friendship signed with the Soviet Union in 1971 was undermined, then cancelled in 1976, as Sadat moved closer to the USA. Sadat visited the USA in 1975 after Nixon's visit to the Middle East, and US–Egyptian relations grew even warmer when Carter became President. Sadat's most memorable achievement, however, was his peace initiative towards Israel. Though this was to win him, jointly with Begin, the Nobel Peace Prize of 1978, it was to cost Egypt most of its allies in the Arab world.

The uselessness of the Yom Kippur War and the busy shuttle diplomacy of Henry Kissinger, as well as the costs of the military burden, helped persuade Sadat of the need for real peace with Israel. At Geneva in 1975 agreement was reached on new demarcation lines around the Suez Canal, and the Canal was reopened. In November 1977 Sadat then made a startling announcement to Egypt's People's Assembly:

> I say now that I am ready to go to the ends of the earth [in pursuit of peace]. Israel will be astonished when it hears me saying now . . . that I am ready to go to their house, to the Knesset itself, and to talk to them.

Israel was astonished but Begin responded at once: later in November Sadat duly addressed the Knesset. The peace process had been opened. Sadat was bitterly accused of betrayal by Gadafy and Assad, leaders of Libya and Syria respectively, and by many members of the PLO. In both Egypt and Israel there were hard-liners hostile to any concessions that might be made. Begin nevertheless visited Cairo and, when negotiations began to lose momentum, Carter invited the leaders to Camp David in Maryland, where a framework for an Egyptian–Israeli settlement was agreed in September 1978. Sadat offered full recognition to Israel, a momentous breakthrough. In return Begin agreed to return Sinai to Egypt. At the same time Sadat felt obliged to bargain on behalf of the Palestinians, to try to secure them a homeland, at least Gaza and the West Bank. The PLO felt that this was too little; hard-line Israelis felt that it was too much. Carter worked vigorously to bring about agreement though confiding to his diary some exasperation with Begin, 'who is acting in a completely irresponsible way' (18 September). Members of the Arab League formed the Steadfastness Front, resolving 'to break off political and economic relations with the Egyptian regime' and to remove League headquarters from Cairo. But the Egyptian–Israeli Peace Treaty was nevertheless signed in March 1979. Sinai was evacuated and returned to Egypt on schedule in 1982.

By then, however, much had changed. Sadat was assassinated in October 1981 by Muslim fundamentalists who disliked his ties with Israel and with the West, whose values penetrated Egypt in 'the plastic invasion'. They also identified Sadat as the man who gave shelter to the Shah of Iran, deposed by fundamentalists (see section 20.2.1). Though he had brought peace to Egypt, Sadat's rule had often been authoritarian and had brought little improvement in Egypt's economy or in the lot of its people, while leaving the country isolated in the Arab world. Carter had meanwhile lost office in the USA, partly because he too had fallen victim to Islam, being unable to do much to resist anti-Americanism in Iran, to the dismay of the American public. In Israel, Dayan resigned from office, angered by the obstruction of hard-liners critical of the treaty he

Fig. 18.2 With President Carter applauding, Israeli Prime Minister Begin and Egyptian President Sadat embrace in the White House on 17 September 1978 after the Camp David summit was concluded with the signing of a 'Framework for Peace' in the Middle East.

had helped Begin to make. He died very soon after Sadat.

Begin's role now seemed ambiguous. In spite of treaty concessions regarding the future 'self-governing authority' of the West Bank and Gaza, Israel seemed in no hurry to make changes there. Indeed, in the West Bank, Israeli settlement not only continued but accelerated. In 1981 Begin declared that the Golan Heights would never be restored to Syria and in 1982 he launched ferocious new strikes against PLO bases in Lebanon. When he retired in 1983, the Palestinians had gained virtually nothing.

Vice-President Hosni Mubarak succeeded Sadat. At home he restored a multi-party parliament in 1984, his conservative National Democratic Party winning an impressive victory over the even more right-wing New Wafd, while parties of the left were routed. Mubarak nevertheless faced unrest and violence from militant supporters of Islam and he had to tread carefully, especially when the army threatened rebellion in 1986. The economy meanwhile began to benefit from Sadat's development of oil production, though the trade balance continued to be adverse. Hussein of Jordan restored relations with Egypt in 1984 and moved cautiously towards Sadat-like relations with Israel. By 1986 it seemed that other Arab states were preparing to readmit Egypt to the Arab League, though deep differences remained. Syria and Libya were well to the left of Egypt and Jordan: Syria was virtually a one-party state of the National Progressive Front, led since 1971 by President Assad and with close links with the Soviet Union, whereas Jordan was governed by the monarchy, without political parties, and still markedly pro-British. The divisions in the Arab world were reflected in the disarray that persisted among the Palestinians, now much scattered as well as homeless.

18.2.4 Palestine and Lebanon: a nation denied and a state destroyed

The setting up of the PLO failed to cloak divisions among Palestinians as to how a Palestinian state might be achieved. Al Fatah came to dominate the PLO, and Arafat was widely regarded as the leader of Palestinian nationalism, even gaining UN recognition in 1976. Some Palestinians disputed his leadership, however. From early dissenters like Black September to the Abu Nidal group in the mid-1980s there were those who demanded more extreme action than Arafat seemed to offer: nothing less than a wave of terror against Israelis and all who supported them. The Lydda airport raid of 1972 was followed by other attacks on airports, aircraft, property and people, not just in Israel but throughout Europe, and further outrages occurred in efforts to secure the release of terrorists who had been captured. In 1976 the Popular Front for the Liberation of Palestine hijacked a plane to Entebbe in Uganda where Amin seemed welcoming. Israeli commandos rescued the Israeli hostages, a raid into Africa showing boldness and skill as well as Israel's determination to match violence with violence. Amin's reputation sank lower and terrorists were temporarily taken aback. But the terrorists were not long deterred and the hijacking, kidnapping, murder and explosions went on.

It was usually argued that the terrorism was counter-productive, alienating world sympathy even while drawing attention to the plight of the Palestinians, many of whom suffered in squalid refugee camps. Expelled from Jordan in 1971, many Palestinians moved to Lebanon and the PLO made its main base in southern Lebanon. This development automatically made the area a target for Israeli counter-strikes, the ferocity of which in the mid-1970s helped reduce Lebanon to civil war. Yet again the scale of the Middle East tragedy increased.

From the start of its independence, the politics of Lebanon were delicately balanced (see section 15.2.1). The President was usually a Christian and the Prime Minister a Muslim, reflecting the main, roughly equal religions in Lebanese society. But the Muslims were divided between Sunni and Shiite sects and their differences were eventually inflamed by controversy about the liberation of Palestine. Of the two, the Shiites were the more militant. The Christians too developed a militant force, the Phalange. The multi-party Assembly elected in 1972 included 20 Sunni Muslims, 19 Shiites, 6 Druse (a minority people), 30 Maronite (Roman Catholic) Christians and 24 Christians of various other sects. The Israelis bombed Palestinian bases in Lebanon as early as 1968 and when the PLO arrived in force after 1970 the strikes became more frequent. Civil war broke out in 1975 when Palestinians were ambushed in a Christian part of Beirut, Lebanon's capital, and Shiites fought back against Christian Phalangists. Syria sent in troops to protect fellow Muslims and restore peace, but peace was not restored and during the next dozen years the conflict – into which Israeli forces soon entered – claimed over 100 000 lives. United Nations forces also arrived to try to keep the factions apart, especially in Beirut which became

Table 18.1 The Palestinians: a scattered nation, 1982

Host country	Palestinian people and refugees	PLO guerillas after expulsion from the Lebanon
Israel*	1 235 000	—
Jordan	1 161 000	260
Kuwait, Gulf States and Arab Emirates	384 400	—
Lebanon	347 000	—
Syria	215 000	6 450
Saudi Arabia	127 000	—
USA	c. 100 000	—
Egypt	45 000	—
Libya	23 000	—
Iraq	20 000	130
Yemen (Aden)	—	1 100
Tunisia	—	1 000
Yemen Arab Republic	—	850
Algeria	—	600
Sudan	—	500
Elsewhere	140 000	—

* In addition to the population listed, Israel had a population of c. 600 000 Palestinian Arabs in the occupied territories (West Bank, East Jerusalem and Gaza - occupied from 1967 onwards).

Adapted from M. Kidron and D. Smith, *The War Atlas* (Pluto Press and Pan Books, 1983)

divided by a UN 'green line' between the Muslim West and the Christian East.

In 1978 Israel had begun occupation in a corner of south Lebanon where a Christian militia a year later was encouraged to proclaim 'Free Lebanon'. In 1982 Begin went further, occupying much of southern Lebanon in ferocious pursuit of the PLO, many of whose fighters were eventually trapped in West Beirut and their expulsion insisted on by the Israelis. Syria meanwhile held much of north and east Lebanon, while the rest was in the hands of various sectarian militias. Only token unity was maintained by the politicians jostling for power in government. Americans and Europeans became involved, combining peace-keeping with the protection of their interests and their nationals, and becoming targets for Islamic attacks and hostage-taking. Efforts to mediate often seemed less than even-handed and neither Syrians nor Americans could do much to heal Lebanese divisions. Ceasefires and truces lasted at best only months: from 1975 to 1984 there were 179. The expulsion of PLO guerillas from West Beirut in 1982 did little to halt the anarchy, and bitterness simply increased when Phalangists massacred Palestinian refugees later that year in the

Israeli-supervised camps of Chabra and Chatila in West Beirut.

The election of Amin Gemayal as President of Lebanon in 1982 brought a flicker of hope. The Gemayal family had long been involved in Lebanese politics and was prominent in the Phalange, but Amin Gemayal, a parliamentarian since 1970, was a respected moderate. He appealed for the withdrawal from Lebanon of Syrians, Israelis and Palestinians but for a continued UN presence, while he tried to bring about a coalition government which would represent all sections. Violence continued to erode whatever was achieved, even causing the withdrawal from Beirut of some UN peace-keepers. Israel began a rather grudging withdrawal after Begin retired, calling on the USA to ensure that Syria withdrew too. But Syria stayed and Israel continued retaliatory strikes into Lebanon in response to Palestinian and Muslim raids, and in defence of the nine-mile security zone in southern Lebanon which the Israelis insisted on holding.

Terror seemed only to intensify in and around Lebanon and the Middle East. In 1985 alone there were related attacks and killings at Frankfurt, Rome and Vienna airports, while hijacking took a new turn when gunmen seized and held for several days the cruise liner *Achille Lauro* in the eastern Mediterranean. Thirty-nine US hostages were seized in Beirut and released only through the good offices of Assad of Syria. Other foreign hostages had been held since 1984, however, and the continuing attacks not only on Israelis but also on Americans and Europeans undermined Arafat's standing and angered the moderate governments of Egypt and Jordan. The PLO condemned much of the terror but seemed unable to control it; Israel nevertheless bombed the Organization's new headquarters in Tunisia, apparently with the connivance of the USA.

Palestinians and the Islamic world in general were convinced that Israel was a creation of the West, an atonement for the West's own crimes against the Jews but one secured, conveniently, at the expense of the Palestinian Arabs. Sadat's initiative had not even brought about self-government for the Palestinians in the West Bank and Gaza, which had remained the occupied territories of Israel since 1967. As more Jewish settlers moved in and their own future remained bleak, the Palestinians in the occupied territories grew more restless. By the end of 1987 they were beginning to express their opposition to Israeli rule in an *intifada* or uprising, Palestinian youths in particular taking to the streets to hurl stones and abuse. Though the demonstrators were poorly armed, the riots began to seem like a rebellion, ambushes and other outrages endangering Jewish lives. Shamir sent in more Israeli troops. But Israeli soldiers were not trained in police work nor in handling civilian demonstrators, and their sometimes vicious counter-attacks with live ammunition as well as rubber bullets and clubs took a steady toll of Palestinian lives. The film taken of brutal reprisals against Palestinians, many of them only youngsters, incensed the outside world and further divided Israeli Jews, emphasizing the divisions within the government between the hard-line Shamir and more conciliatory Peres. United States backing for Israel diminished, though in January 1988 the USA still vetoed a

UN Security Council resolution condemning Israeli attacks upon Lebanese territory.

George Shultz, the US Secretary of State, embarked on another round of shuttle diplomacy early in 1988 to try to bring peace to Israel, Lebanon and the Middle East as a whole. Reagan had earlier taken the view that terrorists were waging an Islamic war against Americans, masterminded by Iran, Syria and Libya (see Unit 20), and in 1986 he had singled out Libya for special 'retribution' – always a ready excuse for further killing. But his Presidency would end in some triumph if the USA were able to bring about a settlement of the problems of the Palestinians, and the release of hostages still held in Lebanon. Though most of the hostages were American they now included Terry Waite, the envoy of the Archbishop of Canterbury. Waite had won a reputation as a negotiator with various sectional groups in Lebanon and had secured the release of a few hostages before he himself was held early in 1987. Not unusually, who held him and where was a mystery: it was one of the difficulties in Lebanon that no one group nor any government – not even that of Syria – was able to exercise authority over the country as a whole. Those jostling for power included rival Palestinian factions and Islamic groups, whose precise allegiances were shadowy but some of whom seemed to have close links with Iran.

Shultz took some encouragement from his contacts with Egypt, Jordan and Syria. In Israel, while Peres seemed willing to make concessions, Shamir stood by the traditional Likud policy of not giving in to the Arabs. Like others before him, Shultz found universal agreement hard to come by even within governments, let alone among the many unofficial organizations and factions. Shamir visited Washington in March 1988. At that time *Tikkun*, a Jewish newspaper in the USA, reflected the anxieties of American Jews about the brutal confrontations between Shamir's government and Palestinians in the occupied territories when it spoke of 'the greatest crisis facing the American Jewish community since the Holocaust'. Shamir was unrepentant. He gave little or no encouragement to the US peace plan though Reagan and Shultz refused to abandon it. Reagan still hoped to make his final year as President a year of agreements which would include a round-table conference in Geneva on the Middle East. Shamir merely tightened the Israeli grip on Gaza and the West Bank and curbed the activities of news reporters there. Before the end of March, Israelis also advanced from their security zone in southern Lebanon to inflict more punishment on what they claimed were Shiite bases.

Like South Africans, many Israelis saw themselves as defending their country against a host of enemies, against whom they struck out viciously. They also became suspicious of the media and of foreign reporters, who drew attention not only to the ferocity with which Shamir dealt with Palestinian demonstrators in the occupied territories, but also to the squalor in which Palestinians lived there. The Israeli judiciary also jailed Mordechai Vanunu for eighteen years in 1988 on the charge of treason. Vanunu had a bad conscience about his work in Israel's nuclear research centre at Dimona and, after resigning, he had given information about it to the *Sunday Times* in London. The newspaper cal-

Table 18.2 States in the Middle East: some comparative statistics

State	Population: Estimated, 1985 (millions)	Population: Annual growth, 1980–5 (%)	Income per head, 1983 (US dollars)*	Number of people per doctor, c. 1980	Percentage of population literate over age 15, c. 1980
Cyprus					
Greek	0.4	1.2	3 720	1 060	93
Turkish	0.2	—	1 558‡		
Egypt	48.5	2.5	730	815	44
Iran†	45.0	3.1	3 830	2 590	43
Iraq†	15.7	3.3	2 300‡	1 772	24
Israel	4.3	1.9	5 340	403	93
Jordan	2.6	2.7	1 710	1 711	68
Kuwait†	1.9	6.6	18 180	686	67
Lebanon	2.7	−0.2§	1 750	530	77
Libya	3.8	5.1	7 500	660	58
Saudi Arabia†	11.2	4.0	10 440	2 606	25
Syria	10.3	3.3	1 680	2 236	66

* At current market prices
† Major oil producers and members of OPEC (Egypt, an associate member of OPEC)
‡ 1981
§ Population fell mainly because of emigration and civil war

Iran and Iraq were at war from September 1980 (see section 20.2.3).

Statistics from *Encyclopaedia Britannica*

culated that Israel was beginning to stockpile nuclear weapons and already had 200 by 1986. Though not too dismayed at this further warning to the Arabs, the Israeli authorities had seized Vanunu illegally and brought him back for trial.

In November 1988 the most significant political development yet in the long saga of conflict between Palestinians and Arabs took place. The Palestine Liberation Organization declared itself willing to accept a two-state solution to the conflict, and issued a declaration of independence for the new state of Palestine, to be based on the West Bank and Gaza strip. It also implicitly recognized the validity of the state of Israel, by accepting previous United Nations resolutions on the controversy, and also renounced acts of terrorism, pending an appropriate Israeli response. The Israeli government dismissed this initiative as a propaganda exercise, and when elections in Israel in the same month brought the right-wing Likud party back to power the venture seemed doomed to fail because of Israeli intransigence. However, the rest of the world, with the notable exception of the United States, either welcomed the PLO's initiative or moved rapidly, as did the Arab states (including Jordan and Egypt), to recognize the new state, which still of course remained under illegal Israeli occupation. It remained to be seen whether the new administration of President Bush, recently elected in the United States, would be as friendly to Israel as the Reagan administration had been. Many external observers believed that time seemed to be running out for Israel to accommodate Palestinian aspirations, and warned of yet another Middle East war if it refused to budge.

18.3 Cyprus

Cyprus, like Lebanon, was divided between Christians and Muslims with disastrous results. The Greek Orthodox Christians spoke Greek and out-numbered the Turkish-speaking Muslims by about four to one. The cultural conflict was made worse by the campaign for *enosis* (union with Greece) waged by *Ethniki Organosis Kyprion Agonista* (EOKA). In 1955, under the leadership of George Grivas who had served in the Greek army, EOKA launched a campaign of guerilla action against British rule and the Turkish minority. When Archbishop Makarios III, the spiritual leader of the Greek Cypriots and another advocate of independence, was suspected of encouraging EOKA, the British deported him to the Seychelles in 1956. But EOKA's violence and the bloodshed roused a response from Turkish Cypriots. They set up a similar organization which in 1958 called for the partitioning of the island. A pamphlet was circulated to the Muslims:

> The day is near when you will be called upon to sacrifice your life in the PARTITION struggle . . . All Turkdom, right and justice and God are with you. PARTITION OR DEATH.

It was to Makarios that the British had to turn to settle their Cypriot problem. He was brought back to negotiate for Cypriot independence, but the seeds of future division had already been planted.

Makarios was elected President at the end of 1959 and in August 1960 Cyprus became an independent republic within the Commonwealth. Fazil Kutchuk became Vice-President and every effort was made to reassure the Turkish community with generous Turkish representation in the government, the civil service and the police. Each community had the right to veto unfavourable laws. The concessions displeased EOKA but Makarios had turned his back on enosis and for a short time there was uneasy peace. The safeguards in the constitution threatened to make it unworkable, however. When Makarios tried to amend it, EOKA renewed its violence, and in 1963 the island plunged into civil war. United Nations forces arrived to restore peace: it was the start of a long vigil. Greece and Turkey took the side of their respective communities, threatening to go to war themselves in 1967 and seriously weakening NATO to the anxiety of their allies. UN mediation averted open war but Cyprus remained disturbed. Makarios was trapped between militant EOKA and apprehensive Turks, and several attempts were made to assassinate him. In 1970 the Turks elected their own assembly in the north of the island and rejected the authority of the Cypriot parliament. Grivas returned to Cyprus to launch a new offensive and, though Grivas died in 1974, Makarios in that year was driven into exile by a military coup partly engineered in Athens.

Only Makarios could command widespread support in Cyprus and he returned to power within six months. By then it was too late to reassure the Muslims. Turkey had sent troops to the island and helped set up the Turkish Federated State of Cyprus in the north, claiming more than a third of the country. Almost 250 000 Greek Cypriots had fled southwards while immigrants from Turkey reinforced the new Federated State. UN forces helped to curb conflict but Makarios died in 1977 before he could reconcile the two Cypruses. The new President, Spyros Kyprianou, was no more successful and in 1983 the Turkish area was renamed the Turkish Republic of Northern Cyprus under the leadership of Rauf Denktash. Only Turkey recognized it and – Northern Cyprus being much the poorer part of the island – provided economic aid. Some 3000 UN troops remained as peace-keepers while Perez de Cuellar, like earlier UN Secretaries, searched for a settlement. He set up a summit in 1985 between Kyprianou and Denktash but talks broke down without agreement on the reunification of Cyprus. The problems were by now even more severe. On top of Muslim fears and Greek resentment at the 25 000 Turkish soldiers on the island, there was now the problem of resettling Greeks from Northern Cyprus. Constitutional wrangling made less progress than in 1959–60, and separation persisted.

Each part of Cyprus meanwhile practised its own multi-party parliamentary democracy. Kyprianou's conservative supporters were returned to power in 1981, though there was a vote of over 30 per cent for the Communist Party which seemed more sympathetic than the President to the Turkish case. Further elections in 1985 kept Kyprianou's supporters in power. In Northern Cyprus, the National Turkish Party was the largest, and Denktash himself was hardly challenged.

EOKA declined after the death of Grivas, and support for enosis seemed to evaporate. Cyprus was quieter after the partition of 1975, though the UN green line between the rival communities seemed essential to keep it so. Like that of Lebanon, the Cypriot economy was set back by the troubles, the flow of tourists reduced. A deficit persisted on the balance of trade, even in the more prosperous Greek part of the island which exported textiles and a little machinery as well as Cyprus's traditional fruit and vegetables. In curbing inflation and unemployment, however, Cyprus was even more successful than much of Europe in the years after 1975. But proximity to Lebanon and to Israel also involved Cyprus in the troubles of the Middle East, as it became a staging-post for the West and for Arab guerillas alike. For the USA and Britain, moreover, Cyprus was an important listening-post, since it was close to the Soviet bloc, and bases had been kept there even after independence. Confronted by all these factors, state-building in Cyprus was fraught with difficulties - even its capital, Nicosia, was divided in the mid-1980s in much the same way as Beirut.

The UN Secretary-General had meanwhile kept up the pressure for reconciliation between the two Cypruses. A federal solution began to seem likely during 1987 but it was rejected by Kyprianou. Only Turkey had yet recognized the Republic of Northern Cyprus but outside opinion was growing more sympathetic towards Turkish Cypriots, especially when 1988 brought repaired relations between Greece and Turkey, easing the anxieties within the NATO alliance. In February 1988 Greek Cypriots chose not to re-elect Kyprianou to the Presidency, returning instead the little-known George Vassiliou, an economist who had been educated in Hungary and who had the support of the left. Vassiliou seemed likely to adopt a more conciliatory attitude towards Turkish Cypriots, though his electoral majority was not sufficient for him to move other than cautiously. Turkey expressed some willingness to reduce its army of about 30 000 in Northern Cyprus. The UN prepared to launch a new initiative to restore unity to Cyprus, and at last hopes grew of the settlement of at least one of the problems of the eastern Mediterranean.

18.4 The war in Vietnam and the rest of Indo-China

18.4.1 Escalation: the domino theory

The Geneva Agreements of 1954 might have enabled Indo-China to make a fairly normal attack on the problems of nation-building in spite of the temporary division of Vietnam (see section 15.2.2), but United States intervention helped to ensure that this would not be the case. Not until 1975 did the last US forces leave Vietnam after years of horrendous warfare, during which US politicians, generals and the CIA all did their best to stop communism without much regard for the consequences for the people of Indo-China. Underlying US policy was the 'domino theory', developed by Eisenhower and explained by one of his spokesmen:

> If we let South Vietnam fall, the next domino Laos, Cambodia, Burma, and on into the sub-continent would go, the Philippines would go and possibly even Australia and New Zealand.

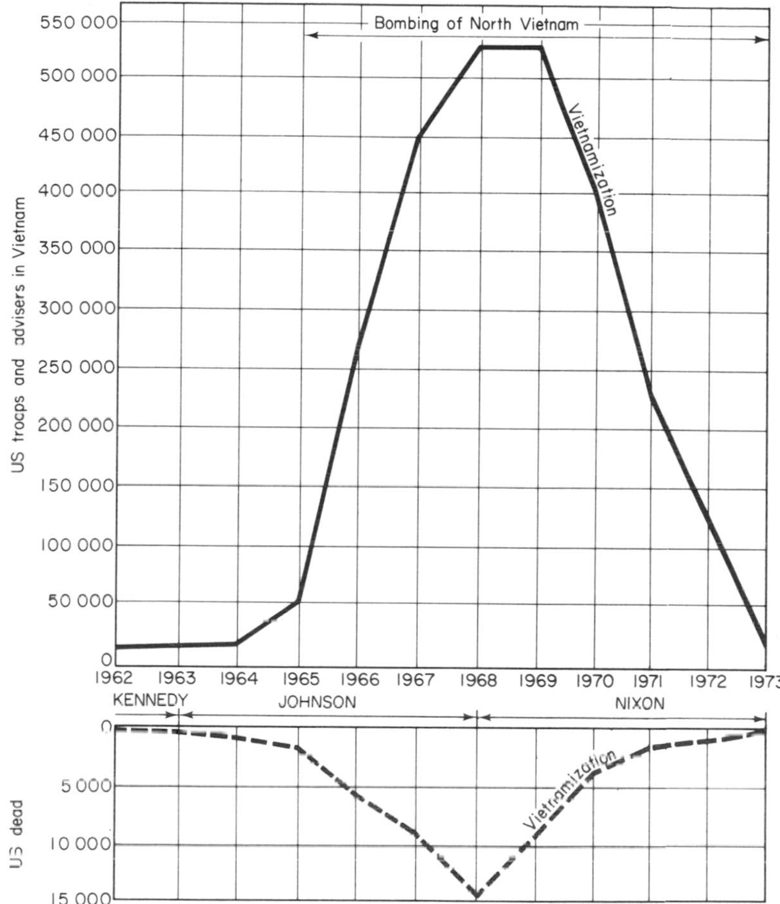

Fig. 18.3 US involvement in Vietnam, 1962–73

Having conjured up this vision of communism knocking over one domino after another the Americans dragged all of Indo-China into their nightmare. They started from the joint assumptions that, whatever the case in North Vietnam (see section 11.4.3), the people of South Vietnam did not want to become communist, and that the USA should support any government there that was not Marxist. When South Vietnam in 1955 rejected Bao Dai in favour of a republic, this meant supporting President Ngo Dinh Diem.

The rule of Diem, a Roman Catholic, was corrupt, repressive, and offensive to the majority Buddhist population. From 1960 the President faced a National

Liberation Front (NLF), not wholly communist but in favour of a united Vietnam, better government and the withdrawal of foreigners – especially the Americans that Kennedy sent to advise Diem. The fighting wing of the NLF came to be known as the Vietcong, which was encouraged by the North and its Vietminh and which by 1963 could muster about 25 000 guerillas. Diem was overthrown and murdered in 1963 by a military coup at which the CIA seemed to have connived. Only a few weeks later Kennedy was assassinated in the USA.

There followed a crucial period in the development of Vietnam's tragedy. President Johnson seemed to accept the domino theory as readily as had Eisenhower and Kennedy, while military leaders jostling for power in Saigon (South Vietnam's capital), who represented Washington in Indo-China, also influenced decisions. The Vietcong grew stronger and the USA sent in men and supplies to try to keep the domino upright. By August 1964 the Vietcong con-

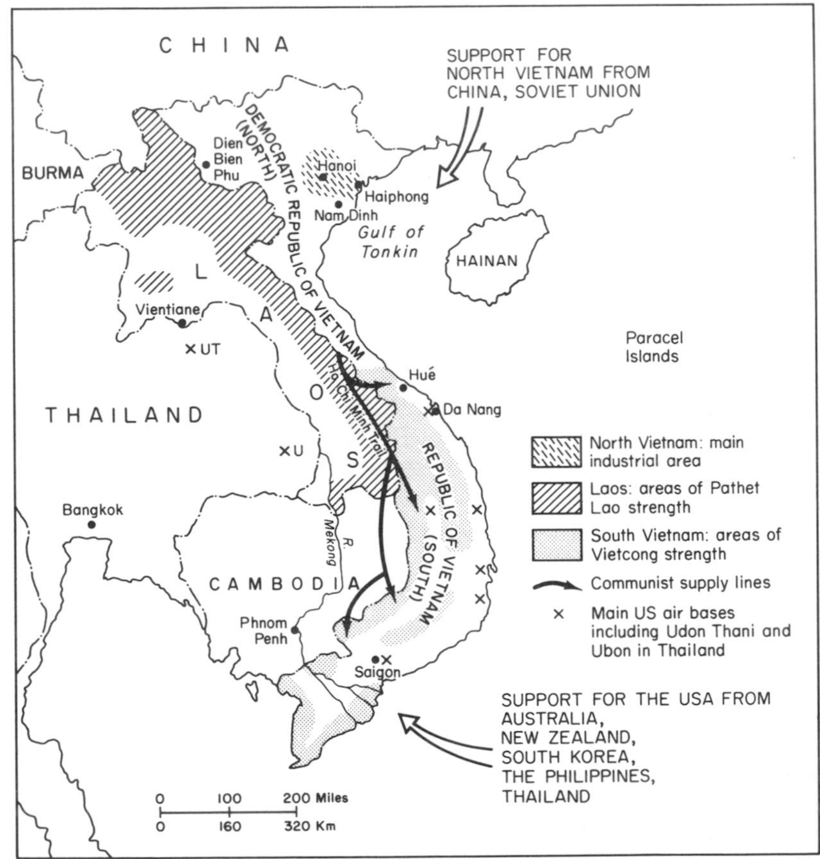

Fig. 18.4 Indo-China in the mid-1960s

trolled perhaps 40 per cent of South Vietnamese villages, and US anxiety grew. North Vietnamese patrol boats in that month ambushed two US destroyers in the Gulf of Tonkin. An alleged second attack a few days later led to massive support in Congress for President Johnson's demands for 'all necessary steps, including the use of armed forces' against Ho Chi Minh and North Vietnam. Thus began the large-scale build-up of US forces, the US bombing of the North and, in effect, the Vietnam War where there had been previously only civil war in the South. It later appeared that no second attack on US warships in the Gulf of Tonkin had taken place at all: the naval officers misread their sonar equipment and opened fire into the darkness. President Johnson was alleged to have told George Ball, Under-Secretary of State:

> Hell, those dumb stupid sailors were just shooting at flying fish.

Johnson was nevertheless willing enough to use the occasion to strengthen presidential power. Congress co-operated and the USA poured forces into Vietnam, assisted by Australia, New Zealand and South Korea. In 1966 the USA and the Vietcong both had around 300 000 troops in the field.

General Nguyen van Thieu was meanwhile emerging from the power struggle in Saigon. In 1965 he led the National Leadership Committee with the chief of the air force, Nguyen Cao Ky, as Prime Minister. When elections were held in 1967, Thieu became President and Ky Vice-President, winning the most votes though hardly more than a third of those cast. The war now dominated everything. North Vietnam sent men and supplies to the South, many along the Ho Chi Minh Trail, while the US bombing of North Vietnam was so intensive that, in weight of bombs dropped, it soon exceeded the bombing of Germany in the Second World War. Early in 1968 General Giap organized the Tet Offensive against Saigon, Huć and other South Vietnamese towns, stretching the combined forces of the three-quarters of a million by now in the South Vietnamese army, the half a million Americans and 50 000 other allies. The Tet Offensive had little long-term success but the communists' ability to mount such an attack in spite of the massive air superiority of the Americans simply added to the demands now growing both within and beyond the USA to end the war.

The communist war effort was sustained by supplies from the USSR and China, but it was the Vietnamese themselves who frustrated the USA, no matter what the cost. Massive bombing, anti-personnel weapons, napalm and other terror weapons, and the use of chemicals to defoliate trees the better to expose Vietcong guerillas could still not win the war for Thieu and the Americans. Already widely condemned, Washington dared not use nuclear weapons. Johnson chose not to seek re-election in 1968, though he halted the bombing and began exploring the possibilities for peace before he left office. He also recalled General Westmoreland who, to the end, had kept his glowing faith in the US mission in Vietnam and in the likelihood of eventual victory. Westmoreland blamed the press for the USA's lack of success. Deep in gloom in this final year in office, Johnson tended to blame the fickleness of the American public, many of whom now denounced the war. Americans were being killed in Vietnam at a rate of about a thousand a month and many Americans were also deeply disturbed by the horrors against civilian Vietnamese for which the USA seemed responsible: investigations later revealed an incident at My Lai early in 1968 when US troops ran amok, murdering more than a hundred Vietnamese including women and children. It was already suspected that such incidents were occurring on a wide scale, on top of the almost conventional wartime atrocities to be seen on television. Nixon's success in winning the Presidency at the end of 1968 owed a good deal to hopes for an end of the involvement in Indo-China.

18.4.2 The American withdrawal

Nixon wanted peace, but he also wanted to beat the communists. The people of Indo-China again suffered from American policy. The key to Nixon's policy was Vietnamization – that the Vietnamese should undertake their own defence against communism, allowing the Americans to come home. Unfortunately Thieu's government seemed no more fitted to achieve this than was Diem's. So Nixon's strategy revolved around more bombing, not only of the North but also of Cambodia where the communists had bases and supply lines and where the Americans became enamoured of Lon Nol's anti-communist government. By

Fig. 18.5 June 1972: the horror of the war in Vietnam. This photograph was taken at Trang Bang in South Vietnam, immediately after an ill-targeted napalm strike by a US Skyraider plane. The child in the centre had torn off burning clothing, and the children were joined in flight by South Vietnamese soldiers.

the end of 1970, half of the US troops had left Vietnam but the fighting and bloodshed in Indo-China were spreading.

Throughout the conflict in Vietnam there had been parallel struggles between communists and anti-communists in Laos and Cambodia. In Laos, the main contest was between the royalists, led by Souvanna Phouma, and the communist Pathet Lao, led by Souphanouvong, a deserter from the royal family. Army officers spiced the conflict with abortive military coups, trying to follow in the footsteps of Thieu and gain American allies. The CIA intrigued against the communists but Laotians were generally left to deal with their own problems. Like the Vietcong, the Pathet Lao made steady progress in the countryside.

In Cambodia, Prince Norodam Sihanouk preserved a more stable regime from independence in 1953 to 1970. He took a neutralist stance, critical of US activities in Vietnam but anti-communist. On a visit to him in early 1968, an American observer reported to his government:

> I came away deeply convinced . . . that Sihanouk's decisions and attitudes, however bizarre, are shaped by intense and deeply rooted nationalism in which ideology has little or no part.

Cambodian armed forces were weak and Sihanouk could do little to stop the North Vietnamese and the Vietcong using the Ho Chi Minh Trail in the east of his country, but he objected to US counter-attacks in that area and US–Cambodian relations were consequently strained. In 1970 Sihanouk was overthrown by anti-communist and anti-Vietnamese republicans, encouraged by the CIA. General Lon Nol became Prime Minister but needed South Vietnamese army support to keep him in power. Nixon sent US forces for a brief time to help him root out the communist opposition, the Khmer Rouge. American bombers also struck viciously into Cambodia in his support. The Khmer Rouge nevertheless grew quickly and spread throughout the country, while the South Vietnamese forces, as so often in Vietnam, resorted to pillaging and looting in preference to more dangerous engagement.

Sihanouk was meanwhile welcomed by Mao Tse-tung in Peking and, though condemned to death by Lon Nol in Phnom Penh, he set up an alternative government in exile. Many of the Khmer Rouge seemed to want neither Sihanouk nor Lon Nol but a Marxist system, however, and the USSR refused to recognize Sihanouk.

Plunged into civil war, Cambodia faced economic ruin. US bombing destroyed many of its rubber plantations; rice paddies became battlefields; and the tourist trade collapsed. The destruction of Cambodia went on steadily and later commentators had no hesitation in laying the blame on Nixon and on Kissinger, the President's Special Adviser on National Security until promoted to Secretary of State in 1973. For their part the US leaders calculated that Vietnamization would be effective if there were pro-American regimes in the neighbouring states, and they assumed that their operations in Cambodia were therefore justified though Kissinger had asserted, soon after Sihanouk was deposed:

> we had nothing to do with what happened in Phnom Penh.

Meanwhile, Nixon and Kissinger continued withdrawal from Vietnam. Bombing North Vietnam and Cambodia failed to stop communist pressure and US planes now mined the waters around North Vietnam's ports. When bombing raids were officially halted in 1972 – the year Nixon visited Peking and Moscow – raids went on unofficially, the air crews apparently unwilling to stop. Indiscipline in South Vietnam was not unusual and, when the war ended, serious drugs problems remained among both Americans and Vietnamese, many of whom were scarred and brutalized amid the carnage. After a final crescendo of bombing, a ceasefire was secured at Paris in January 1973 and Kissinger was given the Nobel Peace Prize for his efforts to end the Vietnamese War. North Vietnam's negotiator, Le Duc Tho, refused to share the prize. Nixon hurriedly withdrew the last US combat troops in February 1973, though American advisers remained at Thieu's side until 1975.

Except for the Americans, the ceasefire in practice meant very little. Canada, Hungary, Poland and Indonesia reluctantly provided a thousand truce supervisors, and agreed to join the two Vietnams and the permanent members of the UN Security Council in trying to find a final Vietnamese settlement. Vietnamization had failed utterly, however: the North Vietnamese made steady inroads into the South and defeated the South's army. Thieu resigned, the last Americans were evacuated and Saigon fell in April 1975. It was renamed Ho Chi Minh City soon afterwards and in 1976 the whole of Vietnam was proclaimed the Socialist Republic of Vietnam. The domino had fallen after all.

Problems of reconstruction were now immense. Devastation was widespread. Much of the countryside had been polluted by chemical weapons and in South Vietnam, especially in the towns, Western culture, with money, drugs and prostitution, had helped create huge social problems. The military dead were estimated at about a million on the communist side, 180 000 South Vietnamese troops and nearly 50 000 Americans. Perhaps 400 000 South Vietnamese civilians had died, with unknown numbers killed in the bombing of the North.

In Cambodia, Lon Nol fell from power in April 1975, a few weeks before Thieu. His American supporters left hurriedly and the civil war ended in victory for the Khmer Rouge. In May 1975 the Khmer Rouge seized the *Mayaguez*, a US container ship, which American marines recaptured while the communists were attacked with further bombing. The end of the civil war theoretically made Sihanouk Cambodia's head of state again, but after a brief visit to Phnom Penh he returned to China and resigned office in 1976. Cambodia was now in the hands of radical communists far to the left of Sihanouk, and Pol Pot, Secretary-General of the Communist Party, emerged as the new Prime Minister in 1976.

Laos meanwhile had a ceasefire in 1973, when an uneasy coalition of royalists and communists was set up. Thao Ma, once an air-force commander and in exile for a previous attempted coup, lost his life in a new effort to seize power. Souvanna Phouma remained Prime Minister but the settlement always looked fragile. In 1975 the Pathet Lao took over, driving out the last American advisers, and Souphanouvong became President of a communist republic. Two more dominoes had fallen, but Indo-China still faced a stormy future.

18.5 Indo-China since 1975

18.5.1 The Socialist Republic of Vietnam

Nation-building in Indo-China was even more difficult after 1975 than in 1954. Border disputes occurred between Cambodia and South Vietnam when Lon Nol came to power, and it was never likely to be easy to define the territories of the Lao, Khmer and Vietnamese peoples. The Americans had furthered the ideological discord in the area and when they withdrew there was rivalry for influence between China and the Soviet Union. The whole of Indo-China also faced grave economic problems and the task of repairing the ravages of war, and the new governments had also to cope with the anxieties of minority groups, especially people of Chinese descent in Vietnam.

Vietnam was far larger than Laos and Cambodia (see Table 12.2 and section 11.4.3). Its people tended to be assertive towards their neighbours though, at the same time, there were pressures on Vietnam itself from China, its mammoth neighbour to the north. These pressures led the Vietnamese Communist Party to turn to the Soviets, signing a treaty of friendship and joining Comecon in 1978. Lavish Soviet aid helped reconstruction and, tightly controlled under its one-party system, Vietnam began to overcome its many difficulties. Le Duan as Communist Party Secretary, Ton Duc Thang as President and Pham Van Dong as Prime Minister provided a leadership similar to that in the USSR, and Le Duan and Dong remained in office for a decade after unification, providing continuity of leadership by 'old-guard revolutionaries'. Le Duan died in 1986, and in 1987 Pham Van Dong retired aged 80 to become a 'comrade adviser' to younger leaders.

Impressive growth in food production was achieved in the early 1980s and there was progress towards extending economic co-operation throughout Indo-China where, eventually, the Vietnamese would probably like to see a three-nation federation in being. The Vietnamese economy was nevertheless burdened with debt and by the mid-1980s neither inflation nor unemployment were fully under control. Progress towards prosperity was retarded by further conflicts after 1975 which brought isolation as well as strain, though Vietnam was admitted to the UN in 1977 after initial obstruction by the USA.

On Christmas Day 1978 the Vietnamese invaded Cambodia. This led to an attack on Vietnam by China and and a brief war in 1979 in which China intended to teach the pro-Soviet Vietnamese a lesson. At the same time, Vietnam's Chinese minorities – many nurturing bourgeois and capitalist ambitions – were persecuted, thousands fleeing the country in perilously overloaded small craft. Known as 'the boat people', the refugees quickly won the sympathies of the West. They came mainly from South Vietnam where many people had suffered hardship, and some death, for their earlier closeness to the Americans.

The exodus of refugees (over 100 000 in all) continued into the 1980s, ridding Vietnam of many ideologically alien influences, but putting great strain on those states, especially Hong Kong, to which they fled.

18.5.2 Vietnam and its neighbours

Vietnam's involvement in Cambodia owed a good deal to the rule there of the Khmer Rouge and Pol Pot. Even in 1975 the new regime had begun to evacuate Phnom Penh in what became a bizarre and bloody reorganization, seemingly aimed at escaping from twentieth-century technology into a world of primitive agrarian communism. There were Cambodian claims to, and attacks on, Vietnamese teritories in 1977, and Vietnam gave support to Heng Samrin and the Kampuchean National United Front which aimed to resist Pol Pot. War followed, and the Vietnamese soon entered the ghost city of Phnom Penh in January 1979 to set up the People's Republic of Kampuchea with Heng Samrin as Prime Minister. In spite of the Khmer Rouge's bloody record and suspected genocide in Cambodia on a scale similar to that of Nazi Germany, China, the USA and much of the West continued to insist that Pol Pot was the country's rightful ruler, though he was now only a guerilla leader among Khmer Rouge rebels. Pol Pot's record was not unknown: as early as 1976 Kissinger had defended US policy in the early 1970s by asserting that:

> in the six years of the war, not ten per cent of the people had been killed in Cambodia that had been killed in one year of Communist rule.

By the end of the decade it seemed likely that half of Cambodia's population had died in the conflicts, most of them victims of Khmer Rouge purges or of famines caused by the successive wars.

China's attack on Vietnam in 1979 did nothing to dislodge the Vietnamese from Kampuchea (see section 11.3.2). On the other hand both Vietnam and the Soviet Union felt the strain of trying to repair Kampuchea's economy and society. Pol Pot continued to wage war against the Republic, and Heng Samrin and the Vietnamese tried to hunt down his guerillas. Meanwhile, refugees fled to Thailand from the war and from famine. Floods and drought as well as war hampered the new government's efforts to restore food output.

In 1982 the opposition to the People's Republic was broadened when Sihanouk, with US and Chinese encouragement, set up another government in exile. The guerillas were now an uneasy coalition of Khmer Rouge and anti-communists resisting Heng Samrin and the Vietnamese in the name of Democratic Kampuchea. By 1986 they claimed to have 60 000 troops, mainly on the Thai borders, operating from refugee camps which survived mainly due to aid from the USA, the West and Japan. China meanwhile kept up the pressure on Vietnam to withdraw from Kampuchea, a demand also voiced by the United Nations. The Vietnamese demanded international guarantees that the Khmer Rouge and Pol Pot would never be allowed to return to government. In any case they still wanted to make Heng Samrin and the Kampuchean Communist Party strong enough to resist their enemies before Vietnamese forces were totally withdrawn.

By 1987, however, there seemed to be some prospect of change. The influence of Gorbachev and perhaps the end of the old leadership in Vietnam led to the suggestion that the Vietnamese were now more ready to withdraw from Kampuchea. Heng Samrin's government had taken root, though it faced formidable problems in rebuilding the Kampuchean state after the damage done both during the rule of Pol Pot and in resistance to its own rule. The economy relied heavily on Soviet support and only a few small-scale private businesses seemed to thrive. The rebuilding of services such as education and health care was handicapped by acute shortages. On the other hand, 1986 had brought successes against the Khmer Rouge and other guerillas and Vietnam forecast the withdrawal of all its forces by 1990. China still demanded their more immediate removal and 1987 opened with renewed fierce fighting on the Sino–Vietnamese borders. Outside support for the rebels of Democratic Kampuchea persisted in 1987–8. Whatever the hopes of Moscow and of Vietnam's new collective leadership for the peace in Indo-China which might at last permit real economic advancement, the region's problems were still far from solved.

The People's Republic of Laos meanwhile proceeded more quietly after 1975. Souphanouvong remained President but the Laotian government was strongly influenced by Vietnam and the USSR. It was, however, a government freer from corruption than many elsewhere and one intent on advancing the well-being of the people. Rigid Marxist ideology was gradually modified to fit the needs of a small Indo-Chinese state whose people depended on subsistence farming and rice production and some 60 per cent of whom were Buddhists. Soviet-style collectivized farming failed and was abandoned. By the mid-1980s the country was wellnigh self-sufficient in food though few peasants had joined the now voluntary co-operatives. Laos was developing as a distinctive Lao nation, albeit a neighbour of the more powerful and influential Vietnam and an ally of the Soviet Union.

Little was left in Indo-China of what the Americans so persistently fought for. Conditions were changing fast. SEATO had decayed along with the USA's reputation: France withdrew from it in 1974 and the Organization was wound up in the late 1970s. The independent states of the region preferred the non-military Association of South East Asian Nations (ASEAN), founded in 1967 by Indonesia, Malaysia, Singapore, Thailand and the Philippines. ASEAN aimed to bring about a 'Zone of Peace, Freedom and Neutrality', by diplomatic means and without resorting to anti-communism. Thailand and Singapore were nevertheless alarmed by the growing influence of Vietnam, though other members were perhaps more fearful of China. ASEAN pressed the United Nations to refuse to recognize the Heng Samrin regime in Kampuchea and to prefer Democratic Kampuchea. ASEAN wanted no more falling dominoes and was apprehensive about a united Indo-China dominated by Vietnam. But the members of ASEAN were all Asian, young countries taking on the responsibilities of statehood and eager to settle the affairs of their region without the superpowers and former colonial masters. The settlement of the affairs of Indo-China had already been too long delayed by interfering US Presidents and ideological missionaries from Moscow and Peking.

UNIT 19

Legacies of empire: 4 – race relations and minorities

19.1 Racial equality

It was broadly true that colonial empires graded people according to their colour. The whites, the Europeans, were in authority and privileged. Blacks were usually cast in subservient, often menial roles, in some societies (until emancipation) even as slaves. Those of other colours, brown and yellow, sometimes occupied in-between roles such as clerks, overseers and administrative assistants, and those of mixed race seemed uneasily to belong to neither governing nor governed. Decolonization and independence were part of a process of change perhaps well represented by the Commonwealth, which was evolving into a multiracial association, blind to differences of colour (see section 14.4). But many of the privileged found the change difficult to accept, especially where independence, as in Africa, brought black governments intent on redressing the gross racial inequalities of the past (see Units 14 and 15). The attitudes and values of colonial empires had nevertheless to be adjusted to a new age. This was part of the process of nation-building in which majorities and minorities needed to learn to coexist in mutual respect. Needless to say, harmony was seldom achieved overnight: in some areas the struggle for racial and ethnic equality was long and painful.

This unit will consider some examples of this struggle, beginning with South Africa around which the fiercest controversies raged. South Africa's system of apartheid for the separate development of its races was the outstanding example of an attempt to institutionalize and to preserve the power and privileges of a white minority, based on theories of white superiority and racial supremacy, *baaskap*. The theories were enthusiastically developed by academics and leaders of the Dutch [Afrikaans] Reformed Church. By 1945 South African whites were well entrenched in power and for many years their authority seemed impregnable, the mass of black South Africans quiet, their leaders ruthlessly jailed, sometimes killed. But the rest of the world was changing and outrage grew that apartheid persisted. Black nationalist governments came to power ever closer to South Africa's frontiers, reinforcing the traditional *laager* (literally, 'encampment') mentality of white South Africans, especially the Boers of Dutch descent. They saw themselves beset by uncivilized and unchristianized blacks – like the early settlers and their wagon trains besieged by the *kaffirs* (a dismissive Afrikaans term for native Africans, mainly Bantu). For good measure, they also saw communists and communist agents among their bogeymen, and proclaimed the justice of their own cause, apartheid, as a bastion of the Western way of life and of Christianity.

Few outside South Africa saw it that way. African liberation movements took time to grow, however. Taking their example from Gandhi, part of whose early life was spent in South Africa where he came into painful conflict with racial prejudice as early as 1907, black nationalists for many years relied on passive resistance: organized violent resistance came later. Outside pressures were also weakened by the USA, Britain and France who persistently obstructed calls for action against South Africa at the United Nations. World patience grew thin, and boycotts multiplied in spite of the obstructions. In 1964 South Africa was barred from the Olympic Games, and sport became one area for pressures against apartheid. Cricket test matches were stopped between England and South Africa and New Zealand and South Africa from 1965, Australia applying the boycott soon afterwards. But sporting contacts and tours, many unofficial, were difficult to stop entirely. South African whites were willing to spend heavily to tempt boycott-busting, and international sport was torn with disputes, for example when New Zealand rugby teams insisted on playing in South Africa in the 1970s.

Members of the Commonwealth, meeting in Britain in 1977, produced the Gleneagles Agreement, to combat apartheid in sport:

> by withholding any form of support for, and taking every practical step to discourage, contact or competition by the nationals with sporting organisations, teams or sportsmen from South Africa.

The Agreement helped to preserve the Commonwealth but boycotts were far from total. Many governments claimed they had no control over the freedom of their subjects to earn money where they could. Similar holes were to be seen in any sorts of boycott – commercial, financial or cultural – South Africa's enemies tried to impose. It became a ritual to claim opposition to apartheid but to assert a belief in the freedom to go along with it. World indignation nevertheless mounted and, as Les Gibbard's cartoon (fig. 19.3) suggests, it was not much cooled by the slow reforms President Botha introduced in South Africa in the 1980s against a background of, by now, looming civil war. By then, apartheid had existed for almost 40 years though its roots went back much further than that.

19.2 South Africa

19.2.1 The Nationalists and apartheid

South African elections in 1948 produced enthusiastic support for Daniel Malan and the Nationalists with their warnings of the 'black menace'. A former preacher, Malan had opposed South Africa's part in the Second World War against Nazi Germany, and he condemned the internationalism of Jan Smuts, the outgoing Prime Minister who had joined that war as well as helping to found the League of Nations and the British Commonwealth of Nations. Malan believed in 'God's elect' – especially white South Africans. He feared the country's growing black population and had a vision of apartheid as the key to a secure future. South Africa's 2.4 million whites were outnumbered in 1948 by about 8 million blacks. There were also about 300 000 Asians and almost a million 'coloureds' (of mixed race) in the country. Non-white populations were growing faster than white and Malan promised to be tougher than Smuts in keeping non-whites in their place.

Smuts was hardly a liberal and 'their place' was already well defined. A few blacks in Cape Province had the right to vote, given to them by South Africans of English descent. But the Boers were becoming more dominant than the English and in 1960 all Bantu representation in parliament, a handful of seats, was abolished. In 1971 all coloured representation ceased similarly. One of the first principles of apartheid was that whites should keep and make total the power they had had in South Africa since independence in 1910. The Bantu were already in 1948 confined mainly to labouring work and a further aspect of apartheid was to organize them as the whites' work-force, while keeping them separate from the whites' living spaces. The Nationalist Party's Manifesto in 1948 put its policy this way:

> Either we must follow the course of equality, which must eventually mean national suicide for the white race, or we must take a course of separation ('apartheid'), through which the character and future of every race will be protected and safeguarded, with full opportunities for development and self-maintenance in their own ideas, without the interests of one clashing with the interests of the other.

The white electorate supported the 'course of separation'. Successive elections returned Nationalist governments and even English South Africans seemed to grow more supportive of Boer (Afrikaans) racism. Smuts died in 1950 and the opposition United Party grew weaker. Nationalist Prime Ministers followed one another into office: Johannes Strijdom when Malan retired in 1954; Hendrik Verwoerd when Strijdom died in 1958; Johannes Vorster when Verwoerd was assassinated in 1966; then Pieter Botha when Vorster became ill in 1978. South Africa had become a republic outside the Commonwealth in 1961 (see section 14.4.1), and in 1984 Botha became President as well as Prime Minister. Elections in 1981 had given him and the Nationalist Party their usual backing with 131 of the 165 parliamentary seats, well ahead of the Progressive Federal Party which tried to keep liberal ideas alive among a minority of South African whites.

Under Nationalist rule after 1948 laws multiplied, and apartheid took shape as a system for organizing the lives of all races – in theory for the benefit of each, in practice and most of all for the benefit of whites. One of the fundamentals was the possession of land. About 87 per cent of South Africa was already earmarked for the whites, and they intended to keep it that way. The

Group Areas Act of 1950 classified the country's racial groups and allocated areas to them for settlement and for owning property. The Population Registration Act at the same time required passes to be carried to provide an instant check on the owner's race and to make the stringent control of movement more effective. This control was furthered in the Natives Act of 1952 and it operated along with labour laws which, where practicable, reserved skilled work for whites, kept non-whites in the employment essential to white prosperity (for example in mines), forbade strikes and, from 1952, restricted non-whites to living away from the white communities. The shanty towns around most urban communities therefore grew, and many were organized by the authorities into black townships such as Soweto and Sharpeville near Johannesburg and Uitenhage in Eastern Cape, from which workers commuted daily to work in the white areas.

Separating the races was almost an obsession. The Prohibition of Mixed Marriages in 1949 was one of the first laws brought in by Malan. The Immorality Act (1950) forbade all sexual relations between the races. Where races were likely to mix, separate facilities were provided. Figure 19.1 shows a footbridge with separate approaches for whites and non-whites, a division common on public transport, at sporting events and in places such as cafés, theatres, post offices, parks and beaches. The Bantu Education Act of 1953 provided for the separate state-run education of blacks, to prepare them for their working lives and the place in society mapped out for them: apart from

Fig. 19.1 Apartheid in practice: separate development meant whites and non-whites would even cross a railway line separately.

education in native languages, for example, black children were to learn enough Afrikaans and English 'to follow oral and written instructions'. Yet some Bantu were educated to university standards: in 1959 universities were segregated so that only very rarely after that did white and non-white students follow courses together. Part of the purpose of Bantu education was to encourage the children to look less to white South Africa and more to their 'homelands', native and tribalized reserves assigned to the blacks and covering about thirteen per cent of South Africa's soil. In due course, blacks living in the townships would be encouraged to go 'home' to these tribal lands, just as an effort was made to persuade Asians, whether born in South Africa or not, to go 'home' to India – to the anger of Indian governments.

To support its system the state developed its own power. The Suppression of Communism Act of 1950 provided all-purpose protection against all sorts of opposition: only the mere assumption of 'communism' was necessary for the law to be invoked, making it easy to disband organizations and to arrest individuals threatening apartheid. A Public Safety Act authorized the suspension of civil liberties in any emergency, and the Criminal Law Amendment Act (1953) increased the punishments for civil disobedience. South Africa's armed forces became easily the most powerful in Africa. Some defence experts even believed that South Africa secretly co-operated with Israel in the development of a nuclear bomb and exploded it in the Indian Ocean in 1979. Certainly South Africa had a strong police force, and a close and sinister watch on all possible opposition and subversion was kept by the Bureau of State Security (BOSS).

The Bantu Self-Government Act of 1959 was a logical development of the system. Its aim was to develop for the homelands eight 'Bantu units' *(bantustans)* where, a government spokesman explained:

> hitherto dependent Bantu peoples can achieve their autonomy without jeopardising the independent nationhood of the Whites. The ultimate aim is the co-operative association of independent Bantu states and a White nation – a Commonwealth of South Africa.

The first self-governing bantustan was Transkei with its Xhosa-speaking people whose parliament met in 1963. Prime Minister Kaiser Mantanzima affronted South Africa by complaining that the lands allocated to Transkei were inadequate. Transkei became independent in 1976 and other bantustans followed – Bophuthatswana, a collection of six scattered, mainly Tswana territories, in 1977; Venda in 1979; and Ciskei in 1981. To the disappointment of the government in Pretoria, the world refused to recognize any of these states as genuinely independent of South Africa, while Chief Buthelezi of the Zulu expressed a fundamental black criticism of the bantustans:

> It is objectionable to us as the aborigines of South Africa that a white minority should prescribe where we may have a stake in our own land, and where we may not.

Meanwhile, hundreds of thousands of Bantu lived in the townships around South Africa's cities or in barracks at the country's mines, dependent on work there to support their families. As well as South African blacks, others came from neighbouring countries such as Malawi. Whites rightly claimed that they provided job opportunities and incomes above what could be got elsewhere, but the whites also needed the cheap labour to sustain their own economy and living standards, and the conditions in which the black workers lived were far from enviable. Though many townships had solid houses and basic amenities including electricity, shops and schools, they were usually drab and spartan - temporary dormitories in which to dump the blacks while they were not at work and before they were sent away to their homelands. Though apartheid claimed to aim at good race relations, it bred racial discontent. Soon the authorities faced anger at home and abroad, and BOSS found plenty to occupy its agents.

19.2.2 Internal dissent

Organized opposition among non-whites was systematically destroyed by the Nationalist South African government. Albert Luthuli, a Zulu chief and from 1952 President of the African National Congress (ANC), preached non-violence and passive resistance which won him acclaim outside South Africa and the Nobel Peace Prize of 1960. Inside South Africa he was persistently harassed and then banished to a remote area of Natal. The ANC was banned in 1960 and Luthuli was reported killed by a train in 1967 soon after writing his autobiography, *Let My People Go*. Critics of apartheid meanwhile formed the Pan-African Congress (PAC) which in 1960 organized a demonstration at Sharpeville against the pass laws. Jet aircraft flew low over the demonstrators, and the police opened fire, killing 69 and wounding three times that number. This was the worst such clash so far. A white farmer wounded Verwoerd a few weeks later and, outside South Africa, the events at Sharpeville caused outrage. BOSS was too firmly in control for sustained open protest to develop inside South Africa, but sabotage increased and black nationalists questioned the effectiveness of merely passive protest.

Leaders were nevertheless arrested as soon as they had a following, and protest of any sort was made difficult. Nelson Mandela, a lawyer who tried to revive the ANC, was in 1962 jailed for five years and then imprisoned for life under new charges brought under the Suppression of Communism Act. Much of his time was spent on Robben Island, a notorious place of detention, and his reputation grew. Winifred Mandela, his wife, continued the struggle for the people's rights, though she was constantly harassed - and from time to time detained - by the authorities. Meanwhile, the PAC was banned and many turned to a new movement, Black Consciousness, born in 1970. It was non-violent and educational and came to be led by Steven Biko. The authorities forced Biko to give up his medical studies, arrested him several times and in 1977 announced his death in police custody from 'accidental' head wounds and brain injuries. When Vorster resigned in 1978, many blacks had begun to despair of peaceful political change.

On the other hand, African trade unionism had made some limited gains during this period. Improved wages and other concessions were won during the 1970s by industrial action which threatened the white economy, though the authorities were not unwilling to open fire when industrial disputes turned ugly, and eleven black miners were killed in 1973 at Western Deep Levels mine in Transvaal. Setbacks to white regimes in other parts of southern Africa also encouraged South African blacks, and students especially grew more restless. In 1976 schoolchildren in Soweto began a boycott of their government-run schools where teaching in Afrikaans was compulsory. Soweto had nearly a million inhabitants by now. Tension mounted, the police opened fire on the demonstrators, killing two children and four adults, and the blacks killed two whites. Waves of arson and destruction and more killings followed, spreading far beyond Soweto before order was eventually restored. The explosion served notice of the deep dissatisfaction in the townships. The black population was unlikely to be stilled for long by the few minor reforms which this time helped to pacify Soweto and which included the ending of Afrikaans teaching. ANC guerillas were beginning to slip back into South Africa from training grounds to the north and sabotage spread. Botha, Vorster's successor, now faced a critical period in South Africa's history.

19.2.3 External pressures and Namibia

South Africa's resignation from the Commonwealth in 1961 had made plain the determination of the Nationalists to ignore both Africa's 'wind of change' and outside opinion and to persist with apartheid (see section 14.4.1). Hostility towards South Africa was increased by Nationalist policies towards Namibia, which South Africans continued to call South West Africa. This former mandate of the League of Nations had been entrusted to South Africa after the First World War but in 1948 Malan refused to accept United Nations authority there. South Africa simply had vague and non-urgent plans for South West Africa's eventual self-government – seeing it almost as an enormous bantustan. Its fairly sparse population (rising to about a million in 1980 and mainly Ovambo) was subjected to the South African economic and social system, and its minerals, especially diamonds and eventually uranium, were extracted by South African and international companies. Inevitably, African resistance movements developed: the South West Africa National Union (SWANU) in 1959 mainly among the minority tribes, and the South West Africa People's Organization (SWAPO), mainly Ovambo, in 1960. By 1966 passive resistance was giving way to armed struggle led by Sam Nujoma, President of SWAPO. The liberation struggle was encouraged by the OAU and boosted by a judgment in 1971 in the International Court of Justice that South Africa's occupation of South West Africa was illegal. Not until the Portuguese left Angola in 1975, however, did the guerillas have secure bases. Independent Angola supported SWAPO, its legality now recognized by the UN, and South Africa took reprisals, fomenting disorders in Angola (see sections 15.4 and 17.5.2).

The independence of Angola and Mozambique and the mounting guerilla action which promised to speed up the independence of Rhodesia left South Africa more exposed and quickened world interest in the affairs of southern Africa. The UN repeatedly condemned apartheid as an attack on human rights. In 1973 South African membership of the UN was virtually suspended and in 1976 the Security Council backed a demand for free elections in Namibia under the supervision of Britain, France, West Germany, Canada and the USA. South Africa had other ideas, preferring to negotiate an 'internal settlement' with approved moderates and to that end holding the Turnhalle Talks from 1975 to 1977. SWAPO was denounced as an Ovambo force, the South Africans playing on tribal rivalries. Walvis Bay was declared part of South Africa, not of South West Africa, and delays over the freedom of the latter continued into the late 1980s. The constitution that South Africa devised for South West Africa found no favour with the UN, since it offered almost nothing to blacks. Meanwhile, transnational companies like Rio Tinto Zinc gathered up the area's minerals while South Africa withheld independence 'for as long as Cuban troops remain in Angola'. UN initiatives were still frustrated. Reagan in the USA and Thatcher in Britain were reluctant to press South Africa too hard, and the Namibian issue remained unresolved into 1988.

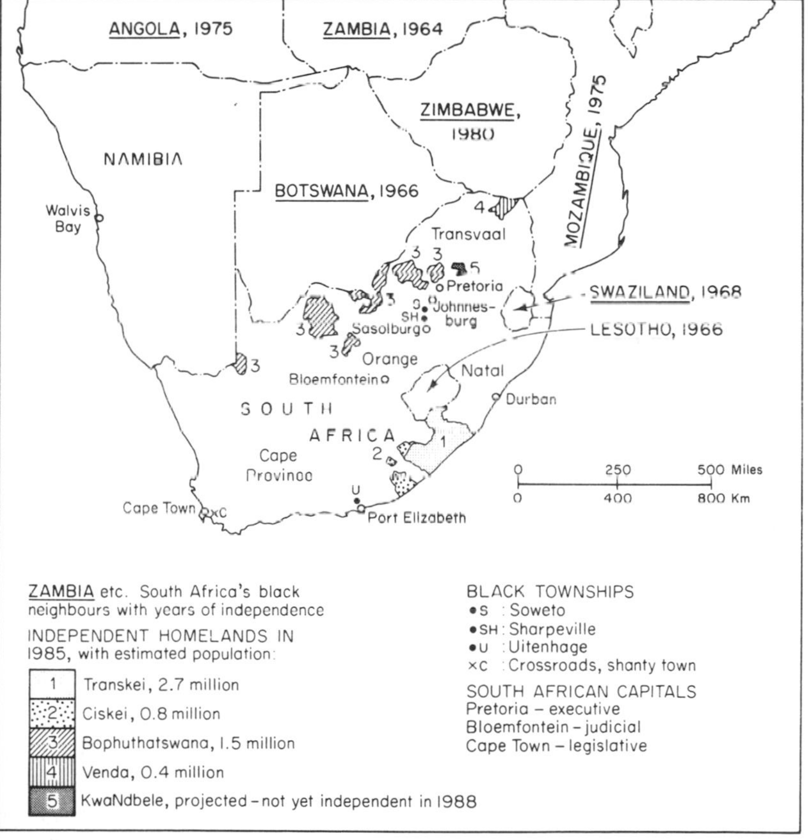

Fig. 19.2 South Africa in the 1980s

The fourteen black African states who issued the Lusaka Manifesto on southern Africa in 1969 – clearly influenced by Nyerere and Kaunda – had no doubts about the racism of South Africa:

> The whole system of government and society in South Africa is based on the denial of human equality. And the system is maintained by a ruthless denial of the human rights of the majority of the population and thus, inevitably of all.

But even they were not unaware of South Africa's economic importance in southern Africa, providing employment, markets and supplies. With a few exceptions such as Malawi, black Africans nevertheless did their best to put pressure on Pretoria to end apartheid, and they were supported by the communist powers and most of the non-white world. The opposition to South Africa was nevertheless watered down by US and western-European abstentions and vetoes at the UN, and the readiness of transnational companies and other organizations to ignore the boycotts that black Africans and others tried to impose. Many in the West were unwilling to lose an important (though not indispensable) trading partner, extensive investments in industry and banking, a surviving white stronghold in Africa, and an anti-communist ally strategically placed in the southern hemisphere. But the West was not united. The question of the supply of arms to South Africa led to bitter debate between left and right in Britain and, along with other links with South Africa, caused widespread argument. France was among the slowest to give up the profitable South African arms market. Always it was argued that continuing dialogue with South Africa would be more effective in bringing about changes in the system of apartheid than would total isolation. Until Botha came to office in 1978 there were few signs that change would happen, however, and by then the National government in Pretoria faced new pressure from spreading black and coloured unrest within South Africa itself.

19.2.4 Botha's balancing act

Further acts of sabotage included a spectacular attack in 1980 on oil storage tanks at Sasolburg. Government ministers began tentatively to show interest in modifying some of the laws connected with apartheid, and Botha began with constitutional changes. These were not designed to reduce white control, though he hoped to appease Asians and coloureds by consulting them in a new President's Council. The elections of 1981 reminded him, however, that change was likely to be perilous. The Nationalist vote fell, partly due to increased support for the liberal Progressive Federal Party whose seats increased from 18 to 27. But the very right-wing Herstigte National Party (HNP) won fourteen per cent of the votes in a strong protest against any concessions. The Nationalists kept a comfortable parliamentary majority but it was apparent that even limited changes were likely to alarm and alienate many white voters. Botha had to walk a difficult tightrope.

The Constitution Act of 1983 nevertheless set up three separate houses of parliament, for whites, Asians and coloureds. Blacks were left out, though Botha declared that the country now had:

> a new foundation for national unity . . . for reform in an evolutionary way. . . . The time for building lies ahead.

When elections were held in 1984, about 80 per cent of Asians and coloureds boycotted them, seeing the policy simply as one of 'divide and rule', the better to preserve apartheid. Botha allowed co-operative Asians and coloureds a small say in government but, for blacks, the policy was still to send them to the homelands, giving them no place in South Africa except as migrant workers. Black anger grew.

ANC guerilla activity increased in South Africa and in Namibia, and Pretoria hit back strongly against ANC and SWAPO bases to the north, especially in Mozambique and Angola where black governments were forced into uneasy agreements with South Africa to limit hostile operations. Within South Africa, support for Mandela and the ANC spread, though young blacks especially grew more extreme and more impatient than the ANC leadership. Sabotage, disturbances, arrests and killings multiplied during 1984. The twenty-fifth anniversary of the shootings at Sharpeville brought many demonstrations in March 1985, and at Uitenhage the police again shot peaceful protestors – killing nineteen and bringing new eruptions of violence. South Africa was censured at the UN and there was bitter external condemnation. Since the new constitution had been introduced the police had killed about 200 blacks and the country now drew nearer to civil war. Reforms, like South Africa's version of an independent constitution for Namibia in 1985, were dismissed as merely cosmetic. In 1985–6 the death toll mounted in the townships, the victims falling both to the security forces and to fellow blacks in flare-ups over collaboration and betrayal. Boycotts of businesses, added to arson and the general disruption, began to undermine the country to such an extent that a once strong economy began to falter and in 1986 the South African currency was in deep trouble.

Botha was ready, he said, to end 'petty apartheid' and the irksome segregation of the races began to be eroded. There were certainly changes. In 1985 the Immorality Act was dismantled and the ban on mixed marriages lifted. Louis Stofberg for the HNP complained that:

> the government has let loose a tiger that it won't be able to control.

When the pass laws were scrapped in 1986, the tiger seemed rampant, all the more so since black unrest was now spreading beyond the townships to the rural areas. There was serious unrest in KwaNdebele, one of the smallest bantustans but due shortly to be the next to achieve 'independence'. Riots and killings in South Africa now occurred with sickening regularity. Catholic, Anglican and Methodist leaders in the South African Council of Churches grew even more outspoken. Many like Bishop (from 1986, Archbishop) Desmond Tutu, an Anglican, took a stance similar to that of Martin Luther King in the USA, preaching and practising civil disobedience. Tutu himself said:

> I cannot help it when I see injustice. I cannot keep quiet.

This was a voice like that of Trevor Huddleston, an anti-apartheid missionary long since expelled from South Africa, and now echoed by many Anglican and

Fig. 19.3 Gibbard's cartoon of August 1985 comments on South African President P.W. Botha's reforms which seemed designed to placate his country's external critics while ignoring the principal internal causes of unrest.

Roman Catholic churchmen who crusaded against the system. Voices outside South Africa were also growing more urgent, many in support of the economic sanctions for which Tutu called. The issue was hotly debated by Commonwealth leaders in 1985 and, compromising, they sent a group of Eminent Persons to try to persuade Pretoria to negotiate with the ANC and make real concessions.

For South African blacks, as for Archbishop Tutu, 'real concessions' would have to include the end of attempts to fragment the lands of South Africa on ethnic lines. Botha was willing to extend the property rights of blacks. In 1986 he was negotiating for a National Council, multiracial and including blacks, which could advise on a new South African constitution which blacks might find acceptable. But 'independent' homelands like Transkei were to be excluded and there was no sign that Botha was ready to abandon the system of bantustans, the very heart of apartheid. Winifred Mandela asserted the unequivocal ANC view:

> Apartheid cannot be reformed. It must be destroyed.

That meant change more fundamental than any Botha yet visualized.

Many whites believed reform had already gone too far. South African forces made new strikes in Botswana, Zambia, and then Angola again, all in 1986, in an effort to reassure Nationalists that the government was not weakening. This was not enough for the fanatical right-wing whites, now rallying not so much to the HNP as to Eugene Terreblanche ('White Earth') and his neo-Nazi *Afrikaner Weerstandsbeweging* (AWB, Afrikaner resistance). The use of tear gas against the AWB was a measure of Botha's growing difficulties. A small white minority, on the other hand, now gave open support to the blacks. The blacks were being steadily politicized, though fierce conflict in 1986 in Crossroads – a vast shanty town near Cape Town – showed internal divisions between conservatives and radicals, in effect often between the old and the young. About four and a half million whites in South Africa were now outnumbered by blacks by about four to one (by far more if the homelands were included). Disturbances were widespread and persistent, with all sides, white, black and coloured, increasingly divided among themselves. In June 1986 the government imposed a state of emergency.

It seemed unlikely, however, that time was on the side of apartheid. Pressures on the government mounted almost daily and, as the toll of lives grew, even the transnational companies began to waver in support of it. Barclays Bank, long regarded as a staunch upholder of the South African regime, announced its withdrawal from the country in November 1986, following the example of important American companies. Pressures increased now on Shell and others to turn off the taps which enabled South Africa to supplement its own coal-produced oil. Congress overruled President Reagan to insist on sanctions against South Africa, though Thatcher and Kohl in Europe still doggedly resisted the effective restrictions recommended by the Commonwealth Eminent Persons. British policy led to angry boycotts of the Commonwealth Games in Edinburgh in 1986. At the end of that year, Botha announced new elections for whites in South Africa, perhaps to test opinion concerning further reform.

The elections returned the Nationalists to power but Botha could take little comfort from them. The South African Conservative Party (CP), only recently created as a right-wing alliance and raucously supported by the AWB, won over a quarter of the votes and replaced the Progressives as the main Opposition. Early in 1988 by-election results showed a dramatic increase in support for the CP and especially for its neo-Nazi wing, the AWB. Local government elections in 1988 showed much the same pattern: the vast majority of blacks boycotted the proceedings, whereas the Conservatives expanded at the expense of the Nationalists. The warning against further reform of the apartheid system and against any talk of power-sharing with blacks was so clear that Botha began even fiercer repression of black dissent and of all liberal opinion. The silent vigils by women of the liberal Black Sash were dispersed. The arrest, detention, beating and torture of blacks and of more troublesome agitators went on. Children as young as eight were declared 'enemies of the state', safe from neither detention nor even killing. Censorship was tightened even further and extensive restrictions were imposed on reporting and filming even by foreign news gatherers. Little freedom of expression remained in South Africa either for blacks or for whites, and it was left to Archbishop Tutu and other religious leaders to defy the state by speaking out against injustice and brutality. Church–state relations grew tense and in March 1988, in St George's Cathedral in Cape Town, Tutu asserted:

> We refuse to be treated as the doormat for the government to wipe its jackboots on.

The churchmen were derided as 'political clergy' and were persistently harassed.

South Africa was indeed being brutalized. Savage clashes between security forces and (mainly black) demonstrators, and between blacks themselves, seemed to occur with dreadful regularity. Killing by hanging burning tyres round the necks of victims ('necklace killings') was horrific even by South African standards, but was used by black militants to take revenge on those suspected of collaborating with the state. The state itself led the way in violence, however. The security forces gained a reputation for bringing about the deaths of those, like Biko, in their custody. In the 1970s and 1980s South Africa also regularly recorded the highest number of hangings in the Western world. Judicial hanging was possible merely for being present at riots where members of the security forces were killed. Botha seemed to feel compelled to be ruthless in order to reassure potential CP supporters that white privileges were safe in his hands.

Commonwealth leaders met again at Vancouver in 1987, and again the demand for economic sanctions against South Africa was almost universal. It was again Mrs Thatcher who resisted it. She had once used Tutu's doubts about the value of sanctions to support her own opposition to them, but she ceased to quote his opinions when the Archbishop came out in favour of sanctions to put pressure on the South African government. President Kaunda of Zambia expressed the general despair when he complained, 'there is no way of moving her'. Britain was neither the chief supplier of South Africa's imports nor the chief customer for its exports (see Table 19.1). But British investment in South Africa and Britain's historical influence there constantly spotlighted the alleged comfort Thatcher's stance on sanctions gave to the Botha regime. Her ritual verbal denunciations of apartheid and claims that she might influence Botha through 'dialogue' merely added to the frustration. Trevor Huddleston, now

Table 19.1 South Africa's main trading partners in the mid-1980s

	Investment in South Africa (£s billion)	Exports to South Africa (US dollars billion)	Imports from South Africa (US dollars billion)
Britain	12.0	1.6	0.7
USA	10.0	2.3	1.4
West Germany	2.0	2.3	0.6
France	1.5	0.6	*
Switzerland	1.0	*	1.1
Japan	†	1.8	1.4
Italy	†	0.5	0.4

* below 0.4 billion dollars
† below 1.0 billion pounds

Source: OECD

President of the British Anti-Apartheid Movement, branded her 'a political pariah'. But though sanctions against South Africa were still only patchy, the country's economy was no longer flourishing. It was sustained by the country's gold production, but GDP growth rates in the 1980s averaged little more than an annual one per cent. With a rapidly rising non-white population and a heavy security budget, this was insufficient to meet the aspirations of either the privileged or the underprivileged, though the need to keep the largest share of the national cake in the hands of the whites reinforced the argument against significant changes in the apartheid policy.

Some 3.5 million South Africans, most of them black, were forcibly shifted about the country in the years 1980–3 to separate the races. The 'independent' homelands of Transkei, Bophuthatswana, Venda and Ciskei were intended by the Nationalists eventually to remove much of the black population from white South Africa. But for the present they still depended heavily on grants from Pretoria and on what their migrant workers could earn in South African mines and other enterprises. Even so they were not immune from the unrest in South Africa. Plans for making KwaNdbele 'independent' were shelved in 1986 when the proposal brought the homeland close to civil war. There were riots and sabotage in other homelands too, sparked off by repression, economic despair and resentment of interference from Pretoria. Transkei underwent upheaval in 1987 when the Transkei Defence Force overthrew the government of Mantanzima. Elections brought to power Mrs Stella Sigcau who thus became the first woman Prime Minister in Africa, but her success was short-lived. Her government was toppled by another military coup within three months, amid accusations of bribery and corruption. Botha's government, it seemed, was beset with problems on all sides.

South Africa in 1988 still relied on force to resolve its difficulties. The murder in Paris of Mrs Dulcie September, an ANC leader, angered the French government and seemed to fit into a pattern of assassinations of black South Africans abroad whom Pretoria found troublesome. About the same time, South African forces raided an allegedly ANC target in Botswana, adding that country to the list of neighbours of South Africa who suffered 'reprisals'. Botswana's government condemned the attack as 'dastardly', murdering 'innocent people', and it urged yet again that the South African government should:

> engage in negotiations with the genuine leadership of the oppressed majority in the country.

There now seemed little prospect of that. Nelson Mandela remained in detention on Robben Island in spite of a worldwide chorus in favour of his release. BOSS remained supreme and, fearful of further defections to the CP, Botha had ceased even to talk of power-sharing with South Africa's blacks.

19.3 Nation-building in the West Indies

Figure 19.4 shows the ethnic composition of three English-speaking states which gained independence in the 1960s: Jamaica, Guyana, and Trinidad (see section 14.3.1). The black Afro-Caribbean communities and the Indian (Asiatic) communities were the result of slave-trading and the importing of labour in earlier centuries to make the colonies profitable for Britain, mainly in the cultivation of sugar-cane. One among many of the problems of independence was to achieve racial harmony and avoid friction more successfully than had been the case in Haiti and the Dominican Republic (see section 9.3.4). Another was to develop – albeit with a strong anti-Marxist bias in Guyana – the parliamentary democracy Britain had tried to plant. A third was to improve standards of living and move forward from the high unemployment, low incomes and squalor inherited from the colonial past. For all three states, struggle was needed to achieve successful nationhood, an aim expressed in Guyana in the slogan. 'One People, One Nation, One Destiny'. But the largest of the three states, Jamaica, had a population in the early 1980s of little more

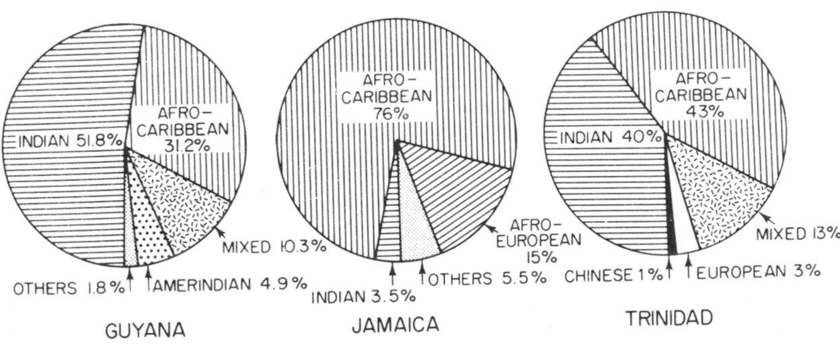

Fig. 19.4 The ethnic composition of three Caribbean states in the 1960s

than two million and inter-state co-operation was clearly desirable. The West Indies Federation had broken down in 1962, and the English-speaking Caribbean then developed Carifta and Caricom (see section 9.4). These organizations, even more than the Commonwealth, helped the new nations to find their place in the modern world. Each state nevertheless sought its own national identity.

19.3.1 Trinidad and Tobago

The roughly equal division of Trinidad's population between Afro-Caribbean and Indian made it important that political parties should not develop on racial lines. Eric Williams, sociologist, historian and independent Trinidad's first Prime Minister, led the People's National Movement (PNM), founded in 1955 on deliberately non-racial principles. Once the West Indies Federation collapsed, Britain saw no reason to delay Trinidad's independence under Williams and his elected PNM government. The new state also included the small nearby island of Tobago.

Williams remained in power in Trinidad and Tobago until he died in 1981 and PNM rule gave the new nation a measure of continuity and stability. Unrest was not uncommon, however, and the government from time to time imposed a state of emergency. Critics complained that Trinidad was almost a one-party state, though this situation owed a good deal to the divisions among the opposition. In 1971, for example, the PNM won all the seats in the House of Representatives with the support of only a third of the electors, the opposition boycotting the elections. Williams stressed the need for 'Discipline, Production and Tolerance' in building the nation, and in 1965 said, 'a small country like ours only has principles.' But Trinidad also had oil and asphalt, offering more hope of prosperity than existed for many of its neighbours.

The way was not easy, even so. Unemployment remained high, partly because the population grew. Asian sugar workers resented their persistently low incomes. Blacks grew militant under the influence of Black Power, with its ambitions for revenge for past injustices to their race; industrial relations were often stormy; protest was violent. Williams also had to grapple with corruption in the PNM government, and Trinidad and Tobago found racial harmony and shared prosperity elusive. Williams persevered, remaining Prime Minister when the country became a republic in 1976. The elections that year restored a parliamentary opposition, mainly composed of members of the United Labour Front, and the balance remained at elections in 1981 when the PNM was again confirmed in power, now with George Chambers as Prime Minister. By now there was another difficulty, however. A separatist movement in Tobago had not been stilled by the granting of a separate assembly in 1980, and the status of Tobago remained typical of the problems involving the drawing of frontiers in the post-colonial world.

The struggle for economic development and social stability went on during the 1980s, racial rivalries and other sorts of disunity surfacing from time to time. Williams had helped lay good foundations, however, and Trinidad had avoided stark political confrontations on racial lines. In elections at the end of

1986, Chambers offered PNM 'stability, continuity and experience'. By now, however, voters were ready for change. They preferred the National Alliance for Reconstruction, and the PNM lost office for the first time since independence.

19.3.2 Jamaica

Figure 19.4 shows that Jamaica was less racially divided than Trinidad. Its reserves of bauxite produced less wealth than Trinidad's oil, however. The political history of Jamaica after independence was one of changing elected governments but of considerable violence outside parliament, with fierce clashes between left and right. Elections on the eve of independence in 1962 brought to power the Jamaica Labour Party (JLP) under Alexander Bustamante, snatching victory from the People's National Party (PNP) with its more socialist policies. The JLP was re-elected in 1967 and remained in office until 1972, though Bustamante – already 78 years old in 1962 – retired before the election of 1967, a widely respected veteran of the island's Labour movement.

Michael Manley became the PNP Prime Minister in 1972. The son of Norman Manley, who had helped found the Party, Michael Manley had radical ideas for the reform of the world economic order to help the poor, and his readiness to co-operate with Castro in neighbouring Cuba displeased the USA. The PNP seemed to move to the left, welcoming Cuban help with Jamaica's pressing housing problems. The JLP meanwhile came to be led by Edward Seaga, who preferred close ties with Washington and favoured private enterprise above Manley's state enterprises. The gulf between the parties widened and some 200 Jamaicans were killed in the violent elections of 1976. Manley won a decisive victory, with the voters supporting the PNP's socialist policies – part of what seemed at the time a general Caribbean movement towards the 'New Left' with its admiration of Castro (see Unit 10).

The PNP faced problems, however. Impatient expectations led to unrest on the left. The two movements of Rastafarianism and Black Power attracted followers with their emphasis on racial identity, and violence sometimes erupted. Others turned to violence in anti-Castro and anti-PNP outbursts. The government replied with emergency powers and set up a special Gun Court. A violent society was not Manley's only difficulty, however. Soaring oil prices and inflation in the 1970s increased the already high levels of Jamaican unemployment. The trade deficit worsened and debt grew. When Jamaica sought help from the IMF, Western financiers imposed conditions which handicapped PNP policies. As elections approached in 1980, unemployment affected about one Jamaican in three. Manley wanted the voters to agree to defy the IMF and seek help among the world's non-aligned nations. Seaga and the JLP denounced such ideas, looking for support to the USA.

The elections took place amid turbulence and bloodshed with reports of some 600 political killings in Jamaica during 1980. The PNP was accused of godlessness and communism, and the JLP took 51 parliamentary seats to the PNP's nine. Seaga became Prime Minister and promptly made peace with the IMF, first cutting down Cuban influence in Jamaica and then breaking off

Table 19.2 States in the Caribbean: some comparative statistics

State	Population		Income per head, 1983 (US dollars)*	Number of people per doctor, c. 1980	Percentage of population literate over age 15, c. 1980
	Estimated, 1985 (millions)	Annual growth, 1980–5 (%)			
Barbados†	0.3	0.3	4 060	1 245	99
Grenada†	0.1	0.1	1 220	2 882	98
Guyana†	1.0	1.8	460	8 170	92
Jamaica†	2.3	1.1	1 290	3 061	96
Trinidad and Tobago†‡	1.2	1.9	6 850	1 450	92
Cuba	10.1	1.0	1 590	637	95
Dominican Republic	6.2	2.7	1 370	2 624	67
Haiti	5.3	1.9	330	5 994	35
Puerto Rico (USA)	3.3	1.0	3 930	848	83

* At current market prices

† English-speaking; founder-members of the Caribbean Free Trade Area (Carifta) (1968) and the Caribbean Community and Common Market (1973–4) (see section 9.4)

‡ Gross national product boosted by oil output

Compare Table 10.1

Statistics from *Encyclopaedia Britannica*

relations with Castro's government at the end of 1981. When Reagan became President of the USA, Seaga was welcomed to Washington as his first overseas visitor. The PNP boycotted new elections in 1983 and the JLP took all 60 parliamentary seats. Political violence subsided, though society was still turbulent as Jamaica continued to be plagued by severe economic problems. The IMF's conditions for help meant currency devaluations, austerity and hardship in the effort to balance the island's finances.

A mature nation was nevertheless being built in Jamaica with genuine political debate and the PNP was once more ready to contest elections. The PNP had sweeping successes in local government elections in 1986, but violence occurred again when Seaga ignored demands for a new general election. Jamaica's violence had seldom been racial but, like many new nations, the island endured social unrest alongside economic deprivation. Geography placed Jamaica uncomfortably close to the USA and to Cuba which, given Washington's deep suspicions of Castro, jeopardized total independence. There were strong suspicions that Jamaica under Manley and the PNP was destabilized by American influences in ways hardly more subtle than those used by South Africa against its black neighbours.

Jamaica's economy was not only vulnerable to financial manipulation, it also relied heavily on tourists, especially from the USA. At the same time, however, the tourist industry itself created strains. The contrast between luxury tourist hotels and the wretched conditions of many Jamaicans was a constant reminder of persisting inequalities, while the tourist–servant relationship, usually white–black, echoed the days of slavery, so much a part of Jamaican and Caribbean history. In coming to terms with the late twentieth century, Jamaica had done much to diversify its economy and to move away from its traditional dependence on sugar cultivation. In the early 1980s, aluminum and bauxite earned far more foreign currency than did sugar and bananas. But, as Manley argued to the Brandt Commission, the economic scales were still weighted heavily against developing nations (see sections 21.1 and 21.3).

19.3.3 Guyana

The timing of Guyana's independence, in 1966, showed clear evidence of British discrimination against Cheddi Jagan and the People's Progressive Party (PPP). It was to Forbes Burnham and a government mainly of the People's National Congress (PNC) that Britain granted independence (see section 14.3.1), Burnham remaining in power until his death in 1985. British opposition to Jagan was based on his pro-Soviet Marxism, and with some justification Jagan complained that his government had been deliberately destabilized while independence was withheld during the 1960s. The PNC gained an overall majority in 1968, and kept it. An outside commission under Lord Chitnis reported unflatteringly on the elections of 1985, however, and documented:

> the historical record of the Guyanese electoral system, showing how, since 1964, that system has been undermined and brought under the control of the ruling PNC.

Guyana had not avoided the racial division in politics which Williams had worked to prevent in Trinidad. Jagan and the PPP, from which Burnham and the PNC had broken away in the 1950s, were supported mainly by Guyana's Asian population; Burnham and the PNC were supported mainly by blacks. Political bitterness widened the racial divide in spite of all the talk of 'one nation' and racial harmony. Moreover, the Asians worked mainly in agriculture while many of the blacks were urban industrial workers, and racial conflict flared all too readily.

Guyana became a republic in 1970 and Burnham became President ten years later after constitutional changes and another much-criticized election. Like Botha in South Africa, however, he kept executive power, whether as Prime Minister or President. Whatever the British might have hoped, the PNC government also adopted strongly socialist policies and in 1978 Guyana became an associate member of Comecon. In Caribbean co-operation, Guyana joined Carifta and Caricom and took the lead in the 1970s in restoring relations with Castro and persuading the Organization of American States to lift its boycott of Cuban trade. Burnham tried to play a leading role in developing the non-aligned movement and joined the African, Caribbean, Pacific (ACP) group and the Latin American Economic System (SELA). But most of Guyana's trade was still conducted with the capitalist world, especially Britain and the USA, and all these overseas links failed to enable Guyana to fulfil its economic potential.

Racial and industrial unrest at home resulted in an exodus of Guyanese, especially to Canada. The population climbed only slowly towards a million and much of the country's interior remained sparsely populated and undeveloped. Bauxite provided some wealth and Burnham nationalized US and Canadian-owned mining enterprises. Sugar cultivation remained important and much of that was also nationalized along with the Booker–McConnell holdings in a variety of enterprises. Per-capita income failed to take off, however, though Guyana's balance of trade, while depending on fluctuating commodity prices for bauxite and sugar, was often better than that of many developing nations. Electrification, the improvement of communications and social services, land resettlement and better housing all showed some successes during the twenty years after independence, but bankruptcy threatened in the 1980s. Like Jamaica, Guyana had to try to meet IMF conditions in order to get external aid. Links with Comecon weakened. To economic disappointment was added disquiet concerning Burnham's authoritarianism. The mysterious killing in 1980 of Walter Rodney, a left-wing lecturer, author and political opponent, increased the disquiet. Burnham was succeeded in 1985 by Desmond Hoyte, and there was renewed dismay when the elections which followed seemed as firmly under PNC control as those which Burnham had conducted. Unrest persisted, holding back development and underlining the grave disservice that had been done to Guyana in the 1950s when the PNC and PPP divided on racial lines.

19.4 Legacies for Britain

19.4.1 Northern Ireland

(a) The double minority and the tyranny of the majority The bulk of Ireland, 26 of its 32 counties, seceded from the United Kingdom in 1922. The Irish Free State was granted Dominion status in the Anglo-Irish Treaty signed that year, and gradually evolved towards complete independence, proclaiming a new constitution in 1937 which effectively removed the last British controls over Irish sovereignty. Ireland, or Eire as it is known in the Gaelic language, remained neutral during the Second World War and proclaimed itself an independent Republic in 1949, when it also left the British Commonwealth. The Irish struggle for cultural and political independence was not untypical of other decolonization episodes. What was untypical, and seemingly insoluble, was the problem posed by the remaining six counties of Ireland, Northern Ireland, which had formerly been part of the northernmost Irish province of Ulster.

Northern Ireland was created in 1920, and granted home rule as a province of the UK with its own devolved Parliament established in Belfast. It was created because of the resistance of a majority of the inhabitants of the area (about 66 per cent of a population of one and a half million) to the idea of home rule and independence for the whole island of Ireland. The roots of this resistance lay in the historically established ethnic, cultural, economic and political differences between the north-eastern part of Ireland and the rest of the island. At the end of the nineteenth century the bulk of the Irish population claimed descent from the native Gaelic-speaking population who had lived in the island before the successive conquests by Norman, English and British monarchs. They were Catholic by religious belief and primarily engaged in agricultural or small-scale economic activities. This population, with a history of several centuries of domination and maltreatment at the hands of their British colonial rulers, formed the social basis of Irish nationalist movements from the late nineteenth century onwards. They were most vehemently opposed by the population of north-eastern Ireland who claimed descent from the Scotch and English colonial settlers who had been planted in Ulster by English monarchs and landowners from the seventeenth century onwards. The planters were overwhelmingly Protestant in their religious beliefs, and over half of them were Presbyterians. At the end of the nineteenth century a great many of them were also engaged in industrial activities, and consequently felt that their interests would be better served by the maintenance of the union with Britain.

The conflicting ambitions of nationalists and unionists led to political and eventually armed mobilization in the years before the First World War, and the British decision to partition the island owed a great deal to the belief that the unionist/Protestant population would fight rather than accept being ruled by a home-rule government in Ireland. The partition of Ireland may have been a sensible recognition of irreconcilable differences but it was also a badly organized partition. Northern Ireland was created with a large minority of

Catholics (about 33 per cent of the population of one and a half million) who would rather have been part of the Irish Free State. Although this minority was not large enough to pose an electoral threat to unionists, provided they remained united, it was too large to permit the majority to relax and accommodate the minority's interests and values. Northern Ireland's boundaries had been created to give unionists as much Irish territory as they could feasibly control. Not surprisingly, therefore, Northern Ireland soon became a classic example of the tyranny of the majority. By contrast, the Protestant/unionist minority in the Irish Free State was less than 10 per cent of the total population, posed no threat to the stability of the state, and was treated reasonably well by the majority.

Irish nationalists argued, and still do, that the creation of Northern Ireland was a denial of the Irish people's right to self-determination. It was created despite the fact that an overwhelming majority of those who voted in the Irish election in 1918 voted for Sinn Féin (literally, 'Ourselves Alone'), a party which stood for the independence of Ireland from Britain, and for the Irish nationalists. The artificial border of Northern Ireland, which had no clear cultural or geographical rationale, created a sectarian province in which the nationalist minority was permanently subordinated. The failure of the British government to redraw the boundaries of Northern Ireland, as envisaged in the Treaty of 1922, created a political entity which was illegitimate both in the eyes of its minority population and in the eyes of the Irish state, which claimed sovereignty over Northern Ireland in its constitution of 1937. It was not surprising, according to Irish nationalists, that the minority population resorted to civil disobedience or insurrection against their status in Northern Ireland.

By contrast, Ulster unionists argued that the Irish Free State had illegitimately broken the Union with Britain. Northern Ireland was and would remain part of Britain. Unionists were a majority within Northern Ireland and therefore had the right, as its majority, both to govern it and to impose their political and cultural preferences upon the minority. They also feared that were they ever to become part of the Irish Free State, or its successor, the Irish Republic, they would become a minority in their turn. The Northern Ireland conflict thus stems in part from a double minority problem: nationalist Catholics are a minority within Northern Ireland, Protestant unionists fear being a similarly situated minority in a united Ireland.

This difficulty need not have been insurmountable had the unionists treated the minority equitably, and had British governments ensured that British standards of democracy and public administration had prevailed in Northern Ireland. Instead unionists behaved as a tyrannous majority, and British governments in effect ignored events in Northern Ireland, which they left in the hands of the devolved Parliament (which from 1932 sat at Stormont, outside Belfast). Between 1920 and 1972 Northern Ireland was governed by the Unionist party, which won all the elections held in the province. Its in-built majority was reinforced by political measures designed to discriminate against the minority, and to unite the majority into focusing its politics on the single issue of the legitimacy of the border across Ireland. First, the election system, proportional representation[G], introduced by the British in the Government of Ireland Act of 1920 as a safeguard for the minority, was repealed in 1929 and replaced by the 'first-past-the-post' electoral system. The purpose was to ensure that Unionists would remain united in their opposition to nationalists, and the aim was achieved. The change in voting system also increased Unionist dominance in seats held at Stormont and in local government, leading many nationalists to abstain from political competition altogether. Second, the Unionist party engaged in extensive gerrymandering[G] of electoral districts, to reduce the number of seats which nationalists could win, and in some cases to create Unionist 'victories' in areas where its voters were outnumbered by nationalists. Finally, it maintained the unreformed property-based voting system for local government, which was abolished after the Second World War in the rest of the United Kingdom. Under this system, people who paid no rates had no votes, and some businessmen were entitled to multiple votes. Given the relatively more privileged position of Protestants compared to Catholics, this archaic absence of 'one person one vote' further reinforced the position of the majority, and the disaffection of the minority.

The Unionists also presided over a system of economic discrimination against the minority population. Catholics were overrepresented among the unemployed: in 1985 a Catholic was still 2.4 times as likely to be unemployed as a Protestant according to research commissioned by the Standing Advisory Commission on Human Rights set-up by the British government. Catholics were also strikingly underrepresented in high-income and high-status positions in both the private and the public sectors. These differences were largely the result of discrimination, although Unionists claimed, erroneously, that they were entirely due to other factors: the backwardness of (separate) Catholic education, the laziness of Catholics, or the greater presence of Catholics in the poorer, western part of Northern Ireland. In fact Unionist politicians actively encouraged discrimination on sectarian grounds, and not simply in employment. For example, discrimination occurred in the allocation of housing by local government authorities. The Cameron Commission, which was appointed by the British government and reported in 1969, confirmed the validity of minority complaints about discrimination.

Finally, the tyranny of the majority was evident in legal and cultural measures. Northern Ireland had on its statute books one of the most repressive pieces of legislation in any liberal democracy: the Special Powers Act. It enabled the government to arrest and intern people without trial, a power that was used regularly to crush nationalist terrorists, and others who were not guilty of insurrection. It also included a clause which has now become infamous:

> 'If any person does any act of such a nature as to be calculated to be prejudicial to the preservation of the peace or the maintenance of order in Northern Ireland and not specifically provided for in the regulations, he shall be deemed to be guilty of an offence against the regulations.'

The nationalist population were also denied the right to march with symbols of their political and cultural identity, for example to wave the flag of the Irish Republic. They were, however, required to endure triumphalist marches of the Orange Order (a sectarian and exclusively Protestant organization founded in 1795 in memory of King William of Orange, who had defeated Catholic King James II) through the areas in which they lived. Perhaps it was therefore not so surprising that sections of the minority population regularly resorted to violence, supporting the Irish Republican Army (the IRA) which aimed to unite Ireland through force, although it had long been illegal in the Irish Republic. However, such campaigns of armed violence were usually easily crushed by the Unionists, as the IRA's campaign between 1956 and 1962 proved. The combination of the policing and legal powers at the disposal of the Unionist government proved too great. However, these regular outbursts of IRA activity did reinforce the *laager*[G] mentality of the Unionist population, who felt besieged both from without (by the Irish Republic, where the Roman Catholic Church was dominant) and from within (by a recalcitrant minority) and uncertain of continued British support.

(b) The Breakdown of Unionist control The Unionist system of majority control broke down in 1968–9 under the impact of the Northern Ireland Civil Rights Association, which had been organized by middle-class Catholics to protest against the abuse of rights and of democracy within the province. The Northern Ireland Civil Rights Association (NICRA, or CRA for short) organized marches and peaceful protests, modelled on the examples of Martin Luther King and Mahatma Gandhi, aiming to appeal to British and world public opinion to remedy its grievances. The civil-rights movement was a sign of hope. Its supporters initially called for equal citizenship rights, that is they called to be treated as 'first-class' British citizens rather than proclaiming traditional nationalist demands.

However, extreme unionists interpreted the CRA's actions as a nationalist front, pointed to the presence of former IRA supporters among its ranks, and agreed with the Reverend Ian Paisley, a Presbyterian preacher, that 'CRA = IRA'. CRA demonstrations were attacked by the overwhelmingly Protestant police force, the Royal Ulster Constabulary (RUC), and its exclusively Protestant reserve constabulary, the 'B specials'. Attacks on Catholic areas culminated in attempted massacres in Belfast in August 1969. In the era of televised mass communications Unionists were no longer able to crush Catholic dissent while Britain looked the other way. The blaze of international publicity caused by the skeleton in Britain's cupboard prompted the Labour government to intervene. It sent troops to Northern Ireland to keep the peace, and demanded that the Unionist government reform itself.

Unfortunately these moves came too late for an amicable settlement. The reforms came too late to satisfy all Catholics. The IRA, which had been dormant since 1962, split into rival factions: the more extreme Provisional IRA ('the Provos') asserting that only a British withdrawal from Ireland could lead to a reform of the province. During 1970–1 the Provisional IRA began a sustained campaign of violence to force a British departure, killing soldiers, murdering police officers and bombing 'economic targets'. Protestant opinion had also polarized. The reforming Prime Minister, Terence O'Neill, was forced to resign, and more extreme Unionist leaders came to the fore: Brian Faulkner, James Craig and Ian Paisley. Protestant paramilitary organizations had also sprung into life: the Ulster Volunteer Force (UVF) had been active since 1966 in campaigns of murder and provocation, and from 1972 they were joined by the Ulster Defence Association (UDA), a paramilitary organization which managed to remain legal.

The Unionist government and the Conservative government (elected in 1970) played into the hands of the IRA in August 1971 by introducing internment without trial and rounding up large numbers of people who proved to be wholly uninvolved with the IRA. At the same time the government's actions legitimated the actions of the IRA in the eyes of some of the nationalist population. The repressive policy of internment actually increased rather than reduced the level of violence in the province, with over 450 people dying in 1972, the year after it was introduced. In the city of Londonderry on 30 January 1972, during what later became known as 'Bloody Sunday', British soldiers killed thirteen unarmed civilians who were demonstrating, illegally, against the policy of internment. The bad feeling these killings created and the support they generated for the IRA led the British government to change tack. It abolished the Stormont Parliament in March 1972 and introduced direct rule from Westminster. Protestant paramilitaries reacted in anguish: fearful that Britain was about to leave, they increasingly engaged in random assassinations of Catholics, and such murders continued at a high rate until 1976.

(c) The impasse and efforts to solve the conflict From 1972 to 1985 the general policy of successive British governments was to try to create an internal political settlement with Northern Ireland in which nationalists and unionists would agree to share political power within a devolved government. This policy was accompanied by efforts to referee the conflict as a neutral arbiter, to reform the province's sectarian practices and to combat terrorism. The attainment of each of these objectives proved elusive.

In 1973–4 a power-sharing executive was established in which power was shared between some Unionists and the newly formed moderate nationalist party, the SDLP (Social Democratic and Labour Party). However, it collapsed under the pressure of a general strike of Protestant workers. Further efforts by British Secretaries of State to promote power-sharing also proved abortive. A constitutional Convention held by Merlyn Rees failed in 1975; all-party talks under Humphrey Atkins got nowhere between 1979 and 1980; and James Prior's scheme for 'rolling devolution' did not succeed. The latter idea was an attempt to devolve power gradually for those responsibilities where nationalists and unionists were prepared to agree upon what needed to be done in the province.

The efforts to promote power-sharing foundered for many reasons. The continuing campaign of terrorism by the IRA made Unionists very unwilling to contemplate power-sharing. The failure of British governments to eradicate discrimination in Northern Ireland and the repressive systems of legislation, policing and military coercion which they used to combat terrorism made the nationalist minority more rather than less nationalist. Many Unionists believed that provided Britain crushed the IRA it would be possible to return Northern Ireland to what it was like before 1972. The Provisional IRA, and the political party which emerged to support it, Provisional Sinn Féin, believed that after a 'long war' of attrition they would force British government to withdraw from Northern Ireland. These extremist views were hardly likely to be conducive to compromise. Those political leaders, within both the nationalist and unionist traditions, who were prepared to accommodate the other side and favour power-sharing found that they were overthrown from below by their followers. Finally, political competition within each tradition increased the intractability of the conflict.

Nationalists were divided between supporters of Sinn Féin and the SDLP, the former being supporters of the IRA, the latter being firmly opposed to violence. However, the SDLP felt obliged to follow Sinn Féin criticisms of British lack of reforms of Northern Ireland, and the maladministration of justice, or else face the threat of being branded as stooges by Sinn Féin. The competitive pressure from Sinn Féin made the SDLP insist upon some recognition of an 'Irish dimension' (that is, a formal role for the Irish government) in the affairs of the province, a demand which all unionists found unacceptable. Unionists were themselves divided into three main groups after 1972: the Ulster Unionist party (which is internally divided between those who favour the complete integration of Northern Ireland into the British political system, those who want a return to majority rule, and those prepared to countenance power-sharing); the Democratic Unionist party (led by Ian Paisley, which stands for 'no surrender' – that is, no compromises on unionist domination); and the Alliance party (which advocates sharing power and finds support among both the Catholic and Protestant middle classes, but with less than 10 per cent of the electorate behind it cannot shape the politics of the province). These divisions on the unionist side, like those on the nationalist side, meant that those who supported power-sharing were always outnumbered, or fearful of rapidly becoming outnumbered.

Apart from failure to promote power-sharing within Northern Ireland, other British policy objectives were not achieved. Britain's attempt to referee the conflict foundered. To the rest of the world, which generally regarded Northern Ireland as illegitimate, Britain appeared to be supporting unionists against nationalists, a view reiterated by the nationalist population. Within Northern Ireland unionists complained that the British government was soft on terrorism, irresolute in its dealings with the minority and the Irish Republic, and not prepared to declare its permanent commitment to Northern Ireland's status as part of the United Kingdom. As unionists made a point of noting, successive British governments declared that Northern Ireland would remain part of the UK as long as a majority of its inhabitants so wished. This 'guarantee' implied that the British government would allow Northern Ireland to become part of the Irish state if opinion within the province changed. Unionists complained that this 'guarantee' made the status of Northern Ireland different from that of all other regions of the UK.

British efforts to reform Northern Ireland proved equally unsuccessful. Unemployment rose for reasons which had nothing to do with the troubles, but the relatively privileged position of Protestants compared to Catholics remained much as it had been, eventually leading to campaigns in America to prevent investment in Northern Ireland unless firms committed themselves to programmes of affirmative action[G]. The Fair Employment Agency, established in 1976, eight years after the beginning of the current 'troubles', proved ineffective, and in 1987 the British government had to promise to create a new agency.

British efforts to crush terrorism were equally unproductive. Between 1969 and 1988 over 2700 people had died in Northern Ireland as a direct result of political violence. The IRA and other nationalist organizations were responsible for over 60 per cent of the deaths; the rest were attributable to the actions of Protestant paramilitaries or the security forces. The dead included nearly 2000 civilians, over 400 members of Northern Ireland's security forces, and over 400 members of the British Army. Both communities had suffered dramatically in other ways: over 20 000 people had sustained serious injuries, there had been over 30 000 shootings, nearly 9000 explosions and nearly 15 000 armed robberies. Moreover, thousands of people were intimidated out of their homes in successive waves of coercion in the twenty years after 1968. The IRA had been able to gain regular international publicity, and some limited degree of international legitimacy, especially after a hunger-striking IRA prisoner, Bobby Sands, was elected to the Westminster Parliament in 1981, before he died of starvation. The IRA had regularly struck abroad at British troops and at British public figures: killing Christopher Ewart-Biggs, the British Ambassador to the Irish Republic, in 1976 and Lord Louis Mountbatten in 1979, and nearly killing most of the British Cabinet, including Mrs Thatcher, in Brighton in 1984. The INLA (Irish National Liberation Army), another nationalist terrorist organization, killed the Conservative politician Airey Neave, the prospective Shadow Secretary of State for Northern Ireland, in May 1979. However, the IRA had failed in its most important task: it enjoyed the support of only a minority of the minority within Northern Ireland, and almost no support in the Irish Republic. Moreover, its frequent atrocities, like the killing of civilians at a Remembrance Day commemoration at Enniskillen in 1987, and other bombings and shootings which killed men, women and children who had nothing to do with the conflict, undermined its credibility as a national liberation organization.

Yet Britain's way of combatting IRA terrorism won it few friends. In European Courts British governments were regularly found to have breached the European Convention on Human Rights, either in their treatment of suspects or in the legislation they had passed to combat terrorism. The measures taken by successive governments included internment without trial, no-jury (Diplock) courts, the apparent sanctioning of the beating of suspects and endorsement of 'shoot-to-kill' actions; the use of paid informants ('super-

Fig. 19.5 The IRA cortege for Bobby Sands – IRA man and Member of Parliament for Fermanagh and South Tyrone – who died in May 1981 after 66 days on hunger strike

grasses'), holding people in police stations as suspects without access to a solicitor for more than seven days, the use of unprecedented powers to exile people from one part of the United Kingdom to another, restrictions on broadcasting freedoms, and interference with the rules governing the elections of candidates for elected office. These measures not only blotted Britain's reputation as a protector of human rights and the rule of law but also failed to defeat terrorism and brought officially unwelcome visits from Amnesty International and Irish-American politicians.

(d) The Anglo–Irish Agreement and the road to consensus? Recognizing the failures of its Northern Ireland policies, the British government signed an international treaty with the Irish government in November 1985, in an attempt to create a framework for a long-run solution to the difficulties of the province. The Agreement declared that Northern Ireland would remain part of the UK for as long as a majority of the province's inhabitants so wished, but would become part of the Republic of Ireland if a majority were to develop for that objective. The Agreement also created an Inter-Governmental Conference, in which the British and Irish governments were to discuss the formulation of all policies pertinent to Northern Ireland. This part of the Agreement, together with the establishment of a Secretariat at Maryfield in Belfast, outraged Unionists as it gave the Irish government a formal say in the government of Northern Ireland, although it did not give the Irish government any executive or legislative powers. The Agreement also declared that if nationalist and unionist were prepared to share power within a devolved assembly in Northern Ireland then the British and Irish governments would support such moves, and where agreement to share power in specific policy fields was made the London and Dublin governments would formally cease to discuss such fields.

The Anglo–Irish Agreement, an imaginative step embarked upon by Mrs Thatcher, the British Prime Minister, and by the Irish Prime Minister Dr Garret FitzGerald, was designed to achieve many things: to reduce support for the IRA and Sinn Féin (which before the Agreement had risen to over 40 per cent of the nationalist vote within Northern Ireland); to increase British and Irish co-operation against terrorism; to reassure nationalists and the Irish government that Britain was intent upon reforming Northern Ireland and treating nationalists as on an equal footing with unionists; and to coerce unionists into choosing power-sharing in preference to giving the Dublin government a potentially powerful role in Northern Ireland through the Inter-Governmental Conference.

In its first three years, however, the Agreement had only limited successes. The Agreement did stem the rise in support for Sinn Féin, although it did not reduce the levels of IRA violence. Despite a considerable increase in police co-operation between the two states, the British and Irish governments had multiple public rows over the extradition of suspected terrorists. Irish belief in the willingness of Britain to reform Northern Ireland was undermined by failures to alter court procedures and by controversial judicial decisions (such as in the cases of the Birmingham Six and the Guildford Four – people sentenced for terrorist bombing in mainland Britain) and undercover operations (such as the killing of an IRA active-service unit in Gibraltar). The appropriate action to be taken against discrimination in employment in Northern Ireland also remained controversial. Unionists remained persistently hostile to the Agreement, and showed no willingness to contemplate a power-sharing settlement which would be acceptable to the SDLP.

The conflict in Northern Ireland continued, a classic example of a conflict fuelled by ethnic, national and religious tensions, exacerbated by terrorism and the disorders which accompanied decolonization and the end of imperialism throughout the world: a gory illustration of the difficulties states faced in meeting the rights of minorities in the modern world. Power-sharing on the basis of equality seemed impossible to achieve, despite the absence of super-power rivalries over the province, and despite relatively good relations between Britain and the Irish Republic. Whether more drastic measures would eventually be taken, such as a British departure from Northern Ireland or another partition of the island, remained to be seen.

19.4.2 Britain's multiracial society

(a) Immigration The census of 1971 showed that six per cent of Britain's population was foreign-born. The figure included 2.3 per cent (just over 1.1 million) born in the 'New Commonwealth', a euphemism for non-whites from Asia, Africa and the West Indies, and 1.3 per cent born in the Irish Republic. Many non-whites were by this time born in the United Kingdom itself, however: around 40 per cent of the two million or so non-whites in the UK's total population of around 56 million.

Few non-whites lived in Britain before the Second World War. But the war helped to change attitudes and to quicken expectations. Developments in transport made movement easier, and the decades of teaching about the greatness of Britain, the mother country, made it natural that people should move into Britain from the Empire and Commonwealth, especially when Britain had a post-war labour shortage. The newcomers staffed transport and hospital services in ill-paid jobs and operated the night-shifts needed to make new textiles machinery profitable. The British Nationality Act of 1948 confirmed the tradition that subjects of the Empire had British nationality and could enter Britain freely. But the changes in society were noticed in the 1950s, especially in communities in London, the Midlands and the North where non-whites tended to settle near available work and their fellow-countrymen. Opinion divided: while many welcomed the newcomers for their contributions to the economy and the ways in which they enriched British society and culture, others feared that white culture and the country's traditions might be undermined. Thousands from the Indian subcontinent could not speak English but hoped to learn it in the UK and escape the poverty they had suffered. Some in Britain feared having to share their own prosperity with those they considered alien.

A fierce debate began about the influx, severely testing those politicians who preached racial equality abroad, especially in the developing Commonwealth, but found many voters at home nothing like so open-minded. It was claimed that Britain was too small for a bigger population (though emigration usually more than matched immigration), and that difficulties in housing, education, welfare services and employment would be increased (see section 5.5). Action to restrict immigration was resisted during the 1950s but after noting the 'wind of change' in Africa, Macmillan bowed to a different wind at home. About 30 000 non-whites a year arrived in Britain in the 1950s, twice that in 1960 and more than 100 000 in 1961, when ethnic minorities made up one per cent of Britain's population and restrictions seemed imminent. The Commonwealth Immigrants Act of 1962 abolished the right of entry from the Commonwealth except for those with work vouchers testifying they already had a job in Britain, and for the close dependants of those already settled in Britain. The Act did not apply to non-Commonwealth countries, including the Irish Republic. Labour was fiercely critical of the Act, but Wilson's government in 1965 nevertheless tightened the screw, limiting the annual total of work vouchers to 8500.

Further legislation was introduced in 1968 in sudden fear of an influx of Asians from Kenya. They had been allowed to keep their British citizenship and passports when Kenya became independent but were now facing explusion from that country because of Africanization (see section 17.4.3). Home Secretary Callaghan imposed a quota in a new Commonwealth Immigration Act. The UK would admit only 1500 such passport-holders and their immediate families each year, while going cap in hand to other countries such as Tanzania and Canada to beg them to absorb the non-whites. Amin launched a fierce attack on Uganda's British Asians in 1972, and they too sought refuge, only to find Heath's government eager to persuade them to go almost anywhere but Britain. Many countries responded, among them Canada, Australia, New Zealand, India and Malawi and, outside the Commonwealth, Sweden and Iran. The generosity of these other host nations helped Britain evade many of its responsibilities, though the European Human Rights Commission was scathing of British policy.

The influx of former colonial subjects was not unique to Britain. The Netherlands, for example, took in about 300 000 when Indonesia became independent, and such immigration along with temporary 'guest-workers' in countries such as West Germany, France and Switzerland, helped create multiracial communities in many parts of Europe. But Britain continued to fear what some politicians rashly called being 'swamped' by non-white newcomers. Enoch Powell, Conservative and later Ulster Unionist MP, warned that non-white immigration would create tensions which might lead to much bloodshed: Heath excluded him from government office for his outspokenness. Powell nevertheless had a following and, further to the right, the National Front and assorted racists exploited colour prejudice to stir up a Nazi-like 'white backlash'. Governments condemned such extremism but Conservatives nevertheless kept alive the idea that non-white immigration could be further reduced. Heath brought in a new Immigration Act in 1971, making uniform regulations for Commonwealth and foreign immigrants, requiring a period of probation before permanent settlement, but also introducing 'patriality' regulations, mainly to favour would-be immigrants from the white Dominions. Thatcher made more adjustments ten years later, including a new Nationality Act, promising her supporters that the immigration of dependants, especially from the Indian subcontinent, would be scrutinized even more fiercely to prevent admissions on false pretences. Non-whites in 1986 were still only 4.5 per cent of the UK population, but it was something some British seemed still to fret about and the Thatcher government boasted that admissions in 1987 fell to the lowest level since the 1940s.

Immigration law, the debate surrounding it, the activities of racist organizations and some occasional bitter election campaigns undermined confidence in

Britain as a champion of multiracialism. Many Britons found the legacy of the Empire uncomfortable and would have liked to forget how their country had benefited from the past exploitation of its colonies, their ancestors conquering and settling more or less wherever they liked. On the other hand, much constructive effort was put into bettering race relations within Britain, though the results were rather patchy.

(b) Race relations Open conflict between the races in Britain was comparatively rare in spite of the unthinking brutality of hooligans and the malevolent efforts of neo-Nazis in various nationalist movements to stir up hatred. Yet clashes in Nottingham and at Notting Hill, London, as early as 1958 had added to pressures for restrictions on immigration and uneasiness about questions of colour persisted. Wilson's government realized that legislation in itself could not create racial goodwill, but felt that it could point the way towards desirable conduct, indicating practices that are socially acceptable, and this it tried to achieve in the Race Relations Act of 1965. The Act aimed to stiffen UK laws about incitement to disorder and to discourage discrimination against ethnic minorities, for example in hotels and public houses. It set up the Race Relations Board to monitor developments and to encourage equal treatment, by conciliation and, if necessary, prosecution. A second Race Relations Act in 1968 extended the scope of the law to include housing, employment and finance, and outlawed discrimination, including:

> segregating people on grounds of colour, race, or ethnic or national origins.

This Act set up the Community Relations Commission, and local authorities were encouraged to set up matching Community Relations Councils. A third Race Relations Act in 1976 firmly extended the scope of the law to education, trade unions and the police, setting up the Commission for Racial Equality and for the first time allowing individuals to bring to court private cases alleging racial discrimination.

The laws erected helpful signposts but attitudes changed only slowly. Many surveys of housing, employment and incomes showed that non-whites in Britain were likely to suffer poorer conditions than whites, and that improvement was painfully slow. In 1985, for example, while unemployment among white males was about ten per cent, it was more than double that among those whose ethnic origins lay in Pakistan, Bangladesh and the West Indies, and almost twenty per cent among those of Indian origin.

The Runnymede Trust and other interested bodies showed that in 1987–8 it was still especially difficult for non-whites to find and keep jobs in Britain. The problem seemed most acute for Bangladeshis and those of Afro-Caribbean descent, but non-whites generally were inadequately represented in many areas such as banking and the civil service. The authorities began to press for more extensive monitoring of the recruitment of work-forces, the better to obtain accurate information and to increase awareness of imbalance where recruitment was narrow. The trade unions, it was alleged, might also do more to encourage the employment and acceptance of non-whites. There was also concern among liberals that the many schemes which by the mid-1980s existed to help people to set up small businesses achieved comparatively little for Afro-Caribbean applicants. The borough of Lambeth in London reported that in the mid-1980s the banks rejected 74 per cent of Afro-Caribbean applications but only thirteen per cent of Asian and six per cent of white applications. Yet local councils such as Lambeth itself which sought actively to promote the interests of blacks were often the subject of witch-hunts and were derided by government and the media for 'loony-left' activities which wasted money.

Though they could win no parliamentary seat, the neo-Nazis, in spite of the race-relations laws, continued to exploit suspicions and fears, sometimes undermining the efforts of local associations and communities, education and the media to combat prejudice. Attacks on non-whites were common enough in the 1970s and 1980s to cause anxiety. The number of non-whites born in Britain naturally grew and young blacks in particular bitterly resented inequality and ignorant parrot-cries that they ought to 'go home'. Tensions increased in many black 'ghettos', the urban areas of usually high unemployment and sub-standard housing where non-whites congregated from necessity rather than from choice.

Violence erupted in England which had some similarities to that in Northern Ireland, with petrol bombs, blazing buildings and battles against the police, though human casualties were fewer. The first major outbreak was in Bristol (St Pauls) in 1980. In 1981 there were riots in London (Brixton and Southall), Manchester (Moss Side) and Liverpool (Toxteth). Toxteth erupted again in 1982, St Paul's again in 1983, and in 1985 came major confrontations in Handsworth in Birmingham, in Brixton, which was part of Lambeth, and then in Tottenham. Non-whites – and especially young blacks – were prominent in all of these conflicts, but they were by no means simple racial conflicts: many saw them as protests by the underprivileged of all colours in a deeply divided society, and much pent-up anger seemed to be released against the police and the authorities in general. They were a pointed reminder, nevertheless, that Britain in the 1980s had not yet rid itself of racial discrimination, and that this often went hand in hand with great social deprivation. The violence which lurked near the surface of many societies in the late twentieth century was not confined to the emerging nations of the Third World: states like the United Kingdom in the developed world, especially those where notions of white superiority lingered, had just as great a need for enlightened attitudes and enlightened policies with regard to race relations.

UNIT 20

Resurgent Islam

20.1 Islamic fundamentalism

Religion maintained much of its force after 1945, though weakened in the West by scepticism and materialism and discouraged in the communist world by the authorities. Indeed, religious conflict and extremism added bitterness to the problems of divided societies such as that of Northern Ireland (see section 19.4.1). A new militancy in the Muslim world was born from growing eagerness to restore Islamic traditions and to break free from colonialist influences now that the West had been discredited in twentieth-century world wars. Such militancy helped to inflame the Middle East (see section 18.2) where Lebanon in particular suffered grievously from religious enmities. The foundation of Muslim Pakistan in 1947 encouraged the Islamic reawakening, and the resurgence influenced states as far apart as Algeria and Indonesia, sometimes leading to a *jihad* (holy war) in which Muslim believers welcomed sacrifice and death in conflict with Islam's enemies.

The Muslim Brotherhood dated from 1928. It aimed to reawaken a religious and personal identity especially among poor Egyptian workers (the *fellahin*), and to overthrow the European systems which the colonial age had imposed in Egypt and elsewhere. Not all Arab leaders shared the movement's Islamic ideals, however. Nasser favoured his own brand of Arab nationalism and sought to suppress the Brotherhood, and Sadat so angered the believers in the resurgence of Islam that he was assassinated in 1981 by members of the Jihad El Jedid (New Holy War). In Libya, on the other hand, Muammar al-Qadhdhafi (Gadafy) came to power in 1969 with a vision of a crusade against Western godlessness and a speedy return to the purer values of Islam. These included improving the lot of the poor, sharing out wealth more equally, enforcing a strict code of behaviour and upholding against European and non-Muslim influences the teachings of the prophet Muhammad, recorded in the *Koran*. Such Islamic fundamentalism inevitably became entangled in politics and national interests.

Though united against the imperialism of Europe and the superpowers, the

Islamic movement was not undivided, however. Gadafy inclined to the Sunni Muslims while in Iran the Shiites were dominant and, of the two, seemingly the more militant. Muslims also differed over the extent to which they wished to distance themselves from the technology and materialist values that had already spread from Europe. Politicians sometimes found the religious zeal of the mullahs[G] irksome, their religious ideals not always coexisting easily with political realities – in the government of Pakistan, for example. But the outside world found Islamic fundamentalism even more irksome, a destabilizing force which threatened vested interests.

In the eyes of the West, some fundamentalists seemed not much different from Marxists in their zeal for equality and for discipline based on ideology. The fundamentalists were also linked in Western eyes with extremism and terrorism. A Shiite republic was set up in Iran by the Ayatollah Khomeini after the overthrow of the Shah in 1979, and it quickly became the centre-piece of the Islamic resurgence. It was from Iran that Sadat's assassins drew their inspiration for what they believed was their divine mission. Iran symbolized defiance of the USA, holding 53 Americans hostage for more than a year and later seeming to encourage hostage-taking in Lebanon. But the Soviets were also alarmed by the Islamic resurgence and the disturbance of the status quo. The USSR had a large Muslim population, both Sunni and Shiite, especially bordering Turkey, Iran and Afghanistan. It was partly from fear that Islamic fundamentalism could easily grow into anti-Soviet separatism and undermine Soviet security that Brezhnev in 1979 sent Soviet forces into Afghanistan. The Islamic resurgence, therefore, not only sent shock waves through the Middle East and all countries with substantial Muslim populations: it also rocked the superpowers and embroiled Europeans in yet more post-colonial upheavals.

20.2 Revolution and the Islamic Republic in Iran

20.2.1 The overthrow of the Shah

Like King Farouk of Egypt in 1952 and King Idris of Libya in 1969, the Shah of Iran was deposed in 1979. Few of Iran's population of over 35 million regretted the exiling of Shah Mohammad Reza Pahlavi whose family had taken over the Iranian (then Persian) monarchy in 1925 and who himself had reigned since 1941. His early liberalism had failed to last, and his rule had become extravagant and, latterly, autocratic. Nationalists recalled his discouraging attitude towards Mussadiq in the 1950s (see section 1.5.1). They deplored his close links with the West, especially with the USA, and his friendship with Nixon and Kissinger which brought over 20 000 Americans and a flood of American goods into Iran. The masses gained little benefit from Iran's oil wealth and when oil prices rose in the 1970s Iran's economy was weakened by mismanagement and inflation. The Shah, moreover, offended devout Muslims. They were affronted by the Western influences to be seen in Iran: gambling, the consumption of alcohol, and the cinema with its displays of sex and violence, all were vigorously condemned by the Shiite Ayatollah Khomeini and his fellow religious leaders.

They also opposed what the Shah and the Americans thought of as modernization, especially the Shah's attempt to emancipate Iranian women in 1963. At this time the Ayatollah was driven into exile. From Iraq, and later from France, he kept up bitter criticism which made him a focus of opposition to the Shah.

Economic crisis brought matters to a head when the poor and unemployed demonstrated. There were fierce protests against the Shah's autocratic rule, censorship, the *Savak* (secret police) and abuse of human rights. Though he talked of restoring free elections, the Shah imposed martial law in 1978 to deal with the growing demonstrations, strikes and economic disruption. Blood was shed: hundreds were killed in Tehran alone as the rioting became fiercely religious and nationalist, protesters demanding the return of Khomeini and threatening Americans and Europeans and eventually the Pahlavi dynasty. Members of the National Resurrection Party, founded by the Shah himself in 1975 to exercise one-party government, advised him to leave Iran while they attempted to restore stability. The Shah left in January 1979, never to return. After finding brief asylum in the USA and other friendly states, he died in Egypt, a guest of Sadat, some eighteen months later. Meanwhile, on 1 February 1979, Khomeini re-entered Tehran, pledged to make Iran an Islamic republic.

The Ayatollah's prestige was high, especially among the urban poor. He became, in effect, Iran's head of state, replacing the Shah. Yet months of confusion followed. Khomeini had earlier written:

Fig. 20.1 Resurgent Islam, a demonstration on the streets of Tehran, Iran, December 1978. Enthusiastic support (especially among young male Muslims) for the return from exile of Ayatollah Khomeini soon led to the flight of the Shah and the proclamation of the Islamic Republic of Iran of which Khomeini became the Moral Supervisor.

> The fundamental difference between Islamic government . . . and constitutional monarchy and republics . . . is this: whereas the representatives of the people or the monarch in such regimes engage in legislation, in Islam the legislative power and competence to establish laws belongs exclusively to God Almighty. . . . No law may be executed except the law of the Divine Legislator. It is for this reason that in an Islamic government, a simple planning body takes the place of the legislative assembly.

A Revolutionary Council was set up in the holy city of Qom, while Revolutionary Guards hunted down the agents of the old regime. The politicians in Tehran who tried to carry on secular government were simply overwhelmed by the religious fervour. Shahpur Bakhtiar, the Shah's last Prime Minister, was driven from office, unable to rally the army to withstand the Ayatollah, and Khomeini made Mehdi Bazargan Prime Minister, a devout Muslim. But real power rested with the Revolutionary Council until a new constitution formally made Iran an Islamic republic and presidential elections were held in January 1980.

By then, the Islamic Revolution had not only exacted revenge on the Shah's Iranian supporters but had also turned violently against both dissenters and foreigners. Purges of the army, the civil service and even rival religious factions were carried out, and in November 1979 militant students seized the United States embassy and 53 hostages. Foreign participation in Iran's economy, especially in the oil industry, was rapidly run down and 1979 ended with the Revolution bellowing defiance of the USA and the economic sanctions imposed by President Carter. 'Death to America' was a slogan which helped unite the Revolution behind the Revolutionary Council.

20.2.2 The Islamic Republic

Presidential elections brought a decisive victory for Abolhassan Bani-Sadr, himself the son of an ayatollah and a former student of theology who had joined Khomeini in exile and in opposition to the Shah. Khomeini now assumed the role of Iran's Moral Supervisor, ensuring that Islam remained in control of the state. That this was the will of the majority was shown in May 1980 when the Islamic Republican Party won a clear majority in the Iranian parliament. But turbulence continued for some time yet. Carter's efforts to free the US hostages were constantly frustrated. A helicopter rescue-mission in April 1980 ended in casualties, disarray and embarrassment, and not until Carter had been beaten in the US presidential elections did the Iranians agree, at a price, to release their prisoners in January 1981. Bani-Sadr was then removed from office, accused of pandering to the West and forced to flee into exile. There was a new wave of executions in Iran and a further tightening of the rule of Islam, with its unrelenting restrictions on those hankering after Western liberalism, and punishments the West thought were sometimes barbarous for those offending against 'the law of the Divine Legislator'. The new President, Ali Rajai, was assassinated and Iran became quieter only when Ali Khameini became President later in 1981. The strict moral code of the new regime was by now well established and Khameini was re-elected in 1985. Parliament and politics, however, were still subordinated to the religious leadership and Islamic ideal of the Ayatollah Khomeini and his Council of Guardians.

In many ways Iran had become isolated. The Islamic Republic was a source of strength for fundamentalists everywhere who wished to imitate it. It inspired Shiites in Lebanon and fundamentalist agitators such as those active in the mid-1980s in Egypt and Pakistan. The Republic also gave strong backing to the PLO, and the Iranians were dedicated to liberating Jerusalem from the Israelis. But only the governments of Syria and Libya gave enthusiastic support to Iran. Others found its crusading zeal uncomfortable and in 1980 neighbouring Iraq invaded Iran and declared war. Like the upheavals of 1979–81, the war burdened Iran's economy and handicapped the economic objectives of the Revolution on behalf of the underprivileged (see Table 18.2). On the other hand, the war acted as a further binding-force, uniting Iran's 'righteous army' of believers in their single-minded pursuit of the will of Allah.

20.2.3 The Iraqi–Iranian War

The outcome of the Revolution of 1979 was less pleasing to Iran's minorities, such as the four million Kurds in the north-west who wished to join fellow Kurds in Iraq and Turkey to create a separate Kurdistan. Arabs in Iran were also restless, resenting the settlement of their future by a people largely Persian. It was partly in expectation of Arab support in Iran, as well as because of anxiety about the unsettling effects of events there upon Kurdish subjects in Iraq, that Saddam Hussein of Iraq went to war against Iran in 1980. Iraq had a population of only fifteen million and, though most were Muslim, its government was secular and socialist, afraid of Shiite militancy. Iraq had become a republic in 1958, at that time protesting like Iran in 1978–9 at the monarchy's ties with the West. But Shiite leaders in Iraq were hanged in 1980, provoking Iran into border clashes and paving the way for a war in which Saddam Hussein hoped not only to subdue the Islamic Republic but also to settle an old dispute over the Shatt el-Arab waterway.

The war lasted longer than expected, gravely damaging the oil industries of both countries. Iran generally had the better of the military engagements, being able to draw on seemingly limitless volunteers eager for battle. The savage fighting over comparatively small areas of land reminded some observers of the Western Front in the First World War, and casualties and destruction were great. By 1985 Iraqi dead were put at 70 000 and prisoners in Iranian hands at 50 000. Iraq had been kept going partly by aid from Kuwait and Saudi Arabia, both fearful of Islamic militancy and Iran's example, but victory nevertheless began to seem impossible. Each side attacked from the air, bringing chaos to oil installations and shipments in the Persian Gulf. In 1986 Iran reckoned the cost of the damage it had suffered at over 200 billion dollars, a bill the Iranians were determined Iraq should pay on top of its own heavy costs. Iranians also demanded the removal from power of Saddam Hussein, hoping no doubt that a fundamentalist regime might replace him. Meanwhile, the Kurds fought on against the Iranian government, not in support of Iraq but for a free Kurdistan. They too, however, found it difficult to prevail against the determination of Khomeini to deny them even self-government. The regional instability and the disruption of oil supplies spread the anxieties across the world: the

Iraqi–Iranian War was developing into one of the longest and most bitter post-war conflicts.

The war was kept going not only by fierce hatreds which rejoiced in 'mountains of bodies' but also by the ease with which both sides obtained arms. Syrian support for Iran cooled in 1986, partly because of their emerging rivalry in Lebanon, but by then the USA seemed to be supplying both sides. Secret dealings between Washington and Tehran were revealed in the Irangate[G] scandal. But just where most weapons came from was always difficult to establish. There were nevertheless enough for a prolonged 'war of the cities' in 1988, during which Iran and Iraq bombarded each other's capital cities of Baghdad and Tehran with missiles, bringing death and destruction. Neutral states meanwhile suffered considerable casualties and damage in the Persian Gulf, where Iraq repeatedly bombed Iranian oil installations and both sides preyed on shipping in efforts to weaken the other's economy. During 1987 additional US, European and Soviet naval patrols were rushed to the Gulf to convoy oil tankers and other merchant vessels. Iran also raided Arab states across the Gulf such as Kuwait and Saudi Arabia, who were regarded as friends of Iraq. Saudi Arabia had helped Iraq with a new pipeline so that its exports of oil need not rely on shipping in the Gulf. There was always the danger that the war might escalate and in 1988 Washington expressed alarm when its spy satellites discovered that the Saudis were themselves stockpiling missiles, apparently obtained from China.

Spurred on by the 'war of the cities', the UN Security Council early in 1988 demanded a ceasefire, but negotiation was made difficult by Iran's insistence that Iraq must overthrow Saddam Hussein and accept total surrender. The Iranians were contemptuous of the threat that the UN might impose a boycott on supplying weapons to the combatants. Iran regarded the Iraqi government as an evil that Islam must destroy. Tehran had long complained that the Iraqis used chemical weapons in the war, and their complaints rose to a new pitch early in 1988 after the bombing of Halabjeh. Halabjeh was an Iraqi town whose inhabitants were mainly Kurds, and it lay in an area the Iranians had overrun. The bombing made it a ghost-town, dreadful civilian casualties seemingly the result of the use of cyanide and mustard gas. This was alleged to be the worst known attack on civilians with gas-bombs in any war, and it was perhaps intended mainly to take revenge on the supporters of Kurdistan.

International efforts to end the Iraqi–Iranian War gained further impetus. But the regime of Khomeini and Ali Khameini in Tehran was in no mood to make concessions. Tehran had grown more confident since the overthrow of the Shah, and even states that disapproved of the Islamic Revolution – such as the USA and the USSR – seemed to have come round to secret dealings with the Islamic Republic. Iranians regarded their casualties in the war, both military and civilian, as martyrs in a holy cause who were privileged to die for Islam. Most observers regarded the first ceasefire, arranged in the summer and autumn of 1988, as unstable. A stalemate in which neither side had achieved its 'war aims' was not regarded as a sound basis for lasting peace.

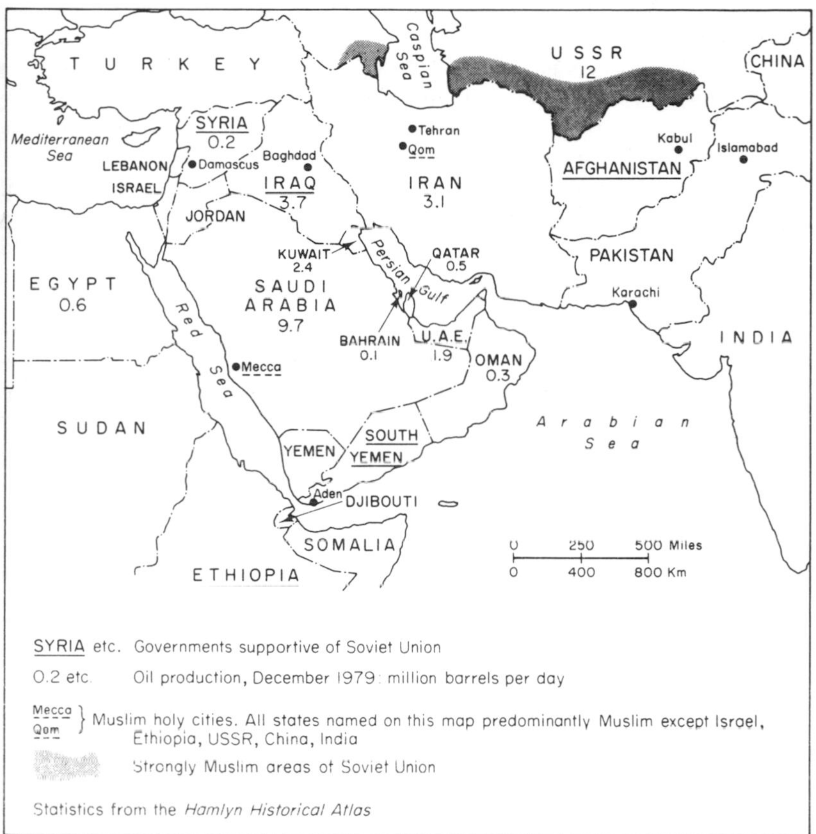

Fig. 20.2 The Middle East in the 1980s

20.3 The Libyan Revolution

20.3.1 The Great Socialist People's Arab Jamahiriya

The military coup which deposed King Idris in September 1969 was also an attack on foreign interests and on the unequal division of Libya's oil wealth. The monarchy had angered its subjects with its pro-Western stance in the Arab–Israeli War of 1967 and its protection of the colonialist interests which had remained in Libya since independence in 1951. The rebel movement was pan-Arab and socialist and the new Revolutionary Council quickly took banks and other businesses into Libyan hands, Arabicized public signs and notices, expressed solidarity with the PLO, and began a campaign to improve the lot of the poor.

Within months it was clear that the strong man in the Council was Colonel Muammar Gadafy, who was not yet 30. Gadafy had a further objective – to promote Islamic fundamentalism. British bases in Libya were closed down and the Friendship Treaty with Britain that King Idris had made was ended in 1972. The oil industry was nationalized and Libya was set on the road to becoming an Islamic, socialist and intensely pro-Arab state which took the name of the Great Socialist People's Arab Jamahiriya. As chief of state, though without a formal title, Gadafy seemed to the outside world to be a dictator, but he ruled in partnership with other military officers and with a People's Congress and People's Committee, presided over by a Prime Minister, who helped formulate and carry out policy.

Within Libya, ambitious development plans coexisted with stern Islamic discipline. The plans made use of immigrant labour from other parts of north Africa and skilled sympathetic personnel from Europe. Oil exports helped to finance modernization, raise standards of living, and improve the provision of services such as hospitals and schools, as well as the levels of nutrition and life expectancy (see Table 18.2). The system was distinctive, with more contradictions than that of the Islamic Republic of Iran, and it was not universally popular. Gadafy's simple life-style (conducting much of his business in a tent), his strong opinions and Islamic fervour attracted critics as well as admirers. His fierce support of Arab interests and the vigour with which Libya pursued its dissenting nationals abroad with 'hit-squads' helped make Gadafy particularly unpopular in the West. At the same time, relations with fellow Arabs were sometimes strained, and plans to unite Libya's population of little more than three million with Egypt, Sudan, Syria and Tunisia all collapsed. Gadafy quarrelled bitterly with Sadat, who courted the USA and sought relations with Israel, and there were skirmishes along the Libyan–Egyptian border in the 1970s.

20.3.2 Competitive terrorism

Relations with other states worsened in the 1980s. The Libyans interfered in Chad and in other parts of black Africa, backing the forces of radical dissent. They backed those whom Gadafy considered freedom-fighters, such as the IRA. They meddled in right-wing Arab states such as Saudi Arabia, and gave staunch support to the Khomeini regime in Iran. At the same time, Gadafy gave backing to the Palestinian cause, usually in alliance with President Assad of Syria. Libyans abroad, hostile to Gadafy, were attacked ruthlessly, with assassinations in 1980 alone in London, Rome, Milan, Athens and Bonn. In 1984 a British policewoman was killed when Libyans clashed at their People's Bureau (embassy) in London.

Relations with the USA became tense. While openly supporting rebels in Northern Ireland and elsewhere, Gadafy condemned America's use of power to destabilize unfriendly regimes such as that in Nicaragua and to uphold governments such as those of Israel and South Africa. Libya claimed sovereignty over the Gulf of Sidra, defying the Reagan administration which claimed the right to send US warships into the Gulf's international waters near Libya's coast.

Several trials of strength took place from 1981 onwards. In Gadafy's view, the USA was at the root of many of the world's problems. In Washington's view, Gadafy was an architect of disorders and Libya, with its self-sacrificing single-mindedness, even asceticism, looked suspiciously like an agent of the Soviets.

Matters came to a head in 1986 following another US foray into the Gulf of Sidra, sending warships across what Gadafy called a 'line of death'. Minor skirmishing resulted, but in April terrorist bombs exploded on a TWA airliner over Greece, killing four Americans, and in a West Berlin night club, killing an American soldier. Reagan declared Gadafy 'the mad dog of the Middle East', alleging to a sceptical world that Gadafy was the force behind a world-wide network of terrorists. Claiming to have proof of Libyan involvement in the recent explosions, Reagan launched bombing raids on Tripoli and Benghazi in Libya which caused civilian casualties and widespread outrage. The raids were denounced as 'state terrorism' not only in Moscow but also in many parts of Europe. Some of the bombers flew from bases in Britain, for which the Thatcher government was also heavily criticized. Gadafy, who may personally have been among the intended targets, survived, but members of his family were injured and an adopted child was killed. Bettino Craxi, Prime Minister of Italy, spoke for many when he said:

> Far from weakening terrorism, this military action risks provoking explosive reactions of fanaticism and criminal and suicidal acts.

Islam rallied to the Libyans in an upsurge of anti-American and anti-British anger.

The Libyan government reasserted its support for 'the People's struggle for freedom', for the PLO, SWAPO and the 'Liberation of the People of South

Fig. 20.3 'Heh! Heh! That goddam insect'll think twice before he stings peace-lovin' folk again!' Gibbard's comment on US bombing raids on Libya in April 1986. Although Margaret Thatcher supported Reagan, many other Europeans were critical of his action and fearful of the consequences.

Africa', rejecting the US charge of terrorism and defying Washington to produce evidence in an international court. Libya's government asserted that:

> We unequivocally reject the charge of terrorism, for we are the victims of official terrorism, economic and psychological, military and political propaganda.

Whatever its contribution to the violence of the late twentieth-century world, it could hardly be maintained that Libya created most of its problems. Gadafy's regime did, on the other hand, represent both another face of the Islamic resurgence and an example of the growing resentment in the South of the arrogance and power of the North. The US bombing raids had not led, as the Americans might have hoped, to Gadafy's overthrow. He remained secure within Libya and soon afterwards embarrassed his neighbours by calling for the overthrow of the pro-Western Mubarak in Egypt and King Hassan II in Morocco. It was also alleged that he was the supplier of arms to the IRA which were intercepted by British security forces; indeed Libyan supplies to the IRA seemed to have increased as a result of Mrs Thatcher's support for Reagan's bombing raids on Tripoli and Benghazi.

20.4 Islam and the Arab World

Libya under Gadafy bridged pan-Arabism and Islamic fundamentalism. Other Arab states were similarly concerned for Arab dignity and pride, making them implacable enemies of Israel, but they were influenced to differing degrees by Islam. Islamic influence ensured the widespread observance throughout the Arab world of a code of traditional practices, for example in worship, in morals and in dress. As Desmond Meiring was later to claim in *Fire of Islam* (Wildwood House, 1982), devout Muslims were 'the water in which the terrorists swam', since they included those who believed it their duty 'to kill the unrepentant deviationist for the sake of a purer Islam', accepting retribution and execution as 'a short-cut to paradise'. This religious fanaticism often merged with Arab nationalism to embitter Middle East conflicts, especially those in Lebanon and concerning Israel (see section 18.2).

The Islamic resurgence which grew in strength in the 1970s was in part a protest against accelerating change. Outside influences seemed to grow as improved communications - especially air travel - increased contacts with the non-Muslim world. For many Muslim societies, such as that of Saudi Arabia, oil wealth brought ambitious programmes of modernization and Western experts and technicians to supervise them. Fears grew that Arab and Muslim identities might be submerged in change towards the slick and lax life-styles that the outsiders brought with them. Saudi Arabia and Syria were among the countries that were staunchly Muslim, both - like Libya - mainly Sunni. Saudi Arabia was enormously rich in oil, vast in area and small in population (about seven million in the 1970s) and was at some distance from Israel and Lebanon. It was ruled by a monarchy without political parties which made only cautious reform in case Islamic fundamentalism should catch fire. Traditions survived: slavery was abolished only in 1962, just two years after the education of women was formally permitted. Official codes tried to reconcile commercial, industrial and administrative development with the principles of Islam. But the Saudi government also maintained close relations with the USA and the West, and Shiite fundamentalism threatened to spread into the east of Saudi Arabia which faced Iran across the Persian Gulf.

Syria was less rich in oil than Saudi Arabia, smaller in area though similar in population (about eight million in the 1970s), and was an immediate neighbour of Israel and Lebanon (see Table 18.2). It was also a republic with a radical tradition from the time of its independence from France. The Ba'ath Party had begun as a pan-Arab movement with crusading slogans such as 'One Arab Nation with an Eternal Mission'. It merged with socialist forces to create an Arab socialism which seemed stronger even than Islam. With Egypt under Nasser, Syria led the Arab resistance to Israel, carrying on relentlessly when Sadat led Egypt in a different direction.

A new constitution was proclaimed in Syria in 1973, declaring the country a 'democratic, popular, socialist state'. By omitting to identify the state as Islamic this so offended the Muslims that rioting broke out. Islam was restored as the state religion, the state legal system was based on Islam and the President was required to be a believer. General Hafez al-Assad had been President since 1970, a member of the Ba'ath Party since his student days and eventually its Secretary-General. Assad remained in power and was re-elected for a third term in 1985, the Ba'ath Party defeating the National Progressive and Communist Parties in parliamentary elections a year later. Assad maintained his radical policies, opposing Israel, supporting Islamic Iran, befriending Gadafy and drawing closer to the Soviet Union than did most Arab states. Policy and geography ensured that Syria was burdened with heavy defence spending, and in the 1980s Syrians prospected anxiously for further reserves of oil with which to finance further social advances and development. Unsurprisingly, the pace of social change in Syria was faster than that in Saudi Arabia, however, and Arab nationalism seemed to burn more fiercely there than Islamic traditionalism.

20.5 Afghanistan, Islam and the Soviets

Almost all the sixteen million people of Afghanistan in the 1970s were Muslim, some 85 per cent Sunni, the rest Shiite. Islamic militants had long been angered by reforms influenced by the West, and King Nadir had been assassinated as early as 1933. But his son kept the throne until 1973 when General Muhammad Daoud set up a republic. Daoud was killed and his government overthrown in 1978 when the Armed Forces Revolutionary Council proclaimed a left-wing Democratic Republic under Muhammad Tarakki, who soon declared his alignment with the Soviet Union. Since the 1950s, Moscow had given aid and support to Afghanistan as a friendly neighbour, but only now did the Soviets become active in its internal affairs.

That year, 1978, was a turbulent one. Tarakki had Soviet and east-European help, but he faced unrest and counter-revolution from dissidents and various tribes restless under government from the capital, Kabul. There was also

Islamic protest which grew in March 1979 into a Liberation Front, encouraged from Islamabad, the capital of Pakistan, and active among Pathan tribesmen on the Afghan–Pakistani border. Tarakki's government also alleged infiltration and incitement from Iran, the Iranians encouraging rebel *mujaheddin* in a developing 'holy war' to rid Afghanistan of communism, Soviet influence and the modernization (such as land reform, female emancipation and social reorganization) which offended against Islamic law. The jihad was encouraged by Ayatollah Khomeini and President Zia who paraded his support for Islam in Pakistan. But the Soviets also claimed that the United States CIA was helping to destabilize Afghanistan and that China too was helping the rebels. The Soviet presence in Afghanistan grew steadily and, in August 1979, 30 Soviets were murdered on a visit to a Muslim shrine, at a time when fundamentalists were proclaiming a rebel government at Patkia.

A month later, Tarakki was deposed in a coup led by Hafizullah Amin, a staunch pro-Moscow communist and earlier colleague of Tarakki. But Amin could not quell the disorders, though sucking Soviet troops and supplies into the country's virtual civil war. In December 1979 the Soviets turned against Amin and helped make Babrak Karmal the new Afghan President; Amin was killed, like Tarakki before him. The new President tried to buy peace with declarations of his sympathies with Islam and international non-alignment, and with offers to slow down social change. At the same time, Soviet troops were now openly committed to the war in Afghanistan.

There was an explosion of international outrage, not only from Iran and Pakistan but also from China, the USA and Britain, and Carter and Thatcher launched a campaign to boycott the 1980 Olympic Games in Moscow. Carter issued a warning that:

> any attempt by any outside power to gain control of the Persian Gulf will be regarded as an assault on the vital interests of the United States of America and such an assault will be repelled by any means necessary, including military force.

Washington seemed to assume the Soviet action was part of a new expansionism, threatening the entire Middle East and oil markets. On the other hand, it seemed likely that Brezhnev's main anxiety was about the turbulence now affecting a previously friendly and fairly stable neighbour, combined with deep unease about the Islamic fervour of the Islamic Republics of Iran and Pakistan. But the Soviet Union found it easier to get into Afghanistan than to get out of it. Brezhnev left to his successors an Afghan dilemma like that the Americans had had in Vietnam. The war was costly and demoralizing though the truth of it was shrouded in the propaganda with which all sides surrounded it. Apart from outside help and encouragement, the rebels were fired by fierce local loyalties, an unwavering devotion to Islam and staunch opposition to alien ideas, such as the education and emancipation of females. On the other hand, they were faction-ridden and handicapped by rivalries. More than 100 000 Soviet troops nevertheless found victory elusive and were worn down by guerilla warfare and ambushes in Afghanistan's rugged and unfriendly terrain.

The war dragged on during the 1980s with few signs that either government or rebel forces could win outright success. Negotiations for an end to the slaughter were complicated by the involvement of others such as Iran and Pakistan, while there was reluctance in Moscow to accept the sort of humiliating withdrawal the USA had had to endure in Vietnam. UN shuttle diplomacy made little progress. Table 12.1 shows, however, how desperately Afghanistan needed peace and development, the state ranking very low in all tables concerning wealth, health, nutrition, education and material well-being. Gorbachev wanted to withdraw Soviet troops as soon as possible, and Babrak Karmal was downgraded and finally stripped of all offices during 1986 in the search for an Afghan government both friendly to the USSR and popular with the Afghan people. His successor, Dr Mohammad Najibullah, Secretary of the Afghan Communist Party, offered a cease-fire at the beginning of 1987, asserting:

> We seek reconciliation with all upright patriots of Afghanistan irrespective of their former political views, wrongs and hostility.

Pravda was now recommending more respect for Afghanistan's age-old traditions as if holding out an olive branch to the mujaheddin. But the rebels were unresponsive. There were deep divisions at their headquarters in Peshawar, Pakistan, where those who might have been willing to negotiate with Kabul jostled for influence with Islamic extremists. By the end of 1987, 12 000 Soviet troops had been killed in Afghanistan and Gorbachev was eager to find a way to withdraw the Soviet army, but he could not leave Najibullah and the supporters of his People's Democratic Party (PDR) government to suffer reprisals from Islamic fundamentalists.

The USA held one of the keys to the future of Afghanistan. Without US support, the Afghan rebels might well be forced to come to terms with Najibullah. Reagan hoped to end his Presidency on a triumphal note. Gorbachev was offering the prospect of another summit meeting in Moscow during 1988 and a string of US–Soviet agreements. A settlement in Afghanistan and the Soviet withdrawal would be helpful in achieving these, and the superpowers worked towards a conference in Geneva to determine Afghanistan's future – a conference parallel to that in Geneva which Shultz was trying to bring about to settle problems in the Middle East. Gorbachev and Najibullah declared their readiness to accept a coalition government in Kabul, with the PDR sharing power with the rebels, and Gorbachev offered to withdraw Soviet forces in May 1988 if progress were made towards this. Washington hesitated, reluctant after all to help the Soviets escape their dilemma but also sceptical as to whether a coalition would work. The PDR had already begun changes in Afghanistan which Islamic fundamentalists considered unacceptable. Najibullah was advancing the rights of women and building secular institutions such as trade unions and a non-Islamic army. In March 1988 the rebels at Peshawar made Gulbuddin Hekmatyar their new leader, a clear indication that they wanted no compromise. Gorbachev decided that May 1988 was too soon to withdraw Soviet forces, but several months later embarked upon a unilateral withdrawal of troops as a gesture of goodwill.

President Zia of Pakistan held another key to Afghanistan's future. He was in no hurry to withdraw support from the mujaheddin whatever the wishes of the USA. Mujaheddin bases in Pakistan and their centre at Peshawar might become a threat to his own authority since he was already under criticism for alleged lack of zeal for Islam. Najibullah launched a new initiative, however, to try to break the deadlock. A general election in Afghanistan was arranged for April 1988, with a guarantee that at least seven of the 28 seats in any new government would be reserved for 'Muslims inside Afghanistan' (who were likely to be more moderate than those organizing the resistance from Peshawar). Seats would be reserved in parliament for the mujaheddin even if they refused to contest the elections. The struggle for a peaceful solution to Afghanistan's problems seemed now to have moved into a new gear, and the West began to nourish a new fear - that even if the elections were fair and free, the PDR might win an overall majority from Afghan voters.

The death of Zia (see section 16.4.2) and Gorbachev's gradual withdrawal of troops in the summer of 1988 seemed to break the deadlock. Hopes for a peaceful internal settlement rose, although it seemed more likely that the civil war between the Soviet-backed regime in Kabul and the mujaheddin in the countryside would be fought to a final conclusion if and when the Soviet withdrawal was completed as promised, by February 1989.

UNIT 21

East–West and North–South: the 1970s and 1980s

21.1 The world economic order: an outline

Increasing wealth throughout the developed world came to be taken for granted in the post-war world. Capitalist countries still experienced the peaks and troughs of the trade cycle and were shaken from time to time by economic crises, but upward trends in output and prosperity continued. The growing economies of the USA, West Germany, Japan and the Scandinavian countries seemed particularly successful, and were often envied by those who found competition in world markets more difficult. The West boasted that competition stimulated output and made capitalist economies more buoyant than the command economies planned and controlled by communist governments. There was unease in the West, nevertheless. Not only was wealth shared out very unevenly, so that poverty persisted even in the USA, but it also seemed that the prosperity of the northern hemisphere was increasing at the expense of the southern, where Third World nations were too weak to escape exploitation by multinational companies and financiers.

Awareness grew of the North–South divide: the states of the South – largely non-white and many newly independent – providing raw materials and foodstuffs at a minimal profit while the richer North prospered on expensive finished products and costly services. The rich provided aid, of course, but non-repayable 'grants' were often 'tied', the receiving country bound by conditions in trade and even in foreign policy laid down by the donors. Countries that were early borrowers, such as Ghana and India, found that loans came only at heavy rates of interest which added to the profits of the North.

In time, concern increased and understanding deepened, and the aid programmes of the North became less self-interested, for example providing interest-free loans. Consideration of the interests of the South brought other piecemeal improvements: there was much discussion of fair commodity prices, to allow the South more stable prices for its output. This was vitally important, especially to those countries that relied heavily on a single export, such as Zambia (copper), Ghana (cocoa) and Jamaica (bauxite). Whether because of accidents of supply and demand or because of deliberate manipulation, such prices sometimes collapsed, threatening to bring down a nation's economy and to overwhelm the state with debt. But international awareness led only slowly to positive action. Aid programmes were reassessed, and more was done to encourage self-help among the poor rather than simply to distribute charity. Goals were re-examined under the influence of men like Nyerere of Tanzania. Many states in the South turned away from attempts merely to imitate the developed nations, preferring an 'intermediate technology' which needed less capital, provided more employment for local people and sought to meet local needs instead of relying on imports. But in the 1980s the North took from the South far more than it put in, finding a variety of opportunities for profit from trade, investment, interest on loans, the provision of expertise and, not least, the sale of armaments. Unable to escape economic dependence on the North, much of the South seemed to draw no nearer to escaping from poverty.

Only fundamental changes in the existing world economic order seemed likely to enable the South to achieve a fairer share of the world's wealth, but the North preferred debating such changes to implementing them. In the 1970s the Organization of Petroleum Exporting Countries (OPEC) administered a severe shock to the existing system, jolting the complacency of the developed world. Resentful of the low prices the West and its oil companies paid for their oil, and urged on by Gadafy of Libya, OPEC members began in 1971 to challenge the existing pricing system. In 1973 the Yom Kippur War further inflamed Arab opinion against the West (see section 18.2.1). As a result, Arab members of OPEC triggered off a world energy crisis. Oil production was cut back and prices rose steeply. OPEC was conscious of fast-diminishing reserves of oil as well as of the unjust distribution of the profits of the industry. From 1971 to 1981, oil prices rose almost twenty-fold, mainly the result of sudden sharp increases in 1973–5 and in 1979. This played havoc with national economies heavily dependent on oil.

The developed countries wriggled uncomfortably as the shock to the system helped bring about a strange combination of inflation and recession. Prices were already tending to rise because of pressures of demand and growing production costs in the North, but they now climbed sharply, for example quadrupling in Britain during the 1970s. At the same time, unemployment became generally more severe than at any time since the Second World War, with uneconomic businesses closing and others seeking to reduce their labour force in a surge towards new technology and greater efficiency. Established patterns of trade were dislocated, the soaring bill for oil a serious burden on all those forced to purchase it. In 1974 Britain had a record deficit on its balance of payments of over £5 billion. The leaders of the USA, Britain, West Germany, France, Italy and Japan met to discuss their problems in an economic summit towards the end of 1975, and met again together with Canada in 1978, after which such summits were held regularly to co-ordinate economic strategies. Hesitant steps were taken to cut down the consumption of oil and other fuels, and individual countries began to devise energy policies. These involved searches for new deposits of oil and, for those who could afford it, for new sources of power such as nuclear energy. Britain and neighbouring countries intensified their drilling operations in the North Sea, and enjoyed considerable success. The Soviet Union stepped up production, and the USA began work in 1975 to bring oil from the Arctic through an Alaskan pipeline.

Most of the poorer nations were less fortunate, though oil-producers such as Nigeria and Trinidad gained higher incomes before oil prices slumped again in the mid and late 1980s. The producers made some effect to help those most savagely hit by fuel costs: an Islamic summit at Lahore in 1974 took steps to channel some oil wealth to the poorest Muslim countries, and oil-producers supported a UN emergency fund. Hardship was nevertheless widespread and the Third World inevitably suffered a further setback to development.

By about 1982 shortages of oil which had temporarily threatened the progress of the USA, Japan and much of Europe had given way to a glut due to reduced demand and new sources of supply. Non-OPEC countries now produced as much oil per day as did members of OPEC. Those, like Britain, with economics geared to oil revenues became anxious about falling oil prices, while economies generally remained unsettled by the uncertainty. Though most developed countries brought inflation under control in the 1980s, unemployment persisted at high levels into the late 1980s, in the North hardly anywhere more so than in Britain and Ireland. Many countries were now involved in the painful transition to high-technology industries which employed fewer workers, and some were moving away from industries such as textile manufacturing, steel production and ship- and vehicle-building where they found it difficult to compete with emerging countries in the Far East. There were now quite wide differences in income between countries previously considered members of the Third World – some like Libya and Venezuela with incomes boosted by oil production, others like Singapore, Taiwan and South Korea following in the commercial footsteps of Japan. But for huge areas of the South, the main legacy of the upheavals of the 1970s was increased debt, leaving them trapped in poverty.

Debt was now a staggering problem. By 1982 countries which had had to renegotiate and defer their repayments included Brazil and Mexico and many other Latin American states, Zaïre and Zambia among African states, Poland in Europe, and Iraq, burdened by war, in the Middle East. The list grew after 1982 to include Vietnam and the Philippines in Asia and even oil-producers such as Venezuela and Nigeria. By 1987 the Third World owed over 900 billion US dollars, almost half being the debt of Latin America. The debtors struggled to repay what they could, but repayments left little with which to buy new goods, further depressing international output and increasing unemployment. The financial world staggered in the face of what the World Bank called 'almost a nightmare', while the price of assistance from the IMF, as in the case of Jamaica and Zambia, was the adoption of policies pleasing to financiers and bankers in the USA and the West.

Even the USA had mounting debts in the mid-1980s, the result, it was alleged, of the administration's pursuit of Reaganomics (see section 2.4.2). The weakness of the US dollar unsettled financial markets throughout the Western world and stock-exchange prices slumped during 1987. Experts could not agree whether a new recession was imminent in the North, but the economic insecurity of the USA was a further factor which added to the confusion.

The interdependence of North and South was examined in the Brandt Report in 1980 (see section 21.3.2). This heavily underlined the imbalance in the world economic order and it was henceforth difficult to ignore the gangrened relations between North and South. Radical solutions gained little support in the North, however, and further shocks seemed inevitable while Northern leaders persisted in pursuing routes of short-term self-interest and national advantage. The world economic system remained part of the status quo against which many terrorists raged, seeking to destroy what could not readily be changed (see sections 20.3.2 and 22.5.2). Meanwhile East–West relations continued to mesmerize the superpowers and their associates, especially in Europe. By the end of the 1970s it seemed that a new East–West Cold War had arrived, perhaps conveniently distracting attention from the deep-rooted problems between North and South.

21.2 The impetus lost and the new Cold War

The drive towards détente faltered soon after the Conference at Helsinki in 1975 (see section 13.4.3). This was partly because of uncertainties in US politics after the disgrace of Nixon. President Carter irritated Moscow with his persistent concern for human rights in the East. A Carter–Brezhnev summit meeting nevertheless took place in Vienna in 1979 and the two leaders agreed on further limits on weapon stocks, broadly pegging them to 1978 levels. The US Senate refused to ratify this SALT 2 agreement, however, and relations grew more frosty, especially when the Soviets invaded Afghanistan at the end of 1979 (see section 20.5). Moscow justified its actions with claims about US intrigue to destabilize Afghanistan, and it was undoubtedly concerned about the effects on the Muslim world of recent developments in Iran, where the USA was even more gravely embarrassed (see section 20.2). The holding of US hostages in Iran, on top of earlier humiliation in Indo-China and a now renewed surge in the price of oil, made Washington nervous about further slights to the USA, and suspicions continued to fester about Soviet intentions throughout the Middle East and in the Horn of Africa. Also in 1979, the Nicaraguans rid themselves of Somoza's dictatorship, an event that Washington was quick to suspect as part of a 'communist plot'.

Fear, suspicion and anger helped swing Americans further to the right, and Ronald Reagan was elected US President, pledged to ensure that citizens of the USA would 'walk tall' again. He took office at the beginning of 1981, rapidly winning admiration from Margaret Thatcher, the 'Iron Lady' who had become British Prime Minister in 1979. Both brought renewed anti-Soviet rhetoric to international affairs. Coexistence and détente had not reduced the ideological gap between East and West, and Reagan referred to the Soviet Union as an 'evil empire'.

The Soviet Union was handicapped in the late 1970s and early 1980s by

Brezhnev's ageing and, after he died, by the deaths of Andropov and Chernenko. When Mikhail Gorbachev came to power in March 1985 a new summit was arranged – the first since 1979 – and Reagan and Gorbachev met in Vienna in November 1985. This was among the most publicized of all summits, helped by Reagan's show-business background and the Soviet Secretary's outgoing personality, and the meeting was remarkably cordial in view of the earlier rhetoric on both sides. Both would have liked to cut back their arsenals of nuclear weapons but negotiations were now bedevilled by Reagan's insistence on US research into a Strategic Defence Initiative (SDI) – 'Star Wars' – to explore a space system which might render existing nuclear missiles ineffective. The Soviets responded angrily and questioned whether the SDI broke the Space Treaty of 1967. They in turn were accused of breaking earlier agreements and were suspected of their own Star Wars research, and it was not surprising that the summit made no obvious progress on further arms limitation. Dangerous escalation of arms continued, but so too did talks. Meanwhile, there were East–West agreements on trade, education, culture and technology, though positions were restated concerning human rights. The USA again protested at Soviet involvement in Afghanistan, and the Soviets made counter-charges about US involvement in Nicaragua where Reagan was intent on helping the Contras to bring down the Sandinista government.

The two leaders agreed to meet again in 1986 and in 1987, and *Pravda* suggested that the end of the winter and a new thaw might be near. In fact, the Reagan–Gorbachev meeting at Reykjavik in Iceland in 1986 ended in recriminations after again foundering on the SDI. On the other hand, detailed discussions continued at a lower level on various possible arms deals, some quite radical since neither the USA nor the USSR could be indifferent to the terrifying destructive power of the accumulating arsenals, and to the wellnigh crippling burden of maintaining them.

Meanwhile, Reagan insisted on trying to live up to his image as the scourge of communists, terrorists and assorted radicals. His determined stance over Star Wars was in keeping with his invasion of Grenada and his interference in Nicaragua (see sections [illegible] and [illegible]). By the mid-1980s his policies had begun to seem negative rather than constructive. Before a surge of activity in 1988, he had little to offer towards advancing the peace process in the Middle East. Along with Thatcher, he tried to dilute international action against the government of South Africa. Though he had lifted Carter's ban on grain sales to the USSR, he tried in 1982 to block supplies for building the pipeline to bring Siberian gas to western Europe. He raged against terrorism but the US bombing of Libya could easily be seen more as the action of a bully than of a statesman (see section 20.3.2).

Late in 1986 Reagan became entangled in mysterious deals which involved the secret sale of arms to Iran and the diversion of the profits to help the Contras in Nicaragua and perhaps also the mujaheddin in Afghanistan. Congress had denied the President the funds he wanted for the Contras and this double dealing caused outrage. Journalists promptly dubbed the affair 'Irangate', recollecting the murky business of Nixon's Watergate. How much

Fig. 21.1 This April 1986 cartoon by Gibbard was one of many reminders of Reagan's acting career in 'Westerns', and allies in Europe as well as critics in the USA suspected that he still nourished simplistic ideas about good and evil in the world and his own crusading mission.

Reagan knew of it was just one of the many questions to be answered. His critics, who included not only most Democrats but also many Republicans, argued that he was treating morality and the US constitution with contempt (if he knew) or was simply incompetent (if he was ignorant of what his aides were up to). Supplying arms to Iran was bad enough after the USA's troubles with the regime there, though the secret deals seemed to be linked with the freeing of US hostages in Lebanon, which some thought justifiable. But what had happened to the money roused greater concern. An inquiry by the US Congress certainly stopped short of acquitting the President of blame, and asserted:

> If the Government becomes a law-breaker it breeds contempt for law.

Investigations continued into 1988. The first result was the prosecution of some of those obviously involved, including Colonel Oliver North, who made no secret of his activities against the government of Nicaragua, and former US Security Adviser John Poindexter. They faced various charges such as fraud and the theft of government property. Further revelations and charges were possible, the scandal threatening to involve Vice-President George Bush, and perhaps to damage his campaign to win election as Reagan's successor in November 1988. However, the major legal inquiries were postponed until George Bush had won the presidential contest against Governor Dukakis and Reagan's term of office had expired. Reagan himself was dubbed 'a Teflon President' to whom scandal could not be made to stick. He remained popular among many Americans, and Thatcher gave him her usual staunch support, perhaps dazzled by their shared enthusiasm for free enterprise and anti-communism. Part of his charm was that he was also readily capable of warm humanitarianism, for example in the relief of famine in Africa, though there was little in his record to suggest he would, or could, give a lead in tackling the daunting root causes of imbalances between North and South.

Soviet policy under Gorbachev was more imaginative than under Brezhnev, and even Thatcher thought him a man she could 'do business with'. He inherited many problems, however. At home, the inertia of the Soviet system hindered glasnost and perestroika and the drive towards increased efficiency and output. Abroad, aside from Soviet relations with the USA, Gorbachev had still to wrestle with the Soviet dilemma in Afghanistan where Amnesty International documented atrocities and breaches of human rights and, blasted by war, the country leaned heavily on economic support from the USSR (see section 20.5). He had also to reckon with the continuing hostility of China. China repeatedly demanded the Soviet evacuation of Afghanistan and the ending of Soviet support for the Vietnamese in Kampuchea. Gorbachev expressed his readiness for change and, like Andropov, was anxious to repair the rift between Moscow and Peking. Peking too seemed to be growing more flexible and, in spite of the persistent problems in Afghanistan and Indo-China, Sino-Soviet relations grew gradually less tense during the 1980s. Border talks were reopened in 1987 and though they had no immediate results, China's relations with the USA seemed the warmer for them. Carter had built on Nixon's overtures, giving full recognition to the Peking government in 1979. Reagan had visited China in 1984, though he had caused some offence there by renewing US support for and sales of arms to Taiwan. China wanted US technology and had therefore continued to develop trade links with the USA and, on the eve of Reagan's visit, had signed an agreement for peaceful nuclear co-operation with the Americans.

Both Reagan and Gorbachev looked forward to further summit meetings in Washington and Moscow before the end of Reagan's Presidency. Both were cautious, however, and no new major initiatives preceded the election of George Bush in November 1988. Gorbachev could not afford to take risks with Soviet security, but he repeated the warnings Khrushchev had given that nuclear war would leave no victors:

> Our earth is a ship on which we are the passengers, and it cannot be allowed to be wrecked. There will be no second Noah's Ark.

In 1987–8 the Soviets and the USA worked industriously to bring about further arms agreements (see section 22.6.3). Gorbachev at the same time published *Perestroika*, a book which reviewed Soviet affairs and criticized the Brezhnev years for their poor leadership. But the Soviet Union could not solve even the problems of Marxist Ethiopia (see section 22.2) and, while condemning the gulf between North and South as a product of capitalism and exploitation, the Soviets showed little inclination to do much about it beyond giving cautious encouragement to socialist revolution. This the USA felt obliged to resist, in case the balance of power should shift to the advantage of the Soviets. Superpower rivalry seemed exasperatingly irrelevant to much of the world, though the horrendous consequences that would follow nuclear conflict threatened all and any retreat from US–Soviet confrontation had almost universal support.

21.3 The North–South dialogue

21.3.1 The North's helping hand

Aid from the wealthy states of the North to the poor nations in the South increased from 3.3 billion dollars in 1956 to almost 21 billion dollars in 1980. Some was bilateral aid, given directly by a donor to a receiver; much was multilateral aid, distributed through agencies such as the IMF, the World Bank and regional development banks. The growth in aid owed a good deal to inflation. In the 1960s the United Nations set an aid target for the prosperous nations of one per cent of national incomes each year, but hardly any achieved it and the UN later reduced the target to 0.7 per cent. Donations from members of the Organization for Economic Co-operation and Development (OECD), a club of the richest capitalist nations, averaged 0.77 per cent in 1968, with Switzerland, West Germany and France among the leaders, Britain and the USA behind them. In 1978 the OECD average was down to 0.35 per cent, while in 1982 Britain managed only 0.11 per cent in aid to the UN-listed poorest nations of the world. OECD members argued, as had usually been the case since the 1950s, that the economic well-being of the developed world must have priority if wealth were ever to be shared more equally between North and South. At the same time, aid was still too often dependent on conditions that reduced its value to the receivers and built in benefits for the donors. OPEC members, on the other hand, increased their aid programmes in the 1970s to average over 1.5 per cent of national incomes.

Aid became more discriminating as more thought was given to its beneficial use – not for prestige projects such as airports, motorways and fine public buildings, but for development schemes which strengthened fragile economies. Statesmen such as Lester Pearson of Canada and Robert McNamara of the USA turned aside from national politics to work for the well-being of the poorer nations, in case, as McNamara put it:

> human nature . . . be frustrated beyond intrinsic limits.

Such men saw the urgency of the need to close the wealth gap between North and South, by increasing output in the developing nations, encouraging improvements in agriculture in the 'Green Revolution', and making it possible for the Third World to earn more from trade. Yet the Third World's share of international trade was slow to grow, sticking at around twenty per cent from the 1940s to the 1970s.

The United Nations Conference on Trade and Development (UNCTAD) was set up in 1964 to encourage Third World industrialization and to press for export markets for Third World output. Too often the developed world had stifled competition from the South, imposing controls on imports into the North in spite of liberal intentions to bring about free trade with the setting up of the General Agreement on Tariffs and Trade (GATT) in 1948 and with the Kennedy Round of tariff cuts, stimulated by President Kennedy, and other such surges towards unfettered trade. The North preferred to take primary products from the South, and it required perseverance on the part of UNCTAD and its sympathizers to bring about increased manufacturing output in the Third World. In the 1980s, however, the less developed countries were increasing trade among themselves, and Asiatic states such as South Korea, Taiwan and Hong Kong were at last making real inroads into the markets of the North. They were given some encouragement by concessions to Third World exports in agreements such as the European Community's Lomé Convention (see section 7.1.2).

Prices were still a bone of contention, however. The North did not expect to pay dearly for the products of the South, especially primary products. Multinational companies had a vested interest in keeping such prices low, and disastrous economic consequences were predicted when prices threatened to rise. In the late 1970s about half of the world's 500 largest industrial companies were based in the USA, a quarter in Continental Europe, and most of the others in Britain and Japan, and their power and influence kept down the costs of their raw materials. The success of OPEC nevertheless encouraged other primary producers to combine to press for higher rewards. An early example of such cooperation was the International Coffee Organization. Copper producers came together in 1967, rubber producers in 1970, banana growers and bauxite producers both in 1974. But not all such organizations enjoyed much success: for example, Zambia, Zaïre, Chile and Peru, as members of the Intergovernmental Council of Copper Exporting Countries ('CIPEC'), had to compete with many non-members such as Canada, and copper prices still fluctuated, as often as not forced down by the manufacturing interests in the North.

The escalating debts of the Third World began to cause alarm (see section 21.1). By 1980 Third World countries owed about 500 billion US dollars at an annual cost of around 50 billion US dollars in charges and interest payments on the debt. In 1981 there was a net transfer of capital from South to North of 7 billion US dollars, rising in 1985 to 74 billion. In the years 1983–8 the world's seventeen poorest nations paid about 100 billion dollars to their creditors, mainly in the West. The 'frustration' of which McNamara had warned still dogged the South, which was trapped in poverty and being left even further behind as other parts of the world increased their riches. In 1980 about a billion people were destitute, living on the edge of starvation. They lived mainly in the South, though it was a feature of the world economic order that, while groups in the North were also impoverished, great affluence existed among élites in the South who managed to profit from the prevailing system, often by identifying with the interests of the North against their fellow nationals. The system encouraged divisions in society, further weakening the ability of the poor – nations and individuals – to improve their lot.

In 1977 an Independent Commission on International Development Issues began work under the chairmanship of Willy Brandt, a former Chancellor of West Germany. It included Edward Heath, a former British Prime Minister,

Shridath Ramphal, Commonwealth Secretary-General, Olof Palme, a later Prime Minister of Sweden, and representatives from all corners of the world. Its members concluded that:

> reshaping worldwide North–South relations had become a crucial commitment to the future of mankind.

Their recommendations were published in 1980 in the Brandt Report, *North–South, A Programme for Survival.*

21.3.2 The Brandt Report and its aftermath

The Brandt Commission did not hesitate to assert the interdependence of the economic problems of North and South, and it appealed not only to the North's humanitarianism but also to its self-interest: while so much of the South was too poor to buy the North's products, recession and unemployment were likely to be worldwide – as indeed they already were. Moreover, while states spent such vast sums on armaments, economies were bound to be distorted and urgent problems unsolved at the cost of enormous human misery. Urgent steps were essential to develop a world strategy for human betterment.

> None of the important problems between industrialised and developing countries can effectively be solved by confrontation: sensible solutions can only result from dialogue and co-operation.

The Report identified many serious faults in the existing system, among them factors which hindered growth, such as the IMF's insistence on 'orthodox' and deflationary policies as a prerequisite for help, to please the West's bankers. States in the South were urged to put their own houses in order by weeding out corruption and inefficiency and ensuring they could at least feed themselves. This involved realistic and fair policies in relation to land ownership, and priority for irrigation and education in productive farming. In many parts of the South the drift towards the towns needed to be checked and the quality of rural life improved. Intermediate technology and less ambitious manufacturing were recommended in preference to capital-intensive and costly high-technology plant, which was beyond local resources. But the Commission also insisted that a massive transfer of wealth was needed to enable the South to grow. Countries in the developed world were urged to meet the UN aid target of 0.7 per cent of national income by 1985, with the further intention of raising this target to one per cent. It seemed unlikely that such money would be found while East and West committed so much of their resources to armaments. But even if the money were forthcoming, Brandt recommended a partnership of North and South to decide its use, a 'shared responsibility for improving the lot of the poorest in the world'. For the North it was not only a matter of increasing aid and improving its quality: fairer prices and better marketing opportunities for the output of the South were essential, though this would require a revolution in thought. On the other hand, the long-term advantages in terms of the prosperity of both North and South were vast.

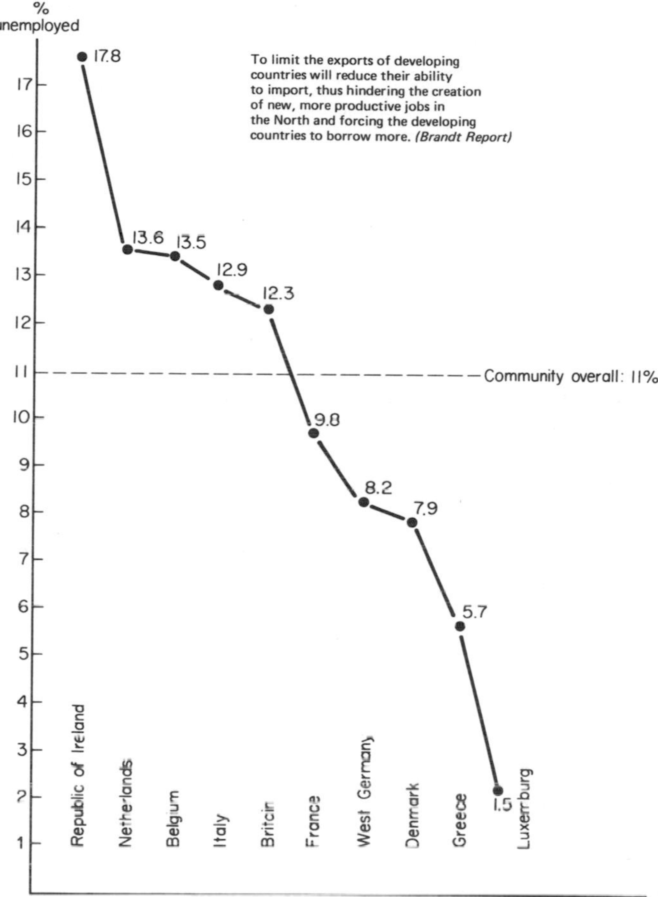

Fig. 21.2 Unemployment in the European Community (percentage of work-force unemployed, July 1985)

The Report did not pull its punches, and it started from the realities of a world in economic disarray in the late 1970s:

> The abolition of poverty is itself not only a moral obligation. It is against everyone's interests to allow poverty to continue, with the insecurity, suffering and destruction which it brings. In the meantime military spending, now at a pace of over 400 billion dollars a year, is wasting still more resources and energies which could be devoted to world development.

The Commission explained at length the philosophy behind its recommendations and set out in detail both a long-term strategy and an immediate programme for action. The latter dealt with four areas:

1 A large-scale transfer of resources to developing countries.
2 An international energy strategy.
3 A global food programme.
4 A start on some major reform in the international economic system.

The Commission was in no doubt that the problem was urgent if the world was to survive crisis and avoid catastrophe in relations between North and South.

Public interest in the Brandt Report varied – it was considerable in Britain and in Scandinavia, for example, but very limited in the USA. Governments responded tardily. The East–West Cold War still sapped the energies of politicians, who shrank from the challenge of the problems the Commission presented to them, and feared that short-term votes might be lost through changing their priorities. Right-wing governments resented Brandt's criticisms of the IMF and his demand for the regulation of the activities of transnational companies. The leading communist states were critical that Brandt's remedies assumed keeping the capitalist system afloat, and they remained aloof. Mexico and Austria gave a lead, however, bringing over twenty nations to a Conference at Cancun, Mexico, in October 1981 to open the North–South dialogue. There was much talk but little agreement and it was perhaps an indication of the general lack of vision that Reagan attended only on condition that Castro was excluded. By 1982 so little that was positive had been done that the Brandt Commission was revived in an attempt to stimulate action with a further report. Yet again, much of the North preferred excuses, and Britain rejected those sections of the new report which seemed to threaten Britain's interests, for example those relating to the Law of the Sea (see section 22.3.2).

Horrific famine in Africa in 1985–6 brought a surge in public concern and reinforced Brandt's warning about the need for 'a global food programme'. People in Britain and elsewhere responded generously with huge private donations to help the suffering (see section 22.2). Consciences were stirred at the United Nations too, and the General Assembly in 1986 launched an Agreement on Africa with a five-year programme for urgent development. But it was the Africans themselves who made the specific commitments – to concentrate on agriculture, improve education, develop transport and reduce bureaucracy. Governments in the developed world agreed that:

> the international community commits itself to make every effort to provide sufficient resources to support and supplement the African development effort.

Such wording was vague enough and far enough from specific pledges by individual countries to anger and frustrate Third World delegates, one of whom expressed his views:

> I came here with cancer and they have given me a sugar-coated aspirin.

At the same time, US and British pressure ensured that Africans had to pledge themselves to promoting free enterprise and dismantling regulations such as those designed to subsidize production and provide employment. The Soviets meanwhile seemed more concerned to word resolutions putting the blame for Africa's problems on past colonial rule.

Dialogue between North and South was still an unequal one, and the North still wasted its energies in the East–West propaganda war. The years from 1980 to 1985 had passed with little of the urgent action the Brandt Report had advised, though events continued to indicate a deepening crisis. Such imaginative initiatives as there were came mainly from pop star Bob Geldof and other individuals who crusaded in Band Aid, Live Aid and Sport Aid, raising money and making efforts in scores of ways to help those in need. But what they could do inevitably fell far short of the global and constructive programme of the Brandt Commission. Government aid programmes in the mid-1980s had hardly grown at all since the previous decade. The developed countries averaged 0.36 per cent of national income in aid, only Norway topping one per cent in keeping with Brandt's recommendation. Of the others, only the Netherlands, Sweden, Denmark and France met the UN target of 0.7 per cent. One of the few encouraging developments found by Robert Cassen and his colleagues (*Does Aid Work?* OUP, 1986) was that in 1982–3 bilateral aid without ties had grown to 46 per cent of total aid compared with 37 per cent in 1976. Cassen concluded that the aid given played an important part in assisting the poor nations and that much of it reached those in greatest need. But not only did some rich nations lag badly behind in what they gave as a percentage of national income – for example, the USA gave only 0.24 per cent – but also distribution was poorly related to the populations of areas in the South. Asia, with 70 per cent of population, gained only about 30 per cent of international aid, with comparatively little for China and India, whereas sub-Saharan Africa (little more than ten per cent in population) secured almost 35 per cent of aid. Increasingly each year, moreover, the South was sending more money to the North than was flowing in the opposite direction.

Speaking for much of Latin America towards the end of 1986, Luis da Silva, a Brazilian trade unionist, said:

> The Third World War has already started – a silent war, not for that reason any less sinister. This war is tearing down Brazil, Latin America and practically all the Third World. Instead of soldiers it is children who are dying, instead of the destruction of bridges there is a tearing down of factories, hospitals and entire economies ... It is a war over the foreign debt, a war which has as its main weapon 'interest'.

21.4 Non-alignment and the voice of the Third World

Non-alignment with either East or West had begun to appeal to independent countries almost as soon as the Cold War began in the mid-1940s. To remain apart from the East–West conflict and to tackle problems of more immediate interest seemed sensible to men like Tito of Yugoslavia and Nehru of India. That was never going to be easy, however. The superpowers had little respect for those who were not their supporters. The non-aligned states lacked economic power, and the economic help they needed could often be had only at the price of glossing over principles. In any case, the non-aligned could not entirely divorce themselves from the ideologies over which East and West disputed. The

West viewed Tito as a communist and Nehru as a socialist, and the world generally sought to simplify its problems by attaching such labels to all its statesmen. Moreover, events soon showed that the massive nuclear stockpiles of the superpowers threatened not only themselves but the whole of mankind.

In 1955, 29 Afro–Asian states were represented at a conference in Bandung, Indonesia, under the chairmanship of Sukarno. Their twin aims were to resist continuing colonialism and to seek a 'non-aligned and neutral position' in relation to the Cold War, in the hope of creating an 'area of peace' in Africa and Asia. The power blocs of East and West were suspicious. Much of the Soviet Union lay in Asia but Moscow was not invited to the conference. Europe and the USA were uneasy about the condemnation of various sorts of colonialism and imperialism, especially when it was seen that Chou En-lai was present in Bandung, speaking for Communist China. Indian–Chinese rivalry soon weakened solidarity in Asia, however, and it became obvious during the next 30 years that Afro–Asian unity was, at best, ramshackle.

A start had been made, however, on providing an alternative voice to those of East and West. A wider movement of Uncommitted Nations held a conference at Belgrade in 1961 at the suggestion of Tito, Sukarno and Nasser of Egypt. Only those not tied to great-power alliances were admitted. Tito gave a lead in condemning the effects of the East–West struggle:

> As a result of the experience acquired in the post-war period, when groupings of individual states began to emerge, all the countries outside these groupings have become profoundly convinced that increasing tensions in the world have been, and still are, arising precisely from this division of the world.

The delegates tried to keep a balance between criticisms of East and West, while calling for negotiations between Kennedy and Khrushchev to improve international relations. Anti-colonialism and anxieties about the development nevertheless made the conference seem, at times, unfriendly to the West.

The Uncommitted Nations, calling themselves non-aligned states, met again in Cairo in 1964 where Nasser helped to get a declaration of support for the Palestinians. But the recent death of Nehru overshadowed the conference, and the quarrel between Indonesia and Malaysia caused strains. The non-aligned movement was now taking shape, however, in spite of its own divisions, and its members met at Lusaka, Zambia, in 1970. In 1973 Egypt, India and Yugoslavia took the lead in bringing about a fourth non-aligned summit in Algiers, now with 57 heads of state. OPEC's growing importance boosted their confidence, and Boumédienne, President of Algeria, claimed that:

> the economic, political and military weapons are now in the hands of the Arabs.

The conference reached few specific agreements, however, beyond agreeing to meet again in 1976 and to set up a Co-ordinating Committee.

The definition of non-alignment still caused problems. Castro of Cuba argued that the Third World must be hostile to Western capitalism which so damaged emerging nations, and thus should be friendly to the Soviet Union. Gadafy was one who resisted this view. When the fifth summit met in Colombo,

Sri Lanka, in 1976 the movement was far from being united, and the conference was now overshadowed by grave economic difficulties.

Ninety-two countries attended the next non-aligned summit in Havana, Cuba, in 1979, the start of three years of Cuban chairmanship which Castro used to urge support for socialism against capitalist exploitation. The movement's support for Nicaragua and for SWAPO in Namibia, as well as for the Palestinians, certainly suggested that the movement was now radical, but the extent of its influence was uncertain, many members still being conservative. The intended Baghdad meeting in 1982 was put off because of the Iraqi–Iranian War, and the next conference therefore assembled in New Delhi, India, in 1983. Priority was now given to promoting the North–South economic dialogue which the Brandt Commission had called for, and to demanding progress towards East–West disarmament.

Disarmament was again prominent in discussion at the non-aligned summit held in 1986 at Harare, Zimbabwe. Inevitably, so too was apartheid, which was roundly condemned. The non-aligned states set up the Africa Fund to speed the development of those African states vulnerable to South African economic reprisals against the anti-apartheid measures demanded by the Harare Special Declaration. Most members pledged aid for SWAPO and for the ANC in South Africa itself. They were less united, however, on the proposal that the next summit be held in Nicaragua, and a decision on this had to be deferred. The non-aligned movement was clearly gaining in stature nonetheless. A total of 101 states were represented in Harare, and the agenda was well filled with matters of concern to the Third World and not simply to the superpowers. When the US State Department denounced Robert Mugabe's opening speech as 'highly offensive', the anti-Americanism of many delegates was simply inflamed.

The growing size of the non-aligned movement was the result of the increasing number of new nations emerging from colonial empires. The presence of these nations in the UN General Assembly and their clamour for economic equality, freedom from interference and more radical solutions to problems such as those of southern Africa sometimes embarrassed and exasperated the superpowers. The USA especially resented the fact that, while being the main financier of the United Nations, it was exposed to criticism and hostility. The Third World, critical of superpower propaganda, demanded a 'new world information order'. The USA in turn fiercely attacked the United Nations Educational, Scientific and Cultural Organization (UNESCO), alleging that it:

> politicised virtually every subject it deals with . . . exhibited hostility towards the basic institutions of a free society . . . and . . . demonstrated unrestrained budgetary expansionism.

Reagan withdrew the USA from UNESCO in protest at the end of 1984, and Thatcher in Britain followed his example a year later.

Third World influence, even at the United Nations, was still limited, however. Many emerging nations were unstable as well as poor, and there were many divisions among them. Major wars in Europe were avoided during the 40 years after 1945, but it was sometimes argued that Cold War rivalries were pursued elsewhere as the superpowers manoeuvred for clients whom they then armed to the teeth. Europeans and Americans seemed ready to sell arms to almost any one who would buy them. Great-power interests were always likely to dilute the constructive work of bodies such as UNCTAD and to frustrate that of world-wide environmental reformers (see Unit 22). It was not surprising that many emerging nations merely copied the examples of self-interest that the developed world so often provided.

Yet the Third World could not be ignored. The removal of Waldheim, a European, as UN Secretary-General in 1981 in favour of Peru's Perez de Cuellar was evidence of influences other than those of the developed world (see section 1.4.2). The new Secretary-General warned in 1983 of the dangers of imposing East–West quarrels on top of regional conflicts, a warning echoed by Olof Palme and Willy Brandt who campaigned for 'international order' based on the UN, and not on the many billion dollars a year governments were spending on their own armaments. In 1985 Perez de Cuellar reminded the UN's now 158 members of their responsibilities to the world as a whole, with its:

> vast, silent majority which wants peace with justice and dignity, with freedom from fear and the hope of a better tomorrow.

The people of the world – including the Third World – were now finding a voice in support of constructive effort to bring about new world 'orders' and to co-operate in solving world problems. Dismally, however, UN delegates in 1985 could not agree on wording the text of a declaration to celebrate the United Nations' fortieth birthday.

UNIT 22

The human environment

22.1 Population

At the end of the Second World War the population of the world was approaching 2.5 billion. In 1971 it was some 3.7 billion and, at the end of the 1970s, the Brandt Commission estimated it had risen to 4.3 billion and was likely to reach 6 billion or more by the end of the century. This was in spite of the growing use of birth-control methods, continuing high levels of infant mortality and comparatively low levels of life expectancy in many of the poorer nations.

Figure 22.1 shows birth and death rates by geographical area at the beginning of the 1970s, which reveal the fastest rates of population increase to be those of Latin America and Africa, followed by that of Asia, and the slowest to be those of the Soviet Union and Europe. One result was that, while emerging nations faced severe problems in educating, finding work for and harnessing the energies of comparatively young populations, societies in the developed world were having to cope with relatively more elderly people who were living longer. In 1980 about 40 per cent of the populations of the developing countries were aged fourteen or under, compared with only 20 per cent in the developed countries. The latter had some 17 per cent aged over 60, compared with only 7 per cent in the developing countries. Younger populations meant, of course, the likelihood of greater population growth in the future. It also became clear in the 1960s, 1970s and 1980s that, while the developed world (especially North America and Europe) was able to produce vast food surpluses, hunger and famine stalked much of the rest of the world. Oxfam calculated that in the 1980s some 500 million people were malnourished and that a person in the North consumed, on average, five times as much grain as a person in the South.

The year 1974 was designated World Population Year, and the World Population Conference met in Bucharest. Problems were debated, but most delegates insisted that they were for national governments to deal with individually. Many nevertheless signed the Statement from Bucharest, recognizing that 'the world situation is potentially disastrous' and the rate of population increase likely to:

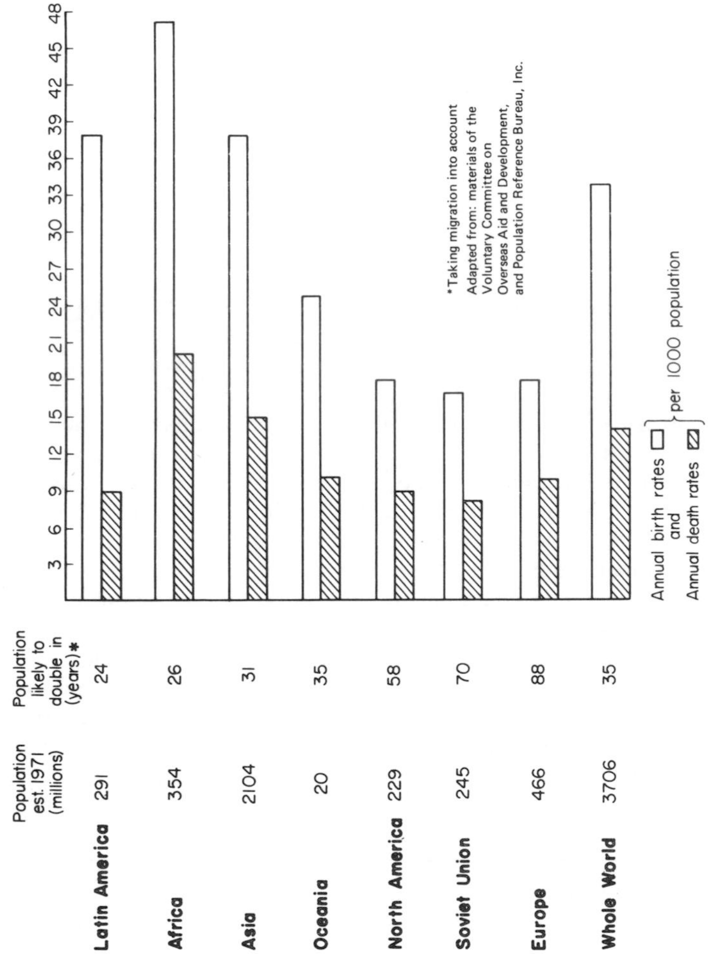

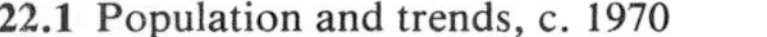

Fig. 22.1 Population and trends, c. 1970

> strain the environment and man's social, political and economic institutions to breaking point.

The Statement went on:

> Some countries consume and waste the earth's resources at a rate that cannot be maintained. Others have densely-settled regions and population growth rates of 2 or 3 per cent a year that will exert demands on the international community which may not be met. The urgency of the global crisis must not be ignored nor submerged beneath national ambitions.

Individual governments coped as best they could. Lee Kwan Yew in Singapore gave one sort of lead, withdrawing state medical and educational support from children after the third in one family. In other states, targets for married couples were commonly set at not more than two children, to discourage population growth. But opinions differed as to how to impose this. Family-planning education became widespread, but birth control won favour only slowly in primitive and superstitious societies. China followed in Singapore's footsteps, sternly discouraging both early marriages and enlarged families and eventually setting a target of only one child per married couple. This reduced its annual growth rate in the early 1980s to little over one per cent (see section 11.2.2). Some countries such as the Soviet Union and Japan took readily to abortion, but this was discouraged in Catholic states among which Venezuela's acceptance of abortion was unusual. Sterilization was also favoured by some governments, often with official incentives, but few governments dared to follow the example of Sanjay Gandhi in India, who made sterilization in some cases compulsory. The modest growth rates of the developed world probably owed most to the high standards of living which large families would erode. But for the poor in the Third World, large families could often mean extra labour on the land, more income and more secure support in old age, and living standards were already too low to be seriously jeopardized by more children. In some states minorities deliberately sought to increase their numbers for greater protection against victimization.

Growth rates therefore fluctuated even within regions, but there was little prospect in the 1980s of any early halt. Wars, famines and natural disasters took a toll, along with genocide such as that of the Khmer Rouge in Kampuchea. But trends were still upwards, population sometimes growing by over three per cent a year, for example in the Middle East and parts of Africa by 1988. Few countries outside Europe had yet dropped below an annual one per cent. Prosperity required that wealth production should outstrip population growth and this was by no means uncommon in the North. In the South, however, economic advances were often cancelled out by larger populations. Frustration and despair seemed inevitably to follow, threatening the stability of nations. At the same time, traditional balances were changing: the South grew faster than the North; the population of Africa caught up with that of Europe; non-whites already outnumbered whites and the gap between them was widening steadily. In 1985 the two superpowers together included only some ten per cent of the world's population, and the proportion was shrinking. Since the

Statement from Bucharest in 1974, 'the global crisis' seemed only to have deepened.

22.2 Food and famine

The 'Green Revolution' which the UN Food and Agriculture Organization (FAO) and others encouraged in the 1960s certainly increased output. New varieties of seed and improved techniques so increased yields that, by the end of the 1960s, the world had doubled its production of food since about 1950. In 1974 Henry Kissinger declared to the World Food Conference in Rome

> Within a decade no child will go to bed hungry . . . no family will fear for its next day's bread and no human being's future and capacity will be stunted by malnutrition.

A decade later, Oxfam advisers calculated that 40 000 children a day were actually dying through malnourishment. When the World Food Conference met again in Brussels in 1988, hunger among the poor was in no way less than in 1974.

The world's food problems were far from simple. Overall, the world produced enough food both in 1974 and in 1988 to feed the growing population. The United Nations in 1975 agreed to build an emergency food reserve of half a million tonnes, mainly cereals. The stockpile began slowly but by 1988 it reached 400 000 tonnes. Yet hunger on an enormous scale persisted. On paper, it seemed that the South exported food that it needed to feed itself, and that the North, especially Europe, imported food while already in possession of food mountains such as those resulting from the European Community's Common Agricultural Policy. Of the 77 mainly Third World countries whose food exports exceeded their imports, at least a third suffered famine during the years 1950–88. These countries were dependent on the income from selling food, largely to markets in the North. They therefore grew export crops such as cocoa, coffee, tea and fruits rather than the grain and other foodstuffs needed locally. Susan George, the author of *A Fate Worse than Debt* (Pelican, 1988), was one of many whose researches showed that this situation was due to outside pressures, such as those of the IMF, which insisted that the poor must export to 'pay their way'.

What the poor exported was then bought at the lowest prices the North could stage-manage. In the mid-1980s, for example, the USA forced down the price of rice from Thailand from 230 dollars to 170 dollars a tonne. Another effect of this imbalance in the availability of food was that the Green Revolution was only patchy: it often benefited the well-to-do farmers who had access to capital, but bypassed the poor whose subsistence agriculture was still highly inefficient. Transport was also a difficulty. Surpluses sometimes rotted before they could be moved, or were sold – like EEC dairy produce to the Soviet Union – at knock-down prices to those near at hand. In the Third World, especially in Africa, poor communications hampered the distribution of food, even that imported by purchase or as aid.

Singapore, Hong Kong and the two Koreas were among the very few developing countries which did not rely on exporting primary products for at least 40 per cent of their foreign earnings. Those with oil and mineral reserves relied heavily on them, but the majority had to export agricultural produce, many being forced to work the land intensively without the capital to buy fertilizers and advanced equipment. Land deteriorated, scarred by poor farming methods and, in some cases, by a hostile climate, drought and flood. Thus, during the years 1974–88, the world as a whole and especially the developed nations increased food output and ate better than ever before, while the poorest produced less food per head of population and suffered further malnutrition. Reviewing one short period alone, early in 1984, Oxfam recorded the devastating effects of drought and flood across the South. At that time, the weather brought hunger, misery and crippling damage to Bolivia, Peru and north-east Brazil; to West Africa south of the Sahara, the Horn of Africa and southern Africa, especially Mozambique; to many parts of India and Pakistan; and to much of Indo-China.

Famine in Ethiopia, the Sudan and other parts of sub-Saharan Africa on a

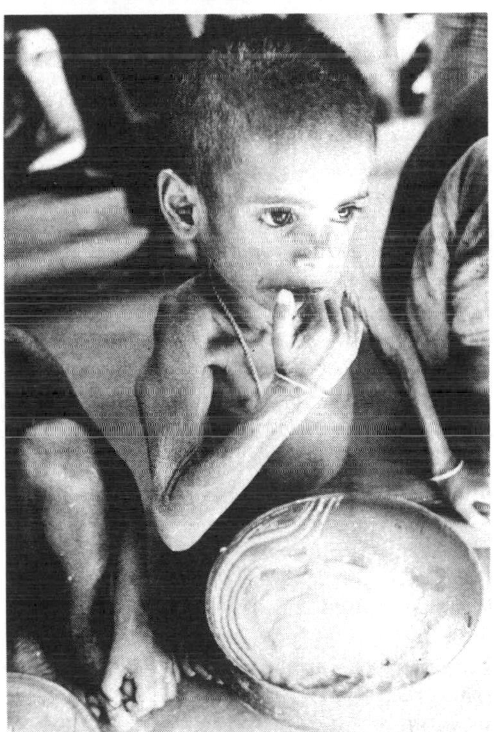

Fig. 22.2 A malnourished child in Bangladesh at the end of 1975

scale horrendous even in the Third World brought the problem home to hundreds of millions in the North, especially through their television sets. Emperor Haile Selassie had ruled Ethiopia until he was deposed in 1974. He had left a country little touched by twentieth-century developments, vast in size with an estimated population of only about 30 million, and one of the poorest states even in Africa. Exports were almost entirely agricultural, such as coffee, pulses and hides. Political change brought to power in 1977 the socialist-inclined Colonel Haile Mengistu, who welcomed to Ethiopia Soviet and Cuban advisers to assist the country's development and 'struggle against imperialism' but whose presence in the Horn of Africa alarmed the West. History had also left Ethiopia with problems of nation-building. Eritrea, a former Italian colony, had become part of Ethiopia in 1952 under the recommendation of the UN, and Haile Selassie had soon withdrawn self-government from the Eritreans, who set up the Eritrean Liberation Front in 1963 and clamoured for independence. Thus began a long-running guerilla war against the government in Addis Ababa, a war which in turn encouraged a similar secessionist movement in the province of Tigre. In the south of Ethiopia, secessionists in Ogaden Province were backed by Somalia and frontiers were disputed. Somalia itself had been a client of the Soviet Union before flirting with the USA. The Soviets and the Cubans helped Ethiopia to win the Ogaden War in 1978 but the area remained restless, and these problems of tribalism and national disunity sapped Ethiopia's strength.

Drought from 1983 to 1985 combined with long-term soil erosion to produce famine in Ethiopia, and the problems were made worse by crop diseases in the south and disorder in the north due to the continuing independence struggles of the Eritreans and the Tigreans. It is difficult even to estimate the number of deaths over this period, but there were many. International authorities estimated in 1985 that some nine million of Ethiopia's population of 43 million needed urgent help, and relief workers struggled to cope with the millions of sick and starving in search of food. Governments were tempted to make political capital of Ethiopia's tragedy, the West being quick to criticize the Marxist administration, though seemingly less outspoken about Eritrean rebels who repeatedly destroyed trucks carrying food to the starving. But universal relief operations were mounted, supplies being rushed to Ethiopia by aircraft from – among others – the USA and the USSR, both Germanies, Britain, Italy, Poland and Libya. Most spectacularly, there was a surge of public concern resulting in vigorous fund-raising in the West, and anger against governments which seemed reluctant to use the resources they alone could command. Imaginations were fired by Bob Geldof, an Irish pop star, who began mobilizing show business and youth in massive fund-raising for relief work, some of which he supervized personally. In July 1985, for example, a televised sixteen-hour pop festival, Live Aid, raised over £50 million in the British Isles and America, the Irish Republic giving most per head of population.

Emergency relief was essential but so too were both short-term and long-term constructive aid. The Ethiopian government embarked on resettlement programmes, moving people to more fertile regions, though it was criticized for interfering with individual freedoms and disrupting tribal patterns. In 1984 the FAO had identified 21 African states on a famine danger list, and two years later Ethiopia and the Sudan in particular still struggled with starvation and disrupted rural economies. In the Sahel region, just south of the Sahara Desert, food production remained precarious. Moreover, famine threatened as far south as some of the overcrowded homelands in South Africa. In other parts of Africa the rains had begun to bring better crops, thus relieving immediate danger. But disaster was never far away: in 1988 Morocco, Algeria and Tunisia needed emergency help to cope with huge swarms of desert locusts which were moving northwards. Meanwhile, basic problems remained. It was important that the world community should change the international order so that the poor should not have to go on relying on importing food that they could ill afford. This was one of the messages of the Brandt Report (see section 21.3.2). The International Fund for Agricultural Development (IFAD) already existed to bring about such change, but in the 1980s it estimated that to achieve it would cost around 12 billion dollars each year.

22.3 Medicine and health

Despite the persistence of famine and malnutrition in the Third World and the increase of heart disease and cancer in more affluent countries, medical advances in the twentieth century played a big part in lengthening human life and increasing the world's population. Alexander Fleming discovered penicillin in 1929, though its enormous value as an antibiotic was not fully realized until the 1940s. Improved communications then rapidly spread its use across the world, along with most advances in knowledge, and by the end of the 1950s the USA alone was producing over 400 tons of penicillin a year. Numerous voluntary organizations, government agencies and the World Health Organization (WHO) tackled with considerable success diseases which had long persisted, including tuberculosis, leprosy and smallpox. In 1975, for example, Bangladesh was declared free from smallpox which now survived only in isolated pockets, in states such as Ethiopia. On the other hand, other diseases persisted in the South where measles still killed two million children a year in the late 1980s.

Pioneers in the richer countries meanwhile pushed forward the frontiers of medical science. Steady progress was made in radiotherapy and anaesthetics, and surgeons now began transplanting human organs – kidneys in the 1940s, livers in the 1960s, and in 1967 the first transplantation of a human heart was carried out by Christiaan Barnard in South Africa. It took time for success rates to grow and the scale of such front-line operations was limited by lack of resources and of sufficiently skilled surgeons, but by the late twentieth century the possibilities in medicine, even to the point of artificially assisting conception, began to seem boundless.

Such advances raised serious moral questions and prompted world-wide debate about issues such as the implanting of human eggs, abortion, euthanasia and even of the definition of death (with regard to the removal of organs for transplants). There was also disquiet about the extent to which millions in the developed world had become dependent on medicines and drugs, both 'uppers' to stimulate and 'downers' to tranquillize. It was the increasing pace and growing complexity of life in the richer nations which helped to increase cancers and heart disease and which boosted the consumption of alcohol, tobacco and drugs. Thalidomide was one example of a drug which had horrific consequences: a sleeping pill thought safe in 1956, it was the cause of major deformities in children born to the pregnant women who had taken it.

Drugs took another form, however. Improved communications made easier the traffic in substances from marijuana to heroin for sale to those seeking their own refuge from stress, resulting in personal fortune for those dealers who escaped detection but bringing untold misery and premature death to many who became addicted to the more dangerous drugs like heroin and cocaine. From the 1960s the number of addicts seemed to escalate alarmingly, especially in the developed world and its urban centres. Awareness and anxiety brought official action against the drug-pushers, and publicity campaigns were launched against dangers to health, which in the 1980s embraced cigarette-smoking, alcohol and unwholesome foods as well as drugs.

Addicts who injected their drugs with shared needles now faced another peril, however. AIDS (acquired immune deficiency syndrome) was first identified in 1981 and, in its rapid spread, threatened a new plague for which doctors had no immediate antidote. AIDS breaks down the body's defences against infection, with wasting and death eventually following for most. Nearly 7000 died of AIDS in the USA alone before the end of 1984. The developed world thought of the disease as sexually transmitted, prevalent especially among homosexuals and also likely to strike at those exposed to infected blood such as drug addicts and the victims of early untested blood transfusions. But AIDS was especially widespread in Africa where it was known as SLIM and where malnutrition, poor health and the inability to finance health care and full-scale blood-testing placed millions at risk who were neither homosexuals nor drug-users. The WHO estimated that in Africa in 1987 there were between two and five million people carrying the disease who might be expected in due course to die of it. The number infected seemed to be doubling every six months and the epidemic was of crisis proportions. Moreover, the disease was beginning to take different forms, while no cure for it seemed yet within sight. Britain in 1987 had about 30 000 carriers according to a government estimate, and deaths from AIDS were approaching one a day in the UK. But the true scale of the problem across the world and in individual areas was still unknown, and its threat to the future of mankind a matter of controversy.

22.4 Resources and pollution

22.4.1 The consumption of finite resources

Economic, usually industrial, development was an almost universal goal, but its achievement was not without cost. The cost in terms of exhausted resources had already by the late twentieth century fallen heavily on the Third World. Walter Rodney, a Caribbean Marxist, wrote of the damaging effects on Africa of colonization and the policies of the North in *How Europe Underdeveloped Africa* (Bogle–L'Ouverture Publications, 1972). Others also documented 'the pillaging of the Third World' of resources from slaves to gold and spices, calculating that 25 billion pounds' worth of resources (at 1982 prices) had already been stripped by the middle of the nineteenth century (Open University, *Third World Atlas*, 1982), since when pillaging had continued. The North needed fuel, minerals and timber to feed its development, needs which persisted even when colonial empires came to an end. This not only caused resentment as wealth was transferred northwards: alarm at the speed with which the developed world consumed natural resources increased in the 1960s, and questions were asked about how long finite resources could last and what would be left of the earth's resources for future generations to inherit. The cost now threatened to fall on the whole of mankind.

In the 1970s OPEC aimed at changes which were partly designed to conserve oil reserves at a time when demands for energy were escalating. The markets for oil were predominantly in the North, and among Third World countries only China, India, Argentina and Brazil consumed more than 0.5 per cent of world oil production in 1979. The Third World seemed sure to need more oil as development spread, however. The energy crisis of the 1970s stimulated exploration, and the discovery of new oil reserves more than met short-term needs (see section 21.1). But that did not remove the underlying fear that oil reserves were being used up and that producers would eventually have nothing left to market. The exhausting of regional reserves was already a familiar story as deposits of minerals – from coal to tin, chromium to phosphates – were worked out. New industries produced new demands, quickening the search for and mining of deposits of uranium ores and rare metals like molybdenum. Forests were stripped to meet the world's insatiable demands for paper. Wildlife was endangered through the demand for furs, ivory and trophies. The sea was pillaged, fish stocks were diminished through over-fishing and the whale was threatened with extinction.

The International Whaling Commission (IWC) was set up as early as 1946, partly to preserve endangered species, but vested interests in the whaling industry frustrated effective action. The Conference on the Environment at Stockholm in 1972 voted for a ten-year moratorium on commercial whaling to give stocks a chance to recover from excessive slaughter. But demands for whale meat and sperm oil apparently could not be denied, and Japan and the Soviet Union were among those who insisted on defying international opinion. IWC scientists advised a total ban on hunting sperm whales, but that too was resisted. Environmentalists nevertheless kept up the pressure. The European Community responded with restrictions on all whale products, and the USA began to put pressure on countries such as Japan and Norway which defied the IWC by hunting minke whales. Most countries agreed to impose a ban on commercial whaling from the start of 1986, though this was still resisted by the Soviet Union, Japan and Norway, while Iceland and South Korea claimed the right to continue killing whales 'for scientific research'. Under further pressure, the Japanese agreed to consider ending whaling in 1988.

The struggle to protect whales was just part of the spreading support for the World Conservation Strategy (WCS), launched in 1980 by international organizations concerned about the environment, natural resources and wildlife. The Strategy pointed out the paradox that peoples in the South were being forced, for short-term survival, to sell and exhaust the very resources they needed to escape from poverty. The WCS therefore joined with the Brandt Report in warning of the urgency of conserving resources, both for environmental and for economic reasons. Once again, however, the international order was very slow to change.

22.4.2 Fouling the nest

Development exacted another cost: the human environment suffered increasing pollution, both the fall-out of industrialization and the refuse of urbanization. Spillages of oil and leakages (some radioactive) from industrial plant seemed more numerous even than terrorist outrages as the twentieth century wore on. Individual tragedies such as that at Bhopal in 1984 caused outrage (see section 16.2.2(b)), and controversy raged about nuclear installations almost wherever they were built (see section 22.5). But behind the specific crises and disputes general pollution spread, poisoning many areas in the North with sulphur dioxide and choking coastal waters throughout the world with a dangerous

Fig. 22.3 A dying guillemot, its plumage encrusted with crude oil from the oil tanker Torrey Canyon, wrecked in 1967

cocktail of tar, chemicals and sewage. In Tokyo, Los Angeles and other cities in the 1970s the air was often so fouled by motor exhausts and industrial pollution that 'smog' masks needed to be worn and reserves of oxygen kept on hand, though countries like Britain fought back – not ineffectively – with clean-air legislation.

Pollution was not simply a national problem, however. In the 1970s and 1980s anxiety grew over 'acid rain', industrial pollution with a strong sulphuric-acid content, blown from one country to another. In Europe such rain was blamed in the mid-1980s for damaging half the trees in West German forests, for polluting Swedish lakes and killing fish, for endangering wildlife such as the osprey, and for causing erosion which threatened parts of Europe's architectural heritage such as St Paul's, London, and the Colosseum, Rome. Britain was identified as responsible for much of the fall-out on the Continent. The environmental group, Friends of the Earth, called it the 'world's worst air polluter', its 'exports' of sulphur dioxide being far greater than those of the next worse offenders, Italy and Spain. The European Community demanded a clean-up.

Awareness of another danger also grew in the 1980s. The widespread use of chlorofluorocarbons (CFCs) in aerosol sprays, plastic foam and refrigerators was suspected of thinning the ozone layer in the earth's atmosphere. This resulted in less protection against radioactivity from the sun and a marked increase in skin cancers in the 1970s and 1980s. UN investigators confirmed the role played by CFCs in this new hazard in a report in 1988, but an international conference at Montreal the previous year had already persuaded some 30 nations to try to reduce their use. Among the countries so far most affected by changes in ozone protection were the USA, most European states, Australia and New Zealand, and it seemed that this was another hazard traceable to more affluent life-styles.

The poisoning of rivers, inland seas and the oceans was another cause for alarm. By the 1970s the Great Lakes in North America, Lake Constance in Europe and Lake Baikal in the USSR were all heavily polluted. Lake Baikal, for example, suffered as the result of the opening of new lead and zinc mines further to develop Soviet resources. Clean-up operations made slow progress, sometimes – but not always – offset by further damage in the rush to create more wealth.

While Britain had already done a good deal to clean up the waters of the River Thames, allowing fish to breed there again, other rivers still contributed significantly to the threat to the ecosystem of the North Sea. Toxic waste from the Rhine, originating in Switzerland it was alleged, caused fury in 1986. The seas were affected by acid rain, by spillages from tankers and by a good deal of dumping, both of waste from industry and of sewage. Some of what was dumped – either buried or merely discharged as effluent – was radioactive, leading not only to anger about coastal waters but also to anxiety about marine life and the seas generally. The poisoning of the land was also disturbing, outrages ranging from the deliberate use of poisons in the Vietnam War and the burying of dangerous waste such as cyanide, storing up unknown hazards for the future, to the widespread and excessive use of pesticides harmful to insects, wildlife and human beings.

The UN Conference on the Human Environment at Stockholm in 1972 faced formidable problems. Development itself was questioned, but the British representative spoke for most when he said:

> We believe that the pressing need is to create more of the right kind of wealth and to use it more wisely: to clean up rivers, to quieten engines, and above all, on a global scale, to get rid of poverty, illiteracy and disease.

Technological progress and industrial expansion were assumed to hold the key to prosperity for both North and South, but the Conference needed to rescue the environment from the already apparent harmful results of this drive towards prosperity. The problems were too massive for any simple master plan, however. A rather vague Declaration identified dangers, among them the pressing threat to 'the non-renewable resources of the earth', though individual countries hastened to protect their own interests as they saw them (Japanese whaling, for example, and Chinese testing of nuclear bombs in the earth's atmosphere). But committees and projects were launched – to survey the earth's remaining resources, to monitor levels of pollution, and to protect plants and wildlife – and the United Nations soon afterwards set up its own Environmental Programme (UNEP).

Considerable attention now focused on the seas. More than 50 nations agreed in 1972 to stop dumping certain types of waste in the sea, and soon afterwards the United Nations Conference on the Law of the Sea (UNCLOS) got to work on a range of problems, from preserving fish stocks to the mining of the sea bed and rights of passage. It took nine years to frame the Law-of-the-Sea Treaty which 117 nations – including the Soviet Union, Canada and France – signed in Jamaica in 1982. The Treaty declared the oceans 'the common heritage of mankind' beyond twelve miles of territorial waters and an economic zone extending 200 miles from each national coastline. Perez de Cuellar called the Treaty:

> possibly . . . the most significant international legal instrument in this century.

But it was also significant that 45 nations declined to sign it, including the USA, Britain and West Germany – nations with reservations about restrictions on mining the sea bed for their own profit. The USA refused to help finance further investigations on this issue. By the end of 1984 more countries had accepted the Treaty, but the USA, Britain and West Germany continued to resist in a display of self-interest.

Such self-interest was still a problem. France insisted on continuing to test nuclear weapons in the Pacific, to the dismay of local islanders, New Zealanders and others living close by. When Greenpeace environmentalists threatened to obstruct further tests, French agents in 1985 sank their vessel, *Rainbow Warrior*, in a New Zealand harbour, showing contempt for a 'nuclear-free Pacific'. Radioactive pollution became so bad on Mururoa atoll, the site of a hundred French tests, that it had to be abandoned in 1988 – the French simply moving to another island 25 miles away. Gradually, however, international agreements had multiplied. UNEP worked vigorously, one of its more recent achievements being a Treaty to protect the eastern Indian Ocean, agreed in 1985. Data was accumulated concerning pollution and its longer-term effects on land and sea, and individual countries and groups such as the European Community were prodded into action, not only by the weight of evidence but also by ecology parties ('Green' parties in many European countries) which were intent on bringing the issues before the electors to whom politicians were answerable.

22.5 Social change

22.5.1 Women's rights

The idea of equality between the sexes attracted much interest in the years after 1945, though the results in practice often disappointed its supporters. In two world wars women had shown their ability to do many of the jobs previously done by men, while women's movements had campaigned against all kinds of discrimination, and socialist and communist ideologies had embraced principles of equality. Women became prominent in revolutionary movements such as those in Algeria and Cuba, though revolutionary regimes there did not fulfil all their hopes. Indeed, progress towards equality varied from one culture to another and the role of women in society was viewed differently in countries such as the USA and the USSR and in Islamic states such as Iran. Few developed countries denied women the vote after 1946 (though Switzerland delayed until 1971), and new states such as India and Pakistan were quick to grant them electoral equality. This equality also applied when voting ages were lowered, as they were in Britain (to eighteen) in time for the election of 1970. Moreover, women such as Sirimavo Bandaranaike, Indira Gandhi, Golda Meir and Margaret Thatcher attained the highest political office of their respective countries in the second half of the twentieth century. But in all societies, East and West, North and South, women in general found total equality of opportunity and of rewards elusive.

A *Handbook of International Data on Women* by Elise Boulding and others (Sage Publications, 1977) concluded that job opportunities were greater in eastern than in western Europe, and that women were most disadvantaged in the Islamic states of the Middle East. Syria had given the vote to women in 1949 and Iran in 1963, but this did little to bring other forms of equality. It was another measure of female disadvantage that in the 1970s women seldom had greater representation in a national parliament than their 21 per cent in Sweden and 15 per cent in Poland. (In Britain and the USA, for example, this figure was closer to a mere 4 per cent.) Equal representation in decision-making institutions and posts of responsibility remained almost everywhere a still distant goal.

Interest in women's rights had been greatly stimulated by the publication in 1949 of Simone de Beauvoir's *The Second Sex*, quickly translated into a further twenty languages from the original French. Women's liberation movements became prominent in many parts of the world, especially in the 1960s. They campaigned for educational and job opportunities, equal pay, legal independence, and social-security benefits for mothers including rights for the unmarried. They also campaigned against all sexual discrimination and sexual harassment, and many members advocated legalized abortion and supported sexual freedom and the rights of lesbians, dividing women themselves as well as communities in general on these sensitive issues. 'Women's Lib' was condemned by critics as too radical and too aggressive, though others welcomed its outspokenness and vigorous promotion in publications such as the magazine *Spare Rib* and the books of the Women's Press. The year 1975 was named International Women's Year but even a decade later women in few countries other than the Soviet Union, the Philippines and Sweden had yet to fill half the jobs in the professions, a measure of what still had to be achieved.

22.5.2 Violence and crime

The attempt to blow up the British Prime Minister and much of her Cabinet at the time of the Conservative Party Conference in Brighton in October 1984 was one of the most audacious modern-day terrorist onslaughts. As a result of this plot, hatched by the IRA, five Conservatives were killed and others were badly injured. Yet other bombings had caused heavier casualties during the previous twenty years, especially in the United Kingdom which had the highest level of political violence in Western Europe. By the 1980s terrorist attacks on lives and property were almost daily events across the world, attracting anger and despair but seldom surprise. Violence bred violence, and governments themselves, as well as those seeking to put pressure on them, sometimes promoted it (see section 20.3.2). Society seemed to have become numbed, perhaps brutalized, by twentieth-century wars and by the horrors and atrocities now reported regularly by the media.

The causes in support of which 'the men of violence' thought murder and destruction fitting means were many and varied, as earlier units in this book have shown, but they could be broadly linked with growing awareness of injustice and, especially through television, of examples which could be copied. The transport revolution of the years after 1945 also played a part, allowing for readier movement between countries and vastly increasing air travel – aircraft being especially tempting and vulnerable targets for bombers and hijackers. In 1985 in one ten-day period alone, an aircraft was hijacked near Athens, bombs exploded at airports in Frankfurt and Tokyo, and an Air India jet broke up over the Atlantic killing 329 people, probably the result of a bomb planted by Sikhs. The authorities, of course, struck back with suffocating security measures and, in many countries, ruthless, sometimes brutal, security forces and riot police ready to engage the enemy – in pitched battle, if necessary.

It was not always easy to draw clear lines between 'wars' and other atrocities. The 'official' conflicts which took place in the Middle East, in Indo-China, and in Afghanistan were not very different from the liberation movements which had freed countries like Mozambique from colonial rule. Many whom the authorities called 'terrorists' were 'freedom-fighters' in the eyes of their supporters, struggling to liberate minorities from their oppressors or peoples from hated governments. While they might operate in guerilla armies in Namibia or Eritrea, Nicaragua or the Philippines, they might be more fragmented elsewhere, operating in scattered groups of bombers, kidnappers and assassins such as the members of the Red Brigade in Italy and the Baader-Meinhof Group in West Germany. Numerous organizations and individuals were at war with society. Within weeks in 1981 President Reagan of the USA and Pope John Paul II were both wounded by would-be assassins. A few years later, Indira Gandhi, Prime Minister of India, and Olof Palme, Prime Minister of Sweden, were murdered, adding to the list of politicians assassinated since 1945. There were, of course, uncounted victims of the violence of vicious governments such as those of Amin in Uganda, Pol Pot in Kampuchea and Pinochet in Chile.

There was also violence which seemed spontaneous, erupting from frustration and despair, like the clashes in the inner cities in Britain in the 1980s (see section 19.4.2(b)). These confrontations occurred in deprived areas with substantial non-white communities, and seemed to have parallels with riots in cities in the USA in the 1960s (see section 2.3.3). But injustices and inequalities other than those inspired by racial hatred provided the mainspring for these disturbances, and urbanization provided the setting for outbreaks of protest and violence, mainly against property and the police who were the agents of authority. Urban unrest was a world-wide problem in fact. In the North it was often linked with the decay of cities and inner cities, once prosperous but now ageing and in decline as a result of economic change. The growth of cities in the South often brought with it social and economic problems with which the authorities were unable to cope. In both cases, the speed and scale of twentieth-century change brought instability. In some areas, like the Indian subcontinent, communal rivalries increased the unrest and the urban violence. Urbanization nevertheless seemed an inescapable part of development, and huge cities grew, sucking in people from rural communities eager for more rapid progress towards prosperity. By the early 1980s Tokyo, Shanghai, Buenos Aires, Mexico City, Peking, Moscow and New York were all more heavily populated then Greater London. Other cities like Bombay were growing fast. It was unsurprising that such cities were often centres of unrest and of crime, disturbing even the governments of China and the Soviet Union, which prided themselves on their disciplined societies.

Crime was believed to be increasing across the world in the late twentieth century, and much of it was violent. Perhaps taking their example in part from the gun-carrying traditions of the USA as well as from terrorists, criminals in Britain and elsewhere armed themselves more readily in the 1970s and 1980s and seemed to turn more willingly to violence. The criminal statistics of different countries remain difficult to compare, and are also subject to difficulties in interpreting movements over time, but the North and more especially the West showed general alarm about escalating crime and violence with widespread hooliganism and vandalism. Prisons, especially in Britain, became severely overcrowded as societies groped for solutions to the disorders. Greed, alienation and violence seemed to be companions in yet another assault on society. In the South, such problems particularly affected the cities, especially those where slums festered and expansion was difficult to control, and where Northern-style affluence often coexisted with Third World deprivation. It was in the cities, some like New York now notorious, that the human environment seemed most obviously to have become despoiled in the late twentieth century. Millions lived in squalor even in the North, and worried about crime and violence as well as about work and incomes.

22.6 Technological change and the nuclear industry

22.6.1 High-speed technology

The massive technological change in the second half of the twentieth century was at its most marked in the fields of transport, electronics and energy. In 1945 jet aircraft were still comparatively new, with mainly military uses. Forty years later, not only did huge jet airliners service a bewildering network of international routes, which brought them thundering in to crowded national airports, but jet propulsion had also enabled man to penetrate into space and even to reach the moon. No less important in its consequences was the development of the helicopter. Though invented as early as 1907, it was not until after the Second World War that the helicopter's uses multiplied dramatically. The Korean War revealed its military usefulness, and its civil uses now extended spectacularly to include short-distance transport, rescue, crop-spraying and surveillance. Increasing speed seemed an essential feature of modern living: motorway traffic, high-speed trains, hovercraft and helicopters moved people and freight rapidly over comparatively short distances, and fast transcontinental air travel was now so developed that the world was often described as a sort of 'global village'.

Developments in electronics brought revolutions in the home and in communications. A luxury for a tiny minority before the Second World War even in the richest countries, television spread steadily after 1945 to become commonplace by the 1980s in all but the poorest countries and most isolated areas. In the developed world, homes became crammed with machines such as vacuum cleaners, washing machines, freezers and automated cookers, while electronic entertainment began to extend from television and gramophones to video recorders and compact-disc players. The first electronic high-speed digital calculating machine was built in the USA in the mid-1940s and computers too developed, spreading by the 1980s to become essential in business and popular in the home. Their uses multiplied to include the storing and communicating of information, automated manufacture and design, and games for personal entertainment. The Americans launched *Telstar* – the first communications satellite in space – in the early 1960s, the start of a revolution in the international transmission of information and entertainment, often by television pictures.

These improved communications both in travel and in spreading information

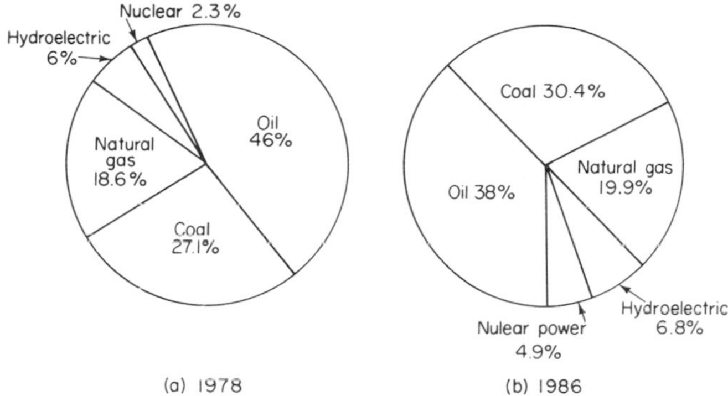

Total world consumption of energy (million tonnes of oil equivalent) was 6714 in 1978 and 7589 in 1986.

Fig. 22.4 The world's consumption of energy: 1978 and 1986

helped to shrink the world and threatened to increase uniformity, for example in dress, recreation, shopping and urban life. Optimists hoped there might also be a spread of knowledge and, in turn, a reduction in prejudice and narrow-minded intolerance. For millions, however, increased stress was the price that had to be paid and stress-related diseases grew markedly in the developed world (see section 22.3). Technological development brought other problems too, not only dangers to the environment (see section 22.4) but also a growing demand for energy in both North and South. Figure 22.4 shows how the world produced the energy it consumed in 1978. Nuclear power was then still a newcomer, but its future role was already the subject of fierce debate.

22.6.2 The nuclear industry: enthusiasm and doubts

Optimists hoped that in the second half of the twentieth century nuclear weapons would guarantee the peace of the world and nuclear energy would supply it with cheap power. Others had doubts about both, fearful of the dangers of such energy and the still largely unknown perils of radioactivity. The USA pressed forward, however. Truman set up the Atomic Energy Commission in 1946 and offered technological help in the peaceful development of nuclear power. The first nuclear reactors were made operational in 1956–7 in Illinois and Pennsylvania in the USA. Twenty years later some five per cent of the world's total electricity was generated in nuclear power stations, a percentage which the energy crisis of the 1970s helped to increase. Nuclear power, it was claimed, was cheaper than that produced from coal or oil – a claim contested in the 1980s and subsequently shown to be false. The largest number of reactors in the 1970s was in the USA, but they were spreading fast in Europe, Japan and the Soviet Union and had already been introduced in parts of the South, such as India and Pakistan, Argentina and Brazil, Iran and South Africa. The USA, Sweden, Belgium and West Germany already depended on nuclear energy for more than ten per cent of their electricity.

Along with the power stations came controversy and protest. There were doubts about the safety of the plant, about the dangers of transporting fissile material between sites and about the disposal of waste. The potential hazards from accident or sabotage seemed alarming, and many found the connections between nuclear power plant and nuclear weapons morally disturbing. In Austria, public opinion stopped the government putting into operation plant at Zwentendorf, near Vienna, and almost all countries building nuclear plant faced repeated anti-nuclear demonstrations. The authorities usually maintained considerable secrecy around the industry but suspicion and rumours abounded. In some cases, high levels of leukemia were detected around plant such as that at Windscale in England, and numerous reports circulated about leaks of radioactivity and radioactive discharges into the sea. A fire at Windscale in 1957 and subsequent leakages of radioactivity were not fully reported until much later, but in 1983 poisonous discharges from Windscale (now renamed Sellafield) led to emergency action to close nearby beaches. Three years later, after yet another accidental discharge of radioactive waste into the Irish Sea, Sellafield was under even fiercer criticism – so much so that Dick Spring, Energy Minister in the Republic of Ireland, demanded that it be closed. Referring to the dangers to the Irish people, Spring said:

> This installation at Sellafield, badly run and incompetently managed for virtually its entire period of operation, has posed and continues to pose a real threat.

Spectacular accidents in the USA and the USSR had by now intensified anti-nuclear concern. The first was at Three Mile Island, Harrisburg, Pennsylvania, in 1979. Errors caused the reactor there to overheat and the danger of explosion and a subsequent release of radioactivity was such that 140 000 people were evacuated before the crisis was brought under control and a major disaster narrowly averted. A reactor at Chernobyl, near Kiev in the Soviet Union, did explode in 1986. Local short-term casualties were measured in dozens rather than thousands, but radioactivity was carried into Poland and Scandinavia and eventually to almost all of Europe as well as across much of the Soviet Union, and the long-term consequences could only be argued over. The Soviets carried out mass evacuations and mobilized a huge effort (and a courageous labour force) to bury the crippled and leaking reactor in concrete, while nuclear experts on all sides hastened to reassure their publics that nuclear power was comparatively safe and that development programmes should continue. But as far away as Britain radioactive fall-out led to temporary but protracted bans on home-produced milk and meat. Local economies were widely disrupted across much of northern Europe. Laplanders, for example, found the reindeer herds on which they depended heavily contaminated. Doubts increased about the costs, especially in terms of future cancer cases, by which the economic advantages of nuclear energy would be obtained, and environmentalists stepped up their anti-nuclear campaigns.

The disposal of nuclear waste was a problem even given the safe operation of power stations. The low-level radioactivity of the material discharged from Sellafield into the Irish Sea was deplored, but far worse was the waste expected to be radioactive for tens of thousands of years. This needed specialist handling and burial underground or under the sea in what were claimed to be leak-proof containers. The transportation and disposal of such containers aroused both anger and alarm, with claims and counter-claims about the future perils of the waste they held. Britain's involvement in specialist waste disposal, treating the waste of other states, was heavily criticized, but such business was profitable and in 1985 both the Soviet Union and China began to seek a part of it.

The plant at Three Mile Island was reopened in 1985 after closure since 1979, but nuclear-energy programmes generally had suffered setbacks in the 1980s. Few countries turned their backs on nuclear energy, however. Some indeed pressed on enthusiastically. In 1984 Belgium produced more than half its energy from nuclear fuel, and France and Sweden more than 40 per cent of theirs. The Swedes, however, had already decided in a referendum in 1980 that they would phase out nuclear power by 2005, a decision reinforced by a fire at their reactor at Oskarshann in 1982. Britain's nuclear output in 1984 rose to almost twenty per cent. With a far bigger total production of energy, the USA and the USSR had not greatly increased the part of it that was nuclear-generated – some thirteen and ten per cent respectively. But nuclear power was no longer confined to the developed countries. Taiwan produced almost half its power from nuclear plant in 1984, and the nuclear industry was growing in India and Pakistan. Austria was one of very few states with the wealth and expertise to build nuclear power stations which continued to refuse to operate them, but of its near neighbours Poland was the only one without nuclear plant.

Sweden had no reserves of coal, oil or gas but expected by 2005 to find alternative sources of energy. Experiments with wind power, wave power and solar energy were already being conducted in many countries from North America to Japan. In the early 1980s the biggest solar plant in the world was on the west coast of the USA, in the Mojave Desert. Japan had a similar plant at Kagawa, near Hiroshima. Others experimented in other directions: New Zealand tapped the geothermal heat of hot springs; Brazil used ethanol, produced from sugar cane, to fuel motor vehicles. The one certainty was that world demand for energy would continue to grow.

22.6.3 Weaponry

Great-power manoeuvring meanwhile continued while nuclear-weapons stockpiles grew. Though the US Senate did not ratify SALT 2, both superpowers nevertheless observed its provisions (see section 21.1). In 1986, however, Reagan increased the number of United States B-52 bombers armed with Cruise missiles, deliberately breaking the agreement in an attempt to put pressure on the Soviets to make new concessions. Gorbachev claimed to want a nuclear-free world and to be ready to negotiate for it. Reagan, still enthusiastic about SDI, was deeply suspicious, hindering progress towards new agreements on intercontinental ballistic missiles (IBMs).

Fig. 22.5 As early as January 1950 in the *Evening Standard*, Low presented a view of post-war scientists that became all too familiar. Whatever the benefits of science for civilisation, it contributed dramatically to the war games of the major powers, breeding weapons and weapon systems which grew ever more terrifying.

Negotiations at Geneva about missiles and at Vienna about reductions in forces dragged on into 1987. Gorbachev insisted that agreements on intermediate-range missiles as well as on IBMs should be linked with a settlement on SDI. Intermediate-range missiles - intermediate nuclear forces (INFs) - were mainly weapons such as Western Cruise, American Pershings and Soviet SS-20s. Both sides could see advantages in removing these from Europe. Two years' talk on 'Disarmament in Europe' produced the Stockholm Declaration in September 1986. This was a modest agreement for more openness between the major powers about troop movements in Europe, the Soviets at last conceding the on-site inspections that the West had long demanded. Negotiations on chemical weapons, nuclear stockpiles and the reduction of conventional forces were to go on. Willy Brandt was not alone in continuing to criticize the thousand billion dollars estimated to have been spent in 1985 alone on weapons and military forces as a shameful misuse of the world's resources, and one for which the major powers bore a heavy responsibility in setting an example for other states. This was mounting criticism of which neither Reagan nor Gorbachev was unaware.

In the mid-1980s it was estimated that the stockpiled weapons were already potentially a million and a half times more destructive than the single bomb dropped on Hiroshima. Environmentalists also worried about the continuing test explosions in the development of yet more nuclear weapons. The Soviet Union suspended such tests in September 1985 but felt obliged to resume testing during 1987 since the West had not followed suit, the USA alone conducting more than twenty tests within twelve months. Nuclear forces, it was argued, had to be modernized unless new technology were to render earlier weapons obsolete (though even a fraction of existing arsenals was more than enough to destroy the world). Both France and China had eventually accepted the ban on testing bombs in the atmosphere (see section 13.3.2). France last tested above ground in 1974 and China in 1980, but there could be no claim that underground tests were entirely safe: many released radioactivity into the atmosphere.

The danger also persisted that more countries would join the nuclear 'club' and even that nuclear weapons might get into the hands of terrorists. Latin America declared itself a nuclear-free zone in 1967 in the Treaty of Tlatelolco, but the example was not followed by other regions. Nor did any country hasten to follow India's example in openly declaring its nuclear capability in 1974, though by 1985 South Africa, Israel and Pakistan were believed secretly to have developed that capacity.

Gorbachev gave way again: he agreed to the INF Treaty in December 1987 without any United States concessions on SDI. Shultz and Eduard Shevardnadze, the Soviet Foreign Minister, put the final touches to the Treaty after the long negotiations in Geneva. Reagan and Gorbachev signed it in Washington before the end of the year. Under the Treaty, US and Soviet intermediate-range weapons were to be removed from the whole of Europe. There were only about 2000 such weapons in all (some four per cent of the nuclear stockpiles), but the Treaty was the first to require the actual destruction of existing nuclear weapons. Each superpower agreed to on-site verification by the other that the missiles were, in fact, destroyed. 'The security services will have a jolly time,' Shevardnadze joked.

Gorbachev had given way on another issue too. British and French weapons were excluded from the deal. Thatcher and Mitterrand insisted that such weapons were an insurance policy as well as being symbols of national status. The Americans would remove from their British bases their Cruise missiles – disparaged by their critics as only rather erratic 'flying-bombs' in any case – but Thatcher had set her heart on equipping Britain's own arsenal with Tridents, more advanced INFs. In her opinion it was only 'strength' which had persuaded the Soviets to make concessions, and she was adamant that her Trident programme would go ahead into the 1990s. There were also nagging worries that the US Senate might yet refuse to ratify the INF Treaty, though the Soviets began removing their INFs from eastern Europe early in 1988.

Hopes were nevertheless raised that the superpowers could go on to an agreement on IBMs in time for another summit meeting in Moscow before Reagan retired from office. Gorbachev offered a 50 per cent cut in long-range missiles over a five-year period, but he demanded US concessions on SDI which the American President still refused to give. Reagan would give no guarantee that the USA would not deploy nuclear missiles in space. On the other hand, the cost of Star Wars was now seriously alarming both Congress and the Pentagon. Twelve billion dollars had already been spent on researching SDI and it was

Table 22.1 Military spending, 1981: the countries spending most during the year on weapons and armed forces

	Million US dollars
USA*	134 390
USSR*	118 800
China*	37 200
West Germany‡	25 509
France*	23 633
Saudi Arabia	22 458
Britain*	19 901
Japan‡	9 461
Italy‡	8 184
Iran§	5 092
Netherlands‡	4 931
East Germany‡	4 394
Canada‡	4 227
India†	3 991
Iraq§	3 759
Belgium‡	3 690
Spain‡	3 682
Libya§	3 670
South Korea§	3 519
Australia	3 508
Turkey‡	3 442
North Korea	3 424
Sweden‡	3 175
Yugoslavia‡	2 936
Czechoslovakia‡	2 900
Israel†	2 750
Poland‡	2 467
Taiwan§	2 456
South Africa†	2 254
Argentina§	2 241
Greece	2 184
Syria	2 166
Nigeria	2 037
Kuwait	2 031
Switzerland‡	2 000
World total	520 000‖

* Possessing stockpiles of nuclear weapons.

† Capability to manufacture nuclear weapons known.

‡ Capability to manufacture nuclear weapons likely but production unlikely.

§ Capability to manufacture nuclear weapons imminent and production not unlikely. Brazil and Pakistan seemed likely soon to produce nuclear weapons though in 1981 spending less than 2000 million US dollars on weapons and armed forces.

‖ This represented more than 100 US dollars for each human being throughout the world, at a time when 100 US dollars was more than the average annual income per head in the poorest countries.

Source: M. Kidron and D. Smith, *The War Atlas* (Pluto Press and Pan Books 1983) now estimated that it would cost around 150 billion dollars to operate it by 1996. Attention focused on Strategic Arms Reduction Talks (START) but it was not only SDI which hindered them. The technical details of IBMs, the need for verification over an area far larger than Europe and of missiles based on submarines also led to massive difficulties. The superpowers had also still to resolve their differences over Afghanistan, Nicaragua, Indo-China and Angola, and perhaps also over human rights. The Cold War rhetoric which could still be heard from time to time in Washington and London showed the depth of suspicion which remained. Nor did Gorbachev have a completely free hand in Moscow, where not all the members of the CPSU were convinced supporters of glasnost and of deals with the West.

The Iraqi–Iranian War meanwhile showed yet again that non-nuclear war could be devastating and horrifying, especially when chemical and biological weapons were deployed (see section 20.2.3). Deploring the violence being done to the human environment in the mid-1980s, Brandt, in *World Armament and World Hunger* (Gollancz, 1986), called for 'a new realism':

> that takes our responsibility for our own heritage and a common future equally seriously.

In his view it was 'an outworn realism' to allow:

> the breakneck arms race to rush on while world hunger is ignored.

Brandt castigated governments which still pursued:

> a policy of confrontation [which had already] brought the world to the brink of an economic and military catastrophe.

The INF Treaty was evidence that constructive co-operation was still possible even between the superpowers, but it was just one small step towards the saner world for which unnumbered millions yearned. This unit has shown just some of the ways in which those working for sanity were engaged in a desperate race against time.

UNIT 23

Towards the 1990s

23.1 Peace and goodwill

For more than 40 years after 1945 Europe enjoyed a period of peace between nations which was almost unknown in earlier centuries. The peace of Europe owed a good deal to changes brought about by the Second World War – the shame of a civilization which had given birth to Nazism, the terrifying development of weaponry, the balance between the now dominant superpowers, and the movement towards unity, at least in western Europe.

In the late 1980s the twelve members of the European Community (EC) were well on course to achieve the totally common market scheduled for 1992, when the last internal tariffs were to be abolished. Turkey was already preparing its application for membership of the EC which would further expand the Community, though Turkey's record on human rights was an obstacle to its admission. The pending application did, however, prompt the EC to reconsider how its own members treated the millions of Turks already resident in the Community, where they provided a pool of cheap labour. The six partners of the European Free Trade Association (EFTA) were also beginning to discuss future membership of the EC, though they agreed in 1988 to act together and not individually to leave EFTA in favour of the Community. Within the EC, Britain continued to toy with the idea of joining the European Monetary System. In contrast, there was movement in 1988 towards merging the armed forces of France and West Germany, recalling the plans for the European Defence Community which had failed in the 1950s. In the first half of the twentieth century, France and Germany had been implacable enemies. In the second half of the century, France and West Germany led the way towards the new concord between the nations of western Europe. When in 1987–8 France and Britain began actively to co-operate in plans for a Channel Tunnel there was further movement towards western European unity.

The Soviet bloc in eastern Europe had achieved a similar unity since 1945. The West tended to underestimate the individuality of eastern-European states, whose cautious search for 'different roads to socialism' had gone on since the days of Malenkov and Khrushchev and was now given renewed impetus by Gorbachev's policies of glasnost. The political, economic and social systems of eastern Europe in the late 1980s nevertheless still differed considerably from those in the West. On the other hand, the danger of conflict between East and West had receded. Contact across the Iron Curtain had increased steadily in the wake of Brandt's Ostpolitik and achieved new vigour with glasnost and the INF Treaty of 1987. Some sort of association between the EC and Comecon no longer seemed unthinkable. In spite of the rhetoric of politicians warning of the continued 'need for vigilance', late twentieth-century Europe had moved a long way towards freeing itself from 'the scourge of war' which had been such a feature of its earlier history.

Europe, however, is a comparatively small area of the world as a whole, and the world was far from achieving a similar freedom from war. At the beginning of 1988 wars of one sort or another still raged in all continents except Europe and Australasia. Some of them were 'proxy' wars in which the superpowers were in indirect confrontation, though in 1988 the superpowers were in the mood for agreements and hopes for peace between them were higher than they had been for some time.

In April 1988 Gorbachev agreed with Najibullah that Soviet forces would leave Afghanistan within the next nine months. An accord was patched together in Geneva for signature by the USSR, the USA and Pakistan. It eased the consciences of the superpowers but did little to resolve the future of Afghanistan. The Soviets reserved the right to go on supplying arms to the government in Kabul, and the USA and Pakistan reserved the right to supply arms to the mujaheddin. President Zia of Pakistan called it 'symmetry of continuation' and, even before the ink was dry on the Geneva agreement, Pakistan insisted that it had not agreed to deprive the rebels of their bases on Pakistani soil. The Geneva agreement might prove no more than a formula for ensuring that the Afghan civil war would continue.

Central America meanwhile balanced on a knife-edge. The ceasefire and peace talks in 1988 brought some hope of a settlement in Nicaragua, but even while those talks proceeded there was an anti-government outburst in neighbouring Honduras, which the authorities blamed on left-wing refugees from El Salvador. There were also disturbances in Panama, where the military regime of General Manuel Noriega offended both Panamanians and the USA. Noriega had seized power in a coup and the USA feared both for human rights and for the security of the Panama Canal. The Arias Peace Plan for the whole of Central America had made some headway, but it still faced formidable difficulties.

Negotiations to bring peace to Angola and to Kampuchea were as yet only in their infancy. Gorbachev would prefer disengagement but could not abandon governments which relied on Soviet support; and, however ready President Reagan might now be to co-operate in agreements, the USA would have a new President in January 1989. There were also other areas of bitter conflict – such as Lebanon and the Iraqi–Iranian War – where the superpowers seemed to have little influence, though there seemed no shortage of American and Soviet weapons with which combatants could fight.

23.2 Fury and conflict

23.2.1 International banditry

Direct conflicts between independent nations, such as the Korean War and the wars between Israel and its Arab neighbours, were not, in fact, very numerous in the second half of the twentieth century. The Iraqi–Iranian War was the longest lasting. But a great many bloody conflicts took place within states, from time to time spilling over into neighbouring territories as occurred all too frequently in southern Africa in the 1970s and 1980s. Murders, bombings, hostage-taking and hijackings extended such conflicts still further until few countries remained untouched by the terrorism and political violence of the late twentieth century. Seeking revenge or simply publicity for their cause, terrorists struck where their victims were most exposed and they showed little regard for international frontiers. Each year added to the list of outrages, for only a few of which has there been space in this book. In 1980 alone, for example, there were about 1200 political assassinations, at least some of which were encouraged by governments as well as by protest movements.

In 1971, 60 aircraft hijackings occurred. Tighter security at airports then reduced the yearly number, but such incidents could not be eliminated completely. Consideration was given to setting up an international agency with the expertise to handle hijacking, hostage-taking and ransom demands - perhaps with an international jail for terrorists whose liberty other terrorists sought to secure by taking new hostages - but nothing had come of it by 1988. The circumstances of the outrages were too diverse and the involvement of national interests too complex for any tidy solution to international banditry. Individual nations set up their own apparatus, including anti-terrorist commando units whose methods were likely to be as ruthless as those of the individuals and organizations with whom they had to deal. Daring rescue attempts sometimes succeeded: Israeli forces successfully stormed an Air France plane which had been hijacked by PLO agents to Entebbe in 1976, and West German forces were also successful in storming a Lufthansa plane held by the Baader–Meinhof group at Mogadishu a year later. On other occasions operations went badly wrong. In November 1985 some 60 people died, most of them passengers held hostage, when Egyptian commandos stormed an EgyptAir Boeing 737 hijacked to Malta by gunmen thought to be Palestinians. A year later there were 62 deaths in a gun-battle at Arar in Saudi Arabia where a hijacked plane had crash-landed. More usually, patient negotiators talked the hijackers into peaceful surrender, though the ordeal for captive passengers and aircrew was often a protracted one. In June 1985 it took seventeen days to negotiate the release of hostages from a TWA airliner hijacked from its Athens–Rome flight to Beirut in Lebanon.

Lebanon in the late 1980s was a land reduced to a state of anarchy by complex political and religious rivalries. The numerous contending parties were faction-ridden and neighbours such as Israel and Syria interfered continually. Even the militant Shiites were divided between the Syrian-backed Amal group and the Iranian-backed Hizbollah. As a result, it was sometimes wellnigh impossible

Fig. 23.1 Beirut, Lebanon, January 1976: this attack was by Christian Phalangists on one of the city's Muslim quarters where there were Palestinian refugees. And an appeal for mercy in a city where civilians suffered repeatedly and hideously from warring militias in the 1970s and 1980s.

accurately to identify the groups who seized hostages such as Terry Waite and committed other terrorist actions. Such was the case when a Kuwaiti Boeing 747 was hijacked by Shiites in 1988, first to Iran and then to Cyprus. Yasser Arafat, leader of the PLO, was one of those called in to negotiate, boosting the prestige of the PLO but winning only limited concessions – a few hostages were released, and the aircraft flew on to Algeria. The hijackers aimed to secure the release of other terrorists held in Kuwait and, as was often the case, expressed their sympathy for the dispossessed Palestinians, whose cause seldom seemed far removed from upheavals in the Middle East. Even while the Kuwaiti hijack continued, however, the Palestinians suffered new setbacks. Abu Jihad, second-in-command to Arafat in the PLO, was brutally killed in Tunisia – murdered, the Organization claimed, by agents of Mossad (the Israeli secret service). Jihad had helped to organize protest in the West Bank and Gaza, Israeli-occupied territories from which Shamir's government had recently begun uprooting and deporting Palestinian agitators. Such Israeli policy was heavily criticized, even by Western friends of Israel's government. Along with Jihad's murder, the deportations inflamed the occupied territories further, and fierce policing almost immediately claimed another dozen lives there. Such was the climate of fury and conflict in just one of the world's most troubled regions.

Algerian negotiators brought an end to the Kuwaiti hijack a few days later. Passengers and crew were released after a sixteen-day ordeal. The hijackers had not succeeded in their aims but, though they had murdered two passengers before leaving Cyprus, they went unpunished and were given passage perhaps to Lebanon or Iran. A good deal of suspicion focused on Iran's involvement in the hijack but this was strongly denied in Tehran. Before the hijack ended, however, there was skirmishing in the Persian Gulf between Iranian and US forces, ostensibly because of renewed Iranian interference there with neutral shipping and the laying of mines, one of which had damaged a US gunboat.

23.2.2 Minorities and dissidents

Earlier units in this book have identified many nationalist aspirations in the second half of the twentieth century, though few problems had as many ramifications as those of the Palestinians. Among the nationalities which aimed to secede from existing states hardly any had achieved their goal by the late 1980s. Bangladesh in 1971 was a rare exception - and even Bangladesh now included restless minorities such as the Biharis. Governments generally preferred the status quo and resisted change. As in the case of Katanga in the Congo in 1960–4 and Biafra in Nigeria in 1967–70, established authorities were fearful of altering boundaries in case the floodgates of change should be opened. But the discontent of minorities was still a world-wide problem in the late 1980s. Polisario in Sahara; Eritreans in Ethiopia; Kurds in Iraq, Turkey and Iran; Sikhs in India; Tamils in Sri Lanka; and the people of East Timor in Indonesia were among those aspiring to set up their own states. The extent of mass support for such aspirations was not easy to assess, but grievances undoubtedly were deep-rooted.

Nowhere were grievances stronger than in South Africa and Namibia, where in 1988 the Pretoria regime continued to uphold white privilege and where prospects for a peaceful future grew increasingly bleak. Northern Ireland seemed to present a similarly intractable problem, with the death toll mounting steadily. Moreover, minority unrest seemed to spread. In the Soviet Union in 1987–8 Armenians demonstrated and went on strike, dissatisfied with the boundaries of the Armenian Republic which left some of their people in Azerbaijan. Like other governments, the Soviet government in Moscow resisted change. Tibetans were also restless, though the Dalai Lama in 1988 accepted that hopes for their independence were unrealistic and that they should aim at a more modest goal - more genuine self-government within the Chinese People's Republic.

Only a few would-be nations had yet to gain independence from the once vast European colonial empires in the late 1980s. France still held New Caledonia, where nationalist Kanaks were engaged in a struggle with white settlers (*caldoches*) reminiscent of that in Algeria 30 years earlier. In 1986 the UN asserted its support for 'the inalienable right of the people of New Caledonia to self-determination and independence'. France was in no hurry to concede it, however. Over 30 per cent of New Caledonia's population of around 150 000 were Europeans whose future the French wanted to safeguard, and in 1988 New Caledonia was one of the remaining small colonies whose future had still to be decided.

Some minorities had no hope at all of achieving an independent national state or even a self-governing one. Their struggle was for recognition of their culture and the redress of injustices. Amerindians in the USA numbered about a million, half of whom lived in tribal reservations. In 1969 they founded the American Indian Movement to seek equality of opportunity – for example in employment – and protection of mineral rights in their tribal lands. Indians in Canada were fewer than a quarter of a million and they sought to secure their rights in the National Indian Brotherhood. But Indians remained among the poorest sections of society in both the USA and Canada. Governments tended to prevaricate: they made some attempts to protect the Indian heritage but spasmodically urged total assimilation and the virtual elimination of special treatment such as the guaranteeing of reservations. Amerindian problems had no high priority with the authorities, and at the end of the 1980s even these advanced countries had failed to resolve the grievances of their aboriginal peoples.

Amerindians in Latin America numbered about 1.5 million in the 1980s, and many of them too suffered discrimination and hardship. Oil companies and agricultural combines tended to regard them as obstacles to development and profit. National governments such as that of Brazil made occasional efforts to follow the example of the USA and to protect the forest regions of the Indians, but they seldom gave priority to the welfare of their aboriginal population. Outbreaks of violence – by resentful Indians, by government forces and by mercenaries in the pay of transnational companies – erupted from time to time but attracted little international concern.

Aborigines made up about one per cent of Australia's population of some 16 million and they too protested at their treatment. After complaints had been made to the UN and to the British Anti-Slavery Society, the Australian government in 1988 set up an investigation into the deaths in police custody in recent years of more than a hundred Aborigines – deaths which seemed uncomfortably similar to those among blacks in South Africa. In spite of occasional expressions of concern for their welfare by the authorities, Australian Aborigines considered themselves an oppressed minority which had little reason in 1988 to join in the celebration of Australia's bicentennial, marking the arrival of the country's first white settlers two hundred years earlier.

In the late twentieth century very few countries had populations that were not composed of peoples of diverse ethnic origins, and very few countries could claim that they had overcome completely the difficulty of ensuring that all ethnic groups were contented. Fiji provided an example of the tensions which often existed and which might well erupt into conflict. Britain gave independence to the Fijian islands in 1970 and left the new nation with parliamentary democracy. Elections were contested mainly by the Alliance Party and the National Federation Party. Just as in Guyana, however, the parties divided on ethnic lines: the Alliance was largely Fijian with Melanesian and Polynesian support, while the National Federation had largely Indian support and represented those whose ancestors had come to Fiji as workers during the years of colonial rule. In 1987 Fiji's population of about 720 000 was about 50 per cent

Indian and 46 per cent Fijian. For the first time in 1987 the Alliance failed to win the elections. The Fijian Ratu Mara, Prime Minister since 1970, lost power to Tomici Bavadra. Bavadra was a Melanesian like Mara, but his support was mainly Indian and his left-wing government alarmed conservative and pro-West opinion.

Right-wing Melanesian opinion seized on fears that Fijian affairs might be dominated by the Indians. The result was a military coup led by Colonel Sitiveni Rambuku who, after briefly considering caretaker governments and coalitions, settled for a military dictatorship fronted by Prime Minister Ratu Mara. Melanesian nationalism took on a new impetus. Indians were deprived of official appointments and there was an ugly cry that they should 'go home', regardless of the fact that most were descended from people who had left India many generations ago. Rambuku poured out rhetoric about the birthright of Melanesians, and recruited more of them to the armed forces. His ministers spoke of the ways in which 'newcomers' had overwhelmed Aborigines in Australia, Maoris in New Zealand and Amerindians in North America, and argued that native Fijians were reclaiming their own country. This was the language of the racial intolerance which blighted the late twentieth-century world. The Australian and New Zealand governments were deeply offended; Queen Elizabeth II was distressed. Late in 1987 Rambuku proclaimed Fiji a republic and, at about the same time, the Commonwealth suspended Fiji's membership for its flagrant disregard of constitutionalism and lawful elections and for the racialism of its self-appointed rulers. When Ratu Mara visited Britain in 1988 to try to win support, he achieved little except Thatcher's agreement to renew the military training of Fiji's soldiers. Fiji's economy faltered, jeopardizing the country's per capita income which – at 1770 US dollars in 1983 – was far higher than those of Papua New Guinea and Indonesia.

23.3 Awareness and leadership

The dramatic expansion in the twentieth century of the mass media (newspapers, radio and television) made millions of people better informed about and more aware of the contemporary world than ever before. Television especially brought the world and its problems into private homes, though the images it presented were often distorted, even in countries which prided themselves on their freedom of expression. In every country those in authority did their best to protect existing systems, and the media, even in Britain and the USA, were for the most part in the hands of members of the establishment who had no desire fundamentally to change the political, economic and social status quo. The Soviets argued that the freedoms of the West were less real than people in the West supposed, since debate took place almost entirely within the framework the 'capitalist' and 'democratic' authorities themselves safeguarded. Opinion was therefore shaped, though its manipulation in one-party states was often more blatant, the official line more readily apparent and 'enemies of the state' more readily stigmatized. In the 1980s, partly because of terrorism and outspoken dissidence, governments generally seemed to show an obsessive concern for security and official secrecy. At the same time, they developed more sophisticated ways of shaping public opinion, berating opponents with carefully selected and sometimes 'massaged' statistics, for example. Those among the population who sought to be informed had need to be on their guard.

To increase people's awareness of the world in which they lived was assumed, nevertheless, to be one of the keys to creating a more just society and a more balanced world community. Black Consciousness, the movement that Steve Biko helped to found, aimed to spread awareness among South African blacks of their inheritance and their present status. This was seen as sufficient reason for heavy-handed retaliation by those in power in South Africa whose entrenched interests were being challenged. Throughout the world blacks had developed similar movements during the twentieth century, especially after 1945. In the Americas they built on foundations laid by Marcus Garvey and the Universal Negro Improvement Association, founded in 1914. In the USA in the 1950s and 1960s the National Association for the Advancement of Colored People stepped up its campaign for civil liberties and equal opportunities for blacks, and found a charismatic leader in Martin Luther King until racial bigotry brought about his assassination. Intolerance could not halt the growing interest in black culture, in black history and in improving the self-image of black people. Indeed, such interest was fuelled by the martyrdom of spokesmen such as Biko and Luther King: awareness of the conditions in which blacks lived grew more intense.

Parallel movements developed in the second half of the twentieth century among other groups who, like blacks, seemed to have been condemned in many societies to positions of inferiority. Feminist movements spread rapidly, especially in the developed world where literacy was more advanced. Along with deepening anxiety about women's rights went an interest in women's history, women's self-image and the forces which had created societies where male interests seemed paramount. Local communities stirred in similar ways, concerning themselves with local history and present-day local issues and attempting to force often remote governments to pay more attention to the many communities over which they presided and to devise regional policies. A greater concern for minorities inevitably resulted from the growing awareness among the minorities themselves of their own identity.

Such awareness seemed sometimes merely to add to the innumerable divisions with which the world had to wrestle. The resurgence of Islam, for example, led to a new-found militancy which at its most extreme was one of the most disruptive forces across the world in the 1970s and 1980s. The divisions had already existed, however. It was the resentment of them which grew and which brought such discomfort to those whose cosy world was now threatened.

The late twentieth century brought a different (and dismaying) awareness – that of children. The photograph in fig. 23.2 was taken in 1962, just a year after the building of the Berlin Wall. Children playing in the shadow of the Wall acted out the conflict which they took for granted and which was their heritage. In Berlin, Northern Ireland, South Africa and countless other places, children grew up already hardened to strife, inhumanity and violence. In many areas,

Fig. 23.2 In 1962, a year after the building of the Berlin Wall, children playing in its shadow mimic the world in which they live.

indeed, for example in parts of Africa, the Middle East and Indo-China, even very young children were recruited as soldiers. Not only was childhood blighted by awareness of the world's political tragedies: for some children childhood was lost altogether by active involvement in the killing and maiming which were part of the conflicts.

The decolonization of empires was perhaps the most far-reaching upheaval in the second half of the twentieth century. This was itself the product of increased awareness of imbalance and exploitation. By the 1980s little remained of white colonial rule, but the change left more than half the world – in the North as well as in the South – struggling to come to terms with a new age. That the transition was a painful one was much less remarkable than the fact that so much was achieved comparatively smoothly in dismantling old empires and building new nations. The change did, however, focus attention on the huge and growing gulf between the prosperous North and the South which so often lacked even the basic necessities of life. Not that the North was free from poverty and deprivation: on a visit to England in 1988 Mother Teresa was horrified by the destitution she found among the homeless in central London. Her Christian and humanitarian work among the poorest people of India, in Calcutta and other cities, was already legendary but she found it shocking that even a relatively small number of people should be living on the streets of Britain's capital and sleeping in cardboard boxes.

Awareness of the suffering of countless millions of hungry and destitute people in the Third World brought increasing concern in the North. Many individuals were moved to help, actively joining or generously supporting the agencies which worked to bring relief and assistance to the disadvantaged. Such agencies, both those within institutions such as the United Nations and the Commonwealth and those outside, operated in the 1980s on a scale greater than ever before. But few national governments matched the concern and vigour of the agencies with programmes that were both urgent and comprehensive. Almost without exception political leaders took refuge in short-term crisis management and readily pleaded the pressure of other problems and priorities, among which could be counted staying in power. In spite of the widespread concern, there was still little electoral advantage to be had in addressing global issues such as the North–South divide: growing awareness had yet to overcome the parochialism and self-interest of masses of voters even in the best-educated countries. Only after retiring from the hurly-burly of national politics did a handful of statesmen such as Willy Brandt address themselves whole-heartedly to major questions such as the gross imbalance in the world economic order, the deterioration of the human environment and the wretchedness of the disadvantaged. In the late 1980s the UN had existed for more than 40 years, and its agencies had achieved a great deal. But the UN was made up of member states (156 in 1986, 'the International Year of Peace') and its collective will could be no more than that of the national governments which directed its policy and financed its operations. In the social and economic field, over 40 years of effort still left much to be desired.

The potential for eliminating famine and malnutrition had long existed by the late 1980s in spite of poorly controlled population growth. For many, especially in the North, successive decades had brought increasing prosperity and material wealth. Some perils had receded, such as the danger of nuclear war between the superpowers. Tens of thousands of conferences since 1945 had increased awareness of the world's problems and a good many, indeed, had produced piecemeal solutions to some of them and contributed to 'progress'. Almost inevitably the media focused attention on the summit meetings of the superpowers, such as that between Gorbachev and Reagan in May 1988, and they seized repeatedly on the apparent energy and dynamic thinking of new leaders whose style – like Gorbachev's – seemed encouragingly constructive. By 1988, however, it had long been clear that the world consisted of far more than self-interested superpowers, and that the North–South problem was more immense than that of East and West.

Nations throughout the world by now grappled both with their own problems and with problems on a global scale, more than ever aware in the late 1980s that the two could seldom be divorced. The pace of change was now frenzied, but awareness of the scale of the problems and of their urgency had still to bring consensus on how best to proceed. In some ways, of course, the world edged closer to consensus on at least some issues. The divisions between capitalism and communism were far less stark in 1988 than 40 years earlier. Even China was moving further towards a mixed economy under Zhao Ziyang and Li Peng, its new Prime Minister. One economic zone in which the PRC experimented with capitalism in 1988 was the island of Hainan, where outsiders such as the Japanese and even the Taiwanese could buy land and make other investments. For China as a whole, however, the CCP had still to decide how much further to move towards modernization and adapting to the outside world. Zhao and Li Peng were again encouraging warmer relations with the Soviet Union, part of the unending re-examination of positions.

It is too soon to place the developments of the years since 1945 in a true historical perspective, and all judgments in a book such as this must be cautious and transitional. For the world as a whole as it looks forward to the 1990s and then to the twenty-first century, it is apparent, however, that peace, tranquillity and the scrupulous respect of one nation for another and of one human being for another are still distant goals. It is open to debate how much nearer to these goals the world has moved since the Second World War ended in 1945. But it is undoubtedly a significant achievement that nations have for more than 40 years avoided a Third World War.

One aspect of growing awareness in the last quarter of the twentieth century was disappointment with the leadership that governments provided. Human achievements in medicine, the arts, science, technology and specific areas such as agricultural development seemed seldom to be matched by political achievement which was neither short-term nor motivated by self-interest. Cynicism about politics grew, especially among the young. Politics and even the image of the UN were not helped by revelations concerning Kurt Waldheim which soured the 1980s. Waldheim had been Austria's Foreign Minister, then Secretary-General of the UN from 1972 to 1982, and in 1986 he was elected President of Austria. By then he should have been a respected elder statesman but suspicions had been raised about his past. Investigations by journalists, historians and others uncovered murky details about the part he had played as a Nazi officer in the Second World War, and about the blatant lies with which he tried to hide information placing him uncomfortably close to a variety of war crimes. Some governments seemed to have connived in his promotion to high office, even though aware at the time of at least something of Waldheim's past. They included those of the Soviet Union, Tito's Yugoslavia and countries in the West, and it was strongly suspected that they had seen national advantage in making him UN Secretary-General. Only in the late 1980s did pressures mount to isolate him, partly at Washington's instigation.

For a Nazi officer suspiciously close to offences against humanity to become UN Secretary-General was, of course, remarkable. The deals which had helped him to achieve that appointment were inevitably shrouded in secrecy – the sort of secrecy governments made it their business to preserve. That Waldheim persistently lied about his past, in his memoirs and elsewhere, was perhaps less surprising, however, and not all that far removed from the distortions of the truth which many cynics had come to believe were inseparable from politics. This book has had occasion to notice many leaders infinitely more evil than Waldheim – leaders whose fanaticism and bloodlust brought widespread misery and disfigured the history of the twentieth century. But the case of Waldheim was still dismaying. Robert Rhodes James, a diplomat, historian and British Conservative MP, and a former colleague of Waldheim at the UN, berated the Austrian President as:

> volcanic in temperament, and single-mindedly personally ambitious, obsequious to the mighty and often poisonous to the lowly.

He considered him 'a mediocrity', and it was mediocrity which at times seemed to characterize those who ruled in the second half of the twentieth century as they wrestled with problems of awesome proportions. The reputations of comparatively few survived their passing, and few, indeed, could be considered 'men [or women] of vision'. Readers will decide for themselves how far they think this judgment an appropriate one and which statesmen or women they would themselves exempt from it.

Main abbreviations used in this book

This list does not include most political parties in individual countries. See also explanations in the text and Glossary, as well as the Index.

ACP African, Caribbean and Pacific (states)
ANC African National(ist) Congress (in South Africa and other states)
ANZUS (Defence pact between) Australia, New Zealand and the US
ASEAN Association of South East Asian Nations

CAF Central African Federation (of the Rhodesias and Nyasaland)
CDC Commonwealth Development Corporation
CIA Central Intelligence Agency (USA)
CP Communist Party (for example, CCP - Chinese Communist Party or Cuban Communist Party; CPSU - Communist Party of the Soviet Union)
CREEP Campaign to Re-Elect the President (Nixon)
CSCSE Conference on Security and Co-operation in Europe

EC European Community
ECOSOC Economic and Social Council (UN)
ECOWAS Economic Community of West African States
ECSC European Coal and Steel Community
EDC European Defence Community
EEC European Economic Community
EFTA European Free Trade Association
EMS European Monetary System
EOKA Ethniki Organosis Kyprion Agonista, organization for the freedom of Cyprus and its union with Greece
ERP European Recovery Programme
ETA Euzkadi ta Azkatasuna, organization for Basque independence

FAO Food and Agriculture Organization (UN)

FLN Front de la Libération Nationale (see NLF)
FRELIMO Frente de Libertação de Moçambique
FRG Federal Republic of Germany (West Germany)

GATT General Agreement on Tariffs and Trade (UN)
GDP Gross domestic product
GDR German Democratic Republic (East Germany)
GNP Gross national product

IBM Intercontinental ballistic missile
ICAO International Civil Aviation Organization (UN)
IFC International Finance Corporation (UN)
ILO International Labour Organization (UN)
IMF International Monetary Fund (UN)
INF Intermediate nuclear force
IRA Irish Republican Army
IRO International Refugee Organization (UN)
ITU International Telecommunications Union
IWC International Whaling Commission

KGB Committee for State Security (USSR)
KMT Kuomintang

LAFTA Latin American Free Trade Association

MPLA Popular Movement for the Liberation of Angola
MTS Machine Tractor Station (USSR)

NAACP National Association for the Advancement of Colored People (USA)
NATO North Atlantic Treaty Organization
NAZI (Supporter of the) Nationalsozialistische Deutsche Arbeiterpartei (NSDAP) (National Socialist German Workers Party), led by Adolf Hitler
NCB National Coal Board (UK)
NHS National Health Service (UK)
NIBMAR No Independence Before Majority Rule (Rhodesia)
NLF National Liberation Front (see FLN and FRELIMO)

OAS (1) Organization of American States; (2) Organisation de l'Armée Secrète (Algeria/France)
OAU Organization of African Unity
OECD Organization for Economic Co-operation and Development
OEEC Organization for European Economic Co-operation
OPEC Organization of Petroleum Exporting Countries

PLO Palestine Liberation Organization
PRC People's Republic of China

RUC Royal Ulster Constabulary

SALT Strategic Arms Limitation Talks
SDI Strategic Defence Initiative, 'Star Wars' (USA)
SEATO South East Asia Treaty Organization
SELA Latin American Economic System
SHAPE Supreme Headquarters Allied Powers Europe (NATO)
START Strategic Arms Reduction Talks
SWAPO South West Africa People's Organization (Namibia)

UAR United Arab Republic (Egypt/Syria)
UDI Unilateral Declaration of Independence (by Rhodesia, for example)
UK United Kingdom
UN United Nations Organization
UNCLOS United Nations Conference on the Law of the Sea
UNCTAD United Nations Conference on Trade and Development
UNEF United Nations Emergency Force
UNEP United Nations Environmental Programme
UNESCO United Nations Educational, Scientific and Cultural Organization
UNICEF United Nations International Children's Emergency Fund
UNRRA United Nations Relief and Rehabilitation Organization
UNSCOP United Nations Special Commission on Palestine
UPU Universal Postal Union (UN)
USA United States of America
USSR Union of Soviet Socialist Republics (Soviet Union)

WASP White Anglo-Saxon Protestant (USA)
WCS World Conservation Strategy
WEU West European Union
WHO World Health Organization (UN)
WMO World Meteorological Organization (UN)

Glossary

The use of *italics* indicates a separate glossary entry. For further explanation of terms marked *, reference should be made to the Index of this book.

Affirmative action Programmes designed to ensure that groups that have been discriminated against are fairly represented in employment.

Afrikaans The modified form of the Dutch language used in South Africa.

Afrikaner An *Afrikaans*-speaking white South African.

Amerindian The original native population of the Americas.

Amnesty A pardon, usually of political offenders.

Anti-Semitism Hostility to Jews, and to their economic and political influence.

Apartheid A discriminatory system of segregating people of different race, colour or ethnicity into distinct residences, places in the labour market and citizenship rights. The word is *Afrikaans* in origin, and became notorious as a result of the South African policy of promoting apartheid as a system of 'separate but equal development'.

Authoritarian Not liberal; usually applied to a ruler or government and to the practice of strict discipline and repression.

Autocracy Absolute rule by one man, a *dictatorship*.

Balance of payments The relationship between a country's international income and expenditure in a given period, usually a year. If more is earned than spent, the country has a surplus. If the reverse, a deficit.

Balance of power The distribution of power, usually between states, such that no one power nor group of allies can dominate. A state's concept of the ideal balance of power usually means a balance in which the state does not feel itself threatened.

Basic democracy A limited form of *democracy* in which the people are allowed to elect only area councils, though these may go on to choose representatives to higher councils with greater powers, such as regional councils or a national parliament. This is a system of *indirect elections*. Ayub Khan introduced 'basic democracy' in Pakistan, intending to educate and guide the people towards less limited democracy. A similar system in Indonesia was called guided democracy.

Billion As used in this book, a thousand million.

Bloc A grouping of states which share common interests and have similar political, economic and social systems, for example the Eastern bloc in Europe. A bloc may or may not be linked by formal alliances.

Bolsheviks Members of a highly disciplined Marxist party founded in 1903 when divisions occurred in the Russian Social-Democratic Party. The Bolsheviks seized power in Russia in October 1917 – November according to the calendar in the West.

Bourgeoisie The middle classes.

Cadre Originally an exclusively military term to describe the officers and personnel forming the permanent core of a military organization. The term is now widely used to describe full-time Communist Party officials, especially those responsible for ensuring adherence to the party's ideology.

Capitalism A system based on the pursuit of private ownership, profit and the influence of private wealth.

Caste A hereditary class, leading to a rigid hierarchical ranking of members of society according to the caste into which they are born. In a caste system it is not possible for an individual to rise into a higher caste or fall into a lower one (at least in this world). Contact with members of a lower caste is also regarded as degrading, and impure. Caste systems were typical of all pre-industrial societies, but especially extreme in the Hindu culture of the Indian subcontinent – where the influence of caste remains very strong.

Central Intelligence Agency (CIA) The external secret service of the United States of America.

Centre Used of political parties to mean middle-of-the-road – between *left* and *right*.

Civil liberties The freedom of citizens and their right, for example, to express themselves to form associations and to travel without the interference of the authorities. Compare *human rights*.

Coexistence A state of international relations in which rivals tolerate one another and exist side by side despite continuing dislike and differences. Compare *détente*.

Cold war* A war fought with propaganda and economic weapons, stopping short of military confrontation – as between the USA and the USSR after 1945.

Collective security International security and stability achieved by the joint effort of several countries to deter those threatening to disturb the peace.

Collectivism A policy of co-operation, community effort and communal ownership, usually under state direction, in preference to private enterprise: for example, collective/collectivist farming.

Colonialism The policy of establishing and maintaining colonies directly ruled by the mother country, that is by the colonizing power. See *imperialism* and *neo-colonialism*.

Command economy An economy in which the government sets targets for economic attainment and plans their fulfilment, a planned economy such as that of the Soviet Union.

Communism* An egalitarian political philosophy, embracing *collectivism* and rooted in the writings of Karl Marx and *Marxism*: dedicated to the well-being of the masses, especially the *proletariat*.

Conscription The compulsory enlistment of individuals for military service.

Conservatism Political philosophy/practice of the *right*, often concerned with preserving traditions, institutions and the *status quo*, including traditional privileges.

Constitution A system of government, usually with liberal characteristics such as an assembly and perhaps the protection of human rights.

Containment The building of strength and of alliances to prevent the expansion of a rival power.

Corporate state An idea still associated with fascists, notably the Italian dictator Mussolini. The corporate state sought to incorporate all organized interests (capital and labour) under its direct control. Under this system, known as authoritarian corporatism, the state controls and grants representational monopolies to approved employers' and labour organizations. The idea of the corporate state should be carefully distinguished from the modern idea of liberal corporatism where state officials in liberal democracies bargain with free employers' organizations and free trade unions in order to establish a national consensus on complex policy matters.

Coup d'état A sudden and illegal change of government; a seizure of power.

Democracy Rule by the people: a system of government which permits some effective control to the masses. 'Bourgeois democracy' in the West, growing from the rise of the middle classes, operates on the basis of competition between rival political parties. 'People's democracy' in the East, growing from ambitions for the masses, tends to operate on the basis of only one political party, embracing all approved interests.

Détente The easing of strained relations between states; a state of relations rather less negative than *coexistence*.

Dictatorship Rule by one leader, a dictator: *autocracy*.

Dissidents* Those disapproving of, and obstructing, the established system.

Dogmatism Rigid adherence to ideas and policy and the rejection of alternatives. 'Dogmatism' was alleged against those who resisted *revisionism* in arguments about the interpretation of *Marxism*: authorities in the USSR accused China's leadership of 'dogmatism'.

Dominion status The given to the constitutional status of self-governing states of the British Empire (and subsequently British Commonwealth), which had formerly been colonies. The term is no longer used. In 1926 the self-governing Dominions were all white-dominated societies: the Irish Free State, Canada, Australia, New Zealand, South Africa and Newfoundland.

Ireland (in 1949) and South Africa (in 1961) subsequently left the Commonwealth, and Newfoundland joined Canada in 1949.

Domino theory If dominoes are stood behind each other, pushing one down will cause the next in line to fall, and so on. This 'domino effect' was applied in the 'domino theory' to countries 'pushed' by communism: to allow one to fall would lead to others falling. Eisenhower popularized the theory.

Enosis Movement for the union of Greece and Cyprus, alarming to Turkish Cypriots.

Eskimo A people living in Arctic areas, for example in Alaska, Canada and the USSR, with a common language and culture. Nowadays often referred to as Innuit.

Federation A union of states with a central authority, for example the short-lived West Indies Federation (1958–62). The central authority administering the federation (for example the federal governments of the USA and the USSR in Washington and Moscow) may be so strong that the federal nature of the union may be overlooked, to the disadvantage of individual state governments such as those of California (USA) and Kazakhstan (USSR).

Flying picket Picket (person or group aiming to discourage strike-breaking) mobile enough to move from one centre of crisis to another.

Franchise The right to vote.

Freedom-fighter A term used to describe a fighter, often a *guerilla*, serving a cause of which the speaker or writer approves. The same fighter may be described as a *terrorist* by those who disapprove of his or her actions.

Free trade Trade free from restrictions such as *tariffs*.

Friedmanite This literally means a follower of the ideas of Milton Friedman, hostile critic of Keynesian economics and *guru* of the monetarist faith. Friedman argued that inflation was always and everywhere a monetary phenomenon, controllable only through reductions in the money supply. He has also argued that unregulated capitalism is the best protector of people's freedoms. His ideas became deeply influential in the late 1970s and early 1980s, affecting government policy notably in the UK, USA and Chile, and also the work of international agencies like the IMF.

GDP/GNP Gross domestic product/gross national product. The money value of a country's total output from all units of production. GDP is the measure of output within the country; GNP is the measure of total output wherever production is situated. This measurement, divided by the country's population (i.e. *per capita*), makes possible rough comparisons in the production of wealth of different countries, for example as in Table 7.1.

Gerrymandering The deliberate manipulation of electoral districts to maximize the prospects of one party winning seats and another winning as few as possible. The easiest way to achieve this objective is to concentrate all one's opponents' voters into large constituencies with few representatives, and to distribute one's own supporters in a large number of smaller constituencies where they are sure to win. The term comes from an American Governor Gerry's manipulation of electoral districts in Massachusetts. He created one district which looked like a salamander, and 'Gerry's salamander' became 'gerrymander'.

Glasnost A Russian word meaning 'openness'. Used frequently by Mikhail Gorbachev after his rise to power in the Soviet Union, the term signified tolerance of greater freedom of expression and room for criticism in Soviet public life.

Growth rate A measure of growth, for example of population or of output, over a given period, often a year, commonly expressed as a percentage of the total at the start of the period.

Guerilla A fighter engaged in irregular warfare, often as a member of a fairly small body resisting authority. 'Guerilla warfare' is often associated with resistance movements using sabotage and hit-and-run tactics. 'Urban guerillas' operate in towns.

Guided democracy See *basic democracy*.

Guru An influential teacher/adviser. The word has Hindu origins.

Hegemony A term which originated with the Greeks and is used to describe leadership or domination, especially by one state over others. The term also has Marxist usages: for example, ideological hegemony refers to the domination of a particular set of ideas in the minds of a population.

Herrenvolk Master race/dominant people. German Nazis saw themselves as the Herrenvolk.

Human rights* The basic rights and liberties of human beings in relation to society and government, though the precise definition of such rights varies. Compare *civil liberties*.

Impeachment A charge before a court or tribunal, usually in connection with the misuse of official authority.

Imperialism Empire-building, the gaining of colonies. Also known as 'formal imperialism', as distinct from 'informal imperialism', in which influence and power is gained over other states without direct colonization, for example economic control. Compare *neo-colonialism*.

Independence Freedom: specifically, the freedom granted to former colonies when the mother country gives up control.

Index numbers Indicators of change in the value of economic variables. An index number may be used to indicate the relative level of a price or quantity at a given date compared with its value at a date set as standard. The point of reference is usually set at 100, and variations are expressed as figures above or below 100. Index numbers can also be used to compare relative achievement, for example for different countries, using the achievement of one country as 100 and expressing that of others as figures above or below 100.

Indicative planning A name given to many types of state intervention in decentralized economic systems, where the objective of state officials is to offer inducements to producers to agree investment, productivity, profit and income targets. Such planning has been found in places as diverse as Sweden, Britain, Japan and Yugoslavia.

Indirect elections There are many differing systems for electing representatives. Elections are said to be 'indirect' when voters choose others to make further elections on their behalf. *Basic democracy* and *guided democracy* use this system. It is also used in the election of the US President, in that voters choose members of an electoral college who in turn elect the President.

Inflation An economic term which is often loosely used to refer to rising prices, but is used by economists to refer to circumstances where money incomes are rising faster than productivity, thus leading to a general rise in prices (as opposed to relative price increases for certain goods and services). Economists differ dramatically over the causes and consequences of inflation, over how to measure it, and over the best ways of dealing with it.

Innuit See *Eskimo*.

International Monetary Fund* (IMF) A specialized agency of the United Nations set up in 1945. The IMF provides loans to assist countries in difficulty, especially those in debt and with serious balance-of-payments problems. The USA provides a large proportion of the IMF's funds and exercises influence over its activities. Third World and socialist critics have repeatedly argued that the IMF is an instrument for the defence of *capitalism*.

Invisible (as of exports, trade) Payments for services which do not include the transfer of goods are said to be 'invisible', for example payments connected with insurance, lending, transport and tourism.

Irangate The ironic name given to a scandal in American politics under Ronald Reagan's Presidency, also known as the Iran-Contra affair. Lieutenant Oliver North and other close advisers to President Reagan sold arms to the Iranians in order to secure the release of Western hostages, and illegally used the proceeds of the arms sales to fund Contra terrorists in Nicaragua, specifically violating Congressional legislation. Whether Reagan knew of these activities remained uncertain: he was either guilty of illegality or of incompetence. What was certain was that high American officials had once more repeated the pattern exhibited in the Nixon years: systematic law-breaking in the executive office of the Presidency, similar to that which had occurred in the Watergate scandal.

Iron curtain* A term popularized by Churchill after 1945 to describe the dividing line in Europe between East and West.

Islam The religion of Muslims, revealed through Muhammad, Prophet of Allah; the term is also used for the Muslim world where the force of religion in the second half of the twentieth century has been strong enough to constitute an Islamic 'revival' or 'resurgence', vigorously supported by 'fundamentalists' who adhere strictly to Islamic codes of behaviour, and led by 'priests' including ayatollahs and *mullahs*.

Jihad A holy war and crusade for Islamic objectives, to which believers give unwavering support.

Junta A Spanish or Italian word meaning 'council'. The term is used frequently to describe the ruling body in South and Central American military dictatorships.

Keynesian This literally means a follower of the economic arguments of the English economist John Maynard Keynes, whose book *The General Theory of Employment, Interest and Money*, published in 1936, revolutionized the way economists understood the dynamics of a capitalist economy. Keynes argued that economic depressions were not necessarily self-correcting through the operation of market forces. He argued that policymakers should manipulate government expenditures or taxation levels in order to achieve a desirable level of economic demand for goods and services. His ideas have subsequently been used and abused. For example, many policymakers hostile to Keynes' criticisms of a capitalist economy advocate 'tax-cutting' to stimulate economic demand yet do not realize that they are advocating Keynesian policies.

KGB The Soviet Committee for State Security set up in 1954 after the downfall of Commissar for Internal Affairs, Lavrenti Beria. In addition to supervising the secret police and maintaining internal security, the KGB is an intelligence agency similar to the US *Central Intelligence Agency*.

Kremlin The buildings in Moscow which house the Soviet government: thus the Soviet government itself.

Laager To attribute a laager mentality refers to the tendency of a group to retreat to its favoured beliefs, to rely upon itself alone, and to regard itself as a righteous but besieged minority. The term comes from an *Afrikaans* word: when the *Afrikaners* fought the Zulus they protected themselves behind a circle of wagons (the laager).

Left A relative term to describe political leanings. Those on the 'left' are more inclined to reform and to political change than those with whom comparison is made. Compare *centre* and *right*.

Lend-Lease A device of the US government for assisting the Allies in the Second World War. Congress gave President Roosevelt authority in March 1941 to 'lend' war materials to be returned after the war should they still exist: in effect these war supplies were given without charge.

Liberalism A political philosophy which usually emphasizes liberty, parliamentary government and *human rights*, and supports *capitalism*.

Literacy The ability to read and write, though the extent of this ability may vary widely and some authorities may accept evidence of literacy far more readily than others. Table 7.1 and others in this book need to be read with this reservation in mind.

Mandates* Mandated territories: colonial areas placed under the control of selected powers after the First World War and subject to League of Nations' supervision until *independence* was achieved. Most that remained after 1945 became UN *trusteeship territories*, for example Tanganyika.

Maoism* The philosophy of Mao Tse-tung, much of it a Chinese adaptation of *Marxism*.

Marxism The philosophy of Karl Marx (1818–83), often regarded as the father/founder of *communism*.

Marxism-Leninism The philosophy of Lenin, an adaptation of *Marxism* to conditions in Russia in the early twentieth century.

Ministerial responsibility The responsibility of government ministers to parliament, to which they must answer for their actions. This is regarded in many countries as an essential element of *democracy*.

Mixed economy An expression used to mean either (1) an economy which combines elements of *capitalism* (private property rights and free markets) with elements of *socialism* (social justice, planning and a welfare state) or (2) an economy which combines the operation of free markets with state regulation of and intervention in those markets. Most real-world economies are mixed in both these senses: arguments centre on what the mix is and how it should (or should not) be altered.

Modus vivendi An arrangement between contending parties - generally an agreement to differ. Compare *coexistence*.

Monetarism The belief that national economies can be controlled by managing the money supply: made fashionable at the end of the 1970s by the work of *Friedmanite* economists.

Mullahs Muslim divines and organizers of prayers. The term is especially common in Iran and Pakistan.

Multinational companies Companies operating in several countries besides that in which they are based, for example multinational oil companies such as Shell. The interests of these companies cross national boundaries (*transnational companies*) and may well differ from the interests of the individual countries in which they operate.

Multiracial Involving several races: a multiracial society includes several different races; a multiracial association such as the Commonwealth represents several different races. See *Race*.

National income Similar to *GNP* with an allowance made for depreciation.

Nationalization Converting into national property: placing under public (state) ownership and supervision, for example the nationalization of railways.

Neo-colonialism The pursuit of objectives similar to those of colonialism. Compare *imperialism*. Neo-colonialism is similar to informal imperialism but is usually applied to the period after formal colonization has ended: thus, the term has come to refer to the use of economic and other means of exerting influence over countries that are no longer colonies.

Non-aligned* Not linked with the two rival power blocs: seeking to stand apart from both. Section 21.4 examines the non-aligned movement which distanced itself from the East–West rivalries of the superpowers and their supporters.

Oligarchy A word of Greek origin, meaning the rule of the corrupt few, as opposed to the rule of the best (aristocracy). The term is now most widely used in South and Central American regimes to describe the malign political and economic dominance of privileged landowners who often claim descent from the aristocracies of the Old World.

One-party state A state in which only one political party is allowed to exist. This is the ruling party, and political debate takes place within the limits it lays down; for example, the Communist Party of the Soviet Union is the one party in the USSR.

Ostpolitik Eastern policy, policy towards the East. Commonly applied to the policies of West German politicians (such as Brandt) towards East Germany and eastern Europe.

Pentagon The five-sided headquarters of the US defence forces in Washington: thus, United States defence interests.

Per capita Per head, as when a total figure (such as a country's *GNP*) is divided by total population to produce an average for each member of the population.

Perestroika A Russian word meaning restructuring, reorganization or renewal. The word used by Mikhail Gorbachev to describe his reform programme for the Soviet Union, especially his programme of economic reforms.

Plebiscite The direct vote of electors on a specific issue in a *referendum*.

Populist One who seeks to please the people, win their favour and represent their interests: perhaps pandering to popular prejudices.

Privatization The opposite to *nationalization*: transferring publicly owned property into private ownership.

Proletariat The masses, who depend on their earnings and lack capital.

Proportional representation A voting system designed to ensure that the percentage of votes cast for a political party is matched by the percentage of seats it wins in an elected assembly.

Protection The opposite to *free trade*: a system of *tariffs* to protect home industries against foreign competition.

Race A group of persons of common descent, of distinctive ethnic stock. Strictly speaking, mankind is divided into five races: for example Caucosoids and Negroids. Caucosoids include Europeans and subdivisions can be made, such as Nordic and Mediterranean. 'Race' is often used inaccurately, to refer to further subdivisions similar to nationalities. See *multiracial*.

Radical Enthusiastic for major change, for reform.

Reactionary Backward-looking, opposed to change.

Real (as of wages, growth) The measure after allowance has been made for distorting factors due to *inflation*. For example, wages may rise in a given period from, say, 100 dollars to 200 dollars, an apparent rise of 100 per cent; but if prices also rise in this period by 100 per cent, *real* wages are unchanged, since there has been no change in purchasing power.

Referendum Direct consultation of the people who vote on a specific issue.

Revisionism This literally means the propensity to revise or change ideas. The term is now almost exclusively used as a Marxist term of abuse: socialists who do not adhere to orthodox Marxist–Leninist conceptions of the laws of history, dialectical materialism, the primacy of class struggle, the necessity of revolution, the role of the working class in liberating mankind, and so on, are labelled 'revisionists'.

Right A relative term to describe political leanings. Those on the 'right' are more inclined to *conservatism* and to resisting change than those with whom comparison is made. Compare *centre* and *left*.

Russia The name given to the Empire ruled by the tsars up to 1917 and by the Bolsheviks up to the constitution of 1923. This constitution established the USSR (Union of Soviet Socialist Republics - Soviet Union). One Republic within the USSR is the Russian Soviet Federated Socialist Republic (RSFSR) (see fig. 3.3). The Soviet Union is a country of many nationalities of whom Russians are the most numerous - about 53 per cent in the 1980s. Most Russians live in the RSFSR.

Sanctions Penalties, methods with which to put pressure on those who commit unpopular acts. Economic sanctions are likely to involve restrictions on trade (such as were used against Rhodesia in the 1960s and 1970s). Military sanctions involve the use of armed force (as, for example, against North Korea in 1950).

Secession Separation, breaking away: within any union (of states, tribes or nationalities) one part may wish to secede (for example many Tamils in Sri Lanka in the 1980s).

Secular state A state relatively free from the political influence of the church and churchmen. India is usually considered a *secular state*, in contrast to Pakistan, which became an Islamic Republic in 1956.

Self-determination Freedom to choose: commonly used for the freedom of a people to choose its own system of government without outside interference.

Separatism A movement in favour of breaking away, usually in support of *secession*.

Shuttle diplomacy Diplomacy conducted by a mediator 'shuttling' between the various parties to a dispute. A style of mediation favoured by Henry Kissinger, US Secretary of State 1971–7, in the Middle East, southern Africa and elsewhere.

Socialism* An egalitarian political philosophy with some similarities to *Marxism* and *communism*, but commonly considered to be less revolutionary and less extreme. *Socialism* in the West seeks change through the parliamentary *democracy* common in the West. In the East, those seeking to achieve *communism* regard *socialism* as a transitional phase in development.

Social wage The benefits to individuals from publicly provided services which have the effect of adding to what wages may purchase: for example educational and health services, public-authority assistance with housing and fuel costs, and social-security benefits.

Sovereignty A political and legal term meaning supreme power or authority. Every state claims to be sovereign within its territorial boundaries. Some political systems concentrate sovereignty (in a *unitary state*); others divide it (as in a *federation*).

Soviet Council, committee. Since 1905 in Russia, commonly associated with revolutionary purposes.

Status quo Loosely, the existing state of affairs. Policy may seek to restore the status quo, such as the 'status quo ante bellum' (the state of affairs existing before the war).

Summit meeting* A meeting of leaders who hold the highest positions, such as heads of government.

Tariffs Levies (duties, taxes) on imports. See *protection*.

Terrorist A term used to describe a person, perhaps a *guerilla*, who seeks to achieve his or her objectives by outrages of which the speaker or writer disapproves. The same person may be described by sympathizers as a *freedom-fighter*.

Third World A term of French origin, now widely used, for those states not classified as members of the developed capitalist world (first world) or the industrialized communist world (second world). The term therefore covers most of the regimes of Latin America, Africa, the Middle East, and South, East and South East Asia. These regimes share a common colonial past, hostility towards European and American imperialism, and economic underdevelopment or undevelopment. Critics argue that the term is too loose, ignores the wide variations within the developing and undeveloped world, and is simply a residual category for non-western and non Soviet regimes.

Totalitarian Permitting no rival parties or opposition, involving total control by the authorities.

Transnational companies Companies operating across international boundaries and to some extend overriding the interests of individual countries. Compare *multi-national companies*.

Tribalism Loyalty to the tribe, often taking precedence over other loyalties such as those to the nation or state.

Trusteeship territories Colonial areas under the control of selected powers and subject to UN supervision. Most had been *mandates* before the Second World War.

Ultimatum A final warning, usually with conditions which must be met to prevent a threat (for example of war) being implemented.

Unilateral Declaration of Independence (UDI) A declaration of *independence* from the mother country made by a colony without the consent of the mother country, such as Rhodesia's UDI in 1965.

Unitary state A country with one central government and without the state governments of a *federation*. Among the countries vast in size, China is unusual in being a 'unitary state' whereas the USA, the USSR and India are all federal republics. Almost all smaller countries such as Britain and France are unitary states.

Visible (as of exports, trade) Trade in merchandise is said to be *visible* trade. Compare *invisible*.

Welfare state A state with comprehensive social services and a social-security system – one providing health and education services, for example, and a system (often financed by National Insurance) to provide benefits in sickness, old age and during unemployment.

White House The building in Washington which houses the US President: thus, the United States government itself.

Zionist A supporter of Zionism, the body of secular, nationalist and socialist ideas, founded by Theodor Herzl, which sought support for a Jewish nation in Palestine from the late nineteenth century onwards. Defenders of Zionism argue that the doctrine is universalist: that is, committed to egalitarian relations with the native Palestinian Arab inhabitants. Critics contend that Zionism is committed to creating an Israeli state in which Jews dominate Arabs.

Bibliography

The following list of further reading will be of help to those who wish to delve more deeply into selected aspects of world history since 1945. Books marked * are particularly suitable for study by students in colleges.

General

Topics and areas

Buchan, A., *The End of the Post-War Era* (Weidenfeld & Nicolson, 1974)
Caute, D., *Sixty-Eight, the Year of the Barricades* (Hamish Hamilton, 1988)
Gatland, N., *Space Technology* (Salamander, 1981)*
Hayes, D., *Terrorists and Freedom Fighters* (Wayland, 1980)*
Kohler, J.A., and Taylor, J.K.G., *Africa and the Middle East* (Edward Arnold, 1985)*
Lane, P., *Europe since 1945, an Introduction* (Batsford, 1985)*
Ranelagh, J., *The Rise and Fall of the CIA* (Simon & Schuster, 1986)
Rayner, E.G., *International Affairs* (Edward Arnold, 1983)*
Short, P., *The Dragon and the Bear: Inside China and Russia Today* (Abacus, 1982)
Taylor, J.K.G., *Asia and Australasia* (Edward Arnold, 1983)*
Taylor, J.K.G., and Kohler, J.A., *Africa and the Middle East* (Edward Arnold, 1985)*

Map books and reference books

Catchpole, B., *A Map History of our own Times* (Heinemann, 1983)*
Crow, B., and Thomas, A., *Third World Atlas* (Open University Press, 1983)*
Dempsey, M., *The Daily Telegraph Atlas of the Arab World* (Daily Telegraph Nomad, 1983)*
Kidron, M., and Segal, R., *The New State of the World Atlas* (Pluto Press and Pan Books, 1984)*
Kidron, M., and Smith, D., *The War Atlas* (Pluto Press and Pan Books, 1983)*

Palmer, A., *Penguin Dictionary of Twentieth-Century History, 1900–1982* (Penguin, 1983)*
Pick, C., *What's What in the 1980s* (Europa Publications, 1982)*
Richards, I., Goodson, J.B., and Morris, J.A., *A Sketch-Map History of the Great Wars and After* (Harrap, 1965)*
Wheatcroft, A., *World Atlas of Revolutions* (Hamish Hamilton, 1983)*
Williams, N.A., *A Chronology of the Modern World* (Penguin, 1975)*
Wilson, D., *A Student's Atlas of African Affairs* (OUP, 1971)*

Documentary collections

Breach, R.W., *Documents and Descriptions, the World since 1914* (OUP, 1966)*
Brownlie, I., *Basic Documents on African Affairs* (OUP, 1971)
Grenville, J.A.S., *The Major International Treaties, 1914–1973* (Methuen, 1974)
Wroughton, J., and Cook, D., *Documents on World History, 1919 to the Present Day* (Macmillan, 1976)*

Self-testing

Rayner, E., Stapley, R., and Watson, J., *Evidence in Question: International Affairs since 1919* (OUP, 1980)*
Rayner, E., Stapley, R., and Watson, J., *Evidence in Question: World Affairs from the Russian Revolution to the Present* (OUP, 1984)*
Watson, J., Rayner, E., and Stapley, R., *Evidence in Question: European History, 1815–1949* (OUP, 1980)*

Further reading for individual units

Unit 1

Botting, D., *In the Ruins of the Reich, Germany 1945–1949* (Allen & Unwin, 1985)*
Conot, R.E., *Justice at Nuremberg* (Weidenfeld & Nicolson, 1984)
Dukes, P., *The Emergence of the Super Powers* (Macmillan, 1970)*
Feis, H., *Between War and Peace: the Potsdam Conference* (OUP, 1960)
Gibbons, S.R., and Morican, P., *The League of Nations and UNO* (Longman, 1970)*
Laqueur, W., *Out of the Ruins of Europe* (Alcove Press, 1972)*
Liddell Hart, B.H., *History of the Second World War* (Cassell, 1970)
Nicholas, H.G., *The UN as a Political Institution* (OUP, 1967)*
Watson, J.B., *Success in Twentieth Century World Affairs, from 1919 to the 1980s* (Murray, 3rd edn 1984)*

Unit 2

Ambrose, S.E., *Eisenhower, the President 1952–1969* (Allen & Unwin, 1984)
Ambrose, S.E., *Rise to Globalism: American Foreign Policy since 1938* (Penguin, 1983)*

Bassett, M., *The American Deal* (Heinemann, 1976)*
Catchpole, B., *A Map History of the United States* (Heinemann, 1972)*
Caute, D., *The Great Fear: The Anticommunist Purge under Truman and Eisenhower* (Secker & Warburg, 1978)
Gardner, L.C., *A Covenant with Power: America and World Order from Wilson to Reagan* (Macmillan, 1984)
Issel, W., *Social Change in the United States, 1945–1983* (Macmillan, 1985)
Mooney, P.J., and Bown, C., *Truman to Carter* (Edward Arnold, 1979)*
Parmet, H.S., *JFK, the Presidency of John F. Kennedy* (Penguin, 1984)*
Snowman, D., *America since 1920* (Heinemann, 1978)*

Unit 3

Brown, A., and Kaser, M., *The Soviet Union since the Fall of Khrushchev* (Macmillan, 1979)
Catchpole, B., *A Map History of Russia* (Heinemann, 1974)*
Hosking, G., *A History of the Soviet Union* (Fontana, 1985)*
Hyland, W., and Shryok, R.W., *The Fall of Khrushchev* (Pitman, 1970)*
Khrushchev, N., *Khrushchev Remembers* (Little, Brown & Co., 1971)*
McCauley, M., *The Soviet Union since 1917* (Longman, 1981)*
Medvedev, R., *Khrushchev* (Anchor Press/Doubleday, 1983)
Mooney, P.J., *The Soviet Superpower, 1945–80* (Heinemann, 1982)*
Munting, R., *The Economic Development of the USSR* (Croom Helm, 1983)
Nove, A., *An Economic History of the USSR* (Penguin, 1972)*
Nove, A., *Stalinism and After* (Allen and Unwin, 1975)*
Taaffe, R.N., and Kingsbury, R.C., *An Atlas of Soviet Affairs* (Methuen, 1965)*
Walker, M., *The Waking Giant, the Soviet Union under Gorbachev* (Abacus, 1987)*
Werth, A., *Russia, the Post-war Years* (Robert Hale, 1971)

Unit 4

Bown, C., and Mooney, P.J., *Cold War to Detente, 1945–80* (Heinemann, 1981)*
Halle, L.J., *The Cold War as History* (Harper & Row, 1971)
Hastings, P., *The Cold War, 1945–1969* (Benn, 1969)*
Higgins, H., *The Cold War* (Heinemann, 1974)*
LaFeber, W., *America, Russia and the Cold War, 1945–75* (Wiley, 1976)*
McCauley, M., *The Origins of the Cold War* (Longman Seminar Studies, 1983)*
Price, H.B., *The Marshall Plan and its Meaning* (OUP, 1955)
Salvadori, M., *NATO* (Anvil, 1957)*

Unit 5

Bartlett, C.J., *A History of Post-war Britain, 1945–1974* (Longman, 1977)
Harris, J., *The Welfare State* (Batsford, 1973)*

Lane, P., *Documents and Questions, British History 1914–1980* (Murray, 1981)*
Lane, P., *Documents in British Economic and Social History Book 3, 1945–1967* (Macmillan, 1968)*
Sampson, A., *The Changing Anatomy of Britain* (Hodder & Stoughton, 1982)
Seabrook, J., *Unemployment* (Quartet, 1982)*
Seaman, L.C.B., *Post-Victorian Britain, 1902–1951* (Methuen, 1966)*
Sked, A., *Britain's Decline* (Blackwell, 1987)*
Sked, A., and Cook, C., *Post-war Britain* (Penguin, 1979)*
Watson, J.B., *Success in British History since 1914* (Murray, 1983)*
Wroughton, J., *Documents on British Political History, 1914–1970* (Macmillan, 1972)*

Unit 6

Absalom, R., *France, the May Events 1968* (Longman, 1971)*
Childs, D., *Germany since 1918* (Batsford, 2nd edn 1980)
Clark, M., *Modern Italy, 1871–1982* (Longman, 1984)*
Cobban, A., *A History of Modern France, 1871–1962* (Penguin, 1965)*
Crozier, B., *De Gaulle, the Statesman* (Eyre Methuen, 1973)*
Hanley, D.L., Kerr, A.P., and Waites, N.H., *Contemporary France, Politics and Society since 1945* (Routledge & Kegan Paul, 1980)
Kloss, G., *West Germany, an Introduction* (Macmillan, 1976)*
Seaman, R.D.H., *Britain and Western Europe* (Edward Arnold, 1983)*
Swann, D., *The Economics of the Common Market* (Penguin, 1978)
Tint, H., *France since 1918* (Batsford, 2nd edn 1980)
Urwin, D.W., *Western Europe since 1945* (Longman, 3rd edn 1981)
Watson, J.B., *Western Europe, 1945–81* (Harrap, 1982)*
Wiskemann, E., *History of Italy since 1945* (Macmillan, 1971)

Unit 7

Arbuthnott, H., and Edwards, G., *A Common Man's Guide to the Common Market* (Macmillan, 1979)*
Fanning, R., *Independent Ireland* (Helicon, 1983)*
Farr, W., *Daily Telegraph Guide to the Common Market* (Collins, 1972)*
Graham, R., *Spain, Change of a Nation* (Michael Joseph, 1984)
Knapp, W., *Unity and Nationalism in Europe since 1945* (Pergamon, 1969)*
Mowat, R.C., *Creating the European Community* (Blandford, 1973)*
Vaughan, R., *Post-war Integration in Europe* (Edward Arnold, 1976)*
The European Community in Maps (European Commission wallet, 1974)*

Unit 8

Allan, P.D., *Russia and Eastern Europe* (Edward Arnold, 1983)*
Chapman, C., *August 21: the Rape of Czechoslovakia* (Cassell, 1968)
Childs, D., *Germany since 1918* (Batsford, 2nd edn 1980)*
Fetjö, F., *A History of the People's Democracies of Eastern Europe* (Penguin, 1975)

Franchere, R., *Tito of Yugoslavia* (Macmillan, 1971)*
Graham, L.S., *Rumania, A Developing Socialist State* (Westview Press, 1982)
Halecki, O., and Polonsky, A., *A History of Poland* (Routledge & Kegan Paul, 1983)
Johnson, A.R., *Yugoslavia in the Twilight of Tito* (Sage, 1974)
Morris, L.P., *Eastern Europe since 1945* (Heinemann, 1984)*
Pryce-Jones, D., *The Hungarian Revolution* (Benn, 1969)*
Rachwald, A.R., *Poland between the Superpowers* (Westview Press, 1983)
Scharf, C.B., *Politics and Change in East Germany* (Westview Press, 1984)

Unit 9

Bourne, R., *Political Leaders in Latin America* (Penguin, 1969)*
Burns, E., *Latin America* (Prentice-Hall, 1977)
Ferris, H.S., *Argentina* (Benn, 1969)*
Graham-Yooll, A., *A State of Fear: Memories of Argentina's Nightmare* (Eland, 1986)*
Gunther, J., *Inside South America* (Hamish Hamilton, 1967)
Lancaster, A.B., *The Americas* (Edward Arnold, 1984)*
Logan, W.R., *Haiti and the Dominican Republic* (OUP, 1968)
McNaught, K., *The Pelican History of Canada* (Pelican, 1982)
Wellington, R.A., *The Brazilians: How They Live and Work* (David & Charles, 1974)*

Unit 10

Ambursley, F., and Dunkerley, J., *Grenada, Whose Freedom?* (Latin America Bureau, 1984)*
Bonsal, P.W., *Cuba, Castro and the United States* (University of Pittsburgh Press, 1971)
Christian, S., *Nicaragua* (Random House, 1985)
Debray, R., *The Chilean Revolution* (Pantheon Books, 1971)
Draper, T., *Castroism, Theory and Practice* (Praeger, 1965)*
Erisman, H.M., *Cuba's International Relations* (Westview Press, 1985)
Fish, J., and Sganga, C., *El Salvador, Testament of Terror* (Zed, 1987)
Jara, J., *Victor, an Unfinished Song* [Chile and Allende] (Cape, 1983)
LaFeber, W., *Inevitable Revolutions: the United States in Central America* (W.W. Norton, 1983)
Melrose, D., *Nicaragua, the Threat of a Good Example* (Oxfam, 1985)*
Szulc, T., *Fidel, A Critical Portrait* (Hutchinson, 1986)*
Thomas, H., *The Cuban Revolution* (Weidenfeld & Nicolson, 1986)

Unit 11

Bonavia, D., *The Chinese* (Allen Lane, 1981)
Bown, C., *China, 1949–1976* (Heinemann, 1980)*
Catchpole, B., *A Map History of Modern China* (Heinemann, 1976)*
Crankshaw, E., *Moscow v. Peking, a New Cold War* (Penguin, 1963)*
Dures, A., and K., *Mao Tse-tung* (Batsford, 1980)*

Halbertson, D., *Ho* (Barrie & Jenkins, 1971)*
Heng, L., and Shapiro, J., *Son of the Revolution* (Fontana Collins, 1984)
Kennett, J., *The Rise of Communist China* (Blackie, 1970)*
Lacouture, J., *Ho Chi Minh* (Allen Lane, 1968)
Lawrence, A., *China's Foreign Relations since 1949* (Routledge & Kegan Paul, 1975)
Tarling, N., *Mao and the Transformation of China* (Heinemann, 1977)*
Tregear, T.R., *The Chinese: How They Live and Work* (David & Charles, 1973)*
Quotations from Chairman Mao Tse-tung ['The Thoughts of Chairman Mao'] (Foreign Languages Press, Peking, 1966)

Unit 12

Allen, D., *A Short Economic History of Modern Japan* (Allen & Unwin, 1981)*
Kennedy, M.D., *A History of Japan* (Weidenfeld & Nicolson, 1963)*
Nish, I., *The Story of Japan* (Faber & Faber, 1968)*
Schaller, M., *The American Occupation of Japan* (OUP, 1986)
Sims, R., *Modern Japan* (Bodley Head, 1973)*
Storry, R., *A History of Modern Japan* (Penguin, 1976)*
Williams, B., *Modern Japan* (Longman, 1969)*
Zepke, N., *The Hundred Year Miracle* (Heinemann, 1977)*

Unit 13

(See also further reading, Unit 4)
Abel, E., *The Missile Crisis* (J.B. Lippincott, 1966)*
Beggs, R., *The Cuban Missiles Crisis* (Longman, 1971)*
Edmonds, R., *Soviet Foreign Policy, 1963–73* (OUP, 1975)
Hersh, S.M., *Kissinger, the Price of Power* (Summit Books, 1983)
Joyce, J.A., *The War Machine* (Quartet, 1980)*
Urban, G.R., *Détente* (Temple Smith, 1976)*

Unit 14

Bolitho, H., *Jinnah – the Creator of Pakistan* (Murray, 1954)
Bolton, G., *Britain's Legacy Overseas* (OUP, 1973)*
Collins, L., and Lapierre, D., *Freedom at Midnight* [India] (Collins, 1975)
Copley, A., *Gandhi* (Blackwell, 1987)*
Ingram, D., *The Commonwealth at Work* (Pergamon, 1969)*
Kaunda, K., *Zambia Shall Be Free* (Heinemann, 1962)*
Lapping, B., *End of Empire* (Guild Publishing, 1985)*
Loney, M., *Rhodesia* (Penguin, 1975)*
Pandey, B.N., *The Break-up of British India* (Macmillan, 1969)*
Purcell, V.C., *Malaysia* (Thames and Hudson, 1965)*
Sithole, N., *African Nationalism* (OUP, 1969)*
Watson, J.B., *Empire to Commonwealth, 1919–1970* (Dent, 1971)*
Wills, A.J., *An Introduction to the History of Central Africa: Zambia, Malawi and Zimbabwe* (OUP, 1985)

Unit 15

Cameron, N., *From Bondage to Liberation, East Asia 1860–1952* (OUP, 1978)
Chamberlain, M.E., *Decolonization – the Fall of the European Empires* (Blackwell, 1985)*
Dayal, R., *Mission for Hammarskjöld* (OUP, 1976)
Fischer, L., *The Story of Indonesia* (Hamish Hamilton, 1959)
Fryer, D.W., and Jackso, J.C., *Indonesia* (Benn, 1977)*
Kennedy, H., *Asian Nationalism in the Twentieth Century* (Macmillan, 1968)
Marr, D., *Asia, the Winning of Independence* (Macmillan, 1981)
Meredith, M., *The First Dance of Freedom* (Hamish Hamilton, 1984)*

Unit 16

Bhatia, K., *Indira, a Biography of Prime Minister Gandhi* (Angus and Robertson, 1974)*
Bhatia, K., *The Ordeal of Nationhood, A Social Study of India since Independence* (Atheneum, 1971)
Caldwell, M., *Indonesia* (OUP, 1968)*
Edwardes, M., *Nehru, a Political Biography* (Penguin, 1973)*
Johnson, B., *India, Resources and Development* (Heinemann, 1979)*
Selbourne, D., *An Eye to India: the Unmasking of a Tyranny* (Penguin, 1977)
Spear, P., *A History of India, Volume 2* (Penguin, 1978)*
Stephens, I., *The Pakistanis* (OUP, 1968)*

Unit 17

Buah, F.K., *A History of Ghana* (Macmillan, 1980)
Busia, K., *Africa in Search of Democracy* (Routledge & Kegan Paul, 1969)*
Davidson, B., *Black Star, Kwame Nkrumah* (Penguin, 1973)*
Hatch, J., *Africa, the Rebirth of Self-rule* (OUP, 1967)*
Hodder, B.W., *Africa Today* (Methuen, 1978)*
Isichei, E., *A History of Nigeria* (Longman, 1983)*
Jones, P., *Kwame Nkrumah and Africa* (Hamish Hamilton, 1965)
Jorgensen, J., *Uganda, A Modern History* (Croom Helm, 1981)
Nyerere, J., *Ujamaa, Essays on Socialism* (OUP, 1968)*
Pedler, F., *Main Currents in West African History, 1940–1978* (Macmillan, 1979)
Rodney, W., *How Europe Underdeveloped Africa* (Bogle–L'Ouverture Publications, 1972)*
Wallbank, T.W., *Documents on Modern Africa* (Anvil, 1964)*
Wallerstein, I., *Africa, the Politics of Independence* (Knopf, 1961)
Williams, B., *Modern Africa* (Longman, 1970)*

Unit 18

Becker, J., *The PLO: the Rise and Fall of the Palestine Liberation Organisation* (Weidenfeld & Nicolson, 1984)
Browne, H., *Suez and Sinai* (Longman, 1971)*

Buttinger, J., *Dragon Defiant, Short History of Vietnam* (David & Charles, 1973)*
Cobban, H., *The Making of Modern Lebanon* (Hutchinson, 1985)*
Dodd, C.H., *Israel and the Arab World* (Routledge & Kegan Paul, 1970)*
Fraser, T.G., *The Middle East, 1914–1979* (Edward Arnold, Documents of Modern History, 1980)*
Higgins, H., *Vietnam* (Heinemann, 1975)*
Maclear, M., *Vietnam, the Thousand Day War* (Thames Methuen, 1981)
Mandle, B., *Conflict in the Promised Land* (Heinemann, 1976)*
Nussbaum, E., *Israel* (OUP, 1968)*
O'Ballance, E., *The Wars in Vietnam* (Ian Allan, 1975)
Polyviou, P., *Cyprus, Conflict and Negotiation 1960–1980* (Duckworth, 1981)
Regan, G.B., *Israel and the Arabs* (Cambridge UP, 1983)
Sachar, H., *A History of Israel* (Blackwell, 1977)*
Said, E., *The Question of Palestine* (Routledge & Kegan Paul, 1980)*
Shawcross, W., *Side-Show: Kissinger, Nixon and the Destruction of Cambodia* (Fontana, 1980)*

Unit 19

Arthur, P., *The Government and Politics of Northern Ireland* (Longman, 1984)
Benson, M., *Nelson Mandela* (Hamish Hamilton, 1986)
Black, C.V., *The Story of Jamaica* (Collins, 1965)*
Brookes, E., *Apartheid* (Routledge & Kegan Paul, 1968)*
Buckland, P., *The Northern Ireland Problem, 1921–1986* (Blackwell, 1987)*
Daly, V.T., *The Making of Guyana* (Macmillan, 1974)*
Davenport, T.R.H., *South Africa, a Modern History* (Macmillan, 1977)*
Hiro, D., *Black British, White British* (Penguin, 1973)*
Lowenthal, D., *West Indian Societies* (OUP, 1973)
Marquard, L., *Peoples and Policies of South Africa* (OUP, 1962)
Runnymede Trust and Radical Statistics Race Group, *Britain's Black Population* (Heinemann, 1980)*
Sorrenson, K., *Separate and Unequal* (Heinemann, 1977)*
Teague, P., (ed.) *Beyond the Rhetoric: Politics, Economics, and Social Policy in Northern Ireland* (Lawrence & Wishart, 1987)*
Troup, F., *South Africa* (Penguin, 1975)*
Tutu, D., *Hope and Suffering* (Collins Fount, 1984)*
Watson, J.B., *The West Indian Heritage* (Murray, 2nd edn 1982)*
Williams, E., *History of the People of Trinidad and Tobago* (Deutsch, 1964)*

Unit 20

Bakhash, S., *The Reign of the Ayatollahs: Iran and the Islamic Revolution* (Tauris, 1985)
Griffiths, J.C., *Afghanistan, Key to a Continent* (Deutsch, 1981)
Halliday, F., *Iran, Dictatorship and Development* (Penguin, 1979)*
Jones, D., *The Arab World* (Hamish Hamilton, 1965)
Mansfield, F., *The Arabs* (Penguin, 1980)*

Mottahedeh, R., *The Mantle of the Prophet* (Chatto & Windus, 1985)*
Saikal, A., *The Rise and Fall of the Shah, 1941–1979* (Angus and Robertson, 1980)
Sarwar, G., *Islam, Beliefs and Teachings* (Muslim Educational Trust, 1980)*
Tames, R., *Approaches to Islam* (Murray, 1982)*

Unit 21

Brandt, W., *World Armament and World Hunger* (Gollancz, 1986)*
The Brandt Report: North-South, A Programme for Survival (Pan, 1980)*
Frankel, J., *International Relations in a Changing World* (OUP, 1987)
George, S., *A Fate Worse than Debt* (Penguin, 1988)*
Girling, J., *America and the Third World* (Routledge & Kegan Paul, 1980)
Odell, P., *Oil and World Power* (Penguin, 1981)
Vaizey, J., *The Squandered Peace, the World 1945–1975* (Hodder & Stoughton, 1983)
Waterlow, C., *Superpowers and Victims, Outlook for the World Community* (Prentice-Hall, 1974)
Third World File (Third World First Group)*
Trade/Aid/Rich World and Poor World (VCOAD Publications: Voluntary Committee on Overseas Aid and Development)*

Unit 22

Banks, O., *Faces of Feminism* (Blackwell, 1981)*
Cottrell, A., *How Safe is Nuclear Energy?* (Heinemann, 1981)*
Cottrell, R.B., *Energy, the Rude Awakening* (MacGraw-Hill, 1977)
Jenkins, I.M.L., *Science and Technology* (Hamish Hamilton, 1966)*
Jones, C., Gadler, S.J., and Engstrom, P.H., *Pollution, the Population Explosion* (Dent, 1972)*
Kincarde, W.H., and Bertram, C., *Nuclear Proliferation in the 1980s* (Macmillan, 1982)
Wilson, E., *Only Halfway to Paradise: Women in Britain, 1945–1968* (Tavistock, 1980)*
Population Growth (VCOAD Publications)*

Unit 23

Lateef, N., *Crisis in the Sahel* (Westview Press, 1980)
Vincent, T.G., *Black Power and the Garvey Movement* (Ramparts Press, 1971)
Williams, R., *Towards 2000* (Chatto & Windus, 1983)

Index

Note Italic numbers indicate references to maps, tables or illustrations. '[G]' after a heading indicates an entry in the Glossary under that heading or a heading derived from it. The following abbreviations are commonly used in the Index: EC = European Community; EEC = European Economic Community; NI = Northern Ireland; SWW = Second World War; UK = United Kingdom ('Britain'); UN = United Nations Organization; US/USA = United States/of America.